Users of this publication are requested to forward information regarding newly discovered dangers, changes in aids to navigation, the existence of new shoals or channels, printing errors, or other information that would be useful for the correction of nautical charts and hydrographic publications affecting Canadian waters to:

**Director General
Canadian Hydrographic Service
Fisheries and Oceans Canada
Ottawa, Ontario
Canada
K1A 0E6**

The Canadian Hydrographic Service produces and distributes *Nautical Charts*, *Sailing Directions*, *Small Craft Guides*, *Tide Tables* and the *Atlas of Tidal Currents* of the navigable waters of Canada. These publications are available from authorized Canadian Hydrographic Service Chart Dealers. To obtain information on ordering, please contact:

**Hydrographic Chart Distribution Office
Fisheries and Oceans Canada
1675 Russell Road, Unit 19
P.O. Box 8080
Ottawa, Ontario
Canada
K1G 3H6**

**Hydrographic Chart Distribution Office
Fisheries and Oceans Canada
Institute of Ocean Sciences
9860 W. Saanich Road
P.O. Box 6000
Sidney, British Columbia
Canada
V8L 4B2**

**Phone: (613) 998-4931
Fax: (613) 998-1217
E-mail: chs_sales@dfo-mpo.gc.ca**

**Phone: (250) 363-6358
Fax: (250) 363-6841
E-mail: chartsales@pac.dfo-mpo.gc.ca**

or visit the CHS web site at:

www.charts.gc.ca

for dealer location and related information

© Minister of Fisheries and Oceans Canada 2004
Catalogue No. Fs 72-3/15-2004E
ISBN 0-660-19350-7
Ottawa, 2004

SAILING DIRECTIONS

BRITISH COLUMBIA COAST
(SOUTH PORTION)

VOL. 1 SEVENTEENTH EDITION 2004

Fisheries and Oceans Canada
Ottawa, Canada

Cover Photograph: Nanaimo Harbour

AMENDMENTS

A mendments published in *Notices to Mariners*, up to and including monthly edition No. 9 of 2004, have been incorporated in this edition.

Between New Editions, *Sailing Directions* must be kept up to date by amendments published in Section IV of Canadian *Notices to Mariners* (www.notmar.com). This is a legal requirement under the *Canada Shipping Act*.

A list of amendments is compiled at the end of each year for each volume of *Sailing Directions* and is available free from:

Hydrographic Chart Distribution Office
Fisheries and Oceans Canada
P.O. Box 6000, 9860 West Saanich Road
Sidney, B.C. Canada V8L 4B2
Telephone: (250) 363-6858
E-mail: chartsales@pac.dfo-mpo.gc.ca

Record of amendments to this *Sailing Directions* volume from monthly *Notices to Mariners*.

N/M Ed. No.	Inserted by:	N/M Ed. No.	Inserted by:	N/M Ed. No.	Inserted by:	N/M Ed. No.	Inserted by:	N/M Ed. No.	Inserted by:

Preface

The Seventeenth Edition of *Sailing Directions, British Columbia Coast (South Portion)*, 2004, has been compiled from Canadian Government and other information sources. Hydrographic terms used are in accordance with meanings given in *Hydrographic Dictionary (Special Publication No. 32)*, published by the International Hydrographic Bureau (http://www.iho.shom.fr/).

Sailing Directions supplement charted information and provide important navigation information which may not be found on charts or other publications. *Sailing Directions* are intended to be used in conjunction with charts quoted in the text.

General information is in *PAC 200 — General Information, Pacific Coast*. It contains navigational information and a brief description of main port facilities as well as geographic, oceanographic and atmospheric characteristics. A geographical index at the end of the booklet should also be consulted.

Tide and current information revised by the Canadian Hydrographic Service.

Photographs are by the Canadian Hydrographic Service unless otherwise indicated.

Meteorological information supplied by the Atmospheric Environment Service, Environment Canada.

Comments about format, content, or any other matter relating to *Sailing Directions* or other CHS products would be greatly appreciated and should be forwarded to:

Director General,
Canadian Hydrographic Service,
Fisheries and Oceans Canada,
Ottawa, Ontario, Canada K1A 0E6.

Telephone: (613) 995-5249
Fax: (613) 996-9053
E-mail: chsinfo@dfo-mpo.gc.ca

Related Publications:

Canadian Hydrographic Service (www.charts.gc.ca/pub/)
• *PAC 200 — Sailing Directions — General Information — Pacific Coast*
• *PAC 205 — Sailing Directions — Inner Passage — Queen Charlotte Sound to Chatham Sound*
• *PAC 206 — Sailing Directions — Hecate Strait, Dixon Entrance, Portland Inlet and Adjacent Waters and Queen Charlotte Islands*
• *Catalogue of Nautical Charts and Publications 2 Pacific Coast*
• *Chart 1 — Symbols, Abbreviations, and Terms*
• *Canadian Tide and Current Tables, Volumes 5, 6 and 7*
• *Canadian Tidal Manual*

Canadian Coast Guard (www.ccg-gcc.gc.ca)
• *Pacific Coast List of Lights, Buoys and Fog Signals*
• *Radio Aids to Marine Navigation (Pacific and Western Arctic)*
• *Notices to Mariners 1 to 46 Annual Edition*
• *The Canadian Aids to Navigation System*

National Oceanic and Atmospheric Association (www.chartmaker.ncd.noaa.gov)
• *United States Coast Pilot 7*

Contents

Explanatory Notes

Bearings and Courses refer to True North (geographic), and are given in degrees from 000° clockwise to 359°. Bearings of conspicuous objects, lights, ranges and light sectors are given from seaward. Courses always refer to the course to be "made good".

Buoys are only described in detail where they have special navigational significance, or where chart scale is too small to clearly show details.

Chart references normally refer to the largest scale Canadian chart. Occasionally a smaller scale chart may be quoted where its use is more appropriate.

Clearances under bridges, overhead cables, etc., are those at HHWLT.

Conspicuous objects, natural or artificial, are those that stand out clearly from the background and are easily identifiable from a few miles offshore in normal visibility.

Dead-weight tonnage and mass are expressed in metric tonnes of 1,000 kilograms. The kilogram is used for expressing relatively small masses.

Depths, unless otherwise stated, are referred to Chart Datum. As depths are liable to change, particularly in dredged channels and alongside wharves and floats, it is strongly recommended that when critical they are confirmed by enquiry to the appropriate authority.

Distances unless otherwise stated, are expressed in nautical miles. For practical purposes, a nautical mile is considered to be the length of one minute of arc, measured along the meridian, in the latitude of the position. The international nautical mile, which has now been adopted by most maritime nations, is equal to 1,852 metres.

Distance tables contain approximate distances only based on tracks usable by most vessels consistent with safe navigation.

Elevations on land are given above HHWLT. Elevations of wooded islands, points, etc., are to tops of trees. **Heights** of objects, as distinct from elevations, refer to heights of structures above ground.

Facilities available to the general public are described. Floats and wharves not described can be assumed to be private.

Figures in brackets given after those denoting fathoms or feet are their equivalent in metres. Those following lights and light buoys are their Canadian Light List number.

Latitudes and Longitudes given in brackets are approximate and intended to facilitate reference to the general area on the chart quoted.

Magnetic Compass Roses must be corrected for annual change in variation.

Names have been taken from the Canadian Permanent Committee on Geographical Names. Unofficial locally used names are given for some features.

Small craft is the term used to designate pleasure craft and small vessels with shallow draught.

Tidal information relating to the vertical movement of water is not given and *Canadian Tide and Current Tables, Volumes 5, 6 and 7*, should be consulted. However, abnormal changes in water level are mentioned.

Tidal streams and currents are described by the direction toward which they flow. The **ebb stream** is caused by a falling tide and the **flood stream** is caused by a rising tide.

Time, unless otherwise stated, is expressed in Pacific Standard or Pacific Daylight time.

Winds are described by the direction from which they blow.

Wreck information is included where drying or submerged wrecks are relatively permanent features having significance for navigation or anchoring. Vessels sunk as **artificial reefs** or having historic significance may also be described.

Definitions

A-frames are derricks generally constructed of logs formed in the shape of the letter "A". They are used for lifting bundles of logs from logging trucks to water and are usually conspicuous.

Booming grounds can be either areas where logs are yarded and formed into sections, or areas where booms and sections are stored. They are generally private areas, holding water leases, which restrict public usage. These areas are subject to frequent change.

Deadheads/Sinkers are logs that have become so waterlogged that they are almost entirely submerged. They usually assume a vertical position and if water is shallow enough for their bottom end to be aground, they can cause massive hull damage. They are invisible even in daylight unless a slight swell causes them to break the surface.

HHWLT (Higher High Water, Large Tide) is the highest predictable tide during an average year in the 19 year lunar cycle.

HW (High Water) refers to the highest water level achieved during one tidal cycle.

LLWLT (Lower Low Water, Large Tide) is the lowest predictable tide during an average year in the 19 year lunar cycle.

LW (Low Water) is the lowest water level achieved during one tidal cycle.

Logbooms are collections of logs formed into units suitable for towing. They are generally oblong and can range up to 76 m wide and 360 m long. Logbooms are encircled and contained by **boomsticks** formed by logs chained together end to end.

Log dumps are areas where logs are dumped either from A-frames or log ramps. Usually the area is blocked off by boomsticks and pilings.

Public wharf is available for general use though fees may be charged by local authorities. Some wharves may give berthing priority to local fishing fleets or other agencies.

Radar beacons (Racon) are beacons which respond to radars. A full description is given in *Radio Aids to Marine Navigation (Pacific and Western Arctic)*.

CHAPTER 1

Juan De Fuca Strait, including Esquimalt, Victoria and Port Angeles Harbours

General

Charts 3461, 3606, 3602

1   This chapter includes approaches to Juan de Fuca Strait, on the south between Cape Alava and Cape Flattery, and on the north between Cape Beale and Carmanah Point. The United States coast of Juan de Fuca Strait as far east as Ediz Hook is briefly described. For complete information see *United States Coast Pilot 7*.

2   **Traffic** through Juan de Fuca Strait is considerable. In addition to local coasting vessels, large tankers from Alaska and freighters operating across the Pacific Ocean or through the Panama Canal have destinations in Puget Sound and Strait of Georgia. Canadian and United States surface and submarine navy vessels transit and exercise in this area. Large car carrying ferries, smaller high speed passenger ferries and cruise ships frequent these waters. Fishing boats and recreational small craft are numerous.

Juan de Fuca Strait and Approaches

3   **Juan de Fuca Strait** *(48°25'N, 124°40'W)* separates the SW part of Vancouver Island from the State of Washington. The west boundary of the Strait is a line between Carmanah Point, B.C. and Cape Flattery, Washington. The north boundary follows the shoreline of Vancouver Island to Gonzales Point, continues directly to Sea Bird Point (Discovery Island) and Cattle Point (San Juan Island). The boundary continues along a line from Cattle Point to Iceberg Point (Lopez Island) to Point Colville (Lopez Island) to Rosario Head (Fidalgo Island), then SW along Whidbey Island to Point Partridge and south to Point Wilson (Quimper Peninsula). The Washington mainland forms the south border of the Strait.

4   Juan de Fuca Strait was discovered in 1592 by a Greek mariner named Apostolos Valerianos, but commonly known as Juan de Fuca. In 1787, it was rediscovered by Charles William Barkley, an Englishman employed by the Austrian East India Company.

5   At its entrance and as far east as Race Rocks, a distance of about 50 miles, the Strait is about 12 miles wide, and for a further 30 miles to Whidbey Island it has a width of about 16 miles.

6   At the east end of the Strait, see *Charts 3461* and *3462*, a number of channels lead north to the Strait of Georgia and the inland waters of British Columbia, and south to Admiralty Inlet, Puget Sound and Hood Canal.

7   **Aspect**. — On the north or Vancouver Island side, hills rise gradually and are for the most part densely wooded, although there are some large bare patches where extensive logging operations have been carried out, or where there has been devastation by fire. These hills do not attain any great elevation. On the south side are the Olympic Mountains, summits are generally snow covered.

8   **Traffic Separation Schemes (TSS)**. — A compulsory routeing system for Juan de Fuca Strait and its approaches has been adopted by the International Maritime Organization (IMO) and is listed in *Notices to Mariners 1 to 46 Annual Edition*. All vessels are required to use the TSS and comply with *Rule 10 (Traffic Separation Schemes)* of the *Collision Regulations*. This system is part of the Canadian/United States Co-operative Vessel Traffic System.

9   **A revised Traffic Separation Scheme** in Juan de Fuca Strait came into force at 0000 Coordinated Universal Time (UTC) on 1 December, 2002. Major changes to the traffic separation scheme are:

    a) re-configuration and extension further offshore of traffic lanes at the entrance to Juan de Fuca Strait;

    b) modification of location, orientation and dimensions of existing Traffic Separation Scheme in Juan de Fuca Strait;

    c) re-location of the Pilot Area and re-configuration of traffic lanes and precautionary area off Port Angeles.

10   **A two-way route** has been established south of the Traffic Separation Scheme in Juan de Fuca Strait for smaller, slower moving vessels that normally do not use the separation scheme in the Strait.

11   **Caution**. — In Canadian waters and fishing zones, provided it does not impede the passage of any vessel following a traffic lane, a vessel engaged in fishing may depart from certain provisions of *Rule 10* of *International Regulations for Preventing Collisions at Sea* and fish in any direction in a traffic lane. A vessel engaged in special operations such as buoy tending or hydrographic surveys, provided it does not prevent any vessels using the route from navigating safely, may also depart from certain provisions of *Rule 10*. For details see Traffic Separation Schemes and Collision Regulations in *PAC 200*.

12   The Traffic Separation Scheme in United States waters of Juan de Fuca Strait, east of Port Angeles, is part of the mandatory *Puget Sound Vessel Traffic Service*.

13   **Light buoys. — Racon**. — Juan de Fuca Traffic Lane Separation light buoy "J" *(180.8)*, 13 miles WNW of Cape Flattery, is fitted with a Racon (— — —).

14   Juan de Fuca Traffic Lane Separation light buoy "JA" *(180.9)*, 5 miles south of Bonilla Point, marks a turn in the Vessel Traffic Lanes.

15   Juan de Fuca Traffic Lane Separation light buoy "PA" *(187.5)*, Race Rocks South Cautionary light buoy "VF" *(189.5)* and Race Rocks East Cautionary light buoy "VG" *(192)*, mark the limits of Traffic Separation Zones south and SE of Race Rocks. Give a wide clearance to and avoid contact with these buoys.

16   The **International Boundary** between Canada and the United States of America runs along the west part of Juan de Fuca Strait, then north and eastward through Haro Strait and Boundary Pass into the Strait of Georgia.

17   **Vessel Traffic Services (VTS)**. — Canadian waters in the approach to Juan de Fuca Strait west of Longitude *124°40'W* are in the *Tofino Traffic Zone*. Frequency is 156.725 MHz, Channel 74.

18   A **Co-operative Vessel Traffic System**, between Canada and the United States of America, is in the waters to seaward of and

Charts 3461, 3606, 3602

through which the International Boundary runs. These waters include Juan de Fuca Strait, Haro Strait, Boundary Pass and the south end of the Strait of Georgia.

19 ***Seattle CVTS Zone: Juan de Fuca Strait***, containing all Canadian and United States waters east of Longitude *124°40'W*, and south of a line from Church Point to Race Rocks light, to the intersection of the Canada/U.S. Border at *48°17'06"N, 123°14'51"W*, then NE to Hein Bank light buoy, then to Cattle Point, is administered by *Seattle Traffic*. Frequency is 156.25 MHz, Channel 5A. Calling-in points are:

20 ***Calling-in Point 1***, *Zone Limit*, is the meridian of Longitude *124°40'00"W*. This calling-in point is for changing from the *Tofino Traffic Zone* to *Juan de Fuca Strait*.

21 ***Calling-in Point 3***, *Race Rocks*, is a line running 090°–270° through Race Rocks light *(189)*. This calling-in point is for changing from *Juan de Fuca Strait* to *Sector One* of the *Vancouver Traffic Zone* administered by *Victoria Traffic*.

22 ***Sector One*** of the ***Vancouver Traffic Zone*** consists of the waters through which the International Boundary runs north of a line joining Church Point, Race Rocks light, to the intersection of the Canada/U.S. Border at *48°17'06"N, 123°14'51"W*, then NE to Hein Bank light buoy, then to Cattle Point. This sector is administered by *Victoria Traffic*. Assigned frequency is 156.55 MHz, Channel 11. Calling-in points in Juan de Fuca Strait are:

23 ***Calling-in Point 4***, *Buoy "VH"*, is a line running 000°–180° through Victoria Harbour Cautionary light buoy *(203)*.

24 ***Calling-in Point 5***, *Hein Bank*, is a line joining Hein Bank light buoy and Cattle Point light *(221)*. This calling-in point is for changing from the *Vancouver Traffic Zone*, administered by *Victoria Traffic*, to *Seattle Traffic* and the *Puget Sound Vessel Traffic Service*.

25 A brief description of Vessel Traffic Services (VTS) is given in *PAC 200*. Full details are given in *Radio Aids to Marine Navigation (Pacific and Western Arctic)*.

26 **Puget Sound Vessel Traffic Service**, in United States waters east of Port Angeles, is mandatory and consists of three major components, a Traffic Separation Scheme, radar surveillance and a Vessel Movement Reporting System. Details of this service are given in *United States Coast Pilot 7*. Proper operating procedures are contained in the Puget Sound Vessel Traffic Service Operating Manual, available free from:

Commanding Officer,
U.S. Coast Guard,
Puget Sound Vessel Traffic Service,
1519 Alaskan Way S.,
Seattle, Washington, U.S.A. 98134-1192.
http://www.uscg.mil/d13/units/vts/manual.html

27 **Regulated Navigation Area**. — Because of heavy vessel concentrations, United States waters of Juan de Fuca Strait east of New Dungeness, San Juan Islands, Strait of Georgia, Puget Sound, and all adjacent waters, are a Regulated Navigation Area. To enhance vessel traffic safety during congested periods, the U.S. Coast Guard may establish Temporary Special Traffic Lanes. For details see *United States Coast Pilot 7*.

28 **Military exercise areas** in the approach to and in Juan de Fuca Strait are charted. For details of the limits of these areas and other information concerning them consult *Notices to Mariners 1 to 46 Annual Edition*. Observe due caution when navigating in the vicinity while exercises are in progress.

29 **Wreck**. — A wreck (depth unknown) at *48°28'57"N, 125°17'06"W* may be hazardous to nets and towed underwater equipment.

30 **Subsurface mooring**. — A current meter has been moored in the western approach to Juan de Fuca Strait since 1983. Its position and depth below surface are changed and advertised via *Notices to Shipping*. It is presently (2003) located at *48°31'43.8"N, 126°12'06.5"W* and has 28 m over it.

31 **Ferries**. — A ferry service crosses Juan de Fuca Strait between Victoria and Port Angeles and a catamaran ferry services operate between Victoria and Seattle. Mariners are cautioned that the Port Angeles/Victoria ferry may deviate from charted standard route due to bad weather, traffic conditions, navigational hazards or other emergency conditions.

32 **Pilot boarding stations**. — Two pilot boarding stations are in Juan de Fuca Strait.

33 The boarding station for the **Pacific Pilotage Authority**, covering Canadian waters, is at Victoria Harbour Cautionary light buoy *(203)*.

34 The pilot boarding station for United States waters is off Port Angeles, about 1.4 miles NNE of Ediz Hook light *(190)*.

35 For details on how to obtain a pilot see *PAC 200*.

36 **Meteorological information** for Juan de Fuca Strait is given in *PAC 200*. Meteorological tables for Pachena Point, Sooke, Victoria, a frequency of fog table for Victoria and wind frequency tables for Cape Beale and Race Rocks are given in the Appendices.

37 **Tides**. — Tidal predictions in Juan de Fuca Strait are given for Port Renfrew (Index No. 8525), Sooke (Index No. 7020), Victoria (Index No. 7120) and Port Townsend (Index No. 7160) in *Tide Tables, Volume 5*.

38 **Tidal differences for the west end of Juan de Fuca Strait**, referenced on Port Renfrew (Index No. 8525) are given for Neah Bay (Index No. 8512) in *Tide Tables, Volume 6*.

39 **Tidal differences for the central portion of Juan de Fuca Strait**, referenced on Sooke (Index No. 7020), are given for Point No Point (Index No. 7010), Sooke Basin (Index No. 7024), Becher Bay (Index No. 7030), Crescent Bay (Index No. 7050) and Port Angeles (Index No. 7060). Tidal differences for the central portion of Juan de Fuca Strait, referenced on Victoria (Index No. 7120), are given for Pedder Bay (Index No. 7080), William Head (Index No. 7082), Esquimalt (Index No. 7110) and Clover Point (Index No. 7115) in *Tide Tables, Volume 5*.

40 **Tidal streams** in the approach to Juan de Fuca Strait, south of La Pérouse Bank, are rotary, but effects of the California Current and wind on streams tend to give a predominant NW flow in winter. In summer predominant flow is reversed and sets SE.

41 In *48°11'N, 125°55'W* the tidal stream sets 325° at 1 kn in winter and 160° at ½ kn in summer.

42 In *48°16'N, 125°46'W* the tidal stream sets 320° at 1 kn in winter and 130° at 1 kn in summer.

43 In *48°22'N, 125°35'W* the tidal stream sets 315° at 1 kn in winter and 115° at 1 kn in summer.

44 In *48°28'N, 125°23'W* the tidal stream sets 270° at 1 kn in winter and 270° at 1 kn in summer.

45 **In vicinity of Swiftsure Bank** *(48°35'N, 125°00'W)* tidal streams are distinctly rotary and, under conditions of equal rise and fall, set east at HW, circling clockwise through south to west at LW, and continuing round through north to east again at HW. Direction of stream, as well as its strength, depends upon range of tide. With

Charts 3461, 3606, 3602

a strong ebb stream out of Juan de Fuca Strait the stream, from about 2 hours after one HW to 4 hours before the next, sets between SW and west, when it gradually changes, through west until at HW it is running nearly due north. From HW until 2 hours after, the stream is nearly slack, and changes quickly, through east, to south and west. See table and diagram *Chart 3602*. Observations give evidence of a permanent west-going current with an average velocity of ½ kn. This causes the NW stream to be considerably stronger than the one setting SE. Direction and strength of prevailing winds have some effect on velocities. SE streams do not exceed 1 kn except under the influence of strong west or NW winds, when an increase up to 1½ kn can occur, whereas NW-setting streams of 2 kn or more frequently occur with strong east or SE winds. Greatest velocity observed in the area is 3 kn.

46   **In vicinity of Umatilla Reef** *(48°11'N, 124°48'W)* tidal streams are only slightly rotary, the flood stream setting 345°, and the ebb 165° at about ½ kn. Non-tidal current shows a very distinct variation; during winter months it sets north at nearly ¾ kn, while in summer it sets south at less than ½ kn. Prevailing wind is east or SE in winter and west or NW in summer; south winds cause a stronger current than north ones. With strong SE winds the combined tidal and non-tidal currents attain 2 to 3 kn in a north direction. Greatest observed velocity at Umatilla Reef is about 3 kn.

47   **Within Juan de Fuca Strait** times and rates of maximum current and time of slack water are predicted and tabulated as daily tables for current stations Juan de Fuca – West (Index No. 9000) *(48°27'N, 124°35'W)*, Juan de Fuca – East (Index No. 1100) *(48°14'N, 123°32'W)* and for Race Passage (Index No. 1200) *(48°18'N, 123°32'W)*. Secondary current station River Jordan (Index No. 1110), referenced on Juan de Fuca (East), is about 7 miles south of Jordan River *(48°19'N, 124°05'W)*.

48   **Predictions for Juan de Fuca (West)** are in *Tide Tables, Volumes 5 and 6*. Predictions for Juan de Fuca (East), Race Passage and River Jordan are in *Tide Tables, Volume 5*.

49   *Current Atlas, Juan de Fuca Strait to Strait of Georgia* is available from Canadian Hydrographic Service Chart Distribution Offices and authorized chart dealers.

50   **Fluctuations in horizontal movement of** water due to meteorological conditions can prolong the duration and increase flow of current in one direction, and have the opposite effect when direction is reversed. The current therefore may not turn exactly when predicted, but at these times the rate will be relatively weak.

51   In the **central portion of Juan de Fuca Strait, Sooke Inlet to Race Rocks**, the flood stream attains a greater rate along the Canadian shore than it does along the American shore. The main flood stream runs south of Race Rocks, then turns north in a wide sweep and heads in the general direction of Victoria Harbour. On the flood, between River Jordan on the Canadian side and Pillar Point on the American side, the tidal stream runs at 2½ kn. The turn to flood takes place on both sides of the Strait at about the same time.

52   Between River Jordan and Pillar Point the ebb stream at spring tides runs at 3 kn on the north side of the Strait, and at 2½ kn on the south side, with the turn to ebb about 30 minutes later on the north side.

53   **When wind and swell oppose the tidal stream** a short choppy sea is raised near the west entrance of the Strait.

54   **Tide-rips** occur off prominent points and in vicinity of banks. They are especially heavy off Cape Flattery, Race Rocks, New Dungeness, Point Wilson, along the north shore between Beechey Head and Esquimalt, and off Clover Point, Trial Islands and Discovery Island. Under certain conditions these tide-rips can be dangerous to small vessels.

55   **Fishing vessels**. — From April 15 to September 30 numerous fishing vessels can be encountered inside the 100 m line on La Pérouse and Swiftsure Banks and in the approach to Juan de Fuca Strait. A smaller winter fishing season is also underway. Vessels may be trolling, towing nets or particularly at night, they may be at anchor. Because of the prevalence of fog and low visibility in this vicinity, vessels approaching these areas from any direction are advised to pass to the south and clear of the banks. Mariners obliged to cross these banks should navigate with extreme caution to avoid risk of collision with fishing vessels. Radar derived information concerning the locations of concentrations of fishing vessels can be obtained from the Marine Communications and Traffic Services at *Tofino Traffic*.

56   **Within Juan de Fuca Strait**, numerous fishing vessels using drift nets or purse seine nets can be encountered day and night from approximately July 1 to November 1. Drift nets can extend up to 552 m in length from the end that is attached to the operating vessel. The free end is marked by a white light. See *PAC 200* and *Notices to Mariners 1 to 46 Annual Edition*.

57   **Driftwood**. — Because logging is one of the main industries, free-floating logs and deadheads are a constant source of danger in Juan de Fuca Strait. Danger is increased during freshets.

58   A **submarine cable** (fibre optic) is laid in Juan de Fuca Strait leading south from Fleming Bay *(48°25'N, 123°25'W)* then east along the north side of the strait across the approach to Haro Strait. Submarine cables are laid in U.S. waters of Juan de Fuca Strait.

59   **Navigation**. — Loran-C coverage in the open waters of Juan de Fuca Strait is good, but it is not reliable close to shore. In the area east of Cape Beale and through Juan de Fuca Strait mariners can experience incorrect cycle acquisition and tracking problems with 5990X because of weak signal strength from the secondary at Shoal Cove, Alaska. For details regarding the best signal strength and position fixing geometry see *PAC 200*.

60   **Racons** are located on Juan de Fuca light buoy "J", in the entrance of the Strait, Victoria Harbour Cautionary light buoy "VH" and Hein Bank light buoy. For details see *Radio Aids to Marine Navigation (Pacific and Western Arctic)*.

61   In the NW approach, between Carmanah Point and Cape Cook *(50°07'N, 127°56'W)*, the set of the tidal stream tends toward land and is accentuated by in-draught into the large sounds, especially during strong winds from SE to SW. This part of the coast of Vancouver Island should be given a wide berth.

62   **Approaching Juan de Fuca Strait from the south** there is no inducement to hug the coast on to which a long rolling swell frequently breaks. This swell meeting SE gales of winter raises a confused sea. Cape Flattery and its off-lying dangers should be given a berth of at least 3 miles because of tidal streams and currents.

63   **In thick or foggy weather** it is very important to strike soundings on the outer edge of the bank which is well defined. Approximate distance from land will then be known. When within 25 or 30 miles from Cape Flattery and the Vancouver Island coast, the steady NW set across the entrance of the Strait should be particularly guarded against, especially during winter when SE and S winds prevail.

Charts 3461, 3606, 3602

64   **During SW or west gales**, it is more desirable to run into the Strait and seek shelter than to remain outside.

Juan de Fuca Strait — South Approach

Charts 3602, 3606

65   **Area to be avoided**. — In order to reduce risk of a marine casualty and resulting pollution and damage to the environment of the **Olympic Coast National Marine Sanctuary**, all ships and barges carrying cargoes of oil or hazardous materials, and all ships 1,600 gross tons and above solely in transit should avoid this area. Mariners are advised that expanded boundaries and applicability of the area to be avoided came into force at 0000 Coordinated Universal Time (UTC) on 1 December, 2002.

66   **Cape Alava** *(48°10'N, 124°44'W)* is the site of a year-round archaeological operation that was established in 1970. **Ozette Island** is flat topped with steep sides. Low, black rocks lie off its south and SE sides. **Bodelteh Islands** have high, bold seaward faces. Close west of the outer island is a whitish rock, 40 m high. **Umatilla Reef** consists of small, low, black rocks and some breakers. A breaker has been reported 1.1 miles NNE, and a rock with 1 m over it lies 0.3 mile east of the reef.

67   **Anchorage** can be obtained off the SE end of Ozette Island, it provides fair protection from prevailing NW winds but the area is small and requires local knowledge to enter.

68   **Light buoy**. — Umatilla light and whistle buoy "2UR" *(US 750)*, 1.5 miles west of Umatilla Reef, is a starboard hand buoy.

69   **Point of Arches** *(48°15'N, 124°42'W)* has cliffs extending 1.5 miles south from it and is fronted by numerous reefs. **Father and Son** are two rocks, 20 and 51 m high, connected by a low reef. **Spike Rock** is sharp, bare, and the outermost of a chain of rocks that can be identified by their arch formations. A drying rock lies 0.3 mile WSW and a dangerous wreck lies about 0.3 mile ENE of Spike Rock.

70   **Portage Head** *(48°17'N, 124°41'W)* has bold, irregular cliffs about 125 m high and 1 mile long. A rock with less than 2 m over it usually breaks, and lies 1.3 miles NW from the point. **Strawberry Rock** is 2 m high.

71   **Makah Bay**, between **Anderson Point** and **Waatch Point**, has numerous rocks awash in its south part and affords indifferent shelter in north and east winds with a smooth sea, but is seldom used. Shores are low and sandy. **Waatch River** enters the north part of the bay through a low valley that is one of the features for identifying Cape Flattery.

72   **Cape Flattery** *(48°23'N, 124°44'W)* has bold, rocky cliffs, 37 m high that are reported to give a good radar echo. **Fuca Pillar**, a 48 m high rock column leaning slightly NW, stands about 0.1 mile from the foot of the cliffs. It is more prominent from north than from south. Numerous rocks and reefs border the cliffs east and south of the Cape. The land rises from the Cape to an elevation of 454 m at **Bahokus Peak** on which there is a radar dome, conspicuous from seaward. Cape Flattery and Bahokus Peak usually first appear as an island when viewed from south because of low land along the Waatch River valley.

73   **Tatoosh Island** is 33 m high with almost perpendicular sides and a bare, flat top. Several islets and reefs lie close-off its west side. The passage between the Island and Cape Flattery is dangerous and constricted by two rocks awash near its centre. Although sometimes used by local small craft it is not recommended. Currents are strong and treacherous.

74   A **reef**, 1.5 miles SW of Tatoosh Island, has a least depth of 13.7 m over which the sea occasionally breaks in a west swell.

75   **Duncan Rock**, small, low and black and **Duntze Rock** with 5.9 m over it, are the two principal dangers NNW of Tatoosh Island. The passage between Duncan Rock and Tatoosh Island is constricted to less than 0.5 mile by reefs. Strong tidal streams and tide-rips make it hazardous.

76   **Light. — Fog signal**. — Cape Flattery light *(181)*, on the west side of Tatoosh Island, is shown at an elevation of 50 m from a white conical tower 20 m high. It is fitted with an emergency light. The fog signal consists of two blasts on a horn every minute.

77   **Light buoy**. — Duntze Rock light and whistle buoy "2D" *(181.4)*, NW of the rock, is a starboard hand buoy.

Juan de Fuca Strait — South Side

78   The south shore of Juan de Fuca Strait is heavily forested and rises to considerable height. Except in a few places the shore is bold and rugged. Generaly water is deep until close to shore and there are few off-lying dangers.

79   **Tides**. — Tidal differences for Neah Bay (Index No. 8512), referenced on Port Renfrew, are in *Tide Tables, Volume 6*.

U.S. Chart 18484

[from U.S. Coast Pilot 7]

80   ***Neah Bay**, about 5 miles E of Cape Flattery, is used extensively by small vessels as a harbor of refuge in foul weather. Its proximity to Cape Flattery and ease of access at any time make the anchorage very useful. It is protected from all but E weather.*

81   ***Baada (Baadah) Point**, the E entrance point to Neah Bay, is rocky and grass-covered for some distance back from the shore. **Waadah Island**, 0.3 mile N of Baada Point, is 0.5 mile long, high, and wooded. A rubblestone breakwater extends from the W side of the bay to about the middle of Waadah Island. A reef and foul ground extend 0.2 mile from the SW side of the island. A wharf, used by the Coast Guard, is on the S end of the island. A light is at each end of the island. A fog signal is at the S end of the island. A reef that bares, marked by a lighted bell buoy, extends 500 yards NW from **Dtokoah Point**, SE of the entrance.*

82   *The buildings of **Neah Bay Coast Guard Station**, 0.4 mile SW of Baada Point, are prominent from the entrance.*

83   *The buoyed entrance to the bay is between Waadah Island and Baada Point. Depths of 14 to 16 feet can be carried into the bay. The careful navigator can carry 16 feet through the entrance by use of the chart and by favoring the S side of the entrance, passing close aboard the end of the Makah Indian T-head pier about 375 yards W of Baada Point. After passing the pier let the chart be the guide to the best water. Anchorage is in 20 to 40 feet, sandy bottom.*

84   *The W shore of Neah Bay is high and precipitous, and bordered by craggy rock outcroppings. The shore E of the village of Neah Bay is a low sand beach to Baada Point. Unmarked sunken wrecks are in the W part of the bay in about 48°22'22"N., 124°37'15"W., and in the NE corner of the bay in about 48°22'39"N., 124°36'20"W. Caution is advised when anchoring in the vicinity of the wrecks.*

85   *The Indian village of **Neah Bay**, on the SW shore of the bay, is the site of considerable sport fishing.*

U.S. Chart 18484

86   *Neah Bay is a* **customs port of entry***. The customs officer also performs immigration duties.*

87   *The Makah Indian T-head pier with a 300 foot face and privately marked at each end by a light, and the ruins of a T-head pier no longer visible, are about 375 and 500 yards SW of Baada Point. Caution is advised in the vicinity of the pier in ruins, as submerged piles may exist. The Coast Guard pier is 0.5 mile SW of Baada Point.*

88   *Two cooperative fish piers, 1 mile and 1.2 miles SW of Baada Point, have facilities for icing and supplying fishing boats. Limited berthage, electricity, gasoline, diesel fuel, water, and ice are available. Both piers have reported depths of 12 feet off the ends. There are many small-craft floats extending along the S shore of the bay. Neah Bay has no public haulout or repair facilities.*

89   *A paved highway extends along the Strait of Juan de Fuca to Port Angeles.*

Chart 3606

90   **Seal Rock** *(48°22'N, 124°33'W) is conspicuous, light coloured and has a flat top sloping east.* **Sail Rock***, 0.3 mile SE, is lower in elevation and has a pointed summit. The wreck of the* Andalucia *just off these rocks is completely covered.*

91   **Sekiu River***, 7 miles SE of Sail Rock, has some logging operations. A bridge over the river shows prominently through trees.*

92   **Clallam Bay** *(48°15'N, 124°16'W), a broad open bight east of* **Sekiu Point***, affords anchorage in 11 to 18 m, sand bottom. It is occasionally used in south winds or thick weather.*

93   **Slip Point** *is high, wooded, and has a light coloured streak down its face that is visible for a long distance. A reef extending west from Slip Point is marked by a port hand light and bell buoy.*

94   **Sekiu***, a resort and sport fishing town at the west end of Clallam Bay, has berths, gasoline, limited supplies and a launching ramp. The town of Clallam Bay, on the east side of the bay, has no waterfront facilities.*

95   **Pillar Point** *(48°13'N, 124°06'W) is about 213 m high, bold and wooded to its summit. A dark pillar-shaped rock close under its east face is over 30 m high and prominent from the west.*

96   **Anchorage** *can be obtained about 0.8 mile SE of Pillar Point, in 16 to 22 m, sticky mud bottom. It offers good shelter from the heavy west swell but gives no protection from the brisk east and NE winds prevalent in winter.*

97   **Military exercise area***. — A U.S. Navy exercise area lies between Pillar and Tongue Points.*

98   **Twin Rivers** *(48°10'N, 123°57'W) are two small streams flowing into the Strait. An earth-filled barge loading facility, 0.3 mile west of* **West Twin River***, has a reported depth of 4.6 m alongside. It is used for barging clay to Seattle.*

99   **Low Point** *(48°09'N, 123°49'W) has numerous drying boulders west of it and should not be approached closer than 0.8 mile. Marine farm facilities, 2.4 miles west of the point, are marked by two private light buoys.*

Chart 3461

100   **Crescent Bay** *(48°10'N, 123°43'W) provides limited anchorage suitable only for small vessels. It is not a good landing place in north weather. The remains of a wharf on the west shore*

should be avoided. **Crescent Rock** is marked by a starboard hand bell buoy and the channel between it and shore is not recommended. A drying reef extends from **Tongue Point** and a wreck lies north of the point. **Striped Peak** is 1 mile ESE of the point.

101   **Tides**. — Tidal differences for Crescent Bay (Index No. 7050), referenced on Sooke, are in *Tide Tables, Volume 5.*

102   **Freshwater Bay**, a broad open bight with 10 to 40 m depths, is designated as an **emergency explosives anchorage**. For limits and regulations see *United States Coast Pilot 7*. **Observatory Point** has a 6 m high rock close east of it, the rock is almost joined to the point at LW. **Angeles Point** (48°09'N, 123°33'W) is low, sandy and covered with alders. A prominent microwave tower, with air obstruction lights, is on the point. Starboard light buoy "4" *(US 16224)* is 3 miles ENE of Angeles Point.

103   **Restricted Area. — Caution**. — The U.S. Navy advises that the precautionary area, located within a 1 nautical mile radius about *48°15'36"N, 123°15'48"W*, approximately 9 nautical miles NNE of Ediz Hook, is used by naval vessels to conduct equipment calibration tests. Surface vessels or submerged submarines will occasionally be maneuvering in circles in this area for several hours or days. When these operations are in progress, the test facility located on the east end of Ediz Hook will be manned and reference lights consisting of a lazy "T" bar, 1 second flashing yellow, 2 seconds flashing red, and a high intensity spot will be lit. The group of lights is visible from the north side of Ediz Hook with the "T" bar to the west and spot light to the east. The naval vessels will be participating in the Seattle Vessel Traffic System on Channel 5A. The Navy Test Facility Port Angeles will monitor VHF Channels 16 and 69. Mariners transiting this area are requested to proceed with caution.

104   **Vessel Traffic Services** are established in U.S. waters east of Port Angeles. This service is mandatory, see *United States Coast Pilot 7*.

105   **Tides**. — Tidal differences for Port Angeles (Index No. 7060), referenced on Sooke, are in *Tide Tables, Volume 5.*

U.S. Chart 18468

U.S. Coast Pilot 7

106   **Port Angeles***, 6.5 miles E of Freshwater Bay and 56 miles from Cape Flattery, is entered between* **Ediz Hook***, a low and narrow, sandspit 3 miles long, and the main shore to the S. The harbor, about 2.5 miles long, is easy of access by the largest vessels, which frequently use it when refueling, making topside repairs, waiting for orders or a tug, and when weather-bound.*

107   *The harbor is protected from all except E winds, which occasionally blow during the winter. During SE winter gales, the wind is not usually felt but some swells roll in. The depths are greatest on the N shore and decrease from 30 to 15 fathoms in the middle of the harbor; from the middle, the depths decrease regularly to the S shore, where the 3-fathom curve in some places in the E part is nearly 0.2 mile from the beach. A rock covered 19 feet is reported in the approach to the harbor in about 48°07'25"N., 123°23'00"W. A depth of 25 feet is off the easternmost pier on the waterfront, and a shoal with a least depth of 3 fathoms lies 350 yards NW of the NW corner of the pier. A buoy is 225 yards off the NW corner of the pier.*

108   *Extra caution in navigating the waters inside Ediz Hook should be exercised because of the large number of submerged*

U.S. Chart 18468

deadheads or sinkers in the area. Deadheads or sinkers are logs that have become adrift from rafts or booms, have become water-logged, and float in a vertical position with one end just awash, rising and falling with the tide.

109   The best **anchorage** is off the wharves, in 7 to 12 fathoms, sticky bottom.

110   A **nonanchorage area** has been established in the E part of Port Angeles Harbor. (See 110.1 and 110.229, chapter 2, for limits and regulations.)

111   Extensive log booming grounds in the N part of the harbor extend more than 1 mile from the W shore. Care must be taken when anchoring at night to avoid the rafted logs; the booming grounds are charted.

112   **Ediz Hook Light** (48°08'25"N., 123°24'08"W.), 60 feet above the water, is shown from a skeleton tower, 0.3 mile W of the E extremity of Ediz Hook. A 170-foot Coast Guard VTS radar tower is about 0.1 mile WSW of the light. A fog signal is near the E end of the point. Shoals extend to about 75 yards E of the E extremity of Ediz Hook. A lighted buoy is about 150 yards E of the outer limits of the shoals. Coast Guard radio station NOW is at the air station. An unmarked shoal with a least depth of 44 feet is about 3.4 miles WNW of Ediz Hook Light. An aquaculture site, marked by private lights, is off the S side of Ediz Hook about 800 yards WSW of the light.

113   **Port Angeles** is on the S shore of the harbor. Logs, lumber, plywood, newsprint, pulp, shakes and shingles, and petroleum products are the principal commodities handled.

114   Pilotage is compulsory for all vessels except those under enrollment or engaged exclusively in the coasting trade on the W coast of the continental United States (including Alaska) and/or British Columbia. Pilotage for Port Angeles is provided by the Puget Sound Pilots. They monitor VHF-FM channel 13. (See Pilotage, Strait of Juan de Fuca and Puget Sound, indexed as such, early this chapter.) http://www.puget-sound-pilots.com/ The pilot station is about 0.7 mile W from Ediz Hook Light. A pier for berthage of the pilot boats is on the S side of Ediz Hook, adjacent to the pilot station.

115   **Towage**. — Tugs to 1,200hp are stationed at Port Angeles, and tugs to 5,000hp are available from Seattle with advance notice.

116   Port Angeles is a **customs port of entry**.

117   **Coast Guard**. — Port Angeles Coast Guard Air Station is on Ediz Hook, about 0.3 mile W of the E extremity.

118   **Harbour regulations**. — The Port of Port Angeles Terminal Manager's office is at the foot of Cedar Street.

119   **Wharves**. — The major piers described, both private and port operated, extend along the S and W sides of the harbor. For a complete description of the port facilities refer to Port Series No. 37, published and sold by the U.S. Army Corps of Engineers. (See appendix for address.) The alongside depths of the facilities described are reported depths. (For information on the latest depths contact the port authorities or the private operators.)

120   **Supplies**. — Water, ice, and marine supplies are available. Groceries are nearby. Diesel oil and gasoline are available at the port boat haven. Bunkering available by barge.

121   **Repairs**. — Port Angeles has several companies and facilities to perform major topside repairs to large oceangoing vessels. The nearest drydocking facilities are in Seattle/Tacoma, WA.

122   **Communications**. — Port Angeles is served by a U.S. highway. It is connected by ferry to Victoria, B.C. The airport is 2.5 miles W of the city.

Juan de Fuca Strait — North Approach

Chart 3602

123   **La Pérouse Bank** (48°45'N, 125°55'W), in the NW approach to Juan de Fuca Strait, extends 35 miles west and 30 miles SW of Cape Beale. **Amphitrite Bank** between Amphitrite Point and La Pérouse Bank has 37 m over it.

124   **Light buoy**. — La Pérouse Bank ODAS light buoy "46206" (176.5) (48°50'N, 126°00'W) is a weather buoy.

125   **Soquel Bank** (48°42'N, 125°10'W) consists of two shoal areas about 2 miles apart. The west part has a least depth of 23.4 m and the east part has 19.2 m over it.

126   **Swiftsure Bank** (48°33'N, 125°00'W) has a least depth of 34 m. The area 4 miles SSW of Swiftsure Bank, known locally as the Chicken Ranch, is frequented by many small sport fishing boats from June to September. These boats may not be well equipped, for example lacking radar, and may have inexperienced crews. They may not be maintaining an adequate lookout or radio watch. Vessel movement in this area may be unpredictable. Extra caution must be exercised in this vicinity to avoid collision and possible loss of life.

127   **Pachena Bay**, 2.8 miles SE of Cape Beale, is exposed to the heavy swell that is usually present and should not be used as an anchorage. Shelter for small craft can be found inside the **Pachena River** entrance, but local knowledge is advised for entering the river.

128   **Seabird Rocks** off the entrance to Pachena Bay are bare. **Pachena Point** 3 miles SE of Seabird Rocks is steep-to.

129   **Lights**. — Seabird Rocks light (177), on the largest rock, is shown at an elevation of 20.1 m from a white tower, with a red band at the top.

130   Pachena Point light (178) is shown at an elevation of 46.9 m from a white tower, 6.1 m high. It operates only at night. A prominent white house with a red roof is close west of the light.

131   **Meteorological information** for Pachena Point is given in the Appendices.

132   **Tsusiat River**, 7 miles ESE of Pachena Point, has **Tsusiat Falls** at its mouth that can be seen for a considerable distance. As the only feature of its kind on this part of the coast, these falls are useful as an aid in fixing position.

Chart 3647

133   **Nitinat Narrows** (48°40'N, 124°51'W) entered between **Tsuquanah Point** and **Whyac Point** leads about 1 mile north into **Nitinat Lake**. **Nitinat Bar**, with depths of 0.9 to 2 m, extends across the entrance of the Narrows. Saw Tooth Rocks, a local name, lie south of Tsuquanah Point and are the visible part of the Bar. A large 1 m high rock lies on the NW side of the approach.

134   A short distance within the entrance the channel narrows to about 30 m and several rocks, covered less than 2 m, lie in the fairway. Entry should be attempted only by those with local knowledge. Nitinat Lake is often used as a harbour of refuge by fishing vessels and tugs of moderate draught. Most of the buildings in the Indian Reserve are in ruins. It is reported that there are numerous deadheads in Nitinat Lake. **Nitinat River** flows into the north end of Nitinat Lake.

Pachena Bay and River (1985)

Tsusiat Falls (1985)

Nitinat Bar and Narrows (1985)

Nitinat Bar and Narrows (1988)

Chart 3647

Carmanah Point Light (1985)

135   **Caution**. — Being exposed to the ocean swell, and especially with an ebb tidal stream, the sea on Nitinat Bar becomes very heavy and confused under adverse weather conditions. Under these circumstances no vessel should attempt to enter.

136   **Tidal streams**. — Secondary current station Nitinat Bar (Index No. 9102), referenced on Tofino, is in *Tide Tables, Volume 6.*

Juan de Fuca Strait — North Side

Chart 3606

137   **Carmanah Point** *(48°37'N, 124°45'W)* is the NW entrance point to Juan de Fuca Strait.

138   **Light**. — Carmanah Point light *(180)* is shown at an elevation of 55.6 m from a white tower 9.1 m high.

139   **Bonilla Point**, about 2 miles SE of Carmanah Point, slopes gradually to the sea. Reefs extend about 0.6 mile west and south from it. Inland of the Point mountains attain elevations in excess of 1,000 m.

140   **Light**. — Bonilla Point Fisheries light *(180.5)* is shown at an elevation of 17 m from a skeleton tower with a red triangular slatwork daymark. It is seasonal.

Chart 3647

141   **Port San Juan**, entered between **Owen Point** *(48°33'N, 124°30'W)* and **San Juan Point**, is easily identified from seaward,

appearing as a gap between two mountain ranges. It affords the first anchorage on the north shore within Juan de Fuca Strait. The Port extends about 3.5 miles inland terminating in a muddy sand beach.

142   Port San Juan is exposed to SW winds and a heavy sea rolls in when a moderate gale blows from that direction. A swell is nearly always present in the outer part of the Port. Although it is possible for a vessel with good ground tackle to ride out a gale if anchored in the most sheltered part of the Port, it is recommended that immediately the approach of a SW gale is indicated, the vessel should seek shelter in Neah Bay.

143   **Light**. — San Juan Point light *(183.5)* is shown at an elevation of 16.8 m from a white tower, with a red band at the top, on the corner of a white rectangular building.

144   **Light buoy**. — Port San Juan light and whistle buoy "YK" *(183)*, 0.7 mile SE of Owen Point, is a fairway buoy.

145   **Kellett Rock**, on the west side of the entrance about 0.5 mile NE of **Owen Island**, dries 0.9 m. **Quartertide Rocks** dry 0.9 to 2.3 m. The shoreline NE of Owen Point is fringed with islets and rock ledges.

146   **Cerantes Rocks**, on the east side of the entrance, consist of one large rock 15 m high, and several smaller rocks. **Hammond Rocks** are a group of above-water and drying rocks, the highest has an elevation of 9 m. **Woods Nose** is a small point fringed by several low islets. The shoreline NE of San Juan Point is fringed with rocks and shoals.

147   An abandoned **submarine cable** runs from close SE of San Juan Point to close NE of **Adze Head**.

Gordon River (1985)

San Juan River (1985)

Port Refrew public wharf (1985)

Chart 3647

148   **Anchorage** can be obtained anywhere in the Port in 10 to 16 m, sand bottom. A good small craft anchorage is in **Thrasher Cove** off the mouth of **Hobbs Creek**, or off the east shore about 0.4 mile NE of the public wharf.

149   **Gordon River** at the north end of Port San Juan, has a bar across its entrance with a drying spit extending from its east entrance point. In 1979 a depth of 0.4 m could be carried across this bar by keeping close to the west entrance point. Close inside the entrance anchorage for small craft can be obtained in 4 m. A gravel boat launching ramp is on the south shore just before the drying section. Private buoys mark the drying section of the channel leading to **Browns Creek**.

150   A **marina** occupies the north end of Browns Creek. A camp ground is on the north side of Browns Creek. A speed limit sign 5 MPH is posted onshore near the marina entrance.

151   **San Juan River** south of Gordon River is fronted by an extensive drying flat and has a bridge with a vertical clearance of 4 m across its entrance. The deepest route across the bar in 1979 was close to the south shore, drying 0.4 m. A submarine pipeline on the south shore 0.2 mile west of the bridge is marked by an outfall sign.

152   A gravel boat launching ramp and a float not connected to shore, are close west of the bridge.

153   **Overhead cables** with a vertical clearance of 8 m, cross the river 0.6 mile east of the bridge. Piles line the south shore of the river between the bridge and the overhead cables.

154   **Port Renfrew** in **Snuggery Cove** on the SE side of Port San Juan is the western terminal of Highway 14 that connects it to Victoria. Restricted logging roads connect Port Renfrew to Cowichan Lake. The settlement has a post office (V0S 1K0) and groceries are available in small quantities.

155   **Wharf**. — The public wharf has an approach 161 m long leading to a 33.5 by 15.2 m wharfhead with a depth of 4.5 m alongside the north face.

156   Ruins of a logging wharf are 0.3 mile ENE of the public wharf. A rock breakwater lies close east of these ruins. A float is attached to the east side of the breakwater and a concrete boat launching ramp is close east.

157   **Private mooring buoys** lie NE of the breakwater.

158   **Tides**. — Tidal predictions for Port Renfrew (Index No. 8525), are in *Tide Tables, Volumes 5 and 6*.

Chart 3606

159   **Military exercise area**. — A Canadian Forces firing and practice exercise area commences at **Sombrio Point** *(48°29'N, 124°17'W)* and extends to Sheringham Point. For details see *Notices to Mariners 1 to 46 Annual Edition*.

160   **Jordan River**, 2 miles east of **San Simon Point**, has a prominent bridge across its entrance. **River Jordan** village close east of the river mouth has a post office (V0S 1L0).

161   **A submarine pipeline** extends 0.6 mile offshore in a SSW direction from River Jordan.

162   **Tidal streams**. — Secondary current station River Jordan (Index No. 1110), referenced on Juan de Fuca Strait (East), is in *Tide Tables, Volume 5*.

163   **Tides**. — Tidal differences, referenced on Sooke, are given for **Point No Point** (Index No. 7010) *(48°24'N, 123°58'W)*, in *Tide Tables Volume 5*.

164   **Orveas Bay** lies between **Sheringham Point** *(48°23'N, 123°55'W)* and **Otter Point**, 4 miles SE.

165   **Light**. — Sheringham Point light *(186)* is shown at an elevation of 21.9 m from a white tower, 19.5 m high.

Chart 3410

166   **Sooke Bay** *(48°22'N, 123°46'W)* has a small lagoon at its head, which is a booming ground. The entrance channel to the lagoon is privately maintained. A conspicuous building is on the west side of the lagoon. A boat launching ramp and float lie west of the lagoon entrance, and another launching ramp is 0.2 mile SE of the lagoon entrance.

167   The coast between **Muir Point** on the east side of Sooke Bay and Parsons Point, the west entrance point of Sooke Harbour, is known locally as **Sooke Bluffs**.

168   A **Radio tower** with a red air obstruction light is on Muir Point.

Sheringham Point Light (1985)

Chart 3410

169   **Possession Point** *(48°20'N, 123°43'W)* should be given a fair clearance when rounding it to avoid off-lying rocks. **Secretary (Donaldson) Island** is rugged and treed. An area about half way between Secretary (Donaldson) Island and **Beechey Head** a bold wooded cliff, is known locally as Beechey Trap.

170   **Tidal streams** flowing in and out of Becher Bay, to the NE of Beechey Head, run strongly at 3 kn or more. They cause tide-rips and overfalls in the vicinity of Beechey Head.

Sooke Harbour and Approach

Chart 3411

171   **Sooke Inlet** *(48°21'N, 123°43'W)*, the entrance to Sooke Harbour and Sooke Basin, is entered between **Parsons Point** and **Company Point. Parsons Spit** extending offshore from Parsons Point has drying and below-water rocks on it.

172   **Sooke Harbour** is used extensively by commercial and sports fishing vessels. The entrance to Sooke Harbour is not visible from small craft until nearly up to **Simpson Point**, as the entrance is almost closed by Whiffin Spit and Grant Rocks.

173   **Whiffin Spit** is low and sandy with small trees and bushes on it.

174   **Grant Rocks** SE of Whiffin Spit is an extensive shoal area with several heads. The shoalest dries 1.4 m.

175   **Light. — Fog signal.** — Whiffin Spit light *(188)*, on the east end of the spit, is shown at an elevation of 6.6 m from a white tower with a green band at the top. A fog signal operated by request only to Victoria Coat Guard Radio VAK, consists of one blast on a horn every 30 seconds.

176   **Light ranges.** — Sooke Harbour Outer range lights *(188.1, 188.12)* in line bearing 049½°, lead west of Grant Rocks.

177   Sooke Harbour Inner range lights *(188.2, 188.22)* in line bearing 007½°, lead clear of the reef east of Whiffin Spit.

178   Sooke Harbour range lights *(188.4, 188.5)*, in line bearing 300½°, mark the channel leading to the public wharf.

179   **Buoys.** — South cardinal buoy "VA" and east cardinal buoy "VB" mark the SE corner of a drying area in the centre of the harbour. Port and starboard hand buoys mark the channel leading to the public wharf, the channel west of **Woodward Point** leading north to Sooke Basin and the channel west of **Middle Ground**.

Sooke Harbour and Whiffin Spit (1985)

Entrance to Sooke Basin (1985)

Chart 3411

180   Private mooring buoys lie along the edges of some drying areas.

181   **Submarine cables**. — A power cable crosses the entrance to Sooke Harbour extending east from the east extremity of Whiffin Spit. A telephone cable extends WNW across the harbour commencing from 0.1 mile SW of **Eliza Point**.

182   **Marine farm** facilities lie WNW of Harrison Point.

183   Piles lie NE of **Christie Point**. Many of the old pilings between **Harrison Point** and Whiffin Spit have rotted away.

184   **Meteorological information** for Sooke is given in the Appendices.

185   **Tides**. — Tidal predictions for Sooke (Index No. 7020) are in *Tide Tables, Volume 5*.

186   **Tidal streams** run with considerable strength around the extremity of Whiffin Spit, attaining 4 kn during large tides. Slack water, about 20 minutes duration, occurs at or near HW at Sooke.

187   **Directions**. — When entering Sooke Inlet and Sooke Harbour, exercise caution as there are navigational hazards and many vessels run into difficulties from not taking adequate precautions. Line up Sooke Harbour Outer range before crossing the bar. There is a least depth of 4.2 m over the bar extending across the entrance between Parsons and Simpson Points. In the narrow part of the channel, east of Whiffin Spit, there is a sharp turn in the channel and care has to be taken to avoid being carried onto Grant Rocks by strong tidal streams. When proceeding to the public wharf follow the channel marked by buoys and Sooke Harbour range lights. The harbour is shallow in many places but they are usually marked by kelp in summer months.

188   **Anchorage**. — No particular area is set aside as an anchorage. Open anchorage can be obtained outside the bar, about 0.5 mile offshore, in depths of about 20 m. During the fishing season vessels are often anchored in the area just north of Whiffin Spit.

189   The community of **Sooke** on the west side of the harbour has a post office (V0S 1N0) and a good variety of retail stores including hardware and laundromat. Stores are within walking distance of the public wharf.

190   **Wharves**. — The **Sooke Harbour Marina** wharf is 100 m north of Sooke Harbour range lights.

191   A series of old dolphins extend about 200 m SSW from the ruins of a fish packers wharf.

192   The **public wharf**, immediately NE of the above-mentioned wharf, has an approach 74 by 4 m leading to a 15 by 18 m wharfhead. Finger floats, each approximately 90 m long, are attached to the north side of the wharfhead. These floats have about 3 m alongside. Power, fresh water and garbage disposal facilities are available on the wharf. A public telephone is at the head of the wharf approach. An ice plant and fish buying operation are alongside.

193   Numerous small private wharves and floats, some with breakwaters, line the shore.

194   **Harbour services**. — Sooke Marine Industries can provide hull and engine repairs. Their marine ways are in Sooke Basin.

195   **Supplies**. — Fuel, water and most provisions are obtainable in Sooke.

196   **Communications**. — Sooke is connected by road with Victoria, bus service is available.

197   **Sooke Basin** is entered from the NE side of Sooke Harbour, between **Trollope Point** and **Hill Head**. The entrance to Sooke Basin requires careful navigation because of the narrow channel and extensive drying areas created by silting from the **Sooke River**. **Billings Spit** extending south from **Billings Point** is part of the above-mentioned drying areas.

198   **Facilities**. — A marine ways, belonging to Sooke Marine Industries, is 0.4 mile NE of Billings Point. A marina is 1.3 miles NE of Billings Point, close west of Goodridge Peninsula.

199   **Submarine cable and pipelines**. — A cable and a pipeline cross the entrance channel to Sooke Basin in the vicinity of Billings Point. A water pipeline crosses Sooke Basin about 0.3 mile east of Hill Head.

200   **Fishing floats**. — Numerous small fishing floats attached to fishing gear can be encountered in Sooke Basin.

201   **Tides**. — Tidal differences for Sooke Basin (Index No. 7024), referenced on Sooke, are in *Tide Tables, Volume 5*.

202   **Directions**. — To enter Sooke Basin keep in deep water along the east side of Sooke Harbour, heading toward Eliza Point. It is advisable to enter Sooke Basin after LW and during daylight hours when the drying banks are visible. There are two routes:

203   The first route is to follow the buoyed channel leading NW of Middle Ground. After passing the last spar buoy, continue parallel with shore until two floats have been passed and a double gabled house with a red roof is abeam, then turn SE and bring the island off Trollope Point ahead.

204   The second route is to follow the coast between Eliza and Trollope Points at a distance of slightly less than 0.1 mile and just outside the kelp that fronts the shore during summer months. Between Trollope Point and Hill Head, the south shore should be favoured, as Billings Spit extends south to mid-point of the channel. On large tides strong tidal streams can be encountered between Trollope Point and Hill Head.

205   **Goodridge Peninsula**, 1.5 miles NE of Billings Point, has a water tower 37 m high at its west end. Numerous piles and dolphins lie in the approach to **Cooper Cove**, which is entered east of the peninsula. An area of foul ground, with numerous snags, is in the entrance to Cooper Cove and wharves in the cove are in disrepair.

206   **Hutchinson Cove**, entered east of **Lorimer Point**, is a good anchorage but open to SW winds.

207   **Kellett Point**, 0.7 mile south of Hutchinson Cove, is the north entrance point to **Roche Cove**. A bridge 0.2 mile inside the entrance to Roche Cove has a vertical clearance of 4 m and restricts the channel to a width of 5 m. **Kellett Reef**, 0.2 mile west of Kellett Point, has two drying heads.

208   **Beacon**. — Kellett Reef daybeacon, on the west head of the reef, has a bifurcation/junction daymark, preferred channel to the right.

209   **Goodridge Islands** lie about 0.4 mile west of Kellett Point and south of them is the entrance to **Anderson Cove**.

210   **Marine farm** facilities lie around Goodridge Islands and SE of Hill Head. Oyster beds protected by leases are in Anderson Cove.

Becher Bay and Approach

Chart 3410

211   **Becher Bay** *(48°19′N, 123°37′W)*, entered between **Alldridge Point** and **Smyth Head**, is open to Juan de Fuca Strait and has several islands and numerous rocks within 0.1 mile of its

Chart 3410

Becher Bay (1991)

shores. Deadheads are likely to be encountered in the Bay. Indian Reserves are on the north and east shores and on several islands within the Bay. **Bedford Islands** lie close south of its east entrance point, and **Frazer Island** with several smaller islands lie off its east shore.

212   **Tides**. — Tidal differences for Becher Bay (Index No. 7030), referenced on Sooke, are in *Tide Tables, Volume 5*.

213   **Tidal streams** in Becher Bay are particularly strong and close attention should be paid to charted information.

214   A **submarine pipeline** (sewer outfall) is laid down the east side of Becher Bay to a discharge point SE of Frazer Island.

215   **Marinas**. — Pacific Lions Marina is on the west side of Becher Bay, in Campbell Cove and the floats are removed during winter months. Cheanuh Marina on the north side of Becher Bay NE of **Caffery Point** is protected by a floating breakwater.

216   **Campbell Cove**, on the west side of Becher Bay, is entered between **Creyke Point** and **Wolf Island**. A rock 0.2 mile NNW of Creyke Point dries 1.7 m and is marked by a private **daybeacon**.

217   **Anchorage** with good shelter can be obtained in **Murder Bay** on the north side of Campbell Cove. Several ruined cribs lie off the west side of Wolf Island and close west of these cribs is a private buoy.

218   **Buoys**. — A private mooring buoy is 0.25 mile SE of **Hoskyn Point**. Private mooring buoys are east of Yates Point.

219   The east side of Becher Bay between **Yates Point** and **John Parker Islands** is a booming ground. Numerous piles and dolphins are NE of Yates Point.

Approach to Race Rocks

Charts 3410, 3440, 3461, 3606

220   **Race Rocks** *(48°18'N, 123°32'W)* are a group of low, bare rocks. **Great Race Rock**, 9 m high is the largest of the group, the others being considerably lower. **Rosedale Rock**, 0.4 mile SE of Great Race Rock, has 1.2 m over it and is the outer danger in that direction. **West Race Rocks**, **North Race Rock** and numerous drying and below-water rocks, on which heavy dangerous overfalls and races occur in bad weather, lie within a 0.4 mile radius of Great Race Rock. Race Rocks and the surrounding area are an **Ecological Reserve** and a **Pilot Marine Protected Area**.

221   A **wind frequency table** for Race Rocks is given in the Appendices.

222   **Light. — Fog signal**. — Race Rocks light *(189)* on Great Race Rock is shown at an elevation of 36 m from a tower with black and white bands, 24.4 m high. It has a heliport. The fog signal consists of three blasts on a horn every minute.

223   **Light buoy**. — Rosedale Rock light buoy "V15" *(189.1)*, close south of the rock, is a port hand buoy.

224   **Caution**. — Wind conditions and/or wave sequences can cause tide-rips, back eddies or tidal currents to suddenly become very dangerous. Large swells can develop with little warning.

225   **Tidal streams**. — Predictions of times and rates of maximum current and times of slack water are tabulated as daily tables for current station Juan de Fuca – East (Index No. 1100), which is 4 miles south of Race Rocks *(48°14'N, 123°32'W)*. These predictions are in *Tide Tables, Volume 5*.

226   **Military exercise area**. — The Canadian Forces have established a demolition range on **Bentinck Island** *(48°18'42"N, 123°32'36"W)*. Periodic tests of small explosive charges may result in flying objects falling into the surrounding area. When red flags are flown on the Island indicating testing is in progress, keep at least 1 mile clear. Do not land on this island. For details see *Notices to Mariners 1 to 46 Annual Edition*. A private mooring buoy on the east side of the Island marks the wreck *Bernard Castle*.

Chart 3410

227   **Church Hill** *(48°19'N, 123°35'W)*, which rises NE of **Church Point**, has steep cliffs on its SE side. **Church Island**, **Little Church Island** and **Swordfish Island** are bare.

228   **Foul ground** 1.5 miles SW of Church Point contains heavy steel wire mesh.

Chart 3410

Race Rocks Light (1991)

229   **Christopher Point** is low, steep, and has the remains of a gun emplacement on it. **Whirl Bay** offers temporary anchorage during favourable conditions.

230   **Eemdyk Passage** separates Bentinck Island from Vancouver Island to the NW.

231   **Tidal streams** through Eemdyk Passage are very strong and attain 6 kn.

232   An **overhead cable** (power), with a vertical clearance of 9.8 m, crosses Eemdyk Passage.

233   **Race Passage** lies between the dangers surrounding Race Rocks and those fringing Bentinck Island. It can be used by small craft in good weather provided they have the power to offset the tidal stream that flows through it. When using this passage, favour the Bentinck Island side keeping just outside the line of kelp, as the outermost danger on the south side of the channel is covered at HW and the strongest eddies are found near it. Although the passage is deep it should not be used by ocean-going vessels.

234   **Tidal streams** in Race Passage attain 7 kn on the flood and 7.5 kn on the ebb. Dangerous tide-rips are formed. Severe tide-rips are often encountered at Christopher Point and in the vicinity of the islands off Church Point. Predictions of times and rates of maximum current and time of slack water are tabulated as daily tables for current station Race Passage (Index No. 1200) in *Tide Tables, Volume 5.*

Race Rocks to Victoria Harbour

Charts 3410, 3440

235   **Coast**. — Pedder Bay, Parry Bay, and Royal Roads, which are separated by William Head and Albert Head, form the coast between **Edye Point** *(48°19'N, 123°32'W)* and the west entrance point of Esquimalt Harbour. The shores are generally high and wooded, and in Parry Bay and Royal Roads there are sandy beaches, backed by steep cliffs in places. Esquimalt Lagoon is at the north end of Royal Roads.

236   **Caution**. — Numerous marinas and concentrations of small craft can be encountered in the vicinity of Pedder Bay and Victoria. Vessels may be engaged in sailing races, fishing or cruising.

237   **Military exercise area**. — Mariners are cautioned that a Canadian Forces exercise area is established in the approach to Esquimalt and Victoria Harbours. For details see *Notices to Mariners 1 to 46 Annual Edition.*

Chart 3410

238   **Controlled Access Zone** – Exists between **Fossil Point** and **Helgesen Point**. For details see *Notices to Mariners 1 to 46 Annual Edition.*

239   **Pedder Bay** *(48°20'N, 123°33'W)* affords anchorage in 10 to 12 m about 0.3 mile ENE of **Manor Point**. Although the

Race Passage on ebb looking west (1991)

Race Passage on flood looking east (1991)

Chart 3410

Pedder Bay (1991)

holding ground is good it is exposed to SE winds, and a gale from that direction would make it neither safe nor a desirable anchorage.

240   **Submarine cables and pipelines** restrict anchorage inside Pedder Bay. A cable and pipeline cross Pedder Bay in the vicinity of **Watt Point**. Sewer pipelines run down the centre of Pedder Bay from **Point Ash** to Helgesen Point and a pipeline extends 0.2 mile ESE from Helgesen Point.

241   **Tides**. — Tidal differences for Pedder Bay (Index No. 7080), referenced on Victoria, are in *Tide Tables, Volume 5*.

242   **Lights**. — Two lights are shown from the outer end of the Department of National Defence (DND) jetty.

243   **Beacon**. — A daybeacon, 0.1 mile NW of Manor Point, has a fluorescent orange diamond-shaped slatwork daymark.

244   **Buoys**. — A DND buoy marked "NAVY", about 0.3 mile ENE of **Fossil Point**, lies in the approach to Pedder Bay and two "NAVY" buoys lie off the north shore in the vicinity of **Anchor Rock**.

245   Port hand buoy "V11" marks the rocks extending west from Watt Point.

246   **Berths**. — The DND wharf is for handling ammunition. Its north face has a berthing length of 80 m with a least depth of 7.6 m alongside. Permanent mooring lines extend from the outer end of the wharf to Manor Point.

247   The Lester B. Pearson College of the Pacific float is on the north shore of Pedder Bay about 0.5 mile NW of **Weir Point**.

248   A **marina** near the head of Pedder Bay was dredged to 1.8 m in 1976.

Charts 3410, 3440

249   **William Head** *(48°20'N, 123°32'W)* is a comparatively low promontory on which the red brick buildings of a Federal Penitentiary are conspicuous.

250   **Tides**. — Tidal differences for William Head (Index No. 7082), referenced on Victoria, are in *Tide Tables, Volume 5*.

251   **Mary Hill**, 0.8 mile west of William Head, has grassy slopes on its south side. **Quarantine Cove** fronts onto the penitentiary grounds.

252   **Parry Bay** affords sheltered anchorage in west winds. **Haystock Islets** are bare and almost joined to shore at LW by drying mud flats at the mouth of **Witty's Lagoon** which is a bird sanctuary.

253   A **submarine cable** is laid down the length of Parry Bay.

254   A **measured distance** of 1,849 m in a 027°41' – 207°41' direction is in Parry Bay. Limits are marked by **daybeacons** with fluorescent orange diamond-shaped slatwork daymarks. The front beacon of the north transit is on the east Haystock Islet.

255   **Anchorage** can be obtained in about 12 m 0.5 mile north of William Head. This anchorage should only be used in fine weather or when sheltering from strong west winds.

256   **Prohibited anchorage**. — In the north part of Parry Bay.

257   **Foul ground**, considered hazardous to vessels fishing or towing underwater bodies lies within a 0.5 mile radius of *48°21'44"N, 123°29'15"W*.

258   **Albert Head** *(48°23'N, 123°29'W)* is a moderately high projection that slopes down to the water's edge; its extremity is

Charts 3410, 3440

bare, but the remainder is wooded. A DND pier with a float attached is in a small bay on the west side. A seasonal yellow buoy deployed May to October and marked "NAVY" is on the east side of the 6.1 m shoal 0.4 mile north of Albert Head.

Chart 3440

259 **Wrecks.** — A wreck 1.8 miles ESE and another wreck 2.1 miles east of Albert Head *(48°23′N, 123°26′W)*, at depths of about 70 m, are considered a hazard to nets and towed underwater equipment.

260 A **radio tower**, with two red air obstruction lights disposed vertically, is on **Triangular Hill** *(48°25′N, 123°31′W)* about 2.5 miles NW of Albert Head.

261 **Constance Bank**, with depths less than 30 m, is about 2 miles long and about 1 mile wide and lies with its NE extremity about 5.5 miles ESE of Albert Head. Several shoal patches are on the bank and the least depth 15.5 m is near its NW side. Vessels should not anchor on the bank, as its bottom is rocky. Heavy tide-rips sometimes occur over the bank.

262 **Light buoy. — Racon.** — Victoria Harbour Cautionary light buoy "VH" *(203)* *(48°22′32″N, 123°23′29″W)* is in the approach to Esquimalt and Victoria Harbours. It is fitted with a Racon (— • —).

263 **Pilot boarding station.** — The boarding and disembarking station for the Pacific Pilotage Authority lies within a 2 mile radius of Victoria Harbour Cautionary light buoy.

264 **Spoil ground.** — An ocean dump site *(48°22.5′N, 123°21.8′W)* used for dumping mud, clay, rock, wood wastes and concrete blocks was discontinued from active use in 1997.

265 **Conspicuous dome.** — The white Dominion Astrophysical Observatory dome, on **Observatory Hill** *(48°31.2′N, 123°25′W)*, is conspicuous from the approach to Victoria and Esquimalt Harbours.

266 **Controlled Access Zone** – Exists in the approach to **Esquimalt Harbour**. For details see *Notices to Mariners 1 to 46 Annual Edition.*

267 **Anchorage** in **Royal Roads** *(48°25′N, 123°28′W)* is prohibited except in the designated positions shown on the chart.

268 **Fishing prohibited.** — Fishing is prohibited in the area of Royal Roads, about 1.7 miles NE of Albert Head and in the entrance to Esquimalt Harbour between Fisgard Island and Duntze Head.

269 **Submarine cables**, some with power running through them, are laid in the approach to and in Esquimalt Harbour.

270 **Buoys.** — Several orange or yellow unlit buoys maintained by DND are in Royal Roads.

271 **Coghlan Rock**, east of Albert Head, is 1 m high and a shoal with 6.1 m over it lies 0.4 mile north of Albert Head.

272 A **pier** for barges and a conspicuous gravel pit are 1.2 miles north of Albert Head.

Charts 3419, 3440

273 **Esquimalt Lagoon**, partially separated from Royal Roads by **Coburg Peninsula**, is entered close south of **Gotha Point** *(48°26′N, 123°27′W)* by a shallow channel. The channel passes under a timber bridge with a vertical clearance of 2.6 m and a horizontal clearance of 5 m. Esquimalt Lagoon is a bird sanctuary.

Esquimalt Harbour

Chart 3419

274 **Controlled Access Zones** – Exists in the approach to **Esquimalt Harbour** and inside the harbour. For details see *Notices to Mariners 1 to 46 Annual Edition.*

275 **Esquimalt Harbour** *(48°26′N, 123°26′W)* is a Canadian Forces Navy base and a port for repairing large commercial vessels. Repair and refit facilities are used by bulk carriers, tankers and passenger vessels. The largest vessel to use these facilities in recent years was approximately 244 m long with a draught of 13 m.

276 **Conspicuous objects.** — Conspicuous tower cranes are visible from the approach to Esquimalt Harbour. Two are on the south side of Constance Cove at the Naval Dockyard, and one is on the north side of Constance Cove at the Esquimalt Graving Dock. They have red air obstruction lights.

277 **Harbour limits.** — Esquimalt Harbour limits are defined as: "All the tidal waters northward from a line running east and west through the southernmost tip of the southernmost of the Brothers Islands".

278 **Regulations** for Esquimalt Harbour are the *Practices and Procedures for Public Ports* with the addition of several special rules that govern towing and the length of tow, speed limits in specific areas, prohibited anchorages, prohibited fishing areas and rules regarding mooring. The harbour is administered, for Transport Canada, by the Harbour Master whose office is at 12 Erie Street, Victoria, B.C. V8V 4X5 telephone (250) 363-3578.

279 The Harbour Master's office and the harbour patrol craft are equipped with VHF radios and monitor Channel 73.

280 **Radio report.** — All vessels inward or outward bound are requested by the Harbour Master to advise the Queen's Harbour Master Operations on Channel 10 of their position before transiting the area between Fisgard Island and Duntze Head.

281 **Customs.** — Vessels proceeding direct to Esquimalt should report their estimated time of arrival to the Collector of Customs at Victoria by radio. By giving as much notice as possible officials can board on arrival.

282 **Tides.** — Tidal differences for Esquimalt (Index No. 7110), referenced on Victoria, are in *Tide Tables, Volume 5.*

283 **Tidal streams** in Esquimalt Harbour and for some distance outside are weak. At the entrance, between Scroggs Rocks and Macaulay Point, the west entrance point of Victoria Harbour, tidal streams run parallel with shore at ½ to 2 kn. The flood sets SE and the ebb NW.

284 **Brothers Islands**, SE of the entrance to Esquimalt Harbour, consist of two groups of islands and islets. The largest island is 12 m high with some bushes near its north end, the others are bare. The passage between the islands and shore is foul.

285 **Scroggs Rocks**, NW of Brothers Islands, are two drying rocks south of the east entrance to Esquimalt Harbour.

286 **Light.** — Scroggs Rocks light *(196)* is shown from a white tower with a red band at the top.

287 **Fisgard Island**, the west entrance point of Esquimalt Harbour, is bare and connected to **Rodd Point** by a causeway.

288 **Light.** — Fisgard Sector light *(197)*, on the island, is shown at an elevation of 21.6 m from a white tower 14.6 m high and is floodlit at night. A two storey red building is attached to the light tower.

Major Port Facilities — Esquimalt Harbour

Berth	Wharf Length (m)	Least Depth (m)	Elevation (m)	Remarks
Jetty A – North Face	230	8.3-8.9	1.8	Berthing dolphin 30 m off west end. Tower crane, fresh water, power, telephone and shore gangway. Designed to berth "Provider" class vessels at a velocity of 0.19 m/sec.
Jetty A – East Face	60	3.2-4.3	1.8	Tower crane, fresh water, power, telephone and shore gangway.
Jetty B – East Face	183	4.2-10.7	1.5	Tower crane, fresh water, power, telephone and shore gangway.
Jetty B – West Face	90	3-11	1.5	Tower crane, fresh water, power, telephone and shore gangway.
Jetty C (inside piers)	139	8.9	2.3	Mobile crane serves all berths.
Jetty C – West Face West Pier	200	6.6-11.3	2.3	
Jetty C – East Face East Pier	200	2.7-9.6	2.3	
MCDV Jetty	57	4-6		Fresh water, power, telephones and shore gangway.
Jetty E (Public Works and Government Services Canada)	290	7.4-10.2	2.1	Fresh water, power, telephones and shore gangway.
Esquimalt Graving Dock North Wall Outing Wharf (Public Works and Government Services Canada)	244	9.1	1.3	150 and 50 tonne travelling cranes.
Jetty D – North Face	137	7.9	1.4	Used for handling Naval stores and equipment.
Jetty D – East Face	137	4-5.7	1.4	8,129 m² open storage.
Jetty F – North Side	230	5.6-10	1.7	Bunkering jetty – bunker fuel loaded at 3,000 bbls/hour. Diesel fuel loaded at 91 kl/hour. Fresh water, telephones and shore gangway. Port hand daybeacon marks drying reef at inner end.
Jetty F – South Side	198	7-9	1.7	Bunkering jetty – bunker fuel loaded at 3,000 bbls/hour. Diesel fuel loaded at 91 kl/hour. Fresh water, telephones and shore gangway. 30 m float at inner end.
Fuel Float				North of Jetty F. Used for fuelling Naval auxiliary vessels.
Jetty G (Colwood Jetty)	60	7.9		Four mooring dolphins and four mooring buoys, two at each end. Fresh water, power, telephone and shore gangway.

289   **Light buoy**. — Fisgard Island light buoy "V17" *(198)*, off the east edge of the shoal area fringing the island, is a port hand buoy.

290   **Duntze Head**, the east entrance point of Esquimalt Harbour, is the extremity of a peninsula on which the Canadian Forces Base is located. The point, 0.2 mile SE of Duntze Head, is known locally as **Black Rock**. It has a gun turret on it. A cream-coloured building, 0.2 mile SE of Duntze Head, is conspicuous. An abandoned signal tower on **Grant Knoll** north of Duntze Head is not conspicuous from the outer approach.

291   **Light range**. — Inskip Islands range lights *(199, 200)*, on the largest of the **Inskip Islands**, in line bearing 015° lead through the entrance of Esquimalt Harbour.

292   **Fishing prohibited**. — Fishing is prohibited in the entrance to Esquimalt Harbour between Fisgard Island and Duntze Head and in an area east of **McCarthy Island**.

293   **Military exercise area** WM extends across the harbour from Jetty F to **Munroe Head**.

294   **Village Rocks**, in **Constance Cove**, are a small group of drying rocks. **Pilgrim Cove** and **Lang Cove** are at the head of Constance Cove. **Malacca Patch** lies in the entrance to Pilgrim Cove.

295   **Light buoy**. — Village Rocks light buoy "V20" *(201)* is a starboard hand buoy.

296   **Lights**. — Fixed red lights are shown at an elevation of 69 m from the top of cranes at the Naval Dockyard. Lights are on the outer ends of most jetties.

297   **Canadian Forces Sailing Association floats** protected by breakwaters are at **Munroe Head**.

298   **Paddy Passage** leads between the Inskip Islands and **Ashe Head**.

299   **Whale Rock**, 0.2 mile WNW of Inskip Islands, has 1.7 m over it.

300   **Light buoy**. — Whale Rock light buoy "VC" *(202)* is a starboard bifurcation buoy.

301   **Beacon**. — A daybeacon with a port hand daymark marks a drying ledge on the north side of Jetty F.

302   **Booming grounds** lie north of Inskip Islands in **Plumper Bay**.

303   Safe **anchorage** can be obtained in the inner harbour north of a line joining **Yew Point**, Grant Knoll and Ashe Head with the exception of the prohibited area off McCarthy Island.

304   **Caution**. — Log debris and deadheads on the bottom are in the area north of a line joining Ashe Head, Whale Rock and McCarthy Island.

305   **Wharves and jetties** in Constance Cove and along the west shore of Esquimalt Harbour are part of Canadian Forces Base Esquimalt. Used for berthing Canadian Navy, Government, and visiting Navy vessels.

306   **Supplies**. — Provisions of all kinds are obtainable in quantity from Victoria. Fresh water is laid to all wharves and jetties.

307   **Fuel**. — Fuelling facilities are for naval vessels only. Bunker fuel can be supplied by tanker or barge by arrangement with oil companies in Victoria. Gasoline and diesel fuel can be supplied by tank truck by arrangement.

308   **Repair facilities**. — There are two dry docks and a marine railway. Esquimalt Graving Dock is the largest non-military graving dock on the West Coast of the Americas. It can handle 90% of

Chart 3419

all vessels operating on the West Coast of North America and most vessels up to 100,000 dwt. It is owned and operated by Public Works and Government Services Canada and contracted out to a number of private companies for ship repair and refitting. It has been modified to allow cruise ship stabilizer repair.

Esquimalt Graving Dock (250) 363-3526
Extreme length: 357.8 m
Breadth at entrance: 41.1 m
Depth over sill at MHWS: 12.2 m
Depth over blocks: 12 m
Equipment: 150 and 50 tonne traveling cranes on north wall, 30 tonne on south wall

Canadian Forces Dry Dock
Extreme length: 146.6 m
Breadth of bottom of dock: 19.8 m
Depth over sill at MHWS: 8.8 m
Depth over blocks at entrance: 7.8 m
Depth over blocks at head: 7.5 m
Used by military and auxiliary vessels only.

Marine Railway south of Pier C
Lifting capacity: 181 tonnes
Extreme length of cradle: 39 m
Bearing length of cradle: 33 m
Depth forward: 4.6 m
Depth aft: 5.2 m
Capable of end handling and side transfer
Used by military and auxiliary vessels only.
Caution. — Track is approximately 1 m above seabed.

Victoria Harbour

Chart 3412

309   **Saxe Point** *(48°25'N, 123°25'W)* is fringed with cliffs. A park is on the point. **Gillingham Islands** are bare. The passage between Gillingham Islands and **Royal Point** is not recommended because of underwater rocks. A seasonal yellow buoy, deployed May to October and marked "NAVY", is close SW of the islands. **Fleming Bay**, protected by a **breakwater**, is only used by small craft. It has several floats and a launching ramp.

310   **Beacons**. — Gillingham Islands daybeacon, on the SE drying reef, has two port hand daymarks.

311   Fleming Bay daybeacon, on the end of the breakwater, has two starboard hand daymarks.

312   **Submarine cables** cross the entrance to Fleming Bay and a cable (fibre-optic) is laid south through the bay then east along the north side of Juan de Fuca Strait. **Submarine pipelines** extend from the north shore of the bay.

313   **Brotchie Ledge** *(48°24'N, 123°23'W)*, in the SE approach to Victoria Harbour, has a rock bottom and is marked by kelp.

314   **Light**. — Brotchie Ledge light *(205)* is shown from a white tower, with a green band at the top.

315   **Light buoy**. — Victoria Harbour Entrance light buoy "V21" *(204.5)*, 0.2 mile south of Harrison Island, is a port hand buoy.

316   **Victoria Harbour** (www.victoriaharbour.org) is entered between **Macaulay Point** and Ogden Point breakwater. East of a line joining Colvile Island and Shoal Point up to the Johnson Street Bridge is known as **Inner Harbour**.

317   **Aspect**. — The harbour entrance is easily recognized by the breakwater and a long, low grey building close north on the east side of the entrance. **McLoughlin Point**, on the west side of the entrance, has conspicuous white buildings and oil storage tanks on it. At night the illuminated sky-line of Victoria is conspicuous.

318   **Harbour limits**. — Victoria Harbour is a Public Harbour and its limits, see *Chart 3440*, are defined as: "All the waters of Juan de Fuca Strait north of a line drawn from the southerly tip of Trial Island to the southerly extremity of Albert Head and including Selkirk Water and the navigable streams flowing into Victoria Harbour. Excluded from this area will be Esquimalt Harbour".

Fleming Bay (1994)

Chart 3412

Victoria Harbour approach (1997)

319   **Regulations** for Victoria Harbour are *Practices and Procedures for Public Ports* with the addition of several special rules that govern fuelling procedures, towing and the length of tow, speed limits in specific areas, prohibited anchorages, prohibited fishing areas, sewage discharge and mooring. The Harbour is administered for Transport Canada by the Harbour Master whose office is at 12 Erie Street, Victoria, B.C. V8V 4X5 telephone (250) 363-3578.

320   The Harbour Master's office and harbour patrol craft are equipped with VHF radios and monitor Channel 18A.

321   **Victoria Harbour Traffic Scheme**. — Victoria Harbour is home to many activities including international ferry services, commercial tugs and barges, fishing fleets, harbour ferries and water taxis, whale watching operations, seaplanes and numerous power driven and non-power driven recreational craft such as kayaks and sculls. There are also numerous "Special Events" that have an impact on harbour traffic and general operations.

322   **Aviation and marine traffic** in Victoria Harbour has increased over the past few years and co-operation is needed to ensure efficient operations and safety in the harbour. The following rules, special procedures and restrictions apply to all vessels and seaplanes operating in Victoria Harbour.

323   **Harbour Characteristics**. — For the purposes of this traffic scheme, Victoria Harbour may be considered in four parts:
- **Outer Harbour** extending from the breakwater to Shoal Point
- **Middle Harbour** extending from Shoal Point to Laurel Point
- **Inner Harbour** extending from Laurel Point to the Johnson Street Bridge
- **Upper Harbour** extending north of the Johnson Street Bridge

324   Located in the middle of the Middle Harbour and extending into the Outer Harbour are two unmarked *Seaplane Take Off and Landing Areas*.

325   Located on the south of the Middle Harbour and extending into the Outer Harbour are two **Inbound/Outbound Traffic Lanes**. The eastern portion of the division between the outbound and the inbound traffic lanes is marked with four cautionary **light buoys** *(208.2, 208.4, 208.6, 208.8)*. A white and orange information buoy is located south of the Songhees Point shoreline. It marks the eastern most limit of the seaplane area and separates non-power driven vessel traffic from seaplanes.

Rules and Restrictions

326   **Speed Limit**. — The speed limit is 5 kn in Victoria Harbour inside a line from Shoal Point to Berens Island, and 7 kn outside the line.

327   **Minimize Wake**. — All vessels are required to minimize their wake in order to prevent damage to shore facilities and other vessels.

328   **No Sailing**. — Sailing is prohibited in the Middle, Inner and Upper Harbour. All sails must be lowered even when under power.

329   **Anchoring** is prohibited without permission of the Harbour Master.

330   **Note**. — Persons failing to comply with these rules and restrictions may be subject to summary conviction and/or fines. The Victoria Harbour Traffic Scheme is not a 'traffic separation scheme' as defined in *Rule 10* of the *Collision Regulations*. Authority is derived from the *Canada Marine Act*.

Vessel Operating Procedures

331   **Power driven vessels less than 20 m in length**, including sailboats, are to transit the Outer Harbour and the Middle Harbour via the vessel *Inbound/Outbound Traffic Lanes*, as indicated on the chart.

332   **Power driven vessels of 20 m in length** or greater are to transit the Middle Harbour via the *Seaplane Take Off and Landing Areas*.

333   **Non-power driven vessels** such as rowboats, rowing sculls, kayaks and canoes are permitted to use the Outer, Middle, Inner and Upper Harbour for recreational purposes. Non-power driven vessels are requested, whenever possible, to avoid the centre channel under the Johnson Street Bridge by remaining between the fender piles and the shore on either the east or west side when transiting to and from the Inner Harbour. When entering the Middle Harbour from the Inner Harbour non-power driven vessels are to remain north of the white and orange information buoy located south of the Songhees Point shoreline. While in the Middle Harbour, or in transit to the Outer Harbour, non-power driven vessels are requested to operate north of Pelly Island and to remain close to the north shore until west of Colvile Island. While in transit from the Outer Harbour to the Upper Harbour, non-power driven vessels may transit by using the *Inbound Traffic Lane* or by

remaining close to the north shore. Non-power driven vessels should use **extreme caution** when operating in larger vessel docking areas such as the Huron Street Public Port Facility.

334   **All Vessels** entering or exiting the *Inbound/Outbound Traffic Lanes* should merge gradually into the appropriate traffic lane. All vessels should avoid crossing traffic lanes. However, if crossing a traffic lane is unavoidable, vessels should cross at right angles to traffic lane. All vessels are reminded that there is a black water dumping prohibition in effect for waters in Victoria Harbour north of Ogden Point Breakwater. Pump out facilities are located at the Coast Harbourside floats and at Village Marina north of Johnson Street Bridge.

335   **Caution**. — All vessels navigating in the area between Songhees and Laurel Points, near the *Inbound/Outbound Traffic Lanes* should use extreme caution. Additional caution is also required in the area between Berens Island and Shoal Point where traffic from West Bay, the Middle Harbour and the Outer Harbour all converge near the north/south *Seaplane Take Off and Landing Area*.

336   **Three short blasts** of a large ferry's whistle (*MV Coho*) means it is in astern propulsion. Stay well clear. Never cross in front of a ferry or in its wake.

Rules of the Road — Collision Avoidance

337   **A seaplane on the water** shall, in general keep well clear of all vessels and avoid impeding their navigation. In circumstances, however, where risk of collision exists, vessels (including seaplanes) are required to comply with the *Collision Regulations*.

338   Mariners are reminded that *Part B, Steering and Sailing Rules*, of the *Collision Regulations* describe responsibilities between vessels in all conditions of visibility.

Seaplanes

339   **Aviation procedures** request that pilots take-off southbound in the north/south seaplane take off and landing area. Landings will most likely occur either eastbound in the east/west seaplane take off and landing area or northbound in the north/south take off and landing area. However, wind, water and aircraft load conditions may be such that aircraft will take off or land in either area, in either direction.

340   **Seaplane Inclement Weather Operating Area** in the West Bay area may be used for take off in some high wind conditions. Because of varying weather conditions, boat operators should not count on pilots always being able to operate completely within the designated areas. Therefore, boaters must remain vigilant at all times. To aid boaters white strobe lights located at Berens Island, Shoal Point, Laurel Point and Pelly Island, are activated by the Flight Service Station up to 60 seconds prior to a seaplane taking off or landing. Seaplanes will normally activate on board landing/pulsating lights prior to take off.

341   Aircraft may have to leave the *Seaplane Take Off and Landing Areas* to make way for other planes and may use the *Inbound/Outbound Traffic Lanes* until being able to return to the *Seaplane Take Off and Landing Areas*.

342   **Aircraft Holding Area** is located SE of Laurel Point and has been designated for one seaplane to hold for short periods while waiting for a berth at one of the seaplane docks.

343   **Aircraft operate** in Victoria Harbour from 0700 local time until 30 minutes past sunset.

344   **Contact the Harbour Master** for general harbour information or to report marine incidents such as navigational hazards or pollution on VHF Channel 73 or (250) 380-8177. For berthing information call the Harbour Master or Wharfinger on VHF Channel 73 or (250) 363-3578.

345   **Heliports** are at the Coast Guard base south of Shoal Point, south of Camel Point and at hospitals.

346   A **submarine pipeline** (sewer outfall) extends 1 mile offshore from west of Macaulay Point.

347   **Submarine cables**, some with power passing through them, cross the harbour in several locations.

348   **Customs**. — Victoria is a port of entry, the customs office is at the corner of Wharf and Government Streets. A customs wharf is on the east side of Inner Harbour, close SW of the foot of Fort Street telephone (250) 363-3339 or 1-888-226-7277.

349   **Meteorological information** and a frequency of fog table for Victoria are given in the Appendices.

350   **Tides**. — Tidal predictions for Victoria (Index No. 7120) are in *Tide Tables, Volume 5*. In Portage Inlet, near the NW extremity of Victoria Harbour, there is a great variation in time differences with Victoria. A long stand at HW is followed by a small drop to the next LW. The latter, at Portage Inlet, occurs at or near 1.8 m on the rising tide at Victoria. Range of tide is about 50% of that at Victoria.

351   **Tidal streams** of 2 kn can be encountered flowing across the entrance to the harbour, between Macaulay Point and Brotchie Ledge. The flood sets SE and the ebb NW. In the Inner Harbour tidal streams do not present any difficulties. Only in Upper Harbour and Gorge Waters will significant velocities be encountered. Secondary current station Gorge-Tillicum Bridge (Index No. 1305), referenced on Victoria, is given in *Tide Tables, Volume 5*.

352   **Ogden Point** *(48°25'N, 123°23'W)*, the east entrance point to Victoria Harbour, has the main harbour breakwater extending west from it. The waters around Ogden Point breakwater are a Marine Sanctuary and closed to divers for taking or killing many marine species. Because of the large number of persons fishing from the breakwater, the **Harbour Master requests all vessels reduce speed and wash**, and give extra clearance when passing this area.

353   **Special precautions**. — During strong SE or SW winds very great care is necessary in going alongside the wharves at Ogden Point and it is desirable to have an anchor in readiness. At times with a SW gale, the wharves are unapproachable. In such cases it is recommended that the vessel proceed to an anchorage to await improvement in conditions.

354   **Light**. — Ogden Point breakwater light *(204)*, on the outer end of the breakwater, is shown from a white tower with a red band at the bottom.

355   Immediately north of Ogden Point breakwater are the **Pacific Pilotage Authority** floats and Westcan Terminals. Pier A has a prominent, long, low grey building on it. Lights on Westcan Terminals are privately operated.

356   A **wreck** lies close offshore about 85 m north of Westcan Terminals.

357   **Foul ground** hazardous to surface navigation lies NE of Camel Point.

358   Between Westcan Terminals and **Shoal Point** are the facilities of the Coast Guard Victoria Base. Fixed red lights are

Chart 3412

Ogden Point Wharves (1997)

Victoria Inner Harbour (1997)

shown from the SW corner of the Coast Guard wharf and their heliport. The hovercraft ramp is close SE of the light. Cautionary **buoy** "VQ" is south of Shoal Point.

359   **Light. — Aeronautical light**. — Shoal Point light *(207)*, west of the point, is shown from a dolphin.

360   **Rose Bay** between McLoughlin Point and **Work Point** has a rockfill breakwater protecting some floats extending from its west side. Two rocks lie in the centre of the bay.

361   **Work Island** and **Berens Island** lie close south and east of Work Point. Berens Island has a rock ledge extending east from its NE point.

362   **Light. — Aeronautical light**. — Berens Island light *(206)* is on the SE extremity of the island.

363   **West Bay** is entered between Berens Island and **Colvile Island**. A channel dredged to a depth of 1.5 m leads NW through West Bay to the marinas. The outer end of the channel is marked by port hand buoy "V23", and the north side of this channel is marked by dolphins.

364   **Pelly Island**, on the north side of Inner Harbour about 0.3 mile ENE of Berens Island, is about 1 m high and bare. **Sleeper Rock**, close west of Pelly Island, is a drying rock marked on its south end by a port hand daybeacon.

365   **Light. — Aeronautical light**. — Pelly Island light *(208)* is on the south extremity of the island.

366   Condominiums and a hotel line the north shore between **Lime Bay** and **Songhees Point**. **Tuzo Rock** close east of Songhees Point dries.

367   **Light**. — Tuzo Rock light *(210)* is on the rock.

368   **Beacon**. — **Discovery Rock** daybeacon, about 0.1 mile NE of Tuzo Rock on the SE extremity of a drying spit, is a white tower with a green band around the top.

369   **Light. — Aeronautical light**. — Laurel Point light *(209)* is on the NW extremity of the point.

370   **James Bay**, SE of Laurel Point, has the Provincial Parliament Buildings near its south end and the Empress Hotel near its east end. Ferry wharves form the SW side of James Bay NW of the Undersea Gardens. Public floats along the east side of James Bay provide facilities for pleasure craft. Ship Point wharf is on the north side of James Bay. It is used by pleasure craft and small commercial vessels.

371   **Victoria** is the seat of the Provincial Government. The fort and foundation of the city were established in 1843 and given the name Fort Albert, which was soon changed to Fort Victoria. The name Victoria was adopted in 1852 when the townsite was laid out.

372   **Wharves**. — Only wharves, on the east side of the harbour, between Ogden and Shoal Points can accommodate ocean-going vessels. Details are given in the adjacent table.

373   **Island Research and Development wharf**, close east of Shoal Point, has a least depth of 4.6 m alongside.

West Bay marinas (1997)

Fishermen's Floats (1997)

James Bay (1997)

Major Port Facilities — Victoria Harbour

Berth	Wharf Length (m)	Least Depth (m)	Elevation (m)	Remarks
Westcan Terminals Ltd Ogden Point Docks Pier A – South Side	305	10.7		Used by cruise ships May to October. Freshwater at 18 tonnes/hour. Power 120v/100 amps. 11,612 m² covered storage, 6 ha open storage.
Ogden Point Docks Pier A – North Side	244	9.8-10.7		As above
Ogden Point Docks Pier B – North Side	244	10.7-12.5		As above
Ogden Point Docks Pier B – South Side	244	9.4-11.3		As above
Canadian Coast Guard	220	3.1-9		
Imperial Oil (Esso)	50	6.2		3 berthing dolphins at wharfhead. Bulk loading and discharging company's products.

374 The **Tanker wharf**, close east of Island Research wharf, is 30 m long on its outer face and has a depth of 5.8 m alongside. A fuel float is at the east end.

375 **Public finger floats** east of the above-mentioned L-shaped wharf are generally used by the fishing fleet. Between May 30 and August 31 when the fishing fleet is at sea, they are used by pleasure craft. Coast Guard vessels use the westernmost float.

376 A **ferry wharf**, on the west side of James Bay, is 148 m long. The extension of this wharf to the SE is 162 m long and used by Black Ball Ferry providing daily service to Port Angels for vehicles and passengers.

377 **Public finger floats**, on the east side of James Bay, have depths on the outside of 3.2 m and 2 m along the inside of the main float. These floats are used by pleasure craft.

378 **Ship Point wharf**, on the NE side of James Bay, is 155 m long on its south face and was dredged (1982) to a depth of 6 m alongside. Depths of 5.8 m lie about 15 m off the wharf face. The north face is 64 m long and has a least depth of 4.9 m alongside.

379 North of Ship Point wharf are small craft floats, a seaplane terminal, and the Customs wharf.

380 **Public floats** close north of the Customs wharf consist of a large T-shaped float with numerous finger floats extending from it. Seaplane floats are close north of the public floats. Additional public floats protected by a floating breakwater are close south of Johnson Street Bridge.

381 **Supplies**. — Provisions of all kinds are available in quantity and fresh water is laid on most of the wharves. Bunker fuel can be delivered by barge, provided sufficient notice is given. Diesel fuel, stove oil, gasoline and a variety of lubricants can also be supplied.

382 **Repairs**. — Hull and machinery repairs can be undertaken in either Victoria or Esquimalt. Larger vessels have to go to the dry dock in Esquimalt for underwater repairs.

383 **Salvage. — Towage**. — Seaspan International Limited maintains fully equipped ocean-going tugs for towing and salvage, as well as smaller tugs to assist in docking and undocking.

384 **Communications**. — B.C. Ferries operates frequent service to Vancouver through Swartz Bay, 27 km north of Victoria. Black Ball Transport Company of Seattle maintains regular passenger and car ferry service to Port Angeles throughout the year. Victoria Clipper operates a passenger catamaran between Victoria and Seattle. Coastal freight is handled mainly by tug and barge.

385 Frequent **bus services** are available to Vancouver and points on Vancouver Island.

386 Regular **air services** to Vancouver and Seattle, with connections to the North American continent and other parts of the

world, are available from the Victoria International Airport, 24 km north of Victoria. Seaplane flights to Vancouver and waypoints are available from Inner Harbour. Helicopter service to Vancouver is available from the heliport at Camel Point.

387 **Rail transportation** is limited to service between Victoria and Courtenay.

388 **Johnson Street Bridge** at the NE end of Inner Harbour consists of separate road and rail spans. It is manned 0800 to 1600 hours daily. It will not be opened except for an emergency between 0700 to 0900 hours and 1600 to 1800 hours on weekdays. Communication with the bridge is made on Channel 12, 156.6 MHz, call sign VAH20, telephone (250) 385-5711. Application for bridge openings outside these hours must be made in advance. A fee is charged for this service. Give as much notice as possible through the City Fire Department telephone (250) 385-5711. The signal for opening the bridge is three blasts on a ships horn.

389 **Mariners must maintain watch on Channel 12** while transiting the bridge. The purpose of this instruction is to enable the bridge operator to advise transiting traffic of any change in vessel traffic in vicinity of the bridge.

390 **Flashing amber light** at the top of the bridge structure indicates the bridge operator has received the signal. Should the operator be unable to lift the bridge, the amber light will be switched to flashing red.

391 White strobe light, at the lift ends of both spans, are to alert aviators the bridge is being raised.

392 **Vertical clearance** under the Johnson Street Bridge at HW is 5.5 m and the width of the channel between fender pilings is 37 m.

393 **Upper Harbour**, between Johnson Street and Point Ellice Bridges, is surrounded by an industrial complex. Residential development is gradually replacing many of the old industries.

394 **Point Ellice Bridge** at the north end of Upper Harbour has a vertical clearance of 8.9 m.

395 **Selkirk Water** extends from the Point Ellice Bridge to Chapman Point.

396 **Beacon. — Sister Rocks** daybeacon with a port hand daymark marks the north end of these rocks.

397 **Halkett Island** has shoal water extending SW from it marked at its outer end by starboard hand buoy "V24". Small craft floats are east of Halkett Island.

398 **Selkirk Trestle** crosses Selkirk Water. This is a former railroad bridge now used by pedestrians and cyclists. The navigation channel under the bridge has a vertical clearance of 1.8 m and a width of 4.9 m. The bridge is usually in a closed position but will

Chart 3412

Public floats - foot of Fort Street (1997)

Public floats - Johnson Street Bridge (1997)

be opened upon request by contacting the Johnson Street Bridge operator from 0800 to 1600 daily.

399   **A submarine cable** crosses Selkirk Water midway between the Selkirk Trestle and Chapman Point.

400   **Submarine pipelines** cross Selkirk Water at **Chapman Point**. A pipeline extends toward Gorge Waters from the south shore SSW of Chapman Point.

401   **Gorge Waters** leads NW from Chapman Point to **Portage Inlet**. Numerous private floats line the shores.

402   **Bridges. — Gorge-Tillicum Bridge** crosses Gorge Waters at **The Gorge** and has a vertical clearance of 7.3 m. **Craigflower Bridge** at the entrance to Portage Inlet has a vertical clearance of 2.4 m.

403   **Tidal streams** through The Gorge are extremely strong, with maximum rates of 5 kn on the flood and 7 kn on the ebb. Secondary current station Gorge-Tillicum Bridge (Index No. 1305), referenced on Victoria, is in *Tide Tables, Volume 5*.

404   **Tides.** — The range of tide in Portage Inlet is about 50% of that at Victoria. There is also a great variation in the time differences with Victoria. A long stand at high water is followed by a small drop to the next low water. This low water occurs at about 1.8 m on the rising tide at Victoria.

405   **Caution. — The Harbour Master reports rescuing a number of overturned vessels from this location every year.**

Victoria to Discovery Island

Chart 3440

406   Between Victoria and Cadboro Point *(48°27'N, 123°16'W)* the coast is fronted by numerous off-lying islands and rocks. Ocean-going vessels destined for Vancouver or New Westminster proceed outside these dangers following the Traffic Separation Scheme, and pass east of Discovery Island. Coastal vessels and others with moderate draught sometimes pass through the islands via Mayor Channel, Baynes Channel or Plumper Passage.

Chart 3424

407   **Clover Point** *(48°24'N, 123°21'W)* is a low point, bare of trees and can be identified by a large parking area on it. It is lit with streetlights at night.

408 **Tides**. — Tidal differences for Clover Point (Index No. 7115), referenced on Victoria, are in *Tide Tables, Volume 5*.

409 **Submarine pipelines and cables**. — A sewer outfall extends 0.3 mile offshore from the east side of Clover Point. Abandoned submarine cables cross the entrances to **Ross Bay** and **Gonzales Bay**. A submarine cable, with an anode array at its outer end, extends about 130 m from the NE shore of Ross Bay. Submarine pipelines (storm drains) extend south into Ross and Gonzales Bays.

410 **Conspicuous objects**. — The flagstaff on **Beacon Hill** *Chart 3440* is prominent. A grey cylindrical water-tower, 1.3 miles NNE of Clover Point, can be identified by a conspicuous apartment building close north. A white dome and historic monument are on **Gonzales Hill** north of **Harling Point**.

411 **Trial Islands** *(48°24'N, 123°18'W)*, rocky and bare, appear as a single island from most directions. The largest island has **Staines Point** at its south extremity. Trial Islands are an Ecological Reserve.

412 **Light**. — Trial Islands light *(212)*, close to the extremity of Staines Point, is shown at an elevation of 28.3 m from a white tower 10.2 m high.

413 **Radio towers** 56 m high are in the centre of the largest Trial Island. Two red air obstruction lights disposed vertically are shown from each tower.

414 **Tidal streams** attain 3 to 6 kn, in vicinity of Trial Islands, and heavy tide-rips occur off Staines Point, particularly with the flood stream. When a strong wind opposes the tidal stream a heavy, steep sea, dangerous to small vessels is raised. Staines Point should be given a wide berth.

415 **Enterprise Channel**, locally known as Trial Island Pass, lies between Trial Islands and the south coast of Vancouver Island. Local knowledge is advised before attempting this channel. The fairway is tortuous and less than 0.1 mile wide in its narrowest part. Tidal streams run at 3 kn and there is a considerable amount of kelp. **Mouat Reef**, which dries 0.9 m, lies on the north side of the east entrance and has a depth of 1.5 m about 0.1 mile SW of it. This reef is marked by south cardinal buoy "VE" and by kelp in summer and autumn.

416 **Submarine pipelines and cables**. — A sewer outfall, west of **McMicking Point**, extends 0.1 mile south into Enterprise Channel. An abandoned submarine cable extends across the channel from close east of **Kitty Islet** to the north end of Trial Islands. Other cables cross the west entrance between Harling Point and Trial Islands.

417 **Brodie Rock** *(48°24'N, 123°17'W)* is a pinnacle with 5.5 m over it rising from a ridge in 20 m of water.

418 **Gonzales Point** *(48°25'N, 123°18'W)*, known locally as **Golf Course Point**, is low, rocky, bare of trees and fairly steep-to on its east side. Green fairways of the Victoria Golf Club NW of Gonzales Point are conspicuous.

419 **Chain Islets**, a group of scattered rocks and islets on an extensive shoal, lie 1 mile NE of Gonzales Point. **Great Chain**

Trial Islands Light (1991)

Chart 3424

Enterprise Channel from south of Harling Point (1988)

Enterprise Channel from Brodie Rock (1988)

Discovery Island Lighthouse from SW (1979)

Island the largest of the group is bare. Kelp fringes shoal areas in this vicinity. Chain Islets and surrounding area are an Ecological Reserve.

420   **Discovery Island** *(48°25′N, 123°14′W)* lies at the junction of Juan de Fuca and Haro Straits. It is wooded and rises to 38 m at **Pandora Hill**. **Discovery Island Marine Park** consists of the south half of the island.

421   **Light**. — Discovery Island light *(216)*, on the east extremity of the island, is shown at an elevation of 28.3 m from a white tower 10.7 m high.

422   **Tidal streams**. — Heavy tide-rips, often dangerous to small craft, are formed in vicinity of Discovery Island particularly near **Sea Bird Point**, and off foul ground fronting **Commodore Point**.

Channels West of Discovery Island

423   **Mayor Channel** west of Great Chain Island is the passage generally used by coastal vessels. It is entered from the south between **Thames Shoal** *(48°25′N, 123°17′W)* and the reefs extending south from Great Chain Island. The north entrance is between **Lewis Reef** and **Fiddle Reef**. The passage between Lewis and Fiddle Reefs is known locally as the Goal Posts.

Mayor Channel from south (1979)

Oak Bay approach (1988)

Oak Bay Entrance (1988)

Chart 3424

Oak Bay (1988)

Baynes Channel from NE (1988)

424   **Tidal streams** follow the fairway of Mayor Channel at 2 to 3 kn. The flood sets north and the ebb south.

425   **Mouat Channel**, on the west side of Mayor Channel, separates Thames Shoal from **Lee Rock**. **Harris Island**, **Robson Reef**, **Emily Islet** and **Tod Rock** lie on the west side of Mayor Channel in the approach to Oak Bay.

426   **Buoy**. — Port hand buoy "V25" lies close south of Lee Rock.

427   **Lights**. — Lewis Reef light *(213)* and Fiddle Reef Sector light *(215)* are on the reefs.

428   **Beacons**. — Harris Island North daybeacon has a port hand daymark.

429   Robson Reef daybeacon has a bifurcation/junction daymark, preferred channel to the right.

430   Tod Rock daybeacon has a starboard hand daymark.

431   **Oak Bay** to the west of Mayor Channel has a large marina on its south side. It is entered between the breakwater at **Turkey Head** and the breakwater projecting south from **Mary Tod Island**.

432   **Speed limit**. — A speed limit of 4 kn is prescribed in the *Boating Restriction Regulations* for that part of Oak Bay west of Mary Tod Island.

433   **Light. — Buoys**. — Mary Tod Island light *(214)* is on the south extremity of Mary Tod Island breakwater.

434   **Starboard hand buoy "V26"** marks the outer end of a reef extending west from Mary Tod Island. Numerous private mooring and cautionary buoys lie to the west.

435   **Tides**. — Tidal differences for Oak Bay (Index No. 7130), referenced on Victoria, are in *Tide Tables, Volume 5*.

436   **Prohibited boating area** at the north end of Oak Bay fronting **Willows Beach** is reserved for swimmers.

437   **Cattle Point** *(48°26′N, 123°17′W)* is the site of a park with boat launching ramps. A speed limit of 5 kn applies in this area.

438   **Beacon**. — Cattle Point daybeacon on a drying rock close north of the point has a bifurcation/junction daymark, preferred channel to the left.

439   **Cadboro Bay**, though open to the SE, is not subject to heavy seas. Tugs and rafts shelter here. A rock breakwater on the west side of the bay shelters the **Royal Victoria Yacht Club**. Cadboro Bay and its approach are often used for yacht races, various buoys and markers are likely to be encountered. Several private mooring buoys are in the bay.

440   **Hecate Passage** *(48°25′N, 123°15′W)* separates **Spencer Ledge** from **Virtue Rock**, about 0.2 mile east.

Chart 3424

441   **Plumper Passage**, which separates Discovery and Chatham Islands from the Chain Islets, is entered from the south between Virtue Rock, with 0.6 m over it, and Commodore Point 0.6 mile east. The north entrance is between **Carolina Reef** *(48°25'N, 123°16'W)*, which dries 1.2 m, and **Heritage Point** 0.6 mile NE.

442   **Tidal streams** of 3 to 5 kn can be expected within Hecate and Plumper Passages. The flood stream begins almost immediately after LW, it runs for about 3 h 45 min after which, there is a period of slack water. The ebb stream then runs until LW, or for about 7 hours.

443   **Baynes Channel** *(48°27'N, 123°16'W)* leads to Haro Strait between the NW part of the Chatham Islands group and the islands and shoals extending from **Cadboro Point**. The area surrounding Cadboro Point is an Ecological Reserve.

444   **Depths. — Dangers.** — The channel has no dangers in the fairway with the exception of the 4.6 m shoal lying 0.5 mile south of Cadboro Point.

445   **Light.** — Baynes Channel North light *(216.3)* is on an islet 0.1 mile ESE of Cadboro Point.

446   **Tidal streams** set along the axis of Baynes Channel, at 4 to 6 kn in the north entrance, between Strongtide Islet and Cadboro Point, and at 2 to 3 kn in its south entrance. Secondary current station Baynes Channel (Index No. 1225), referenced on Race Passage, is given in *Tide Tables, Volume 5*. The flood sets NE and the ebb SW. Winds can be very changeable in Baynes Channel. A strong wind opposing the tide will cause heavy tide-rips with short steep seas.

447   **Submarine cables** cross Baynes Channel from **Maynard Cove** to Chatham Islands.

448   **Chatham Islands** *(48°26'N, 123°15'W)*, on the east side of Baynes Channel, are a compact group of islands and rocks. The islands are low, wooded and almost connected at LW. **Alpha Islet**, **Griffin Island** and the surrounding area are an Ecological Reserve.

449   **Strongtide Islet** about 15 m high is the NW island of the Chatham Islands. It is rocky, wooded and moderately steep-to on its NW side.

450   **Radio towers.** — Radio towers 9 m high with red air obstruction lights are on Strongtide Islet. A radio tower 47 m high is on **Vantreight Island**. The largest of the Chatham Islands has radio towers 62 m high with red air obstruction lights.

451   **Jemmy Jones Island**, 0.5 mile SW of Cadboro Point on the west side of Baynes Channel, is bare and is an Ecological Reserve.

CHAPTER 2

Haro Strait, Boundary Pass and Gulf Islands

General

Charts 3461, 3462, 3463

1 This chapter describes Haro Strait, Boundary Pass, the passages leading west from Haro Strait and the east coast of Vancouver Island between Cadboro Point *(48°27′N, 123°16′W)* and Round Island *(49°07′N, 123°48′W)*. Channels leading through the Gulf Islands, south of Dodd and False Narrows, are also described.

2 United States coasts of the San Juan Islands bordering the east side of Haro Strait and the south side of Boundary Pass are briefly described. For complete information see *United States Coast Pilot 7*.

3 **The main shipping route** connecting Juan de Fuca Strait to the Strait of Georgia is via Haro Strait and Boundary Pass. Several channels leading through the Gulf Islands can be entered from the north end of Haro Strait and the north side of Boundary Pass. Satellite, Swanson, Trincomali, and Stuart Channels lead to ports along the Vancouver Island coast. Active Pass and Porlier Pass connect channels within the Gulf Islands to the Strait of Georgia. Active Pass is used by large fast ferries that connect the mainland to Vancouver Island. Porlier Pass is generally used by large freighters bound from the Strait of Georgia to ports along Vancouver Island.

4 **The most frequented routes used by tugs and barges and pleasure craft**, when proceeding between Juan de Fuca Strait and the Strait of Georgia, is through Sidney Channel and its continuation Moresby Passage on the west side of Haro Strait. From the north end of Moresby Passage the route leads through Swanson and Trincomali Channels and enters the Strait of Georgia through Active Pass. To avoid busy ferry traffic through Active Pass, the route through Captain Passage, Trincomali Channel and Porlier Pass is frequently used. This route is more sheltered than the Haro Strait/Boundary Pass route and there are several good anchorages along it.

5 **Pleasure craft** are encountered in large numbers throughout the area. Sport and commercial fishing craft are also encountered, they usually congregate near the entrances to narrow passages and off prominent headlands where fishing is good.

6 **Gulf Islands National Park Reserve** is comprised of sites scattered throughout the southern Gulf Islands. It includes sites from D'Arcy Island north to Prevost Island, and Portland Island east to Tumbo Island. The park office is in Sidney. Waters surrounding or adjacent to park lands, generally 200 m perpendicularly distant from the natural boundary of the land, are a protected marine zone managed by Parks Canada. Camping is permitted in designated areas only; no camping on islets. Dogs must be leashed on park lands.

7 **Meteorological information** for Victoria International Airport and Cowichan Bay, and a wind frequency table for Saturna Point Light (East Point) are in the Appendices.

Haro Strait and Boundary Pass

Charts 3440, 3441, 3461, 3462

8 **Haro Strait** *(48°35′N, 123°19′W)* lies between Juan de Fuca Strait and Boundary Pass, encompassing the waters between San Juan Island and Vancouver Island. The southern limit is between Sea Bird Point (Discovery Island) and Cattle Point (San Juan Island). On the west, limits are between Cadboro Point (Vancouver Island) and the northern end of the eastern Chatham Island, then to the northern shore of Discovery Island. The north limit is a line from the northernmost extremity of Saanich Peninsula through Harry Point (Piers Island) to Kanaka Bluff (Portland Island). Then from the north extremity of Portland Island to Reynard Point (Moresby Island), and from Point Fairfax (Moresby Island) to Turn Point (Stuart Island). The eastern limit is from the south extremity of Stuart Island to McCracken Point (Henry Island), then from the south point of Henry Island to the SW entrance point of Mitchell Bay on San Juan Island.

9 **Boundary Pass**, between Haro Strait and the Strait of Georgia, encompasses the area from Stuart Island to Patos Island. The southern limit is between Turn Point (Stuart Island) and Point Fairfax (Moresby Island). The NW limit is between Pelorus Point (Moresby Island), to Wallace Point (North Pender Island), then to Tilly Point (South Pender Island), and then from Teece Point to Taylor Point (Saturna Island). The north limit is between East Point (Saturna Island) and Alden Point (Patos Island). The SE limit is between Alden Point (Patos Island) and Point Hammond (Waldron Island), then from Sandy Point (Waldron Island) to Charles Point (Stuart Island).

10 **The main shipping route to Vancouver** follows the Traffic Separation Scheme east of Discovery Island, then through the portion of Haro Strait lying east of Sidney Island, through Boundary Pass entering the Strait of Georgia between East Point (Saturna Island), and Alden Point (Patos Island).

11 Haro Strait and Boundary Pass are deep and for the most part wide. Great caution and vigilance are necessary because of reefs in some parts and the rate and varying directions of tidal streams.

12 The **International Boundary** between Canada and the United States runs along the centre of Haro Strait and Boundary Pass.

13 A **Traffic Separation Scheme** in the south approach to Haro Strait leads SW in Canadian waters toward Victoria. It is recommended for use by all ships. Mariners are advised that a revised Traffic Separation Scheme in Rosario Strait came into force at **0000 Coordinated Universal Time (UTC) on 1 December, 2002**. Major changes to the traffic separation schemes are:

 a) expansion of precautionary area "RB" at the south end of Rosario Strait; and

 b) re-alignment of the existing Traffic Separation Scheme with the Separation Scheme north of Rosario Strait, and their linkage with a new precautionary area off East Point.

Charts 3440, 3441, 3461, 3462

Mariners should familiarize themselves with changes shown on charts.

14 The Traffic Separation Scheme leading SE in United States waters leads into the mandatory Puget Sound Vessel Traffic Service. Details and regulations are in *United States Coast Pilot 7*.

15 **Turn Point. — Special Operating Area (SOA).** — Turn Point Special Operating Area has been established to enhance order and predictability, efficient and safe movement of goods and services, and to further reduce risk of accidents with respect to vessels transiting boundary waters of Haro Strait and Boundary Pass in vicinity of Turn Point.

16 Turn Point Operating Area consists of those waters contained within a four sided area connected by a line drawn from Turn Point light *(255)* to 48°42.4'N, 123°13.967'W to Arachne Reef light *(254.3)* to Tom Point light *(225)*.

17 **Movement Procedures**. — The following operating standards apply to all VTS participant vessels within or approaching Turn Point Special Operating Area from Haro Strait northbound for Boundary Pass or Swanson Channel and from Boundary Pass southbound for Haro Strait. They do not apply to vessels southbound out of Swanson Channel.

(a) A VTS participant, if towing astern, do so with as short a hawser as safety and good seamanship permits.

(b) A VTS participant of 100 m or more in length will make best efforts consistent with safety and industry practices:

  (i) Not to enter the Turn Point SOA when another VTS participant of 100 m or more in length is already located in the SOA, unless:

    1) When following astern a minimum .5NM (5 cables) separation is maintained with the vessel ahead;

    2) When overtaking in the SOA with the concurrence of MCTS Victoria that there is no opposing traffic and a CPA of at least .5NM (5 cables) is maintained;

    3) If outbound from Boundary Pass and meeting an inbound vessel from Haro Strait already in the SOA, enter only after the outbound vessel is past the vector heading of the inbound vessel engaged in the turn and maintain at least a .5NM (5 cables) CPA;

    4) If inbound from Haro Strait and meeting an outbound vessel from Boundary Pass already in the SOA, enter only after the outbound vessel has crossed a bearing line between Turn Point and Arachne Reef and maintain at least a .5NM (5 cables) CPA.

  (ii) Maintain a distance off of Turn Point of at least .3NM (3 cables).

18 All VTS participants are expected to report to *Victoria Traffic* northbound at *Calling-in Point 4* Brotchie Ledge and *Calling-in Point 5* Hein Bank, and southbound at *Calling-in Point 7* East Point. *Victoria Traffic* will provide the necessary traffic advisory information for *Calling-in Point 6* Turn Point.

19 All VTS participants are expected to report to *Victoria Traffic* at *Calling-in Point 6* (3 miles from Turn Point). *Victoria Traffic* will provide the traffic advisory information for Turn Point SOA and the next Calling-in Point. This traffic advisory will include opposing vessels name, ETA for Turn Point, and vessels speed.

20 All VTS participants approaching Turn Point SOA are expected to make safe passing arrangements with other VTS participants at either Monarch Head or Blunden Islet southbound; and Lime Kiln Light *(LL222/US19695)* or Kellett Bluff Light *(LL229/US19720)* northbound. These arrangements should be made no later than reaching CIP 6 at Gowlland Point *(LL253/US19800)* southbound, and approximately abeam Danger Shoal Light and Horn Buoy *(US19775)* northbound.

21 **Vessel Traffic Services** (VTS). — Haro Strait and Boundary Pass are in *Sector 1* of the *Vancouver Traffic Zone*, administered by *Victoria Traffic*. Assigned frequency is 156.55 MHz, Channel 11.

22 *Calling-in Point No. 5*, *Hein Bank*, is a line joining Hein Bank light buoy with Cattle Point light *(221)*. Administered by *Victoria Traffic* and *Seattle Traffic*.

23 *Calling-in Point No. 6*, *Turn Point*, is when approaching Turn Point light *(255)* and is a circle with a 3-mile radius centred on Turn Point light.

24 *Calling-in Point No. 7*, *East Point*, is a line joining Saturna Island Sector light *(264)* to Patos Island Sector light *(265)*.

25 A brief description of the *Vancouver Traffic Zone* is in *PAC 200*. Details are in *Radio Aids to Marine Navigation (Pacific and Western Arctic)*.

26 **Racons** are fitted to light buoys at Hein Bank and Rosenfeld Rock.

27 **Magnetic anomaly**. — A local magnetic anomaly, as much as 4° from normal variation, has been observed on the east side of Haro Strait in the vicinity of **Bellevue Point** *(48°32'N, 123°11'W)*.

28 **Tides**. — Tidal differences along Haro Strait and Boundary Pass, all referenced on Fulford Harbour (Index No. 7330), are given for Finnerty Cove (Index No. 7140), Saanichton Bay (Index No. 7255), Sidney (Index No. 7260), Swartz Bay (Index No. 7270), Narvaez Bay (Index No. 7345) and Bedwell Harbour (Index No. 7350) in *Tide Tables, Volume 5*.

29 **Tidal streams**. — Secondary current stations Haro Strait (Index No. 1230) *(48°35'N, 123°14'W)*, Boundary Pass (Index No. 1260) *(48°45'N, 123°05'W)* and Sidney Channel (Index No. 1232) *(48°37'N, 123°20'W)* referenced on Race Passage (Index No. 1200), are in *Tide Tables, Volume 5*.

30 **Between the south entrance of Haro Strait and Turn Point** the tidal stream sets fairly through the main channel of Haro Strait on the ebb, but on the flood stream a huge gyre is present to the east of Discovery Island, see diagram. The main flood stream that runs along the south shore of Discovery Island sets NE toward San Juan Island resulting in a strong set to the north along San Juan Island, and a southerly set in the west portion of Haro Strait off Discovery Island.

31 This tendency of the flood stream to confine itself to a narrow band along the Canadian shore, from Staines Point (Trial Islands) to Sea Bird Point (Discovery Island), results in the gyre at the south end of Haro Strait and delay in the turn of the tidal stream to ebb off Sidney Island, which can be anywhere from 1 h 10 min to 2 h 30 min later than the turn predicted at Race Passage.

32 **On the United States side of Haro Strait**, when tidal streams off Kellett Bluff reach their maximum velocity, direction on the flood is about north and on the ebb about 170°. Maximum rate, generally greater on the ebb stream, can amount to 4 kn. On reaching Turn Point, the flood stream divides, the main current continuing toward Active Pass in a direction about 340° while the

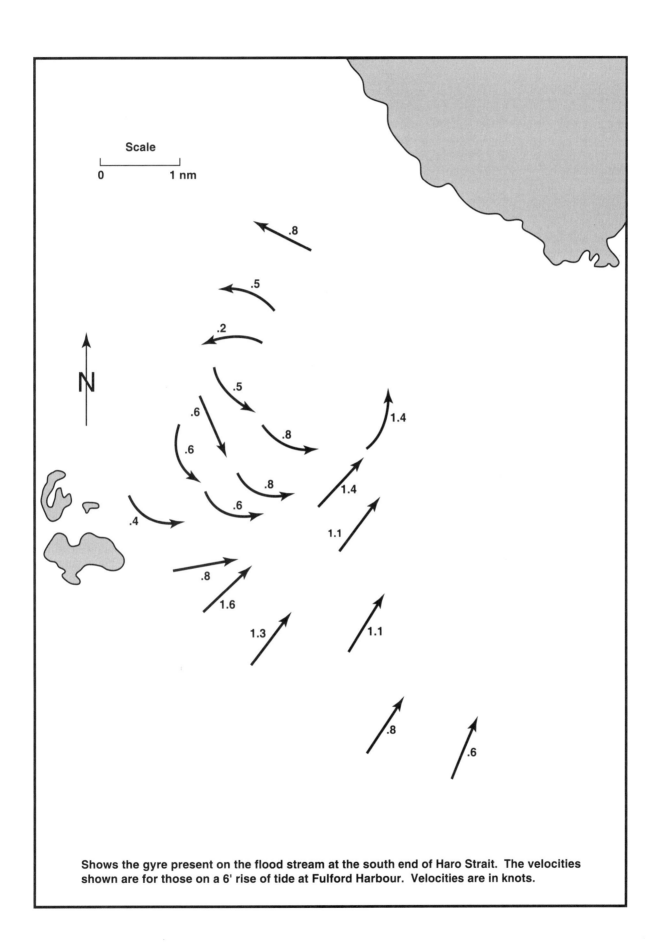

Scale

0   1 nm

N

.8

.5

.2

.5

.6

.6

.6

.8

.8

.6

.4

1.4

1.4

1.1

.8

1.6

1.3

1.1

.8

.6

Shows the gyre present on the flood stream at the south end of Haro Strait. The velocities shown are for those on a 6' rise of tide at Fulford Harbour. Velocities are in knots.

Charts 3440, 3441, 3461, 3462

weaker current branches off into Boundary Pass. Consequently at Turn Point the flood is variable in direction, sometimes setting toward the east end of South Pender Island and frequently curving round the north side of Stuart Island. During the strength of the flood, the current runs up the centre of Boundary Pass in the direction of Patos Island.

33　　At a position with Turn Point bearing 216°, distant 1.3 miles, the ebb begins promptly and for the first hour the direction is about 284°, then becoming 260°. On large tides the maximum velocity on the ebb is 4 kn.

34　　**Heavy tide-rips** are formed round Discovery Island, between Henry Island and Turn Point, and on the south-going tidal stream round Turn Point. In bad weather, there are heavy tide-rips on the small banks lying in mid-channel east and NE of Fulford Reef *(48°26'N, 123°14'W)*.

35　　Near the east end of Boundary Pass, at secondary current station Boundary Pass *(48°45'N, 123°05'W)*, during the first hour of flood the direction of the current is 014° changing to 070° at about the time of maximum velocity. The ebb begins in a 195° direction, changing to 216° at maximum velocity. Duration of slack at both HW and LW is 10 to 12 minutes. On the ebb the current runs in surges, forming eddies, whereas the flood runs more evenly.

36　　Between Saturna and Patos Islands tidal streams are strong and somewhat erratic with tide-rips and eddies. Care should be observed when navigating in this area. The passage between Patos Island and Sucia Islands is almost free of tide-rips and the tidal currents set more fairly through it. They are less strong and more regular than those between Saturna and Patos Islands.

37　　**Submarine cables**. — A cable (fibre optic) crosses the south approach to Haro Strait. A submarine cable crosses Haro Strait from 1 mile north of Ten Mile Point to San Juan Island 1.2 miles north of Bellevue Point. A cable (fibre optic) is laid from Cordova Bay then north and east through Haro Strait, Boundary Pass and across the Strait of Georgia.

38　　A **ferry** crosses the north end of Haro Strait running between Sidney, B.C. and Anacortes, Washington via Friday Harbor. Charted ferry routes are general indications of the route followed.

Haro Strait — South Approach

Charts 3440, 3461, 3462

39　　**Hein Bank** *(48°21'N, 123°03'W)* lies in Juan de Fuca Strait and the approach to the south entrance to Haro Strait, it has a least depth of 4.1 m.

40　　**Light buoys**. — Hein Bank isolated danger light buoy "DH" *(US 16361)* is on the bank.

41　　Hein Bank light buoy "1" *(US 16362)*, 1 mile NNE of the bank, is a port hand buoy fitted with a Racon (— • —).

42　　**Middle Bank** *(48°25'N, 123°06'W)* has a least depth of 19.8 m over it. In heavy weather tide-rips occur on and in vicinity of this bank.

43　　**Cattle Point** *(48°27'N, 122°58'W)* is the south extremity of San Juan Island. **Salmon Bank**, a shoal spit, extends 1.5 miles SSW from Cattle Point.

44　　**Light**. — Cattle Point light *(221)* is shown at an elevation of 28.7 m from a tower. The fog signal consists of one blast on a horn every 15 seconds.

45　　**Light buoy**. — Salmon Bank light and gong buoy *(US 16365)*, at the south end of the bank, is a port hand buoy.

46　　**San Juan Island**, on the east side of Haro Strait, is rugged and partially wooded. **Mount Dallas** *(48°31'N, 123°08'W)*, the highest of several hills, rises abruptly from the west shore to an elevation of 329 m.

47　　**Eagle Point** is 3 miles WNW of Cattle Point. The shore NW of Eagle Point is steep-to and rocky. **Pile Point** is 2.7 miles WNW of Eagle Point. **Kanaka Bay**, close east of Pile Point, is a small cove used by fishing vessels.

48　　**Fishing vessels**. — During the fishing season, June to October, many fishing vessels anchor close inshore at night, generally between Cattle and Pile Points.

Haro Strait — South End

Chart 3440

49　　**Light**. — Lime Kiln light *(222) (48°31'N, 123°09'W)*, on a headland on the north side of **Deadman Bay**, is shown at an elevation of 16.8 m from an octagonal tower. The fog signal consists of one blast on a horn every 30 seconds. Two buildings are SE of the light.

50　　**Alpha Islet**, the outermost islet of the Chatham Islands group, is 5 m high and bare.

51　　**Fulford Reef**, 0.8 mile NW of Alpha Islet, consists of a group of drying reefs. The highest dries 1.5 m.

52　　**Light buoy**. — Fulford Reef light buoy "VK" *(215.5)* is a north cardinal buoy.

53　　**Beaumont Shoal** *(48°27'N, 123°11'W)*, in the centre of the traffic separation zone, has 17.1 m over it. Several shoal pinnacles lie in the separation zone to the north and south of Beaumont Shoal. A shoal with a least depth of 13.4 m lies 1.1 miles north of Beaumont Shoal.

54　　**Light buoy**. — Haro Strait light buoy "VD" *(216.4)*, close south of Beaumont Shoal, is a south cardinal buoy.

55　　**Ten Mile Point** is 1.2 miles WNW of Fulford Reef.

56　　**Telegraph Cove**, **Finnerty Cove** and **Arbutus Cove** lie between Ten Mile Point and **Gordon Head**, 3 miles NNW. **Cormorant Point** is 0.3 mile west of Gordon Head. **Gordon Rock**, 0.15 mile north of Gordon Head, dries 1.5 m.

57　　A **submarine pipeline** (sewer outfall), close south of Finnerty Cove, extends 0.2 mile offshore. Another pipeline is in the south part of Finnerty Cove.

58　　**Tides**. — Tidal differences for Finnerty Cove (Index No. 7140), referenced on Fulford Harbour, are in *Tide Tables, Volume 5*.

59　　**Johnstone Reef**, 1 mile east of Finnerty Cove, dries 0.6 m. Port hand buoy "V29" lies close-off the reef.

60　　The **wreck** of a former refugee carrying vessel "Black Dragon" sank 0.9 mile NW of Johnstone Reef in December 2003. This steel hulled vessel is 42 m long, 7 m wide and has a draft of 5 m.

61　　**Zero Rock**, 1.8 miles NNE of Gordon Head, dries 3 m. It lies in the south approach to Cordova and Sidney Channels. Shoal pinnacles and a rock with less than 2 m over it lie within 0.5 mile north of Zero Rock.

62　　**Light**. — Zero Rock light *(223)* is shown at an elevation of 8.5 m from a white tower with a green band at the top.

Chart 3440

63   **Little Zero Rock**, 1 mile WNW of Zero Rock, dries 2.4 m and is steep-to on its east side. Shoal pinnacles and a rock with less than 2 m over it extend 0.6 mile WNW from Little Zero Rock.

64   **Light buoy**. — Little Zero Rock light buoy "V30" *(222.8)*, 0.6 mile WNW of Little Zero Rock, is a starboard hand buoy.

65   **Anchorage** can be obtained in the south part of **Cordova Bay**, about 1 mile NNW of Gordon Head. The holding ground is good and depths are 15 to 16 m.

66   **Military exercise area**. — Located in the north end of Cordova Bay and extends north to Cordova Spit. For details see *Notices to Mariners 1 to 46 Annual Edition*.

67   **Cowichan Head** *(48°33'N, 123°22'W)* has conspicuous white cliffs that gradually decline in elevation on either side.

68   **Kelp Reefs** *(48°33'N, 123°14'W)*, in the centre of Haro Strait, consist of a group of below-water and drying rocks. The main shipping channel through Haro Strait lies between Kelp Reefs and San Juan Island.

69   **Light**. — Kelp Reefs light *(224)*, on a drying reef at the east side of the reefs, is shown at an elevation of 10.7 m from a white tower.

Haro Strait — North End

Chart 3441

70   **Little D'Arcy Island** *(48°34'N, 123°16'W)*, 1.5 miles NW of Kelp Reefs, is wooded.

71   **Unit Rocks**, 0.5 mile SE of Little D'Arcy Island, consist of a group of drying and below-water rocks, the highest rock dries 1.8 m. Part of Gulf Islands National Park Reserve.

72   **Hughes Passage** separates D'Arcy Island from Sidney Island to the north and leads west from the main shipping channel of Haro Strait into Sidney Channel. On its south side it is encumbered with drying and above-water rocks extending 0.3 mile north from D'Arcy and Little D'Arcy Islands. **Sallas Rocks**, extending 0.5 mile south from Sidney Island, encumber the north side of this passage; the highest rock of this group has an elevation of 10 m.

73   **Wymond Point**, 0.9 mile ENE of Sallas Rocks, is the south extremity of Sidney Island.

74   **Halibut Island**, 1.1 miles NNE of Hamley Point, is wooded and has shoal areas south and SE.

75   **Light buoy**. — Mandarte Island light buoy "UT" *(225.1)*, 0.4 mile north of Halibut Island, is an east cardinal buoy.

76   **Gooch Island** *(48°40'N, 123°17'W)* is wooded. A conspicuous red and white watch-tower and a house beside it are on the NW part of the island. **Rum Island** lies close-off the east end of Gooch Island, its east extremity is **Tom Point**. Rum Island, also known as Isle-de-Lis, is part of Gulf Islands National Park Reserve. Camping in designated areas only.

77   **Light**. — Tom Point Sector light *(225)*, on an islet east of the point, is shown at an elevation of 6.4 m from a white tower with a green band at the top.

78   **Artificial reef**. — *HMCS Mackenzie* was sunk close north of Gooch Island as an artificial reef for divers. It is marked by cautionary/information buoys and has mooring buoys.

79   **Cooper Reef**, 0.5 mile north of Tom Point, dries 2.1 m. **Arachne Reef**, 1 mile NW, has three drying heads and lies in the centre of the east entrance of Prevost Passage.

80   **Light**. — Arachne Reef light *(254.3)*, on the north side of the reef, is shown at an elevation of 5.8 m from a white tower with a green band at the top.

81   **Spoil ground**. — A non-active ocean dump site is centered at *48°41'N, 123°16.4'W*.

82   **Moresby Island** *(48°43'N, 123°19'W)* has a prominent hill near the middle of its south end. **Point Fairfax** is the south extremity of Moresby Island. A bare rock 4 m high and steep-to lies close SE.

83   **Light**. — Point Fairfax light *(254.5)*, on the bare rock close SE of the point, is shown at an elevation of 8.8 m from a white tower.

84   **Kellett Bluff** *(48°35'N, 123°12'W)*, the SW extremity of Henry Island, is steep, rocky and prominent from north and south. **Henry Island** is separated from San Juan Island by **Mosquito Pass** and **Roche Harbor**.

85   **Light**. — Kellett Bluff light *(229)* is shown at an elevation of 24.4 m from a small white building with a black and white diamond-shaped daymark.

86   **McCracken Point** is the north extremity of Henry Island. **Battleship Island**, 0.2 mile WNW of McCracken Point, is small and 9 m high. **Danger Shoal**, 0.9 mile north of Battleship Island, has 1.8 m over it and is marked by kelp.

87   **Light buoy**. — Danger Shoal light and horn buoy *(US 19775)* is a port bifurcation buoy.

88   **Stuart Island** *(48°40'N, 123°12'W)* is wooded and has two prominent hills in its central part. **Turn Point**, the NW extremity of Stuart Island, is a bold, steep-to bluff.

89   **Light**. — Turn Point light *(255)* is shown at an elevation of 13.4 m from a white tower. The light is obscured from 260°30' to 357°. The fog signal consists of two blasts on a horn every 30 seconds. A white building with a red roof is close SE.

Boundary Pass — North Side

90   **Pelorus Point** *(48°43'N, 123°17'W)* is the east extremity of Moresby Island and the SW entrance point to Swanson Channel. **Tilly Point**, 3.5 miles ENE of Pelorus Point, is the SE entrance point to Bedwell Harbour and Swanson Channel. The shore of South Pender Island between Tilly Point and **Gowlland Point**, 1 mile east, is fringed with rocks and should not be approached within a distance of about 0.2 mile.

91   **Light**. — Gowlland Point light *(253)* is shown at an elevation of 10.7 m from a white tower with a green band at the top.

92   **Plumper Sound**, entered between **Blunden Islet** and **Taylor Point**, 2 miles NE, is described later in this chapter. Blunden Islet is rocky with a few trees and is part of Gulf Islands National Park Reserve, no camping.

93   **Tide-rips** are encountered in the vicinity of Blunden Islet.

94   A **conspicuous television tower**, 1.7 miles WNW of Taylor Point, is near the summit of **Mount Warburton Pike**. The tower has an approximate height of 62 m and is marked by three red air obstruction lights disposed vertically.

95   **Java Islets**, 0.8 mile east of Taylor Point, are bare and rocky and part of Gulf Islands National Park Reserve.

96   **Narvaez Bay**, entered east of **Monarch Head**, is free of dangers. It is not recommended as an anchorage except in fine weather as it is exposed to the east. With strong winds from that direction a heavy sea rolls in. Uplands on the south side of the bay,

Chart 3441

and most of the lands at the head of the bay are part of Gulf Islands National Park Reserve.

97   **Tides**. — Tidal differences for Narvaez Bay (Index No. 7345), referenced on Fulford Harbour, are in *Tide Tables, Volume 5*.

98   **East Point**, the SE extremity of **Saturna Island**, is moderately steep-to but should be given a wide berth because of heavy tide-rips, overfalls and eddies. Waters surrounding East Point and encompassing Boiling Reef are a protected marine zone managed by Parks Canada.

99   **Lights**. — Saturna Island Sector lights *(264)*, on East Point, are shown from a skeleton tower 13.7 m high. The upper light, shown at an elevation of 36.9 m, is visible all round the horizon. The lower light, shown at an elevation of 31.1 m, is a sector light.

100   A **wind frequency table** for Saturna Island Light is in the Appendices.

101   **Boiling Reef** extends 0.4 mile NE from East Point; a rock 2 m high stands in the centre of the reef.

Boundary Pass — South Side

102   **Prevost Harbor** *(48°41'N, 123°12'W)* affords good shelter and anchorage. **Satellite Island** lies within Prevost Harbor and the entrance to the harbour is west of the island.

103   **Waldron Island** *(48°42'N, 123°02'W)* is steep and rocky on its east side but flat with sandy beaches on its north and west sides. The highest part of the island is near **Point Disney**, its south extremity.

104   **Cowlitz Bay**, on the SW side of Waldron Island, affords anchorage in fair weather. **Mouatt Reef**, in the south part of the bay, lies 0.5 mile north of Point Disney.

105   **Skipjack Island**, north of Waldron Island, is 37 m high and wooded. The passage between Skipjack Island and Point Hammond should be avoided because of strong tidal streams.

106   **Light**. — Skipjack Island light *(US 19805)*, on the NW side of the island, has two black and white diamond-shaped daymarks. The light is obscured from 261° to 347°.

Boundary Pass — East End

Charts 3441, 3462

107   **Point Hammond** *(48°43'N, 123°00'W)*, the north extremity of Waldron Island, is a high, yellow, sand bluff. **Bare Island**, 0.5 mile NNW of Point Hammond, is grassy and bare of trees.

108   **Light buoy**. — Boundary Pass Shoal light and bell buoy "DB" *(264.5)*, 2.1 miles NE of Skipjack Island, is an isolated danger buoy.

109   **Patos Island** *(48°47'N, 122°58'W)* is wooded except near **Alden Point** at its west extremity. **Active Cove**, at the SW extremity of the island, is reported to be a good anchorage for small vessels, local knowledge is advised. There is a tidal race in the approach.

110   **Light**. — Patos Island Sector light *(265)*, on Alden Point, is shown at an elevation of 16 m from a white tower on a building. The fog signal consists of one blast on a horn every 30 seconds. White buildings with red roofs stand nearby.

111   **Sucia Islands** lie 1.4 miles SE of Patos Island. Reefs extend 1.5 miles west of Sucia Islands to **West Bank**. **Clements Reef**, 0.5 mile north of Sucia Islands, is marked at its NW end by a starboard hand buoy and at its SE end by a danger buoy.

112   **Tidal streams** between Saturna and Patos Islands are strong and somewhat erratic, with tide-rips and eddies. The passage between Patos Island and Sucia Islands is almost free of tide-rips and the tidal streams set more fairly through it.

113   **Savage Point** *(48°48'N, 123°04'W)*, the north extremity of **Tumbo Island**, is in the Strait of Georgia in the approach to Boundary Pass. **Tumbo Reef** extends 0.6 mile ENE from Savage Point and has less than 2 m over it. **Tumbo Point**, the east extremity of Tumbo Island, has foul ground extending 0.5 mile east.

114   **Rosenfeld Rock**, 0.7 mile NE of Tumbo Point and about 1 mile NNE of East Point, has 2.7 m over it and is usually marked by kelp. It should be given a wide berth because of strong tide-rips and eddies.

115   **Light buoy**. — Rosenfeld Rock light buoy "U59" *(263)*, east of the rock, is a port hand buoy fitted with a Racon (— • — •).

Channels on NW Side of Haro Strait

Chart 3441

Cordova Channel

116   **Cordova Channel** *(48°36'N, 123°22'W)* separates James Island from **Saanich Peninsula**.

117   **Tidal streams** in Cordova Channel attain 2-3 kn on the flood, and 1-2 kn on the ebb. The flood sets north and the ebb south.

118   **Submarine cables** cross Cordova Channel between Cordova Spit and James Island. A submarine cable area (power) crosses the channel between **Ferguson Cove** and James Island.

119   A **submarine pipeline** is laid at the south end of Cordova Spit and two submarine pipelines extend 0.9 mile offshore at **Bazan Bay**.

120   **James Island** has a conspicuous white earth cliff extending across the width of its south coast, its east side is low and sandy. It is privately owned.

121   **James Spit**, with less than 5 m over it, is a sandy spit extending 1.8 miles SSE from the south coast of James Island.

122   **Cordova Spit**, on the west side of the channel, is low with clumps of stunted bushes and a row of utility poles.

123   **Saanichton Bay**, entered between Cordova Spit and **Turgoose Point**, affords anchorage open to SE winds. Tidal streams are not significant. The south side of the bay and the south end of Cordova Spit is an Indian Reserve.

124   **Tides**. — Tidal differences for Saanichton Bay (Index No. 7255), referenced on Fulford Harbour, are in *Tide Tables, Volume 5*.

125   **Wharf**. — The public wharf, close south of Turgoose Point, has an approach 35 m long leading to an 18 by 9 m wharfhead with a depth of 4.6 m at its outer end. A float 10 m long, and mooring dolphins are on the south side of the wharf approach. Garbage disposal is available at the head of the wharf.

126   **Buoys**. — Private mooring buoys are in Saanichton Bay. Charted buoys are for securing logbooms and barges.

127   **Lights**. — A private light is at the north end of the islet close-off the SW side of James Island.

Cordova Channel from south (1979)

Sidney Channel from south (1979)

Sidney Channel

Sidney Spit, Gulf Islands National Park Reserve, from south (1979)

Chart 3441

128   James Island light *(227)*, off the NW extremity of the island, is shown from a dolphin.

129   **Radio towers** on **Mount Newton** *(48°37'N, 123°27'W)* have flashing red air obstruction lights.

Sidney Channel and Approach

130   **D'Arcy Island** *(48°34'N, 123°17'W)* is wooded. Part of Gulf Islands National Park Reserve, camping is permitted in designated areas only. Mooring buoy for park staff only.

131   **Light**. — D'Arcy Island light *(226)*, on the SW side of the island, is shown at an elevation of 7.9 m from a white tower with a red band at the top.

132   **Fairway Patch**, 0.7 mile SW of D'Arcy Island, has a least depth of 9.1 m over it. **D'Arcy Shoals**, 0.7 mile west of D'Arcy Island, consist of two rocky heads.

133   **Light buoy**. — D'Arcy Shoals light buoy "U1" *(226.3)*, east of the shoals, is a port hand buoy.

134   **Clearing marks**. — Cadboro Point in line with Zero Rock light structure *(Chart 3440)*, bearing 165°, leads west of Fairway Patch and D'Arcy Shoals.

135   **Sidney Channel** is entered from the south between James Spit and D'Arcy Island; its north entrance is between the north extremities of James and Sidney Islands.

136   **Tidal streams**. — Secondary current station Sidney Channel (Index No. 1232), referenced on Race Passage, is in *Tide Tables, Volume 5.*

137   A **submarine cable** crosses the north entrance of Sidney Channel from the north end of Sidney Island to the Vancouver Island shore close south of Sidney.

138   **Wharf**. — The wharf on the east side of James Island is 37 m long with 6 m depths alongside. A private mooring buoy is north of the wharf.

139   **Sidney Island** has earth cliffs and banks on the SW side which become white and conspicuous toward their south end. This side of the island is fringed with a drying mud flat extending up to 0.2 mile offshore.

140   **Munroe Rock**, 0.4 mile west of the SW end of Sidney Island, is 1 m high.

141   **Two detached shoals**, 0.3 mile west of the NW part of Sidney Island, have 1.5 and 2.4 m over them.

142   **Light buoy. — Buoy**. — Sidney Channel light buoy "U2" *(228)*, west of the shoals, is a starboard hand buoy.

143   Port hand buoy "U3" is on the east side of the shoals.

144   A **measured distance** of 1,838 m in a 142°48' – 322°48' direction, on the west side of Sidney Spit, is marked by two pairs of white slatwork triangular daymarks.

Chart 3476

145   **Sidney Spit** *(48°39'N, 123°20'W)*, a low sandy spit, extends about 1 mile north from Sidney Island. The northern third of Sidney Island is part of Gulf Islands National Park Reserve and has picnic and camping facilities. Mooring buoys and a landing float for small craft are on the west side of the spit.

146   **Light**. — Sidney Spit light *(230.3)* is at the north end of the spit.

Miners Channel to Moresby Passage

Chart 3441

147   **Miners Channel**, entered between **Hamley Point** *(48°36'N, 123°16'W)* and Halibut Island, 1 mile north, leads NW along the NE coast of Sidney Island and is sometimes used by small commercial vessels. The Sidney-Anacortes ferry passes through the north end of Miners Channel.

148   **Mandarte Island**, 0.7 mile NW of Halibut Island, is bare with the exception of a few stunted trees at the NW end. It is an Indian Reserve and a nesting area for sea birds. Shoals extend SE and NW of the island.

149   **Light**. — Mandarte Island North light *(225.2)* is on the bare rock 0.3 mile NW of the island.

150   **South Cod Reef** *(48°39'N, 123°18'W)* dries 0.3 m and **North Cod Reef** dries 1.8 m, they lie south of the west end of Gooch Island.

151   **Light buoy**. — South Cod Reef light buoy "US" *(225.3)* is a south cardinal buoy.

152   **Light**. — Forrest Island light *(225.4)* is on an islet 0.2 mile SE of the island.

Charts 3441, 3476

153   **Forrest Island** *(48°40'N, 123°20'W)*, 0.1 mile east of North and South Cod Reefs, is wooded and surrounded by drying reefs. A breakwater is on the NE side of the island. **Sunk Rock** lies 0.3 mile NW of Forrest Island.

154   A **submarine cable** (power) crosses the channel from Forrest Island to Roberts Point.

155   **Dock Island** *(48°40'N, 123°21'W)*, the east island of Little Group, lies on the west side of the passage leading north from Sidney and Miners Channels to Moresby and Shute Passages. Dock Island and unnamed islets west and south of it are part of Gulf Islands National Park Reserve, no camping.

156   **Light**. — Dock Island light *(230)* is on the east side of the island.

157   **Clearing marks**. — Beaver Point *(48°46'N, 123°22'W)*, seen midway between the east extremity of Portland Island and the west Pellow Islet, bearing 355°, leads about 0.1 mile west of Sunk Rock *(Chart 3441)*.

158   **Greig Island**, 0.7 mile north of Forrest Island, is bare. Part of Gulf Islands National Park Reserve, no camping.

159   **Beacon**. — Greig Island daybeacon, on a drying rock close north of the island, has a starboard hand daymark.

Chart 3441

160   **Domville Island** *(48°40'N, 123°19'W)* and **Brethour Island**, NE of Forrest Island, are separated by a narrow channel. **Rubly Island** lies close SE of Domville Island and **Sheep Island** lies off the NW extremity of Domville Island. A chain of above-water and drying rocks extends NW of Brethour Island with **Reay Island** at the extremity. Reay Island is part of Gulf Islands National Park Reserve; no camping.

161   A **breakwater** and private float are on the NW side of Brethour Island. Another breakwater is on the SE side of Sheep Island.

162   **Prevost Passage** connects the main shipping channel of Haro Strait to Moresby Passage.

163   **Comet Island** lies 0.3 mile north of Gooch Island. The passage between the islands is almost completely obstructed by drying reefs and shoals.

164   **Joan Rock**, 1 mile west of Arachne Reef and 0.4 mile north of Brethour Island, has 0.6 m over it. Starboard bifurcation buoy "UH" is on the NW side of Joan Rock. **Imrie Island**, 0.7 mile

Chart 3441

NW of Joan Rock, is grassy and part of Gulf Islands National Park Reserve.

Moresby and Shute Passages

Charts 3441, 3476

165   **Moresby Passage** *(48°43'N, 123°20'W)*, between Moresby and Portland Islands, is a continuation of the route north from Sidney Channel. Ferries leaving Swartz Bay use this passage.

166   **Tidal streams** run fair through the constricted north entrance of Moresby Passage at 2 to 3 kn. The flood sets north and the ebb south.

Chart 3476

167   **Seymour Point** *(48°43'N, 123°20'W)* is the west extremity of Moresby Island. **Reynard Point**, 0.7 mile NNE of Seymour Point, has a drying rock ledge extending 0.2 mile WNW from it.

168   **Canoe Rock** *(48°44'N, 123°20'W)* is a drying rock lying in the north entrance of Moresby Passage.

169   **Light**. — Canoe Rock light *(256)* is shown at an elevation of 5.9 m from a white tower with a red band at the top.

170   **Portland Island**, on the west side of Moresby Passage, is surrounded by drying and below-water rocks extending up to 0.5 mile offshore.Also known as Princess Margaret, the island is part of Gulf Islands National Park Reserve which encompasses the whole of Portland Island as well as Pellow Islets and Tortoise Islets. a 400 m zone surrounding the island is a protected marine zone managed by Parks Canada..

171   **Artificial reef**. — The *G.B. Church* was sunk close south of Pellow Islets as an artificial reef for divers. It is marked by cautionary/information buoys and has mooring buoys.

172   **Pellow Islets** are on a drying reef extending from the east extremity of Portland Island. They have a few stunted trees on them and are conspicuous from north and south. Part of Gulf Islands National Park Reserve.

173   **Light buoy**. — Pellow Islets light buoy "U15" *(256.5)*, about 0.25 mile SE of the islets, is a port hand buoy.

174   **Turnbull Reef**, north of Pellow Islets, consists of several drying heads surrounded by shallow water extending 0.4 mile NE from Portland Island. Kelp is present on the reef during summer but is often drawn underwater by the strength of tidal streams.

175   **Leading marks**. — The west side of Imrie Island in line with the west side of Reay Island, bearing 165°, leads through the deepest part of Moresby Passage. It has been reported that in certain light conditions, Reay Island cannot be observed on the above bearing because of an unfavourable background *(Chart 3441)*.

176   **Shute Passage**, south of Portland Island and north of Coal, Pym, Knapp and Piers Islands, leads NW into Satellite Channel. **Celia Reefs** and some drying reefs close-off the islands on the south side are the only dangers.

177   **Light buoy**. — Celia Reefs light buoy "U14" *(240.5)*, south of the reefs, is a starboard hand buoy.

178   **Ferries** from Swartz Bay frequently cross Shute Passage coming from Gosse Passage to the south and bound for Active Pass.

179   A **submarine cable** is laid across the NW end of Shute Passage.

180   **Hood Island** *(48°43'N, 123°22'W)* is joined to the south end of Portland Island by a drying ledge. **Princess Bay**, entered north of **Tortoise Islets**, provides anchorage for small craft.

181   **Brackman Island**, off the SW side of Portland Island, is wooded and cliffy on its east side. Part of Gulf Islands National Park Reserve.

Sidney, Tsehum Harbour and Approach

182   **Little Group** *(48°40'N, 123°22'W)* is a group of islands and rocks surrounded by drying ledges and shoals lying in the approach to Sidney and Tsehum Harbour. **Little Shell Island** is separated from **Ker Island** by **Byers Passage**. Some piles lie close north of Little Shell Island.

183   **Light**. — Little Group Rock light *(230.5)*, in the centre of the passage between Coal and Ker Islands, is shown at an elevation of 4.9 m from a white tower.

184   **Sidney** *(48°39'N, 123°24'W)* *www.sidneybc.com* is a town with a wide variety of stores including a post office (V8L 3S2). There are a number of marine hardware stores as well as dental and medical offices, restaurants, and a laundromat. It is

Princess Bay - Portland Island (1988)

Public Wharf

Sidney (1997)

Port Sidney Marina (1997)

Sidney Public Wharf (1997)

Entrance - Port Sidney Marina (1997)

Chart 3476

the terminal of the Washington State Ferry that runs to Anacortes. **Victoria International Airport** is close west.

185   **Shoals. — Buoys**. — Two shoals, with less than 2 m over them, lie in the approach to the public wharf. One, 0.2 mile SE of the public wharf, is marked by port hand buoy "U5", the other, 0.2 mile NE of the same wharf, is marked by starboard hand buoy "U6".

186   **Lights**. — Sidney Breakwater light *(230.7)*, on the south extremity of the north breakwater, is shown at an elevation of 6.3 m from a white tower with a red band at the top.

187   Two private lights are shown from the seaward end of the public fishing and recreation pier.

188   Victoria Aero Beacon light *(235)*, west of Sidney, is shown from Victoria International Airport control tower and is private.

189   Washington State Ferries terminal has two private flashing lights on the outermost dolphins.

190   **Radio towers**, close west of the ferry wharf, display red air obstruction lights.

191   **Submarine pipelines**. — A pipeline, commencing close north of the ferry wharf, extends 0.4 mile seaward. Another pipeline south of the ferry wharf extends 91 m offshore.

192   **Submarine cables**. — A cable, about 0.1 mile south of the ferry wharf, is laid across the north entrance of Cordova and Sidney Channels to Sidney Island. A power cable crosses from Roberts Point to Forrest Island.

193   **Tides**. — Tidal differences for Sidney (Index No. 7260), referenced on Fulford Harbour, are in *Tide Tables, Volume 5*.

194   **Tidal streams** off Sidney are strong, the flood setting north and the ebb south. Currents alongside the public wharf are variable and during SE weather berthing is difficult; it is advisable to berth at or near slack water.

195   **Meteorological information** for Victoria International Airport is in the Appendices.

196   **Customs**. — A customs office for pleasure craft, with a direct telephone line to the main customs office, is located at Port Sidney Marina.

197   **Wharves**. — The public wharf extends about 122 m off shore, its seaward face is 46 m long with a least depth of 4 m alongside. The wharf is equipped with a 3-tonne crane; garbage disposal facilities are available on the wharfhead. A float extending south from the public wharf is used by a passenger ferry that operates to Tsehum Harbour and Sidney Island.

198   A **rock breakwater** extending 250 m north from close north of the public wharf and a second rock breakwater extending south from drying ledges 0.3 mile north of the public wharf, protect a marina. The entrance between the breakwaters is about 30 m wide with two private buoys used for traffic separation and there are depths of about 2 m alongside the floats.

199   A **public fishing and recreation pier** extends 90 m offshore close south of the public wharf. Artificial reefs lie on the north and south side of the pier which is not designed for berthing.

200   The **Washington State Ferry landing** is 0.4 mile south of the public wharf.

201   A **float and launching ramp**, protected by a rock breakwater, are at **Tulista Park**, 0.5 mile SW of the public wharf.

202   **Supplies**. — Marine supplies are available locally, fuel is obtainable in Tsehum Harbour.

203   **Graham Rock** lies off the entrance to **Roberts Bay** and on the south side of the approach to Tsehum Harbour.

204   **Beacon**. — Roberts Bay daybeacon, on Graham Rock, has a port hand daymark.

205   **Tsehum Harbour**, known locally as **Shoal Harbour**, is entered between **Armstrong Point** and **Curteis Point**. Several marinas are in the harbour and it is used extensively by pleasure craft. The channel into the harbour and to the marinas is well marked by lights, daybeacons and buoys.

206   **Customs** clearance for pleasure craft can be obtained at the customs float in All Bay.

207   A **speed limit** of 8 km/h (4 kn) is prescribed by the *Boating Restriction Regulations* for Tsehum Harbour west of a line drawn between Armstrong and Curteis Points.

208   **Dangers**. — Shoals extend 0.25 mile ESE from Curteis Point. The north shore of Tsehum Harbour, between Curteis Point and **Kingfisher Point**, is fringed by drying and below-water rocks.

209   **All Bay** is on the south side of Tsehum Harbour, west of **Thumb Point**. **Blue Heron Basin** is at the west end of Tsehum Harbour.

210   A **submarine pipeline** runs from the shore north of Nymph Point seaward through central Tsehum Harbour to a point 0.3 mile west of Little Shell Island.

211   **Lights**. — Tsehum Harbour light *(233)*, 0.3 mile SW of Curteis Point, is shown from a dolphin with a starboard hand daymark.

212   Tsehum Harbour Entrance light *(234.1)*, about 0.1 mile WNW of the above light, is shown from a mast with two starboard hand daymarks.

213   Blue Heron Basin Entrance light *(234.3)*, 0.1 mile SW of Kingfisher Point, is shown from a dolphin with a port hand daymark.

214   Blue Heron Basin light *(234.5)*, at the entrance to the south boat basin, is shown from a dolphin with a port hand daymark.

215   A private light is shown from the outer end of the breakwater extending north from Thumb Point. Two private lights are on the outer end of the wharves at the marina west of All Bay. Private lights are on the outer ends of the breakwaters extending south from the north entrance point of Blue Heron Basin.

216   **Light range**. — The light range at the north end of the harbour leading to the Royal Victoria Yacht Club is private.

217   **Beacons. — Buoys**. — Daybeacons mark the entrance to All Bay, the channel leading to the marina west of All Bay, and the channel leading into Blue Heron Basin. Daybeacons and buoys mark the channel leading north from Blue Heron Basin Entrance light.

218   **Wharf**. — The public wharf, in All Bay, has two wharfheads and floats with depths of 2.4 m alongside. Power is laid on the floats and fresh water and garbage and used oil disposal facilities are at the wharfhead.

219   **Supplies**. — Diesel fuel, gasoline, fresh water and provisions can be obtained from marinas.

220   **Repairs** to hull and engine can be carried out by several boatyards. Marine ways capable of hauling out craft up to 24.3 m long, 5.2 m beam and 2.4 m draught are available.

Channels West of Coal Island

221   A **speed limit** of 8 km/h (4 kn) is prescribed by the *Boating Restriction Regulations* for Page Passage, Canoe Bay and Iroquois Passage.

Tsehum Harbour approach (1997)

Tsehum Harbour - All Bay (1997)

Tsehum Harbour - NW of All Bay (1997)

Chart 3476

Tsehum Harbour - Blue Heron Basin (1997)

Tsehum Harbour - north arm (1997)

222   **Page Passage** is entered from the south between Curteis Point and **Kamaree Point**. **Fernie Island** and **Johnson Islet** are on the east side of the passage and **Kolb Island**, with **Harlock Islet** close SE, form its west side. **Rose Rock** lies in mid-channel, at the north end of Page Passage. Three rocks, two with less than 2 m over them and one that dries 0.2 m, lie in or near mid-channel. The north rock is marked by a daybeacon with two port hand daymarks.

223   An **overhead cable**, vertical clearance 8.8 m, crosses between Kolb Island and Harlock Islet.

224   **Submarine cables** cross Page Passage in several locations.

225   **Canoe Bay**, locally known as Canoe Cove, is approached between Kolb Island and **Musclow Islet**. Numerous drying reefs and below-water rocks lie to the north and west of Musclow Islet.

226   **Customs** clearance for pleasure craft can be obtained at the float at the east end of the marina.

227   **Beacon**. — A private daybeacon is in the north part of Canoe Bay.

228   **Marina** facilities in Canoe Bay afford extensive berthing for small craft. Repairs and supplies are obtainable.

229   **Anchorage** for small craft can be obtained between the marina and Kolb Island. A **submarine cable** and a **submarine pipeline** cross the south part of the bay to Kolb Island and several private mooring buoys are in the bay.

230   **Iroquois Passage**, entered from the south between **Goudge Island** and Fernie Island, leads NW passing east of Musclow Islet; it enters Colburne Passage between **Swartz Head** and Goudge Island light. A reef of above-water and drying rocks extends NNW from Musclow Islet to Swartz Head. The wharves and breakwater on the west side of Goudge Island are private.

231   **Submarine cables** and a **submarine pipeline** cross the north end of Iroquois Passage.

232   **Lights**. — Goudge Island light *(237)* is on a reef close NW of the island.

233   **John Passage** separates **Coal Island** from Goudge Island and is entered from the south between **Killer Whale Point** and Fernie Island. **Cap Rocks** lie close-off Killer Whale Point and several drying reefs lie in the fairway. **John Rock**, off the SE end of Goudge Island, dries 1.7 m and is the south rock of the drying reefs.

Page Passage from south (1988)

Canoe Bay (1988)

John Passage from south (1988)

Chart 3476

Colburne Passage looking west (1979)

Colburne Passage looking east (1979)

234   **Submarine cables** cross John Passage close south of Carney Point and across the north entrance from Lewis Bay.

235   **Light**. — Fernie Island light *(236)*, on a drying ledge extending SE from the island, is shown at an elevation of 6.7 m from a white tower with a green band at the top.

236   **Beacons**. — John Passage daybeacon, on a drying reef close north of John Rock, has a port hand daymark.

237   Coal Island daybeacon, on a drying reef 0.1 mile north of John Passage daybeacon, has a starboard hand daymark.

238   **Lewis Bay**, in the north part of Coal Island, is entered between **Carney Point** and Fir Cone Point. A reef of drying rocks extends 0.1 mile NW from Carney Point. A rock with 1.3 m over it lies in the centre of the bay. A breakwater and privately owned floats close east of it are at the head of the bay.

239   A **submarine cable** is laid down the centre of Lewis Bay.

240   **Light**. — A private light is on a dolphin north of the above-mentioned breakwater.

241   An **overhead cable** clearance unknown crosses the fore-shore at the north end of Goudge Island.

242   Coal Island forms the south side of the east entrance to Colburne Passage. Its north side is cliffy and moderately steep-to.

Colburne Passage

243   **Colburne Passage** is entered from the east between **Fir Cone Point**, the NW extremity of Coal Island, and **Pym Island** *(48°42′N, 123°23′W)*. It leads west to Satellite Channel between Coal Island, Goudge Island and Saanich Peninsula on the south and Pym, Knapp and Piers Islands on the north. Stranger and Gosse Passages lead from its north side into Shute Passage; John and Iroquois Passages lead south from its south side.

244   **Ferries**. — Large fast ferries, continually arriving and departing from the terminal at Swartz Bay, usually use Gosse Passage, but at times they use the east or west entrances to Colburne Passage. Charted ferry routes are general indications of the route followed. Ferries can be encountered anywhere within vicinity of the route shown. **Caution. — Ferries are limited in their ability to maneuver especially during docking. Vessels should give ferries a wide berth and be sure to maintain a vigilant look out especially near ferry routes and terminals.**

245   **Tidal streams** of 1 to 2 kn can be expected in Colburne Passage; the flood sets west and the ebb east.

246   **Submarine cables** and a **submarine pipeline** cross Colburne Passage.

Chart 3476

247 **Light**. — Coal Island light *(238)* is on Fir Cone Point.

248 **Light buoy**. — Coal Island light buoy "U8" *(240)*, 0.2 mile N of Coal Island light, is a starboard hand buoy.

249 **Swartz Bay** *(48°41'N, 123°24'W)* is on the south side of Colburne Passage, about 1 mile west of Fir Cone Point. It is the site of a large ferry terminal and connected by highway to Victoria.

250 **Tides**. — Tidal differences for Swartz Bay (Index No. 7270), referenced on Fulford Harbour, are in *Tide Tables, Volume 5*.

251 **Ferry landings**. — The Swartz Bay Terminal is operated by the British Columbia Ferry Services Inc. Regular and frequent passenger and vehicle service is maintained to and from Tsawwassen, on the mainland, and to places in the Gulf Islands.

252 The ferry berth close east of the B.C. Ferry terminal is for freight ferries operating from the Fraser River.

253 **Lights**. — Swartz Bay lights at the ferry terminal are private and fitted with radar reflectors. The fog signal is operated by ferry personnel when required for ferry movements.

254 **Float**. — A public float, east of the ferry landings, is 26 m long at the end of a trestle approach ramp. The outer end of the float has a depth of 0.6 m. The bottom surrounding the float is mainly rock ledges with sand and gravel patches between; a depth of 0.6 m lies 10 m NE of the float. This float is intended for vessels loading and unloading; use of the float is restricted to 2 hours.

255 **Wilhelm Point**, 0.7 mile north of Swartz Bay, is the SE extremity of Piers Island. Numerous private piers and floats line the shores of Piers Island.

256 **Wharf**. — A public wharf, close NW of Wilhelm Point, has floats attached to its outer end. The floats, each 21 m long, form a triangle and have depths of 1.2 to 2.1 m alongside.

257 **Indian Point**, the SW extremity of Piers Island, has a drying ledge extending 0.1 mile SW from it. **Patrol Island** on the drying ledge is 5 m high.

258 **Shoals** lie in the west entrance of Colburne Passage, south and SE of Indian Point; the fairway through these shoals is marked by the following light buoys and light.

259 **Light buoys. — Light**. — Colburne Passage light buoy "U18" *(248)*, 0.3 mile S. of Piers Island, is a starboard hand buoy.

260 Patrol Islet light buoy "U16" *(248.2)*, 0.2 mile south of Patrol Island, is a starboard hand buoy.

261 Colburne Passage South light *(248.1)* is on a shoal about 0.3 mile south of Patrol Island.

Stranger Passage

262 **Stranger Passage**, between Pym and Knapp Islands, connects Colburne Passage to Shute Passage. Its south end is obstructed by a drying ledge extending east from Knapp Island, and by a rock with 1.6 m over it in the centre of the fairway.

263 **Submarine cables** cross the south end of Stranger Passage.

264 **Beacon**. — A private daybeacon is on the above-mentioned drying ledge.

265 A **breakwater and floats** are in **Trader Bay**, on the west side of Stranger Passage.

Gosse Passage

266 **Gosse Passage**, between **Knapp Island** *(48°42'N, 123°24'W)* and **Piers Island**, connects Colburne Passage to Shute Passage. It is encumbered with **Clive Island**, the rocks and shoals extending 0.1 mile south from it and by a shallow ridge extending west from Knapp Island. The NE coast of Piers Island, between **Schmidt Point** and **Harvey Point**, is encumbered with several off-lying drying reefs. **Peck Reef** is the only named reef of this group.

267 **Ferries** continually arriving and departing from Swartz Bay use Gosse Passage.

268 A **submarine cable** is laid down the centre of Gosse Passage.

269 **Light**. — Clive Island light *(246)* is on a drying ledge extending SE from the island.

270 **Light buoys**. — Knapp Island light buoy "U10" *(247)* is a starboard hand buoy.

271 Gosse Passage light buoy "U9" *(247.3)* is a port hand buoy. These buoys mark the fairway on the SE side of Clive Island.

272 Piers Island light buoy "U12" *(245)*, about 0.3 mile NE of Clive Island, is a starboard hand buoy.

273 **Beacon**. — Peck Reef daybeacon has a port hand daymark.

Satellite Channel

Chart 3441

274 **Satellite Channel** *(48°44'N, 123°22'W)*, entered from Swanson Channel at its east end, leads around the south end of **Saltspring Island** to Fulford Harbour, Saanich Inlet, Cowichan Bay and the south end of Sansum Narrows. Shute and Colburne Passages enter the south side of Satellite Channel.

275 **Meteorological information** for Cowichan Bay (Cherry Point) is in the Appendices.

276 **Ferries**. — The east end of Satellite Channel is frequently used by large ferries going between Swartz Bay, at the north end of Saanich Peninsula, and Tsawwassen on the mainland. Smaller ferries cross Satellite Channel between Swartz Bay and Fulford Harbour. Charted ferry routes are general indications of the route followed.

277 **Tides**. — Tidal predictions in Satellite Channel are given for Fulford Harbour (Index No. 7330). Tidal differences, referenced on Fulford Harbour, are given for Cowichan Bay (Index No. 7310); predictions and tidal differences are in *Tide Tables, Volume 5*.

278 **Tidal streams** attain 1 to 2 kn in Satellite Channel. In the vicinity of Cape Keppel the flood sets NW and the ebb SE.

279 **Submarine cables** cross the east end of Satellite Channel from close SW of Beaver Point to Shute Passage. The shore end of the cables, SW of Beaver Point, is marked by an orange square daymark and cable sign. Another cable crosses Satellite Channel from about 1 mile west of Isabella Island to the north end of Saanich Peninsula, both ends are marked by cable signs.

Beaver Point to Fulford Harbour

280 **Beaver Point** *(48°46'N, 123°22'W)*, the NE entrance point to Satellite Channel, is the site of a park and campsite. **Eleanor Point**, 1.3 miles SW of Beaver Point, has a rock 0.3 m high close SE of it.

281 **Light**. — Beaver Point light *(257)* is on the point.

282 **Chesil Bank** *(48°45'N, 123°22'W)*, in the east entrance of Satellite Channel, has a least depth of 8.3 m.

Satellite Channel looking east (1979)

Fulford Harbour (1991)

Fulford Harbour (1991)

Chart 3441

283 **Chads Island**, 0.4 mile SW of Chesil Bank, is separated from the north side of Portland Island by a narrow channel, almost entirely blocked by above-water and drying rocks. **Royal Cove** is reported to afford anchorage for small craft; a dinghy float is at the head of the cove. **Kanaka Bluff**, the west extremity of Portland Island, is moderately steep-to.

284 **Light**. — Kanaka Bluff light *(241)* is shown at an elevation of 7.6 m from a white tower with a red band at the top.

Fulford Harbour and Approach

Chart 3478

285 **Russell Island** *(48°45'N, 123°24'W)* lies in the approach to Fulford Harbour, and is part of Gulf Islands National Park Reserve, no camping. The main approach to Fulford Harbour is between Russell Island and **Isabella Point**. The harbour can also be approached north of Russell Island but care should be taken to avoid **Louisa Rock** and other detached shoals off the Saltspring Island shore. A detached shoal, with 4.3 m over it, lies 0.2 mile south of the east extremity of Russell Island. **Cecil Rock**, 0.2 mile south of Russell Island, has less than 2 m over it.

286 **Kingfisher Cove**, NE of Louisa Rock, has a breakwater, with a private daybeacon, extending from its west entrance point.

287 **Fulford Harbour**, entered west of **Jackson Rock**, penetrates the south shore of Saltspring Island for 1.5 miles. It is used mainly by pleasure craft and B.C. Ferries that run between Saltspring and Vancouver Islands. **Fulford Harbour** village, at the head of the inlet, has a post office (V0S 1C0), store and restaurant. It is connected to Ganges by road. Numerous private floats and moorings are in Fulford Harbour.

288 **Tides**. — Tidal predictions for Fulford Harbour (Index No. 7330) are in *Tide Tables, Volume 5.*

289 **Lights**. — Jackson Rock light *(243)* is on a drying rock about 0.2 mile W of Jackson Rock.

290 Fulford Harbour light *(244)*, and Fulford Harbour Dolphin light *(244.1)*, at the ferry landing, are private. The fog signal is operated by ferry personnel when required for ferry movements.

291 **Ferry**. — A scheduled ferry operates between Fulford Harbour and Swartz bay at frequent intervals.

292 **Anchorage** can be obtained clear of the ferry route in 18 to 26 m.

293 **Wharves**. — The public wharf is 24 m long with a depth of 3 m alongside. A float 16.6 m long is attached to the west end of the wharf.

294 The **ferry wharf** is close north of the public wharf.

295 A **marina** is north of the ferry landing.

Fulford Harbour to Cowichan Bay

Chart 3441

296 **Isabella Island** *(48°44'N, 123°26'W)* and a small islet close west of it are connected to the Saltspring Island shore by a drying ridge. Isabella Island is part of Gulf Islands National Park Reserve.

297 **Light**. — Isabella Island light *(242)* is on the SE extremity of the island.

298 **Cape Keppel** is the south extremity of Saltspring Island. The land rises steeply from Cape Keppel to the summit of **Mount Tuam**, 0.9 mile NE.

299 **Shute Reef** *(48°43'N, 123°26'W)* dries 1.2 m. **Arbutus Island** is grassy with a few arbutus trees.

300 **Light**. — Shute Reef light *(248.3)* is on the reef.

301 **Radio towers** with red air obstruction lights are on the summit of **Cloake Hill** on the south side of Satellite Channel. On the north side of the channel radio towers, with red air obstruction lights, are on the summit of Mount Tuam.

302 The Saltspring Island shore west of Isabella Island and an area covering approximately 1 square mile at the junction of Satellite Channel and Saanich Inlet are **Ecological Reserves**.

303 **Patey Rock** *(48°42'N, 123°31'W)* dries 2 m.

304 **Light**. — Patey Rock light *(249)* is shown at an elevation of 7 m from a white tower with a green band at the top.

305 **Hatch Point**, the west entrance point to Saanich Inlet, has a ruined conveyor and overturned barge on it. Private lights are shown from the wharf NW of Hatch Point.

306 **Wharf**. — A wharf, 0.4 mile NW of Hatch Point, has a pipeline system and is used by coastal oil tankers.

307 A **floating breakwater**, protecting a private pier with a float, is close south of the wharf.

Cowichan Bay and Approach

Charts 3478, 3441

308 The west end of Satellite Channel *(48°43'N, 123°22'W)* forms the south approach to Cowichan Bay and Sansum Narrows.

309 **Anchorages**. — Designated anchorages are in Cowichan Bay and its south approach. Anchorages 1 to 5 *(Chart 3478)* lie within Cowichan Bay. Anchorages 6 to 8 *(Chart 3441)* lie in the west part of Satellite Channel. The bottom is mud.

310 **Cherry Point** is 1.5 miles NW of Hatch Point. **Boatswain Bank** extends east from the drying flats between Cherry and Hatch Points; it has a sand bottom.

311 **Musgrave Rock**, 1.5 miles north of Cherry Point, has 2.1 m over it and is marked by starboard hand buoy "U26".

Chart 3478

312 **Separation Point** *(48°45'N, 123°34'W)* is the north entrance point to Cowichan Bay and the SW entrance point of Sansum Narrows.

313 **Light**. — Separation Point light *(250)* is shown at an elevation of 6.1 m from a white tower.

314 **Mount Tzouhalem** *(48°46'N, 123°37'W)*, with **Skinner Bluff** forming its SE side, is conspicuous from all directions.

Major Port Facilities — Cowichan Bay

Berth	Wharf Length (m)	Least Depth (m)	Elevation (m)	Remarks
Wescan Terminals Berth 1 (southern)	155	9.3 (9.9 3 m off dockface)	0.5	Handles lumber and forest products. Forklifts. Power and telephone.
Wescan Terminals Berth 2 (northern)	198	8.3 (9.7 3 m off dockface)	0.5	Handles lumber and forest products. Mooring dolphin 15 m north connected by walkway. 8 hectares paved storage. Forklifts, lumber carriers. Power and telephone.

Chart 3478

Cowichan Bay lumber wharf (1988)

Cowichan Bay wharves from NW (1988)

315　　**Cowichan Bay**, entered south of Separation Point, has a large drying mud flat, about 0.8 mile wide, at its west end. **Cowichan River** and **Koksilah River** discharge into the bay across these flats.

316　　**Cowichan Bay settlement**, on the south shore, is a resort for sportsmen who take part in the fishing for which the bay has achieved a wide reputation. The port exports significant quantities of lumber and forest products. The largest vessel to use the port was 196 m long with a draught of 10.4 m.

317　　A licensed inn, restaurants, post office and garbage disposal facilities are available. A RCMP detachment is at Duncan, about 6 km NW of the community. Medical, dental, hospital and pharmacy facilities are also available at Duncan.

318　　**Pilotage** is compulsory. For information on obtaining a pilot when arriving or departing see *PAC 200*.

319　　**Tides**. — Tidal differences for Cowichan Bay (Index No. 7310), referenced on Fulford Harbour, are in *Tide Tables, Volume 5*.

320　　**Meteorological information** for Cowichan Bay is in the Appendices.

321　　**Lights**. — Private lights are shown from the north and south extremities of the Lumber wharf and from a dolphin 70 m south of the barge slip.

322　　**Wharves**. — Lumber wharf, at the outer end of the mud flats, is connected to shore by a causeway and used as a lumber storage area. The wharf has two berths on its outer side and a barge slip on its south end; it is of timber construction, on wooden piles. Details are given in the adjacent table.

323　　The **barge slip**, at the south end of the wharf, has berthing dolphins on its east and west sides. A dolphin is 70 m south of the barge slip.

324　　The **public wharf**, at the settlement on the south shore, is protected from east weather by a pile and timber breakwater; several floats are attached to its east and west sides. The area inside the breakwater and east of the wharf was dredged to 3 m (1966). The wharf is equipped with a 3 tonne crane and a tidal grid is on

Chart 3478

Entrance to Genoa Bay (1988)

Genoa Bay facilities (1988)

the east side of the wharf approach. Power, fresh water and garbage and used oil disposal facilities are available at the floats.

325 Private wharves, floats and **marinas** lie west of the public wharf.

326 A **submarine pipeline**, 0.3 mile west of the public wharf, extends about 0.2 mile offshore.

327 **Genoa Bay**, on the north side of Cowichan Bay, has a drying reef in the centre of its entrance. The bay affords good anchorage, mud bottom, for small craft. The east side of the bay is a booming ground with private mooring buoys. A marina is on the west side of the bay. A wharf with sheds is on the west side of Genoa Bay a short distance inside the entrance.

328 **Beacon. — Buoy**. — A daybeacon on the drying reef in the entrance to Genoa Bay has a starboard hand daymark.

329 Port hand buoy "U27" marks the drying rock on the west side of the entrance.

Saanich Inlet

Chart 3441

330 **Saanich Inlet** (*48°40′N, 123°30′W*), entered between Hatch Point and **Moses Point**, extends 13 miles south from

Chart 3441

Satellite Channel. **Malahat Ridge**, along the west side of Saanich Inlet, is steep and heavily wooded on its lower slopes. The east shore, as far south as Tod Inlet, is low and wooded. South of Tod Inlet it is steep and heavily wooded. The head of Saanich Inlet is known as Finlayson Arm.

331 A deep trough runs down the centre of the inlet, but close offshore there are several isolated rocks and reefs. Private floats, boathouses, rubble breakwaters and mooring buoys line the shores.

332 **Military exercise area**. — About 1 square mile in extent is in the middle of Saanich Inlet NW of Yarrow Point. For details see *Notices to Mariners 1 to 46 Annual Edition.*

333 **Ferry**. — A regular passenger and vehicle ferry service crosses Saanich Inlet from McPhail Point on the west side, to Brentwood Bay on the east side. Charted ferry routes are general indications of the route followed.

334 **Submarine cables** cross Saanich Inlet from Coal Point to south of Hatch Point. Near Brentwood Bay two submarine cables cross Saanich Inlet.

335 **Tides**. — Tidal differences in Saanich Inlet, referenced on Fulford Harbour, are given for Patricia Bay (Index No. 7277), Brentwood Bay (Index No. 7280) and Finlayson Arm (Index No. 7284) in *Tide Tables, Volume 5.*

336 **Wain Rock**, 0.2 mile WSW of Moses Point, dries 2 m.

337 **Light**. — Wain Rock light *(248.6)* is on the rock.

338 **Deep Cove**, entered between Moses Point and **Coal Point**, has the remains of a public wharf in its south part, it cannot be used for berthing. A marina is close east of the public wharf. Several pilings and a rubble breakwater are at the head of the cove.

339 A daybeacon on a drying rock, in the south part of Deep Cove, has a starboard hand daymark.

340 Numerous private mooring buoys are in Deep Cove.

341 **Patricia Bay**, known locally as **Pat Bay**, about 1.5 miles south of Deep Cove, is fringed by drying flats. Victoria International Airport is east of the bay.

342 **Tides**. — Tidal differences for Patricia Bay (Index No. 7277), referenced on Fulford Harbour, are in *Tide Tables, Volume 5.*

343 A **submarine cable area** (power) is laid in the vicinity of the mooring buoys in Patricia Bay. Navy vessels use this area to conduct acoustic testing.

344 A **submarine cable** (fibre optic) extends from the end of the Institute of Ocean Sciences wharf in a WSW direction for approximately 1.4 mile and ends in water 100 m deep. This is part of the Victoria Experimental Network Under the Sea (VENUS). Various oceanographic instruments will be deployed from a node at the end of the cable which should be given a wide clearance from any type of seabed activity.

345 Patricia Bay is a **water aerodrome**. The Victoria Airport seaplane base is on the north side of the Institute of Ocean Sciences wharf.

346 **Buoys**. — Orange and white mooring buoys marked "NAVY" are in Patricia Bay SW of **Warrior Point**.

347 Pat Bay ODAS light buoy "46134" *(251.3)* lies in Patricia Bay.

348 **Anchorage** in 20 to 50 m depths can be obtained in Patricia Bay.

349 **Wharves**. — Wharves of the Institute of Ocean Sciences are in the SE corner of Patricia Bay. These facilities are for government vessel or vessels visiting the Institute of Ocean Sciences. The main pier consists of an approach causeway extend-

ing 170 m NW from shore; a concrete pier extends 244 m WNW from the outer end of the causeway. A float for small vessels fronts the north side of the main pier extending from the causeway to the L-shaped pier. All berths are equipped with large rubber fenders and the elevation of the wharves is 1.8 m.

350 On the north side of the main pier, and 120 m from its outer end, an L-shaped concrete pier forms a dock 39 m wide. The berth on its north side is 92 m long with a least depth of 6.1 m alongside; depths inside the dock are generally in excess of 7 m. The berth on its south side is 120 m long with a least depth of 5.4 m alongside.

351 The berth on the north side of the L-shaped pier is 103 m long and has a depth of 5.2 m at its east end and 6.2 m at mid-length.

352 The south side of the main pier has a berthing length of 226 m with depths ranging from 4.1 m at its inner end to 6.5 m at its outer end.

353 A **rock breakwater** extends 100 m south from the inner end of the main pier and another rock breakwater, close west, extends 107 m north from the south shore protecting a small boat harbour with floats. This is used by government vessels only.

354 The **seaplane base** on the north side of the wharves is protected by a floating breakwater.

355 **Lights**. — Two private red and two green lights are shown from the outer ends of the above-mentioned piers.

356 Patricia Bay breakwater light *(251.5)*, on the north end of the south breakwater, has a starboard hand daymark.

357 **Mill Bay** on the west side of Saanich Inlet, opposite Patricia Bay, is entered south of **Whiskey Point**. A shoal pinnacle lies in the centre of the bay. A marina protected by a floating breakwater, and launching ramp are close north of the public wharf.

358 A **submarine pipeline**, at the NW end of Mill Bay, extends about 0.25 mile offshore.

359 **Wharf**. — The public wharf in Mill Bay has a float with 30 m of berthing and depths of 1.2 to 3 m alongside.

360 **Anchorage** for small vessels can be obtained in Mill Bay, but it is open to the SE. Numerous private mooring buoys lie between the marina and public wharf.

361 **Verdier Point**, south of Mill Bay, has a row of dolphins close south of it. A conspicuous gravel pit is close north.

362 **Tanner Rock**, 0.3 mile SSE of Verdier Point, dries 1.8 m. **Tozier Rock** lies 0.8 mile SSE of Tanner Rock and about 0.3 mile offshore.

363 **Beacons**. — Tanner and Tozier Rocks are marked by daybeacons with starboard hand daymarks.

364 **McPhail Point** is situated 0.5 mile SSW of Tozier Rock.

365 The **ferry wharf**, 0.3 mile north of McPhail Point, is used by the ferry that plies to and from Brentwood Bay.

366 **Lights**. — Private lights are shown from the ferry wharf.

367 Mill Bay Ferry Fog Signal *(252.5)* is operated by ferry personnel when required for ferry movements only.

368 **Bamberton**, 1.3 miles south of McPhail Point, is the site of a former cement works with berthing facilities for freighters and barges. The works were closed in 1980 and plans for residential redevelopment have yet to produce results. A cluster of silos and other buildings remain and are conspicuous.

369 **Wharves**. — The north wharf is 76 m long with depths of 9 m alongside; it can berth vessels up to 160 m long. The south wharf is 122 m long with depths of 4.6 m alongside.

Chart 3441

Brentwood Bay (1991)

Brentwood Bay ferry landing (1991)

370   **Coles Bay** *(48°38'N, 123°28'W)* affords anchorage in 20 to 30 m. **Dyer Rocks**, 1 m high, lie close SW of **Yarrow Point** on the west side of Coles Bay. A rock, with 1.8 m over it, lies 0.3 mile WSW of Yarrow Point; it is marked by port hand **buoy** "U23". Approaching Coles Bay from the north give Dyer Rocks a berth of at least 0.5 mile to avoid shoals extending south from them.

371   **Thomson Cove** has a private warning buoy marked *"Electric cables — No anchoring within 50 feet"* near its head. A flagpole is on **Henderson Point**.

372   **Brentwood Bay** is entered between Henderson Point and **Willis Point**. **Senanus Island** lies in its entrance. Brentwood Bay village, several marinas, numerous private floats and mooring buoys are in the SE corner of the bay.

373   A **speed limit** of 8 km/h (4 kn) is prescribed by the *Boating Restriction Regulations* for Brentwood Bay.

374   **Light**. — Senanus Island light *(252)*, on the NW extremity of the island, is shown at an elevation of 8.5 m from a white tower.

Sansum Narrows looking north (1988)

Sansum Narrows looking south (1988)

375   **Anchorage** in 60 to 80 m can be obtained east of Senanus Island.

376   A **submarine cable** crosses the south end of Brentwood Bay and another submarine cable is laid from the south shore to **Daphne Islet**.

377   **Tides**. — Tidal differences for Brentwood Bay (Index No. 7280), referenced on Fulford Harbour, are in *Tide Tables, Volume 5*.

378   The **ferry wharf** from which the ferry to McPhail Point operates is close south of **Sluggett Point**; this is known as the Mill Bay Ferry.

379   **Fog signal**. — Brentwood Bay Ferry Fog Signal *(252.3)* is operated by ferry personnel when required for ferry movements only.

380   **Buoy. — Beacon**. — Starboard hand buoy "U22" marks a drying rock close SW of the ferry landing.

381   A daybeacon, on a drying rock 0.1 mile north of Daphne Islet, has a bifurcation/junction daymark, preferred channel to the right.

382   **Caution. — Do not approach the marina close south of the ferry wharf between the above-mentioned buoy and daybeacon; drying rocks lie between the buoy and shore.**

383   **Float**. — The public float, 0.3 mile SE of the ferry landing, is 22 m long with a depth of 4.2 m alongside.

384   **Supplies**. — Diesel fuel, gasoline, lubricants, provisions, ice and fresh water are obtainable.

385   **Tod Inlet**, at the south end of Brentwood Bay, has a narrow entrance, less than 0.1 mile wide. Port hand buoy "U21", on the east side just inside the entrance, marks a rock on the outer edge of a small gravel spit. This is the site of a former cement works though little remains except one chimney and piles from a ruined wharf. The inlet is surrounded by **Gowlland Tod Provincial Park**. Facilities are limited, but this is a very popular destination

for small craft especially in summer when the anchorage can become quite crowded.

386   **Anchorage** and shelter for small craft can be obtained inside Tod Inlet in about 5 m, mud bottom.

387   **Squally Reach** is the portion of Saanich Inlet from Willis Point to **Elbow Point**, 2.7 miles SW.

388   **Repulse Rock**, 0.1 mile SW of Elbow Point, is a drying rock marked by a daybeacon with a bifurcation/junction daymark, preferred channel to the right.

389   **Finlayson Arm** extends 3.5 miles south from Repulse Rock and forms the south end of Saanich Inlet.

390   **Tides**. — Tidal differences at the south end of Finlayson Arm (Index No. 7284), referenced on Fulford Harbour, are in *Tide Tables, Volume 5*.

391   **Overhead cables**. — A power line, vertical clearance 55 m, crosses Finlayson Arm at **Christmas Point**. Power lines on pylons, vertical clearance 113 m, cross Finlayson Arm at the south end of **Sawluctus Island**. A power line, vertical clearance 21 m, crosses the mud flats at the head of the inlet.

392   **Conspicuous greenhouses** and pipelines of an abalone farm are on the hillside about 0.5 mile north of Christmas Point.

393   A **submarine cable** crosses the drying flat in the entrance to Goldstream River close south of the overhead cable.

394   **Goldstream River** flows into the head of Finlayson Arm, across an extensive drying mud flat. A marina is on the west side of Finlayson Arm close north of the mud flats.

Sansum Narrows

Chart 3478

395   **Sansum Narrows** *(48°45′N, 123°34′W)* leads from Satellite Channel to Stuart Channel, its narrowest part is about

Chart 3478

0.3 mile wide. Wind tends to funnel along the axis of the narrows and down valleys leading into it and tends to be directionally erratic.

396   Numerous sports and commercial fishermen are likely to be encountered in the narrows, especially near Burial Islet, **Bold Bluff Point** and **Sansum Point**.

397   **Speed limit**. — In the narrowest parts of the fairway, or within 300 m of shore, a speed limit of 7 kn is prescribed.

398   **Marine farm** facilities are in several locations along the shores of Sansum Narrows. Reduce speed to avoid damaging these facilities.

399   **Tides**. — Tidal differences for Maple Bay (Index No. 7315), at the north end and on the west side of Sansum Narrows, referenced on Fulford Harbour are in *Tide Tables, Volume 5*.

400   **Tidal streams** flood north and ebb south through Sansum Narrows. In narrower parts of the fairway the tidal stream seldom exceeds 3 kn, in wider portions 1 to 2 kn can be expected.

401   **Whirlpools and tide-rips** occur around Burial Islet, also between Sansum and Bold Bluff Points. **Under some conditions of wind and tide these can be hazardous to small craft.**

402   Secondary current station Sansum Narrows (Index No. 3050), referenced on Active Pass, is in *Tide Tables, Volume 5*.

403   **Mountains** on the east and west sides of Sansum Narrows (*Charts 3441, 3442*) are: **Bruce Peak** (*48°46'N, 123°30'W*) is the highest of three peaks at the south end and on the east side of the narrows; **Baynes Peak** (*48°48'N, 123°31'W*) is a remarkable mountain on Saltspring Island, it has a conspicuous precipice on its south side near the summit; **Mount Erskine** (*48°51'N, 123°33'W*) has some precipitous sides near its summit; and **Maple Mountain** (*48°50'N, 123°36'W*) has a rounded summit conspicuous from all directions. Several towers with red air obstruction lights are on the ridge between Bruce Peak and Mount Tuam.

404   **Musgrave Landing** (*48°45'N, 123°33'W*), on the north side of **Musgrave Point**, has public floats on the N shore 70 m long extending west from an approach ramp. Depths alongside range from 1.8 to 6.7 m. Private floats protected by a floating log breakwater are on the S shore.

405   **Burial Islet**, 1.3 miles NNW of Musgrave Point, is 2 m high with a grassy top.

406   **Light**. — Burial Islet light (*251*) is on the NW corner of the islet.

407   **Burgoyne Bay**, entered north of Bold Bluff Point, terminates in a mud and sand drying flat. A public wharf, on the north side of the bay, has a float on its NW side with a berthing length of 10.5 m. A notice on the wharf reads *"No vessel may berth at this wharf more than 2 hours in a period of 24 consecutive hours when not seeking refuge from inclement weather"*. Private mooring buoys are on the north side of the bay. A submarine cable is laid from the public wharf across Sansum Narrows in a NE direction to the launching ramp in Maple Bay.

408   **Octopus Point** is on the west side of Sansum Narrows, about 1 mile north of Sansum Point. **Paddy Mile Stone**, 1.2 miles NW of Octopus Point, is the south entrance point of Maple Bay. A conspicuous boulder 2 m high lies close north of the point.

409   **Light**. — Octopus Point light (*276.1*) is on the point.

410   **Maple Bay** has the community of Maple Bay on its west side. Public floats in the west part of the bay have depths of 4.6 to 8.2 m alongside. A swimming float is north of the public floats. There is a boat launch and a rowing club.

411   **Caution. — A rock with less than 2 m over it, and a shoal with a depth of 2.1 m over it, lie close SE of the public floats.**

412   In most parts of Maple Bay depths are too great for anchorage. Temporary anchorage can be obtained in 40 to 60 m SE of the public floats.

413   **Tides**. — Tidal differences for Maple Bay (Index No. 7315), referenced on Fulford Harbour, are in *Tide Tables, Volume 5*.

414   **Birds Eye Cove**, the south arm of Maple Bay, is a major pleasure boat centre with marinas and a yacht club. Moorage with all services and facilities including showers, laundry, restaurant and internet centre are available. There are fuel floats and repair facilities including a 100 ton marine railway and 15 ton lift. Harbour Air provides scheduled float plane service to Vancouver.

415   **Light buoy**. — Maple Bay Speed Control light buoy (*276.12*) lies in the entrance of Birds Eye Cove. A speed limit of 8 km/h (5 kn) is prescribed by the *Boating Restriction Regulations* for Birds Eye Cove.

416   A **submarine cable** is laid across the entrance to Birds Eye Cove.

417   **Breakwater**. — A floating concrete breakwater, on the west side of Birds Eye Cove near the entrance, borders the facilities of the Maple Bay Yacht Club. Signs posted on the breakwater read *"Warning Anchoring Lines Extend 8 m Do Not Anchor, Max Draft at Float 2 m"*.

418   **Lights**. — Private lights are shown from north and south ends of the breakwater.

419   **Overhead cables** (power), a short distance north of **Arbutus Point** (*48°49'N, 123°35'W*) and **Maxwell Point**, cross Sansum Narrows. They are suspended from towers and have a minimum vertical clearance of 52 m. Red spheres are attached to the cables to increase visibility and towers are marked by red and white chequered discs.

420   **Grave Point** (*48°51'N, 123°36'W*) and **Erskine Point** are the north entrance points to Sansum Narrows. A conspicuous red cliff and a booming ground with a breakwater are close south of Grave Point.

421   **Light**. — Grave Point light (*276.3*) is on the point.

Stuart Channel

Charts 3442, 3443

422   **Stuart Channel** (*48°55'N, 123°37'W*) leads from the north end of Sansum Narrows to Dodd Narrows and is bounded on its east side by Saltspring, Kuper, Thetis, Ruxton and De Courcy Islands. Harbour facilities of Crofton, Chemainus and Ladysmith are on the west side of the channel. Houstoun Passage leads north of Saltspring Island and connects Stuart Channel with Trincomali Channel. Trincomali Channel joins Stuart Channel between Thetis and Pylades Islands.

423   **Tidal streams** in Stuart Channel ebb in a general south direction, following the contour of the channel. A velocity of 1 kn can be expected. The flood stream is weak and variable. At the north end of Stuart Channel in the approach to Dodd Narrows, both the flood and ebb attain 3 kn.

Charts 3442, 3443

424   **Tides**. — Tidal differences in Stuart Channel, all referenced on Fulford Harbour, are given for Crofton (Index No. 7450), Chemainus (Index No. 7455), Ladysmith (Index No. 7460) and Preedy Harbour (Index No. 7471) in *Tide Tables, Volume 5.*

425   **Ferries**. — A regular ferry service crosses the south end of Stuart Channel connecting Crofton, on Vancouver Island, to Vesuvius Bay on Saltspring Island. Farther north, a ferry crosses Stuart Channel connecting Chemainus to Thetis and Kuper Islands. Charted ferry routes are general indications of the route followed.

426   **Submarine cables** cross Stuart Channel in the following locations: 0.4 mile north of Grave Point; from Houstoun Passage to Hospital Point in Chemainus; from the entrances of Telegraph and Preedy Harbours to Hospital Point; and from the west side of Thetis Island to the coast of Vancouver Island, 0.3 mile north of Coffin Point.

Osborn Bay and Approach

Chart 3475

427   **Osborn Bay** *(48°52'N, 123°38'W)*, on the west side of Stuart Channel, is entered between **Sherard Point** and Crofton light 1.2 miles NNW. The south and SW shores of the bay are fronted by a mud and sand drying bank extending 0.1 mile offshore. The north shore of the bay is formed by the south end of a drying bank and the Shoal Islands.

428   **Booming grounds**. — A large dry-land log sorting area and causeway are on the north shore of Osborn Bay. Booming grounds surround the sorting area, mooring buoys and numerous dolphins are located in the booming ground and it is floodlit at night. A booming ground is along the south shore.

429   **Approach**. — The smoke plume from the pulp mill can usually be seen for a considerable distance. A good lookout should be kept for deadheads and floating logs.

Nos. 1, 2 & 3 Docks - Crofton (1988)

Crofton public and ferry wharves (1988)

Chart 3475

Major Port Facilities — Crofton

Berth	Wharf Length (m)	Least Depth (m)	Elevation (m)	Remarks
NorskeCanada Berth 1	170	12		Handles pulp, paper and lumber. 1,040 m² covered storage. Lift trucks, pulp and paper handling equipment. Power.
NorskeCanada Berth 2	152	12.2		Handles pulp, paper and lumber. 2,600 m² covered storage. Lift trucks, pulp and paper handling equipment. Power.
Timber West Forest Ltd Stuart Channel Wharves Berth 3	138	12		Common user terminal handles pulp, paper and lumber. Accepts largest forest products carriers. Mooring dolphins. 843 m² covered storage. 9.2 hectares paved storage. Lift trucks, container lift truck. Power.

430　　**Lights**. — Crofton light *(277)* on the SE end of the Shoal Islands, is shown at an elevation of 5.8 m from a white tower.

431　　Lights on the outer end of wharves and the light and radar reflector at the ferry landing are private.

432　　**Indian Reef**, 0.5 mile north of Crofton light, dries 1.2 m, it is marked by a daybeacon consisting of a white tower with a green band around the top. Towers, 0.3 mile NW of Indian Reef, are 12.2 m high and mark the seaward end of sewer pipelines that cross the mud flats. They have port hand daymarks.

433　　**Submarine pipelines** between the public wharf and Stuart Channel Wharves extend 230 m offshore.

434　　**Tides**. — Tidal differences for Crofton (Index No. 7450), referenced on Fulford Harbour, are in *Tide Tables, Volume 5*.

435　　**Crofton**, in the SW part of Osborn Bay, is a community and port engaged in processing and shipping forest products, it has a post office, bank, accommodation, stores and restaurants. In addition to cargo ships and tankers bringing fuel for local industry, the harbour is used by tugs and barges and fishing vessels. Bus service is available to Victoria and Nanaimo and a ferry service operates to Vesuvius Bay on Saltspring Island. The nearest hospital, dentist and pharmacies are in Duncan, a short distance inland.

436　　**Pilotage** is compulsory. For information on obtaining a pilot see *PAC 200.*

437　　**Berths**. — Approaches to berths are deep and free of dangers but occasional strong east winds can make berthing difficult and necessitate use of tugs. Berths suitable for deep-sea ships are at the pulp and paper mill, details are given in the adjacent table.

438　　**Barge loading** facilities are north of Deep-sea Dock and at the south end of Berth No. 3.

439　　The **public wharf**, 0.2 mile south of Berth No. 3, has a berthing length of 18 m with a depth of 4.2 m alongside, it is connected to shore by a causeway. A 3 tonne crane is on the wharfhead. Power, washrooms, showers laundry and garbage disposal are available. The ferry landing is at the head of the wharf on its south side.

440　　A **small craft basin**, close south of the public wharf, has approximately 137 m of berthing. The basin, sheltered by a breakwater, was dredged to a depth of 2.1 m (1976).

441　　**Facilities**. — Tugs are available by prior arrangement. Minor hull repairs can be effected.

442　　**Supplies**. — Fuel and provisions are available in small quantities.

Osborn Bay to Chemainus Bay

Chart 3442

443　　**Shoal Islands** *(48°54′N, 123°40′W)*, north of Osborn Bay, consist of a number of islands, islets and rocks on a large mud and sand drying flat extending 1 mile offshore. **Bonsall Creek** flows into the south end of this drying flat and **Chemainus River**, with **Mainguy Island** in its entrance, flows into the north end of the drying flat. **Willy Island** is the largest of the Shoal Islands.

444　　**Booming grounds** surround the dry land sorting area at the south end of Shoal Islands. Another booming ground is at the north extremity of Shoal Islands.

Chemainus Bay and Approach

Chart 3475

445　　**Chemainus Bay**, on the west side of Stuart Channel, is entered between **Bare Point** *(48°56′N, 123°42′W)* and **Hospital Point**. The east and south shores of the bay are occupied by booming grounds in which there are numerous piles and dolphins. The west side of the bay is occupied by wharves and floats.

446　　**The B.C. Hydro and Power Authority generating station**, on the east side of the peninsula of which Bare Point forms the north extremity, is conspicuous. Oil storage tanks are north of the generating station. An oil wharf is on the east side of Bare Point.

447　　**Lights**. — Bare Point light *(280)* is on the point.

448　　A private light on a standing boom, within the entrance of Chemainus Bay, marks the outer extremity of the booming grounds along the east side of the bay.

449　　Private lights are shown from the sawmill wharf; yellow lights are shown from the vicinity of the ferry wharf and a fixed red light with a radar reflector is shown from a dolphin nearby.

450　　**Light range**. — Chemainus Bay range lights *(282, 283)*, in line bearing 199°, lead east of Hospital Rock to the north end of the sawmill wharf.

451　　**Hospital Rock**, 0.3 mile west of Bare Point, has 3 m over it.

452　　**Light buoy**. — Hospital Rock light buoy "U30" *(281)*, close east of the rock, is a starboard hand buoy.

453　　**Bird Rock**, 0.2 mile north of Hospital Point, dries 3 m and is connected to shore by drying mud flats. It is marked by a daybeacon consisting of a white tower with a red band around the top.

454　　**Submarine cables**, commencing from the north side of Hospital Point, cross the entrance to Chemainus Bay and lead across Stuart Channel to Telegraph and Preedy Harbours and to Houstoun Passage.

455　　**Submarine pipelines** extend 0.3 mile offshore from the north side of Hospital Point.

456　　**Anchorage** in Chemainus Bay is not advisable because of extensive booming grounds and congestion inside the bay. Vessels awaiting a berth usually anchor in Houstoun Passage.

Chart 3475

Chemainus public wharf (1988)

Slag Point

Woods Islands

Ladysmith Harbour (1979)

457   **Tides**. — Tidal differences for Chemainus (Index No. 7455), referenced on Fulford Harbour, are in *Tide Tables, Volume 5*.

458   The community of **Chemainus**, on the west side of Chemainus Bay has a hospital, post office (V0R 1K0), stores and motels. Bus service is available to Victoria and Nanaimo and a ferry service operates to Thetis and Kuper Islands. Rail service connects to Victoria and Courtenay. Nanaimo Airport is about 32 km north. A sawmill is on reclaimed ground in the SW corner of the harbour.

459   **Pilotage** is compulsory, for information on obtaining a pilot see *PAC 200*.

460   **Berths**. — All berths within Chemainus Bay are along the west shore.

461   The **Chemainus Sawmill wharf** has one berth 150 m long capable of taking deep draught vessels.

462   South of the sawmill wharf are **barge loading** facilities and conveyor belts.

463   The **public wharf** close north of the sawmill wharf has floats on its south side for small craft. This wharf has fresh water, a 3-tonne crane, telephone and garbage disposal facilities.

464   **Thetis Island ferry wharf** is close north.

465   **Facilities**. — Tugs are available but not normally necessary. Underwater inspection and minor repairs can be effected. A marine railway, owned by Chemainus Towing, is available for small vessels in an emergency.

466   **Supplies**. — Fresh water, provisions, lubricants, diesel fuel and gasoline are usually available. Bunker fuel is not normally available.

Ladysmith Harbour and Approach

Charts 3475, 3442, 3443

467   **Ladysmith Harbour**, also known as **Oyster Harbour**, is entered between **Boulder Point** *(48°58'N, 123°45'W)* and **Sharpe Point**, 1.5 miles NNW. Boulder Point has a large conspicuous boulder close-off its extremity and Sharpe Point has a long wooded hill above it that rises to an elevation of 64 m.

468   **Anchorages**. — Designated anchorages lie within close vicinity of Ladysmith Harbour. Anchorage berths 1 to 4 are on *Chart 3475*; anchorage berths 5 to 7, in Stuart Channel, are on *Chart 3442*; anchorage berths 8 and 9, in Kulleet Bay, are on *Chart 3443*.

469   **Tides**. — Tidal differences for Ladysmith (Index No. 7460), referenced on Fulford Harbour, are in *Tide Tables, Volume 5*.

Chart 3475

470   **Evening Cove**, between Sharpe Point *(48°59'N, 123°46'W)* and **Coffin Point**, has **Collins Shoal** in the centre of its entrance. **Coffin Island** lies 0.2 mile east of Coffin Point and **Nares Rock**, with 0.3 m over it, lies 0.1 mile east of Coffin Island.

471   **Light**. — Coffin Island light *(297)* is shown at an elevation of 5.8 m from a white tower with a green band at the top.

472   **Davis Lagoon** *(48°58'N, 123°46'W)* has marine farm facilities near its entrance.

473   **Holland Bank**, 1.3 miles NW of Davis Lagoon, is an extensive drying mud flat. **Slag Point**, 0.7 mile NNW of Holland Bank, is steep sided. A large conspicuous blue conveyor near Williams Point is for loading barges.

474   A **submarine pipeline** commences from a 9 m high tank onshore and crosses Holland Bank to a prominent pipeline notice, at the outer end of the bank; it then extends 0.3 mile east into Ladysmith Harbour.

475   **Beacon**. — Holland Bank daybeacon, on the outer edge of Holland Bank and close north of the pipeline, has a port hand daymark.

476   A **measured distance** of 1,846 m NW of Sharpe Point is marked by a pair of beacons at each end and laid out for courses 118½°–298½°.

477   **Dunsmuir Islands**, 0.6 mile NE of Holland Bank, are wooded. **Cluster Rocks**, 0.1 mile south of Dunsmuir Islands, dry 1.2 m at their highest point and are marked by starboard hand **buoy "U36"**.

478   **Sibell Bay**, east of Dunsmuir Islands, and the bay to the north with **Bute Island** in it, have marine farm facilities.

479   **Booming grounds** occupy a large portion of **Burleith Arm** and the west side of **Woods Islands**. On the west side of Ladysmith Harbour, booming grounds are north and south of **Williams Point**.

480   **Beacon**. — Ladysmith Boat Basin daybeacon 0.3 mile NW of Slag Point has a port hand daymark.

481   **Lights**. — Private lights are on the extremities of Doman Forest Products wharf.

482   A **submarine cable** crosses Ladysmith Harbour about 0.2 mile NW of **Page Point**.

483   **Marine farm** facilities occupy drying flats at the head of the harbour NW of **Wedge Point**.

484   **Ladysmith**, on the SW side of the harbour, is a town with a post office (V0R 2E0), hospital, pharmacy, doctors, dentists and several stores. The main industry is logging.

485   The public wharf, 0.35 mile NW of Slag Point, consists of a pier with floats attached to it; each float is 61 m long. These floats are protected by a rock breakwater on the SE side and a timbered breakwater on the NW side. The area around the floats has been dredged to 3 m. Power is laid on the float; water, garbage and used oil disposal facilities are available on the wharfhead. A tidal grid is on the south side of the wharf.

486   **Doman Forest Products wharf** is NW of Williams Point.

487   **Marinas** are N of Slag Point, NW of Williams Point and at Page Point.

488   **Supplies** of diesel fuel, gasoline and lubricants can be obtained in small quantities from the marina at Page Point. Provisions and fresh water are also obtainable.

489   **Communications**. — Ladysmith is connected with Victoria and Nanaimo by road and rail. Nanaimo Airport is 8 km north.

Chart 3443

490   **Kulleet Bay** *(49°01'N, 123°46'W)* is entered south of **Deer Point**. It is a good anchorage in fine weather only as it is exposed to east winds. Recommended anchorages are designated Numbers 8 and 9. Number 8 anchorage is in 33 m and Number 9 is in 53 m, both with mud bottom.

Booth Bay to False Reef

Chart 3442

491   **Booth Bay** *(48°52'N, 123°34'W)* has shoals near its head that extend 0.1 mile offshore. Marine farm facilities are in the bay. Temporary anchorage can be obtained, 0.3 mile from the head of the bay in a depth of 22 m, mud, but being exposed to prevailing wind is not recommended.

492   **Vesuvius Bay**, close north of Booth Bay, has a public wharf with a depth of 2.4 m alongside. Regular ferry service is maintained between Vesuvius Bay and Crofton on Vancouver Island. The settlement has a hotel, stores and is on the main Saltspring Island road system.

493   **Light**. — A private light and radar reflector are shown from the ferry wharf.

494   **Dock Point** has a drying ridge extending 0.1 mile NW from it. **Parminter Point**, the most prominent point on the west side of Saltspring Island, has a prominent house and flagpole on it.

495   **North Reef** *(48°55'N, 123°38'W)* is a narrow ridge of sandstone 1 m high.

496   **Light**. — North Reef light *(284)* is on the reef.

497   **Josling Point** *(48°56'N, 123°38'W)* is the south extremity of **Kuper Island** which is an Indian Reserve.

498   **Escape Reef**, 2 miles NW of North Reef, is a narrow drying rock ridge. It is marked by a daybeacon consisting of a white tower with a red band around the top.

499   **Scott Island**, 2.2 miles NW of Escape Reef, is joined to Dayman Island by drying ledges.

500   A **submarine cable** crosses from Scott Island to Crescent Point.

501   **False Reef** *(48°59'N, 123°42'W)*, in the NW approach to Preedy Harbour, is marked by a daybeacon with a bifurcation/junction daymark, preferred channel to the left.

Chart 3442

502   A **submarine cable** crosses Stuart Channel 1 mile north of False Reef.

503   **Marine farm** facilities lie off the west shore of Thetis Island close north of the cable sign.

Telegraph and Preedy Harbours

Chart 3477

504   **Telegraph Harbour** *(48°58′N, 123°40′W)* entered between **Alarm Rock** and **Active Point** lies between the NW side of Kuper Island and the SE extremity of **Thetis Island**. Pleasure craft congregate in the harbour and a ferry that plies between Kuper Island and Chemainus makes frequent calls. The post office (V0R 2Y0) is near the head.

505   **Lights.** — Alarm Rock light *(294)* is shown at an elevation of 5.2 m from a white tower.

506   Private lights and a radar reflector are on the outer end of the ferry landing.

507   Kuper Island Ferry Landing Fog Signal *(296.5)* is operated by ferry personnel when required for ferry movements.

508   **Submarine cables.** — A cable commencing from the public wharf on the east side of the harbour passes down the centre of the entrance. Another cable runs from close west of Foster Point to Hudson Island.

509   A **booming ground** lies between the public wharf and **Donckele Point**.

510   **Beacons.** — Two daybeacons, about 0.5 mile north of **Foster Point**, are on the north and south ends of a breakwater fronting the marina; they have port hand daymarks.

511   A daybeacon in the entrance to The Cut has a starboard hand daymark. A tide scale fitted to this piling is not referenced to Chart Datum.

512   **Anchorage** can be obtained in Telegraph Harbour for vessels of moderate size, in a depth of 13 m, mud, NW of the public wharf and submarine cable.

513   **Wharf.** — The public wharf, 0.3 mile NNE of Donckele Point, is 18.3 m long with a depth of 3 m alongside. A float 12.2 m long is attached to the SE side of the wharf.

514   The **ferry landing** close north of the public wharf is used by the Chemainus to Kuper Island ferry.

515   **Marinas** are in the harbour; one on the west side and the other near the head.

516   **Preedy Harbour** fronted by **Hudson Island** and **Dayman Island** has three entrances. The entrance from Telegraph Harbour, between Hudson Island and Foster Point, has drying reefs along its centre line; the fairway that lies between the drying reefs and Hudson Island has a least depth of 3 m.

517   **Light. — Beacons.** — Hudson Island North light *(294.5)* is on the south extremity of the drying reefs between Hudson Island and Foster Point.

518   Two daybeacons with starboard hand daymarks are on the drying reefs.

519   **Entrance channel** between Hudson and Dayman Islands has a least depth of 4.3 m between drying ledges extending from both islands.

520   **Buoys. — Lights.** — Port hand buoys "U33" and "U35", off Dayman Island, are on the NW side of the channel.

521   Preedy Harbour light *(295)* is on the drying ledge extending NW from Hudson Island.

522   Private lights are shown from the outer end of the ferry landing and from a dolphin close SW.

523   **Fog signal.** — Thetis Island Ferry Landing Fog Signal *(296)* is operated by ferry personnel when required for ferry movements only.

524   The NW entrance to Preedy Harbour is between Dayman Island and **Crescent Point**; shoal soundings extend at least 0.1 mile from both sides of this channel but it has 11 m through the centre of the fairway.

525   **Submarine cables.** — A cable crosses the south side of Preedy Harbour and continues SW along the centre of the channel between Dayman and Hudson Islands. Another cable crosses the harbour from south of the ferry landing to Dayman Island.

526   **Tides.** — Tidal differences for Preedy Harbour (Index No. 7471), referenced on Fulford Harbour, are given in *Tide Tables, Volume 5.*

527   Preedy Harbour affords good **anchorage**, mud bottom, in its north part avoiding the submarine cables.

528   **Wharf.** — The public wharf in the NE corner of Preedy Harbour is 18.3 m long with a depth of 5.5 m alongside. A float attached to the west corner of the wharf is 11 m long with a depth of 2.4 m.

529   The **ferry landing** close north of the public wharf is used by the ferry that runs to Chemainus.

530   **Caution. — A rock with 0.3 m over it lies about 45 m due south of the head of the public wharf.**

Charts 3477, 3442

531   **Directions.** — False Reef can be passed on either side, but the preferred side is to the north taking care to avoid foul ground in its vicinity. A mid-channel course should be steered through the entrance between Crescent Point and Dayman Island.

532   When entering Preedy Harbour through the passage between Hudson and Dayman Islands, favour the north side of the fairway to avoid drying reef extending from Hudson Island.

533   Using the SE entrance from Telegraph Harbour keep on the SW side of Hudson Island North light and the two daybeacons that mark the mid-channel reefs. Maintain a mid-channel course until Preedy Harbour light is well abaft the beam.

Thetis Island to Dodd Narrows

Chart 3443

534   **North Cove** *(49°01′N, 123°42′W)*, at the north end of Thetis Island, lies between **Fraser Point** and **Pilkey Point**. A rock breakwater and a private float lie in the SW part of the cove. **Cufra Inlet**, in the SE corner of North Cove, has a breakwater near its entrance that extends out from its east shore; the breakwater affords good shelter to small craft, but most of Cufra Inlet dries.

535   A **submarine cable** crosses Cufra Inlet.

536   **Anchorage** in a depth of 13 m, mud, can be obtained in the middle of North Cove; the cove affords shelter from south winds.

537   **Ragged Islets**, 0.4 mile NW of Pilkey Point, consist of three islets on a drying rock ledge; the middle islet has some bushes on it.

538   **Beacon.** — A daybeacon on the NW end of the drying ledge of Ragged Islets has a starboard hand daymark.

Telegraph Harbour looking north (1988)

The Cut from Telegraph Harbour (1988)

Chart 3443

Preedy Harbour - south entrance (1988)

Preedy Harbour - north entrance (1988)

Preedy Harbour public and ferry wharves (1988)

539 **Miami Islet** *(49°02′N, 123°43′W)* is 2 m high, bare and rocky. Reefs, with less than 2 m over them, extend NW and SE from the islet.

540 **Wrecks**. — A wreck lies 0.3 mile SSE of Miami Islet and another, visible at LW, is 0.2 mile NW of the islet, near the north edge of the reef.

541 **Buoy**. — Starboard hand buoy "U40" is at the NW extremity of the reef extending NW from Miami Islet.

542 **Danger Reefs** consist of several below-water rocks and drying reefs, the highest of which dries 1.2 m.

543 **Light**. — Danger Reefs light *(292)*, on the north end of easternmost rock, is shown at an elevation of 6.7 m from a white tower. **Caution. — When using the passage between Miami Islet and Danger Reefs give Danger Reefs light structure a clearance of at least 0.5 mile to avoid the shoal water south of Danger Reefs.**

Chart 3443

Boat Harbour anchorage (1988)

Herring Bay (1988)

544   **Tree Island** *(49°04′N, 123°42′W)* has some stunted trees on it. **Pylades Island** has some broken cliffs about 24 m high on its west side.

545   **Whaleboat Passage**, between Pylades Island and **Ruxton Island**, has a least depth of 2.1 m in mid-channel and is only suitable for small craft. Several private mooring buoys lie close to shore. **Whaleboat Island** lies in the NE approach to Whaleboat Passage; **Whaleboat Island Marine Park** is undeveloped.

546   **Yellow Point** *(49°02′N, 123°45′W)* is low and grassy but immediately inland it rises to a wooded summit, with an elevation of 73 m. A resort on the point, and another in **Nicholson Cove** have floats and private mooring buoys.

547   **Beacon**. — The daybeacon on a drying rock in the entrance to Nicholson Cove has a starboard hand daymark.

548   **Boat Harbour**, entered between **Flewett Point** and **Reynolds Point**, is often used as a temporary anchorage for vessels awaiting slack water in Dodd Narrows. The cove in the south part of Boat Harbour, west of Flewett Point, is **Kenary Cove**. Floats in Boat Harbour are private.

549   **Beacon**. — A daybeacon, on the SE end of a drying reef extending from the north entrance point of Boat Harbour, has a starboard hand daymark.

550   **Anchorage** can be obtained in the entrance of Boat Harbour, in 15 m, mud bottom. Small craft can obtain well-sheltered anchorage in Kenary Cove, in 3 to 5 m, mud bottom.

551   **Submarine pipelines**, 0.2 mile north of Reynolds Point, extend seaward to the 20 m contour.

Chart 3475

552   **Ruxton Passage** *(49°05′N, 123°44′W)*, between Ruxton Island and **De Courcy Island**, connects Stuart Channel to Pylades Channel. A shoal with 7.6 m over it lies in the east entrance, otherwise the fairway is deep.

553   **Beacon**. — Ruxton Passage daybeacon, on a drying reef on the south side of Ruxton Passage, has a starboard hand daymark.

554   **Herring Bay**, at the NW end of Ruxton Island, offers good anchorage for small craft. **Caution** is advised because of the drying reefs. Mooring buoys in the bay are private.

555   **Link Island** is connected to the north end of De Courcy Island and the south end of **Mudge Island** by drying ridges.

556   **Round Island** *(49°07′N, 123°48′W)*, in the south approach to Dodd Narrows, is surrounded by drying ledges and shoals.

Houstoun Passage

Chart 3442

557   **Houstoun Passage** *(48°56′N, 123°36′W)* connects Stuart Channel to Trincomali Channel. Entered from Stuart Channel

Chart 3442

Houstoun Passage looking NE from Stuart Channel (1991)

between Parminter Point and North Reef it leads north between the NW end of Saltspring Island and the east side of Kuper Island. At the north end of Saltspring Island it turns SE and leads between the NE side of Saltspring Island and the SW sides of Secretary Islands and Wallace Island. It enters Trincomali Channel between Fernwood and Panther Points.

558   **Tidal streams** within Houstoun Passage are generally weak. The flood sets NW and the ebb SE.

559   **Submarine cables**. — A cable is laid down the centre of Houstoun Passage. A power cable crosses the passage from SE of Southey Point to Jackscrew Island.

560   **Anchorage** can be obtained in the western portion of Houstoun Passage in 24 to 40 m, mud bottom. Anchorages are designated Numbers 1 to 4.

561   **Tent Island** *(48°56'N, 123°38'W)* is connected to Josling Point by a drying ridge. North Reef lies 0.5 mile south. **Sandstone Rocks** lie close SE of Tent Island.

562   **Beacon**. — Tent Island Reef daybeacon, on a drying rock 0.1 mile NE of Sandstone Rocks, is a white tower with a green band around the top.

563   **Idol Island** lies 1 mile east of Sandstone Rocks. **Stone Cutters Bay** is surrounded by houses. **Grappler Rock** has three drying heads. **Southey Point** is the north extremity of Saltspring Island. **Jackscrew Island** lies 0.5 mile NE of Southey Point. A breakwater and private float are in the small bay north of the light.

564   **Lights**. — Grappler Rock light *(285)* is on the west side of the rock.

565   Southey Point light *(286)* is shown at an elevation of 6.1 m from a white tower.

566   Jackscrew Island light *(293.5)*, on the south extremity of the island, is shown at an elevation of 5.8 m from a white tower with a red band at the top.

567   **Secretary Islands**, north of Jackscrew Island, are connected to one another by a drying sand and gravel ridge.

568   **Mowgli Island**, NW of Secretary Islands, is known locally as Spike Island. A narrow chain of wooded islets and drying reefs, 0.4 mile long, lies 0.2 mile south of Mowgli Island. The channel between Mowgli Island and **Norway Island** to the north is 0.15 mile wide; it connects the north end of Houstoun Passage to Trincomali Channel.

569   **Buoy. — Beacons**. — South cardinal buoy "UV" is at the SE extremity of the chain of islets and drying reefs.

570   Houstoun Passage daybeacon on the NW extremity of the chain of islets and drying reefs has a starboard hand daymark.

571   Norway Island daybeacon on an islet close south of Norway Island has a port hand daymark.

572   **Wallace Island**, SE of Secretary Islands, is separated from them by a narrow channel that has a drying reef and below-water rocks in the centre of its fairway. A narrow chain of rocky islets, drying rocks and shoals lies parallel with and about 0.2 mile from the SW shore of Wallace Island. **Conover Cove** within **Wallace Island Marine Park** affords good shelter for small craft and has a small float. **Princess Cove** affords anchorage in the centre and along the SW side where stern lines are usually attached to trees or metal rings. **Panther Point** has a drying ledge extending 0.2 mile SE from it.

573   **Light buoy**. — Panther Point light buoy "U44" *(293)*, at the SE extremity of the shoals, is a starboard hand buoy.

574   **Beacon**. — Panther Point daybeacon, on the drying ledge, has a bifurcation/junction daymark, preferred channel to the right.

575   **Light**. — Saltspring Island Sector light *(291.1)* is 1 mile NW of Fernwood Point. The white sector indicates the preferred channel for approaching the east entrance of Houstoun Passage.

576   **Wharf**. — A public pier with a float attached to its outer end extends over the tidal flats at **Fernwood Point**. This float has 24.4 m of berthing space with 3 m alongside.

Swanson Channel

Charts 3441, 3442

577   **Swanson Channel** *(48°45'N, 123°18'W)* leads north from Boundary Pass and Satellite Channel to Trincomali Channel, Active Pass and Navy Channel. North Pender Island forms the east side of Swanson Channel. Moresby, Saltspring and Prevost Islands form its west side. Satellite Channel leads west between Moresby and Saltspring Islands. Captain Passage, between Saltspring and Prevost Islands, leads to Ganges Harbour and connects with Trincomali Channel. It offers no saving in distance to vessels proceeding up Swanson Channel for the upper reaches of Trincomali Channel but by taking this passage ferry traffic entering and leaving Active Pass is avoided.

Charts 3441, 3442

Bedwell Harbour (Resort) (1988)

Skull Islet

Bedwell Harbour anchorage (1988)

578 **Vessel Traffic Services (VTS)**. — Calling-in points of the *Vancouver Traffic Zone*, administered by *Victoria Traffic*, are in Swanson Channel. Assigned frequency is 156.55 MHz, Channel 11.

579 ***Calling-in Point No. 6***, *Turn Point*, is when approaching Haro Strait and is a circle with a 3-mile radius centered on Turn Point light *(255)*.

580 ***Calling-in Point No. 9***, *Portlock Point*, is a line running 090°–270° through Portlock Point light *(267)*.

581 A brief description of the *Vancouver Traffic Zone* is given in *PAC 200*. Details are in *Radio Aids to Marine Navigation (Pacific and Western Arctic)*.

582 **Tidal streams** flood NW and north through Swanson Channel, but a branch flows into Navy Channel; the ebb flows SE. At the north end of Swanson Channel, there is another division of flood stream, one part going through Active Pass, the other through Trincomali Channel. Toward Enterprise Reef there is a significant increase in the velocity of the flood stream, and, at the entrance to Active Pass 5 to 7 kn can be expected with large tides; 3 to 5 kn on smaller tides.

583 Secondary current station Swanson Channel (Index No. 1240), referenced on Race Passage, is given in *Tide Tables, Volume 5*.

584 **Submarine cables** cross Swanson Channel from close north of Beaver Point to Otter Bay and Willey Point on North Pender Island.

585 **Ferries**. — The north part of Swanson Channel is used by ferries operating between Swartz Bay, Tsawwassen and Gulf Islands. Tracks are usually mid-channel. However, inter-island ferries cross Swanson Channel between Captain Passage and Otter Bay. Charted ferry routes are general indications of the route followed.

Bedwell Harbour

Chart 3477

586 **Bedwell Harbour** *(48°45'N, 123°14'W)*, an inlet formed by the overlap of **North Pender Island** and **South Pender Island**, is entered between Tilly Point and **Wallace Point**. The harbour is used mainly by pleasure craft. Gulf Islands National Park Reserve occupies the NE shore of the harbour and adjacent islets, including Skull Islet, and has mooring buoys. No camping on Skull Islet. Strong south winds funnel through the harbour, but no heavy sea is raised. Pender Canal at the north end connects Bedwell Harbour to Port Browning.

587 Bedwell Harbour is a **water aerodrome**.

588 An **abandoned submarine cable** (telephone) crosses Bedwell Harbour from 0.3 mile NW of Wallace Point to the public wharf north of **Hay Point**.

589 A **submarine pipeline** (sewer outfall), close south of the public wharf, is marked by a sign.

590 **Anchorage**, with the exception of in the vicinity of the submarine cable and pipeline, can be obtained almost anywhere in Bedwell Harbour. The best position is 0.2 mile SE of **Skull Islet** in 13 to 15 m, stiff mud bottom.

591 **Tides**. — Tidal differences for Bedwell Harbour (Index No. 7350), referenced on Fulford Harbour, are given in *Tide Tables, Volume 5*.

592 **Drew Rock**, near the head of the harbour, has 2.1 m over it. Several rocks, with less than 2 m over them, lie between Drew Rock and the head of the harbour.

593 **Light**. — Hay Point light *(254)* is on the point.

594 **Beacon**. — Skull Islet daybeacon is a white tower with a red band around the top.

595 **Bedwell Harbour** settlement, on the east side of **Egeria Bay**, is a resort. A breakwater extending from **Richardson Bluff** protects the berths in Egeria Bay from north winds. The resort is connected to other settlements on South and North Pender Islands by road.

596 **Customs** service is provided during summer months.

597 **Berths**. — The public float, at the head of Egeria Bay, is 24 m long with depths of 3.7 to 6 m alongside.

598 **Public floats**, attached to the south side of the main public float, are reserved for vessels entering and clearing customs. They are 12 to 49 m long, in a T-formation, with 4.6 to 7.6 m alongside.

599 A **marina** is on the north side of Egeria Bay.

600 **Public mooring buoys** are in the area east of Skull Islet. Private mooring buoys are in **Peter Cove** and the bay north of it.

601 **Pender Canal** leads north from the head of Bedwell Harbour into Shark Cove and Port Browning. It is about 23 m wide with a least depth of 2.2 m through it and is fringed on both sides by drying ledges. In the south entrance a drying rock and a rock awash are marked by starboard hand buoy "U54" and port hand buoy "U53".

602 A **speed limit** of 10 km/h (5 kn) is prescribed by the *Boating Restriction Regulations* for Pender Canal.

603 A **highway bridge** crosses Pender Canal near its north end. It has a vertical clearance of 8.5 m and a width between piers of 12.2 m.

604 **Overhead cables**, close north of the bridge, have a vertical clearance of 11 m; those close south of the bridge have a vertical clearance of 15 m.

605 **Tidal streams** in Pender Canal attain 3 to 4 kn at springs; the flood sets north and the ebb south.

Pelorus Point to Mouat Point

Chart 3441

606 **Parkin Point** is the NE extremity of Moresby Island. Beaver Point and its light, 3.3 miles NW of Parkin Point, have been described with Satellite Channel.

607 A **conspicuous telephone tower**, with a red air obstruction light, is on **Cramer Hill** *(48°47'N, 123°18'W)*.

608 **Oaks Bluff** *(48°45'N, 123°16'W)* are high cliffs along the SW side of North Pender Island, between Wallace Point and Boat Nook. **Beddis Rock** dries 3.7 m and lies off the north entrance point of **Boat Nook**.

609 **Thieves Bay**, 0.5 mile NW of Beddis Rock, is shallow with depths of 0.6 m. A rockfill and piling breakwater protects private floats and a launching ramp.

610 **Light**. — Mouat Point light *(257.5)*, on the peninsula forming the south side of Thieves Bay, is shown at an elevation of 6.7 m from a white tower with a red band at the top.

611 **Mouat Point**, 0.6 mile NNW of the above-mentioned light, is fairly steep-to and forms the south side of **Shingle Bay**. The ruins of an old wharf are on the east side of the bay. A private float is at the head of the bay.

612 **Anchorage** can be obtained in the centre of Shingle Bay in depths of 20 to 27 m. It is exposed to west winds.

Mouat Point to Portlock Point

Chart 3442

613 **Otter Bay** *(48°48'N, 123°19'W)* has a ferry landing on its north shore, the light and radar reflectors are private. A marina is on the north side of Otter Bay, in **Hyashi Cove**. Port hand buoy "U57" is close SE off the point south of the marina. On the south shore of Otter Bay, **Roe Islet** and adjacent uplands above Ella Bay are part of Gulf Islands National Park Reserve.

614 **Anchorage** for small vessels can be obtained in Otter Bay, in 13 to 17 m, mud bottom.

615 **Grimmer Bay**, the approach to Port Washington, has a chain of above-water and drying rocks extending 0.2 mile WNW from the middle of its east shore. **Boat Islet** is at the outer extremity of these rocks. **Port Washington** is a small settlement with summer resorts. **Percival Cove** is on the north side of Grimmer Bay.

616 **Light**. — Port Washington light *(266.5)* is on Boat Islet.

617 The approach to Port Washington is a **water aerodrome**.

618 **Wharf**. — The public wharf is 15.8 m long at its outside face, with 4.6 to 5.8 m alongside. A 21 m float is on the south side of the wharf, with a 12 m seaplane float attached to it. A 24 m float is attached to the north end of the wharf.

619 **Danger**. — A rock with less than 2 m over it lies about 46 m south of the SE end of the public wharf.

620 **Stanley Point** *(48°49'N, 123°20'W)* the NW extremity of North Pender Island lies at the junction of Swanson, Navy and Trincomali Channels.

621 **Prevost Island** *(48°50'N, 123°23'W)* is moderately high, thickly wooded, and separates Captain Passage from Swanson and

Chart 3442

Pender Canal from Bedwell Harbour (1988)

Pender Canal from Port Browning (1988)

Trincomali Channels. **Point Liddell**, the SE extremity of Prevost Island, has a reef of drying and below-water rocks extending 0.2 mile SE from it. Much of the lands above James Bay and Selby Cove are part of Gulf Islands National Park Reserve.

622 **Beacon**. — Point Liddell daybeacon, on the outermost of the drying rocks, is a white tower with a green band around the top.

623 **Ellen Bay** affords fair anchorage near the middle in 27 m, mud bottom, or about 0.1 mile from the head of the bay in 18 m.

Chart 3442

624   **Diver Bay** is entered between **Red Islets** and **Bright Islet**. Small craft can obtain anchorage in 9 to 13 m, sand and mud; it is exposed to the SE. Red Islets and Bright Islet are part of Gulf Islands National Park Reserve.

625   **Portlock Point**, the east extremity of Prevost Island, lies at the junction of Swanson and Trincomali Channels. Portlock Point, excluding the light, is part of Gulf Islands National Park Reserve.

626   **Light**. — Portlock Point light *(267)* is shown at an elevation of 15.5 m from a white tower. A windmill generator is close WNW.

Captain Passage

Charts 3478, 3442

627   **Captain Passage** *(48°48′N, 123°23′W)*, entered from Swanson Channel between Beaver Point and Point Liddell, leads NW between Prevost and Saltspring Islands to Ganges Harbour and Trincomali Channel.

628   **Tidal streams** within Captain Passage attain 2 to 3 kn on the flood and 3 to 4 kn on the ebb. The flood sets mainly toward Trincomali Channel and the ebb sets directly onto the south shore, with tide-rips in the vicinity of Nose Point. Tidal streams in Ganges Harbour are generally weak.

629   **Ferries**. — BC Ferries operating from Tsawwassen, on the mainland, pass at frequent intervals through Captain Passage and call into Long Harbour, at the NW end of the passage. Charted ferry routes are general indications of the route followed.

Yeo Point to Peile Point

Chart 3478

630   **Yeo Point** *(48°48′N, 123°24′W)* can be identified by white sandy beaches, on either side of it. Wooded cliffs, about 60 m high, extend 1.3 miles NW from Yeo Point. North of these cliffs there are no distinguishing features.

631   **Marine farm** facilities are in **Cusheon Cove** and China Cove (a local name), 0.4 and 0.6 mile west of Yeo Point.

632   **Channel Islands**, 0.3 mile NE of Yeo Point, consist of three islands. The largest island is 24 m high; the other two islands, 4 and 11 m high, are grassy. They are part of Gulf Islands National Park Reserve. **Deep Ridge** is a shoal spit extending 0.4 mile SE from Channel Islands. **Acland Islands**, 0.6 mile north of Channel Islands, consist of two islands lying close-off the SW coast of Prevost Island.

633   **Light**. — Channel Islands light *(258)*, on N end of North Channel Islands, is shown at an elevation of 8.8 m from a white tower.

634   **Light buoys**. — Deep Ridge light buoy "UN" *(257.9)*, SE of Channel Islands, is a port bifurcation buoy.

635   Acland Islands light buoy "U60" *(258.2)*, SW of the islands, is a starboard hand buoy.

636   **Batt Rock**, 1.8 miles NW of Channel Islands, has less than 2 m over it and is marked by port bifurcation buoy "UC".

637   **Horda Shoals**, 0.8 mile NNE of Batt Rock, has less than 2 m over its north part.

638   **Light buoys**. — Horda Shoals light buoy "UD" *(258.5)*, close SE of the shoals, is a port bifurcation buoy.

639   Captain Passage light buoy "U62" *(258.4)*, SE of Annette Point, is a starboard hand buoy.

640   **Secret Island** is separated from **Glenthorne Point** on Prevost Island by a very narrow passage. **Glenthorne Passage** has several private mooring buoys and floats along its shores. **Annette Inlet** and **Selby Cove**, on the NW side of Prevost Island, are narrow and shallow but afford sheltered anchorage to small craft. Annette Inlet has a drying rock in its approach and shoal depths on the north and south sides of its entrance. A private daybeacon is on the south entrance point to Annette Inlet. **James Bay**, north of Selby Cove, is sheltered from the south but open to the NW.

641   **Welbury Bay** *(48°51′N, 123°27′W)* is entered between **Welbury Point** and **Scott Point**. A shoal extending 0.6 mile SE from Welbury Point is marked at its outer end by port hand buoy "U49". A pier near the head of Welbury Bay is in poor condition, and its associated lumber mill is in ruins.

Long Harbour (1988)

Chart 3478

Chain Islands - Ganges Harbour (1988)

642   **Long Harbour**, entered between Scott Point and **Nose Point**, extends 2 miles NW terminating in a mud flat. A group of islets, connected to the north shore by a drying ridge, lie 0.4 mile NW of Nose Point. A rock, with less than 2 m over it, lies close WNW of the above islets and is marked by starboard hand buoy "U50". **Clamshell Islet**, in the middle of Long Harbour, has foul ground extending north marked by port hand buoy "U55".

643   **Lights**. — Nose Point light *(259)* is on the point.

644   Long Harbour light *(260)* is on a rock close south of Clamshell Islet.

645   **Ferries** call into Long Harbour at frequent intervals; the ferry landing is 0.2 mile west of Long Harbour light.

646   A **submarine cable** crosses Long Harbour 0.6 mile NW of Long Harbour light.

647   **Anchorage** can be obtained in Long Harbour, north of the ferry route and midway between the group of islets, near the entrance, and Clamshell Islet in the middle of the harbour, in 17 to 18 m, mud bottom. Small craft can find anchorage near the head of the harbour, clear of the submarine cable. The basin at the NW end of the harbour has foul ground in the centre. The wreck of a small cement hulled power boat is on the south side of the basin and is marked by a buoy and pole.

648   **Private facilities** of the Royal Vancouver Yacht Club protected by a rock breakwater are 0.6 mile NW of Scott Point. Numerous private wharves and floats lie in the upper reaches of Long Harbour.

Ganges Harbour

649   **Ganges Harbour** entered from Captain Passage is free of dangers in the fairway, with the exception of **Ganges Shoal** which has 4 m over it.

650   **Speed limit**. — A speed limit of 10 km/h (5 kn) is prescribed by the *Boating Restriction Regulations* for Ganges Harbour.

651   Ganges Harbour is a **water aerodrome**.

652   **Tides**. — Tidal differences for Ganges Harbour (Index No. 7407), referenced on Fulford Harbour, are in *Tide Tables, Volume 5*.

653   **Chain Islands** lie on the NE side of Ganges Harbour; named ones are **Second Sister Island**, **Third Sister Island**, **First Sister Island**, **Deadman Islands**, **Goat Island** and **Powder Islet**. **Money Maker Reef** extends 0.3 mile NW of Third Sister Island.

654   A **wreck** with 3.9 m over it lies close SW of Goat Island.

655   **Light**. — Ganges Harbour light *(261)* is on the south end of Second Sister Island.

656   **Light buoy**. — A private light buoy, in the centre of Ganges Harbour, is fitted with a speed limit sign and a radar reflector.

657   **Beacons**. — Ganges Harbour daybeacon No. 1, on a drying reef 0.1 mile NE of Deadman Islands, has a bifurcation/junction daymark, preferred channel to the right.

658   Ganges Harbour daybeacon No. 2, on a drying reef NW of Goat Island, has a starboard hand daymark.

659   **Walter Bay**, on the SE shore of Ganges Harbour, has private floats and a mooring buoy. Saltspring Island Sailing Club floats, protected by a floating breakwater, are close NW of Walter Bay.

660   **Lights**. — Private lights are shown from the breakwater.

661   **Grace Islet**, 0.4 mile west of Goat Island, is joined to a narrow peninsula, on the west side of Ganges Harbour, by a drying sand bar.

662   **Light**. — Grace Islet light *(262)* is on the low water rock E of the islet.

663   **Beacons** mark the entrance to the boat basin west of Grace Islet. Two daybeacons have starboard hand daymarks and four have port hand daymarks. The outermost port hand beacon has a radar reflector.

664   A **submarine pipeline** (sewer outfall) runs, along the centre of Ganges Harbour, from the boat basin to a discharge point approximately 0.5 mile ESE of Ganges Harbour light.

665   **Money Makers Rock**, close-off the marina near the head of Ganges Harbour, has less than 2 m over it.

666   **Ganges**, near the head of Ganges Harbour, is the agricultural centre for Saltspring Island. The community has a post office (V0S 1E0), hospital with a heliport, dental and pharmacy facilities, banks and several stores.

667   **Breakwater. — Wreck**. — A floating breakwater, NW of the public wharf, protects a marina. A wreck with 4.1 m over it lies close-off the breakwater.

668   **Berths**. — The public wharf, 0.2 mile NW of Grace Islet light, has a berthing length of 41 m and depths of 2.8 to 4.7 m alongside; it can be identified by its white shed with red trim. A 3-tonne crane is on the wharf and garbage disposal facilities are

Chart 3478

available. The L-shaped float, attached to the north end of the wharf, is for the exclusive use of aircraft and Coast Guard vessels.

669   **Public floats** for small craft are about 45 m NW of the public wharf. Gulf Islands Water Taxi operates from a float attached to these floats.

670   The **boat basin**, west of Grace Islet, is protected on its east side by a breakwater. The channel leading to the basin was dredged to 3 m (1964). Public floats with a common connection to shore are at the north end of this boat basin providing berthing space of 300 m. Power is laid on the floats; garbage and used oil disposal facilities are at the head of the floats. Private floats are east of the public floats.

671   **Marinas** are near the head of Ganges Harbour.

672   **Coast Guard has a year-round rescue unit with a launch based in Ganges.**

Plumper Sound and Navy Channel

Charts 3477, 3441, 3442

673   **Plumper Sound** *(48°46'N, 123°13'W)* has Saturna, Samuel and Mayne Islands on its east side; North and South Pender Islands form its west side. Easy of access and entered from Boundary Pass between Blunden Islet and Taylor Point it leads NW to Navy Channel which in turn leads to the junction of Swanson and Trincomali Channels. Vessels using Boundary Pass frequently use Plumper Sound as an anchorage.

674   Georgeson Passage and Winter Cove, on the NW and SE sides, respectively, of Samuel Island, lead into the Strait of Georgia. Port Browning and Pender Canal, between South and North Pender Islands, lead into Bedwell Harbour and Swanson Channel.

675   **Tides.** — Tidal differences in Plumper Sound, referenced on Fulford Harbour, are given for Hope Bay (Index No. 7360) and Samuel Island south shore (Index No. 7370) in *Tide Tables, Volume 5.*

676   **Tidal streams** flood NW and north through Swanson Channel and NW through Plumper Sound, but a branch flows east into Navy Channel, meeting that flowing through Plumper Sound off Hope Bay, where tide-rips are formed. From this position the combined stream flows east and north through narrow channels at both ends of Samuel Island into the Strait of Georgia. The ebb tidal stream runs in the reverse direction. Maximum flood tidal stream is 2 to 3 kn, at the east end of Navy Channel. Maximum ebb tidal stream is 2 to 3 kn off Croker Point, and 1 to 2 kn in Navy Channel. Blunden Islet usually has strong tide-rips in its vicinity.

677   **Submarine cables.** — A cable crosses Plumper Sound between Razor Point and Breezy Bay. Another cable crosses the sound about 0.5 mile NW of Fane Island. A submarine cable area lies in the north part of Plumper Sound, from north of St. John Point on Mayne Island to Digby Point on Saturna Island.

678   **Anchorage** in Plumper Sound is safe, convenient and easy of access to Boundary Pass. There is ample swinging room and depths range from 10 to 26 m, mud and sand bottom. Designated anchorages are in Plumper Sound; anchorages 1 to 5 are on *Charts 3442 and 3477,* and anchorages 3 to 5 are on *Chart 3441.*

679   A **conspicuous television tower** *(48°46'N, 123°10'W),* near the summit of Mount Warburton Pike, has an approximate height of 62 m and is marked by three red air obstruction lights.

680   **Ferries.** — BC Ferries operating from Tsawwassen on the mainland or Swartz Bay on Vancouver Island pass at frequent intervals through Navy Channel and Plumper Sound, and call into Lyall Harbour, on the west side of Saturna Island. Charted ferry routes are general indications of the route followed.

Plumper Sound

Chart 3477

681   **Croker Point** *(48°46'N, 123°12'W)* has a drying rock, an above-water rock and two rocks with less than 2 m over them close west of it.

682   **Lights.** — Croker Point light *(265.2),* on the above-water rock close west of the point, has a starboard hand daymark.

683   Fane Island light *(265.8)* is on the east extremity of the island.

684   **Clearing marks.** — The NE extremity of North Pender Island bearing 310° and open south of Fane Island, and the SE extremity of Lizard Island bearing 351° and open west of Elliot Bluff, lead south and west, respectively, of the dangers lying within 0.3 mile of Croker Point.

685   **Breezy Bay** lies between Croker Point and **Elliot Bluff. Saturna Beach,** in the south part of Breezy Bay, has private floats and mooring buoys off it.

686   **Razor Point,** 1.5 miles WSW of Croker Point, has a drying reef and shoal spit extending 0.2 mile east from it; its outer end is marked by starboard hand buoy "U56".

687   A **booming ground** protected by a floating breakwater lies on South Pender Island 0.8 mile SE of Razor Point.

688   **Perry Rock,** 0.8 mile NNW of Razor Point, has 2.1 m over it. **Bald Cone,** 1.4 miles NW of Razor Point, is a curious bare topped hill rising steeply from shore.

689   **Hope Bay** *(48°48'N, 123°16'W),* entered between **Auchterlonie Point** and **Fane Island,** has a public wharf and float. Hope Bay is connected to other settlements on North and South Pender Islands by road.

690   **Tides.** — Tidal differences for Hope Bay (Index No. 7360), referenced on Fulford Harbour, are in *Tide Tables, Volume 5.*

691   **Anchorage** can be obtained in Hope Bay, about 0.2 mile south of Fane Island, in 13 to 16 m, mud bottom.

Port Browning

692   **Port Browning** *(48°46'N, 123°15'W),* entered south of Razor Point, is an inlet formed by the overlap of North and South Pender Islands. The bottom is mainly mud and a convenient anchorage is 0.4 mile from the head in about 8 m.

693   **Shark Cove,** on the south side of Port Browning, is sheltered by **Mortimer Spit.** Pender Canal at the south end of Shark Cove leads into Bedwell Harbour.

694   **Hamilton Cove,** at the head of Port Browning, has a marina on its south side protected by a floating breakwater. When entering keep close to the breakwater. Rocks off the north entrance point are marked by starboard hand buoy "U52". Several stores and the Pender Island Post Office are close by. **Brackett Cove** is close north.

695   **Float.** — The public float ENE of Hamilton Cove is 15 m long with a depth of 2.4 m alongside.

Navy Channel and Plumper Sound anchorage (1981)

Saturna Point ferry landing (1988)

Boot Cove looking NNW (1988)

Lyall Harbour

696 **Lyall Harbour** *(48°48'N, 123°12'W)*, on the west side of Saturna Island, is entered between **Payne Point** and **King Islets**. **Saturna Point**, 0.5 mile ENE of Payne Point, can be identified by the conspicuous ferry landing.

697 **Crispin Rock**, 0.2 mile NE of Saturna Point, has less than 2 m over it. A rock with 3.4 m over it lies in the approach to Boot Cove, about 0.15 mile west of Saturna Point; it is marked by starboard hand buoy "U58".

698 **Light buoy. — Lights**. — Crispin Rock light buoy "UJ" *(265.5)* is a starboard bifurcation buoy.

699 Private lights with radar reflectors are shown from the ferry landing.

700 A **submarine cable area** crosses Lyall Harbour from the vicinity of King Islets to east of the public wharf.

701 A **submarine pipeline** alongside the ferry wharf extends 91 m offshore.

702 **Anchorage** in Lyall Harbour is sheltered from all but west winds and can be obtained, clear of the submarine cable area, in depths of 13 m in the entrance decreasing to 5 m about 0.1 mile from the mud flat at the head.

Chart 3477

Winter Cove entrance (1988)

Boat Passage (1988)

703   **Saturna** community, close east of Saturna Point, has a general store and post office.

704   **Wharves**. — The public wharf on Saturna Point is 34 m long at its outside face with a depth of 7.8 m alongside. Floats attached to the east side of the wharf have a combined length of 60 m with a depth of 5.5 m alongside.

705   The **ferry wharf** is close west of the public wharf.

706   **Boot Cove**, entered between Saturna Point and **Trevor Islet**, affords anchorage for small craft on a mud bottom. When entering the cove favour the starboard side to avoid a rock with 0.6 m over it. Because of hills on both sides of the cove, winds from the north or south funnel through and attain a fair strength. Marine farm facilities and private mooring buoys are in the cove.

707   A **submarine cable** crosses the entrance of Boot Cove.

Winter Cove, Georgeson Passage and Approach

708   **Samuel Island** and **Curlew Island** lie between the NW side of Saturna Island and the east side of Mayne Island.

709   **Tides**. — Tidal differences for Samuel Island (south shore) (Index No. 7370), referenced on Fulford Harbour, and tidal differences for Samuel Island (north shore) (Index No. 7515), referenced on Point Atkinson, are in *Tide Tables, Volume 5*.

710   A **submarine cable area** crosses the south approach to Winter Cove and Georgeson Passage from north of King Islets to close north of **St. John Point**.

711   **Minx Reef** is a drying reef extending 0.3 mile NW from **Mikuni Point**, the south entrance point of Winter Cove.

712   **Irish Bay**, on the south side of Samuel Island, provides good anchorage for small craft. Floats in the bay are private.

713   **Winter Cove**, between the NW side of Saturna Island and the SE side of Samuel Island, is shallow and has several drying reefs and below-water rocks in it. It affords shelter for small craft and a route from Plumper Sound to the Strait of Georgia. Private floats and mooring buoys are in the cove. The Winter Cove component of Gulf Islands National Park Reserve is on the east side of the cove. A portion of the waters of Winter Cove are a protected marine zone managed by Parks Canada.

714   **Boat Passage**, between **Ralph Grey Point** and **Winter Point**, leads into the Strait of Georgia. The passage has a least depth of 2.1 m and two drying rocks lie close-off Ralph Grey Point. It is only suitable for small craft at or near slack water, local knowledge is advised.

715   **Tidal streams**. — Secondary current station Boat Passage (Index No. 3012), referenced on Active Pass, is in *Tide Tables, Volume 5*. The flood sets E, and the ebb W through Boat Passage.

716   **Georgeson Passage** entered from Plumper Sound between the SE extremity of **Lizard Island** and the SW side of Samuel Island, leads NW then north between Curlew and Samuel Islands into the Strait of Georgia. The least depth through the fairway is 10.4 m but dangerous shoals and rocks lie in the north entrance.

717   **Tidal streams**. — Secondary current station Georgeson Passage (Index No. 3010), referenced on Active Pass, is in *Tide Tables, Volume 5*. The flood sets NW and the ebb SE through Georgeson Passage.

Georgeson Passage (1979)

Georgeson Passage (1988)

Georgeson Passage from Campbell Point (1988)

Horton Bay entrance via Robson Channel (1988)

Horton Bay entrance from north (1988)

Horton Bay public wharf (1988)

Chart 3477

Trincomali Channel looking north from Enterprise Reef (1988)

Trincomali Channel - SE part from vicinity of Governor Rock (1972)

718   **Robson Channel**, between the south end of Curlew Island and Mayne Island, leads into the south part of Horton Bay. A rock, with less than 2 m over it, lies in the east entrance to Robson Channel and a drying ledge extends south from the south extremity of Curlew Island.

719   **Horton Bay** affords snug anchorage for small craft; it should be entered at or near slack water. Entering Horton Bay from the north **Paddon Point** can be passed reasonably close-to but **Aitken Point** should be given a reasonably wide berth to avoid the piles extending from it. A rock with less than 2 m over it lies 0.1 mile off the head of the bay. Marine farm facilities are in the west end of the bay.

720   A **submarine cable** crosses the north entrance to Horton Bay.

721   **Float**. — The public float, on the south side of Horton Bay, is 24 m long with 1.8 to 3.7 m depths alongside.

Navy Channel

Chart 3442

722   **Navy Channel** *(48°49′N, 123°18′W)* leads WNW between **Mayne Island** and North Pender Island and connects Plumper Sound to the north end of Swanson Channel, and the south end of Trincomali Channel.

723   **Submarine cables** cross Navy Channel in several locations.

724   **Tidal streams** in Navy Channel are described earlier with Plumper Sound.

725   **Conconi Reef**, about 0.1 mile off the Mayne Island shore, dries 2.4 m at its highest part.

726   **Light**. — Conconi Reef light *(266)* is shown at an elevation of 6 m from a white tower with a red band at the top.

Trincomali Channel

Charts 3478, 3473, 3442, 3443

727   **Trincomali Channel** *(48°51′N, 123°23′W)* leads NW from Navy Channel, Swanson Channel and Active Pass to Pylades and Stuart Channels. The channel is deep throughout and presents no navigational difficulties. It is 0.8 mile wide at its narrowest part.

728   Captain Passage leads west and south of Prevost Island. Houstoun Passage leads around the north end of Saltspring Island,

Charts 3478, 3473, 3442, 3443

to Stuart Channel. Porlier Pass, on the NE side of Trincomali Channel, leads through to the Strait of Georgia. At the NW end of Trincomali Channel, Stuart Channel is entered between Thetis Island and Pylades Island.

729   The NE side of Trincomali Channel is formed by Galiano Island and Valdes Island; Prevost, Saltspring and Thetis Islands form its SW side.

730   **Vessel Traffic Services (VTS).** — Three calling-in points of the *Vancouver Traffic Zone*, administered by *Victoria Traffic*, are in Trincomali Channel. Assigned frequency is 156.55 MHz, Channel 11.

731   *Calling-in Point No. 9*, *Portlock Point*, is a line running 090°–270° through Portlock Point light *(267)*.

732   *Calling-in Point No. 10*, *Peile Point*, is a line running 045°–225° through Peile Point light *(268)*.

733   *Calling-in Point No. 13*, *West Porlier Pass*, is 3 miles before entry or after exit of Porlier Pass.

734   A brief description of the *Vancouver Traffic Zone* is in *PAC 200*. Details are in *Radio Aids to Marine Navigation (Pacific and Western Arctic)*.

735   **Anchorages.** — Designated anchorages lie between Valdes and Thetis Islands and are on *Chart 3443*. Anchorage 1 is also on *Chart 3473*, and 1 and 2 are on *Chart 3442*.

736   **Tides.** — Tidal differences in Trincomali Channel, referenced on Fulford Harbour, are given for Village Bay (Index No. 7414), Montague Harbour (Index No. 7420) and Porlier Pass (Index No. 7437) in *Tide Tables, Volume 5*.

737   **Tidal streams** in the SE and wider part of Trincomali Channel attain 1½ kn, but north of Wallace Island there is an increase in velocity and up to 3 kn can be expected.

738   Secondary current station Trincomali Channel (Index No. 1275), referenced on Race Passage, is located about 1 mile south of Wise Island and given in *Tide Tables, Volume 5*.

739   A **submarine cable area** approximately 2 miles in extent, from the south end of Parker Island to Wilmot Head, its NW extremity, crosses Trincomali Channel to the shore of Saltspring Island. A submarine cable crosses Trincomali Channel from Retreat Cove to south of Panther Point then up the centre of Houstoun Passage.

740   **Ferries.** — The south part of Trincomali Channel is used by large ferries operating between Swartz Bay, on Vancouver Island, and Tsawwassen on the mainland; their route is from Active Pass, west of Enterprise Reef into Swanson Channel. An inter-island ferry calls into Village Bay and crosses Trincomali Channel entering Captain Passage. Charted ferry routes are general indications of the route followed.

Approach to Active Pass

Chart 3473

741   **Enterprise Reef** *(48°51′N, 123°21′W)* consists of two rocky heads about 0.2 mile apart; each dries 0.3 m.

742   **Lights. — Buoy.** — Enterprise Reef lights *(271)*, on the west rock, are shown from a white tower with a red band at the top. The upper light, shown at an elevation of 5.9 m, is visible all round the horizon. The lower light, shown at an elevation of 3.3 m, is a sector light.

743   Port hand buoy "U51" marks the east end of the reef.

744   **Village Bay**, 1 mile SE of Helen Point, affords anchorage in about 15 m north of the submarine cable. A ferry enters the bay at frequent intervals.

745   **Ferry landing.** — A ferry landing is on the north shore of Village Bay. Private lights and radar reflectors are on the ferry dock.

746   **Tides.** — Tidal differences for Village Bay (Index No. 7414), referenced on Fulford Harbour, are in *Tide Tables, Volume 5*.

747   **Collinson Point** *(48°51′N, 123°21′W)* is a steep-to, rugged, rocky point rising steeply to a summit about 0.5 mile NW. **Helen Point**, about 0.4 mile SE, is the termination of a thickly wooded slope that rises gently to the summit of Mount Parke.

748   **Light.** — Helen Point light *(272)* is on the point.

749   **Beacon.** — Helen Point daybeacon, close NE of the light, has a starboard hand daymark.

Portlock Point to Phillimore Point

Charts 3478, 3442

750   **Hawkins Island**, 1 mile NW of Portlock Point, has a few bushes on it. It is part of Gulf Islands National Park Reserve. Waters north, west and east of the island, 200 m perpendicularly distant from the natural boundary of the land, are a protected marine zone managed by Parks Canada. A beach of white shells on the NE side of Prevost Island and close to Hawkins Island is prominent. **Charles Rocks** consist of several drying rocks extending 0.4 mile NW from Hawkins Island.

751   **Marine farm** facilities are on the south side of Hawkins Island.

752   **Peile Point**, the north extremity of Prevost Island, lies at the junction of Captain Passage and Trincomali Channel. **Sutil Mountain**, 1.5 miles NE of Peile Point, is on Galiano Island and rises to an elevation of 300 m, it has prominent cliffs on its south side.

753   **Light.** — Peile Point light *(268)* is shown at an elevation of 7.6 m from a white tower.

754   **Ben Mohr Rock**, 0.8 mile NE of Peile Point, has 4 m over it.

755   **Light buoy.** — Ben Mohr Rock light buoy "UK" *(270)*, NE of Peile Point light, is a starboard bifurcation buoy.

Montague Harbour and Approach

Chart 3473

756   **Parker Island** *(48°53′N, 123°25′W)*, across the entrance of Montague Harbour, has steep cliffs on its SW side. **Julia Island** lies close-off its SE extremity and **Wilmot Head** is the NW extremity of Parker Island. The channel between Wilmot Head and **Sphinx Island** has a depth of 7.3 m through its fairway. Large cable signs are onshore at the NW and SW ends of Parker Island.

757   **Phillimore Point**, about 0.2 mile SE of Julia Island, is the south entrance point of Montague Harbour.

758   **Light.** — Phillimore Point light *(269)* is shown at an elevation of 7.3 m from a white tower with a red band at the top.

759   **Montague Harbour**, on the SW side of Galiano Island, is sheltered by Parker Island and affords a good anchorage for small craft. Its south entrance, between Phillimore Point and Julia Island, is easy of access. The north entrance, between **Gray**

Montague Harbour - south entrance (1988)

Montague Harbour ferry landing and marina (1988)

Wise and Sphinx Islands from Trincomali Channel (1979)

Chart 3473

Houstoun Passage from Trincomali Channel (1991)

Peninsula and the peninsula on the NE side of Parker Island, has a depth of 5.2 m through the centre of its fairway.

760   A **ferry** occasionally calls into Montague Harbour, it generally uses the south entrance and berths on the NE side of the harbour, about 0.4 mile NE of **Winstanley Point**. The ferry landing, with private light and radar reflectors, is close NW of the public float.

761   **Overhead cables** (power) cross both the south and north entrances to Montague Harbour, vertical clearance through both entrances is 38 m. Red spheres are attached to the cables to increase visibility.

762   A **submarine cable area** crosses the south entrance to Montague Harbour from, south of Winstanley Point to the SE side of Parker Island.

763   The **tower** on Gray Peninsula is a useful landmark.

764   **Sewage disposal** in the waters of Montague Harbour is prohibited under the *Pleasure/Non-Pleasure Craft Sewage Pollution Prevention Regulations.*

765   **Tides**. — Tidal differences for Montague Harbour (Index No. 7420), referenced on Fulford Harbour, are in *Tide Tables, Volume 5.*

766   **Payne Bay** north of Phillimore Point offers temporary anchorage, mud and sand bottom.

767   **Buoys**. — Several public mooring buoys are in the north end of Montague Harbour, to the east of Gray Peninsula. They are part of the facilities provided by **Montague Harbour Marine Park**.

768   **Wharves**. — A public wharf and float are at the marine park.

769   **Public floats**, on the east side of Montague Harbour 0.4 mile NE of Winstanley Point, have 97.5 m of berthing space.

770   A **marina** is close south of the public float.

771   Numerous private floats line the south and east shores of the harbour.

Parker Island to Norway Island

Chart 3442

772   **Wise Island** *(48°54'N, 123°27'W)* and **Charles Island** lie NW of Parker Island. **Ballingall Islets**, NW of Wise Island, are low and covered with stunted shrubs. **Ballingall Islets Park** is a nature reserve.

773   **Atkins Reef** *(48°53'N, 123°28'W)*, 1.4 miles SW of Wise Island, dries 2.6 m.

774   **Beacon**. — Atkins Reef daybeacon, on the highest part of the reef, has a bifurcation/junction daymark, preferred channel to the right.

775   **Mount Parke** *(48°50'N, 123°18'W)*, on Mayne Island, has a radar tower with red air obstruction lights on its summit.

776   **Clearing marks**. — The summit of Mount Parke in line with the SW extremity of Galiano Island, bearing about 115°, leads about 0.5 mile NE of Atkins Reef and the dangers SE of it.

777   **Walker Hook** *(48°54'N, 123°30'W)* is a narrow wooded peninsula. A reef with less than 2 m over it extends 0.3 mile ESE. Reasonable anchorage, sand bottom, can be obtained inside the reef during west winds.

778   **Governor Rock**, 1 mile north of Walker Hook, lies nearly in mid-channel and has two heads with less than 2 m over them.

779   **Light buoy**. — Governor Rock light buoy "U45" *(290)*, east of the rock, is a port hand buoy.

780   **Victoria Rock**, 0.8 mile west of Governor Rock, has 4.3 m over it and is marked on its west side by starboard bifurcation buoy "UE".

781   **Victoria Shoal**, 0.3 mile NE of Victoria Rock, has 4.9 m over it.

782   **Light buoy**. — Victoria Shoal light buoy "U43" *(291.3)*, NW of Governor Rock, is a port hand buoy.

783   **Walker Rock**, 1.5 miles ESE of Panther Point, is a narrow drying ledge with shoal water extending 0.2 mile NW.

784   **Lights**. — Walker Rock lights *(291)* are shown from a white tower. The upper light, shown at an elevation of 7.2 m, is visible all round the horizon. The lower light, shown at an elevation of 6.9 m, is a sector light with the white sector indicating the preferred channel leading to Houstoun Passage.

785   **Clearing marks**. — The NE extremity of Thetis Island bearing 310° and open east of the NE side of Wallace Island leads between Governor and Walker Rocks.

786   **Retreat Cove** *(48°56'N, 123°30'W)* has depths of 1.8 to 8.2 m in its SE corner and affords good shelter for small craft. **Retreat Island**, in the middle of the cove, is connected to shore by a drying flat. **Scarrow Reef** dries 2.7 m.

787   **Wharf**. — The public wharf, with a float attached to its outer end, is in the SE part of Retreat Cove. The float is 31 m long with a depth of 4 m alongside.

788   **Quadra Hill** *(48°56'N, 123°28'W)* is prominent. A conspicuous white patch, shaped like a lug sail, is on the cliffy coast under the hill. **Bodega Hill**, 3 miles NW of Quadra Hill, is conspicuous, it has one very large isolated tree on it and rises above some prominent high cliffs.

789   **Spotlight Cove**, 3.3 miles NW of Retreat Cove, has private moorings. **North Galiano**, 1 mile north of Spotlight Cove, has a general store.

The Cut looking west (1988)

The Cut - west end (1988)

Chart 3442

Trincomali Channel from Stuart Channel (1972)

790   **Wharf**. — The public wharf in North Galiano has a depth of 3 m alongside the wharf face. A float on the north side has a depth of 2.4 m alongside.

Clam Bay and Approach

Chart 3477

791   **Light**. — Norway Island light *(286.5)*, on the NW end of Norway Island *(48°59'N, 123°38'W)*, is private and seasonal.

792   **Beacon**. — A private daybeacon on a rock off the NW extremity of Norway Island has a starboard hand daymark.

793   **Penelakut Spit**, 0.3 mile west of Norway Island, is low, white in appearance and composed of broken clam shells. The passage between Penelakut Spit and Norway Island, encumbered with several below-water rocks, is only suitable for small craft; local knowledge is advised. An Indian village at the south end of Penelakut Spit has a conspicuous church spire.

794   **Clam Bay**, between the north end of Kuper Island and the SE part of Thetis Island, is entered between Penelakut Spit and **Leech Island**. **Centre Reef**, in the entrance to Clam Bay, dries 0.6 m and is marked at its SE end by starboard hand buoy "U42". **Rocket Shoal**, 0.2 mile south of Leech Island, consists of several rocks with less than 2 m over them.

795   A **submarine cable** (power) crosses Clam Bay from south of Leech Island to Norway Island.

796   The SW corner of Clam Bay has marine farm facilities which lie off the SW shore.

797   **Anchorage** for small craft can be obtained south of Rocket Shoal in about 9 m, mud bottom.

798   **The Cut**, at the west end of Clam Bay, is a very narrow dredged channel leading to Telegraph Harbour; it is usable by small craft at or near HW. The north side of the passage consists of a revetment formed by dredging overcast, the south side is a drying mud flat.

799   **Caution. — The Cut is not recommended without the aid of local knowledge. Slow speed should be used to avoid excessive wash. Visibility is obscured by a sharp turn at the west end.**

800   **Beacons**. — The upstream direction for the beacons is when proceeding west from Clam Bay to Telegraph Harbour. The north side of The Cut is marked by daybeacons with starboard hand daymarks. The south side is marked at the Clam Bay entrance, by a daybeacon with a port hand daymark. A daybeacon on the north side of the narrows, at the west end, has an orange triangular daymark.

801   **Tide scales** on beacons at both ends of The Cut are not referenced to Chart Datum.

802   **Tidal streams** in The Cut flood east and ebb west.

803   **Submarine cables** (telephone) cross The Cut at its west end.

Trincomali Channel — NW End

Chart 3443

804   **Hall Island** *(48°59'N, 123°36'W)*, **Reid Island** and **Rose Islets** front Clam Bay and form a chain south and west of Porlier Pass.

805   Rose Islets are an **Ecological Reserve**, landing is not permitted without a permit.

806   **Cardale Point** *(49°01'N, 123°36'W)* is a low, sandy projection at the SW end of **Valdes Island**. **Shingle Point**, 2 miles NW of Cardale Point, is also low and sandy.

807   Between Shingle Point and **Blackberry Point**, 1 mile NW, there are high cliffs above which rises **Mexicana Hill**, the highest part of Valdes Island.

808   Stuart Channel can be entered from the north end of Trincomali Channel, between Pilkey Point *(49°01'N, 123°41'W)* and Pylades Island, 2.5 miles north.

Pylades Channel

Charts 3475, 3443

809   **Pylades Channel** *(49°06'N, 123°42'W)* leads NW from Trincomali Channel, between the west side of Valdes Island and the **De Courcy Group** to the SE. From the NW end of Pylades Channel, Gabriola Passage leads east into the Strait of Georgia and False Narrows leads NW into Northumberland Channel.

Pirates Cove Marine Park - south side (1988)

Pirates Cove (1988)

Pirates Cove entrance (1988)

Gabriola Passage looking east (1991)

Gabriola Passage looking west (1991)

Charts 3475, 3443

Degnen Bay public wharf (1988)

810   Whaleboat Passage and Ruxton Passage lead west through the De Courcy Group to Stuart Channel. These passages and the SW sides of the islands are described with Stuart Channel.

811   **Anchorages**. — Designated anchorages, Nos. 7 to 9, lie within Pylades Channel.

812   **Tidal streams** in Pylades Channel attain 2 kn at times; the flood sets NW and the ebb SE.

813   The NE shore of Pylades Channel, between Blackberry Point *(49°03′N, 123°39′W)* and Dibuxante Point, 5 miles NW, is mainly composed of cliffs. **Coal Mine Bay**, 0.7 mile SE of Dibuxante Point, is a booming ground and has mooring buoys in it.

814   **Private mooring buoys** lie close offshore from Ruxton Island.

Chart 3475

815   **Pirates Cove Marine Park** *(49°06′N, 123°43′W)* is on the SE side of De Courcy Island. A drying reef in the entrance of **Pirates Cove** extends NW from the north end of this peninsula; it is marked by a daybeacon with a port hand daymark. Starboard hand buoy "U38" is west of the daybeacon. Pass between the beacon and buoy when entering. A white line painted on a rock, with a white cross on a pole, above it serves as a range to clear the north end of the drying reef. Public dinghy floats are in the cove.

816   **Anchorage** for small craft can be obtained in Pirates Cove; it is sheltered from all but north winds. Ring bolts for stern

mooring are located along the shore of the peninsula on the east side of the cove.

817   **Buoy**. — Port hand buoy "U37" marks the outer edge of the drying reefs extending from the NE extremity of De Courcy Island.

Gabriola Passage

818   **Gabriola Passage**, between Valdes Island and **Gabriola Island**, is narrow, intricate and has numerous dangers in its east approach. This combined with the velocity of the tidal streams does not recommend it for general navigation. It should only be navigated at slack water, by those familiar with local conditions.

819   **Tides**. — Tidal differences for Degnen Bay (Index No. 7445) inside Gabriola Passage, referenced on Fulford Harbour, are in *Tide Tables, Volume 5*.

820   **Tidal streams**. — Predictions of the times and rates of maximum current and the times of slack water are given for Gabriola Passage (Index No. 3300) in *Tide Tables, Volume 5*. The flood sets east and the ebb west through Gabriola Passage; the maximum on the flood is 8½ kn and on the ebb 9 kn.

821   **Dibuxante Point**, the NW extremity of Valdes Island, is the SW entrance point to Gabriola Passage. A drying rock ledge extends 0.1 mile NW of Dibuxante Point.

822   **Light**. — Dibuxante Point light *(433.8)* is on the W. entrance to Gabriola Pass.

Porlier Pass range lights slightly open (1988)

Porlier Pass from SW (1972)

Porlier Pass from east (1979)

Chart 3475

823 **Degnen Bay**, on the north side of Gabriola Passage, affords excellent shelter for small craft. A public wharf on the north shore has a float on its NE side providing 120.4 m of berthing space with a depth of 3 m alongside. A 5-tonne crane, power and garbage and used oil disposal facilities are available on the wharf. There are several private floats close west of the public wharf.

824 **Wakes Cove** offers anchorage for small craft but is exposed to the NW.

825 The three small islets SE of **Cordero Point** *(49°07'N, 123°42'W)* are wooded, the largest of these islets is **Kendrick Island**. The bay formed between these three islets and the east shore of Valdes Island, known locally as Dogfish Bay, offers good sheltered anchorage and is used regularly by towboats with rafts when awaiting tides or are weather-bound. Floats and mooring buoys of a yacht club are on the west side of Kendrick Island.

826 **Light**. — Gabriola Passage East light *(433.5)* is off the NE side of Valdes Island.

827 **Breakwater Island**, 0.7 mile east of Cordero Point, lies across the east approach to Gabriola Passage. **Rogers Reef**, on the north side, at the east entrance to Gabriola Passage consists of a group of drying and sunken rocks.

828 **Lights**. — Rogers Reef light *(433.3)*, on the E entrance of Gabriola Pass, is shown at an elevation of 5.5 m from a white tower.

829 Breakwater Island light *(433.2)* is on the west side of the island, opposite the entrance to Gabriola Passage.

Porlier Pass

Chart 3473

830 **Porlier Pass** *(49°01'N, 123°35'W)* was discovered and named in 1791 by Jose M. Narvaez after Antonio Porlier, an official in Madrid. It is known locally as Cowichan Gap. The pass is entered from Trincomali Channel between **Alcala Point** and **Cayetano Point**, 0.8 mile NNW. It is not less than 0.4 mile wide but the navigable channel is narrow and tidal streams run with considerable strength. The channel can be safely taken by a handy vessel at slack water.

831 **Vessel Traffic Services** (VTS). — Before entering and after leaving Porlier Pass report to *Victoria Traffic* on 156.55 MHz, Channel 11. Calling-in points are:

832 *Calling-in Point No. 13*, *West Porlier Pass*, is 3 miles before entry or after exit.

833 *Calling-in Point No. 14*, *East Porlier Pass*, is 3 miles before entry or after exit.

834 A brief description of the *Vancouver Traffic Zone* is in *PAC 200*. Details are in *Radio Aids to Marine Navigation (Pacific and Western Arctic)*.

835 **Tides**. — Tidal differences for Porlier Pass (Index No. 7437), referenced on Fulford Harbour, and for Dionisio Point (Index No. 7535) at the east end of the pass, referenced on Point Atkinson, are in *Tide Tables, Volume 5*.

836 **Tidal streams**. — Predictions of times and rates of maximum current and times of slack water are given for Porlier Pass (Index No. 3100) in *Tide Tables, Volume 5*. Maximum flood is 10 kn and the ebb is 7 kn; it sets from Trincomali Channel into the Strait of Georgia on the flood and in the reverse direction on the ebb.

837 **Buoyage**. — Upstream direction for buoyage purposes is proceeding NE from Trincomali Channel toward the Strait of Georgia.

838 **Virago Point** *(49°01'N, 123°35'W)* is the extremity of a narrow projection, faced with cliffs on its west side.

839 **Light range**. — Porlier Pass range lights, in line bearing 196°, are on Virago and Race Points. The rear light *(289)*, on Virago Point, is shown at an elevation of 10.3 m from a white tower. The front light *(288)*, on the extremity of **Race Point**, is shown at an elevation of 6.8 m from a white tower.

840 **Boscowitz Rock**, close SW of Race Point, dries 1.2 m.

841 **Lighthouse Bay**, between Virago and Race Points, affords shelter for small craft. Its east shore is cliffy. An overhead cable, vertical clearance 23 m, crosses the drying flats at the head of the bay. A submarine cable (power) is laid across the entrance of the bay.

842 **Anchorage** for small craft can be obtained in Lighthouse Bay, south of the submarine cable.

843 **Romulus Reef**, 0.25 mile SSW of Virago Point light, has depths of 7.3 m.

844 **Black Rock**, which dries 3.4 m, lies about 0.4 mile NW of Virago Point light. A rock, with 2.6 m over it, lies 0.1 mile SE of Black Rock and a rock with 0.5 m over it is about 61 m ENE from the daybeacon on Black Rock.

845 **Beacon**. — Black Rock daybeacon, on the NW end of the rock, has a starboard hand daymark.

846 **Virago Rock**, 0.2 mile NE of Black Rock, dries 0.6 m and lies on a shoal with depths of 1.8 to 2.1 m.

847 **Light**. — Virago Rock Sector light *(289.3)* is shown at an elevation of 6.8 m from a white structure with a green band at the top.

848 **Dionisio Point** *(49°01'N, 123°34'W)* is connected to Galiano Island by a narrow ridge of sand.

849 **Vernaci Point**, at the SE end of Valdes Island, should be given a clearance of at least 0.2 mile. The coast between Vernaci Point and **Shah Point**, 0.65 mile NNW, is fringed with drying reefs and shoals. **Canoe Islet**, 0.3 mile east of Shah Point, is 3 m high with drying reefs extending 0.2 mile SSE from it.

850 **Light buoy**. — Porlier Pass light and bell buoy "U41" *(287)*, off E entrance to pass, is a port hand buoy.

851 Canoe Islet and the drying reefs are an **Ecological Reserve**, landing is not permitted without a permit.

852 **Wreck**. — The historically important wreck of the sidewheel steamer *Del Norte* is located at *49°01'35"N, 123°35'18"W*. Vessels should not anchor in this vicinity to avoid damaging the remains.

853 **Galiano Island**, with Porlier Pass at its north end and Active Pass at its south end, is 14 miles long in a NW/SE direction.

Active Pass

854 **Active Pass** *(48°52'N, 123°20'W)*, between Mayne and Galiano Islands, is a deep, tortuous channel leading from Swanson and Trincomali Channels into the Strait of Georgia. The fairway is about 0.2 mile wide in its narrowest part. Fairway Bank lies in the centre of the north entrance to Active Pass. Local knowledge is advised.

Active Pass looking west (1988)

Active Pass looking east (1979)

Active Pass looking north (1988)

Chart 3473

855　　Active Pass is frequently used by large, fast ferries linking Victoria and Vancouver. A vessel traversing the pass could meet as many as three such ferries in the pass. It is also frequently used by all types of coastal vessels, including tugs towing barges, coastal tankers and freighters. Particulalry during summer months, numerous fishing and pleasure craft are encountered.

856　　Great care should always be taken to avoid the dangers at the west entrance, as well as Fairway Bank and the shoals, on either side of the north entrance to the pass. Active Pass is not recommended for attempting under sail.

857　　**Vessel Traffic Services (VTS).** — Before entering and after leaving Active Pass report to *Victoria Traffic* on 156.55 MHz, Channel 11. Calling-in points are;

858　　*Calling-in Point No. 9*, *Portlock Point*, at the west end of Active Pass, is a line running 090°–270° through Portlock Point light *(267)*.

859　　*Calling-in Point No. 10*, *Peile Point*, at the west end of Active Pass, is a line running 045°–225° through Peile Point light *(268)*.

860　　*Calling-in Point No. 11*, *Active Pass*, at the east end of Active Pass, is 3 miles NE of Active Pass light *(275)*.

861　　For Portlock and Peile Points, both in Trincomali Channel, see *Chart 3442*. A brief description of the *Vancouver Traffic Zone* is in *PAC 200*. Details are in *Radio Aids to Marine Navigation (Pacific and Western Arctic)*.

862　　**Sound signals.** — Visibility is obscured by two bends in the channel. Sound signals prescribed by *Rule 34(e)* of the *Collision Regulations* are used.

863　　**Buoyage.** — Upstream direction for buoyage purposes in Active Pass is proceeding from Trincomali Channel toward the Strait of Georgia.

864　　**Tides.** — Tidal differences in Active Pass, referenced on Point Atkinson, are given for Georgina Point (Index No. 7525) and Miners Bay (Index No. 7528) in *Tide Tables, Volume 5*.

865　　**Tidal streams.** — Predictions of times and rates of maximum current and times of slack water are given for Active Pass (Index No. 3000) in *Tide Tables, Volume 5*.

866　　On the north-going (flood) tidal stream, there is a strong set into Miners Bay along its north shore, and on the south-going (ebb) tidal stream there is a corresponding set into the bay along its south shore. Heavy freshets from the Fraser River increase the rate of the south-going tidal stream.

867　　**Flood streams.** — Approaching from south, the flood stream rapidly gains velocity off Helen Point. Turning east in conformity with the channel, the main stream sets close to Matthews Point. From 0.2 mile south of Mary Anne Point, it sets ENE as far as Laura Point, whence it is deflected to NE and follows close along the east shore. This direction is maintained as far as Fairway Bank, where the influence of the flood in the Strait of Georgia is felt and the stream from Active Pass veers to NW in the vicinity of Gossip Shoals.

868　　A portion of the flood stream turns south from Laura Point creating a large clockwise eddy in Miners Bay. Off Mayne Island wharf, the current attains 2½ kn. It returns to the main stream off Mary Anne Point causing great turbulence on strong tides. A weaker eddy occurs on the flood north of the main stream and NE of Mary Anne Point. It sets anti-clockwise and returns to the main stream close to Mary Anne Point.

869　　Off Georgina Point, a weak current from the east occurs on the flood.

870　　At a point midway between Georgina Point and Fairway Bank, it can set west or even SW at 1 to 1½ kn.

871　　On strong flood tides, violent rips, dangerous to small craft, occur over an area extending from mid-channel, south of Mary Anne Point, to Laura Point. Strong rips also occur near Fairway Bank and are increased in violence during strong winds from the north quadrant.

872　　**Ebb streams.** — From the Strait of Georgia, the ebb appears to set SSE across the entrance to Active Pass. Near Fairway Bank, it is often weak and variable in direction, but on large tides, the set is south at 1 to 2 kn. After passing Laura Point, the main ebb stream veers west and opposite Matthews Point its greatest strength is found somewhat south of mid-channel. Passing over the shoal area north of Helen Point, it sets across the south entrance to Collinson Point, whence the current disperses in Trincomali Channel.

873　　On the ebb an anti-clockwise eddy appears in Miners Bay, which can attain 2 kn, off the Mayne Island wharf on strong tides. An eddy also appears west of Helen Point. The main ebb stream, setting strongly toward Collinson Point, appears to cause this indraught of water from the south that moves anti-clockwise across the entrance. On strong tides, at a point midway between Helen and Collinson Points, the set can be due west at 1 to 1½ kn. No rips of any violence occur on the ebb tide in Active Pass.

874　　**Caution. — On the Strait of Georgia side of Active Pass heavy tide-rips occur in the vicinity of Gossip Island, Lion Islets and Salamanca Point, particularly with the flood tidal stream and a strong NW wind.**

875　　**Submarine cables** (power and telephone) cross Active Pass in the area between Matthews and Mary Anne Points and at Scoones Point.

Helen Point to Georgina Point

876　　Active Pass is entered from Trincomali Channel between Collinson Point *(48°51'N, 123°21'W)* and Helen Point 0.4 mile SE.

877　　**Georgeson Bay**, on the north side of the channel, lies between Collinson Point and **Matthews Point**. Off the west shore is a drying ledge with Galiano light on it, and farther north there are several shoals and rocks with less than 2 m over them. **Salalikum Rock**, which dries 0.6 m, lies close SE of Matthews Point.

878　　**Light.** — Galiano light *(273)* is on the above-mentioned drying ledge.

879　　**Mary Anne Point**, 0.6 mile east of Matthews Point, is steep-to on its south side.

880　　**Light.** — Mary Anne Point light *(274)* is on the point.

881　　**Bellhouse Bay**, between **Scoones Point** and **Burrill Point**, has drying reefs in it.

882　　**Miners Bay**, 0.5 mile SE of Mary Anne Point, affords an anchorage in case of necessity. Mariners must go close inshore to obtain a depth of 20 m, and even there are barely out of the whirl of the tidal streams. **Caution is necessary because of the strong eddies that set into the bay.** Numerous private mooring buoys lie close offshore. Anchorage is prohibited in the submarine cable area.

883　　Miners Bay is a **water aerodrome** known as Mayne Island.

884　　**Mayne**, a settlement in the SE corner of Miners Bay, has a post office and heliport. Communication with neighbouring

Miners Bay public wharf (1988)

Sturdies Bay public wharf and ferry landing (1988)

Whaler Bay entrance (1988)

Chart 3473

communities is maintained by the B.C. Ferries through the terminal at Village Bay.

885   **Wharf**. — The public wharf has a berthing face of 22 m with a depth of 4 m alongside. Floats are attached to the public wharf. The float on the south side is for small craft. Floats are on the north side, one for seaplanes, the other is a fuel float. A surge due to traffic of large vessels and ferries is experienced alongside the wharf.

886   **Sturdies Bay** is shallow with some foul ground extending about 0.1 mile from the head. A combined public wharf and ferry landing has a depth of 4.9 m alongside its head. The public float, 24 m long, is attached to the west side of the wharf. A surge due to traffic of large vessels and ferries is experienced alongside the wharf. The community has stores and resorts.

887   **Lights**. — Private lights and radar reflectors are on the outer end of the Sturdies Bay ferry landing.

888   **Fairway Bank** *(48°53'N, 123°18'W)*, which has a least depth of 9.1 m, lies almost midway between **Rip Point**, north of Sturdies Bay, and **Georgina Point** 0.9 mile ESE. There is no kelp on the bank but except at slack water, its position is marked by tide-rips.

889   **Light**. — Active Pass light *(275)*, on Georgina Point, is shown at an elevation of 17.4 m from a white tower, 10.7 m high. It is fitted with a radiobeacon and has a heliport.

890   **Georgina Shoals** lie about 0.3 mile NE of Active Pass light. The sea occasionally breaks over the shoals where depths are less than 2 m.

891   **Gossip Island**, about 1.3 miles NW of Georgina Point, has drying ledges extending SE from it, into the north approach to Active Pass. **Gossip Shoals**, off the SE end of Gossip Island, consist of drying reefs and several rocks with less than 2 m over them.

892   **Light buoy**. — Gossip Shoals light and bell buoy "U47" *(276)*, E of shoal, off SE end of Gossip Island, is a port hand buoy. **It is very liable to drag off its charted position** owing to its exposed location and the strength of tidal streams.

Whaler Bay

893   The passage between Gossip Island and **Cain Peninsula** leads to **Whaler Bay**; it has rocks and shoals in its SE entrance and a least depth of 10.4 m.

894   **Submarine cables** cross the passage between Cain Peninsula and Gossip Island; they are marked by signs.

895   The north entrance to Whaler Bay lies between Gossip Island and **Twiss Point**. **Lion Islets**, 0.4 mile north of Twiss Point, consist of two islets connected by a drying reef; the passage west of the islets is unusable even for small craft.

896   **Caution. — Heavy tide-rips occur in the vicinity of Gossip Island and Lion Islets, particularly with a flood tidal stream and a strong NW wind.**

897   An **overhead cable**, vertical clearance 11 m, crosses the bay south of Twiss Point.

898   **York Rocks**, off the NW side of Gossip Island, consist of a rock 5 m high and several drying and below-water rocks.

899   **Wharves**. — The public wharf and float are in the south arm of Whaler Bay, about 0.2 mile south of **Cain Point**. Depths of as little as 0.3 m are found in the vicinity of this wharf. There are numerous private wharves, floats and flag staffs along the shores of Whaler Bay and Gossip Island.

900   A **booming ground** and log dump are on the west shore, of the south arm of Whaler Bay.

901   **Tides**. — Tidal differences for Whaler Bay (Index No. 7532), referenced on Point Atkinson, are in *Tide Tables, Volume 5*.

CHAPTER 3

Strait of Georgia (SE Part), Vancouver Harbour, Howe Sound and Nanaimo Harbour

General

Charts 3462, 3463, 3512

1   This chapter describes the SE part of the Strait of Georgia. The south limit is north entrances of Boundary Pass and Rosario Strait. The north limit is between Cottam Point *(49°19'N, 124°13'W)* and Sargeant Bay *(49°28'N, 123°51'W)*. Burrard Inlet, with the facilities of the Harbour of Vancouver, Howe Sound with Squamish Harbour at its head, and Nanaimo Harbour are described.

Strait of Georgia — SE Part

2   **Strait of Georgia (SE part)** *(48°50'N, 123°00'W)* is entered from the south by way of Boundary Pass *(48°48'N, 123°00'W)* or Rosario Strait. The west side of this portion of the strait is formed by the east coasts of Saturna, Samuel, Mayne, Galiano, Valdes, Gabriola and Vancouver Islands. Boat Passage, Georgeson Passage, Active Pass, Porlier Pass and Gabriola Passage lead west through these islands to the channels separating the Gulf Islands. Fairway, Rainbow and Horswell Channels, between Gabriola and Vancouver Islands, are the approach channels to Nanaimo Harbour.

3   **Caution. — The shore between Boundary Pass and Active Pass should be given a berth of at least 2 miles. It is fringed with dangers and lights on Georgina and East Points are obscured over them.**

4   Entering the Strait of Georgia from Boundary Pass or Rosario Strait the promontory of Point Roberts appears as an island or a flat wooded feature and makes an excellent landmark. High piles of coal, shiploaders and container cranes at Westshore Terminals and Deltaport, 4 miles NW of Point Roberts, also make good landmarks. Between Point Roberts and the entrance to Burrard Inlet, 20 miles NNW, the east shore of the Strait of Georgia is fronted by the drying sand and mud flats of the Fraser River delta extending 5 miles offshore. The outer limit of the Harbour of Vancouver, west of these drying flats, extends from the International Boundary to Point Grey, then north across the entrance of Burrard Inlet to Point Atkinson.

5   From Point Atkinson *(49°20'N, 123°16'W)* to Sargeant Bay, 25 miles NW, the coast and islands in the entrance of Howe Sound are mountainous. This stretch of coast and the remainder of the NE side of the Strait of Georgia as far as the north tip of Malaspina Peninsula is known as the **Sunshine Coast**.

6   **Halibut Bank** *(49°20'N, 123°43'W)*, with 20.1 m over it, and **McCall Bank** *(49°21'N, 123°36'W)*, with 29 m over it, lie in the Strait of Georgia SW of the entrance to Howe Sound.

7   **Light buoy.** — Halibut Bank ODAS light buoy "46146" *(447.5)* is on the bank.

8   **International Boundary** between Canada and the United States of America runs from the middle of Boundary Pass, along the SE part of the Strait of Georgia to a position west of Point Roberts.

Then east crossing Point Roberts and the entrance of Boundary Bay, and then into Semiahmoo Bay and the mainland.

9   **Traffic Separation Scheme** in the Strait of Georgia commences north of Boundary Pass and leads north along the east side of the strait into Burrard Inlet. This Traffic Separation Scheme is recommended for use by all ships.

10   Mariners are advised that a revised Traffic Separation Scheme in the Strait of Georgia came into force at 0000 Coordinated Universal Time (UTC) on 1 December, 2002. Major changes are:

   a)   A new precautionary area has been established in the Strait of Georgia west of Deltaport and the Tsawwassen Ferry Terminal;

   b)   Expansion of precautionary area "RB" at the south end of Rosario Strait; and

   c)   Re-alignment of existing Traffic Separation Scheme with Separation Scheme north of Rosario Strait, and their linkage with a new precautionary area off East Point.

11   In Canadian waters and fishing zones, provided it does not impede the passage of any vessel following a traffic lane, a vessel engaged in fishing may depart from certain provisions of *Rule 10* of the *International Regulations for Preventing Collisions at Sea, 1972*, and fish in any direction in a traffic lane. A vessel engaged in special operations such as buoy tending or hydrographic surveys, provided it does not prevent other vessels using the route from navigating safely, may also depart from certain provisions of *Rule 10*. For details see *Collision Regulations* in *PAC 200*.

12   **Traffic Separation Scheme** commencing east of Sucia Islands and leading SE into **Rosario Strait** is part of the mandatory *Puget Sound Vessel Traffic Service*. Details of this service and its regulations are in *United States Coast Pilot 7*.

13   **Vessel Traffic Services (VTS).** — A Co-operative Vessel Traffic System (CVTS) between Canada and the United States of America has been established in the Strait of Georgia through which the International Boundary runs. The SE part of the Strait of Georgia with the exception of the approaches to Howe Sound, Burrard Inlet, Vancouver Harbour and the Fraser River, in *Sector One* of the *Vancouver Traffic Zone*, is administered by *Victoria Traffic* and the assigned frequency is 156.55 MHz, Channel 11.

14   The approaches to Burrard Inlet and Howe Sound in *Sector Three* are administered by *Vancouver Traffic* and the assigned frequency is 156.6 MHz, Channel 12. *Sector Three* is defined as all waters north and east of a line from the Iona Breakwater light *(49°12'18"N, 123°15'50"W)*, thence 270°, 6.6 miles to *49°12'18"N, 123°25'53"W*, thence 000°, 8.15 miles to Cape Roger Curtis light *(417)*, thence 303°, 4.8 miles to Gower Point *(49°23'01"N, 124°32'06"W)*, including all the waters of Howe Sound and Burrard Inlet.

15   The NW part of the Strait of Georgia in *Sector Four* of the *Vancouver Traffic Zone* is administered by *Comox Traffic*. *Sector Four* is bounded on the south by a line from Reception Point light *(448.8)* to Merry Island light *(449)* to Ballenas Islands light *(490)* to Cottam Point *(49°18'15.7"N, 124°12'45"W)*.

Charts 3462, 3463, 3512

16   When approaching designated calling-in points that coincide with a change of sector make a report when 3 miles from the sector change line. On crossing the sector change line change to the new frequency and report at the designated calling-in point.

17   Special operating procedures at Calling-in Point 24, when changing from *Sector One* to *Sector 4* require:

    (a)   Northbound vessels to call *Victoria Traffic* and check out of *Sector One* then call *Comox Traffic*; and

    (b)   Southbound vessels to call *Comox Traffic* and check out of *Sector Four* then call *Victoria Traffic*.

18   A brief description of this VTS is in *PAC 200*. Details are in *Radio Aids to Marine Navigation (Pacific and Western Arctic)*. Calling-in points in the Strait of Georgia (SE part) are:

19   **Calling-in Point No. 8**, *Patos Island*, is a line joining Patos Island Sector light *(265)* with **Alden Bank** light and gong buoy "A" *(US 19910)*. This CIP is administered by *Victoria Traffic* and *Seattle Traffic*;

20   **Calling-in Point No. 11**, *Active Pass*, is 3 miles NE of Active Pass light *(275)* before entry or after exit of Active Pass;

21   **Calling-in Point No. 12**, *Sand Heads*, is a change from *Sector One* to *Sector Two* and is a line running 000°–180° through Sand Heads light *(311)*;

22   **Calling-in Point No. 14**, *East Porlier Pass*, is 3 miles NE of Virago Rock Sector light *(289.3)* before entry or after exit of Porlier Pass;

23   **Calling-in Point No. 15A**, *Iona*, is a change from *Sector One (Victoria Traffic)* to *Sector Three (Vancouver Traffic)* and is a line due west of the Iona Breakwater light *(49°12'18"N, 123°15'50"W)* intersecting with 15B at *49°12'18"N, 123°25'53"W*;

24   **Calling-in Point No. 15B**, *Cape Roger Curtis*, is a change from *Sector One (Victoria Traffic)* to *Sector Three (Vancouver Traffic)* and is a line due south of Cape Roger Curtis light *(417)* intersecting with 15A at *49°12'18"N, 123°25'53"W*;

25   **Calling-in Point No. 15C**, *Gower Point*, is a change from *Sector One (Victoria Traffic)* to *Sector Three (Vancouver Traffic)* and is a line joining Cape Roger Curtis light *(417)* and Gower Point *(49°23'01"N, 123°32'06"W)*;

26   **Calling-in Point No. 23**, *Entrance Island/Five Fingers Island*, is a line joining Entrance Island light *(435)* and Five Finger Island *(49°14'N, 123°55'W)*;

27   **Calling-in Point No. 24**, *Ballenas Island/Merry Island/Welcome Passage*, is a change from *Sector One (Victoria Traffic)* to *Sector Four (Comox Traffic)* and is a line joining Reception Point light *(448.8)*, Merry Island light *(449)* and Ballenas Islands light *(490)*. When northbound mariners shall indicate whether their course is through Malaspina Strait, Sabine Channel, Stevens Passage, or west of Sisters Islets.

28   **Ferries** on frequent regular schedules cross the Traffic Separation Scheme in the Strait of Georgia between Tsawwassen *(49°00'N, 123°08'W)* and Active Pass *(48°53'N, 123°18'W)*, Tsawwassen and Nanaimo (Duke Point) *(49°10'N, 123°54'W)*, and between Fraser River and Active Pass and Nanaimo. Another ferry route across the SE part of the Strait of Georgia is between Horseshoe Bay *(49°23'N, 123°16'W)* and Departure Bay *(49°12'N, 123°58'W)*. Charted ferry routes are general indications of the route followed.

29   **Fishing vessels** can be encountered in large concentrations anywhere within the Strait of Georgia, from approximately July 1 to November 1 and sporadically throughout the year.

30   **Military exercise areas** are charted in the SE part of the Strait of Georgia. Area WE is a non-firing area for general purpose exercises. Area WF is for general purpose and anti-submarine exercises excluding high explosive projectiles. Area WG is for general purpose type exercises and torpedo firing; it has associated air space CYD 107 for surface firing high trajectory and air to sea firing.

31   **Mariners are advised to avoid Exercise Area WG, particularly during hours of darkness or reduced visibility.** Equipment recovery vessels operate by day or night and exhibit a flashing red light in addition to the prescribed lights and shapes. They should not be approached closer than 1,400 m due to outlying unlit buoys. Unlighted buoys and lighted buoys are temporarily deployed in the area and are not charted.

32   The portion of Area WG enclosed by pecked lines is an active area within which torpedo firings are conducted from 0700–1730 Monday to Saturday, during which time vessels will be required to clear the area on demand. Area WG constitutes a defence establishment as defined in the *National Defence Act* to which *Defence Controlled Access Area Regulations* apply. Additional information is available from:

    (a)   VHF Channel 21B (listen only); and

    (b)   Comox MCTS, Winchelsea Island Control VHF Channel 16, or Victoria Traffic VHF Channel 11.

33   For full information on military exercise areas see *Notices to Mariners 1 to 46 Annual Edition*.

34   **Spoil grounds**. — In the SE part of the Strait of Georgia ocean dump sites, under permit through the *Ocean Dumping Control Act*, are located in *49°06'N, 123°20'W* and *49°15'N, 123°55'W*. A disused explosive dumping area is in *49°22'N, 123°57'W*.

35   **Submarine cables**. — A cable (fibre optic) crosses the Strait of Georgia from Point Roberts and passes through Boundary Pass. Submarine cables cross the SE part of the Strait of Georgia, from Point Roberts to Mayne Island about 1 mile SE of Active Pass. A cable area crosses the Strait of Georgia with its south limit being a line between Salamanca Point, on Galiano Island, and a position 0.7 mile north of Point Roberts light; its north limit is a position on Galiano Island 4 miles WNW of Salamanca Point and a position on Roberts Bank 7.5 miles NW of Point Roberts. A submarine cable is laid from a position 5 miles SE of Dionisio Point on Galiano Island to the Middle Arm of the Fraser River. A submarine cable extends from the entrance of Burrard Inlet, in a WSW direction, to the centre of the Strait of Georgia, then leads WNW through the centre of the strait. A submarine cable extends from close west of Jericho Beach, across Spanish Bank, then leads across the Strait of Georgia to Qualicum Beach. Several abandoned cables cross the Strait of Georgia from Burrard Inlet to Nanaimo Harbour.

36   **Tides**. — Tidal predictions in the SE part of the Strait of Georgia are given for Point Atkinson (Index No. 7795). Tidal differences, referenced on Point Atkinson, are given for Tumbo Channel (Index No. 7510), Samuel Island, north shore (Index No. 7515), Georgina Point (Index No. 7525), Whaler Bay (Index No. 7532), Dionisio Point (Index No. 7535), Valdes Island (Index No. 7542), Silva Bay (Index No. 7550), Nanaimo (Index No. 7917), Nanoose Bay (Index No. 7930), Winchelsea Islands (Index No. 7935), Northwest Bay (Index No. 7938), Blaine (Index No. 7570), White Rock (Index No. 7577), Crescent Beach (Index No. 7579), Tsawwassen (Index No. 7590), Sand Heads (Index

No. 7594) and Roberts Creek (Index No. 7824). These tidal predictions and differences are in *Tide Tables, Volume 5*.

37   **Currents**. — *Current Atlas, Juan de Fuca Strait to Strait of Georgia* is available from CHS chart distribution offices and authorized chart dealers.

38   Surface currents in the Strait of Georgia are produced by the combined effect of tides, winds and runoff from the Fraser River. Within the main portion of the strait all three are separately capable of generating surface currents of comparable strength. In connecting passes to the strait however it is the hydraulic head, or difference in tidal height between either end of the pass, which determines speed and direction of currents. Other effects will only become important near slack water. Near shore and in restricted passageways, topography of the bottom and shape of the shoreline will also strongly influence motion of surface waters. Upwellings and backeddies are two of the more common features of such topographic influences.

39   Within the main channel of the Strait of Georgia tidal currents set NW on the flood and SE on the ebb. The effect of the earth's rotation (Coriolis effect), is to turn these currents slightly to the right of their direction of motion so that the flood is somewhat stronger and of longer duration on the eastern side than on the western side of the strait. The ebb on the other hand is somewhat stronger and of longer duration on the western side for the same reason. Tidal currents in the strait reach their maximum of over 2 kn in the southern strait south of a line between Point Roberts and Active Pass. Within the central portion of the strait, between this line and the southern end of Texada Island, tidal currents attain maximums of about 2 kn. In the northern strait, where the tides propagating from the south meet those propagating from the north, tidal currents are less than 1 kn and variable in direction from one flood tide to the next. Only on the flood, within 1 mile of the approach to Discovery Passage, do tidal currents become appreciably greater than 1 kn. There is also an increase in maximum attainable speeds within some of the more confined passages such as Sabine Channel and Malaspina Strait, but these never attain speeds to be found in the southern end of the strait.

40   Because of the nature of the tide in the Strait of Georgia **maximum ebbs and floods** for a particular tide occur about midway between HW and LW. HW slack and LW slack occur within an hour of the local HW and local LW, respectively. Since times of tide over the whole of the strait differs by only 18 minutes at most, from the times of the tide at Point Atkinson, tidal predictions at that station serve as a reference for determining tides and tidal currents elsewhere in the strait. This is not true however of the major passes such as Porlier Pass, Active Pass, Gabriola Passage and First Narrows, in which tidal currents are not related to those within the strait itself. Current predictions for these passages are published under separate headings in the Tide Tables. In addition the jet-like structure of currents flooding through these passages will alter surface motions to about 1 mile or so into the strait.

41   **Fresh water runoff from the Fraser River** is a major factor influencing surface currents in the central portion of the Strait of Georgia. This is particularly so from May to September when the volume of river water flowing into the strait seaward of Sand Heads usually exceeds 2,800 m³ per second. During the peak runoff period in late June a large percentage of the area of this region will be covered by a 1 – 9 m layer of brackish silty water. Under influence of wind and the hydraulic head between the river mouth and the strait, this top layer of relatively light water can

move in a manner that differs considerably from tidal currents in the saltier oceanic water beneath. During periods of light winds it has been observed that the surface plume of fresh water flowing from the main arm near Steveston will on the ebb maintain its SW direction toward Active Pass despite the fact that the tidal currents are to the SE. If the ensuing flood is weak this portion of the plume may then reach the vicinity of the Gulf Islands within one tidal cycle (12½ hours) having drifted across the strait at typical speeds of 1 to 2 kn. If the flood is not weak the plume will move northward during light winds. Fraser River runoff entering the strait on the flood on the other hand immediately begins to curve to the north. It may then reach Burrard Inlet or continue to drift northward in the direction of Sechelt Peninsula. Typical drift speeds of the surface layer at this time are between 1 to 2 kn, which is comparable to tidal currents in this area.

42   During summer speed of river water flowing into the strait can reach over 4 kn near the time of LLW but this is reduced to about 1 kn near times of HHW. The former are slowed to speeds of 1 kn or so within a few miles of Sand Heads. In winter when runoff is low, less than 570 m³ per second, flood tidal currents reverse the river flow such that the resultant currents are upriver as far inland as New Westminster.

43   Off the Fraser River delta, north of the Steveston Jetty, surface currents are often persistently southerly. This near-shore current is usually confined to about 2 to 3 miles west of the shore and attains 1 kn or more. It is most probably a feature of summer and autumn oceanographic conditions, and will be less prevalent in winter and early spring.

44   On the flood tide, and when close to Roberts or Sturgeon Banks, onflow of water onto the banks creates a set toward these banks.

45   Provided they exceed 15 kn winds will also become important in moving the surface layer of light brackish water over the saltier water beneath. Under the influence of such winds the top layer will slide downwind like a lubricated slab of "slippery water". A typical layer 5 m thick for example will drift downwind at about 1 kn under 15 kn winds. When wind speeds exceed 25 kn and there is a fairly widespread surface layer of light water produced by the Fraser River runoff, surface currents will be mainly wind influenced while tides will have only a secondary influence.

46   Finally there are poorly understood drift motions in the Strait of Georgia called "residual currents", which can cause the circulation to differ significantly from that expected from the combined action of the wind, tides and Fraser River runoff. Since they are unpredictable mariners should not expect surface currents to behave in a completely regular manner even when all observable influences have been considered.

47   **Meteorological information** for the Strait of Georgia is in *PAC 200*. Meteorological information for Ballenas Islands, Gower Point, Nanaimo, Vancouver International Airport and White Rock, wind frequency tables for Entrance Island and Sand Heads and a frequency of fog table for Vancouver International Airport are in the Appendices.

48   **Caution for small craft. — Steep confused seas are formed by winds blowing against the flood tidal stream off the entrances to Boundary Pass, Active Pass and Porlier Pass and by winds blowing against the ebb tidal stream off Fraser River and in the approaches to Vancouver Harbour and Howe Sound.**

49   During summer months effects of the freshet from the Fraser River and NW winds that blow strongly nearly every

Charts 3462, 3463, 3512

afternoon cause rough conditions for small craft along the west portion of the Strait of Georgia. Crossings to the mainland or travel along the east shores of the Gulf Islands should be carried out early in the morning, but the most preferred time is late afternoon or early evening when winds die away.

50 In winter Arctic air from the interior surges down Howe Sound creating gale force outflow winds called "Squamish Winds"; they spread out in a jet over the Strait of Georgia. Due to sheltering, Point Atkinson lighthouse reports are not indicative of Squamish Winds.

51 **Navigation**. — Loran-C coverage in the open waters of the Strait of Georgia is good. It is not reliable close to shore, especially near mountainous coastlines such as the approaches to Howe Sound and Malaspina Strait. For details regarding the best signal strength and position fixing geometry see *PAC 200*.

52 **A radiobeacon** is on Georgina Point at Active Pass.

53 **Racons** are fitted to Canoe Pass Light Buoy, Roberts Bank Light, Roberts Bank Cautionary Light buoy, Rosenfeld Rock Light Buoy, Thrasher Rock Light and Vancouver Approach Cautionary Light Buoy.

Boundary Bay — Semiahmoo Bay

Chart 3463

54 **Boundary Bay** indents the mainland between white cliffs forming the east extremity of Point Roberts (*48°58'N, 123°02'W*) and **Kwomais Point**, 6.5 miles NE. Most of the bay is filled with drying flats.

55 **The International Boundary** between Canada and the United States of America passes through Boundary Bay. Note. — For a description of the waters south of the International Boundary see *United States Coast Pilot 7*.

56 **Harbour limits**. — The Canadian waters of Boundary Bay and Semiahmoo Bay, up to the average HW line, are defined in the *Canada Marine Act* as a part of the Harbour of Vancouver.

57 **Fishing vessels**. — Extensive night drift fishing in the area from Point Roberts to Blaine makes night navigation difficult.

58 **Light buoy**. — Point Roberts light and bell buoy "4" *(300)*, at the outer end of a rock ledge extending SE from the SE extremity of Point Roberts, is a starboard hand buoy.

59 **Light**. — International Boundary Obstruction light *(304)* is on the west side of Boundary Bay, at the edge of the drying flats.

60 **Light ranges**. — International Boundary range C lights *(306, 307)* are in Semiahmoo Bay about 2 miles SE of White Rock.

61 International Boundary range B lights *(305, 305.1)* are on the west side of Boundary Bay. A red air obstruction light is shown from the top of the rear tower.

62 **Mud Bay**, in the NE part of Boundary Bay, has narrow, shallow channels leading across its drying flats through which the **Nicomekl River** and **Serpentine River** discharge. These channels converge at **Blackie Spit**.

63 **Lights**. — Crescent Beach light *(299.5)*, at the entrance to the Nicomekl River, is shown from a dolphin with a starboard hand daymark.

64 Crescent Channel light *(299.6)*, 0.4 mile SW of Blackie Spit, is shown from a dolphin with a starboard hand daymark.

65 **Beacons**. — The channel leading to Crescent Beach and the Nicomekl River is marked by port and starboard hand daymarks on dolphins and the above-mentioned lights.

66 A **speed limit** of 4 kn is posted in Nicomekl River.

67 **Crescent Beach**, at Blackie Spit, is a year-round residential community and has a variety of restaurants and shops. The public wharf on Blackie Spit is 58 m long and has a 12 m float attached to its NE side. A marina is in a dredged basin close east of the bridge.

68 **Tides**. — Tidal differences for Crescent Beach (Index No. 7579), referenced on Point Atkinson, are in *Tide Tables, Volume 5*.

69 **Burlington Northern Railway Bridge** has a swing span that shows a red light when closed and a green light when open. The swing span has a vertical clearance of 2.7 m when closed; the trestle has a vertical clearance of 3.7 m. A height clearance gauge is on the NW end of the bridge.

70 The bridge is manned 0630 to 2230 seven days a week. The bridge opening signal is 3 blasts on a horn or telephone the Crescent Beach Marina at least one hour before arrival time and before 1530 hours (604) 538-9666.

71 A **submarine pipeline** is laid across the Nicomekl River close east of the marina.

72 **White Rock** is a seaside community along the north side of **Semiahmoo Bay**. It has a train station, shops, restaurants, schools, and several recreation facilities.

73 **Light**. — White Rock breakwater light *(299.7)*, close west of the breakwater, is shown from a dolphin.

74 **Customs**. — White Rock is a Canadian Port of Entry for customs clearance used by pleasure craft.

75 **Tides**. — Tidal differences for White Rock (Index No. 7577), referenced on Point Atkinson, are in *Tide Tables, Volume 5*.

76 **Wharf. — Breakwater**. — The public wharf is at the outer end of a long jetty projecting south across the drying foreshore. The jetty is 470 m long and 5 m wide. Floats, at the outer end of the jetty, are protected by a rock breakwater.

77 **Meteorological information** for White Rock is in the Appendices.

Point Roberts to Point Grey

78 The coast north of Point Roberts (*48°58'N, 123°05'W*) to **English Bluff**, 3 miles north, consists of bluffs of moderate elevation. North of Tsawwassen the shore merges into the swampy Fraser River delta and is low, featureless and barely discernible from a vessel in the strait. Fronting this portion of the coast are Roberts and Sturgeon Banks. These banks dry in patches, are steep-to and extend up to 5 miles offshore.

79 **Harbour limits**. — The east side of the Strait of Georgia, between the International Boundary and Point Grey, is defined in the *Canada Marine Act* as a part of the Harbour of Vancouver.

Chart 3492

80 **Point Roberts** (*48°58'N, 123°05'W*) is the termination of a remarkable promontory extending south from the Fraser River delta. At the SE extremity of the promontory are white cliffs with trees on their summit; from the trees the land declines gradually to the SW extremity of the promontory terminating in a low shingle point. From a distance, particularly from the south, Point Roberts appears as an island. A rocky ledge that dries in places extends 1 mile SE of the SE extremity of the promontory (*Chart 3463*).

Chart 3492

81 **Light**. — Point Roberts light *(301)*, on the S extremity of the point, is shown at an elevation of 9.1 m from a skeleton tower with a red and white diamond-shaped daymark.

82 A large **marina**, at **South Beach**, 1 mile east of Point Roberts light, is entered to the west of and protected by a detached rock breakwater. The NW side of the entrance channel is marked by dolphins. The outer dolphin and both ends of the breakwater are marked by privately operated lights.

83 **Customs**. — A United States Customs Officer is based at the marina.

84 **Boundary Bluff** *(49°00'N, 123°05'W)* is on the Canada/United States boundary. A granite monument, 7.6 m high, stands on the summit of the bluff.

85 **Light range. — Light**. — International Boundary range A lights *(302, 303)* are on the shore north of Point Roberts. A red air obstruction light is shown from the top of the rear tower.

86 International Boundary light "A" *(US 19969)*, 0.8 mile west of the front light, is shown at an elevation of 7.6 m from a concrete structure.

87 **Submarine pipelines** (storm drains) extend offshore in the vicinity of Boundary Bluff.

88 **Tsawwassen** *(49°00'N, 123°08'W)*, on the north side of English Bluff, is the site of a large prominent ferry terminal.

89 **Ferry landing**. — A causeway extends 1.6 miles in a SW direction from the north side of English Bluff. The Tsawwassen Terminal operated by the British Columbia Ferry Services Inc is at the outer end of this causeway. Regular and frequent passenger and automobile service is maintained to and from Swartz Bay and Nanaimo (Duke Point), on Vancouver Island, and ports in the Gulf Islands. A breakwater, about 0.2 mile long, is a short distance south of the ferry landing.

90 **Tides**. — Tidal differences for Tsawwassen (Index No. 7590), referenced on Point Atkinson, are in *Tide Tables, Volume 5*.

91 **Lights. — Fog signal**. — Tsawwassen Ferry breakwater light *(307.1)* is on the west end of the south breakwater.

92 Tsawwassen light *(307.13)*, 0.4 mile west of the ferry terminal, is privately operated.

93 Tsawwassen Ferry South light *(307.15)*, off S breakwater, is privately operated. The fog signal is operated by ferry personnel when required for ferry movements only.

94 Additional privately operated lights and radar reflectors are shown from the ferry berths.

95 **Light range**. — Tsawwassen range lights *(307.121, 307.122)*, in line bearing 017°, lead to the ferry terminal and are privately operated.

96 Two privately operated light ranges, in line bearing 043°, lead to other ferry berths.

97 **Westshore Terminals** *(49°01'N, 123°10'W)* and **Deltaport**, NW of the ferry terminal, can be identified by conspicuous high piles of coal, shiploaders, and container cranes with air obstruction lights on them. Westshore Terminals is used by bulk carriers loading coal for export and has two deep-sea berths. Deltaport is a container terminal capable of handling two Post Panamax vessels.

98 **Lights** on the extremities of Westshore Terminals berths are privately operated.

Westshore Terminals & Deltaport (1999)

Deltaport & Westshore Terminals (1999)

Chart 3492

Major Port Facilities — Roberts Bank

Berth	Wharf Length (m)	Least Depth (m)	Elevation (m)	Remarks
Westshore Terminals Berth 1	350	22.9		Handles coal and coke. Mooring buoys at east and west ends. Designed for vessels up to 260,000 dwt, Design approach velocity for vessels when 80% loaded is 12 cm/sec. Single travelling shiploader.
Westshore Terminals Berth 2	263	20.8		Handles coal and coke. Designed for vessels up to 150,000 dwt. Two quadrant shiploaders capable of handling 5,442 tonnes/hour. Floating moorings ahead and astern the loaders.
Deltaport Berth 1	335	15.5	2.8	Handles containers. Six gantry cranes capable of handling 50 tonnes each and spanning 18-20 containers wide. On-dock intermodal railyard. Eight loading rail tracks 1,067.5 m each. 40 hectares open storage capacity 25,000 TEU's.
Deltaport Berth 2	335	15.5	2.8	As above

99　　**Light range**. — Roberts Bank Entrance range lights *(307.91, 307.92)*, in line bearing 032°, are inshore of Westshore Terminals on the SE side of Deltaport.

100　　**Beacon range**. — A beacon range bearing 302° is near the inner end of the berths at Deltaport.

101　　**Light buoys**. — The dredged basin at Westshore Terminals and Deltaport is marked by light buoys named Roberts Bank *(307.2, 307.3, 307.4, 307.5, 307.7, 307.9)*, starboard hand "T2", "T4", "T6", "T8", port hand "T1" and cautionary "TB".

102　　**Approach**. — During smaller flood and ebb tides the velocity and direction of tidal streams off the approach to Westshore Terminals and Deltaport may be different from those indicated on the chart. The channel leading to Westshore Terminals Berth No. 2 and Deltaport is dredged to 20.4 m (1994). A turning basin, south of the channel, was dredged to 12.2 m (1994) but has a least depth of 11.6 m.

103　　**Arrival information**. — Westshore Terminals and Deltaport are within the limits of the Harbour of Vancouver, and under the jurisdiction of the Vancouver Port Authority and Harbour Master, telephone (604) 665-9144. Tugs are available for berthing. Port regulations for the Harbour of Vancouver apply.

104　　**Anchorage designated "R"** *(49°00'46"N, 123°12'14"W)* is in a depth of about 70 m. Due to depth and prevailing weather in this area, Pilot must remain onboard at all times while the vessel is anchored.

105　　**Berths**. — Details of berths at Westshore Terminals and Deltaport are given in the adjacent table.

106　　**A barge loading ramp** and float are at the NE end of Deltaport.

107　　**Roberts Bank** extends north from Westshore Terminals to the main channel of the Fraser River.

108　　**Caution. — Mariners navigating along or close to Roberts and Sturgeon Banks on the flood tide are warned to avoid being set toward the banks by onflow of water onto the banks.**

109　　**Light buoy. — Racon**. — Canoe Pass light and bell buoy "T14" *(308)*, at the entrance to the Pass, is a starboard hand buoy fitted with a Racon (— • —).

110　　A shallow channel, marked by private buoys and dolphins, leads from the above buoy across Roberts Bank to Canoe Passage. It is described in Chapter 4.

111　　**Dolphins**. — Two dolphins about 0.6 mile apart, close SE of Canoe Pass light and bell buoy, mark a cable area and have privately operated lights and radar reflectors.

112　　**Light. — Racon**. — Roberts Bank light *(309)*, close south of the entrance to Fraser River main channel, is shown at an elevation of 10.9 m from a white tower with a red band at the top and a concrete building, on piles. It is fitted with a Racon (— •).

Chart 3463

113　　**Sand Heads** *(49°06'N, 123°18'W)* forms the north entrance point to the main channel of the Fraser River. **Sturgeon Bank** fronts the Fraser River commencing from Sand Heads and extends 9 miles north to the NW extremity of North Arm Jetty.

114　　**Light**. — Sand Heads light *(311)*, near the outer end of the Steveston Jetty, is shown at an elevation of 12.7 m from a white tower.

115　　**Light buoys. — Racon**. — Roberts Bank Cautionary light buoy "TA" *(309.5)*, 3.6 miles WSW of Sand Heads light, is a cautionary buoy fitted with a Racon (— — —).

116　　Fraser River Light buoy "S0" *(312)*, about 0.7 mile SW of Sand Heads light, is a starboard hand buoy.

117　　Sand Heads light and bell buoy "S1" *(310)*, about 0.3 mile WSW of the light, is a port hand buoy.

118　　Sturgeon Bank light buoy "T10" *(380.5)*, 4.5 miles north of Sand Heads light, is a starboard hand buoy.

119　　**Tides**. — Tidal differences for Sand Heads (Index No. 7594), referenced on Point Atkinson, are in *Tide Tables, Volume 5*.

120　　A **wind frequency table** for Sand Heads is in the Appendices.

121　　**Iona Breakwater** *(49°12'N, 123°16'W)* extends in a WSW direction across Sturgeon Bank from Iona Island.

122　　A **submarine pipeline** (sewer outfall) extends 1.6 miles west of the breakwater.

123　　**Light**. — A privately operated light with a radar reflector is 0.1 mile west of the breakwater.

124　　**Conspicuous dome. — Lights**. — A conspicuous golf ball-shaped radar dome, with fixed red lights, is at Vancouver International Airport *(49°11'57"N, 123°11'09"W)*. The airport control tower is conspicuous. Air obstruction lights are shown from dolphins on the west side of Sea Island and from towers at the airport.

Boundary Pass to Gabriola Passage

Charts 3441, 3462

125　　**Tumbo Island** *(48°48'N, 123°04'W)* is wooded. Steep cliffs 6 to 15 m high extend along its south side. It is part of Gulf

Charts 3441, 3462

Tumbo Channel looking north (1991)

Tumbo Channel looking south (1991)

Islands National Park Reserve, no camping. Waters surrounding Tumbo Island, Cabbage Island and Pine Islet are a protected marine zone managed by Parks Canada.

126   **Tumbo Channel** is deep but has dangers in both entrances.

127   **Tides**. — Tidal differences for Tumbo Channel (Index No. 7510), referenced on Point Atkinson, are in *Tide Tables, Volume 5*.

128   **Cabbage Island** and **Pine Islet**, both part of Gulf Islands National Park Reserve, lie on a drying reef extending WNW from the NW end of Tumbo Island. Foul ground with several rocky heads extends 1 mile beyond this reef. **Reef Harbour**, between Cabbage Island and the west end of Tumbo Island, can be used as a temporary anchorage for small craft, local knowledge is advised. Mooring buoys are located here and camping permitted on Cabbage Island.

Charts 3477, 3442

129   **Russell Reef**, east of Winter Point, lies about 0.1 mile north of Saturna Island and is part of Gulf Islands National Park

Reserve. **Mount David**, near the north end of Saturna Island, has a rounded summit and is prominent when seen from the north.

130   **Tides**. — Tidal differences for **Samuel Island, North Shore** (Index No. 7515), referenced on Point Atkinson, are in *Tide Tables, Volume 5*.

131   **Belle Chain Islets**, north of and parallel to Samuel Island, consist of a number of islets, drying reefs and below-water rocks, and are part of Gulf Islands National Park Reserve. Anniversary Island, at the south end of the chain, has a few trees on it, no camping. Surrounding waters and north to Campbell Point on Mayne Island are a protected marine zone managed by Parks Canada.

132   **Georgeson Island** *(48°51'N, 123°14'W)* has a chain of islets, drying reefs and shoals extending 2 miles SE from it, they obstruct the east approach to Georgeson Passage. The passage between Georgeson Island and **Campbell Point**, to the NW, is narrow with a depth of 0.3 m through it. Favour the Georgeson Island side to avoid the drying reef extending from Campbell

Charts 3477, 3442

Belle Chain Islets looking north (1991)

Belle Chain Islets looking south (1991)

Passage between Campbell Point & Georgeson Island (1988)

Point. Georgeson Island and Campbell Point are part of Gulf Islands National Park Reserve. Adjacent waters are a protected marine zone managed by Parks Canada.

133   **Bennett Bay**, south of Campbell Point, affords good anchorage for small craft but is exposed to SE winds. The Mayne Inn is conspicuous and has a large sign "Mayne Inn" painted on its roof. Private floats are in the bay.

134   **Campbell Bay**, entered between Campbell Point and **Edith Point**, affords temporary anchorage, mud bottom and it is exposed to the SE.

Chart 3442

135   **David Cove** (*48°52'N, 123°17'W*) is fringed by drying ledges and has a launching ramp and **submarine cables** running through it.

136   The north end of **Mayne Island** is fronted by Georgina Shoals; these shoals, together with Gossip Shoals, Gossip Island and Lion Islets, lie in the north approach to Active Pass.

137   **Salamanca Point** (*48°54'N, 123°21'W*) is a rocky point on which trees grow nearly to the HW line, it is prominent from NW and SE.

138   **Caution. — Heavy tide-rips occur in the vicinity of Salamanca Point, Lion Islets and Gossip Island, particularly with the flood tidal stream and a strong NW wind.**

139   **A submarine cable area** (power) crosses the Strait of Georgia, its limits are between Salamanca Point and a position on Galiano Island 4 miles WNW. Another submarine cable crosses the strait 2.2 miles WNW.

140   **Tides**. — Tidal differences for Dionisio Point (Index No. 7535), referenced on Point Atkinson, are in *Tide Tables, Volume 5.*

Chart 3443

141   Porlier Pass (*49°01'N, 123°35'W*) separates Galiano Island from Valdes Island, it is described in Chapter 2.

Chart 3443

142   Between Porlier Pass and Gabriola Passage, 8 miles NNW, the NE coast of Valdes Island has no distinguishing features. Several shoals lie about 0.3 mile offshore between Shah Point and **Detwiller Point**.

143   **Tides**. — Tidal differences for **Valdes Island** *(49°04'N, 123°37'W)* (Index No. 7542), referenced on Point Atkinson, are in *Tide Tables, Volume 5.*

East Approach to Gabriola Passage

Chart 3475

144   **Thrasher Rock** *(49°09'N, 123°38'W)* is steep to on all but its west side.

145   **Light. — Racon**. — Thrasher Rock light *(433)* is shown at an elevation of 11 m from a white tower with a green band at the top and is fitted with a Racon (— • • —).

146   **Gabriola Reefs**, extending about 1.5 miles SSW from Thrasher Rock, consist of drying and below-water rocks.

147   **Light buoy**. — Gabriola Reefs light buoy "UM" *(433.1)*, at the south extremity of the reefs, is a port bifurcation buoy.

148   Breakwater Island *(49°08'N, 123°41'W)* lies across the east entrance to Gabriola Passage; it is described with Gabriola Passage in Chapter 2.

149   **Flat Top Islands**, north of Breakwater Island, consist of **Bath Island, Saturnina Island, Sear Island, Tugboat Island, Vance Island, Lily Island, Carlos Island, Gaviola Island** and **Acorn Island. Brant Reef**, 0.2 mile NE of Acorn Island, is 1 m high.

150   **Commodore Passage** is formed by Tugboat and Vance Islands on its SW side; Acorn and Gaviola Islands form its NW side. A reef, which dries 4.8 m, lies 0.1 mile SE of Acorn Island and a rock awash lies close south of this reef.

151   **Light**. — Tugboat Island light *(434)* is on a drying reef about 0.2 mile SE of the island.

152   An **overhead cable**, with a vertical clearance of 14 m, joins Tugboat and Sear Islands and is marked by orange spheres.

153   **Submarine cables** cross the passage between Breakwater and Tugboat Islands and between Gabriola and Sears Islands.

154   **Silva Bay** has three passages leading into it and is frequently used by small craft. It is sheltered by Vance, Tugboat and Sear Islands. Silva Bay offers various activities, shops, general store, restaurants, marine repairs and resorts. Silva Bay is the home of a wooden boat building school. Marinas are on the west side of Silva Bay.

155   The main entrance to Silva Bay is between Tugboat and Vance Islands. It is encumbered with a drying reef projecting north from Tugboat Island and **Shipyard Rock** in mid-channel. The least depth in the channel north of Shipyard Rock is 5.9 m.

156   **Lights. — Buoy**. — Silva Bay light *(434.3)*, NW of Tugboat Island, has a port hand daymark.

157   Port hand buoy "U39" marks the NW extremity of the drying reef.

158   A privately operated light is shown from yacht club floats on Tugboat Island.

159   The south entrance to Silva Bay leads between Sear and Gabriola Islands. It is about 30.5 m wide and has a least depth of 1 m.

160   The north entrance to Silva Bay, between Lily and Vance Islands, is entered at its north end between Carlos Island and the shoals north of Lily Island. The least depth through this channel is 3.6 m.

161   **Buoy**. — East cardinal buoy "PA" marks the shoals north of Lily Island.

162   **Tides**. — Tidal differences for Silva Bay (Index No. 7550), referenced on Point Atkinson, are in *Tide Tables, Volume 5.*

Flat Top Islands to Cottam Point

Chart 3443

163   The north coast of **Gabriola Island** between **Law Point** *(49°09'N, 123°42'W)* and **Orlebar Point**, 5.5 miles NW, is bold and thickly wooded.

Chart 3458

164   **Lock Bay** *(49°11'N, 123°49'W)* is exposed and not recommended as an anchorage.

165   The NE approach to Nanaimo Harbour lies between Entrance Island, 0.5 mile NE of Orlebar Point, and Neck Point *(49°14'N, 123°58'W)*; it is described with Nanaimo Harbour.

166   **Icarus Point**, 3 miles WNW of Neck Point, is not well defined and difficult to identify.

Chart 3459

167   **Blunden Point** *(49°15'N, 124°05'W)* is wooded and cliffy. **Edgell Banks**, 0.6 mile east of **Maude Island**, have a least depth of 9.1 m.

168   **Light**. — Maude Island (Nanoose Harbour) light *(486)*, near the E end of island, N side of entrance to the harbour, is shown at an elevation of 9.8 m from a white tower with a red band at the top.

169   A **submarine cable** is laid from 0.3 mile SE of Blunden Point to the north Winchelsea Island.

170   **Nanoose Harbour**, entered between Blunden Point and **Wallis Point**, is a Canadian Forces Base. Wallis Point, the east extremity of a low island, has a number of stunted trees on it. **Nanoose Hill**, on the north side of the harbour, has two summits, which from the south appear as a notched peak. The head of the harbour is low and swampy and its south shore is low with no natural distinguishing features. The north side is bolder in character and fringed with rock cliffs. Marine farm facilities are in several locations around the harbour, some are marked by buoys.

171   **Radio towers** at two locations on the north shore are marked by red air obstruction lights.

172   **Controlled Access Zone**. — Mariners are cautioned that Nanoose Harbour is a Controlled Access Zone. For details see No. 43 of *Notices to Mariners 1 to 46 Annual Edition.*

173   **Harbour limits. — Regulations**. — Nanoose Harbour is a Public Harbour and its limits are defined as "All tidal waters West of a line drawn South from the high water line at Wallis Point to the high water line of the southerly shore of the harbour". It is governed by *Public Harbours Regulations*. The north shore and adjacent waters of the harbour are an Administration Control and Benefit Area of the Department of National Defence. Naval vessels use Nanoose Harbour for exercises and mooring. Shore areas within these limits are restricted and landing is prohibited.

174   **Tides**. — Tidal differences for Nanoose Bay (Index 7930), referenced on Point Atkinson, are in *Tide Tables, Volume 5.*

175   **Mooring buoys**. — Several DND orange and white mooring buoys are in Nanoose Harbour.

Fleet Point - Nanoose Harbour (1990)

176   **Nonooa Rock**, 0.3 mile SW of Wallis Point has 1.8 m over it, is steep-to on its south side, and marked by starboard hand **buoy "P20"**.

177   **Richard Point**, 0.5 mile west of Nonooa Rock, has a drying rock ledge extending east from it.

178   **Lights**. — Nanoose Harbour light *(487)* is on the point SW of Richard Point.

179   A privately operated light, 0.5 mile west of Nanoose Harbour light, is on the outer end of a wharf, it is occasionally shown. Privately operated lights are shown from the wharf at Ranch Point.

180   **Impérieuse Rock**, 0.25 mile SW of Richard Point, has 1.8 m over it. **Entrance Rocks**, 0.1 mile south of Impérieuse Rock, are a group of drying rocks on a mud flat extending north from **Fleet Point**.

181   **Light buoy**. — Impérieuse Rock light buoy "P21" *(488)*, north of the rock, is a port hand buoy.

182   **Breakwater**. — A rockfill breakwater extends north from Fleet Point. **Datum Rock**, 0.1 mile west of the outer end of the breakwater, dries 3.8 m. Port hand buoy "P23" is 0.2 mile west of Datum Rock on the edge of the mud flat.

183   **A marina** is close west of Fleet Point.

184   **Ranch Point**, 1.1 miles west of Richard Point, is the site of a Canadian Forces Base.

185   **Anchorage** can be obtained 0.3 mile WNW of Fleet Point, behind the shelter of the breakwater, in a depth of 24 m. It can also be obtained about 0.2 mile WSW of Ranch Point in a depth of 24 m or closer inshore in a depth of 18 m. Good shelter is afforded from all except infrequent south winds. Anchorage can also be obtained near the head of the harbour but landing is restricted.

186   **Wharves**. — The DND wharf at Ranch Point is T-shaped and its outer face is 155 m long, 16 m wide with a least depth of 16.7 m alongside. The deck elevation is 2.3 m. An L-shaped float, 145 m long, is close NW of the wharf.

187   Another DND wharf and float is 0.5 mile east of Ranch Point. It extends 44 m from the west side of a rock causeway and its south face is 12 m long with a least depth of 7.3 m alongside. A float on the north side of this wharf is 24 m long.

188   **Beacon**. — A private daybeacon, 1.7 miles west of Fleet Point in the SW part of the harbour, has an orange daymark.

189   **Dolphins** and numerous piles front the mud bank to the east and west of the daybeacon. Some cover at HW and could be dangerous.

190   **Nanoose Bay** settlement, at the head of Nanoose Harbour, offers a variety of activities and has a post office, golf course, schools, stores, resorts, a launching ramp and several marinas, one with 400 berths. The Island Highway and E&N Railway pass through the community.

Schooner Cove (1990)

191   **Southey Island** *(49°17'N, 124°06'W)* and **Ruth Island**, to the NW, are surrounded by drying reefs. Local knowledge is advised to pass between these islands and the Vancouver Island shore. The cove on Vancouver Island, 0.5 mile west of Southey Island, affords temporary shelter during strong south or west winds, it is not recommended as the bottom is rocky and it is open to swells during onshore winds and is within the Department of National Defence Administration Control and Benefit Area.

192   **Marine farm** facilities are at the head of the cove.

193   **Ada Islands** together with numerous rocks and shoals lie between Ruth and Southey Islands on the SW and Winchelsea Islands to the NE. A DND yellow spherical buoy is close east of the islands and a similar buoy is close north of a shoal area north of the group.

194   **Winchelsea Islands** *(49°18'N, 124°05'W)* are covered with grass and have a few stunted trees on them. The islands are a Canadian Forces Base, trespassing is prohibited. A conspicuous white building, radar dome, and radio masts with red air obstruction lights are on the north island. **Grey Rock**, 0.2 mile east of Winchelsea Islands, is 0.6 m high. **Rudder Rock**, 0.2 mile SE of Grey Rock, is awash.

195   **Beacon. — Buoys**. — A daybeacon, on Grey Rock, has an orange diamond-shaped daymark.

196   A yellow spherical buoy is close ESE of Rudder Rock.

197   An orange and white mooring buoy lies within 0.1 mile of the south side of Winchelsea Islands.

198   **Float. — Breakwater**. — A float, connected to shore by a ramp, is in the small bay on the south side of the north Winchelsea Island. It is protected by a breakwater that connects the north island with the small island south of it.

199   **Light**. — A privately operated light is on the SW extremity of the north Winchelsea Island.

200   A **submarine cable** is laid from the north Winchelsea Island to Blunden Point on Vancouver Island. A submarine cable area (power) extends from the north Winchelsea Island to a point on Vancouver Island 0.45 mile SW from the east extremity of Ruth Island.

201   **Tides**. — Tidal differences for Winchelsea Islands (Index No. 7935), referenced on Point Atkinson, are in *Tide Tables, Volume 5*.

202   **Tidal streams** between Winchelsea and Ada Islands are weak and irregular.

203   **Military exercise area WG** surrounds Winchelsea Islands, Yeo Islands and Ballenas Islands. It is described at the beginning of this section, and in *Notices to Mariners 1 to 46 Annual Edition*.

204   **Nankivell Point** *(49°17'N, 124°08'W)* is a thickly wooded promontory. **Schooner Reef**, 0.3 mile NE of Nankivell Point, is a group of drying rocks.

205   **Schooner Cove**, on the south side of Nankivell Point, has a rock breakwater across its entrance with a floating log breakwater close west of its seaward end. A dangerous underwater rock of 2 m or less lies 0.06 mile WSW of the breakwater light. The cove affords good anchorage to small craft in depths of 5.5 to 7 m. A large resort hotel and marina are in Schooner Cove.

206   **Lights**. — Schooner Reefs light *(488.5)*, on the reef, has a bifurcation/junction daymark, preferred channel to the right.

207   Schooner Cove breakwater light *(488.3)*, on the north end of the rock breakwater, has a port hand daymark.

208   A **submarine pipeline** (sewer outfall) is laid in a NW direction from the south entrance point of Schooner Cove.

209   Between Nankivell Point and **Dorcas Point**, about 2.5 miles NW, the coast is rugged and cliffy in places. **Yeo Islands, Douglas Island, Gerald Island, Amelia Island** and several reefs and shoals lie within 1 mile offshore, knowledge of local conditions is advised to navigate the area safely.

210   **Beacons**. — Two private daybeacons with orange and white striped masts are on the east extremity of Yeo Islands and on the east extremity of the island 0.4 mile south of Yeo Islands.

211   **Cottam Reef** extends 0.5 mile NNW from Dorcas Point. **Dorcas Rock**, near its north extremity, dries 0.3 m and is marked by port hand buoy "P27".

Chart 3459

212 **Nuttal Bay**, between Dorcas and Cottam Points, has a submarine cable along its east side and a marina near its head. Several private mooring buoys are in the bay.

213 A **submarine cable** (power) is laid between **Cottam Point** and **Mistaken Island**.

214 **Northwest Bay** is completely exposed to NW winds and affords no anchorage for large vessels. Anchorage for small craft can be obtained close to shore near the head of Northwest Bay. Garbage disposal facilities and a launching ramp near the public float complex are located at Northwest Bay.

215 **Tides**. — Tidal differences for Northwest Bay (Index No. 7938), referenced on Point Atkinson, are in *Tide Tables, Volume 5*.

216 The inner west shore of Northwest Bay is a **booming ground** with several dolphins.

217 A **rock breakwater**, 0.9 mile SSE of Cottam Point and on the east side of Northwest Bay, extends south from the shore toward a drying reef. A marina is close east of this breakwater.

218 **Beacon**. — A daybeacon with a port hand daymark is on the drying reef.

219 **Buoys**. — Port hand buoy "P29" is close SSE of the above-mentioned drying reef and starboard hand buoy "P30" is north of a rock awash. Approach the marina between these buoys.

220 **Craig Bay**, between **Madrona Point** and **Brant Point**, is filled with drying flats extending 0.6 mile offshore. Craig Bay is a residential community with several resorts. **Rathtrevor Beach Park** has camping and picnic facilities.

Ballenas Channel

Charts 3459, 3512

221 **Ballenas Channel** *(49°19'N, 124°09'W)*, between Ballenas Islands and the islands between Nankivell and Dorcas Points, is deep and not less than 0.8 mile wide in the fairway.

222 **Military exercise area WG** encompasses the whole of Ballenas Channel. Mariners are advised to avoid Area WG particularly during hours of darkness or reduced visibility. Buoys, lighted and unlighted, are randomly located within Exercise Area WG and are not charted.

Chart 3512

223 **Ballenas Islands** *(49°21'N, 124°10'W)* are two in number. The north island is sparsely wooded. The south island is for the most part bare but its north end is heavily wooded. A white radar dome on the south island is conspicuous from eastward.

224 The narrow passage between the two Ballenas Islands is almost closed and only navigable by small craft at or near HW, local knowledge is advised. In the middle the channel opens out forming a sheltered cove on the north side of the south island, a sandy beach forms its south side. A large sign at the head of this cove reads *"Do Not Anchor in this cove — submerged cables"*.

225 **Light**. — Ballenas Islands light *(490)*, on the N point of North Ballenas Island, is shown at an elevation of 21.3 m from a white tower, 8.2 m high. The light is visible from 040° through east, south and west to 307°.

226 **Meteorological information** for Ballenas Islands is in the Appendices.

227 A **submarine cable** (power) is laid between Ballenas Islands light and the head of Nuttal Bay. Another submarine cable

(power) is laid on the east side of the islands from the lighthouse to the south island.

Gower Point to Sargeant Bay

228 **Gower Point** *(49°23'N, 123°32'W)*, the west entrance point to Howe Sound, is a low rounded point and not well defined. About 2 miles NW of Gower Point, the words "Camp Byng", in large white letters, are prominently displayed and make an excellent reference mark.

229 **Roberts Creek**, 4.5 miles WNW of Gower Point, is a residential area. A rockfill causeway, with two white cylindrical propane tanks on it, and a walkway leading to three sets of dolphins is used by a propane company. Stores, schools, restaurants, marinas, a post office, golf course, and a launching ramp are at Roberts Creek. **Roberts Creek Provincial Park** has camping and picnic facilities.

230 **Danger**. — A group of rocks, with less than 2 m over them, lie about 0.5 mile SE of Roberts Creek.

231 **Tides**. — Tidal differences for Roberts Creek (Index No. 7824), referenced on Point Atkinson, are in *Tide Tables, Volume 5*.

232 **White Islets**, 2.8 miles west of Roberts Creek, are two white, bare, steep-to rocky islets.

233 **Light**. — White Islets light *(448)* is shown at an elevation of 10.7 m from a white tower.

234 **Wilson Creek**, 1.2 miles north of White Islets on the east side of **Mission Point**, is a large rural and residential community with commercial/industrial development. Wilson Creek has a regional airport, camping facilities, and plaza and is the site of fish processing and sawmilling operations. A rock breakwater across the entrance to Wilson Creek protects a booming ground. A marina protected by a breakwater is on the west side of Wilson Creek.

235 A sand and gravel spit, at the mouth of **Chapman Creek**, extends 0.2 mile south of Mission Point. It can be a hazard at LW.

236 **Davis Bay**, close north of Mission Point, has motels, restaurants, and a wharf for unloading bulk oil.

237 **Selma Park**, 1 mile north of Davis Bay, is a quiet residential neighborhood, it has a boat harbour, about 53 m wide, protected by a rock breakwater.

238 **Light**. — Selma Park breakwater light *(448.5)*, on the outer end of the breakwater, is shown at an elevation of 8.2 m from a white tower with a red band at the top.

239 **Wharf**. — A trestle pier, 0.2 mile north of the boat harbour, is 480 m long with dolphins at its outer end providing berthing for barges. It has a loading conveyor on it.

240 **Trail Bay** is an indentation between Mission Point and a point 3 miles NW. Its head is formed by a low isthmus that joins Sechelt Peninsula to the mainland and separates the Strait of Georgia from Sechelt Inlet. A road, about 1 km long, crosses this isthmus. Numerous private mooring buoys are located throughout Trail Bay.

241 A **submarine pipeline** (sewer outfall) extends 0.3 mile from Sechelt into Trail Bay.

242 **Anchorage** can be obtained in Trail Bay in a depth of about 27 m off the village of Sechelt, abreast a bluff in the NE corner of the bay. This anchorage is exposed to south winds.

243 **Sechelt**, at the head of Trail Bay, is a town with a hospital, post office, major shopping centre, galleries, marine repairs, motels,

Chart 3512

restaurants and marinas. A variety of activities are offered at Sechelt. The church at Sechelt is conspicuous. An aircraft landing strip 732 m long with an asphalt runway is 6.4 km east of the village.

244   **Trail Islands**, four in number, lie within 1 mile of the shore. It offers limited shelter and only temporary anchorage. A rockfill breakwater extends from the west extremity of the 47 m high Trail Island.

245   A **submarine cable** (power) and a **submarine pipeline** (water) cross the channel between Sechelt Peninsula and the 58 m high Trail Island.

246   **Anchorage** for small craft can be obtained to the north of Trail Islands, keeping clear of the submarine cable and pipeline. This anchorage is frequently used by tugs with logbooms.

247   **Sargeant Bay**, 2 miles NW of Trail Islands, is deep but offers shelter and anchorage for small vessels close to shore. Drying and below-water rocks lie within 0.2 mile of its west entrance point. **Sargeant Bay Provincial Park** is a bird sanctuary and offers a launching ramp, picnic area and pit toilets.

Burrard Inlet

Charts 3481, 3493, 3494, 3495

248   **Burrard Inlet**, close north of the mouth of the Fraser River, is entered between Point Grey *(49°16'N, 123°16'W)* and Point Atkinson 4 miles north. In 1792, Captain George Vancouver RN, on a voyage of exploration in HMS Discovery, sailed into the Strait of Georgia. Leaving his vessel and its consort HMS Chatham, he proceeded with the ship's boats through the channel now known as First Narrows and entered the sheltered waters of Burrard Inlet. The inlet penetrates 12.5 miles east where it divides into Indian Arm and Port Moody.

249   **Vancouver Harbour** is the portion of Burrard Inlet east of First Narrows.

250   Burrard Inlet differs from most of the great sounds on this coast as it is relatively shallow and depths are suitable for anchorage in all parts, except the north end of Indian Arm.

251   **Harbour limits**. — The **Harbour of Vancouver** is defined in the *Canada Marine Act*. For the purposes of this Act, the Harbour of Vancouver includes Burrard Inlet, with Indian Arm and Port Moody, False Creek and English Bay and all other tidal waters lying east of a line drawn from Point Atkinson light south to the west point of Point Grey *(Chart 3481)*. It also includes a narrow coastal strip in the Strait of Georgia in the approach to Fraser River, Sturgeon Bank, Roberts Bank and Boundary Bay *(Chart 3463)*.

252   **Regulations**. — Vancouver Port Authority regulations are obtainable from:

           Vancouver Port Authority,
           1900 Granville Square,
           200 Granville Street,
           Vancouver, B.C. V6C 2P9
           Telephone (604) 665-9000.

253   Regulations govern vessels manoeuvring or otherwise underway, at anchor, berthing or alongside a berth in the Harbour of Vancouver. The regulations require that no vessel shall move in the harbour at a rate of speed that may endanger life or property or is in excess of any rate of speed authorized by the Port Authority.

254   The Port Authority may order vessels to move, use tugs, berth or anchor in locations that it designates. Certain restrictions

on the times for navigating Second Narrows, anchoring and berthing are included and vessels are required to inform the Corporation of their expected time of arrival and intention to anchor or berth in the harbour.

255   Vessels are regulated with respect to bunkering, cargo-handling operations, and the equipment and lighting employed in these operations. Instructions for signalling, action in the event of accidents, cargo or gear lost overboard and safety requirements are included.

256   There are specific vessel regulations for carrying and handling explosives and dangerous goods, as well as rules to be observed in the prevention of fires.

257   **Ballast Water Exchange Program**. — All vessels destined to arrive at the Port of Vancouver in ballast condition are required to carry out a mid ocean ballast water exchange prior to entering Canadian waters. This is to limit the possibility of transferring non indigenous species into Canadian waters.

258   Any vessel conforming to IMO Resolution A774(18), *Guidelines for Preventing the Introduction of Unwanted Aquatic Organisms and Pathogens from Ships' Ballast Water and Sediment Discharges*, will be in compliance with these procedures.

259   Harbour Masters' representatives will board vessels to conduct ballast checks and obtain the Captain's record of mid-ocean ballast exchange. In the event a ship has not exchanged ballast, samples of ballast water will be drawn and analyzed. Ships in violation of recognized environmental standards will be dealt with accordingly.

260   **Vessel Traffic Services (VTS)**. — Vancouver Harbour and its approach in *Sector Three* of the *Vancouver Traffic Zone* is administered by *Vancouver Traffic* and the assigned frequency is 156.6 MHz, Channel 12. Calling-in points are:

261   *Calling-in Point No. 15A*, *Iona*, is a change from *Sector One (Victoria Traffic)* to *Sector Three (Vancouver Traffic)* and is a line due west of the Iona Breakwater light *(49°12'18"N, 123°15'50"W)* intersecting with *15B* at *49°12'18"N, 123°25'53"W (Chart 3463)*.

262   *Calling-in Point No. 15B*, *Cape Roger Curtis*, is a change from *Sector One (Victoria Traffic)* to *Sector Three (Vancouver Traffic)* and is a line due south of Cape Roger Curtis light *(417)* intersecting with *15A* at *49°12'18"N, 123°25'53"W (Chart 3463)*.

263   *Calling-in Point No. 19*, *Dundarave*, is a line running 000°–180° through Burrard Inlet light buoy "QB" *(388)*. Only eastbound vessels report.

264   *Calling-in Point No. 20*, *Vanterm*, is a line running 358°–178° through the west end of Vanterm *(49°17'23"N, 123°04'33"W)* to *49°18'21"N, 123°04'37"W*.

265   *Calling-in Point No. 21*, *Berry Point*, is a line running 000°–180° through Berry Point light *(411)*. Only westbound vessels report.

266   *Calling-in Point No. 22*, *Roche Point*, is a line running 000°–180° through Roche Point light *(412)*.

267   A brief description of this VTS is in *PAC 200*. Details are in *Radio Aids to Marine Navigation (Pacific and Western Arctic)*.

268   **Anchorage**. — No vessel shall moor or anchor, in the Harbour of Vancouver, without permission of the Harbour Master. *Vancouver Traffic* will on behalf of the Harbour Master assign anchorages within the harbour. In the approach west of First Narrows there are fifteen anchorages in English Bay, designated 1 to 12 and Z, and three on the north shore between Point Atkinson and Dundarave, designated 13 to 15. Seven anchorage berths in the

west portion of the harbour between First and Second Narrows are designated A, B, C, D, E, X and Y. Four anchorage berths east of Second Narrows are designated K, L, M and N.

269   No vessel shall anchor outside a designated anchorage within the limits of the Harbour of Vancouver. It is the responsibility of a vessel to maintain its position within its assigned anchorage and to reposition itself in the event of dragging. Every power driven vessel anchored in the harbour shall have sufficient power and crew available to enable the vessel to move under its own power. Prior authority from *Vancouver Traffic* is required before a vessel at anchor can disable its main propulsion.

270   Mariners are advised that wherever possible *Vancouver Traffic* maintains radar surveillance of anchored vessels. If a vessel drags out of position and does not take immediate steps to recover its position, *Vancouver Traffic* will attempt to establish contact with that vessel on 156.6 MHz, Channel 12. If contact with the vessel cannot be made they may initiate action through the Harbour Master to have that vessel repositioned at the expense of the vessel.

271   Ship's boats used for ferrying crew from ship to shore in English Bay must land and embark only at the south shore on the east side of Burrard Bridge. Ship's lifeboats must not be used in the Inner Harbour.

272   **Meteorological information** for Vancouver International Airport and Ioco and frequency of fog tables for Vancouver Harbour and Vancouver International Airport are in the Appendices.

273   **Tides**. — In the approach to Vancouver Harbour tidal predictions are given for Point Atkinson (Index No. 7795) and tidal differences, referenced on Point Atkinson, are given for False Creek (Index No. 7710).

274   In the west portion of Vancouver Harbour, between First and Second Narrows, tidal predictions are given for Vancouver (Index No. 7735).

275   East of Second Narrows tidal differences referenced on Vancouver are given for Port Moody (Index No. 7755), Deep Cove (Index No. 7765) and Lake Buntzen (Index No. 7771).

276   Tidal predictions and differences are in *Tide Tables, Volume 5*.

277   **Tidal streams**. — Predictions of times and rates of maximum current and times of slack water are given for First Narrows (Index No. 4000) and Second Narrows (Index No. 4100) in *Tide Tables, Volume 5*.

278   **West of First Narrows**, between it and Buoy "QB" 2.5 miles west of Lions Gate Bridge, the ebb current is preceded by a well-defined tide line. Surface currents west of the tide line are slack but at a depth of 10 m a strong west current in excess of 2 kn is usually present.

279   **In First Narrows** the duration of slack water varies and is sometimes considerable. In the narrowest part of the channel the rate of the tidal stream varies greatly and can be as strong as 6 kn. The flood going east through First Narrows is straight and without turbulence as far as Brockton Point, where extensive rips develop on large tides.

280   The ebb follows the fairway from Brockton Point but on passing Lions Gate Bridge it sets in a narrow band along the north shore. The ebb can attain 4 kn 0.2 mile off Navvy Jack Point, but 0.6 mile off this point, in the fairway, it seldom exceeds 1 kn. On strong ebbs a distinct front exists along the junction of the main stream, with the relatively weak currents to the south. It is often

marked by a line of rips, dangerous to small craft, especially in the area near the mouth of the Capilano River.

281   **Freshets from the Capilano River**, caused by heavy rain storms in the mountains, can occur in almost any month. If the river is in flood a considerable set toward Prospect Point can be experienced at certain stages of the tide, therefore great caution should be exercised when passing the mouth of the Capilano River.

282   **In the west portion of Vancouver Harbour**, between First and Second Narrows, the surface current is not always indicative of the current throughout the water column during late spring and summer. On a rising tide strong easterly bottom currents may be present, especially off Neptune Bulk Terminals, even though there is slack water at the surface.

283   **Between Brockton Point and Neptune Bank**, 2.5 miles east, tidal streams tend to circulate anti-clockwise both on the flood and the ebb. On the ebb, the main stream sets west in the central and north parts of the harbour and a weak eddy sets east along the south shore. On the flood, the main stream sets strongly from Brockton Point toward Centerm 1 mile ESE. Currents along the north shore, after a period of weak velocity and variable direction following slack water, form an eddy that continues west and re-enters the main stream opposite Brockton Point.

284   **Between First and Second Narrows** strongest currents occur 3 hours before the turn to ebb when velocities can attain 2 kn setting ESE off Centerm on the south shore, then again 2 hours before the turn to flood when velocities can attain 2 kn setting west along the north shore.

285   **Inshore eddies** within Vancouver Harbour are unpredictable. No reliance should be placed on the anticipated direction of the tidal stream alongside any wharf. Vessels berthing should have anchors in readiness.

Approach to Vancouver Harbour

Chart 3481

286   **Vancouver Harbour Approach** (*49°18'N, 123°16'W*) is between Point Grey and Point Atkinson.

287   The **Traffic Separation Scheme** on the east side of the Strait of Georgia, described at the beginning of this chapter, joins the Traffic Separation Scheme leading into Burrard Inlet west of Point Grey. The Burrard Inlet Traffic Separation Scheme terminates about 2 miles west of First Narrows. It is recommended for use by all ships. For details see *PAC 200* and *Notices to Mariners 1 to 46 Annual Edition*.

288   **Light buoys. — Racons**. — Two light buoys mark the west and east ends of this section of the Traffic Separation Scheme.

289   Vancouver Approach light buoy "QA" (*385.5*), 2.3 miles west of Point Grey, is a cautionary buoy fitted with a Racon (— — •).

290   Burrard Inlet light buoy "QB" (*388*), 2.3 miles west of Prospect Point at the east end of the Traffic Separation Scheme, is a cautionary buoy fitted with a Racon (— • —).

291   **Point Grey** (*49°16'N, 123°16'W*), the west extremity of a wooded promontory terminating in a rounded bluff, is very conspicuous from south. University of British Columbia buildings on the high land above the point are conspicuous.

292   **Spoil ground**. — An ocean dumpsite (*48°15.4'N, 123°22.1'W*) under permit through the *Ocean Dumping Control Act* is actively used for dumping river dredging spoil only.

Chart 3481

False Creek entrance from English Bay anchorage (1999)

293 **Spanish Bank** *(49°17'N, 123°14'W)*, composed of hard sand that dries near LW, extends 0.6 mile north from the west portion of Point Grey. The edge of the bank is steep-to and only visible near LW with strong west winds when there is a line of small breakers.

294 **Light buoy**. — Point Grey light and bell buoy "Q62" *(387)*, 1.5 miles north of Point Grey, is a starboard hand buoy.

295 **Lights**. — Spanish Bank No. 2 light *(386.3)* and Spanish Bank light *(387.01)* are shown from dolphins along the outer edge of Spanish Bank.

296 **Measured distance. — Light**. — Two pairs of beacons, erected on Spanish Bank, mark a measured distance of 1,853 m in a 089½ — 269½° direction. The beacons are dolphins with orange octagonal-shaped slatwork daymarks with a white vertical stripe. The east outer beacon is Spanish Bank Anchorage East light *(387.1)*.

297 **Submarine cables** cross Spanish Bank and then lead across the Strait of Georgia.

298 **English Bay** lies between Spanish Bank and **Stanley Park** 3 miles NE. Yacht races, some of them international, take place in the Kitsilano-Jericho Beach area of English Bay between April and October. Shipping should if possible keep clear of such yacht races. A public fishing and recreation pier is at **Jericho**. The Royal Vancouver and Kitsilano Yacht Clubs are 0.4 and 1.5 miles, respectively, east of **Jericho Beach**. A private mooring buoy lies north of **Kitsilano Beach**. Private buoys mark areas reserved for swimming off Kitsilano Beach, Sunset Beach and Second Beach. A launching ramp and the Kitsilano Coast Guard station are located in English Bay. English Bay community has all amenities and offers a variety of recreational activities.

299 **Light**. — English Bay Anchorage East light *(387.2)*, on the seaward end of the Royal Vancouver Yacht Club breakwater, is shown at an elevation of 4.9 m from a lantern on a railing. It is private.

300 **Elsje Point**, close east of **Kitsilano Point**, is the extremity of a rockfill breakwater, has a privately operated light on it, and protects several small craft floats.

301 **Submarine pipelines** extend from shore close SW and east of Kitsilano Point.

302 **Siwash Rock**, a prominent pinnacle 16 m high, lies close-off the west side of Stanley Park, about 0.5 mile north of **Ferguson Point**. A mooring buoy lies west of the rock. A submarine cable lands close north of Ferguson Point.

303 **Light buoy**. — Ferguson Point light buoy "QC" *(390.5)*, 0.3 mile west of the point, is a west cardinal buoy.

304 **Point Atkinson** *(49°20'N, 123°16'W)* is moderately steep-to. Strong tide-rips, caused by the meeting of the tidal streams from Burrard Inlet and Howe Sound, frequently occur off the point.

305 **Light**. — Point Atkinson light *(386)* is shown at an elevation of 32.9 m from a white tower with six buttresses. The light has a heliport.

306 **Tides**. — Tidal predictions for Point Atkinson (Index No. 7795) are in *Tide Tables, Volume 5*.

307 Between Point Atkinson and Navvy Jack Point, 2.7 miles east, the coast is indented by several coves. A picnic area, public float and mooring buoys are in **Caulfield Cove**. A private mooring buoy is off **Cypress Park**. A submarine pipeline (water intake) extends 110 m offshore on the west side of Sandy Cove.

308 **Dundarave**, 3 miles east of Point Atkinson, has a micro-wave tower north of it. **Navvy Jack Point**, 0.6 mile SE of Dundarave, has several drying rocks SW and NW of it. Dundarave has a variety of services, stores, and restaurants.

False Creek

Chart 3493

309 **False Creek** *(49°16'N, 123°08'W)*, in the SE part of English Bay, is shallow and used by tugs, barges, fish boats and pleasure craft. It can be identified by Burrard Bridge, the Maritime Museum and the Planetarium. The approach to False Creek is relatively shallow and no attempt to enter should be made except in the white sector of the light, on the north pier of the Burrard Bridge. A yacht club, public marina and wharf are located at False Creek; anchorage is prohibited.

310 **Regulations. — Speed**. — *Boating Restriction Regulations* prohibits proceeding under sail and prescribes a speed limit of 5 kn in False Creek. Speed restriction light buoys are at the entrance to False Creek.

311 **Submarine pipelines and cables** cross False Creek in several places, locations are marked by signs.

312 **Tides**. — Tidal differences for False Creek (Index No. 7710), referenced on Point Atkinson, are in *Tide Tables, Volume 5*.

313 **Lights. — Light buoys. — Beacon**. — Kitsilano Base West light *(388.9)* is on the NW corner of the Coast Guard wharf.

Chart 3493

First Narrows from seaward (1999)

First Narrows looking west (1999)

Kitsilano Base light *(389)* is on a dolphin at the SE end of the breakwater.

314   False Creek Sector light *(390)* is on the north pier of Burrard Bridge. The white sector indicates the preferred channel.

315   Kitsilano and English Bay light buoys "Q52" and "Q41" *(388.1, 388.6)*, marking the approach to False Creek, are port and starboard hand buoys.

316   A daybeacon with a starboard hand daymark is on the outer end of a rock groyne on the west side of the entrance to False Creek.

317   Numerous privately operated lights are shown from wharves and floats in False Creek.

318   False Creek is spanned by three fixed span bridges.

319   **Burrard Street Bridge**, the first within the entrance, has a mid-channel vertical clearance of 28 m. Vertical clearance under the south span is 17 m.

320   **Granville Street Bridge** has a vertical clearance of 27 m.

321   **Cambie Bridge**, near the head of the creek, has a vertical clearance of 13 m.

322   **Kitsilano Coast Guard Base** and wharf are on the SW shore just before the Burrard Bridge. A floating breakwater protects floats on the south side of the wharf.

323   **Fishermans Harbour** is operated by the False Creek Harbour Authority. Floats for fishing vessels and other small craft are close south of Burrard Bridge, on the west shore of False Creek in **Brokers Bay**. They vary in length from 67 to 127 m and depths alongside are between 2.6 and 3.2 m.

Chart 3493

324 **Fuel**. — Diesel fuel, gasoline and lubricants can be obtained from fuel barges in False Creek.

325 **Several marinas** are in False Creek.

First Narrows

326 **Hollyburn** *(49°20'N, 123°09'W)* has a breakwater for protecting small craft. A breakwater, pier and wharf are at **Ambleside**. Privately operated lights are shown from the wharf.

327 **First Narrows** forms the entrance to the west part of Vancouver Harbour. The entrance channel between Lions Gate Bridge and Brockton Point, marked by Lions Gate Bridge (South and North) Sector lights, is maintained to a least depth of 15 m.

328 **Fishing prohibited — in the west approach to First Narrows and in First Narrows between the mouth of Capilano River and Burnaby Shoal. Numerous cases have occurred where small craft have come very close to being overrun or swamped by large vessels. In some instances large vessels have nearly run aground in their efforts to avoid sports fishing craft.**

329 **Buoys**. — Unlighted seasonal cautionary buoys, in a line between Navvy Jack Point and First Narrows light, mark the south limit for fishing in the west approach to First Narrows.

330 **Navigation Restriction By-Law** prescribed by the Vancouver Port Authority prohibits, in First Narrows, a vessel greater than 60 m long from overtaking another vessel greater than 60 m long unless the vessel to be overtaken is moving at a speed of less than 6 kn; specific rules for overtaking under the latter condition are prescribed. The By-Law also prescribes, in First Narrows, that a vessel shall keep as near as is safe and practicable to the outer limit of the channel that lies on the vessels starboard side and shall avoid crossing the channel. If obliged to cross the channel it shall cross at as close a right angle to the general direction of traffic flow as practicable. No vessel shall proceed under sail or oars in First Narrows.

331 **Tidal streams**. — Current tables giving daily predictions for First Narrows (Index No. 4000) are published in *Tide Tables, Volume 5*. See remarks regarding tidal streams in Vancouver Harbour at the beginning of this section.

332 **Capilano River** is a mountain stream having its source in the mountains east of Howe Sound, then it flows in a south direction and enters the harbour north of Prospect Point. Owing to the high elevation of its source, and the precipitous nature of its descent down the mountains, freshets are sudden and destructive.

333 **Caution. — Vessels entering or leaving First Narrows in the vicinity of Prospect Point should exercise great caution passing the mouth of the Capilano River. If the river is in flood a considerable set toward Prospect Point can be experienced at certain stages of the tide.**

334 **Lions Gate Bridge**, a suspension bridge, crosses First Narrows close east of Prospect Point. The vertical clearance under the centre of the span is 61 m. Under the remainder of the navigable channel it is 58.5 m.

335 **Bridge lights**. — Fixed red lights are shown from the tops of the main towers. Two fixed white lights are shown on the underside of the bridge to indicate the limits of the channel. Four fixed yellow lights are shown from the centres of the bases of the two main towers.

336 Lions Gate Bridge South Sector light *(392.5)* and Lions Gate Bridge North Sector light *(393)*, both on the bridge, mark the channel east of the bridge to Brockton Point. **White sectors indicate the preferred channel and are not to be used east of Brockton Point.**

337 **Prospect Point** *(49°19'N, 123°08'W)* is a high bluff on the south side of First Narrows.

338 **Lights**. — Prospect Point light *(392)*, at the foot of the bluff, is shown at an elevation of 10.7 m from a white tower, 8.2 m high.

339 First Narrows light *(394)*, 0.35 mile NNW of Prospect Point, at the outer end of the mud flats off Capilano River, is shown at an elevation of 7.5 m from a white tower with a green band at the top on a dolphin.

340 **Calamity Point**, on the north side of First Narrows about 0.4 mile east of Lions Gate Bridge, has a ridge of drying boulders extending from it.

341 A **submarine pipeline** (water intake) at Calamity Point extends 100 m offshore.

342 **Light**. — Calamity Point light *(395)* is shown at an elevation of 5.1 m from a white tower with a green band at the top on a dolphin.

343 A conspicuous tower with a copper roof, 8.5 m high, built over the north shaft of the First Narrows pressure tunnel is on the north side of the narrows, about 0.15 mile SE of Calamity Point.

344 **Light buoy**. — Calamity Shoal light buoy "Q65" *(395.3)*, close south of the shoal spit extending south from Calamity Point, is a port hand buoy.

345 **Brockton Point** is on the south side at the east end of First Narrows. **Parthia Shoal** is 0.3 mile NW of Brockton Point on the south side of First Narrows; the bottom consists of boulders.

346 **Submarine pipelines** extend 0.15 mile offshore in the vicinity of Parthia Shoal.

347 **Light**. — Brockton Point Sector light *(402)* is shown at an elevation of 12.5 m from a white tower with a red band. It is fitted with a neon sign marked *"Speed Limit 5 KTS. Coal Harbour"* that is visible from the west approach.

Vancouver Harbour — West Portion

348 **Vancouver Harbour (west portion)** is the area between First and Second Narrows.

349 **Water aerodrome**. — The west portion of Vancouver Harbour, between Burnaby Shoal and Second Narrows, is a water aerodrome. A good lookout should be kept for seaplanes, particularly in the vicinity of Coal Harbour, where the majority of these seaplanes are based.

350 **Ferry**. — The Vancouver Sea Bus, on a regular schedule, crosses Vancouver Harbour from 0.9 mile SSE of Brockton Point on the Vancouver side to 1.5 miles ENE of Brockton Point on the North Vancouver side.

351 **Sailing is prohibited** in the portion of the harbour west of a line drawn from the west end of Centerm, across the harbour, to the SW end of Lonsdale Avenue.

352 **Burnaby Shoal**, extending 0.3 mile SE of Brockton Point, is usually marked by kelp.

353 **Lights**. — Burnaby Shoal light *(403)* is shown at an elevation of 9 m from a white tower with a red band at the top.

354 A privately operated light is on a dolphin 0.3 mile SW of the above light.

355 Deadman Island light *(403.5)* is on a dolphin at the edge of a drying flat 0.1 mile south of the island.

Chart 3493

Coal Harbour - English Bay anchorage in background (1999)

356   Coal Harbour light *(404)* is on a dolphin at the west edge of a drying bank SW of Deadman Island.

357   Terminal Dock East light *(408.5)* is on pilings 0.8 mile ENE of Vanterm.

358   Privately operated lights are on the extremities of most wharves.

359   **Mooring buoys**, some connected by booms, lie about 0.3 mile off the north shore approximately 0.9 mile NE of Brockton Point.

360   **Loch Katrine Bank** lies in the centre of Vancouver Harbour north of Vanterm. **Neptune Bank**, east of Loch Katrine Bank, lies south of Neptune and Seaboard International Terminals.

361   **Deadman Island**, 0.5 mile SW of Brockton Point, is connected to the mainland close north by a narrow causeway and surrounded by a drying flat with scattered boulders on it.

362   **Submarine cables** extend south from 0.2 mile south of Brockton Point to the marine service station barges. A submarine cable extends from Brockton Point to Burnaby Shoal.

363   **Marine service stations** are on barges moored east of Deadman Island. At night lighted signs are conspicuous.

364   **Anchorages** between First and Second Narrows and regulations governing them are described at the beginning of this section.

365   **Anchorage is prohibited** south of a line drawn from the south end of Deadman Island to Centerm and in Coal Harbour.

366   **Coal Harbour**, which leads NW from the south end of Deadman Island, has a channel about 120 m wide with a depth of 3 m; it affords excellent shelter for small craft alongside any of the numerous floats. Several marinas and berths for aircraft are on the south side of the harbour. The Vancouver Rowing Club headquarters and floats are at the head of the harbour. Rowing shells can be encountered between the headquarters and Centerm. The Royal Vancouver Yacht Club floats are on the north side of the harbour.

367   **Speed limit** of 5 kn in Coal Harbour, south of Burnaby Shoal, is strictly enforced.

368   **Berthing** facilities in the adjacent table are presented in a west to east sequence on the south shore, and east to west on the north shore. Depths alongside were taken in 1995 and 1997 and are subject to shoaling. For latest depths contact the Vancouver Port Authority.

Vancouver Harbour — General Information

369   The city of **Vancouver** owes its existence to the building of the Canadian Pacific Railway. Before the railway was constructed there was a small collection of houses named Granville, but when it was decided that the railway would make this point its Pacific terminus the village sprang into prominence. In 1886 the city was incorporated under the name Vancouver in honour of the man who first explored Burrard Inlet. Vancouver is well provided with hospitals and complete municipal facilities, amenities include a YMCA, YWCA and the Seafarers Society of British Columbia. Consulates for about forty countries are in Vancouver.

370   **Arrival information**. — Vancouver is a port of entry for customs and immigration, officials board on arrival. The Customs House is at 333 Dunsmuir Street. Vancouver is also the Quarantine Station for British Columbia. Tugs are available for berthing and running lines. Linesmen are available through local shipping agents. The Harbour Master's office is at 200 Granville Street, close south of the Vancouver Trade and Convention Centre pier.

371   **Pilotage** is compulsory. Vancouver is in Area 2 of the Pacific Pilotage Region and the pilot boards in the vicinity of the Cautionary Buoy off Brotchie Ledge, near Victoria. For details regarding obtaining a pilot when arriving or departing see *PAC 200*. The Pacific Pilotage Authority office is in Vancouver, telephone (604) 666-6776.

Centerm (1999)

Ballantyne Pier

Centerm

Centerm & Ballantyne Pier (1999)

Vanterm (1999)

Pacific Elevators (1999)

Cascadia Grain Terminal (1999)

Lynnterm (1999)

Seaboard International (1999)

Neptune Bulk Terminals & Saskatchewan Wheat Pool (1999)

James Richardson International (1999)

Pier 94 & Vancouver Dry Dock (1999)

Fibreco Export (1999)

Vancouver Wharves (1999)

Major Port Facilities — Vancouver Harbour Western Portion

Berth	Wharf Length (m)	Least Depth (m)	Elevation (m)	Remarks
Vancouver Port Authority Canada Place East	506	8.5	2.8	Cruise ship terminal. Four automatic tide-sensored gangways. Conveyors and mobile cranes for handling baggage and stores. Baggage area 6,000 m². Dock apron 9,500 m². Fresh water, telephones, garbage disposal and 24-hr tug service.
Canada Place North	274	8.5	2.8	As above
Canada Place West	329	8.5	2.8	As above
Centerm Berths 3 & 4	362	12.2 – 15.5	2.6	Operated by Casco Terminals Ltd (604) 252-2400. Containers, forest products, breakbulk and general cargo. 1 45 tonne container crane 50 m outreach, 3 40 tonne cranes 37-43 m outreach, forklifts, top and side lifters, yard tractors and trailers. On-dock intermodal railyard. 30,000 m² covered storage, 204,380 m² open storage and 12,00 TEU's. 294 reefer outlets. Fresh water at 227 tonnes/hr and telephones.
Centerm Berths 5 & 6	644	12.2 – 15.5	2.6	As above
Vancouver Port Authority Ballantyne Pier North Berth	200	10.0	2.2	General cargo and cruise ships. 18,600 m² covered storage, 4,000 m² open storage and passenger terminal. On-dock rail service, two shore gangways. Baggage area 2,320 m². Dock apron 10,100 m². Fresh water at 181 tonnes/hr, telephones, garbage disposal, 24-hr tug service.
Ballantyne Pier East Berth	366	13-9.5	2.2	As above
Burlington Northern – Santa Fe Deep-sea Berth	200	10.0	3.4	Steel, breakbulk, pulp, newsprint and lumber. Mooring buoys and dolphins. 2,800 m² covered storage, 4,046 m² open storage. On-dock railway. Barge berth. Fresh water at 54 tonnes/hr and telephones.
Burlington Northern – Santa Fe Barge Berth	120	6.5		As above
Rogers Sugar	130	9.1		Bulk raw sugar imports. Storage 31,745 tonnes raw sugar. Maximum discharge rate approx 363 tonnes/day. Fresh water at 27 tonnes/hr and telephones.
United Grain Growers East Berth	213	13.4		Bulk grain and grain products. Seven loading spouts, two belts with loading rate 600 tons/hr per belt. 102,070 tons storage. Fresh water 91 tonnes/hr and telephone.
United Grain Growers West Berth	213	11.7		As above
Vanterm Berths 1 & 2	340	10-9.5	2.5	Operated by Terminal Systems Inc. (604) 251-9200. Containers, forest products, project cargo, bulk liquid and general cargo. Five 40-tonne container cranes, side picks, yard tractors, chassis, lift trucks. On dock intermodal railyard. 288 reefer outlets. Underground pipeline for loading bulk liquid. Storage 11,613 m² covered storage, 22,296 m² open storage, 9,200 full TEUs, 3,000 empty TEUs.
Vanterm Berth 3	91	9.2	2.5	As above
Vanterm Berth 4	183	11.0-9.8	2.5	As above
Vanterm Berths 5 & 6	619	15.6-15.0	2.5	As above
Vanterm Berth 7	228	14.6	2.5	As above
Pacific Elevators Berth 1	185	9.6	1.9	Not currently operational (2003)
Pacific Elevators Berth 2	215	13.7	1.9	Canola, barley, rye, peas, flax and pellets Seven loading spouts at each berth. Loading rates 2,000 tonnes/hour. Fresh water at 91 tonnes/hr, telephones and shore gangway 9 m long.
Pacific Elevators Berth 4	305	10.2	1.9	Not currently operational (2003)

Chart 3494

Berth	Wharf Length (m)	Least Depth (m)	Elevation (m)	Remarks
Cascadia Grain Terminal Berth 1	274	15.0		Wheat, barley, flax, canola and durum wheat. Two belts, 7 spouts, loading rates 3,200 tonnes/hr. Storage 280,000 tonnes. Fresh water at 23 tonnes/hr, power (550v, 3 phase and 100 amps for lighting), telephones and shore gangways 9 and 18 m long.
Lynnterm East Gate Berths 4, 5, 6, & 7	915	15.0	1.9	Operated by Western Stevedore Co. Ltd. (604) 904-2800. Forest products, steel products, general cargo and containers. Equipment to handle cargo up to 42 tonnes. 56,000 m²

Major Port Facilities — Vancouver Western Portion

Berth	Wharf Length (m)	Least Depth (m)	Elevation (m)	Remarks
Dow Chemical Lynnterm Berth 7	200	11.6		Caustic soda solution (40,000 tonnes storage, loading 1,200 tonnes/hr), ethylene dichloride (30,000 tonnes storage, loading 1,000 tonnes/hr) and ethylene glycol (17,000 tonnes storage, loading 800 tonnes/hr)l. 3 dolphins extend from east end, North face of dolphins is for barges. South face of dolphins designed for vessels berthing port side to dock at a velocity not exceeding 0.1 m/sec. Berthing at slack water only with wind velocity less than 15 m/sec. Line pull on bollards not to exceed 75 tonnes. Allowable hull pressure: 20 t/m^2, maximum berthing force: 72.5 tonnes.

Chart 3493

Berth	Wharf Length (m)	Least Depth (m)	Elevation (m)	Remarks
Lynnterm West Gate Berths 1, 2 & 3	600	12.0	1.5	Operated by Western Stevedore Co. Ltd. (604) 904-2800. Forest products, steel products, general cargo and containers. Equipment to handle cargo up to 42 tonnes. 13,935 m^2 covered storage, 183,087 m^2 open storage. Lift trucks and tractor trailers. Railway services warehouses. Power (110v/15amps), fresh water and telephones.
Neptune Bulk Terminals				Coal, potash, agri-products, chemical fertilzers, canola oil and phosphate rock. Open storage 600,000 tonnes coal, covered storage 210,000 tonnes dry bulk, 19,000 tonnes tank storage for oil. Eight tank car unloading stations for oil at Berths 1 and 2, 400 tonnes/hr. Shore gangways at all berths. Fresh water, power (440v 3 phase 30 amps, 110/220v single phase), and telephones.
Neptune Bulk Terminals Berth 1	230	15.2	1.6	Coal and canola oil. Handles ships to 180,000 dwt. Two quadrant ship loaders at 2,700 tonnes/hr. Stacker/reclaimer rated at 3,600 tonnes/hr. Secondary reclaimer 1,000 tonnes/hr. Railcar rotary dumper 3,600 tonnes/hr.
Neptune Bulk Terminals Berth 2	229	13.7	1.6	Potash, fertilizer, dry bulk and canola oil. Handles ships to 80,000 dwt. Two quadrant ship loaders at 2,000 tonnes/hr each.
Neptune Bulk Terminals Berth 3	250	13.1	1.6	Agri-products and phosphate rock. Handles ships to 65,000 dwt. Outbound – linear travelling ship loader 1,200 tonnes/hr agribulk, 2,500 tonnes/hr potash. Inbound – 2 travelling bridges with 50 tonne receiving hoppers. Storage 250,000 tonnes
Saskatchewan Wheat Pool Berth 1	230	15.0	2	Wheat, durum wheat, canola, barley and grain by-products. Loading via two belts at 1,200 tonnes/hr each, five spouts at each berth. Storage 240,000 tonnes.
Saskatchewan Wheat Pool Berth 2	230	12.0	2	As above
James Richardson International	180	14.4	2	Canola and cereal grains. Two Peco loaders at 2,000 tonnes/hr each. Storage 108,000 tonnes.
Vancouver Dry Dock	220			Panamax floating dry dock. Dry docking, ship repair and industrial engineering.
Fibreco Chip Loading Terminal	137	11.5	1.7	Bulk wood chips. Berthing dolphins 73 m WSW and 55 m ENE off wharf. Designed for vessels up to 265 m long with 11.5 m draught, 42,000 dwt. Berthing velocity at 10° approach not to exceed 0.1 m/sec. Loading by conveyor belt and pneumatic blower at maximum rate of 1,200 tonnes/hr. Bulk storage 100,000 bone dry units. Fresh water via 2" pipeline, power (120 v) and telephones.
BCR Marine Vancouver Wharves				Mineral concentrates, canola oil, pulp, sulphur, potash, fertilizer, agri-products and dry bulk commodities. Five deep-sea berths, 45 hectares of land, tracks for up to 400 railcars. Barge slip.
Berth 1	520 (combined with 2 & 3)	13.7		Concentrate rail car unloader and grab bucket ship unloader.
Berths 2 & 3		11.2		Breakbulk handling pulp and paper, and canola oil. Tractors, flat deck trailers and lift trucks. 2,790 m^2 covered storage
Berth 4 & 5	410	11.6		Sulphur and agri-products etc. Two separate dry-bulk systems. Dual purpose rail car dumper. Two quadrant loaders at berth 4 (sulphur, fertilizer and potash). Separate dumper, conveying system and shiploader at berth 5 (agri-products).

³⁷²   **Supplies**. — Fresh water is obtainable at most berths. All types of provisions, as well as deck and engine stores are available. Bunker fuel oil and diesel oil are available in any quantity at oil company wharves or are delivered by tank barge alongside.

³⁷³   **Harbour services**. — Labour is available through local stevedoring firms. Tugs are available for berthing, shifting and running lines. Ships gangways can be easily utilized at most berths. The port is well provided with companies equipped to undertake repairs to all types of marine instruments and for compass adjusting.

³⁷⁴   **Police**. — Vancouver Police have two patrol vessels based in the harbour. They can be reached on Channel 16 or Channel 12, or in an emergency telephone 911.

³⁷⁵   **Heavy-lift equipment**. — For repairs Vancouver Dry Dock has a 15 tonne and two 85 tonne capacity cranes at various piers. It also has two 40 tonne capacity cranes at the dry dock machine shops.

³⁷⁶   **Repairs**. — On the North Vancouver side of the harbour **Vancouver Dry Dock** (604) 988-6361 has the following facilities.

Floating dry dock
Lifting capacity – 36,000 tonnes
Extreme length – 220 m
Length over keel blocks – 204 m
Breadth – 45.8 m
Depth over blocks – 10.65 m

Floating dry dock
Lifting capacity – 8,163 tonnes
Extreme length – 131.2 m
Length over pontoons – 128 m
Breadth – 33.5 m
Depth over blocks forward – 5 m
Depth over blocks aft – 4.5 m

Graving dock
Vessels up to 100,000 dwt
Extreme length – 347.7 m
Breadth – 38.4 m
Cranage to 150 tonnes

Syncrolift
Lifting capacity – 1,500 tonnes
Extreme length – 90 m
Length over keel blocks – 76.2 m
Breadth – 21.34 m
Depth over sill – 5.6 m.
Cranage to 100 tonnes

³⁷⁷   Vancouver Dry Dock is equipped with deep-sea berths ranging from 140 to 168 m long. Facilities for all kinds of repairs are available.

³⁷⁸   **Allied Shipbuilders** (604) 929-2365, on the north side of the harbour close east of Second Narrows, has three small floating dry docks, with a capacity up to 2,000 dwt, several slipways and marine ways with 8.8 x 36.6 m capacity. They have the capability to build new vessels up to 122 m in length and 10,000 dwt. They are also capable of conversions, ship repairs and refits, machinery installation, marine and general machining, and manufacturing hydraulic tow pin units, cable hold down block and stern rollers.

³⁷⁹   In addition there are several smaller ship building and repair shops. Refer to the Vancouver telephone directory.

³⁸⁰   **Communications**. — Several railroads serve the port and provide continent-wide transportation for passengers and freight. The Greater Vancouver Transportation Authority, (Translink) maintains local transit facilities. Bus services are available to all points in Canada and the United States. World-wide air services are available for passengers and freight at the Vancouver International Airport. Local airlines provide passenger services to various places within the province.

Second Narrows from west (1999)

Chart 3493

381   B.C. Ferry Services Inc. maintains regular passenger and vehicle ferry services between Tsawwassen and Swartz Bay and Nanaimo (Duke Point) on Vancouver Island, also between Horseshoe Bay, Howe Sound and Nanaimo (Departure Bay). Regularly scheduled freight and passenger services are maintained between Vancouver and other coastal ports in British Columbia.

382   **Small craft berthing** facilities are available in False Creek and Coal Harbour. In North Vancouver there are small craft facilities in marinas at Mosquito Creek and at Lynnwood Marina, located between Second Narrows and Lynnterm. Marinas for small craft are also at Reed Point in Port Moody and Deep Cove in Indian Arm.

383   **Heliports** are at Children's Hospital, Vancouver Hospital and Health Science Centre and on the south shore of the harbour between Vancouver Trade and Convention Centre and Centerm. Several private heliports are located around the harbour.

Second Narrows

Chart 3494

384   **Second Narrows** *(49°18'N, 123°02'W)*, 4.5 miles east of First Narrows, is similar in character to the latter. The bank along the north shore is caused by deposit brought down by the **Seymour River**, which flows into Burrard Inlet at this point. The fairway at its narrowest part is a little more than 90 m wide.

385   **Best time for large vessels to pass through Second Narrows** is at or near HW slack with the first ebb being best for inbound (east-going) vessels and the last of the flood being best for outbound (west-going) vessels. At LW slack, when tidal stream conditions permit, the last of the ebb for inbound (east-going)

vessels and the first of the flood for outbound (west-going) vessels are considered reasonably good times to transit the narrows.

386   ***Second Narrows Movement Restriction Area (MRA) Standing Orders*** are designed to provide for the orderly and safe flow of traffic through Second Narrows. These orders are promulgated by the Vancouver Port Authority, 1900-200 Granville Street, Vancouver, B.C. V6C 2P9. Telephone (604) 665-9000.

387   Second Narrows Movement Restriction Area comprises an area enclosed within lines drawn 000° from Terminal Dock East light *(408.5)* to the North Vancouver shoreline at Neptune Bulk Terminals and a line drawn 000° from Berry Point light *(411)* to the north shore on the opposite side of the channel.

388   **Control procedures**. — The *Vessel Traffic Service* procedures for the *Vancouver Traffic Zone*, as described in *Radio Aids to Marine Navigation (Pacific and Western Arctic)*, are mandatory for any vessel to which these procedures apply that is intending to transit the MRA. The western boundary for mandatory reporting is the Point Grey/Point Atkinson line. In addition, vessels subject to mandatory reporting should also establish communication on VHF Channel 12 (156.6 MHz) with the CN Railway Bridge Operator upon entering the port limits or prior to departing from a berth or anchorage. The Harbour Master shall be advised of the proposed transit time for any vessel subject to mandatory reporting, as early as possible, and at least 12 hours prior to the proposed transit and of any change thereto.

389   **Restricted periods** for transiting Second Narrows are defined for any vessel required to carry a Pilot, any barge with a displacement of 6,500 tonnes and greater whether or not self propelled, and any small vessel carrying dangerous goods. In general these vessels are restricted to high or low water slack, or stemming the current with a limiting tidal current of 2 kn. These

Second Narrows from east (1999)

periods are in an Appendix to the Standing Orders and are available to port users.

390   **Visibility**. — Unless there is a clear visibility range at, the CN Railway Bridge, of at least 1.5 miles to the east and 1 mile to the west no vessel shall transit through the MRA. In addition no vessel shall attempt to transit the MRA when wind conditions are such that difficulty in manoeuvring can be experienced.

391   **Speed**. — A maximum speed of 6 kn is prescribed in the MRA. If a vessel is unable to navigate safely, at 6 kn or less, it must remain at berth or anchor until adequate tugs and other methods are approved by the Harbour Master for its safe transit through Second Narrows. All small craft in the MRA shall proceed at a safe speed.

392   **Clear Narrows** situations are required for the transit of tankers involved in the movement of petroleum products, and other vessels as specified by the Harbour Master. All vessels shall observe the order of a Clear Narrows and shall not obstruct the passage of a vessel for which a Clear Narrows has been issued.

393   **Attendant tugs**, unless specifically exempted by the Harbour Master, are required for any vessel required to carry a Pilot. The number and required horsepower of attendant tugs is pre-scribed in the Standing Order.

394   **Tugs and tows** shall give way to and not interfere with the movement of any vessel required to carry a Pilot or any barge with a displacement of 6,500 tonnes and greater. In addition to any tug involved in a towing operation, an additional tug of adequate power is required for the transit of dangerous goods, as specified in the Standing Order. Tugs and tows, other than those described as carrying dangerous goods, shall, wherever possible, use the first fixed span south of the CN Railway Bridge lift span. There are special requirements for logbooms and log rafts and, under speci-fied conditions, an additional tug is required. The permissible length of towline is also specified.

395   **Holding areas** are designated areas within the MRA in which tugs and tows can hold themselves in readiness until conditions are such that a transit of Second Narrows Bridges can be made. The four holding areas are charted.

396   **Sailing Prohibited**. — No vessel shall transit the MRA by means of sail and no sail shall be hoisted fully or partially in the MRA.

397   **Bridge**. — **Small craft** that can pass safely under the CN Railway Bridge main lift span or the first fixed span immedi-ately south of the south tower without risking injury to either the vessel or CN Railway Bridge shall do so without signalling for the lift span to be raised.

398   **Tidal streams**. — Current tables for Second Narrows (Index No. 4100) are in *Tide Tables, Volume 5*.

399   **Near HW slack**. — Current is straighter with a more uniform run during the first of the ebb than at any other stage. There are no tide-rips or eddies of noticeable proportions. As far as current conditions are concerned, the first of the ebb is considered the best time for a safe passage inbound (east-going).

400   Current conditions on the last of the flood are reasonably good and the best time for a safe passage outbound (west-going). The current sweeps uniformly into the narrows without turbulence. It is deflected little when opposite Seymour River except on very weak tides. Rips and eddies that appear east of the bridge are less turbulent than at the first of the flood.

401   **Near LW slack**. — During the first of the flood and last of the ebb, stronger rips and eddies will be encountered than at

other times. When tides are large, LW slack is of short duration and velocity increases rapidly. On the first of the flood offset to the south abreast Seymour River is quite noticeable on weak tides, and rips and eddies farther east are very turbulent.

402   On the last of the ebb velocity at the bridge is about 1 kn more than it would be at other stages and rips and eddies west of the bridge can be quite strong. A west-going vessel with a tow may find itself set north here by the main current while the object being towed can be carried south into the weak variable currents off Cascadia Grain Terminal. Towing lines should therefore be as short as possible.

403   Navigators should avoid making passage through the narrows on the first of the flood or the last of the ebb when LW at Vancouver falls below 2 m. If necessary to do so, every effort should be made to arrive at the bridge as near as possible to slack water.

404   **Caution. — Due to disturbances or other causes, the predicted slack and times of maximum current can vary from the actual conditions by as much as 30 minutes. A definite set to the NW of the narrows, during the first half of the flood, should be expected. Freshets from the Seymour River cause a cross current toward the south shore that is most pronounced on the ebb tide.**

405   **Points of maximum velocities**. — During the flood maximum velocity occurs about 0.2 mile east of the bridge and during the ebb at or near the bridge. Flood currents attain 6½ kn but the ebb, due to turbulence west of the bridge, seldom exceeds 5½ kn.

406   **Iron Workers Memorial Second Narrows Bridge** (Ministry of Transportation and Highways) is a fixed span road bridge with a width of 315 m between supports over the channel. It has a minimum vertical clearance of 44 m over the 110 m wide shipping channel.

407   **Lights**. — The highway bridge has six white lights marking the main shipping channel. Two face east *(408.53, 408.7)*, two face west *(408.54, 408.8)* and centre floodlights pointing downward *(408.55, 408.6)*. Bridge piers on both sides of the shipping channel are floodlit.

408   **Second Narrows Railway Bridge** (Canadian National Railways), close east of the highway bridge, has a vertical lift span over the navigable channel. The limits of this channel, which is 137.1 m wide, are indicated by fixed white lights at the base of the piers supporting the lift span. The minimum clearance under the raised span is 46 m and 10.8 m when the span is closed. The first fixed span immediately south of the south tower has a vertical clearance of 10.8 m.

409   **Lights**. — The east and west sides of the lift span are marked by red lights on the south side *(409.1, 409.2)* and white lights on the north side *(409, 409.3)*. Centre green lights *(409.6, 409.7)* indicate the span is raised. Centre red lights indicate the span is lowered *(409.8, 409.9)*. These lights are private.

410   **Bridge operating procedures**. — Vessels requiring an opening of the bridge shall contact the bridge operator on VHF Channel 12 (156.6 MHz) call sign CJU52, and:

(a)   Sound 3 prolonged blasts, this signal to be repeated until acknowledgement has been received from the bridge operator; and

(b)   Remain at a distance of a least 0.25 mile from the bridge until lift span is in a raised position.

411   The bridge operator shall when the vessel's signal has been received:

Chart 3494

(a)   Verbally confirm his understanding on VHF Channel 12;

(b)   Display a flashing red light on that side of the lift span facing the approaching vessel which indicates the lift span is in the process of being raised; and

(c)   Display a flashing green light on that side of the lift span facing the approaching vessel which indicates that the lift span has been raised.

412   No vessel shall approach the CN Railway Bridge when the following signals are displayed:

(a)   2 flashing red lights on that side of the lift span facing the approaching vessel which indicates vessel is to stop at once or if necessary go astern; or

(b)   A vertical row of 4 fixed white lights on the centre of the main lift span which indicates another vessel is approaching from the opposite direction.

413   An **overhead cable**, with a vertical clearance of 65 m, crosses Second Narrows close east of the railway bridge.

414   **Submarine pipelines** cross Second Narrows about 0.2 mile east of the railway bridge.

415   **Lights**. — Second Narrows light *(410)*, 0.7 mile east of the railway bridge, is shown at an elevation of 6.7 m from a white tower with a green band at the top, on a dolphin on the north side of the harbour.

416   Second Narrows East light *(410.5)*, 1.1 miles east of the railway bridge, is on a dolphin on the north side of the harbour.

417   **Berry Point** light *(411)*, on the N extremity of the point, is shown from a white building on a dolphin.

418   **Private mooring buoys** lie off the north shore west of Roche Point and off the south shore between Berry Point and the Terasen Pipelines Terminal.

Vancouver Harbour — East Portion

Chart 3495

419   **Roche Point** *(49°18′N, 122°57′W)*, 2.5 miles east of Second Narrows, is the west entrance point of Indian Arm. A launching ramp is on the west side of Cates Park.

420   **Light**. — Roche Point light *(412)* is on the S extremity of the point.

421   **Port Moody**, the east branch at the head of Burrard Inlet, is entered between **Admiralty Point** *(49°18′N, 122°56′W)* and **Gosse Point** 0.3 mile south.

422   Near **Burns Point**, 0.45 mile SE of Admiralty Point, the inlet is about 0.2 mile wide and free of dangers. **Carraholly Point**, 0.35 mile east of Burns Point, has a drying rock ledge extending SE from it.

423   At **Dockrill Point** a mud flat extends 0.2 mile offshore. Numerous private floats line the shore SE of the point. Mud flats at the head of the inlet are used for log storage.

424   **Regulations**. — Port Moody lies within Vancouver Harbour and is administered by the Vancouver Port Authority.

425   **Overhead cables** (power), with vertical clearances of 44 m, cross the entrance to Port Moody at Burns Point and the channel leading to Port Moody about 0.7 mile east of Burns Point.

426   **Submarine pipelines (oil) and a submarine cable** cross the inlet between **Ioco** and **Reed Point**. A submarine pipeline, 0.7 mile SE of Reed Point, extends 0.1 mile across the drying flat.

427   **A large marina** protected by breakwaters is on the south shore close west of Reed Point.

428   Central and east entrances to the marina are marked by private lights *(415.5, 415.6, 415.7, 415.75)*, located on the floating breakwaters.

Ioco Refinery (1999)

Petro Canada & Reed Point Marina (1999)

429   **Lights**. — Gosse Point light *(413)*, Burns Point light *(414)* and Carraholly Point light *(415)* mark the entrance to Port Moody.

430   Reed Point light *(416)*, on the south shore of Port Moody 1.4 miles east of Carraholly Point, is on a dolphin.

431   A privately operated light on a dolphin, 0.25 mile east of Reed Point, has a sign reading *"Underwater Obstruction Keep Clear 15 Metres"*.

432   Port Moody light *(416.5)*, 1 mile SE of Reed Point at the entrance to a dredged area, is on a dolphin with a starboard hand daymark.

433   Privately operated lights are on most wharves.

434   Beacons, two with a port hand daymark and one with a starboard hand daymark, mark a channel that leads SE from Port Moody light to floats and a boat launching ramp at Rocky Point Park. This has been dredged to 0.3 m.

435   **Light range**. — Port Moody range lights *(416.2, 416.3)*, in line bearing 090½°, are on the north shore about 0.75 mile east of Reed Point.

436   **Port Moody** (city) is at the head of Burrard Inlet. Exports are bituminous coal, sulphur, chemical fertilizers, petrochemicals and petroleum products. The port has the usual facilities of a medium sized community. A museum, launching ramp, swimming pool and picnic area located at Rocky Point Park.

437   **Anchorage** is by arrangement with the Vancouver Harbour Master. Nearest official anchorage berths are in the entrance to Indian Arm. Mooring buoys are SE of Pacific Coast Terminals.

438   **Tides**. — Tidal differences for Port Moody (Index No. 7755), referenced on Vancouver, are in *Tide Tables, Volume 5*.

439   **Inner approach**. — Controlling depth for ships proceeding to Pacific Coast Terminals is 10.4 m. The bottom in Port Moody consists of soft mud and organic silt and charted depths are to the top of this silt layer.

440   **Berthing** facilities east of Second Narrows in the adjacent table are presented in a west to east sequence on the south shore, and east to west on the north shore. Depths alongside are subject to shoaling. For latest depths contact the Vancouver Port Authority.

441   **Oil containment booms**. — Berths at oil refineries and at Pacific Coast Terminals have pollution prevention booms that are deployed only when a ship or barge is alongside. When the ship or barge departs the booms are usually moored to a buoy.

Indian Arm

442   **Indian Arm**, entered between Roche Point and Admiralty Point.*(49°18'N, 122°56'W)*, is entirely different in character from other portions of Burrard Inlet. It is enclosed on both sides by rugged mountains rising to elevations of 609 to 1,524 m. During spring and summer months melting snow falls in foaming cascades down the mountain sides and renders surface water nearly fresh. Several resorts are located in the inlet and numerous private floats line the shores. Resorts are served during summer months by a small

Chart 3495

Pacific Coast Terminals (1999)

passenger vessel operated by Harbour Cruises Limited of Vancouver. Yacht clubs and anchorage are at the head of Indian Arm.

443   **Spoil grounds**. — Non-active ocean dump sites are in *49°18'50"N, 122°56'17"W* and *49°20'45"N, 122°54'37"W*.

444   A **speed limit** of 5 kn is prescribed by the Vancouver Port Authority for Belcarra Bay, Deep Cove, Bedwell Bay and approach to Strathcona Park between White Rock and Cove Cliff.

445   **Dollarton** is a small community on the west shore, about 0.5 mile NE of Roche Point. Many private ramps, floats and boat-houses line the shore.

446   **Boulder Island**, about 0.5 mile NE of Dollarton, has a prominent house on its south end.

447   **Beacon**. — Belcarra daybeacon, on a drying rock 0.25 mile ESE of the south extremity of Boulder Island, is a white tower.

448   **Belcarra** is on the east side of Indian Arm at the south end of **Belcarra Bay**. The public wharf, with an L-shaped float, has a depth of 2.4 m alongside and is for unloading and loading only, overnight mooring is not permitted. **Belcarra Regional Park** is near the entrance of Indian Arm on the east shore.

449   **Turtle Head** *(49°19'N, 122°56'W)* and **Hamber Island**, close west, have cliffs on their south sides.

450   **Beacon**. — Turtle Head daybeacon, off the south end of Hamber Island, is a white tower with a red band around the top.

451   **White Rock**, west of Hamber Island, lies at the extremity of a drying rock ledge extending SE from **Grey Rocks Island**.

452   **Cove Cliff**, a community in the bay NW of Grey Rocks Island, has a public float that dries at LW.

453   A **submarine cable** and **submarine pipeline** are laid from Grey Rocks Island to the mainland.

454   **Deep Cove**, a settlement at the head of the cove with the same name, is a residential area. It has several stores, restaurants and direct highway connection with Vancouver.

455   **Light buoy. — Lights**. — A speed control light buoy is in the entrance to Deep Cove.

456   Privately operated lights are on the ends of the outer float at the yacht club.

457   **Wharf**. — The public float at the end of a long approach structure is 22 m long. The float is for loading and unloading only, overnight mooring is not permitted. Yacht club floats are close north of the public float and a marina is on the north side of the cove.

458   A **submarine pipeline** (sewer) is laid on the south shore of Deep Cove.

459   **Tides**. — Tidal differences for Deep Cove (Index No. 7765), referenced on Vancouver, are in *Tide Tables, Volume 5*.

460   **Whiskey Cove**, **Coombe** and **Cosy Cove** are on the east shore NE of Turtle Head. Two rocks, with 3 and 4 m over them, are in the north approach to Whiskey Cove.

461   An **overhead cable**, vertical clearance 49 m, crosses Indian Arm about 0.6 mile NE of Turtle Head.

462   **Black Shoal**, **Tupper Rock** and **Charles Reef** lie between **Jug Island** and **Racoon Island** in the approach to Bedwell Bay.

463   **Bedwell Bay** *(49°19'N, 122°54'W)* provides one of the few anchorages in Indian Arm. It is exposed to occasional strong NE winds that occur in winter. A drying reef extends from the west entrance point, and 0.2 mile south of this point there is a shoal with 10.4 m over it. Speed limit signs are posted around the shores. Numerous private mooring buoys and buoys marking a water-ski slalom course are in the bay.

464   **Beacon**. — Bedwell Bay daybeacon, on the NE extremity of the reef extending from the west entrance point to the bay, is a white tower with a red band around the top.

465   **Light buoy**. — A speed control light buoy is 0.6 mile SSW of Bedwell Bay daybeacon.

466   An **overhead cable**, vertical clearance 99 m, crosses Bedwell Bay.

467   **Farrer Cove**, NE of Bedwell Bay, is the site of a YMCA summer camp. **Belvedere Rock**, in the entrance to the cove, has 0.6 m over it.

468   **Lone Rock Point**, on the west shore abreast Racoon Island, has a private wharf on its SW side.

Chart 3495

Major Port Facilities — Vancouver Harbour Eastern Portion

Berth	Wharf Length (m)	Least Depth (m)	Elevation (m)	Remarks
Chart 3494				
Chevron Canada Stanovan Terminal	62	11.7		Petroleum products. Berth length 110 m between mooring dolphins. Condition for approaching wharf best on first or last of ebb. Velocity during these periods seldom reach 1 kn and the set is uniformly from east, either at an angle or parallel with wharf. On flood tides the current direction is more uncertain and can reach 2½ kn. Light range at berth.
Berry Point Site	122	12		Variety of forest products. 48,560 m² open storage. Booming grounds and mooring buoys lie off wharf.
Shell Canada Products Shellburn Terminal Outer Berth (north face)	122	12.1		Petroleum products. Mooring dolphins 154 m apart. Designed to accommodate 40,000 dwt tanker vessels. Partially laden vessels to a maximum displacement 52,000 dwt can be accommodated. Dolphins designed for tanker berthing with a velocity of 0.11 m/sec perpendicular to berth face and a maximum berthing angle of 5°.
Chart 3495				
Terasen Pipelines Westridge Marine Terminal	92	11.4	2.8	Crude petroleum, petroleum products and jet fuel. Six mooring dolphins 275 m apart, can accommodate vessels up to 100,000 dwt. Gravity feed crude loading from Burnaby Terminal 3,400 m³/hr, 24" crude oil loading line c/w 2x12" chiksans 10" flexible hose for vapour recovery, 2x8" hoses for jet fuel unloading maximum 1,375 m³/hr. Some crude barges requires distance flanges. Fresh water, power (220-440v/100 amps), telephone and shore gangway.
PetroCanada West Jetty	43	12	1.5	Berth 90 m between mooring dolphins designed for vessels 50,000 dwt. Petroleum products handled via pipelines at 3,637 to 4,546 lmp. Fresh water at 54 tonnes/hr.
PetroCanada East Jetty	40	6	2.9	Petroleum products via pipeline at 3,637 to 4,546 lpm. Fresh water at 91 tonnes/hr and telephone. Fireboat and spill response sea truck moored at float close east.
Pacific Coast Terminals Berth 1	237	12	2.4	Bulk liquids (ethylene glycol). Handles ships up to 70,000 dwt. Loading 800 tonnes/hr. Storage 55,000 tonnes ethylene glycol and 11,200 tonnes unused tanks. Fresh water at 27 tonnes/hr and telephones.
Pacific Coast Terminals Berth 2	165	12.5	2.4	Sulphur. Single quadrant shiploader at 5,000 tonnes/hr. Bulk storage 220,000 tonnes sulphur. Fresh water at 27 tonnes/hr and telephones.
Imperial Oil IOCO Terminal	165	9.2	2.1	Petrochemicals and petroleum products. Mooring dolphins off each end for vessels to 35,000 dwt. Products conveyed by pipeline and hose at 4,000 bbls/hr. Fresh water at 23 tonnes/hr and telephone. Berths for barges and coastal tankers east of main wharf.
Chart 3494				
Nexen Chemicals South Berth	152	9.9-10.1	1.8	Imports bulk sea salt, exports chlor-alkali and hydrochloric acid. Bulk storage 27,000 tonnes salt, two tanks 11,000 tonnes each. Fresh water at 13.6 tonnes/hr and 5 m shore gangway. Two sets range lights mark limit of deep water close to shore.
Nexen Chemicals West Berth	76	6.6-8.5	1.8	As above

469   **Light**. — Woodlands light *(412.3)* is close south of Lone Rock Point.

470   **Woodlands**, close west of Lone Rock Point, has a public float with a 24 hour limit. A rock, with 1.5 m over it, lies close south of the float. **Sunshine**, 0.3 mile NE, has a small public float.

471   A **submarine pipeline** (water) is laid close offshore from Woodlands to Sunshine.

472   **Twin Islands**, close-off the east shore, are joined by a drying isthmus. The channel east of the islands can be used by small craft. A rock, which dries 1.5 m, lies close inshore at the north end of the channel. Twin Islands offers temporary anchorage and the larger of the two islands has picnic and sanitary facilities. The largest Twin Island (northern) has a dinghy float on its east side.

473   **Light**. — Twin Islands light *(412.4)* is shown at an elevation of 9.1 m from a white tower with a red band at the top on the north extremity of the north island.

474   **Indian Arm Marine Park** comprises Racoon Island, Twin Islands, Croker Island and Granite Falls.

475   **Brighton Beach** and **Orlomah Beach** are on the west shore. **Best Point** has a conspicuous three-storey house on its north side.

476   **Light**. — Best Point light *(412.5)* is shown at an elevation of 5.2 m from a white tower on the point.

477   **Buntzen Bay** *(49°23'N, 122°52'W)* is on the east side of the arm. B.C. Hydro power generating stations are at **Lake Buntzen**.

478   **Caution** should be exercised when approaching the power houses as the gates may be opened without warning to discharge huge volumes of water.

479   **Tides**. — Tidal differences for Lake Buntzen (Index No. 7771), referenced on Vancouver, are in *Tide Tables, Volume 5*.

480   **Indian Arm Park** encompasses the waters and shorelines from Buntzen Bay north to the head of the arm.

Chart 3495

Indian Arm (1986)

481   **Coldwell Beach** is north of Best Point. **Silver Falls**, north of Coldwell Beach, is conspicuous from northward. **Johnson** is on the east shore opposite Silver Falls and 0.9 mile north is the site of an old sawmill.

482   **Croker Island** is part of the Indian Arm Marine Park.

483   **Light**. — Croker Island South light *(412.6)*, on the SE extremity of the island, is shown at an elevation of 5.5 m from a white tower.

484   **Bergs**, on the west side of the arm, is the site of an abandoned sand and gravel operation.

485   **Buoy**. — A private buoy, at the north west end of Croker Island, has a sign that reads "*SLOW NO WAKE*".

486   Burrard Yacht Club floats are at the mouth of **Clementine Creek**.

487   **Granite Falls** *(49°27′N, 122°52′W)*, on the east side of the arm, is the site of **Fairy Falls**, a conspicuous waterfall. Ruins of a small float and a house are visible. Granite Falls offers fair anchorage, overnight anchoring is not recommended.

488   **Beacon**. — Granite Falls daybeacon, close south of the falls, is a white tower with a red band at the top, fitted with a radar reflector.

489   **Iron Bay**, north of Granite Falls, has the Deep Cove Yacht Club floats. The coast from Iron Bay north to the mouth of **Indian River** may be used as booming grounds.

490   **Wigwam Inn**, at the head of Indian Arm on its west side, is an outstation for the Royal Vancouver Yacht Club.

Howe Sound

Chart 3526

491   **Howe Sound** is entered between Point Atkinson *(49°20′N, 123°16′W)* and Gower Point, 11 miles WNW. Several islands divide the entrance into four main channels named, from east to west, Queen Charlotte Channel, Collingwood Channel, Barfleur Passage and Shoal Channel. Howe Sound offers few small craft anchorages due to great depths and lack of protected bays. The sound is almost entirely hemmed in by rugged, precipitous mountains rising abruptly from the water's edge.

492   The British Columbia Railway, from its terminus in North Vancouver, runs along the east shore of Howe Sound to Squamish and northern B.C. A main highway runs close to the railway.

493   **Ferries**. — Regular ferry service crosses the entrance to Howe Sound from Horseshoe Bay to Langdale. Another ferry crosses Queen Charlotte Channel from Horseshoe Bay to Snug Cove. Large ferries connecting Horseshoe Bay in Queen Charlotte Channel to Departure Bay on Vancouver Island will be encountered in Queen Charlotte Channel, Collingwood Channel, Barfleur Passage or in the approach to Howe Sound. Charted ferry routes are general indications of the route followed.

494   **Caution. — In the south entrances to Shoal Channel, Barfleur Passage, Collingwood Channel and Queen Charlotte Channel, there can be large quantities of logs and beach refuse that are difficult to see in choppy water.**

495   **Vessel Traffic Services** (vts). — Howe Sound in *Sector Three* of the *Vancouver Traffic Zone* is administered by *Vancouver Traffic* and the assigned frequency is 156.6 MHz, Channel 12. The

Chart 3526

Passage Island

Queen Charlotte Channel from vicinity of Point Grey (1981)

Master of a vessel must request a clearance from *Vancouver Traffic* before proceeding to or leaving any berth within *Sector Three*. Calling-in points for are:

496   **Calling-in Point 15C**, *Gower Point*, is a change from *Sector Three (Vancouver Traffic)* to *Sector One (Victoria Traffic)* and is a line joining Cape Roger Curtis light *(417)* and Gower Point *(49°23'01"N, 123°32'06"W)*.

497   **Calling-in Point 16**, *Halkett Point*, is a line joining Halkett Point *(49°26.7'N, 123°19.2'W)* and a point south of Lions Bay on the east shore.

498   **Calling-in Point 17**, *Grace Island*, is a line joining Grace Islands light *(429)* and a point south of Langdale on the west shore.

499   **Calling-in Point 18**, *Cowan Point/Point Atkinson*, is a line joining Point Cowan light *(418)* and Point Atkinson light *(386)*.

500   **Tides**. — Tidal predictions at the entrance to Howe Sound are given for Point Atkinson (Index No. 7795). Tidal differences in Howe Sound, referenced on Point Atkinson, are given for Gibsons (Index No. 7820) and Squamish (Index No. 7811) in *Tide Tables, Volume 5*.

501   **Meteorological information** in Howe Sound for Port Mellon and Woodfibre is in the Appendices.

Queen Charlotte Channel

Chart 3481

502   **Queen Charlotte Channel** separates Bowen Island from the mainland to the east. Entered between Point Cowan and Point Atkinson the channel extends north to Bowyer Island.

503   From Point Atkinson *(49°20'N, 123°16'W)*, off which there are often tide-rips, the east shore of the channel is indented and a number of islets and rocks lie off it. The west shore is moderately steep-to for the most part and free of off-lying dangers.

504   **Submarine cables** cross Queen Charlotte Channel commencing on the east shore from **Larsen Bay**, **Batchelor Cove**, **Cliff Cove** and **Copper Cove**.

505   **Passage Island** *(49°21'N, 123°18'W)* lies in the middle of the entrance to Queen Charlotte Channel. A bare patch, on the SE part of the island, is visible for a good distance from south. A prominent circular house is on the NE corner. Foul ground extends a short distance from the SE part of the island. A private mooring buoy is 0.3 mile west of Passage Island.

Queen Charlotte Channel — East Side

506   **Grebe Islets**, 0.7 mile NNW of Point Atkinson, have several shoals and drying rocks to the north of them. **Bird Islet**, 1.5 miles NNW of Grebe Islets, has a drying rock close SW and a rock with 1.2 m over it 0.1 mile NE. The channel between Bird Islet and **Kettle Point** is not recommended.

507   **Whyte Cove**, between **Whyte Islet** and **White Cliff Point**, has numerous private mooring buoys in it. **Lookout Point** is 0.3 mile NE of White Cliff Point.

508   **Marine Sanctuary**. — An underwater reserve extends from Whyte Islet to Cliff Cove. Spear fishing and removal of marine specimens are prohibited in this area.

509   **Lights**. — Grebe Islets light *(421.2)* is on the west islet.

510   Bird Islet light *(421.4)* is on the drying rock close SW of the islet.

511   Lookout Point light *(422)* is on the point.

512   **Beacon**. — White Cliff Point daybeacon, on a drying reef close SW of the point, is a white tower with a green band around the top.

Chart 3534

513   **Eagle Harbour** *(49°21'N, 123°16'W)* has a floating breakwater with a private light on its south extremity. The breakwater extends from the NW entrance point and is anchored to the eastern shore. A yacht club with small craft floats lies on the north side of the harbour and private buoys are in the harbour.

514   **Landmark**. — A road cut and bridge, on the Upper Levels Highway behind Fishermans Cove, are conspicuous from SW.

515   **Fishermans Cove**, north of Eagle Harbour, can be entered east or NW of **Eagle Island**. The entrance channel NW of Eagle Island is 20 m wide and has a least depth of 1.2 m, a starboard hand daymark marks the south side of this channel. The entrance east of

Eagle Harbour (1989)

Fishermans Cove (1989)

Horseshoe Bay (1989)

Snug Cove (1989)

Chart 3534

Eagle Island has a least depth of 0.6 m. The West Vancouver Yacht Club and other small craft facilities are in the cove.

516   **Submarine pipelines** cross the channel east of Eagle Island, one is a gas pipeline. A gas pipeline connects Eagle Island to the island west of it. A submarine cable crosses the channel east of Eagle Island and another runs along the centre of the channel NW of Eagle Island.

517   **Overhead cables**. — A cable, with a vertical clearance of 24 m, crosses the NW entrance channel to Fishermans Cove. Another cable (telephone), with a vertical clearance of 3.7 m, connects Eagle Island to the two islands close west.

518   **Light**. — Fishermans Cove light *(421)* is on the north end of a drying reef in the entrance NW of Eagle Island.

519   **Horseshoe Bay** *(49°23'N, 123°16'W)*, entered east of **Tyee Point**, has a residential area of the same name at the head of the bay which offers stores, restaurants and repair facilities.

520   **Light**. — Tyee Point light *(423)* is on a drying reef east of the point.

521   **Wharf**. — The public wharf, with floats attached to its outer end and both sides, is at the head of the bay. There is a depth of 6 m alongside the wharfhead, and a 3-tonne crane on the wharfhead.

522   Close NW of the public wharf is a **marina** protected by breakwaters. Floats, belonging to the marina, also lie SE of the public wharf.

523   **Lights**. — Privately operated lights and strobe lights are on the outer ends of the ferry berths.

524   **Buoy**. — A private buoy is moored close NW of the breakwater at the marina.

525   **Transportation**. — B.C. Ferry Services Inc. maintains regular service to Nanaimo (Departure Bay). Services are also maintained between Horseshoe Bay and Snug Cove and Langdale, the latter providing a through route by road and ferry to Powell River. Frequent bus service is available to Vancouver.

Chart 3526

526   Between Horseshoe Bay and **Alberta Bay** *(49°28'N, 123°15'W)* marinas provide facilities for small craft. One is at **Sunset Beach** 1.8 miles NE of Horseshoe Bay. It is protected by a floating breakwater and has a fuel dock, launching ramp and restaurant. The other at **Lions Bay** is 4.5 miles NNE of Horseshoe Bay.

527   The Vancouver Yacht Club has established a **measured distance** of 1,853 m in the vicinity of **Newman Creek** *(49°26'N, 123°14'W)*.

528   A **submarine pipeline** (sewer outfall) is 0.3 mile south of Lions Bay.

Queen Charlotte Channel — West Side

Chart 3481

529   The west side of Queen Charlotte Channel is formed by **Bowen Island** (east side). **Point Cowan** *(49°20'N, 123°22'W)* is the SW entrance point of Queen Charlotte Channel.

530   **Light**. — Point Cowan light *(418)* is shown at an elevation of 20.4 m from a white tower.

531   **Seymour Landing**, 0.5 mile NE of Point Cowan, has a public wharf and is connected by road to Mannion Bay and Snug Cove. The bay is exposed to ferry wash.

532   **Apodaca Cove Park** is a nature reserve.

Chart 3534

533   **Snug Cove** *(49°23'N, 123°20'W)* is the south and smaller part of a double headed bay. The settlement has restaurants, groceries, stores, gas station, library, and the Bowen Island post office. Anchorage is not recommended in Snug Cove because of the ferry route and submarine cables and pipelines.

534   **Lights**. — Snug Cove light *(419)* and Snug Cove North light *(419.5)* mark the entrance to Snug Cove.

535   Privately operated lights are at the ferry landing.

536   **Landmarks**. — A conspicuous bare red area and a road scar are about 1 mile south of Snug Cove.

537   A **submarine pipeline** (sewer outfall) is laid along the south shore of Snug Cove and extends about 100 m seaward from the south entrance point.

538   **Ferry**. — Regular ferry service is maintained to and from Horseshoe Bay.

539   **Wharf**. — The public wharf and float, near the head of the bay with a ferry landing attached to its inner end, has 107 m of berthing with a depth of 3 m alongside.

540   **Marinas** on each side of the public wharf provide small craft berthing.

541   **Mannion Bay**, formerly known as Deep Bay, is exposed and during SE weather a heavy swell rolls in. Drying and below-water rocks lie on the south side of the bay. Private floats and mooring buoys are in the north part and a boomed off area is on the south shore.

Chart 3526

542   **Millers Landing** *(49°23'N, 123°19'W)*, a short distance north of Mannion Bay, has private floats.

543   **Finisterre Island** *(49°25'N, 123°18'W)* is connected to the NE end of Bowen Island by a drying ledge.

544   **Light**. — Finisterre Island light *(420)*, on the north extremity of the island, is shown at an elevation of 10.1 m from a white tower.

545   The coast on either side of **Hood Point** *(49°25'N, 123°19'W)* is indented and the shore is lined with houses. **Cates Bay**, **Enchanta Bay**, **Columbine Bay** and **Smugglers Cove**, east and west of Hood Point, provide shelter and anchorage for small craft. A rock that dries 3.7 m lies in the middle of Enchanta Bay. A log dump and booming ground are west of Smugglers Cove.

546   **Bowyer Island**, 1.5 miles ENE of Finisterre Island, has a 5.5 m shoal off its south end and a 2.4 m shoal 0.1 mile off its NW part. Private mooring buoys are on these shoals.

Collingwood Channel

547   **Collingwood Channel**, along **Bowen Island** (west side), is entered from the south between **Cape Roger Curtis** *(49°20'N, 123°26'W)* and Worlcombe Island 1 mile WNW. **Mount Gardner** is easily distinguished by its round, partially bare summit.

548   **Conspicuous microwave towers** are on the south side of Bowen Island. Microwave towers with red air obstruction lights are on the summit of Mount Gardner, and a TV tower with red air obstruction lights is 0.7 mile NNE of the mount.

549   **Light**. — Cape Roger Curtis light *(417)* is shown at an elevation of 11 m from a white tower.

Chart 3526

550 A **submarine cable** crosses Collingwood Channel between **Bowen Bay** and **Ragged Island**.

551 **Tunstall Bay**, on the east side of the channel about 1 mile within the entrance, has some drying rocks and an islet in its north part. The bay is too deep for anchorage. Camp Cates, at the head of the bay, has a private float and booming grounds line the south shore.

552 **Beacon**. — Collingwood Channel daybeacon, 1.4 miles SW of Hutt Island, has a bifurcation/junction daymark, preferred channel to the left, it marks a 2.7 m drying rock.

553 **Hutt Island**, on the east side of the north entrance to Collingwood Channel, has a conspicuous quarry (abandoned) with several piles offshore at its NE point. **Hutt Rock**, 0.2 mile SW of Hutt Island, has a rock that dries 0.6 m close north of it. Marine farm facilities marked by a cautionary buoy lie close-off Bowen Island SE of Hutt Rock.

554 **Beacon**. — Hutt Rock daybeacon has a bifurcation/junction daymark, preferred channel to the left.

555 **Galbraith Bay**, east of Hutt Rock, has a public float 18 m long with a depth of 4.6 m alongside. **Mount Gardner** locality, in the south part of the bay, is connected by road to Snug Cove.

556 **Grafton Bay**, east of the north end of Hutt Island, is too deep for satisfactory anchorage. Floats and mooring buoys are private.

557 **Beacon**. — Grafton Bay daybeacon, on a rock in the channel between Hutt Island and Grafton Bay, has a starboard hand daymark. A rock that dries 0.6 m lies close east of the beacon.

558 **Worlcombe Island** *(49°21'N, 123°28'W)* has a few houses on it. The passage between Worlcombe Island and **Pasley Island** is encumbered with reefs and local knowledge is advised.

559 **Beacon**. — Worlcombe Island daybeacon, on a rock in the passage between Worlcombe and Pasley Islands, has a starboard hand daymark.

560 **Mickey Island**, **New Islet** and **Ragged Island** lie north of Pasley Island.

561 **Keats Island** forms the NW side of Collingwood Channel. **Cotton Point** is its NE extremity. **Eastbourne**, 0.5 mile south of Cotton Point, has a public float 15 m long at the end of a long pier and a number of private mooring buoys are in the vicinity. A pedestrian ferry operates between Eastbourne and Langdale.

Barfleur Passage

562 **Barfleur Passage** leads between Keats Island and the group of islands to the south. It is entered from the west between **Popham Island** *(49°22'N, 123°29'W)* and **Home Island** 1.3 miles NNW. Home Island is small, sparsely wooded and joined to Keats Island by a drying ledge. **Little Popham Island** and **Hermit Island** are NE of Popham Island.

563 **Light**. — Popham Island light *(432)* is on the NW extremity of the island.

564 A **submarine cable** crosses Barfleur Passage between Keats and Ragged Islands.

565 **Preston Island**, 1.5 miles NNE of Popham Island, is wooded and conspicuous. Small vessels using the channel to the north of Preston Island should favour the Preston Island shore to avoid islets, fringed with rocks, extending from Keats Island.

Shoal Channel

Chart 3534

566 **Shoal Channel** *(49°23'N, 123°30'W)* separates Keats Island from the mainland. Its south entrance is obstructed by a bar of sand and rock with 2.1 m over it. The bar has depths of 1.5 m over a rock bottom near mid-channel with drying and sunken rocks closer inshore. The sea breaks over the bar when wind opposes tide. This entrance to Shoal Channel should only be used by those familiar with local conditions.

567 **Submarine cables** (power and telephone) cross Shoal Channel in the vicinity of Steep Bluff and Gibsons. A **submarine pipeline**, 0.6 mile SW of Steep Bluff, extends about 91 m offshore.

568 **Steep Bluff**, just within the bar, is fringed with a drying rock ledge. A rocky spit, with drying rocks on it, extends 0.2 mile NNE of Steep Bluff and lies in the south approach to Gibsons. A scow mooring is on the west side of the spit.

569 **Lights**. — Gibsons Landing Rock light *(430)* is on a rock at the north end of the spit.

570 Gibsons Landing light *(431)*, atop the gazebo on the outer end of the north rock breakwater, has a starboard hand daymark.

571 Gibsons Landing Breakwater South light *(431.5)*, on the outer end of the south breakwater, has a port hand daymark.

572 **Tides**. — Tidal differences for Gibsons (Index No. 7820), referenced on Point Atkinson, are in *Tide Tables, Volume 5*.

573 **Gibsons** is a town, on the west side of a bight, on the north side of Steep Bluff. It is a tourist resort and distributing centre for towns on the north side of the Strait of Georgia. A variety of stores, restaurants, lodging, businesses, services and postal office are available. The Sunshine Coast Museum and Archives is located in Gibsons.

574 **Breakwaters**. — A pile breakwater extends NNW from the public wharf and a rock breakwater extends south from the wharfhead. A second rock breakwater extends NNW from the SE shore. The area behind the breakwaters was dredged to 2.2 m (1984).

575 **Wharves. — Floats**. — The public wharf has floats, from 40 to 90 m long attached to it; 14 m of the south finger float is reserved for aircraft. Depths alongside the wharfhead are 2.4 to 6 m at the NE face, and 4.2 to 4.8 m at the SE face. Power is laid on the floats. Water, garbage and used oil disposal facilities and a 3 tonne crane are on the wharfhead.

576 **Marinas** provide additional berthing for small craft.

577 **Supplies**. — Diesel fuel, gasoline, lubricants and fresh water are obtainable.

578 **Repairs**. — Two marine railways, capable of hauling out small craft up to 15 m long, are available and engine repairs can be undertaken by a local machine shop.

579 **Anchorage**, with good holding, can be obtained off the wharf, in a depth of about 17 m, but care should be taken to keep clear of the submarine cable that lands close north of the wharf.

580 **Communications**. — A road connects Gibsons with Langdale, Sechelt, Pender Harbour and Earls Cove (Agamemnon Channel), the latter providing ferry connection with the road leading to Westview, Powell River and north to Malaspina Inlet via Lund.

581 **Keats Island** settlement, on the west side of Keats Island abreast Steep Bluff, consists mainly of summer homes. The public wharf and float have a depth of 4 m alongside. A 3 tonne crane is

Chart 3534

Gibsons (1989)

Gibsons (1989)

on the wharf. A pedestrian ferry operates between Keats Island and Langdale.

582   **Shelter Islets**, off the NW shore of Keats Island, consist of two islets joined by a drying bank; they shelter Plumper Cove.

583   **Plumper Cove**, entered north of Shelter Islets, provides a snug anchorage. However hard it may be blowing in the Strait of Georgia it is usually calm in the cove. **Plumper Cove Marine Park** has public floats and mooring buoys. Drinking water, camping, picnic, pit toilets and garbage disposal facilities are available. Cautionary buoy "QP" marks a shoal area off the floats.

584   **Anchorage** can be obtained in the middle of Plumper Cove, in depths of 13 to 15 m, and though small vessels could lie at single anchor it is recommended to moor with two anchors.

Chart 3526

585   **Granthams Landing** *(49°25′N, 123°30′W)*, on the west side of Shoal Channel north of Gibsons, is a summer resort with stores and a post office. The wharf and floats are private.

586   **Soames Point**, 0.5 mile NE of Granthams Landing, is the NW entrance point of Shoal Channel. A shoal spit extends south

from Soames Point; its outer end is marked by port hand buoy "Q57".

Thornbrough Channel

587   **Thornbrough Channel**, on the west side of Howe Sound, leads west and north of Gambier Island.

588   **Hopkins Landing** *(49°26′N, 123°29′W)* has a public wharf 18 m long at the end of an approach pier. A float, 17 m long with a least depth of 4.6 m alongside, is attached to the north side of the pier. Provisions and fuel are obtainable. A conspicuous row of oil tanks is on the hillside 0.1 mile NW of the wharf.

589   **Langdale**, 0.3 mile NE, is the site of the B.C. Ferries Services Inc. landing for the ferry to Horseshoe Bay. A large Salvation Army summer camp is in the vicinity. A conspicuous orange coloured cliff is 0.5 mile north of the ferry landing.

590   **Lights. — Fog signal**. — Lights and radar reflectors on the ferry landing are private.

591   Langdale Ferry Landing Fog Signal *(428.1)* is operated by ferry personnel when required for ferry movements only.

Port Mellon (1989)

592   **Submarine cables** cross Thornbrough Channel from close north of Langdale to **Avalon Bay** and **Burgess Cove**.

593   **Grace Islands** *(49°26′N, 123°27′W)*, the SE entrance point of Thornbrough Channel, are connected to one another by a drying ledge and fringed with drying and below-water rocks.

594   **Light**. — Grace Islands light *(429)* is on the SW extremity of the islands.

595   **Thornbrough Bay**, 1.1 miles north of the Grace Islands, has several private floats and small mooring buoys. **New Brighton**, at the head of the bay, has a public wharf with a depth of 8.2 m alongside. Attached to it are floats with 119 m of berthing space. A 3 tonne crane is on the wharf. A pedestrian ferry operates between Thornbrough Bay, Keats Island and Langdale.

596   **Booming grounds** are in the bays 0.7 and 1.3 miles NW of Thornbrough Bay.

597   **Williamsons Landing**, 1.3 miles north of Langdale, is fronted by pilings and private floats. A short distance south of Williamsons Landing is a YMCA Camp with a float.

598   **Booming grounds** are south of the YMCA camp and an extensive log sorting area is 0.5 mile NNW of Williamsons Landing. A large mill in this vicinity has a wharf with a covered conveyor for loading barges.

599   **Twin Creeks** is about 1.5 miles north of Williamsons Landing. A private wharf, with a depth of 7.6 m alongside, and extensive booming grounds are in the vicinity.

600   **Buoys**. — Numerous buoys and boomsticks between Williamsons Landing and Twin Creeks provide moorings for logbooms and rafts.

601   **Witherby Point**, about 1.8 miles north of Williamsons Landing, is steep-to and very prominent. **Mariners Rest**, 0.9 mile SE of Witherby Point, is a rock off the west extremity of Gambier Island. **Andys Bay**, NE of Mariners Rest, has a float where diesel fuel, gasoline and fresh water can be obtained. Booming grounds and mooring buoys are in Andys Bay.

602   Between Witherby Point and **Hillside**, 1.5 miles NW, there is a conspicuous row of lights on top of poles, booming grounds, a private light buoy, several mooring buoys and a barge

loading ramp. A gravel quarry and a booming ground are about 0.5 mile north of Hillside.

603   **Spoil ground**. — An ocean dump site under permit through the *Ocean Dumping Control Act* is in *49°31′N, 123°28.3′W*.

604   **Port Mellon** *(49°31′N, 123°29′W)* is the site of a large pulp mill. Its principal exports are wood pulp, newsprint and fertilizers. The port is used mainly by cargo vessels and has a Post Office.

605   A **submarine pipeline** extends about 0.2 mile south from the south entrance point of **Rainy River**.

606   **Approach**. — The inner approach to the port is deep and free of dangers.

607   **Wharves**. — The main wharf is 189 m long with a least depth of 10.6 m alongside. It is used mainly for loading pulp, which is brought alongside by 9 tonne lift trucks. Loading is done by ships gear. Fresh water at 90 psi is available through 2½″ hose. There is no shore gangway, but there is a telephone. The wharf has 5,200 m² of covered storage and 2,045 m² of open storage. It is recommended that vessels berth starboard side to. A wharf with a float for seaplanes is close west of the main wharf.

608   **Rail-car barge ramp** and chip handling facilities for barges are east of the wharf.

609   **Supplies**. — Fuel, lubricants or food supplies are not available in the quantities normally needed by ships; such supplies are obtainable from Vancouver.

610   **Meteorological information** for Port Mellon is in the Appendices.

611   **Seaside Park**, a short distance NE, has barge unloading facilities protected by a breakwater.

612   **Booming grounds** are in the bight ENE of Seaside Park and off the mouth of **Bain Creek**.

613   **Latona Passage**, between **Woolridge Island** *(49°31′N, 123°28′W)* and Gambier Island, is deep and free of dangers in the fairway. Booming grounds are along the east shore of Latona Passage and off the south and north ends of Woolridge Island.

614   **McNab Creek** is in a bight on the north shore of Thornbrough Channel, about 4 miles ENE of Port Mellon. A repair

Chart 3526

building, A-frame, four storage tanks and a log dump and booming ground are located here. Some dredging has been done at the mouth of the creek to facilitate landing for logging equipment and supplies.

615   **Ekins Point** (locality), close SW of **Ekins Point**, has floats owned by a yacht club. **Camp Latona** and a yacht club, SW of Ekins Point landing, have private wharves and floats. A submarine pipeline (sewer outfall) is close north of Camp Latona.

616   **Light**. — Ekins Point light *(428)* is on the point.

617   The junction of Thornbrough and Ramillies Channels is 1 mile east of Ekins Point.

Gambier Island — South Side

618   **Gambier Island**, in the centre of Howe Sound, has four bays indenting its south side.

619   **Halkett Bay**, entered west of **Halkett Point** *(49°27'N, 123°19'W)*, is the east and smallest of the four indentations on the south side of Gambier Island. A cluster of above-water and drying rocks lies in the NW part of the bay, and a detached rock, with less than 2 m over it, lies in the middle of the fairway, near the head of the bay. The east side of the bay is a booming ground.

620   **Halkett Bay Marine Park** has a dinghy float, pit toilets and camping facilities.

621   A **submarine pipeline** (sewer outfall), at the west entrance point to Halkett Bay, extends 93 m offshore.

622   **Wharf**. — The public wharf and float are in the small cove west of the west entrance point to Halkett Bay. The wharf has a shed and derrick on it and the float is 17 m long.

623   **Port Graves**, the principal anchorage in Howe Sound, can be approached from any of the channels, at the entrance of Howe Sound. The most direct route is through Collingwood Channel, however the entrance is not easily identified until within a short distance off **Hope Point** *(49°26'N, 123°22'W)*.

624   **Light**. — Hope Point light *(420.4)*, on a drying ledge 0.1 mile SE of the point, is shown at an elevation of 7 m from a white tower.

625   **Mount Artaban**, east of Port Graves, has a lookout tower at its summit, the tower is only visible from the east. **East Bay**, known locally as Daisy Bay, lies close north of **Gambier Point** and has a breakwater protecting a private wharf. **Potts Point** is fronted by a shingle spit with shallow water for about 90 m beyond its extremity, the point should be given a wide berth. Both sides of Port Graves, north of Potts Point, are booming grounds and private mooring buoys line the shore between East Bay and Potts Point.

626   **Anchorage** can be obtained north of Potts Point in a depth of 15 m or less. A good position is between 0.5 and 0.7 mile north of Potts Point in a depth of 13 m. It has been reported that the bottom is littered with sunken logs, cables and chains.

627   **Camp Artaban**, at the head of Port Graves, is an Anglican Church camp ground. Camp floats are on the east side of the public wharf.

628   **Wharf**. — The public wharf at the head of Port Graves has a float on its west side with a depth of 2 m alongside. It is equipped with a 5 tonne crane.

629   **Centre Bay** is the next indentation west of Port Graves. **Alexandra Island** has an above-water rock and a 2.1 m drying rock close-off its east shore. Yacht clubs have floats on the west side of Alexandra Island, in Elliot Bay (local name) and at the head of Centre Bay. Booming grounds occupy both sides of the bay.

McKenzie Bay (local name) is on the east side of Centre Bay. Drying and below-water rocks lie at the head of the bay.

630   **West Bay** is entered west of **Carmelo Point** *(49°27'N, 123°24'W)*. It is partially obstructed by above-water and drying rocks a short distance within the entrance, but a clear channel about 0.1 mile wide lies along the west shore. The east side of the bay has booming grounds. A summer resort and a public wharf, 50 m long, are on the west side of the entrance to the bay.

631   **Gambier Harbour** *(49°26'N, 123°26'W)*, near the SW point of Gambier Island, has a public wharf with depths of 3 to 4.6 m alongside. A float 30 m long is attached to its west side. A 2 tonne crane and a shed are on the wharfhead. This public wharf and the entire harbour are exposed to the weather. A store is nearby.

Ramillies and Montagu Channels

632   **Ramillies Channel**, separating **Anvil Island** from the NE side of Gambier Island, is entered west of Pam Rock *(49°29'N, 123°18'W)*.

633   **Pam Rock** is conspicuous and has numerous drying and below-water rocks extending north and south from it. **Christie Islet** is bare and conspicuous, the rock and islet are a bird sanctuary.

634   **Light**. — Pam Rock light *(424)* is shown at an elevation of 11.6 m from a white tower.

635   **Irby Point**, 1.4 miles north of Pam Rock, is the south extremity of Anvil Island.

636   Two bays separated by **Daybreak Point** lie NW of Irby Point. **Anvil Island** settlement is on the north side of these bays. A float protected by a breakwater is at the settlement.

637   **Leading Peak**, the summit of Anvil Island, is 754 m high and very conspicuous from most parts of Howe Sound, it resembles the horn of an anvil pointed upwards.

638   **Brigade Bay**, on the west side of the channel, is 1.3 miles west of Pam Rock. **Douglas Bay** is 2 miles NW of Brigade Bay. Temporary anchorage is possible in the south part of Brigade Bay and in Douglas Bay. Care should be taken in Douglas Bay to avoid the drying rock and shallows extending from the mouth of **Gambier Creek**.

639   The bay at the NW extremity of Anvil Island is a **booming ground**.

640   **Domett Point**, the north extremity of Anvil Island, is the NE entrance point to Ramillies Channel.

641   The wharf on the mainland shore, 1.4 miles north of Domett Point and close west of **Potlatch Creek**, belongs to **Camp Potlatch**.

642   **Montagu Channel** separates Anvil Island from the mainland to the east and is the main entrance channel to the head of Howe Sound and Squamish Harbour. **Brunswick Point** is on the east side of the channel.

643   **Light**. — Brunswick Point light *(425)* is on the point, on the E side of Montagu Channel.

644   **Submarine cables** lead from Copper Cove up the centre of Montagu Channel, landing at Minaty and Darrell Bays.

645   **Wharf**. — A B.C. Ferries Services Inc. wharf for emergency use only is at **Porteau Cove**, 2 miles NNE of Brunswick Point.

646   **Light**. — A privately operated light with a radar reflector is shown from the ferry wharf.

647   **Porteau Cove Marine Park** has sunken wrecks and an artificial reef, for the use of divers. The area is marked by buoys.

Chart 3526

Camping facilities, toilets, picnic area and a launching ramp are available at the park.

648   **Defence Islands** lie 2 miles north of Porteau Cove on the west side of the channel.

Squamish Harbour

649   **Squamish Harbour**, at the head of Howe Sound, includes within its limits the facilities at Woodfibre and Squamish.

650   **Ferry**. — A scheduled ferry, operated by Harbour Ferries, crosses Squamish Harbour from Woodfibre, on the north shore, to **Darrell Bay** on the south shore. Both ferry landings have privately operated lights and radar reflectors.

651   **Pilotage** is compulsory. Squamish Harbour is in Area 2 of the Pacific Pilotage Region and the pilot boards in the vicinity of the Cautionary Buoy off Brotchie Ledge, near Victoria. For details regarding obtaining a pilot when arriving or departing see *PAC 200.*

652   **Arrival information**. — Squamish Harbour is not a port of entry and Customs officials from Vancouver deal with Customs formalities. The harbour is under the jurisdiction of Transport Canada whose local representative is the Harbour Master, telephone (604) 892-9433. Tugs are available.

653   There are extensive **booming grounds** within Squamish Harbour.

654   **Tides**. — Tidal differences for Squamish (Index No. 7811), referenced on Point Atkinson, are in *Tide Tables, Volume 5.*

655   **Anchorage** of a short term nature can be obtained in about 50 m, 0.3 mile SW of Squamish Approach light. Due to the strength and suddenness of local winds and the poor holding ground, long term anchorage is not recommended.

656   **Minaty Bay** *(49°37'N, 123°13'W)* is the site of a gravel pit with several loading conveyors and a scow mooring jetty.

657   A **submarine cable** lands at Minaty Bay; it is marked by a sign.

658   **Britannia Beach** was formerly a mining town with facilities for shipping copper ore. The mine is closed and its loading wharf is in a state of disrepair. Harbour Ferries Limited has a float and walkway, protected by a rockfill causeway with a pile pier head and shed at its outer end. The old mine building, on the hillside overlooking the townsite, is a conspicuous landmark and has a large sign "Mining Museum" facing seaward. The community has a post office and store. Two ruined wharves are SW of the Mining Museum. The southern most wharf has the wreck of the Gulf Bird, a tug approximately 14 m long, close off its SE end. The top of the mast is just visible. The submerged wreck of the Cape Swain, a fishing vessel 17.4 m long, is close off the NE end of the same ruined wharf.

659   A **submarine cable** (power) is laid on the south side of the causeway and is marked by a sign.

660   **Watts Point**, 1.5 miles NW of Britannia Beach, has **booming grounds** to the north and south of it. A quarry operation, 0.8 mile NE of Watts Point, has a barge ramp and loading conveyors.

661   **Microwave towers** are 0.6 mile ENE and 0.7 mile east of Watts Point. The east tower has red air obstruction **lights**.

662   **Woodfibre** *(49°40'N, 123°15'W)* is the site of a large pulpmill. Manufacturing wood pulp is the only local industry. Private **mooring buoys** are south of the pulpmill.

663   A **submarine cable** (telephone) lands at Darrell Bay and is marked by a sign. A second **submarine cable** extends from Woodfibre to the north of Britannia Beach.

664   **Wharves**. — **South Pulp Loading Dock** is 137 m long with a depth of 9 m alongside.

665   **North Pulp Loading Dock** is 122 m long with depths of 9 m alongside.

666   Three warehouses have a storage capacity of 22,000 tonnes of pulp. Both docks are equipped with 2.7 and 3.6 tonne forklifts and have loading rates of 23 tonnes/hour. The docks are equipped with telephones and fresh water but they do not have a shore gangway.

667   **Chip Loading Dock**, for barges and railcars, is 110 m long with depths of 4.6 m alongside. Used for handling chips and hog fuel it is equipped with a Colby Crane and a Peco Crane.

Squamish Terminals (1989)

Squamish public wharf (1989)

Squamish floats (1989)

Chart 3526

Major Port Facilities — Squamish

Berth	Wharf Length (m)	Least Depth (m)	Elevation (m)	Remarks
Squamish Terminals Berth 1 (East)	137	11.6		Forest products. Dolphins off both ends of berth to accommodate vessels 195 m long. Barge ramp north of berth. 47,410 m² covered storage.
Squamish Terminals Berth 2 (West)	153	12.2		Forest products. Dolphins at both ends of berth to accommodate vessels 212 m long. 47,410 m² covered storage.
Western Pulp Ltd Woodfibre Pulp Mill South Dock	137	9		Pulp. 3 warehouses capacity 22,000 tonnes. Unloading ramp for railcars and barges, ferry slip. Five mooring buoys in bay for barges.
Western Pulp Ltd Woodfibre Pulp Mill North Dock	122	9		Handles chemical and petroleum barges.

668   **Passenger ferry slip** is to the west of the wharves.

669   **Communications**. — A ferry service connects Woodfibre with Darrell Bay, 3 miles south of Squamish, and the Vancouver highway. A freight car ferry service transports pulp and chemicals.

Chart 3534

670   **Squamish** *(49°41'N, 123°10'W)* is in the entrance to the east arm of the **Squamish River**. The main function of the port is handling forest products. Squamish has a variety of retail stores, restaurants, a post office and a hospital. **Caution. — Numerous wind and kite surfers can be expected in the approaches to Squamish, particularly during summer afternoons.**

671   **Inner approach**. — The approach to Mamquam Blind Channel, between Squamish Approach light and the north end of a disused wharf, was dredged to 9 m but silting has been occurring and in 1990 depths of 7.1 m were encountered in this area.

672   **Mamquam Blind Channel** is the east entrance channel of Squamish River between the disused wharf and Squamish Range lights. The channel, marked by Squamish Range lights, and the continuation of the east arm of Squamish River to within 0.1 mile of the rail bridge, was dredged (1986) to a depth of 2.9 m. Shoaling has developed across the full channel width near the mouth of the Stawamus River. The portion of the range north of the river should not be used, the preferred channel is reported to be to the west of the range.

673   **Lights**. — Squamish Approach light *(425.5)*, on the east side of the entrance to Mamquam Blind Channel, is on a dolphin with a starboard hand daymark.

674   Squamish Terminal No. 1 light *(427.4)* is on a dolphin 0.5 mile WNW of Squamish Approach light.

675   Squamish Terminal No. 2 light *(427.5)* is on a dolphin 0.3 mile WNW of Squamish Approach light.

676   Private lights are on the wharves and on the rock groyne, on the east entrance point of the west arm to Squamish River.

677   **Light ranges**. — Squamish Terminal range lights *(427.1, 427.2)*, west of Squamish Terminal, in line bearing 019½° lead to the west berth of the terminal. **Caution. — Considerable silting has occurred 120 m west of the range line. A shoal extends from the flashing green Squamish Terminal No. 1 light *(427.4)*, 300 m in a south west direction. A 0.3 m sounding is at *49°40.84'N, 123°10.69'W* (2004), however further changes are likely to occur.**

678   Private range lights, east of Squamish Terminals, in line bearing 026° lead to the east berth of Squamish Terminals.

679   Squamish range lights *(426, 427)*, on the east bank of Mamquam Blind Channel about 0.8 mile NE of Squamish Approach

light, bearing 034½° lead through Mamquam Blind Channel to the inner part of the Squamish River.

680   **Private mooring buoys** lie south of Squamish Approach light.

681   **Wharves**. — Details of the deep-sea wharves in Squamish are in the adjacent table.

682   The **public wharf**, on the west bank of the east arm to Squamish River and about 1 mile NNE of Squamish Approach light, has a depth of 2.3 m alongside its outer end. Floats attached to the wharf have a combined berthing length of 330 m and depths of 0.7 to 1.1 m alongside. A 3 tonne crane is on the wharfhead, power and water are available at the floats.

683   **Squamish Yacht Club floats** are on the north side of the public wharf.

684   A **marina** is at the head of the channel.

685   The **ferry wharf** is 0.1 mile north of the public wharf.

686   **Supplies**. — Fuel is available by prior arrangement for tank truck delivery. Fresh water can be obtained at the public wharf and provisions are obtainable in moderate quantities at stores in Squamish.

687   **Harbour services**. — Tugs and small craft repair facilities are available.

688   **Communications**. — Squamish is connected with Vancouver and the interior by road and rail; regular bus service is available. The airport, north of the town, has an asphalt runway 732 m long. A ferry to Woodfibre runs from Darrell Bay, about 1 mile south of the town.

Nanaimo Harbour and Approach

Chart 3458

689   The approach to Nanaimo Harbour *(49°12'N, 123°54'W)* from the Strait of Georgia is between Entrance Island and Lagoon Head, 5.5 miles WNW. The navigable channels in this approach, from east to west, are Fairway Channel, Rainbow Channel and Horswell Channel. These channels, divided by islands and shoals, are deep and well lighted.

690   **Vessel Traffic Services** (VTS). — Nanaimo Harbour in *Sector One* of the *Vancouver Traffic Zone* is administered by *Victoria Traffic* and the assigned frequency is 156.55 MHz, Channel 11.

691   ***Calling-in Point No. 23**, Entrance Island/Five Fingers Island*, is a line joining Entrance Island light *(435)* and Five Finger Island *(49°13'53"N, 123°54'52"W)*.

Chart 3458

692   A brief description of the VTS is in *PAC 200*. Details are in *Radio Aids to Marine Navigation (Pacific and Western Arctic)*.

693   **Pilotage** is compulsory. Nanaimo Harbour is in Area 2 of the Pacific Pilotage Region. For details regarding obtaining a pilot when arriving or departing see *PAC 200*.

694   **Ferries**. — Large, fast, passenger and vehicle ferries on regular schedules between Departure Bay and Horseshoe Bay, in Howe Sound, and Duke Point and Tsawwassen generally use Rainbow or Fairway Channels. A freight ferry operating between Nanaimo and the Fraser River generally uses Fairway Channel and the Gabriola Island ferry operates from Meakin Channel.

695   **Tides**. — Tidal differences for Nanaimo (Index No. 7917), referenced on Point Atkinson, are in *Tide Tables, Volume 5*.

696   **Tidal streams** are strong in the vicinity of Jack Point, especially at spring tides.

697   **Meteorological information** for Nanaimo (Departure Bay) and a wind frequency table for Entrance Island are in the Appendices.

698   **Entrance Island** *(49°13'N, 123°49'W)* is a sandstone rock 9 m high bare of trees with some stunted vegetation on it. Foul ground extends west and SW from the island. Conspicuous white buildings with red roofs, a radio tower and flag staff are on the island. Vessels bound to and from Nanaimo, or passing through the Strait of Georgia, should pass north of this island.

699   **Light**. — Entrance Island light *(435)* is shown at an elevation of 19 m from a white tower 10.7 m high.

700   **Buoys**. — North cardinal buoy "PE" marks the NW extremity of the foul ground extending from Entrance Island. Starboard hand buoy "PO" marks the south edge of the foul ground extending SW from Entrance Island.

701   **Forwood Channel**, between **Orlebar Point** and Entrance Island, is partially obstructed by foul ground extending about 0.2 mile south and west from the island; it should not be attempted without local knowledge. A submarine cable (power) crosses this channel.

702   **Sewage disposal** in the waters of **Pilot Bay** and **Gabriola Sands Park**, at the north end of Gabriola Island, is prohibited under the *Pleasure/Non-Pleasure Craft Sewage Pollution Prevention Regulations*.

Chart 3447

703   **Fairway Channel**, between the NW end of Gabriola Island and Snake Island, has a navigable width of about 0.7 mile. **Snake Island** is a smooth topped, grassy island fringed by drying reefs. A shoal, 0.3 mile SE of Snake Island, has a least depth of 1.5 m over it. Passage between Snake Island and this shoal is not recommended.

704   **Light**. — Snake Island light *(436)*, on the north end of the island, is shown at an elevation of 12.1 m from a white tower with a green band at the top.

705   **Light buoy**. — Snake Island Reef light and bell buoy "P2" *(437)*, south of the shoal lying SE of Snake Island, is a starboard hand buoy.

706   **Artificial reef. — Buoys**. — HMCS Saskatchewan has been sunk close east of Snake Island as an artificial reef for divers. It is marked by cautionary/information buoys and has mooring buoys.

707   HMCS Cape Breton has been sunk SE of Snake Island as an artificial reef for divers. It is marked by cautionary buoys.

708   **Rainbow Channel** lies between Snake Island and Five Finger Island and Hudson Rocks, about 1.5 miles NW. **Five Finger Island** is bare and rugged. It gets its name from five hummocks which on certain bearings resemble knuckles of a clenched fist. **Hudson Rocks** consist of five islets and rocks from 1 to 10 m high encircled by reefs.

709   **Light**. — Hudson Rocks light *(447)* is on the summit of the SW islet.

710   **Horswell Channel** lies between Hudson Rocks and the coast of Vancouver Island. **Clarke Rock**, on the west side of Horswell Channel, is separated from Vancouver Island by a narrow channel in which there is foul ground.

711   **Light**. — Clarke Rock light *(447.2)* is on the rock.

712   **Lagoon Head**, 0.3 mile NW of Clarke Rock, has several drying rocks on its NW side.

713   **Hammond Bay**, entered between Lagoon Head and **Neck Point**, is exposed to NE weather. A submarine pipeline (sewer outfall) passes through the centre of the bay and extends 1.1 miles NE.

714   **Horswell Bluff**, 0.7 mile south of Clarke Rock, is fronted by foul ground. **Horswell Rock**, at the outer end of this foul ground, has 1.8 m over it.

715   **Light buoy. — Buoy**. — Horswell Rock light buoy "PL" *(446.5)*, east of Horswell Rock, is an east cardinal buoy.

716   Port hand buoy "P15", 0.2 mile north of Horswell Rock, marks the edge of the shoal area extending east of Horswell Bluff.

717   **Submarine cables** run from the north side of Departure Bay through Rainbow Channel. Through Fairway Channel there is a cable from Newcastle Island and a cable from Departure Bay. These cables all cross the Strait of Georgia to Point Grey and are abandoned.

Nanaimo Harbour

718   **Nanaimo Harbour** is under the jurisdiction of the Nanaimo Port Authority. The office is at 104 Front Street, near the Commercial Inlet Basin, telephone (250) 753-4146.

719   **Approach**. — The outer approach to Nanaimo from the Strait of Georgia is deep and well lighted. The usual approach is through Fairway Channel. Entry into the inner portion of Nanaimo Harbour is through McKay and Meakin Channels using the Colliery range beacons. Berths for Duke Point Terminal and Harmac are in Northumberland Channel.

720   **Harbour limits**. — Nanaimo Harbour comprises all waters south of a line from a position on Vancouver Island in *49°13'16"N, 123°56'42"W* to a point on Gabriola Island in *49°11'26"N, 123°52'22"W*, including Descanso Bay, Departure Bay, Northumberland Channel, False Narrows as far east as *123°46'38"W*, and Dodd Narrows as far south as *49°08'02"N*.

721   **Regulations**. — *Practices and Procedures* established by the Nanaimo Port Authority apply to all ships within the harbour limits. Copies can be obtained by writing to:

Nanaimo Port Authority,
P.O. Box 131,
Nanaimo, B.C. V9R 5K4

722   A 'ship' means every description of vessel, boat or craft designed, used or capable of being used solely or partly for marine navigation, whether self-propelled or no and without regard to the method of propulsion, and includes a seaplane and raft or boom of log or lumber.

Chart 3447

Approach to Departure Bay (1979)

723   Regulations require persons in charge of ships to make certain reports to the Port Authority and govern ships manoeuvring or otherwise underway, at anchor, berthing or alongside a berth within the harbour limits. No ship shall move in the harbour at a rate of speed that may endanger or injury any person or cause damage to or interfere with any ship, tow, port facility, structure, construction site or work being carried on by the Authority or by any person. No ship shall move in excess of any rate of speed authorized by the Port Authority.

724   Ships are regulated with respect to watch – keeping, bunkering, anchoring, cargo handling operations and lighting. There are specific regulations for carrying and handling explosives and dangerous goods as well as rules to be observed in the prevention of fire.

725   *Practices and Procedures* forbid the discharge of sewage or other pollutants into the waters of the harbour.

726   A **speed limit** of 10 km/h (5 kn) is prescribed by the *Boating Restriction Regulations* for Nanaimo Harbour, excluding Dodd Narrows.

727   **Harbour patrol**. — The Nanaimo Harbour patrol vessel may exhibit two blue strobe lights on either side of the yardarm for identification purposes.

728   **Arrival information**. — Nanaimo is a port of entry and Customs officers board on arrival. The customs office is in the Federal Building near Commercial Inlet. Tugs are available for berthing.

729   **Anchorage** berths in Nanaimo for ships greater than 50 m in length are assigned by the Harbour Master. Anchorage berths, east of Protection and Newcastle Islands, are designated A to G and are for use by large commercial ships. There is a small ship anchorage in Mark Bay north of the seaplane water aerodrome. No ship shall anchor within a designated seaplane water aerodrome in the harbour. The southern limit of the small ship anchorage is marked by "no anchoring" buoys.

730   **Ferries** frequently cross the north entrance of Northumberland Channel in the vicinity of the designated anchorages.

731   **Batchelor Point** *(49°11′N, 123°55′W)* is the NE extremity of Protection Island. **Power Squadron Reef** is 0.2 mile NW of Batchelor Point. **McKay Point** and **Angle Point** form the NE extremity of Newcastle Island.

732   The drying channel between Protection and Newcastle Islands, known locally as Reef Bay, has a private **daybeacon** in its central part.

733   **Submarine cables and pipelines** cross the drying channel between Protection and Newcastle Islands. An abandoned cable lands in the bay south of Angle Point. A pipeline (sewer outfall) extends 0.2 mile offshore, 0.3 mile west of McKay Point.

734   A **yellow mooring buoy** lies 0.4 mile east of McKay Point.

Departure Bay

735   **Departure Bay** *(49°12′N, 123°57′W)*, NW of Newcastle Island, is entered between Horswell Bluff and **Nares Point**, 0.6 mile south. It is well sheltered, however a constant passage of ferries causes large swells which can be a problem to small craft.

736   **Water aerodrome**. — Departure Bay, north of the ferry terminal, is part of Nanaimo water aerodrome. No ship shall anchor within a designated water aerodrome.

737   An **aeronautical strobe light** activated by the aircraft pilot to alert mariners of aircraft landing or taking off is on a piling close-off Shaft Point.

738   **Jesse Island** lies on the north side of the east entrance. The channel to the north of Jesse Island has several **submarine cables** in it.

739   **Light**. — Jesse Island light *(446)* is on the east extremity of the island.

740   **Brandon Islands**, west of Jesse Island, have a **daybeacon** with a starboard hand daymark on their west extremity.

741   **Marine farm**. — A fish holding pen lies off the north shore of Brandon Islands. Mariners are requested to exercise caution when navigating in its vicinity and reduce speed to less than 5 kn.

742   **Inskip Rock**, on a drying ledge 0.2 mile west of Jesse Island, is 1 m high. A shoal, with 1.2 m over it, lies in the centre of the channel between Inskip Rock and Jesse Island.

743   **Buoy**. — Cautionary buoy "PC" marks the west extremity of the shoal extending from Inskip Rock.

Chart 3447

False Narrows from Percy Anchorage (1988)

744   The Pacific Biological Station (Department of Fisheries and Oceans) is on the north shore of Departure Bay abreast Brandon Islands.

745   **Submarine pipelines** (water intakes) extend about 0.1 mile SW from the Biological Station. A submarine cable is laid between the Biological Station and Brandon Islands.

746   **Prohibited anchorage**. — Anchorage is prohibited in the area north of Brandon Islands.

747   **Rafts**. — Swimming area marker floats, diving rafts, are moored off the west shore of Departure Bay during summer months. No ship shall move at a speed greater than 5 kn within 180 m of a swimmer or 365 m of a beach.

748   **Ferry landing**. — A ferry terminal is about 0.2 mile west of **Pimbury Point** in the south part of the bay. The approach has been dredged to a depth of 5.2 m and regular ferry service is maintained with Vancouver (Horseshoe Bay) via Rainbow Channel.

749   **Lights. — Fog signal**. — Lights and radar reflectors on the ferry terminal are private.

750   Departure Bay Ferry Landing Fog Signal *(445.1)* is operated by ferry personnel when required for ferry movements only. A dolphin east of the ferry landing is fitted with a radar reflector.

751   A **barge loading ramp** and dolphins, belonging to a cement company, are between the ferry terminal and Pimbury Point.

752   **Wharf**. — Esso (Imperial) Oil Bulk Plant wharf, at Pimbury Point, is 49 m long with a least depth of 3 m alongside.

753   Pimbury Point and **Shaft Point**, to the NE, form the north entrance to Newcastle Island Passage.

754   **Light buoy**. — Departure Bay light buoy "PW" *(445.5)*, about 0.1 mile NW of Shaft Point, is a west cardinal buoy.

755   **Artificial reef**. — Porta Reef (local name) is a fish haven close ENE of buoy "PW". It consists of concrete pieces, has a least depth of 3 m and is about 85 m long in a NE/SW direction by 40 m wide. Anchorage is prohibited in the vicinity of the reef.

False Narrows

Chart 3475

756   **False Narrows** *(49°08′N, 123°47′W)* leads from Pylades Channel to Percy Anchorage and Northumberland Channel. It is suitable only for boats and small craft; local knowledge is advised. The navigable channel, with depths of 0.9 to 1.5 m, leads north of a long narrow drying ledge near the middle of the passage. Kelp grows profusely in the narrows, during summer and autumn, and is an additional source of danger.

757   **Harbour limits**. — The SE limit of Nanaimo Harbour crosses False Narrows, regulations for Nanaimo Harbour apply west of this limit.

758   **Tidal streams** through False Narrows, in the vicinity of the drying reef, run parallel with the shore on both flood and ebb. The flood sets NW and the ebb SE. At the east end of the narrows at LW the stream runs smoothly along the north shore of Mudge Island, and gradually extends over the whole narrows as the tide rises, on a falling tide the effect is reversed.

759   Secondary current station False Narrows (Index No. 3510), referenced on Dodd Narrows, is in *Tide Tables, Volume 5*.

760   **Beacon ranges**. — False Narrows East Range, on the north side of False Narrows 0.8 mile NW from the east extremity of Mudge Island, in line bearing 326° leads to the channel north of the long drying ledge.

761   False Narrows West Range, on the north side of False Narrows and about 0.3 mile west of the East Range, in line bearing 088° leads to the channel north of the long drying ledge. Drying boulders lie close to the north side of False Narrows, close east of the West Range.

762   A **submarine cable** crosses False Narrows in a NE direction from close west of the West Range.

763   **Directions**. — Logbooms are often towed through False Narrows, usually southbound with the first of the ebb. Mariners intending to navigate the passage should be prepared to give them adequate clearance. Approaching False Narrows from Pylades

Dodd Narrows (1972)

Dodd Narrows (1979)

Channel hold to the Mudge Island shore to avoid the drying area to the north that has a number of large boulders on it. At the west end keep on the West Range until close to the Mudge Island shore to avoid the drying spit extending west of the West Range.

764   **Percy Anchorage**, at the west end of False Narrows, is a convenient place to anchor to wait for slack water in Dodd and False Narrows. On the north shore of Mudge Island, close east of the power line, is a small cove occupied by a yacht club. The public float on the north side of Percy Anchorage has been damaged and is closed to the public (1996).

765   **Tidal streams** in Percy Anchorage are weak.

766   **Overhead cables** with a vertical clearance of 28 m cross the west entrance to Percy Anchorage.

Dodd Narrows

767   **Dodd Narrows**, separated from False Narrows by Mudge Island, connects Stuart Channel with Northumberland Channel. It is used mainly by tugs, barges and logbooms. Because of the narrowness of the channel and velocity of tidal streams, it is not a recommended passage for much larger craft. However, vessels up

to 70 m have passed through without undue difficulty at slack water.

768   **Harbour limits**. — The SW limit of Nanaimo Harbour crosses Dodd Narrows, regulations for Nanaimo Harbour apply north of this limit.

769   **Tidal streams**. — Predictions of times and rates of maximum current, and times of slack water are given for Dodd Narrows (Index No. 3500) in *Tide Tables, Volume 5*. The maximum flood (north) is 9½ kn and the ebb (south) is 8½ kn.

770   When the tidal stream is running at strength tide-rips, formed by the stream and its counterflow, occur off the north entrance on the flood, and in the vicinity of the overhead cable on the ebb. No attempt should be made to alter course out of the main stream until clear of this turbulence. Gradual disappearance of these tide-rips is an indication of slackening in the tidal stream.

771   **Overhead cable** (power), with a vertical clearance of 37 m, crosses Dodd Narrows about 0.2 mile south of Purvis Point.

772   **Purvis Point**, the west extremity of Mudge Island, forms the east side of Dodd Narrows, and **Joan Point**, about 0.1 mile SW, forms the west side.

Chart 3475

773 **Light**. — Joan Point light *(298)*, on the west side of Dodd Narrows, is shown at an elevation of 8.8 m from a white tower with a green band at the top.

774 **Directions**. — Dodd Narrows is more difficult to pass through when entering from north than from south. From north the slight alteration of course necessary when passing through has to be made immediately on entering the narrow part. Also the entrance to Dodd Narrows is difficult to see when approaching from Northumberland Channel.

775 It is recommended that passage through Dodd Narrows be made at slack water. Before passing through Dodd Narrows other than at slack water, be sure the vessel is able to proceed against the tidal stream. If there is any doubt passage should be delayed until slack water.

776 Care should be taken not to hinder tugs with barges passing through, and attention should be given to sound and radio signals for narrow channels.

Northumberland Channel

Charts 3475, 3458

777 **Northumberland Channel** *(49°09′N, 123°52′W)* leads NW from Dodd and False Narrows, between Vancouver Island and the SW coast of Gabriola Island, toward Nanaimo and the Strait of Georgia.

778 **Regulations**. — Northumberland Channel, within the harbour limits of Nanaimo, is regulated by *Practices and Procedures* established by the Nanaimo Port Authority.

779 **Tides**. — Tidal differences for Harmac (Index No. 7913), referenced on Point Atkinson, are in *Tide Tables, Volume 5*.

780 **Tidal streams** in Northumberland Channel are unusual as the set is continually to the east, due to the more rapid progression of the tide in the Strait of Georgia than in the channels south of Dodd Narrows. Maximum of this east-going stream is 1 to 2 kn at springs.

781 **Ferries** on regular schedules cross the north end of Northumberland Channel from the Duke Point Ferry terminal to Tsawwassen and between Nanaimo and Descanso Bay.

782 A **submarine cable** crosses Northumberland Channel from a position 0.5 mile west of Dodd Narrows.

783 A **tower** in *49°09′N, 123°50.5′W* has red air obstruction lights.

784 **Submarine pipelines**. — A sewer outfall, 0.2 mile west of Harmac, extends 0.6 mile north into Northumberland Channel. A salt water intake, constructed of concrete with 14 m over it, from which a pipeline leads shoreward lies close-off the Nexen Chemicals wharf. A pipeline extends 152 m offshore 0.1 mile west of the chemicals wharf.

785 **Supplies and Harbour Services**. — See Nanaimo.

786 **Communications**. — There is highway communication with Nanaimo.

787 **Duke Point**, on the south side of Northumberland Channel about 1.5 miles west of Joan Point, is the site of a large pulp mill. Weyerhaeuser Canada Ltd operate Harmac East Dock and Pope and Talbot Ltd operate Harmac West Dock. The plant has a conspicuous 87 m chimney, which together with its smoke can be seen for many miles.

788 **Lights**. — Privately operated lights are on the east and west extremities of Harmac West Dock, and on the east and west extremities of Duke Point Deep Sea Terminal. The container crane at the terminal is also lit.

789 **Booming grounds** with many mooring buoys lie between Joan Point and Doman Industries. Booming grounds fronting Harmac are flood lit. The north shore of Northumberland Channel is also a booming ground.

790 **Wharves**. — Details of wharves in Northumberland Channel are given in the adjacent table.

Chart 3447

791 **Ferry landing**. — B.C. Ferries Duke Point terminal is at **Jack Point**. Regular ferry service is maintained with Tsawwassen via Fairway or Rainbow Channels. Lights on the ferry terminal are private.

792 **Lights**. — Jack Point light *(438.5)* is on the east side of the point.

Chart 3458

793 **Descanso Bay** *(49°11′N, 123°52′W)*, south of **Malaspina Point**, has a ferry landing in its NE part. Frequent ferry service to and from Nanaimo is maintained. Private lights and a radar reflector are on the ferry landing. Precipitous cliffs extend south from the south entrance point and a large white guano patch on the cliff is near the bay.

794 **Lights**. — Descanso Bay light *(438)*, on the south entrance point to the bay, is shown at an elevation of 6.1 m from a white tower.

Nanaimo Harbour — Inner Portion

Chart 3447

795 The inner portion of Nanaimo Harbour *(49°10′N, 123°56′W)*, entered 1 mile west of Jack Point, has a large mud flat on its south side and is protected on its north and east sides by **Newcastle Island** and **Protection Island**. A private mooring buoy lies 0.5 mile WSW of Jack Point.

796 **McKay Channel**, between Protection Island and **Middle Bank**, is deep and without dangers. **Meakin Channel** leads SW from McKay Channel to the Nanaimo Port Authority Assembly wharf.

797 **Gallows Point**, the south extremity of Protection Island, is surrounded on its seaward faces by a drying ledge. **Satellite Reef**, 0.4 mile NW of Gallows Point, dries 0.7 m.

798 **Lights. — Buoys**. — Gallows Point light *(439)* is on the drying ledge close south of Gallows Point.

799 The edge of the foul ground south of Gallows Point is marked by starboard hand buoy "P4".

800 Nanaimo Harbour Entrance light *(440)*, 0.25 mile SSE of Gallows Point light, is shown from a dolphin.

801 Nanaimo Harbour Entrance Groyne light *(441.5)*, 0.25 mile SW of Nanaimo Harbour Entrance light, is shown from a dolphin.

802 The lights on the Nanaimo Port Authority Assembly wharves are private.

803 Colliery range lights *(442, 443)*, 0.5 mile WSW of Gallows Point light, in line bearing 254° lead through McKay Channel.

804 Nanaimo Harbour Sector light *(441.6)*, at the ferry landing, is private.

805 West cardinal buoy "PS" is on the west side of Satellite Reef.

Harmac (1997)

Nexen Chemicals (1997)

Duke Point Deep Sea Terminal (1990)

Major Port Facilities — Northumberland Channel

Berth	Wharf Length (m)	Least Depth (m)	Elevation (m)	Remarks
Pope & Talbot Ltd Harmac Pulp Operations West Dock	122	10		152 m berthing between dolphins off each end of wharf, mooring buoys off each end of wharf. 8 tonne forklift trucks, 2 18 tonne straddle carriers. Loading rates average 150 tonnes/gang hour. Fresh water at 10.8 tonnes/hour through 1½" hose, power 110v/20 amps.
Weyerhaeuser Canada Ltd Harmac East Dock	137	10.4		Used for loading packaged lumber. Mooring buoys off each end of wharf. Four 15 tonne forklift trucks. 4,273 m² open storage. Fresh water at 10.8 tonnes/hour through 1½" hose, power 110v/20 amps, telephones. No shore gangway.
Nexen Chemicals Wharf	70	11		Used for unloading caustic soda. Mooring buoys off each end of wharf. Submarine pipeline close north of wharf.
Barge Ramp				Used for loading railway freight cars.
Nanaimo Port Authority Duke Point Deep Sea Terminal Berth D	170	13.5	2	Handles forest products, general and project cargoes. Berthing dolphins 50 m NW & SE and connected to wharf by catwalk. 40 tonne container crane, 80 000 lb container lift truck. 6 ha paved open storage.
Nanaimo Port Authority Duke Point Barge Berth		4.2		100-tonne capacity barge ramp. 19.5 ha open storage. Designed for barges 63 m long.
Scow Loading Float	121	3.7		Mooring buoys north of wharf.
Doman Industries South Barge Wharf	140			Used by nearby sawmill for loading scows.
Doman Industries North Barge Wharf	140			Used by nearby sawmill for loading scows. Rockfill breakwater at north end.

806 A **booming ground** with mooring buoys lies between Protection Island and Satellite Reef.

807 **Water aerodrome**. — Nanaimo Harbour, south of Newcastle Island and west of Protections Island, is a water aerodrome. The terminal is at the north end of Commercial Inlet.

808 **An aeronautical strobe light** activated by the aircraft to alert mariners of aircraft landing or taking off is on the central breakwater at the entrance to Commercial Inlet.

809 **Ferry landings**. — A freight ferry and the Gabriola Island vehicle and passenger ferry operate from ferry landings NW of the Nanaimo Port Authority Assembly Wharves. A ferry wharf, close NW of Gallows Point, is protected by a rock breakwater.

810 **Floats**. — A public float is alongside the ferry wharf NW of Gallows Point.

811 A public float and ferry landing are at **Good Point**.

812 **Newcastle Island Marine Park** has public floats and mooring buoys in Mark Bay. Camping, picnic area, garbage drop are available.

813 **Anchorage** for small craft can be obtained in Mark Bay, in 7 m, mud bottom, north of the water aerodrome. The south limit of the anchorage is marked by no anchorage buoys. No ship shall anchor within a designated water aerodrome in the harbour. All ships at anchor shall comply with lights and shapes prescribed in *Collision Regulations*. The anchorage is in an area where other vessels normally navigate.

814 A **speed limit** has been introduced in the waters between Protection and Newcastle Islands. Speed restriction buoys are at the SW and NE entrance to Newcastle Island Passage.

815 **Commercial Inlet** is a small craft basin operated by the Nanaimo Port Authority. Contact with the Nanaimo Wharfingers Office can be made on VHF Channel 67 for general information and berth allocation within the basin. The seaplane terminal is at the north end of the boat basin.

816 **Piers. — Breakwater**. — A Visiting Vessel Pier used by large pleasure craft, small cruise ships and government vessels extends north from Cameron Island (local name) along the east side of Commercial Inlet Basin.

817 A **submarine cable** (power) is laid from the end of the Visiting Vessel Pier to the central breakwater, it is marked by signs.

818 A 50 m long central breakwater lies in the entrance to Commercial Inlet. The entrance south of the breakwater is used by vessels. The entrance north of the breakwater is 50 m wide and for exclusive use of seaplanes. A solar powered small ship sewage reception barge is on the breakwater, a nominal fee is charged for self pump-outs.

819 An L-shaped public fishing pier extends 100 m offshore north of the seaplane terminal.

820 **Beacon Rock**, in the entrance to Commercial Inlet, dries 1.2 m. **Carpenter Rock**, 0.1 mile north of Beacon Rock, is awash.

821 **Lights**. — Private lights are shown from the outer end of the small vessels pier, both ends of the breakwater, and the outer end of the fishing pier.

822 Beacon Rock is marked by private lighted north, south, east and west cardinal aids.

823 A **submarine cable** crosses the harbour from Good Point on Protection Island to the shore west of Carpenter Rock.

824 A **submarine pipeline** crosses the harbour from Good Point to the mouth of **Millstone River**.

825 **Newcastle Island Passage**, between Vancouver and Newcastle Islands, leads north from the inner portion of Nanaimo Harbour to Departure Bay. It is narrow, shallow and suitable only for small vessels. The west shore of the passage has numerous wharves, marinas and fuel jetties.

826 **Speed limit**. — No vessel shall proceed at a speed greater than 5 kn in Newcastle Island Passage between **Bate Point** and Pimbury Point. Buoys 0.1 mile SW of Bate Point have speed caution signs and speed restriction signs are posted along Newcastle Island Passage.

827 **Light buoys. — Lights**. — Bate Point light buoy "P12" *(445)*, south of the drying flat extending from the point, is a starboard hand buoy.

828 Millstone light buoy "P9" *(444)* and Millstone Creek light buoy "P11" *(444.5)*, at the outer edge of a drying flat on the west side of the passage, are port hand buoys.

Nanaimo Assembly Wharves (1997)

Newcastle Island Passage from Nanaimo Harbour (1997)

Newcastle Island Passage from Departure Bay (1997)

Chart 3447

Commercial Inlet from north (1997)

Major Port Facilities — Nanaimo

Berth	Wharf Length (m)	Least Depth (m)	Elevation (m)	Remarks
Nanaimo Port Authority (Westcan Terminals Ltd) Nanaimo Assembly Wharf Berth A	183	10.1		Loading lumber, pulp, plywood, other forest products and general cargo. Eighteen forklift trucks with 15-tonne capacities as well as tractor trailers. 8,333 m^2 covered storage, 15 hectares paved open storage. North end of berth has barge ramp with 60-tonne capacity for vehicle loading and unloading. Fresh water, power and telephone.
Nanaimo Port Authority Nanaimo Assembly Wharf Berth B	183	12.4		As above
Nanaimo Port Authority Nanaimo Assembly Wharf Berth C	183	12.0		As above. Reported dredged to 12.0 m, November 2003.

829   Privately operated lights are shown from the breakwaters at the yacht club.

830   **Oregon Rock**, 0.2 mile NNW of Bate Point, dries 0.3 m and is marked by port hand buoy "P13". **Passage Rock**, close north of Oregon Rock, has 0.1 m over it and is marked by a daybeacon with a port hand daymark. Vessels should not pass between these markers as the channel lies to the east side, off the Newcastle Island shore.

831   **Submarine cables** cross Newcastle Island Passage in the vicinity of Oregon Rock and at **Brechin Point**, 0.6 mile NNW. Submarine pipelines cross the passage close north of Bate Point and near Pimbury Point at the north end.

832   The city of **Nanaimo**, along the west side of the harbour, had its beginning in 1851 when coal was discovered. By 1898 coal exporting had reached its peak and by 1930 most of the coal mines had closed. Today main industries are lumber, pulp, newsprint and fisheries. The city has a full range of municipal services including a post office, hospital with a heliport, shopping centres and recreational facilities.

833   **Wharves**. — Details of the deep-sea wharves in Nanaimo Harbour are in the adjacent table.

834   **Rail ferry wharf**, close SE of the Colliery range beacons, is for handling freight cars and trailers. The ferry wharf for Gabriola Island is close north of the Colliery range beacons.

835   **Visiting Vessel Pier**, at the entrance to Commercial Inlet, is 180 m long with anchor chains extending 30 m from both sides. It is used by small cruise ships, government vessels and large pleasure craft and is lighted at night. A ramp leading from Cameron Island onto the pier has a weight restriction of 9 tonnes.

836   Commercial Inlet, entered between the central breakwater and the visiting vessels pier, is a small craft basin, with 2,800 m of berthing at the public floats and can be contacted on VHF Channel 67 0700-2300 daily. Reservations for moorage must be made at least 24 hours in advance, telephone (250) 754-5053. Power and water are laid on the floats, toilets, showers, laundry, crane, ice, public telephones, garbage and used oil disposal facilities, and sewage pumpout are available. A fuel barge is at the floats. A wharfinger is in charge of these floats.

837   **Public floats** are in Mark Bay and at Good Point.

838   **Marinas** line the west shore of Newcastle Island Passage.

839   **Supplies**. — Ample supplies of fresh provisions are available. Bunkering is limited to delivery by tanker truck or barge, large quantities have to be obtained from Vancouver.

840   **Harbour services**. — Nanaimo Shipyard, on the west side of Newcastle Island Passage, has three sets of marine ways capable of hauling vessels up to 270 tonnes, underwater repairs for larger vessels are done by divers. Propulsion machinery repair is limited to vessels up to about 300 tonnes although auxiliary machinery and electrical repairs can be done by local machine shops, electronic repairs, including radar, can be carried out. Tugs are available.

841   **Communications**. — Nanaimo has bus service to all Vancouver Island points and is connected to Vancouver (Horseshoe Bay and Tsawwassen) and Gabriola Island by regular ferry services. Rail service is available to Victoria and Courtenay. Float plane services are available in the harbour area and the Nanaimo Airport is 9 km south of the city. A small foot passenger ferry operates between Nanaimo and Newcastle and Protection Islands.

CHAPTER 4

Fraser River, Pitt River and Lake, Harrison River and Lake

General

Charts 3463, 3490, 3491, 3492, 3489, 3488, 3062, 3061

1 **Fraser River** *(49°06'N, 123°18'W)*, which rises near Jasper Park, Alberta, 1,370 km NE in the west slopes of the Rocky Mountains, was named after Simon Fraser, who explored it by canoe in 1808. It empties into the Strait of Georgia and is protected from the open ocean by Vancouver Island.

2 **The river is navigable by deep-sea vessels as far as Douglas Island**, 24 miles from the entrance. Upstream from Douglas Island it is navigable by small vessels as far as Hope, 73 miles from the entrance. It is not charted beyond the Harrison River entrance. Pitt River leads NE from Douglas Island to Pitt Lake, and Harrison River leads NW then NE to Harrison Lake. Both are navigable by small vessels and are charted.

3 **Drying banks**. — The large flat delta of the Fraser River is fronted by **Roberts Bank** and **Sturgeon Bank** which extend 5 miles offshore.

4 **Caution. — There is an inflow of water onto Roberts and Sturgeon Banks during rising tide. When navigating along or close to the banks on a flood tide, take care not to be set onto them. A NW wind opposing the flood tide, or a SW wind blowing against the freshet causes short steep seas. Under these conditions numerous small vessels have been swamped.**

5 **South Arm**, also known as the main channel, entered south of Sand Heads *(49°06'N, 123°18'W)*, is used by deep-sea shipping, tugs, barges, logbooms and fish boats.

6 **North Arm**, known to coastal shipping as The Ditch, is entered SW of Point Grey *(49°16'N, 123°16'W)* and is used mainly by tugs with logbooms or barges.

7 **Middle Arm**, south of Sea Island, is used mainly by pleasure craft.

8 **Canoe Passage**, which leads across Roberts Bank south of Westham Island, is used by local fishermen.

9 **Meteorological information** and a **frequency of fog table** for Vancouver International Airport and a **wind frequency table** for Sand Heads are in the Appendices.

Fraser River — Main Channel

Charts 3490, 3489, 3488

10 **Fraser Port**, the main deep-sea shipping facilities, are near New Westminster 18 miles up river.

11 **Vessel Traffic Services (VTS)**. — The south arm of the Fraser River from east of Sand Heads light *(311)* to Shoal Point light *(367)* is in *Sector Two* of the *Vancouver Traffic Zone* and is administered by *Victoria Traffic*. Assigned frequency is 156.725 MHz, Channel 74, calling-in points are:

12 **Calling-in Point No. 12**, *Sand Heads*, is a change from *Sector One* to *Sector Two* and is a line running 000°–180° through Sand Heads light *(311)*.

13 **Calling-in Point No. 12A**, *Woodward Island (Crown Forest)*, is a line running 000°–180° through Woodward Island light *(345)*.

14 **Calling-in Point No. 12B**, *LaFarge*, is abeam LaFarge Cement Plant *(49°09.4'N, 123°00.2'W)*.

15 **Calling-in Point 12C**, *Shoal Point*, is at Shoal Point light *(367)*.

16 A brief description of this VTS is in *PAC 200*. Details are in *Radio Aids to Marine Navigation (Pacific and Western Arctic)*.

17 **Pilotage** is compulsory for vessels with a gross registered tonnage greater than 350 tons. Twelve (12) hours notice of requirement for pilotage services is necessary prior to the vessel's arrival at the Pilot Boarding Station at Brotchie Ledge, Victoria. For details on obtaining a Pilot see *PAC 200*. The Pacific Pilotage Authority office is in Vancouver, telephone (604) 666-6776.

18 **Berthing**. — Most vessels require the assistance of tugs to land and depart berths in the Fraser River Port. The river pilot will determine the number of tugs required based on factors affecting each vessel movement.

19 **Anchoring**. — No vessel is to anchor within the bounds of the Fraser Port without advising the Port Authority of the location, duration, and mitigating conditions, to ensure the safety of the vessel and other Port users.

20 **Rise and fall of the river**. — The river is at its lowest stage during January, February and March. In April it starts to rise from melting of inland snows and throughout May it rises rapidly. The river is at its highest in June and remains up with small fluctuations until the end of July or middle of August. Records show the year's HW mark is reached anywhere between mid May and mid July. During this period the strength of the stream between Mission and Hope is 4 to 7 kn and in narrow parts even more. The usual rise of the river at Fort Langley *(49°10'N, 122°35'W)* due to these floods is about 4.3 m but it has been known to reach 7.6 m.

21 From middle to end of August water begins to subside. September, October and November are favourable months for river navigation as water is sufficiently high for small vessels to reach Hope, and strength of current is considerably abated.

22 **Depths**. — Because of continual changes in depths as a result of silting, scouring and/or dredging charts may not show the latest conditions. Surveys are conducted annually by Public Works and Government Services Canada. The Fraser River Port Authority maintains channel parameters by carrying out an annual maintenance dredging program.

23 **Dredged Channel**. — The Fraser River Deep-Sea Shipping Channel is located within the South Arm of the river entering at Sand Heads and continuing upriver to New Westminster. Deep draught vessels will display three all-round red lights in a vertical line at night or a cylinder during the day to indicate their inability to deviate from the dredged channel.

24 **Outer Channel** is designed for two-way traffic of vessels with 10.7 m draught, it is 200 to 250 m wide. **Inner Channel** is deeper and can accommodate deep-sea vessels with 11.5 m draught, it is only 130 to 170 m wide. There are reaches throughout the channel that allow meeting or overtaking of deep-sea vessels

Charts 3490, 3489, 3488

at the Pilot's discretion. Overall, the shipping channel is designated for two-way deep-sea traffic with an underkeel clearance of 1.5 m from Sand Heads to Steveston Bend, and 0.9 m from Steveston Bend to New Westminster.

25   **Dredging is also carried out at wharves in Fraser Port.** For up-to-date information, particularly when a critical draught is concerned, consult wharf owners.

26   **Aids to navigation**. — The main channel, as far as Douglas Island, is marked by buoys, most are lighted. There are numerous fixed light structures, and most reaches of the river are marked by light ranges. Lights and light ranges are given in the text but buoys are not described.

27   **Caution. — Channels of the Fraser River are continually changing, buoys are moved and the alignment of ranges is changed as required. During freshets, buoys and fixed structures are liable to be washed away.**

28   **Submerged River Crossings**. — Attention is drawn to cables, pipelines and the tunnel in various parts of the river. Locations are marked by signs and mariners are warned to avoid anchoring in their vicinity.

29   **Overhead River Crossings**. — Attention is drawn to cables and bridges in various parts of the river.

30   **Fishing vessels**. — Concentration of fishing vessels using gillnets in the Fraser River may be encountered between late July and mid August. During the fishing season many nets may be set across the channel. Extra caution is required particularly during the first few hours of an opening and during high water slack when catches are best.

31   **Tides**. — Tidal heights and time differences for Steveston, Deas Island and New Westminster are in *Tide Tables, Volume 5*.

32   **Tidal assist**. — Use of tidal assistance to provide more water for vessel transit is a common practice in the Fraser River. Waiting times are reasonably short due to the semi-diurnal tide cycle. Tidal aid at the mouth of the river represents approximately one-third of the mean water depth in the river, which is significantly greater than upstream at New Westminster where the tidal aid represents only one-fifth of the mean water depth. Information on available drafts, draft restrictions, and arrival and departure windows is available from the Vancouver Pilot Dispatch Office (604) 666-6776.

33   **Tidal streams** are affected by weather in the Strait of Georgia, rain, and amount of water in the river. In the channel above Garry Point flow during freshet season is almost continuously toward the mouth of the river, though it may be checked on rise of the tide. During low stage of the river, there is a flood and an ebb tidal stream on all large tides, the flood beginning soon after LW at Sand Heads, and flowing first along the bottom.

34   During freshets the greatest rate of the outgoing stream is approximately 8–10 kn. After the freshet is over it reduces to 5–6 kn.

35   At New Westminster, the incoming tidal stream is unable to reverse river current during freshet. At other times the flow will reverse and a flood current can occur as far as Mission.

36   **Salt intrusion**. — On a rising tide in the Strait of Georgia salt water, being denser than the fresh water, is forced upstream along the bottom in the form of a wedge. During periods of low flow (February and March) this salt wedge can penetrate the main arm as far as New Westminster.

37   In lower reaches of the main arm the salt wedge has been observed to move upstream at a speed of 1 kn. At a falling tide

increasing river slope will halt the wedge's upstream advance and eventually force the salt out of the system. This process can take several hours after tide in the Strait of Georgia starts to fall. As it recedes toward the mouth the wedge disintegrates rapidly and eventually moves out as a homogeneous plug of brackish water.

38   Limits of penetration depend largely on river discharge. However, two successive high tides of almost equal amplitude separated by a high LW can force the salt wedge 1 or 2 miles further upstream than normally expected (i.e. when salt is not completely flushed out by the river after the first high tide).

39   In a fully developed salt wedge, salinity generally ranges between 25‰ at Sand Heads and 5‰ at the upstream limit.

40   **Ice**. — The river is rarely frozen over at New Westminster. Loose pieces of ice sometimes come down river but do not cause damage to shipping.

Fraser River Harbour

Chart 3490

41   **Harbour limits**. — The lower portion of the Fraser River excluding the North Arm and Middle Arm, defined as **Fraser River Harbour**, is under the jurisdiction of the **Fraser River Port Authority**. Limits extend from a line drawn south across the river at Longitude *123°19'22"W* to a line drawn across the river in a SW direction from the mouth of Kanaka Creek *(49°12'N, 122°35'W)* *(Chart 3489)*, and to a line drawn in a SSW direction across the Pitt River at Grant Narrows *(Chart 3062)*. Also included is a small portion of North Arm, extending from its confluence with the main river at New Westminster to the west boundary of the city.

42   **Practices and procedures** established pursuant to Section 56 of the *Canada Marine Act* are available from:

> Fraser River Port Authority
> 500–713 Columbia Street
> New Westminster, B.C. V3M 1B2
> Telephone (604) 524-6655
> http://www.fraserportauthority.com/contact/first.html

Their purpose is to promote safe and efficient navigation in the waters of Fraser Port, while endeavouring to protect the environment.

43   **Practices** includes sections on General Information, Navigation, Fishing in the Lower Fraser River, Loading of Logs, Terminal Berth Activities, Mooring of Vessels, Floating Property and Booms, Towing, Dredging and Other (Deas Slough).

44   **Procedures** includes sections on Anchoring, Bridge Transits, Loading of Logs in Timberland Basin, Ballast Water Exchange Program, and a Fuel Transfer Safety Checklist.

Sand Heads to Steveston

45   Between Sand Heads and **Garry Point** *(49°07'N, 123°12'W)* the north side of the river is bordered by **Steveston Jetty**. Fraser River light buoy "S2" *(314)* is frequently damaged, particularly by tug and tow operators who should ensure they take measures to avoid contact with this buoy.

46   **Caution. — Steveston Jetty has several gaps through which a cross current flows. On ebb tides extremely turbulent water exists in vicinity of the rock groyne at Steveston Bend.**

Chart 3490

47   **Lights. — Beacons. — Light buoys**. — Steveston Jetty is marked by lights *(313.5 to 329)* and daybeacons. The south side of the channel is marked by starboard hand light buoys.

48   Garry Point West light *(333)*, 0.1 mile west of the point, is shown at an elevation of 7.2 m from a white tower with a green band at the top on a dolphin.

49   A port hand daybeacon is on a dolphin close south of Garry Point. A conspicuous monument is on the point 0.1 mile east of the beacon.

50   **Light ranges**. — The channel as far as Steveston is marked by Wing Dam range lights *(323, 324)* and New Cut range 1 lights *(327, 328)*, both located at Steveston Bend.

51   **Scott Pond** (local name) is a private fish boat harbour north of Garry Point. It is well protected.

52   **Reifel Island** *(49°06′N, 123°10′W)*, known locally as Smokey Tom Island, is on the south side of the river entrance. The island is a bird sanctuary. **Albion Dyke No. 2**, NW of Reifel Island, extends along the south side of the river channel.

53   **Steveston**, on the north side of **Cannery Channel**, known locally as Cannery Basin, is the centre of the salmon industry of the Fraser River and is used extensively by commercial fishermen. With the decline of the fishery all canneries have closed and tourism is becoming more important. The Gulf of Georgia Cannery National Historic Site and Britannia Heritage Shipyard are examples of this change. The east end of Cannery Channel is closed by a rock finger.

54   **Facilities**. — Fuel, fresh water, hull and engine repairs, and shopping facilities are available in Steveston. The public wharf complex is at the west end of Cannery Channel. Power and water are laid on the floats and used oil disposal facilities are available.

55   **Anchorage is prohibited** from mid May to the end of October in the approaches to, and the west end of Cannery Channel.

56   **Light**. — Steveston breakwater light *(335)* is on the west end of **Steveston Bar**.

57   **Tides**. — Tidal heights and time differences for Steveston, referenced on Point Atkinson, are in *Tide Tables, Volume 5*.

Steveston to Deas Island

58   **Wing dams** extend into the river channel from the south side of **Steveston Island**, known locally as Shady Island, and from 0.3 mile WNW of **Blair Point**.

59   A **submarine pipeline** and an abandoned **submarine cable** are west of Blair Point.

60   **Woodward Training Wall** borders the south side of the river from abreast Steveston Island and forms the north sides of **Woodward Island** and **No. 1 Island**. **Woodward Dam**, an extension of the training wall, connects to **Rose Island**, the SW part of **Kirkland Island**.

61   **Lights**. — Woodward Island North light *(339)* is on Woodward Training Wall 0.5 mile SW of Blair Point.

62   Woodward Island light *(345)* is at the NW end of Woodward Dam.

63   Kirkland Island West light *(346.5)* is on the NW side of Kirkland Island.

64   Kirkland Island Breakwater light *(348.2)*, on the NE extremity of Kirkland Island, has a starboard hand daymark.

65   Privately operated lights, on the north shore 0.4 mile west of **Gilmour Island**, are on east and west extremities of the Crown Packaging wharf.

66   **Light ranges**. — New Cut range 2 lights *(338, 338.5)*, at the west end of Woodward Training Wall, and Woodward Island Downstream range lights *(340, 341)*, midway along the north side of Woodward Island, lead from Steveston to north of Woodward Island.

67   Woodward Island Upstream range lights *(342, 343)*, close east of the downstream range, and Deas Island range lights *(348.5, 348.6)*, near the west end of **Deas Island**, lead through **Woodward Reach**. Deas Island range lights are visible in line of range only.

68   **Submarine cables** and a **submarine pipeline** cross the river near **Woodwards Landing**.

69   **Dredged basin**. — A private starboard hand buoy, east of Woodwards Landing, marks the entrance to a dredged basin used by the British Columbia Ferry Services Inc.

70   **Prohibited anchorage**. — Anchorage is prohibited in vicinity of **George Massey Tunnel** which crosses from Deas Island to Lulu Island.

71   **Tides**. — Tidal heights and time differences for Deas Island, referenced on Point Atkinson, are in *Tide Tables, Volume 5*.

Sea Reach and Ladner Reach

72   **Sea Reach** leads SE between Westham and Woodward Islands to the north end of Canoe Passage, it is suitable only for small craft.

73   **Beacon range**. — Sea Reach range beacons, close SE of **Ewen Slough**, lead into Sea Reach from the main channel.

74   **Beacon**. — A daybeacon with two port hand daymarks, on a dolphin, is on the SW extremity of **Barber Island**.

75   **Fish buyers floats** and fish processing plants are at several locations on the south shore of Sea Reach and Ladner Reach.

76   **Ladner Reach** leads SSW from Deas Island and east of **Williamson Island** and **Gunn Island** is suitable only for small craft.

77   A **submarine cable** crosses the north end of Ladner Reach.

78   At **Ladner** there are public floats and extensive shopping facilities.

79   **Deas Slough**, suitable only for small craft, has marinas and a public float.

80   **Light**. — Deas Slough light *(348.3)* is on a dolphin in the entrance to Deas Slough.

81   **Submarine cables** and **pipelines** are laid across the entrance to Deas Slough.

82   **Deas Slough Causeway** (Ministry of Transportation and Highways), a fixed span highway bridge, vertical clearance 2.8 m, crosses Deas Slough. **Overhead cables** (power), vertical clearance 9.9 m, cross the channel on the west side of the bridge.

Deas Island to Annacis Island

83   **Gravesend Reach** extends from Deas Island to the SW end of Annacis Island. The deep channel lies along the NW bank.

Chart 3490

Woodward Reach (1999)

Steveston & Cannery Channel (1999)

84   **Conspicuous object**. — A large conspicuous white gas tank is on the south side of the river, SW of Lehigh Northwest Cement.

85   **Submarine pipelines** (gas) cross the river close west of the Chatterton Petro Chemical plant, they are marked by signs.

86   **Light ranges. — Lights**. — Kirkland Island range lights *(348, 348.1)*, on the east extremity of Kirkland Island, and Tilbury range 2 lights *(353, 354)*, on the north bank of the river north of **Tilbury Island**, lead through the SW part of Gravesend Reach. Tilbury range lights are visible in line of range only.

87   Tilbury range 1 lights *(351, 352)*, 0.5 mile SW of Tilbury range 2, and Purfleet Point range lights *(356, 357)* lead through the NE part of Gravesend Reach. Lights of these ranges are visible in line of range only.

88   Privately operated lights are shown from wharves in Gravesend Reach.

89   **Beacon**. — A port hand daybeacon with a radar reflector is 0.6 mile east of Tilbury range 2.

Annacis Island to New Westminster

90   **City Reach**, known locally as St. Mungo's Bend or Mungo Bend, extends around the south side of **Annacis Island**, from **Purfleet Point** to the vicinity of Gundersen Slough.

91   **Overhead cables** (power), vertical clearance 54 m, cross the main channel at Purfleet Point and help identify it. Another power transmission line, vertical clearance 56 m, crosses the river 0.7 mile upstream from Alex Fraser Bridge.

92   **Submarine pipelines** cross City Reach close SW of Alex Fraser Bridge.

93   **Alex Fraser Bridge** (Ministry of Transportation and Highways), a fixed span highway bridge crosses the main shipping

Woodward Training Wall from Steveston (1981)

Woodward Reach (1999)

Gunn Island

Woodward Dam

Rose Island

Williamson Slough

Gravesend & City Reaches from Tilbury Island (1999)

Alex Fraser Bridge looking upstream (1999)

Alex Fraser Bridge from SW of Gundersen Slough (1986)

Annieville Channel from Gundersen Slough (1999)

Chart 3490

channel, vertical clearance 57 m. Flashing red lights are on top of the towers and a fixed white light is on the centre of the span.

94   **Light ranges**. — City Reach range 2 lights *(361, 362)*, on the south shore close west of Alex Fraser Bridge, and City Reach range 1 lights *(359, 360)*, on the south shore 0.5 mile west, lead through the west and NE parts, respectively, of City Reach.

95   **Gundersen Slough** has a public float. Moorage is restricted to 8 hours.

Charts 3490, 3489

96   **Annieville Channel** *(49°11′N, 122°55′W)* extends from Gundersen Slough to Pattullo Bridge at New Westminster. Both sides of the channel have training walls.

97   **Annacis Island Pile Wall** and **Annieville Dyke** form the west side of the channel along the coast of Annacis Island. A break in Annieville Dyke has a submerged weir off **Shoal Point** with 3.4 m over it. **Annieville Channel Pile Wall** and **Annieville Rock Wall** form the east side of Annieville Channel. A break at the north end of Annieville Rock Wall has a submerged weir with 2.6 m over it.

98   Any vessel navigating the Fraser River between the quick flashing green light located on the down stream end of the Annieville Pile Wall and the quick flashing green light located on the Sapperton Dyke shall keep to the side of the main channel that lies to the port side of the vessel.

99   **Light range. — Lights. — Beacons**. — Annieville Channel range lights *(363, 364)*, on the south shore SSW of Gundersen Slough *(Chart 3490)*, lead through this channel.

100   Annacis Island Pile Wall South light *(365)*, at the south end of the wall, has a port hand daymark.

101   Two daybeacons, with port hand daymarks, marking a submerged weir, are on Annieville Dyke.

102   Annacis Island Pile Wall Centre light *(366.4)*, near the middle of Annieville Dyke, has a port hand daymark.

103   A daybeacon, with a port hand daymark, marks the south end of the submerged weir off Shoal Point.

104   Shoal Point light *(367)* marks the east side of the north entrance to Annacis Channel.

105   Annieville Channel Pile Wall South and North lights *(366.1, 366.3)* are at the south and north ends of Annieville Channel Pile Wall.

106   Annieville Rock Wall 1 light *(366.5)*, at the south end of Annieville Rock Wall, has a starboard hand daymark.

107   Annieville Rock Wall 3 and 4 lights *(366.6, 366.7)* and a starboard hand daybeacon mark the north section of the Annieville Rock Wall. Number 3 light has a starboard hand daymark.

108   **Submarine pipelines** cross Annieville Channel in several locations.

109   A **submarine cable area** crosses the main channel in vicinity of SkyBridge.

110   **Submerged weirs**, close NE and 0.1 mile SW of SkyBridge, extend into the fairway from the New Westminster side of the river; they have 11.5 and 11.6 m over them.

111   **SkyBridge** (BC Transit), crossing the Fraser River at New Westminster, is a light rapid transit bridge vertical clearance 44 m. Passage under the span of SkyBridge is marked by a fixed white light on each side and aircraft warning lights are on top of its towers.

112   **Pattullo Bridge** (Greater Vancouver Transit Authority), a high-level highway bridge with a clear span of 137 m across the

navigable channel and vertical clearance 45 m, is close NE of SkyBridge. Passage under the span of the Pattullo Bridge is marked by a fixed white light on each side, visible to vessels approaching from either direction.

113   **New Westminster Railway Bridge** (Public Works and Government Services Canada), close upstream from Pattullo Bridge has a swing span 99 m in length, vertical clearance 6.7 m when closed. It also has a fixed span known locally as the Log Hole, vertical clearance 6.7 m, and horizontal clearance 113.6 m. The swing span will open only for vessels that cannot pass under any part of the bridge.

114   In most conditions, upbound traffic shall transit the draw on the New Westminster (north) side of the Bridge. Downbound traffic shall transit the draw on the Surrey (south) side of the bridge.

115   No vessel shall pass under the bridge or through the swing span unless the vessel and everything that it has in tow are under complete control. No vessel shall overtake or attempt to overtake, or obstruct or attempt to obstruct any vessel that has signalled for the swing span to be opened. A vessel that has signalled for the swing span to be opened shall remain at a safe distance from the bridge until the signal to proceede. Transiting procedures prescribe that tugs towing barges in excess of certain prescribed measurements or tonnages must have assist tugs. Under certain circumstances they may only transit the swing span when stemming the current.

116   Where unusual conditions or circumstances exist, the towing company or the Master of the vessel shall prior to transit, advise Port Authority staff of the precautions that will be taken during the transit. Port Authority may add conditions. The Master of the vessel will advise the bridge operator of precautions to be taken by the vessel during transit.

117   **New Westminster Railway Bridge lights** *(368)* are shown from centre span, extremities of the pier, and from both upstream and downstream extremities of buttresses. Flood-lights on the swing span and piers, which are automatically activated when the span is open, illuminate both north and south navigation channels. Lights may be deactivated upon request by radio.

118   **Bridge operating procedures**. — Vessels requiring an opening of the bridge shall contact the bridge operator on VHF Channel 74 call sign XLZ35, telephone (604) 589-6612. Calling-in points are:

    (a)   Port Mann Bridge;
    (b)   Fraser Surrey Docks;
    (c)   Queensborough Highway Bridge;
    (d)   Prior to departure from a berth or vessel tie-up within the above calling-in points.

119   When calling in vessel will provide the bridge with an ETA, if this changes vessel will advise the bridge operator.

120   Where for safety reasons, vessels must transit the bridge counter to Regulations they will make at least two (2) security broadcasts on VHF Channel 74 advising other users of their intentions.

121   Once radiotelephone contact has been established, a listening watch shall be maintained on Channel 74 until vessel has cleared the bridge.

122   **Signals**. — For the New Westminster Railway Bridge are:

SkyBridge, Pattullo & New Westminster Bridges looking upstream (1999)

New Westminster, Pattullo & SkyBridge Bridges looking downstream (1999)

1. Where a vessel requires the swing span to be opened, it shall signal with three long blasts.

123 **Bridge operator shall use the following signals during the night:**
1. A fixed red light on the side of the bridge facing the vessel to indicate span is closed;
2. A green light on the side of the bridge facing the vessel to indicate the span is open.

124 **When weather restricts visibility bridge operator shall use following signals:**
1. A siren blowing five seconds every twenty-four seconds to indicate span is open.

Annacis Channel

Chart 3490

125 **Annacis Channel** *(49°10'N, 122°57'W)*, between Annacis and Lulu Islands, has **Lion Island** and **Don Island** in its SW entrance; preferred channel is south of Don Island. East of the swing bridge the channel is frequently cluttered with logs.

126 An **overhead cable** (power) across the south entrance to Annacis Channel has vertical clearance 25 m. The **overhead cable** crossing to **Patrick Island** has vertical clearance 28 m.

127 **Submarine pipelines and cables** cross Annacis Channel in several locations.

128 **Annacis Channel West Causeway** (Ministry of Transportation and Highways), about 1.5 miles NE of Purfleet Point, is a fixed span highway bridge, vertical clearance 9 m. Fixed white lights mark centre span.

129 **Annacis Channel East Causeway** (Ministry of Transportation and Highways) is a fixed span highway bridge, vertical clearance 9 m. Fixed white lights mark centre span.

Charts 3490, 3489

130 An **overhead cable** (power), vertical clearance 27 m, crosses the channel 0.3 mile SW of Annacis Channel Bridge *(49°11'N, 122°56'W)*.

131 A **radio tower**, on the north shore 0.2 mile west of the bridge, has red air obstruction lights.

132 **Annacis Channel Bridge** (Ministry of Transportation and Highways), 2.6 miles NE of Purfleet Point, is a single-opening swing road and rail bridge with a navigable width of 33.7 m. The swing span has vertical clearance 2.3 m when closed. The swing span will open only for vessels that cannot pass under any part of the bridge.

133 No vessel shall pass under the bridge or through the swing span unless the vessel and everything that it has in tow are under complete control. No vessel shall overtake or attempt to overtake, or obstruct or attempt to obstruct any vessel that has signalled for the swing span to be opened. A vessel that has signalled for the swing span to be opened shall remain at a safe distance from the bridge until the signal to proceede. Transiting procedures prescribe that tugs towing barges in excess of certain prescribed measurements or tonnages must have assist tugs. Under certain circumstances they may only transit the swing span when stemming the current.

134 **Annacis Channel Bridge Lights**. — Privately operated fixed white lights are shown from each side of the passage through the swing bridge, visible to vessels approaching from either direction. A fixed white light is shown from each end of the centre pier projection.

135 **Bridge operating procedures**. — Vessels requiring an opening of the bridge can contact the bridge operator on VHF Channel 74, telephone (604) 521-0964. Three long blasts on the vessels horn can also be used. Bridge will only open once every half hour.

136 **Bridge operator shall use the following signals**:
1. A fixed red light on each side of the bridge to indicate span is closed;
2. A fixed green light on the side of the bridge facing an oncoming vessel to indicate span is open;
3. A flashing red light visible from each side of the bridge to indicate span is out of order.

137 A **submerged weir**, crossing the NE entrance to Annacis Channel, has a depth of 2.9 m over it.

138 **Public Works and Government Services Canada Annacis Marine Base** wharf is at Shoal Point.

New Westminster — Fraser Port

139 The city of **New Westminster** is on the north bank of the Fraser River with its west boundary adjacent to the North Arm, some 18 miles by river from the river entrance. The city has extensive shopping facilities. Its wide range of amenities includes hospitals and a YMCA.

140 **Fraser Port (Fraser Surrey Docks)**, administered by Fraser River Port Authority, is a year-round port. Vessels in international trade using the port are bulk carriers, automobile carriers, general cargo and container vessels. Shipments include cement, chemicals, fertilizer, food, industrial feed stocks, general cargo, limestone, logs, lumber, motor vehicles, pulp and paper, wood products, salt, sand, gravel, steel and wine.

141 **Tides**. — Tidal heights and time differences for New Westminster, referenced on Point Atkinson, are in *Tide Tables, Volume 5*.

142 **Supplies** are readily obtainable. Bunker fuel, light and heavy diesel oil, gasoline and lubricants can be obtained from various oil companies who have lightering or pipeline services.

143 **Harbour services**. — Machinery repairs and minor hull repairs can be undertaken. Repair facilities for small craft are available. Major hull repairs can be carried out at Vancouver. Harbour tugs are available.

144 **Transportation**. — There is a highway and rapid transit to Vancouver, 13 km away, and direct rail connection with major Canadian and U.S. railroads. World-wide air services are available at Vancouver International Airport about 10 miles down river.

145 **Berthing**. — Numerous wharves, most with warehouses and connection to railways, and sawmills line the waterfront. Details of principal loading and discharging facilities are given in the adjacent table.

New Westminster to Douglas Island

146 **Queens Reach** extends from New Westminster to **Port Mann**. The south shore is lined with piles and dolphins. Georgia Pacific wharf is 0.7 mile east of Pattullo Bridge.

Charts 3490, 3489

Major Port Facilities — Fraser River

Berth	Wharf Length (m)	Least Depth (m)	Elevation (m) (Geodetic)	Remarks
Crown Packaging	152	6.7		Loading ramp used by covered barges for pulp and paper.
Fraser Wharves	154	11.4	4.5	Discharging automobiles from RO/RO carriers. Mooring dolphins 61 m up and downstream from wharf. 25 hectares open storage for 18,000 vehicles. Fresh water and telephones.
Lehigh Northwest Cement Ltd Deep-sea Berth	213	9.8		Handles limestone, shale, cement, gypsum, mill scale, coal, geyserite and slag. Loading rates: main conveyor 1,200 tonnes/hour, gypsum 350 tonnes/hour, cement 450 tonnes/hour. Telephones and power (100/220/575 volts).
Lehigh Northwest Cement Ltd Coastal Vessel Berth	152	9.1		As above.
Seaspan Coastal Intermodal Company Tilbury Terminal				Truck and railcar ferry terminal. 2 ferry slips with ramps and 3 holding berths. 6 ha paved storage.
Rivtow Marine Tilbury Terminal		4.6		End-on loading ramp.
LaFarge Canada	256	6.6		Handles bulk cement and cement clinker via single hatch conveyor. Loading rate 907 tonnes/hour. Unloading rate 543 tonnes/hour. 6.8-tonne Colby elevator. 4 hectares open storage. Fresh water, power (110/220/550 volts), telephone and shore gangway.
Chatterton Petrochemical	91	4.6		Discharging by pipeline liquids from barges and tankers. Telephone.
Annacis Auto Terminal South Berth 1	214	10.0	3.6	Discharging automobiles from RO/RO carriers. Mooring bollards up and downstream. 53 hectares storage for 25,000 vehicles. Rail served. Fresh water and power.
Annacis Auto Terminal North Berth 2	222	10.0	3.6	As above
Fraser Surrey Docks Berths 2, 3 & 4	2 – 168 3 – 183 4 – 183	12.0	2 – 3.6 3 – 3.1 4 – 3.1	Handles containers, lumber, pulp, paper, steel and general cargo Two 40 tonne container cranes, one 65 tonne container crane. Large forklifts, yard tractors, trailers and container handlers. 68 ha paved storage, six fully serviced warehouses three have fully enclosed rail tracks. Fresh water, power and telephone.
Fraser Surrey Docks Berth 6	122	3.0	4.4	Barge berth and hydraulic ramp.
Fraser Surrey Docks Berths 7, 8 & 9	7 – 229 8 – 229 9 – 244	12.5	7 – 3.9 8 – 3.9 9 – 4.1	Handles containers, lumber, pulp, paper, steel and general cargo Two 40 tonne container cranes, one 65 tonne container crane. Large forklifts, yard tractors, trailers and container handlers. 68 ha paved storage, six fully serviced warehouses three have fully enclosed rail tracks. Fresh water, power and telephone.
Fraser Surrey Docks Berth 10	220	11.6		To service vessels not requiring handling of cargo across the dock.
Georgia Pacific	195	11.0	4.1	Unloading bulk gypsum by hopper-feeder conveyor belts with 454-tonnes/hour capacity. Loading plasterboard by forklift at 45 tonnes/hour. Bulk storage 16,326 tonnes gypsum. Covered storage 2,081 m^2. Fresh water, power (110/550 volts) and shore gangway.
Richmond Properties				Being developed. 54 metre barge berth and potential for 4 deep-sea terminals.

147 **City Bank** *(49°13'N, 122°53'W)* is a log storage ground with numerous piles and dolphins. Two training dykes extend from its south side. **Sapperton Bar** extends east from the bank to **Sapperton Dyke**, a V-shaped structure with its apex upstream; each wall is 122 m long and has a pile dolphin at its outer end.

148 **Sapperton Channel** lies on the north side of City Bank and Sapperton Dyke. Wharf and floats for a seaplane base are at the west end of the channel. Numerous piles and dolphins line the north shore.

149 **Lights**. — Port Mann Training Dyke Lower and Upper lights *(369, 370)* are at the south ends of the two training dykes on City Bank.

150 Sapperton Bar Dyke light *(371)* is at the west end of the south wing.

151 **Submarine pipelines** cross Queens Reach at several locations; they are marked by signs.

152 **Overhead cables** (power), vertical clearance 45 m, cross Queens Reach about 0.5 mile west of Port Mann Bridge.

153 **Port Mann Bridge** (Ministry of Transportation and Highways), carrying the Trans-Canada Highway, has vertical clearance 42 m over the navigable channel. Fixed red lights are shown from the lower part of the span on both sides of the bridge. There is extensive flood lighting.

154 **Douglas Island** *(49°13'N, 122°46'W)* is almost in mid-river at the confluence of the Fraser and Pitt Rivers. **Helmcken Point** forms its west extremity and **Sebastian Point** is its east extremity. The channel on the south side of the island is the wider

Charts 3490, 3489

Port Mann Bridge looking upstream (1999)

and deeper. **Tree Island** and **Essondale Islet** together with numerous dolphins are NW of Douglas Island.

155   **Vessels anchoring in the vicinity of the lower end of Douglas Island** should anchor as close to the island as possible. Vessels anchored in this area have posed a hazard to barge traffic moving past the island.

Canoe Passage

Chart 3492

156   **Canoe Passage** *(49°04'N, 123°08'W)* separates the SE side of **Westham Island** from the mainland. South of the swing bridge, favour the mainland (south) side of the channel and north of the bridge favour the Westham Island (east) side. Local knowledge is advised.

157   A channel, marked by private dolphins, leads across Roberts Bank to Canoe Passage. It is used by local fishermen but depths in the channel change and local knowledge is advised. A marina is close south of the swing bridge.

158   **Landmarks**. — A low white tower, on the south side of Westham Island, is reported to be visible about 4 miles from seaward. Ruins of an old fish cannery, on the opposite side of the channel from the tower, are reported to make a good landmark.

159   **Westham Island Bridge** (Greater Vancouver Transit Authority), crosses the NE end of Canoe Passage and connects Westham Island to the municipality of Delta. The swing span has vertical clearance 1.6 m when closed. The swing span will only open for vessels that cannot pass under any part of the bridge.

160   April 1 to November 30 the bridge operator is on duty 24 hours a day. December 1 to March 31 the bridge operator is on duty 0600 to 2200 hours. The bridge is closed to marine traffic between 2200 and 0600 hours but can be opened by appointment. Emergency response time is about 1 hour.

161   **Bridge operating procedures**. — Vessels requiring an opening of the bridge shall contact the bridge operator by VHF Channel 74, telephone (604) 946-0139. Three long blasts of a vessels horn may also be used.

162   No vessel shall pass under the bridge or through the swing span unless the vessel and everything that it may have in tow are under complete control. No vessel shall overtake or attempt to overtake, or obstruct or attempt to obstruct any vessel that has signalled for the swing span to be opened. A vessel that has signalled for the swing span to be opened shall remain at a safe distance from the bridge until the bridge has been fully opened.

163   **Overhead cables**, vertical clearance 23.1 m, cross Canoe Passage close to the bridge

North Fraser Harbour

Chart 3491

164   **North Fraser Harbour** *(49°12'N, 123°08'W)* comprises the waters of the North and Middle Arms and is under the jurisdiction of the North Fraser Port Authority. The harbour is not a deep-sea port but is used by shallow draught vessels and tugs towing logbooms, scows or barges. Marinas for pleasure craft are located in Middle Arm. Numerous industries line the banks of North Arm. Cargoes handled are logs, lumber, wood chips, sawdust, manufactured building materials, steel, iron, sand and gravel.

Chart 3491

North Arm Jetty (1999)

165   **Regulations**. — North Fraser Port Authority regulations can be obtained from:

North Fraser Port Authority,
7911 Grauer Road,
Richmond, B.C. V7B 1N4
Telephone (604) 273-1866.

Their office is on the NE end of Sea Island, at the junction of North and Middle Arms.

166   **Sea Island** *(49°12'N, 123°12'W)* separates the west end of North Arm from Middle Arm and is the site of **Vancouver International Airport**. The airport control tower, and a large white golf ball-shaped radar dome with red air obstruction lights are conspicuous.

167   **Meteorological information** and a **frequency of fog table** for Vancouver International Airport are in the Appendices.

North Arm

168   **North Arm**, locally known as The Ditch, is entered from the Strait of Georgia SW of Point Grey *(49°16'N, 123°16'W)*; it leads north of Sea Island and **Lulu Island** and joins the main channel of Fraser River at New Westminster.

169   **Logbooms** can be expected to be found moored to the banks almost anywhere in North Arm; their numbers and widths are controlled by the Port Authority so they do not obstruct the fairway.

170   **Channel maintenance and dredging**. — A channel width of 90 m is maintained from the entrance, at the Strait of Georgia, to Inner Easterly light, 2.7 miles upstream, and a width of 60 m from there to the main channel at New Westminster.

171   **Depths**. — Attempts are made to maintain channel depths at local LW of 5.5 m from the mouth to North Arm Second light, 0.8 mile upstream, and 4.6 m from there to the main channel at New Westminster. North of Mitchell Island and in Middle Arm as far as Dinsmore Bridge they attempt to maintain 3.6 m.

172   **Tides**. — The range of tide in North Arm, for mean and large tides, respectively, is 3.3 and 5.0 m at the mouth, decreasing with the river slope to New Westminster. Tidal heights and time differences for New Westminster are in *Tide Tables, Volume 5*.

173   **Currents**. — Normal river current on the ebb is not severe although during summer freshet periods it is often strong enough to deter towing. There is a distinct flood stream, providing a definite advantage when towing up river.

174   **Salt intrusion**. — On a rising tide in the Strait of Georgia salt water, being denser than the fresh water of the river, is forced upstream along the bottom in the form of a wedge. During periods of low flow (February and March), this salt wedge can penetrate North Arm to the east tip of Mitchell Island, 10 miles upstream from the entrance at Point Grey. During high river discharge (mid May to mid July) this limit would be reduced to 7 miles upstream (Oak Street Bridge).

175   **Vessel Traffic Services (vts)**. — The Strait of Georgia, at the west end of North Arm, is in *Sector Three* of the *Vancouver Traffic Zone*; before entering the Strait of Georgia make a report to *Vancouver Traffic*.

176   The Fraser River south of Shoal Point light *(367)*, at the east end of North Arm, is in *Sector Two* of the *Vancouver Traffic Zone* administered by *Victoria Traffic*.

177   **Submarine cables** and **pipelines** cross the North Arm in several locations.

178   **North Arm Jetty** borders the SW side of North Arm from 0.7 mile SW of Point Grey to Iona Island. **North Arm Breakwater**, on the north side of the entrance, extends SW from **Noon Breakfast Point**. **Cowards Cove** is the dredged area close SE of North Arm Breakwater; it is used by local fishing vessels. An extensive log storage area, with numerous piles and dolphins for securing logbooms, borders the NE side of the channel for 3 miles.

179   **Lights. — Beacon**. — Westerly light *(381)* is near the NW extremity of North Arm Jetty. Other lights on the jetty (from NW to SE) are North Arm Third light *(384)* with a starboard hand daymark and Inner (Easterly) light *(385)*. A starboard hand daybeacon with a radar reflector is 0.6 mile SE of Westerly light.

180   North Arm Breakwater light *(382)*, on the south end of the breakwater, has a port hand daymark.

Chart 3491

North Arm entrance from Main Arm (1999)

181 **McDonald Slough** separates Sea Island from **Iona Island**. **Deering Island**, known locally as Celtic Island, lies opposite Iona Island and has a housing development on it. **McDonald Beach Launching Basin**, 0.3 mile SE of Deering Island, has public floats and launching ramps. **Richmond Island** is joined to the north shore by a causeway.

182 The area between Arthur Laing Bridge and Marpole Railway Bridge is known locally as Marpole Basin. A fuel float is on the south shore, close west of Arthur Laing Bridge and a marina is close west of the Railway Bridge.

183 **Mitchell Island** comprises three islands, joined by the deposits of dredging overcast, known locally from west to east as Eburne Island, Twigg Island and Mitchell Island. **Poplar Island**, at the east end of North Arm, lies between Queensborough Highway and Railway Bridges, the fairway is on its south side.

184 **Overhead cables**. — Power cables at the west end of Mitchell Island have vertical clearance 28 m. In the channel north of Mitchell Island a cable adjacent to two piers has vertical clearance 24 m. Between the piers and Knight Street Bridge there are two cables, vertical clearance is 23 m for the first and 29 m for the second. In the channel south of Mitchell Island there is a cable close east of Knight Street Bridge, vertical clearance 27 m. A cable, vertical clearance 24 m, crosses the channel 0.1 mile west of Queensborough Highway Bridge.

185 **Bridges**. — Fixed span and swing bridges cross the North Arm. When a vessel has given the appropriate signal to have a bridge opened, and for any reason it is decided not to pass through the swing span, the vessel should signal that the span may be closed by sounding two long blasts followed by two short blasts on its whistle or siren. If the swing span cannot be opened the bridge tender will give a series of short blasts on a horn or whistle and by day raise a red ball and at night swing a red light in circles.

186 **Arthur Laing Bridge**, at the east extremity of Sea Island, is a fixed span road bridge vertical clearance 19 m, channel width 97 m.

187 **Marpole Railway Bridge** (Canadian Pacific Railway), 0.4 mile east of the NE extremity of Sea Island, is a swing span. When closed it has vertical clearance 0.5 m. Channel widths on the north and south sides are 36 m. A radio station for ship traffic control, call sign VGC248 Channel 06, is operated from 0730 to 1500 hours local time, telephone (604) 261-5012. The signal for opening the bridge is three long blasts.

188 **Oak Street Bridge**, close east, is a fixed span road bridge vertical clearance 18 m, channel width 86 m.

189 **Knight Street Bridge**, at the east end of Mitchell Island, is a fixed span road bridge crossing the north and south channels vertical clearance 12 m under the north branch and 19 m under the south branch. Channel width under the north branch is 71 m and 97 m under the south branch. Clearances are under the centre portion of the main span.

190 **Canadian National Railway Bridge**, 3.5 miles ESE of Mitchell Island, is a swing span vertical clearance 6.4 m when closed. Channel widths on the north and south sides are 37 m. The bridge operator can be contacted on VHF Channel 74, telephone (604) 522-5131. The signal for opening the bridge is 3 long blasts. An overhead cable (power) over the south span draw has vertical clearance 21 m.

191 **Queensborough Highway Bridge** (Ministry of Transportation and Highways), 2 miles farther upstream, is a fixed span vertical clearance 22 m, channel width 85 m.

192 **Queensborough Railway Bridge** (B.C. Southern Railway), east of Poplar Island, is a swing span under jurisdiction of the Fraser River Port Authority. When closed it has vertical clearance 2 m. Channel width on north side is 26 m and on the south side 29 m. The swing span will open only for vessels that cannot pass under any part of the bridge.

Chart 3491

193   In most conditions, both upbound and downbound vessels shall transit the draw on the Queensborough (south) side of the bridge.

194   No vessel shall pass under the bridge or through the swing span unless the vessel and everything that it has in tow are under complete control. No vessel shall overtake or attempt to overtake, or obstruct or attempt to obstruct any vessel that has signalled for the swing span to be opened. A vessel that has signalled for the swing span to be opened shall remain at a safe distance from the bridge until the green light to proceede. Transiting procedures prescribe that tugs towing barges in excess of certain prescribed measurements or tonnages must have assist tugs. Under certain circumstances, they may only transit the swing span when stemming the current.

195   Where unusual conditions or circumstances exist, the towing company or the Master of the vessel shall, prior to transit being made, advise Port Authority staff of the precautions that will be taken during the transit. Port Authority may add conditions. The Master of the vessel will advise the bridge operator of precautions to be taken by the vessel during transit.

196   **Bridge operating procedure**. — Vessels transiting the Queensborough Railway Bridge shall make a safety call on VHF Channels 6 or 74 call sign XJJ62, telephone (604) 522-3729 to determine if there is opposing traffic. Once a safety call has been made maintain a listening watch on Channel 74 until a tow has cleared the bridge. Calling-in points are:

    (a)   SkyBridge;
    (b)   Fraser Surrey Docks;
    (c)   Annacis Swing Span;
    (d)   Queensborough Highway Bridge;
    (e)   Prior to departure from a berth or vessel tie-up within the above calling-in points.

197   **Signals**. — For the Queensborough Railway Bridge are:
1.   Where a vessel requires the swing span to be opened, it shall signal with four long blasts.

198   **Bridge operator shall use the following signals:**
1.   A red light on the side of the bridge facing the vessel to indicate span is closed;
2.   A green light on the side of the bridge facing the vessel to indicate span is open;
3.   A red ball displayed during the day on a mast near the centre of the swing span to indicate span is out of order;
4.   A flashing red light displayed at night on a mast near the centre of the swing span to indicate span is out of order.

Middle Arm

199   **Middle Arm** *(49°11'N, 123°09'W)*, between Sea and Lulu Islands, is part of North Fraser Harbour. It is entered from North Arm. Sturgeon Bank obstructs its west end and has no marked channel across it.

200   **Depths** in Middle Arm are suitable for small craft.

201   **Submarine pipelines** and **cables** cross Middle Arm in several locations, they are marked by signs.

202   **Middle Arm Swing Bridge** has vertical clearance 3.6 m when closed. The signal for opening the bridge is three long blasts. Signals prescribed for North Arm swing bridges also apply to this bridge. The bridge will not be opened between 0700 and 0900 or 1600 and 1800 daily except in an emergency. For bridge openings

between 2400 and 0700, telephone (604) 521-0964. Channel widths on the east and west sides are 18 m.

203   **Dinsmore Bridge** is a fixed span road bridge vertical clearance 2 m, channel width 27 m.

204   **No. 2 Road Bridge**, 0.35 mile west of Dinsmore Bridge, is a fixed span vertical clearance 4.3 m.

205   **Morey Channel** is the portion of Middle Arm in the vicinity of Dinsmore Bridge.

206   **Water aerodrome**. — Middle Arm west of No. 2 Road Bridge is a water aerodrome.

207   The **Coast Guard** base is on Sea Island close NE of **Swishwash Island**. It is home to a hovercraft and dive team available 24 hours a day for rescue and other operations.

208   **Marinas** and marine service stations in Middle Arm provide services for small craft.

Pitt River and Pitt Lake

Chart 3062

209   **Pitt River** *(49°15'N, 122°45'W)*, within the Fraser River Harbour limits, is navigable by small craft from its junction with the Fraser River to Pitt Lake. It is used for storing and transporting logs. Logbooms line the river banks and occupy shoal areas in mid-channel as far as Grant Narrows. Numerous piles and dolphins line the river banks and lie in mid-channel from the river mouth to Addington Point.

210   **Caution. — Keep a sharp lookout for loose logs.**

211   **Tidal streams**. — Water flow of Pitt River is affected by tides, and between May and August by the runoff from both Fraser River and Pitt Lake. Under normal conditions the flow reverses according to tidal conditions in the Fraser River, but in freshet season flow is usually outward.

212   **Meteorological information** for Pitt River is in the Appendices.

213   **Port Coquitlam** (city) is on the west bank of Pitt River, near its confluence with the Fraser River.

214   A **marina** is located at the mouth of **Alouette River**.

215   **Pitt River Railway Bridge** and **Pitt River Highway Bridge**, which has 2 spans 76 m apart, cross **Chatham Reach** 2 miles NE of Douglas Island. All three bridges have swing spans.

216   **Pitt River Railway Bridge** (Canadian Pacific Railway), will open only for vessels that cannot pass under any part of the bridge. It is closed to marine traffic from 0530 to 0800, and 1615 to 1930 Monday to Friday. However, the bridge may open providing the vessel is ready to go, no commuter train is waiting to pass over the bridge, and bridge closure can be done for next commuter train.

217   **Bridge operating procedure**. — Vessels requiring an opening of the bridge shall contact the bridge operator on VHF Channel 74, telephone (604) 941-0079. Vessels are requested to call the bridge operator 30 minutes in advance of ETA at the bridge. Once an opening time has been established, a second call must be made to the bridge operator not later than 10 minutes before ETA at the bridge to confirm opening.

218   **Signals**. — For the Pitt River Railway Bridge are:
1.   Where any vessel requires the bridge to be opened it shall signal with three long blasts.

219   **Bridge operator shall use the following signals:**

Entrance to Pitt River (1999)

Pitt River Bridges looking upstream (1999)

Pitt River Bridges looking downstream (1986)

Chart 3062

Entrance to Pitt Lake (1999)

1. A fixed red light on the side of the bridge facing the vessel to indicate span is closed;
2. A green light on the side of the bridge facing the vessel to indicate span is open and in locked position; and
3. A fixed siren facing downstream and capable of being heard for a distance of not less than one-half mile, to indicate span will be opened or closed forthwith.

220   **Pitt River Highway Bridge** (Ministry of Transportation and Highways) is closed to marine traffic from 0530 to 0845 and from 1445 to 1845 Monday to Friday. The bridge will be opened by appointment only from 0100 to 0530. Saturday and Sunday the bridge will be opened between 0830 and 2300 and by appointment only from 2300 to 0830. Emergency openings are possible at anytime.

221   **Bridge operating procedure**. — The bridge operator can be contacted of VHF Channel 74, telephone (604) 240-6468.

222   **Signals**. — For the Pitt River Highway Bridge are:
1. Where any vessel requires the bridge to be opened it shall signal with two short blasts followed by two long blasts.

223   Bridge operator shall use the following signals:
1. A green light at the end of the swing span to indicate span is open;
2. A red displayed at the end of the swing span to indicate span is closed.

224   **Overhead cables** (power), vertical clearance 20 m, cross Chatham Reach between the bridges. A power cable, vertical clearance 22 m, crosses **Fox Reach** about 1.5 miles NW of **Addington Point**.

225   **Submarine pipelines** and **submarine cables** cross Chatham Reach near the bridges and about 1 mile NE of the bridges. They are marked by signs. A **submarine cable** crosses Fox Reach 1.5 miles NW of Addington Point.

226   **Goose Bar**, known locally as Goose Island, is a drying bank in mid-stream about 2 miles up river from the bridges.

227   **Conspicuous quarries** are located near the entrance to **Sturgeon Slough** and east of **MacIntyre Creek**.

228   **Siwash Island** is separated from the mainland by **Widgeon Slough**. The SE side of the island is usually lined with logbooms.

229   **Speed limits** of 5 km/h (3 kn) in Widgeon Slough and 10 km/h (5 kn) in Grant Narrows are prescribed in the *Boating Restriction Regulations*.

230   **Grant Narrows**, connecting Fox Reach and Pitt Lake, is deep and has a dyke along its south side, its north side is formed by extensive flats of mud and weeds. A **breakwater** and floats are on the north side, a float and launching ramp are on the south side.

231   **Grant Channel**, leading east and north from Grant Narrows, is a deep channel through flats at the south end of Pitt Lake. Sides of the channel are steep with very shallow depths along them, it is essential that a good course be made.

232   **Lights**. — Grant Narrows West light *(372)* is at the west end of Grant Narrows.

233   Grant Narrows East light *(373)*, 1.4 miles east of Grant Narrows, has a starboard hand daymark.

234   **Light buoys**. — Pitt Lake light buoys "L11" *(372.5)*, "L15" *(373.1)* and "L23" *(373.4)* are port hand buoys. Pitt Lake light buoy "L20" *(373.2)* is a starboard hand buoy.

235   **Buoys**. — Grant Channel is marked by port and starboard hand buoys.

Pitt Lake

236   The south end of **Pitt Lake** is filled by an extensive shallow area with drying banks. After the light buoys at the north

Chart 3062

end of Grant Channel are passed, depths increase sharply and continue deep to the north end of the lake.

237   **Goose Island**, locally known as Pen Island, is 1 mile north of the light buoys marking the north entrance to Grant Channel. A rock, with 4.1 m over it, lies 0.25 mile NE of the island.

238   **Lights**. — Goose Island light *(373.5)*, is on the SW extremity of the island.

239   Cozen Point light *(373.7)* is on the point.

240   **Little Goose Island** lies close offshore about 1.5 miles NE of Goose Island.

241   **Williams Landing**, east of Little Goose Island, has numerous private floats along its shores.

242   **Subiaco Cove**, about 4 miles NW of Williams Landing, lies between **Deer Point** and **Cacus Point**. Breakwaters protect private floats in the cove.

243   The head of Pitt Lake is about 3 miles north of Cacus Point. Logging camps and booming grounds are at the head of the lake. Several unnamed islands lie in the continuation of Pitt River.

244   **Weather**. — Due to mountains surrounding the lake, weather conditions can differ from one part of the lake to another. For example, warm sunny weather can be experienced in the north part of the lake while squalls are occurring in the south part.

Douglas Island to Hope

Charts 3489, 3488

245   The Fraser River from Douglas Island *(49°13'N, 122°46'W)* to Kanaka Creek is within Fraser River Harbour and the Fraser River Port Authority Practices and Procedures apply.

246   An unmarked navigation channel is maintained between Douglas Island and **Hope**, a distance of 49 miles. The channel is not charted beyond the Harrison River entrance *(49°13'N, 121°57'W)*.

247   **Tidal information**. — The Fraser River is affected by tide as far upstream as Chilliwack. Mean daily variation in water level when the river flow is low is 1.3 m at Port Hammond and 1.0 m at Mission. During freshets, variation in water level decreases to about 0.3 m at Port Hammond and 0.1 m at Mission. See charted Hydrographs showing seasonal variations in water levels for Port Hammond, Whonnock, Mission and Harrison Bay.

248   **Depths. — Caution charted depths are subject to change due to silting, scouring and dredging.**

249   **Booming grounds**. — Logbooms are moored to banks anywhere along the river. Size and location of these areas change frequently. Lumber mills with barge loading facilities lie along the river.

250   **Transportation**. — Communities along the Fraser River are connected to New Westminster and Vancouver by rail and highways. Bus services are available.

Douglas Island to Crescent Island

Chart 3489

251   **Barnston Island** *(49°12'N, 122°42'W)* is 1.3 miles upstream from Douglas Island. **Robert Point** forms its west extremity and **Mann Point** is its east extremity.

252   A **submarine pipeline** (sewer) crosses the river 0.2 mile west of Robert Point.

253   **Bishops Reach** leads north of Barnston Island. **Pitt Meadows Airport** is on the north shore.

254   **Radio towers**, with red air obstruction lights, are 0.5 mile ENE of Robert Point. An aeronautical beacon light is at the airport.

255   **Water aerodrome**. — Bishops Reach is a water aerodrome known as Pitt Meadows. An aircraft float protected by a breakwater is east of the radio towers.

256   **Parsons Channel** leads south of Barnston Island. A passenger and vehicle ferry, operated by the Ministry of Transportation and Highways, crosses the channel. A launching ramp is alongside the ferry dock.

257   A **submarine pipeline** (water) crosses Parsons Channel 0.9 mile WSW of Mann Point *(49°12'N, 122°40'W)*. An **overhead cable** (power), vertical clearance 23 m, crosses the channel close east of the pipeline.

258   **Light**. — A privately operated light is on Barnston Island, 0.4 mile WSW of Mann Point.

259   **Derby Reach** extends from Barnston Island to the west end of McMillan Island.

260   A **submarine pipeline** (water) crosses the river 0.3 mile east of Mann Point.

261   **Port Hammond** *(49°12'N, 122°39'W)* is engaged almost exclusively in processing forest products. Wharves and floats line the waterfront.

262   A **marina** is protected by a floating breakwater.

263   **Haney**, 2 miles up river, is a large community with all amenities including a hospital.

264   The Fraser River Harbour limit is at **Kanaka Creek** *(49°12'N, 122°35'W)*. A conspicuous bridge crosses the entrance to the creek.

265   **Russel Reach** leads north of **McMillan Island**.

266   **Wharf. — Breakwater**. — A public pier, protected by a floating breakwater is at Kanaka Landing (local name) 0.7 mile SSE of Kanaka Creek. Floats, with 195 m of berthing space, are attached to the outer end of the pier, power is laid on the floats. A launching ramp is adjacent to the wharf.

267   A **submarine pipeline** (gas) crosses Russel Reach 0.6 mile SE of **Tavistock Point**, the NW extremity of McMillan Island.

268   **Ferries**. — Two passenger and automobile ferries, operated by the Greater Vancouver Transit Authority cross Russel Reach between **Albion** and McMillan Island to Fort Langley.

269   **Lights**. — Privately operated lights are displayed from both ferry landings.

270   **Wharves. — Breakwaters**. — Albion public wharf, east of the ferry landing, is protected by a floating breakwater. A ramp 46 m long and a float with 95 m of berthing space are attached to the west side. Power is laid on the float and a telephone is nearby. A conspicuous tower with red air obstruction lights is near the head of the wharf.

271   McMillan Island **public wharf**, adjacent to the ferry landing, is at the outer end of a long trestle approach. Floats with 116 m of berthing space are attached to the wharf. A floating breakwater protects the wharf and floats.

272   **Fort Langley** and **Fort Langley Historic Park** are in **Bedford Channel**, which leads south of McMillan Island.

273   A **speed limit** of 10 km/h (5 kn) is prescribed by the *Boating Restriction Regulations* for Bedford Channel.

Chart 3489

274 A **submarine pipeline** (gas) crosses Bedford Channel.

275 **Glover Road Bridge**, vertical clearance 2.7 m, crosses Bedford Channel.

276 **Water aerodrome. — Airstrip**. — The Fraser River east of McMillan Island is a water aerodrome known as Fort Langley. An aircraft float and launching ramp are 0.25 mile east of **Endsleigh Point**. An aircraft landing strip with turf runway is at the east end of Bedford Channel.

277 **Wharf. — Breakwater**. — A public wharf at the end of a long trestle approach, known locally as McIvor's Landing, is 1 mile east of Endsleigh Point. Floats, with 134 m of berthing space, are attached to the west side of the wharfhead. A derrick is on the wharfhead and power is laid on the floats. A floating breakwater protects the wharf.

278 **Whonnock** *(49°10'N, 122°28'W)* is on the north bank of the river.

279 **Wharf. — Breakwater**. — Whonnock public wharf, protected by a floating breakwater, has a float with 56 m of berthing space attached to its east end. Power is laid on the float and a derrick is on the wharfhead.

280 **Plumper Reach** *(49°10'N, 122°26'W)* leads north of **Crescent Island**. **Enterprise Channel**, south of Crescent Island, has a drying bank across it.

281 **Overhead cables** (power) cross Plumper Reach, vertical clearance 33 m, and Enterprise Channel, vertical clearance 14 m.

Charts 3489, 3488

282 **Stave River** *(49°10'N, 122°25'W)* has two bridges across its entrance. The railway bridge has vertical clearance 2.3 m and the highway bridge vertical clearance 3.6 m. An **overhead cable** (power), vertical clearance unknown, crosses the river close south of the highway bridge.

283 **Buoy**. — Crescent Island buoy "S60", 0.4 mile upstream from the island, is a starboard hand buoy.

Crescent Island to Harrison River

Chart 3488

284 **Matsqui Island** *(49°07'N, 122°21'W)* is 2.4 miles upstream from Crescent Island. Submarine pipelines (sewer) cross from the south shore the river 0.1 mile and 0.25 mile east of the island.

285 **Mission Highway Bridge**, 0.8 mile upstream from Matsqui Island, is a fixed span, vertical clearance 19 m.

286 **Mission Railway Bridge**, 0.2 mile upstream, is a swing span, vertical clearance 4.9 m when closed. The bridge operator, on duty 24 hours a day, can be contacted on VHF Channel 74 or 69, telephone (604) 826-3117. The opening signal is 3 long blasts.

287 Calling-in Points for vessels transiting down river which require opening are:

   (a)   Abeam the mouth of the Nicomen Slough;

   (b)   Abeam the mouth of the Lower Hatzic Slough;

   (c)   Prior to departure from a berth or vessel tie up within the above calling-in points.

288 Calling-in Points for vessels transiting up river which require opening are:

   (a)   Abeam of the downstream end of Matsqui Island;

   (b)   Abeam of the upstream end of Matsqui Island;

   (c)   Prior to departure from a berth of a vessel tie up within the above calling-in points.

289 Once contact has been established between the vessel and the bridge operator at the first Calling-in Point, the vessel will provide the bridge operator with an estimated time of arrival (ETA). The bridge operator will check for rail traffic which may coincide with the vessels ETA and advise the vessel of any conflicts.

290 At the second Calling-in Point the vessel will confirm (or revise) their ETA to the bridge. The bridge operator will in turn confirm the availability of the bridge to open.

291 Once a vessel has made radio telephone contact with the Mission Railway Bridge, a listening watch shall be maintained on VHF Channel 69 until the vessel has cleared the bridge.

292 Should vessels from opposing direction wish to transit the bridge at the same time, the vessel proceeding down river shall have the right of way, in accordance with the *Collision Regulations* of the *Canada Shipping Act*.

293 An **overhead cable**, across the swing span of the railway bridge, has vertical clearance 21 m. An **overhead cable** (power), vertical clearance 24 m, crosses the river close west of the railway bridge.

294 **Lights**. — Fixed white lights are shown from both ends of the swing span and from both ends and centre of the protection pier. Red lights are shown on upstream and downstream sides of the swing span when the bridge is closed.

295 **Water aerodrome**. — The Fraser River fronting Mission is a water aerodrome.

296 **Mission**, a community on the north side of the river, has a full range of municipal facilities including a hospital with a heliport, and shopping centres. Several wharves and floats line the waterfront.

297 **Meteorological information** for Mission is in the Appendices.

298 **Supplies** and fuel are readily obtainable.

299 The **public boat basin** is protected by an A-frame and floating breakwaters on the east, and a floating concrete breakwater on its south side. Floats provide 630 m of berthing space. Power and water are laid on and garbage disposal facilities are available.

300 A **submarine pipeline** (sewer) crosses the river near Mission

301 **Hatzic**, about 2 miles upstream from Mission, has no waterfront facilities. **Lower Hatzic Slough** enters the Fraser River east of the community.

302 A **submarine pipeline** crosses the river north of Hatzic.

303 **Nicomen Slough** enters the Fraser River west of **Strawberry Island** *(49°09'N, 122°10'W)*. An **overhead cable** (power), vertical clearance 10 m, crosses Nicomen Slough 0.35 mile NW of **Strawberry Slough**. A highway bridge, vertical clearance unknown, also crosses Nicomen Slough.

304 A **gravel quarrying operation** with loading facilities is across the river from Nicomen Slough.

305 **Nicomen Island**, **Skumalasph Island** and **Queens Island** form the north bank of the river.

306 **Sumas River** *(49°08'N, 122°07'W)* enters the south side of the Fraser River. A railway bridge crosses the Sumas River 1 mile upstream.

307 A log storage basin *(49°08'N, 122°04'W)* has an **overhead cable** (power) across it, vertical clearance 18 m.

Chart 3488

308   Unnamed islands, 38, 42 and 33 m high, 1 mile up river from **Yaalstrick Island** are an Ecological Reserve.

309   Dredging operations can be encountered in the vicinity of **Minto Landing** *(49°12'N, 121°57'W)* from May to September.

Harrison River and Harrison Lake

Charts 3488, 3061

310   **Harrison River** *(49°13'N, 121°57'W)* is navigable by small craft from its junction with Fraser River to Harrison Lake. It is used for storing and transporting logs, booming grounds line the shores.

311   **Harrison Mills Railway Bridge**, 0.8 mile up river from its junction with Fraser River, is a swing span, vertical clearance 3.9 m when closed. The bridge operator is on duty 0600 to 1400 hours daily from April 1 to September 30. The bridge tender monitors VHF Channel 80 or can be reached by telephone (604) 796-2839. During the off season, CP Rail requires 48 hours notice for bridge openings.

312   **Harrison Mills Highway Bridge** is a swing span, vertical clearance 7.7 m when closed. This bridge is unmanned and requires 48 hours notice to be opened, telephone 1-800-667-5122.

313   **Lights.** — Fixed red lights are shown from the ends of the swing spans on both bridges.

314   A **radio tower**, with red air obstruction lights, is at the SE end of the railway bridge.

315   A **submarine pipeline** (water intake) is on the north side of the railway bridge.

316   Several **weirs** along the sandbars contain the river channel across **Harrison Bay**.

317   An **overhead cable** (power), vertical clearance 24 m, crosses the river at Harrison Mills. Towers carrying the cable are in the navigable channel.

318   **Harrison Mills** is the site of a large mill. A store, postal service and fuel float are available.

Chart 3061

319   **Wilson Point** *(49°16'N, 121°55'W)* and **Raake Point** are named features about 1.5 miles upstream of Harrison Mills. **Chehalis River** enters the bay opposite Wilson Point.

320   An **overhead cable** (telephone), vertical clearance 8 m, and towers carrying the cable, cross the foreshore west of Chehalis River.

321   **Morris Creek** *(49°18'N, 121°53'W)* has an overhead cable, vertical clearance 18 m, across it.

322   **McDonalds Bay** *(49°18'N, 121°50'W)* has private floats along its shores.

323   **Overhead cables** (power) cross the Harrison River at **Pirates Point**, vertical clearance 125 m, and at **Spooks Point**, vertical clearance 221 m.

324   **Harrison Lake**, entered at **Whippoorwill Point**, extends 32 miles NNW to the entrance of the Lillooet River. Several logging camps lie along the shores and tugboats towing logbooms can be encountered anywhere on the lake.

325   **Lights.** — Whippoorwill Point light *(378)* has a starboard hand daymark.

326   Harrison Hot Springs light *(379)*, about 1 mile east of the above light, is shown at an elevation of 8.6 m from a dolphin at the outer end of the breakwater.

327   **Buoys.** — Speed control buoys, displaying a 10 km/h (5 kn) speed limit, front Harrison Hot Springs.

328   A **submarine pipeline** (water intake) extends about 0.6 mile offshore south of Whippoorwill Point, it is marked by a sign.

329   **Water aerodrome.** — The south end of Harrison Lake is a water aerodrome.

330   **Harrison Hot Springs**, on the south shore of the lake, is a resort area. Acomodation, campsites, stores and postal services are available. A public swimming area protected by a breakwater is on the waterfront.

331   **Wharf. — Breakwaters.** — The public wharf, on the east shore, has a float with 37 m of berthing space attached to its outer end. A rock breakwater is on the north side of the wharf.

332   **Floating breakwaters** protect floats south of the public wharf.

333   A **marina** with a fuel float, the Harrison Lake Yacht Club and a launching ramp are on the east shore south of the breakwater.

334   **Echo Island** has **Camile Island** and **Marguerite Island** close-off its SE extremity. **McComb Bay**, on the east shore of Echo Island, is a booming ground.

335   **Light.** — Echo Island light *(377)*, on the west side of the island, has a starboard hand daymark.

336   **Echo Bay** is 0.25 mile north of the light.

337   **Celia Cove** and **Camp Cove** are on the west shore of Harrison Lake, opposite Echo Island. **Limbert Rocks**, 1.6 miles north of Camp Cove, dry 1.8 m.

338   **Cascade Bay** lies east of **Cascade Peninsula**. **Lone Tree Island**, at the entrance to the bay, is connected to shore by a rock breakwater. **Blind Bay** and **Lakeberg Bay** are at the head of Cascade Bay. A reef with two islets on it is in Blind Bay and numerous private floats line the shores of the bays.

339   **Rainbow Falls**, on the east shore of Cascade Bay, is marked by a B.C. Forest Service Recreation Site sign.

340   **Sturgeon Bay** and **Beach Bay** are at the north end of Cascade Peninsula. Sturgeon Bay is a booming ground. Private daybeacons mark drying rocks lying in the entrance to Beach Bay.

341   **Macs Cove** and **Cooks Cove** are 1.2 miles NNE of Beach Bay. A B.C. Forest Service Recreation Site sign is at **Bear Creek**.

342   **Sheers Island** *(49°25'N, 121°50'W)* has a booming ground on its NW side.

343   **Light.** — Sheers Island light *(374)*, close north of **Ten Mile Point**, has a port hand daybeacon.

344   **Purcell Point** is the south extremity of **Long Island**.

345   **Light.** — Inkman Island light *(375)*, close-off the SE shore of Long Island, has a port hand daymark.

346   **Scherrer Bay**, extending NNW from Inkman Island, is a booming ground.

347   **Towboat Strait** leads between Long Island and the mainland. **Long Island Bay**, with **Deer Island** in its entrance, is on the west shore of Long Island. Several private floats are in the bay.

348   **Timberman Cove**, west of **Molly Hogan Point**, is at the north end of Towboat Strait. The bay is a booming ground with a dry land sort area and a barge loading ramp.

349   **Light.** — Long Island light *(376)*, on the north extremity of the island, has a starboard hand daymark.

350   **Bear Creek** (locality) *(49°32'N, 121°46'W)* has a log sorting operation and booming ground.

Chart 3061

351 **Silver River** (locality), at the mouth of **Big Silver Creek**, has a log sorting operation and booming grounds protected by breakwaters. **East Bay** is a booming ground.

352 **Light**. — **Vedder Rock** light *(379.3) (49°36'N, 121°56'W)* has a port hand daymark.

353 **Westwood Bay**, **Doctors Point**, **Doctors Bay** and **Doctors Island** are named features NW of Vedder Rock. Westwood Bay is a booming ground.

354 **Light**. — Doctors Point light *(379.5)*, 0.4 mile NW of the point, has a port hand daymark.

355 **Five Mile Bay** *(49°42'N, 122°03'W)* has ruins of a logging operation, broken piles and snags foul the bottom. **Todd Bay** is on the opposite shore.

356 **Conspicuous towers** are along the shore 2 miles NE of Five Mile Bay.

357 **Lillooet River** enters the head of Harrison Lake. Numerous islands lie in the river mouth.

358 **Tipella**, on the south side of the river mouth, is a logging operation with booming grounds and a private gravel airstrip.

359 **Light**. — Port Douglas Channel light *(380)*, on the north entrance point to the channel, has a starboard hand daymark.

360 **Port Douglas Channel**, depth 1.3 m, leads to **Little Harrison Lake** which has booming grounds along its shores. **Port Douglas**, at the head of the lake, has a loading wharf belonging to Metals Research Corporation of America.

CHAPTER 5

Strait of Georgia (NW Part), Baynes Sound, Malaspina Strait, Jervis Inlet

General

Charts 3512, 3513, 3514

1 This chapter describes the NW part of the Strait of Georgia. South limit is between Cottam Point and Sargeant Bay. North limit is between Shelter and Sarah Points. Malaspina Strait and Jervis Inlet on the NE side of the Strait of Georgia, and Baynes Sound on the SW side are also described.

Strait of Georgia — NW Part

Charts 3512, 3513

2 **Strait of Georgia** (NW part) is the portion of the Strait of Georgia north of a line drawn between Cottam Point *(49°19'N, 124°13'W)* and Sargeant Bay *(49°28'N, 123°51'W)*. The main shipping route through the NW part of Strait of Georgia is between Hornby Island and Sisters Islets or by way of Stevens Passage. It then passes between Montgomery Bank and Vancouver Island into the south entrance of Discovery Passage.

3 **Texada Island** *(49°40'N, 124°25'W)* is 27 miles long in a NW/SE direction and approximately 5 miles wide. It separates the main shipping route through the Strait of Georgia from Malaspina Strait. A ridge of rugged mountains runs throughout its length but reaches its greatest elevations near the south end. Lasqueti Island, SW of Texada Island, is separated from it by Sabine Channel.

4 **Achilles Bank** *(49°33'N, 124°30'W)* has a least depth of 26.5 m. **Exeter Shoal** *(49°40'N, 124°39'W)* has a least depth of 14.6 m. **Ajax Bank** *(49°39'N, 124°42'W)* has a least depth of 29 m. These banks lie along the centre of the fairway in the main shipping route.

5 **Montgomery Bank** *(49°54'N, 124°57'W)* lies in the north part of the Strait of Georgia. **Sentry Shoal**, on the NW part of the bank, has a least depth of 7 m.

6 **Vessel Traffic Services** (VTS). — The NW part of the Strait of Georgia is in *Sector Four* of the *Vancouver Traffic Zone* and is administered by *Comox Traffic*. Assigned frequency is 156.575 MHz, Channel 71.

7 Special operating procedures when changing from *Sector One* to *Sector Four* require:

(a) Northbound vessels to call *Victoria Traffic* and check out of *Sector One* then call *Comox Traffic*; and

(b) Southbound vessels to call *Comox Traffic* and check out of *Sector Four* then call *Victoria Traffic*.

8 A brief description of this VTS is in *PAC 200*. Details are in *Radio Aids to Marine Navigation (Pacific and Western Arctic)*. Calling-in points are:

9 **Calling-in Point No. 24**, *Ballenas Island/Merry Island/Welcome Passage*, is a change from *Sector One (Victoria Traffic)* to *Sector Four (Comox Traffic)*. It is a line joining Reception Point light *(448.8)*, Merry Island light *(449)* and Ballenas Islands light

(490). When northbound mariners shall indicate if their route is through Welcome Passage, Malaspina Strait, Sabine Channel, Stevens Passage, or west of Sisters Islets.

10 **Calling-in Point No. 25**, *Cape Lazo/Powell River*, is a line joining Cape Lazo and Powell River Floating Breakwater Entrance South light *(476.3)*. When southbound mariners shall indicate if their route is through Malaspina Strait, Sabine Channel, Stevens Passage, or west of Sisters Islets.

11 **Ferries**. — Regular ferry services cross the Strait of Georgia and the north entrance to Malaspina Strait. Ferry services commence from Westview on the mainland, close south of Powell River. Landings are at Blubber Bay on the north end of Texada Island, and at Little River about 3 miles NW of Cape Lazo on Vancouver Island. Another ferry crosses the Strait of Georgia from False Bay on Lasqueti Island to French Creek on Vancouver Island. Charted ferry routes are general indications of the route followed.

12 **Military exercise areas** include: Area WF, SE of Texada Island, is for general purpose and anti-submarine exercises excluding high explosive projectiles; Area WI, west of Texada Island, is for dropping explosive echo ranging devices from aircraft. For details see *Notices to Mariners 1 to 46 Annual Edition*.

13 **Spoil grounds**. — Ocean dump sites, under permit through the *Ocean Dumping Control Act* are in *49°41.7'N, 124°44.5'W* and *49°57.7'N, 125°05'W*.

14 **Submarine cables** cross the Strait of Georgia from Nile Creek *(49°25'N, 124°38'W)*, on Vancouver Island, to Texada Island in the vicinity of Mount Davies *(49°36'N, 124°19'W)*. The cable area is approximately 1.5 miles wide and passes close north of Sisters and Fegen Islets. Flashing yellow lights maintained by B.C. Hydro are on the Vancouver and Texada Islands shores to mark the landing site of this cable crossing. A cable crosses the Strait of Georgia between Qualicum Beach, on Vancouver Island, and Burrard Inlet and another cable crosses the strait between Qualicum Beach and Spanish Bank. A cable crosses the strait between Qualicum Beach and False Bay on Lasqueti Island. An abandoned cable crosses the strait between Cape Lazo and Powell River.

15 **Submarine gas pipelines** cross the Strait of Georgia from Powell River *(49°51'N, 124°32'W)* to Little River *(49°45'N, 124°56'W)*.

16 **Tides**. — Tidal differences in the NW part of the Strait of Georgia, all referenced on Point Atkinson (Index No. 7795), are in *Tide Tables, Volume 5*. Along the mainland shore they are given for Halfmoon Bay (Index No. 7830), Irvines Landing (Index No. 7836), Pender Harbour (Index No. 7837), Blind Bay (Index No. 7865), Powell River (Index No. 7880) and Lund (Index No. 7885). Along the central islands for False Bay (Index No. 7982), Blubber Bay (Index No. 7875), Welcome Bay (Index No. 7990), Twin Islands (Index No. 7892) and Mitlenatch Island (Index No. 7895). Along the Vancouver Island side for Northwest Bay (Index No. 7938), Hornby Island (Index No. 7953), Denman Island (Index No. 7955), Comox (Index No. 7965) and Little River (Index No. 7993).

Charts 3512, 3513

17   **Tidal streams**. — The tidal stream entering the Strait of Georgia round the SE end of Vancouver Island meets the corresponding tidal stream that flows round the NW end of the island between Cape Mudge *(50°00'N, 125°11'W)* and Cape Lazo *(49°42'N, 124°52'W)*. The meeting usually occurs much nearer Cape Mudge than Cape Lazo but the place varies because of differences in character of opposing tides and the state of weather. At the meeting a considerable race often forms and rips, dangerous to small craft, can occur in this area during strong east or SE winds. For detailed information see Strait of Georgia (SE part) in Chapter 3.

18   *Current Atlas, Juan de Fuca Strait to Strait of Georgia*, is available from the CHS Chart Distribution Office and Authorized Chart Dealers.

19   **Meteorological information** for the Strait of Georgia is given in *PAC 200*. Meteorological tables for Ballenas Islands, Merry Island, Texada Island, Powell River, Comox Airport and Campbell River and frequency of fog tables for Merry Island and Campbell River are in the Appendices.

Craig Bay to Baynes Sound

20   The coast between Craig Bay *(49°19'N, 124°15'W,* Chapter 3), and Baynes Sound, 20 miles NW, consists of a series of wooded bluffs of moderate height that terminate in points of sand and shingle. Mountain ranges, about 6 km inland, rise to considerable elevations and have conspicuous peaks. **Mount Arrowsmith** *(49°13'N, 124°36'W)*, the most conspicuous peak, rises to an elevation of 1,817 m.

Chart 3512

21   **Parksville Bay** *(49°20'N, 124°19'W)* has a drying sand beach extending 0.4 mile from the HW line in places. Under ideal conditions, small craft can find anchorage but allowance must be made for the afternoon onshore wind. The town of **Parksville** surrounds the bay and is a summer resort and retirement community. It has a shopping centre, stores, accommodation, restaurants and a post office. The main highway passes close to Parksville and the E&N railway pass through it.

Charts 3512, 3513

22   **French Creek** *(49°21'N, 124°21'W)*, 2 miles NW of Parksville, has a boat harbour in its entrance that is protected by rock breakwaters. The entrance channel is 49 m wide and the boat harbour is 183 m by 91 m, both were dredged to a depth of 3 m (1965). Public floats with 550 m of berthing space and a private float are in the boat harbour. The three south floats are reserved for commercial fishing vessels. Power, fresh water and garbage and used oil disposal facilities are available on the floats, fuel is obtainable. Accommodation, dining, marine supply store, mechanical repairs, emergency haul out and a tidal grid are available. A privately owned ferry plies between French Creek and False Bay on Lasqueti Island. This service provides transportation for passengers and light freight and is dependent on favourable weather and tidal conditions.

23   **Coast Guard has a year-round rescue unit based at French Creek.**

24   **Light**. — French Creek light *(491)* is shown at an elevation of 5.8 m from a mast near the outer end of the W breakwater.

25   **Beacons**. — The entrance channel is marked by five daybeacons, three have starboard hand daymarks and two have port hand daymarks.

26   A **submarine pipeline** extends 0.6 mile north from the inner end of the north breakwater.

27   **Wreck**. — It was reported (1987) that fishermen foul their gear on a wrecked barge off the 50 m contour north of French Creek.

Chart 3513

28   **Qualicum Beach** *(49°21'N, 124°25'W)* is a town and summer resort with stores, post office, hotels and golf courses. The main highway is close by and the E&N Railway passes through town. An asphalt airstrip is 3.2 km south of Qualicum Beach.

29   **Submarine cables** cross the Strait of Georgia from Qualicum Beach to False Bay, on Lasqueti Island, and to Burrard Inlet.

30   **Numerous private mooring buoys** lie close offshore between Qualicum Beach and Bowser.

Chart 3527

31   **Qualicum Bay** *(49°25'N, 124°38'W)*, between the entrances of **Qualicum River** and **Nile Creek**, has a marine service station. A boat launching ramp is at the Indian Reserve, SE of the bay.

32   A **submarine pipeline** (water intake) extends 0.8 mile offshore, 1 mile south of Qualicum Bay at **Dunsmuir**.

33   **Conspicuous hydroelectric towers** are at the mouth of Nile Creek.

34   **Submarine cables** cross the Strait of Georgia from Nile Creek to Texada Island, the cable area is about 1.5 miles wide.

35   **Light**. — A flashing yellow light maintained by B.C. Hydro, close north of Nile Creek, marks the landing site of the submarine cables.

36   **Bowser**, 2.5 miles NW of Qualicum Bay, has a post office. A prominent microwave tower with red air obstruction lights is on a hill west of Bowser.

Lambert Channel

37   **Lambert Channel** *(49°30'N, 124°42'W)* separates Hornby Island from the SE side of Denman Island. The fairway through Lambert Channel is about 0.5 mile wide but reefs and shoal spits lie close-off the Hornby Island shore. The Denman Island shore is free of dangers beyond a distance of 0.15 mile except near the north end, in the vicinity of **Fillongley Park**, where a drying mud flat extends nearly 0.5 mile offshore. Its outer edge is steep-to and has several large drying boulders on it. Houses lie along the Denman Island shore and along the Hornby Island shore north of Hornby Island settlement.

38   **Tides**. — Tidal differences for Hornby Island (Index No. 7953), referenced on Point Atkinson, are in *Tide Tables, Volume 5*.

39   **Ferry**. — A scheduled ferry crosses Lambert Channel connecting Gravelly Bay on Denman Island to Hornby Island.

40   **Submarine cables** cross Lambert Channel from 0.4 mile NW of **Whalebone Point** and from **Phipps Point**.

Approach to French Creek (1990)

French Creek entrance (1982)

French Creek boat basin (1990)

Chart 3527

Lambert Channel from south (1991)

41   **Eagle Rock** *(49°29'N, 124°41'W)* is 15 m high and connected to the Denman Island shore by a drying ledge.

42   **Gravelly Bay** is the site of **Denman Island East Ferry Landing**. Regular ferry service for passengers and vehicles operates to Hornby Island. A launching ramp is located south of the ferry landing at **Bill Mee Park**.

43   **Light. — Fog signal**. — Denman Island East Ferry Landing light *(496.3)*, on a dolphin with a radar reflector, is private. The fog signal is operated by ferry personnel when required for ferry movements.

44   **Hornby Island** *(49°30'N, 124°40'W)* rises precipitously in terraces on its west side to the summit of **Mount Geoffrey** from which it slopes more gently east. The island is easily identifiable from all angles of approach. Several resorts are on the island.

45   **Norman Point** is the south extremity of Hornby Island, **Toby Island** and **Heron Rocks** lie close SE of it. The channel between **Norris Rocks** and Heron Rocks is not recommended.

46   **Ford Cove** *(49°30'N, 124°40'W)* can be entered north or south of **Maude Reef**. A rock breakwater extends NW from the south entrance point of the cove and a floating breakwater connected to it protects the NW side of the berths.

47   **Light**. — Ford Cove Floating Breakwater North light *(494.5)* is shown from a short white cylindrical mast.

48   **Buoy**. — Port hand buoy "P37" is close to the SE extremity of Maude Reef.

49   **Beacon**. — A daybeacon, on the NW extremity of Maude Reef, has a starboard hand daymark.

50   **Marine farm** facilities line the north side of Maude Reef.

51   **Berths**. — Public floats with a common connection to shore are in the SE corner of Ford Cove. The boat basin within the breakwaters was dredged to a depth of 2.4 m (1960). The SW float is a fuel dock and a 3 tonne crane is on the wharfhead. Power is laid on the floats and garbage disposal is available.

52   **Savoie Rocks** have three heads with less than 2 m over them. **Shingle Spit**, with a clump of trees near its extremity, projects as a drying spit for about 0.15 mile into the channel.

53   **Hornby Island settlement** and ferry landing near Shingle Spit has stores, a motel with a small float, a campsite and launching ramp. The post office is on the east side of the island in the vicinity of Tribune Bay.

54   A **ferry landing**, close SE of Shingle Spit, is protected by a rockfill breakwater. Regular ferry service for passengers and vehicles operates to Gravelly Bay on Denman Island.

55   **Light. — Fog signal**. — Hornby Island Ferry Landing light *(496.4)*, on a dolphin with a radar reflector, is private. The fog

signal is operated by ferry personnel when required for ferry movements.

56   **Anchorage** for small craft can be obtained in the lee of Shingle Spit, taking care to anchor well clear of the submarine cables. Predominating winds during summer months are from NW, which blow strongly at times through Lambert Channel. Larger vessels can obtain anchorage with good holding ground north of Shingle Spit in about 26 m.

Hornby Island to Little River

57   **Tribune Bay** *(49°31'N, 124°38'W)* is low and shelving with drying ledges on its west shore and has bold cliffs on its NE shore. It is entered between **Nash Bank**, marked at its outer end by port hand buoy "P35", and **St. John Point**. The Hornby Island Post Office is at the Co-op store, within walking distance of Tribune Bay.

58   **Anchorage** can be obtained in Tribune Bay in 15 m, sand bottom. It is exposed to ESE and SE winds but sheltered from other winds.

59   **Flora Islet**, close east of St. John Point, is a low, grassy islet surrounded by drying rock ledges extending 0.4 mile SE from it.

60   **Caution should be exercised when rounding Flora Islet, as rocks on the ledge do not always break. Chrome Island lighthouse bearing more than 244° and open south of Norris Rocks leads south of both Nash Bank and this ledge.**

61   **Light**. — Flora Islet light *(494)*, on the north side of the islet, is shown at an elevation of 20.7 m from a skeleton tower, 16.2 m high.

62   **Collishaw Point** *(49°33'N, 124°41'W)*, known locally as Boulder Point, is the north extremity of Hornby Island. Drying rock ledges, studded with boulders, extend 0.8 mile NW from the point.

63   **Komas Bluff** *(49°35'N, 124°48'W)* is formed of sandstone and rises to a height of about 150 m. Comox Bar extends NNW from the north end of Denman Island and is the north entrance to Baynes Sound.

64   **Cape Lazo** *(49°42'N, 124°52'W)*, known locally as Point Holmes, is a prominent headland with a flat summit, its seaward sides are faced with yellow clay. From the SE, this headland appears to be an island and it is not until north of Hornby Island that it can be seen to be part of Vancouver Island. Drying rock ledges surround the cape and **Kye Bay**, on its north side, dries completely.

Chart 3527

65   **Light**. — Comox Aeronautical Beacon light *(508)* is 1.25 miles NW of Cape Lazo.

66   **Buoy. — Light buoy**. — East cardinal buoy "PJ" and Cape Lazo east cardinal light buoy "PB" *(507.5)* mark the outer edge of the shoal area east of Cape Lazo.

67   **Conspicuous towers**. — A large white radar dome, 1.1 miles NW of Cape Lazo at **Comox Airport**, has fixed red lights and is the first identifiable feature when approaching Cape Lazo from north. A microwave tower, 42 m high, and a radio tower are at the north end of Cape Lazo.

68   A **submarine pipeline** (sewer outfall), at the south end of Cape Lazo, extends 1.6 miles seaward.

69   **Ferry landing**. — A ferry landing, 3 miles NW of Cape Lazo, is close east of the mouth of **Little River**. It is operated by the British Columbia Ferry Services Inc. and provides regular service for passengers and vehicles to Westview on the mainland.

70   **Lights** and radar reflectors at Little River ferry landing are private.

71   **Tides**. — Tidal differences for Little River (Index No. 7993), referenced on Point Atkinson, are in *Tide Tables, Volume 5*.

72   **Comox Marine Communications and Traffic Services Centre** VAC *(49°45'00"N, 124°56'39"W)*, 1 mile NW of Little River ferry landing, provides scheduled broadcasts and ship to shore service. For details see *Radio Aids to Marine Navigation (Pacific and Western Arctic)*.

73   A **radio tower** with red air obstruction lights is 0.5 mile WNW of the Comox MCTS Centre.

74   **Submarine pipelines** (gas) cross the Strait of Georgia from close NW of the ferry landing.

75   A **wreck** with 45 m over it lies 1.8 miles ENE of the ferry landing.

Lasqueti Island — South Coast

Chart 3512

76   **Lasqueti Island** *(49°29'N, 124°16'W)* is about 9 miles long and 4 miles wide. The islands and islets lying around it form a shelter area for small craft proceeding to Desolation Sound.

77   **Young Point** *(49°26'N, 124°10'W)* is the SE extremity of Lasqueti Island. **Trematon Mountain** near the middle of Lasqueti Island has a conspicuous turret shaped summit.

78   **Sangster Island** is quite heavily forested and has reefs extending from its NW and SE extremities. **Elephant Eye Point** consists of eroded cliffs and forms the SE side of Sangster Island.

79   **Light**. — Sangster Island Sector light *(490.3)*, on the SW tip of the island, is shown at an elevation of 16.5 m from a white tower.

80   **Beacon**. — A daybeacon with a starboard hand daymark and radar reflector is near the centre of **Seal Reef**.

81   **Boat Cove** has a number of drying and sunken rocks in its SE approach and is exposed to the south and SE. It offers good protection from west winds.

82   **Anchorage** for small craft can be obtained at the head of **Old House Bay** and in **Richardson Cove**.

83   **Jenkins Island** *(49°27'N, 124°17'W)* is separated from Lasqueti Island by a narrow, deep passage. **Sea Egg Rocks** lie 0.3 mile west of Jenkins Island, the highest has an elevation of 8 m.

84   The Lasqueti Island shore between Richardson and Jenkins Coves is an **Ecological Reserve**.

Charts 3512, 3513

85   **Finnerty Islands** *(49°30'N, 124°24'W)* are separated from the west end of Lasqueti Island by a shallow passage, suitable for small craft. Care must be taken to avoid the drying reef east of the largest island. With strong north winds steep seas break in this passage.

86   **Sisters Islets** *(49°29'N, 124°26'W)* consist of two bare, rocky islets the highest of which has an elevation of 2.7 m.

87   **Light**. — Sisters Islets light *(493)*, on the east islet, is shown at an elevation of 21.3 m from a white tower. White buildings are near the light.

88   **Stevens Passage** separates Sisters Islets from Finnerty Islands. It is a deep passage providing Finnerty Islands are given a berth of at least 0.3 mile.

False Bay

Chart 3536

89   **False Bay** *(49°30'N, 124°21'W)*, entered between **Olsen Island** and **Heath Islet**, is open to the *Qualicum*, a strong west wind that blows in from the Pacific Ocean and funnels through the Qualicum Beach area. **Jeffrey Rock**, 0.2 mile south of Olsen Island, has less than 2 m over it. A rock, with less than 2 m over it lies midway between Olsen Island and **Higgins Island**.

90   **Beacons**. — Heath Islet daybeacon has a starboard hand daymark. A private daybeacon is on a drying rock 0.2 mile east of Higgins Island.

91   **Light**. — False Bay light *(492)* is on **Prowse Point** at the S side of the entrance to the bay.

92   **Tides**. — Tidal differences for False Bay (Index No. 7982), referenced on Point Atkinson, are in *Tide Tables, Volume 5*.

93   **Submarine cables**. — A cable commencing from close south of the public wharf passes along the centre of False Bay. A cable crosses the entrance channel to the lagoon SE of Prowse Point, and another cable crosses the lagoon.

94   **Water aerodrome**. — False Bay is a water aerodrome known as Lasqueti Island.

95   A **pier** is SE of Prowse Point and a rock breakwater, dolphins and a pier are in the NE part of False Bay.

96   The lagoon, entered east of Prowse Point, is completely protected and often used by wintering fish boats. A drying reef lies in the middle of the entrance and the entrance channel dries at about half tide. It is best to use this channel only at HW as there is a 3 to 4 kn current when the tide is running. The deepest part of the channel is on its north side but care must be taken to avoid the rock ledges projecting from shore. A rock that dries 3.6 m lies about midway through the channel.

97   **Marine farm** facilities are located at the head of the lagoon.

98   **Anchorage** sheltered from most winds can be obtained in the north part of False Bay east of Higgins Island in a depth of about 13 m. Small craft can find anchorage with good holding ground in shallower water closer to shore.

99   **Lasqueti**, near the SE end of False Bay, has a post office, restaurant and store. Diesel fuel, gasoline and fresh water are

False Bay north end (1985)

Lagoon on south side of False Bay (1985)

False Bay public wharf (1985)

Chart 3536

obtainable. A privately owned passenger ferry plies between False Bay and French Creek on Vancouver Island and is dependent on favourable weather and tidal conditions.

100   **Wharf. — Floats.** — The public wharf in Lasqueti has a depth of 5.4 m alongside. A float 37 m long attached to its south side has a seaplane float at its outer end. A dock attached to the north side of the public wharf is 12 m long. A 3 tonne crane, power and fresh water are available on the wharf. At times, there is a considerable sea at these floats making berths uncomfortable.

Sabine Channel

Chart 3512

101   **Sabine Channel** *(49°31'N, 124°14'W)* separates Lasqueti Island and the islands to the east from Texada Island. The fairway through Sabine Channel is deeper than 200 m. **Rabbit Island**, **Sheer Island** and **Circle Island** lie on the south side and at the east end of the fairway through Sabine Channel, drying reefs lie 0.2 mile north of Sheer Island.

102   **Tidal streams** in Sabine Channel seldom exceed 2 kn but rough seas can be encountered when wind opposes tide.

103   **Upwood Point** *(49°29'N, 124°07'W)* is rugged and precipitous with stunted pines between bare rock crevices, the land behind is more thickly wooded. **Mount Dick**, 1.5 miles NW of Upwood Point, is a very well defined hill. **Mount Shepherd**, 3.5 miles NW of Upwood Point, is the highest summit on Texada Island.

104   **Buoy.** — South cardinal buoy "QT", 0.2 mile south of Upwood Point, marks a rock that dries 4.6 m.

105   **Lights.** — Point Upwood light *(465)*, on the southeastern extreme of Texada Island, is shown at an elevation of 11 m from a white tower with a red band at the top.

106   Texada Island light *(465.5)*, on **Partington Point**, is shown at an elevation of 8.2 m from a white tower with a red band at the top.

107   **Cook Bay**, 1.6 miles NW of Partington Point, is too deep for anchorage. Two islets lie off its west entrance and a drying rock lies off the head of the bay.

108   **Mount Davies** *(49°36'N, 124°19'W)* has conspicuous hydroelectric towers running from the shore up its west face.

109   **Submarine cables** cross the Strait of Georgia, from the vicinity of Mount Davies to Qualicum Bay, on Vancouver Island; the cable area is approximately 1.5 miles wide.

110   **Light.** — A flashing yellow light, maintained by B.C. Hydro, marks the landing site of the submarine cables.

111   **Squitty Bay Marine Park** encompasses the area around **Squitty Bay** *(49°27'N, 124°10'W)*, a small indentation on the east end of Lasqueti Island. The bay has been dredged to a depth of 2.4 m beyond the public float but several rocks lie in the entrance. The public float is 30 m long with 2.2 m alongside. The park is undeveloped except for the float.

112   **Bull Passage**, along the NE shore of Lasqueti Island, is separated from Sabine Channel by **Bull Island**, **Jedediah Island**, **Paul Island** and **Jervis Island**. It is often used by tugs towing logbooms and affords good shelter in all weather, local knowledge is advised. Drying rocks lie close offshore in several locations.

113   A drying rock lies off **Rouse Bay** in the south approach to Bull Passage.

114   A **submarine cable** is laid from Rouse Bay to Thormanby Islands.

115   **Boho Island** lies on the west side of Bull Passage. Small craft can find good anchorage south of Boho Island in **Boho Bay** or west of the island in **Skerry Bay**; a drying rock lies in the middle of the north entrance to Skerry Bay. Marine farm facilities are in the north part of Skerry Bay and along the NW shore of the north entrance to the bay.

116   **Little Bull Passage** separates the steep cliffs on the SW side of Jedediah Island from Bull Island. It is deep enough for small craft to navigate safely. A drying rock lies at the west end of the passage, close to Jedediah Island. Dangerous pinnacle rocks resulting from a rockslide on the Bull Island shore lie about halfway through the passage. **Jedediah Island Marine Park** is one of the largest island parks in the province.

117   **West Point** *(49°31'N, 124°17'W)* is sloping, partially bare of trees and prominent from most directions.

118   **Tucker Bay** is entered between West Point and some easily identified wooded islets off the NW side of Jervis Island. **Avery Reef** and several rocky heads, with less than 2 m over them, lie in the middle of Tucker Bay. **Larson Islet**, close-off **Wells Point**, is 8 m high. **Tuck Rock**, midway between Wells Point and Larson Islet, is awash.

119   **Anchorage** in Tucker Bay is fair in a depth of about 30 m with the NW islet on the east side of the entrance bearing 048° and West Point bearing 313°. With a strong NW wind and a NW going tidal stream, this anchorage though safe would be uncomfortable. Small craft can anchor south of Larson Islet in 9 to 11 m where they will be almost completely sheltered. When approaching this small craft anchorage pass within a distance of 90 m of the west end of Larson Islet.

120   **Marine farm** facilities are SE and west of West Point and between the point and **Jelina Island**.

121   **Scottie Bay**, south of **Lindbergh Island**, is protected from virtually all winds and sea. Enter close to the Lasqueti Island shore to avoid the reef extending south from Lindbergh Island. The wharf and slipway are private.

122   **Fegen Islets** *(49°32'N, 124°23'W)*, off the NW end of Lasqueti Island, should not be approached within a distance of 0.2 mile nor should any attempt be made to pass between these islets and Lasqueti Island.

123   **Light.** — Fegen Islets light *(466)*, on the W entrance to Sabine Channel, is shown at an elevation of 7.9 m from a white tower.

124   **Spring Bay**, east of Fegen Islets, offers good **anchorage** in SE winds but Fegen Islets give only minimal protection from NW winds and sea.

Texada Island — West Coast

Chart 3513

125   **Davie Bay** *(49°36'N, 124°23'W)* is exposed and only suitable for small craft. Two islets lie off its entrance and a rock awash lies NW of the east islet.

126   **Mouat Bay** has **Mouat Islands** lying in its entrance and is fronted by a boulder foreshore. A log dump and breakwater lie close south of **Harwood Point**, another log dump and breakwater are 1 mile SE. **Dick Island** is connected to Harwood Point by a drying boulder bar.

Tucker Bay (1985)

Scottie Bay (1985)

Fegen Islets from SW (1985)

Spring Bay (1985)

Chart 3513

127　　**Gillies Bay** can easily be identified by houses around its shores when approaching from the south. The community has a store, post office, RCMP office, medical clinic and resident doctor. There is no wharf or jetty in the bay. An asphalt airstrip, NW of the bay, is 915 m long.

128　　A **red and white radio mast**, 63 m high, is on the north entrance point of Gillies Bay.

129　　**Anchorage** can be obtained 0.2 mile offshore in Gillies Bay in a depth of about 20 m but it is quite exposed to most winds.

130　　**Meteorological information** for Texada Island is in the Appendices.

131　　**Beale Cove**, 3 miles NW of Gillies Bay, has a wharf and conspicuous orange conveyor belonging to Ideal Cement Company. Inland from the wharf are conspicuous open pit mines, a tower, storage tanks and some buildings. The wharf is 275 m long with a depth of 13 m alongside. **Welcome Bay** is close NW of Beale Cove.

132　　**Light**. — A private flashing amber light is shown from the wharf in Beale Cove.

133　　**Tides**. — Tidal differences for Welcome Bay (Index No. 7990), referenced on Point Atkinson, are in *Tide Tables, Volume 5*.

134　　**Surprise Mountain** rises steeply from shore between Welcome Bay and **Davis Bay**.

135　　**Favada Point** *(49°44'N, 124°38'W)* is moderately steep-to and has a conspicuous house and log dump on it. **Crescent Bay** and **Limekiln Bay**, north of Favada Point, are separated by **Marshall Point** and have extensive shallow beaches. A conspicuous house is reported to be at the south end of Crescent Bay.

Cape Lazo to Shelter Point

136　　From Cape Lazo *(49°42'N, 124°52'W)* to the south entrance to Discovery Passage, 20 miles NW, the shore is fronted by beaches of stones and boulders backed by ranges of thickly wooded hills. Mountain ranges 10 km inland rise to considerable elevations. **Constitution Hill** *(49°47'N, 125°11'W)* makes a good radar target.

137　　**Elma Bay** *(49°51'N, 125°05'W)*, at the entrance to **Black Creek**, has a resort with boat launching ramp.

138　　**Oyster River**, 1.5 miles NW of Elma Bay, is a stream of considerable size with a drying bank of shingle extending 0.3 mile from its mouth. A dredged channel leading to a boat basin and marina in the mouth of Oyster River is marked by a series of piles. Due to storms and unstable shoreline the channel and boat basin require dredging annually, local knowledge is advised before entering the channel.

139　　**Anchorage** open to most winds can be obtained about 0.5 mile from shore midway between Elma Bay and Oyster River in 18 to 30 m.

140　　**Kuhushan Point** *(49°53'N, 125°07'W)* is a low, sandy projection. Trees, which in thick weather can be mistaken for the extremity of the point, are about 0.15 mile inland. Several houses are near the point and close north of the light structure there is a large low building with a conspicuous pyramidal roof marked "Pub", which in daytime, can be seen long before the light structure can be identified. A dredged channel close north of **Oyster Pond** leads to a boat basin and resort. It requires annual dredging therefore local knowledge is advised.

141　　**Light**. — Kuhushan Point light *(509)*, on the point, is shown at an elevation of 17.7 m from a skeleton tower.

142　　**Oyster Bay**, between Kuhushan Point and **Shelter Point** 4 miles NW, is the site of several resorts. A reef extends 0.4 mile SE from Shelter Point and affords considerable protection to the anchorage in the bay.

143　　**Anchorage** with fair shelter from all but SE winds can be obtained in Oyster Bay in 10 to 20 m about 1 mile offshore.

144　　**Montgomery Bank** *(49°54'N, 124°57'W)* lies in the centre of the Strait of Georgia, SE of Mitlenatch Island. **Sentry Shoal**, on the NW part of Montgomery Bank, has a least depth of 7 m. The meeting of the tidal streams mentioned at the beginning of this chapter usually occurs in this locality.

145　　**Light buoy**. — Sentry Shoal ODAS light buoy "46131" *(509.5)* is moored close south of the shoal.

146　　**Mitlenatch Island** *(49°57'N, 125°00'W)* is rocky with two bare peaks separated by a grassy valley. A shoal spit extends 0.5 mile north from its north extremity, otherwise, the island is steep-to. The best landing is in a semi-protected cove at the SE corner of the island, a small cabin is on the shore of this cove. The island and adjacent waters to 305 m comprise **Mitlenatch Island Nature Park**.

147　　**Tides**. — Tidal differences for Mitlenatch Island (Index No. 7895), referenced on Point Atkinson, are in *Tide Tables, Volume 5*.

Algerine and Shearwater Passages

148　　**Harwood Island** *(49°51'N, 124°40'W)* separates Algerine Passage from Shearwater Passage and is flat topped and wooded. Its south extremity is steep-to, its east side is fringed with boulders and drying reefs extending up to 0.5 mile offshore. Its west side is fringed with steep-to banks of stones and boulders.

149　　**Algerine Passage**, between the north end of Texada Island and Harwood Island, is 2.5 miles wide. **Kiddie Point** is the NW extremity of Texada Island and **Rebecca Rock**, 1.2 miles NNW of Kiddie Point, is 2 m high, bare and foul on all sides.

150　　**Light**. — Rebecca Rock light *(471)* is shown at an elevation of 9.1 m from a white tower. A wind-powered generator is close to the light structure.

151　　**Submarine pipelines** (gas) cross the Strait of Georgia and the north end of Malaspina Strait land at Kiddie Point and are marked by a sign.

152　　**Grilse Point**, the NE extremity of Texada Island, has foul ground extending north and east from it. **Cyril Rock**, north of Grilse Point, dries 3 m.

153　　**Light**. — Cyril Rock light *(470)* is on the rock, off Grisle Point.

154　　**Radio towers**, with red air obstruction lights, are on Grilse Point. The north tower has an elevation of 48 m and the other 57 m.

155　　**Alan Bank** lies 0.7 mile NNW and **Oswald Bank** 0.5 mile NW from Grilse Point.

156　　**Blubber Bay**, on the north side of Texada Island, is entered between **Blubber Point** and **Treat Point**; both points should be given a berth of at least 0.1 mile. Blubber Bay settlement has a post office and is connected by road to Van Anda and Gillies Bay.

Oyster River approach (1990)

Oyster River boat basin (1990)

Approach to boat basin north of Kuhushan Point (1990)

Boat basin north of Kuhushan Point (1990)

Chart 3513

Powell River (1990)

157   **Ferry**. — A ferry, operated by the British Columbia Ferry Services Inc., maintains a regular schedule between Blubber Bay and Westview. Take care not to anchor in the route of this ferry.

158   **Anchorage** can be obtained by large vessels, off the entrance of Blubber Bay in 35 m, sand, with Grilse Point bearing 092° distant about 0.6 mile. Inside the bay the bottom is mud and sand but space is restricted and used frequently by the ferry.

159   **Tides**. — Tidal differences for Blubber Bay (Index No. 7875), referenced on Point Atkinson, are in *Tide Tables, Volume 5.*

160   **Lights**. — A private fixed green light is shown from the end of a catwalk that extends NE from the lime works wharves.

161   A private flashing yellow light and radar reflector are shown from the outer end of the floating leads of the ferry landing.

162   **Berths**. — The wharf on the west side of Blubber Bay has had the float permanently removed and access to the shore is no longer possible.

163   The **ferry landing** is close south of the wharf.

164   The **wharf** on the east side of Blubber Bay is in ruins.

165   **Wharves** and barge loading facilities of a lime works are in the south part of Blubber Bay.

166   **Floats** belonging to the Blubber Bay Boat Club are close west of the lime works wharves.

167   **Shearwater Passage** is bounded on its SE side by Harwood Island and on its NW side by Grant Reefs and Mystery Reef. The fairway is about 2.5 miles wide. The south side of Savary Island has conspicuous white sandy cliffs backed by grassy patches. **Stradiotti Reef** extends about 1 mile from the south shore of Savary Island and has numerous boulders on it.

168   **Vivian Island**, 1 mile west of the south end of Harwood Island, is rocky, treeless and almost flat. A drying rock lies close east of it.

169   **Grant Reefs** *(49°53'N, 124°47'W)* have drying rocks and a rock awash near their east end. **Mystery Reef**, 3 miles SE of Savary Island, is a group of drying boulders connected to Savary Island by a shoal spit. It is steep-to on its SW, south and SE sides. Do not pass between Mystery Reef and Savary Island.

170   **Light buoys**. — Grant Reefs light buoy "QM" *(477)*, close south of the east end of the reefs, is a port bifurcation buoy.

171   Mystery Reef light and bell buoy "Q25" *(478)*, NE of the reef, is a port hand buoy.

Powell River and Westview

Chart 3536

172   **Powell River** *(49°52'N, 124°33'W)*, on the slope of a hill SE of a river of the same name, is the site of a paper mill operated by NorskeCanada. It exports newsprint and imports pulp and general supplies. The port has been used by barges only in recent years. Foreign going cargo vessel have used these facilities in the past, the largest being 178 m long with an approximate draught of 10 m. The town has the usual municipal amenities that include a post office and a hospital.

173   **Approach**. — Is deep and without dangers. **Powell Hill**, 1.8 miles NNE of the town *(Chart 3513)*, has a bare summit and is a conspicuous landmark. Close SE of the main wharves an encircling breakwater of floating hulks protects shore facilities.

Chart 3536

Major Port Facilities — Powell River

Berth	Wharf Length (m)	Least Depth (m)	Elevation (m)	Remarks
NorskeCanada Pier A	148	9		Berth 1 (NW side of pier) has a barge ramp and is used for exporting paper rolls. NOTE: SE winds can cause difficulties when docking. Tugs are available. Berth 2 is general purpose. Lift trucks with a loading rate of 27 tonnes/gang hour.
Pier C	50			Used for tugs and vessel maintenance.
Pier D	179	5.8		Used for unloading pulp. Elevators are decommissioned.
Pier E	128			Used for unloading materials and general supplies. Rail barge berth is close north.

174 **Lights**. — Powell River Floating Breakwater Entrance North and South lights *(476.2, 476.3)*, and the white flashing light marking the NW end of the breakwater *(476.35)*, are private.

175 **Light range**. — Powell River range on the west side of Berth A is private.

176 **Submarine pipelines**. — An outfall pipeline extends 0.45 mile in a SW direction from a position NW of the main wharves. Close south of Powell River, two gas pipelines extend seaward to Kiddie Point on Texada Island, and cross the Strait of Georgia. These pipelines are marked by signs.

177 A **submarine cable** (abandoned) commences from close south of the breakwater and extends seaward through Algerine Passage into the Strait of Georgia.

178 **Anchorage** can be obtained SW of the wharves, but it is exposed to west winds.

179 **Arrival information**. — The port is administered by the Corporation of the District of Powell River through a Harbour Master. The office is located in Westview VHF 68, (604) 485-5244.

180 **Meteorological information** for Powell River is in the Appendices.

181 **Tides**. — Tidal differences for Powell River (Index No. 7880), referenced on Point Atkinson, are in *Tide Tables, Volume 5*.

182 **Berths**. — Depths given for berths are subject to silting but are maintained as necessary by dredging. Details are given in the adjacent table.

183 **Harbour services**. — Tugs are available to assist in docking. Underwater inspection and repair can be carried out by local divers. Hull, engine, electrical and electronic repairs can be done by local firms. Small craft repair facilities including a marine railway are available.

184 **Supplies**. — Provisions are available in quantity from local stores, and diesel fuel and gasoline can be obtained at the public wharf at Westview. Bunker fuel in any large quantities has to be shipped by barge from Vancouver.

185 **Communications**. — There is regular daily bus service to and from Vancouver by road and ferries. The airport has an asphalt runway 1,105 m long and maintains scheduled flights to and from Vancouver. There are regular tug and barge freight services between Powell River, Westview, Seattle and Vancouver, and ferry services for passengers and vehicles from Westview to Little River, near Cape Lazo on Vancouver Island, and to Blubber Bay on Texada Island.

186 **Westview**, 2 miles south of Powell River, is a suburb of Powell River. **The Coast Guard has a year-round rescue unit based at Westview.**

187 **Lights**. — Westview Fishing Harbour South light *(472)* is at the seaward end of the south breakwater.

188 A port hand **daybeacon** is on the south extremity of the middle breakwater.

189 Westview Boat Harbour North light *(476)*, at the north extremity of the north breakwater, is shown at an elevation of 7.6 m from a mast.

190 A private light is close south of the ferry landing.

191 A **submarine pipeline**, marked by a sign, is laid close north of the north breakwater.

192 **Berths**. — The public wharf, between the north and south basins, is used mainly for handling petroleum products. It has a berthing length of 59 m on its west side, 46 m at its north end and 30 m at its south end. The least depth alongside is 9 m on the west side.

193 The **ferry landing** extends from the south side of the public wharf.

194 A **boat harbour**, on the north side of the public wharf, is operated as a marina by the municipality of Powell River, there are no transient facilities. Breakwaters protect its north and west sides and the basin was dredged to 2.4 m (1975). Numerous finger floats are in the basin. Water and power are available at the floats.

195 A **public fishing harbour**, on the south side of the public wharf, is protected by breakwaters to the west and south and was dredged to 2.4 m (1975). A long float extending south has a series of finger floats extending SW from it. Water and power are available at the floats.

196 A **barge loading wharf** behind the south breakwater has depths of 3.6 to 4.2 m.

Powell River to Sarah Point

Chart 3513

197 **Sliammon** *(49°54′N, 124°36′W)* is an Indian village near the mouth of **Sliammon Creek**.

198 **Submarine pipelines** (outfalls) extend about 140 m seaward 1 mile SE of Sliammon and 0.25 mile in a SW direction close north of Sliammon.

199 **Anchorage** can be obtained off Sliammon village but it is open. Keep Dinner Rock *(49°57′N, 124°43′W)* bearing more than 308° and open of the point west of the village.

200 **Atrevida Reef**, 2.5 miles NW of Sliammon, extends 0.3 mile from shore. A prominent house and wind-powered generator are on the point 1.5 miles NW of Atrevida Reef.

201 **Light buoy**. — Atrevida Reef light buoy "Q26" *(477.5)* is a starboard hand buoy.

Westview from south (1990)

Westview from north (1990)

Chart 3513

202   **Dinner Rock**, 2.7 miles NW of Atrevida Reef, is 16 m high and bare.

Chart 3538

203   **Hurtado Point** *(49°58'N, 124°45'W)* is bold and cliffy. **Mace Point**, the east extremity of Savary Island, is bold and steep-to. The channel between Hurtado and Mace Points is deep and free of dangers.

204   **Submarine cables** cross the channel from Lund to the NE end of Savary Island.

205   **Lund**, 1.3 miles NW of Hurtado Point, is a small settlement at the northern terminus of the main highway from Vancouver. A post office, store, hotel and marinas are in the settlement.

206   **Tides.** — Tidal differences for Lund (Index No. 7885), referenced on Point Atkinson, are in *Tide Tables, Volume 5*.

207   A **submarine pipeline** (sewer outfall), marked by a sign, is laid near the public floats.

208   **Lights.** — Lund Breakwater South, Centre and North lights *(478.2, 478.3, 478.4)* are on the breakwater. The north light has a starboard hand daymark.

209   **Buoy.** — Port hand buoy "Q29" marks a rock between the public float and public wharf.

210   **Berths.** — The public wharf, with a depth of 11 m alongside its seaward face, is 24 m long. A 3 tonne crane is available on the wharfhead.

211   **Public floats**, south of the public wharf, are 75 m long and have a common connection to an approach structure. Water and power are available on the floats and washrooms and showers on shore. A water taxi float is in the harbour between the public floats and the wharf head. A rockfill breakwater is south and a floating three section concrete breakwater is west of the floats and also used for mooring.

212   Close north of the public floats are **floats** belonging to the hotel, the south float is a fuel dock.

213   **Finn Cove**, 0.4 mile north of Lund, offers protection to small craft from west winds. A new travel lift with repair and dry storage is on the East side of the bay and can accomadate vessels up to 18 m long and 30 tonnes. A mooring for a barge facility is also in the bay, and a 40 m mooring float with no shore access administered by the Lund Harbour Authority.

214   Anchorage in Finn Cove is not recommended due to underwater hazards.

215   A **submarine pipeline** (water) is laid along the East side of Finn Cove and extends from the hotel marina across to Sevilla Island at the mouth of the cove.

216   An **overhead cable** (telephone), with a vertical clearance of 10 m, crosses from Sevilla Island to the SW shore of Finn Cove. Another overhead cable, with a vertical clearance of 8 m, is NE.

217   **Major Islet** *(49°59'N, 124°49'W)* is bare and composed of white granite. A drying ledge extends 0.1 mile from its NE point and a detached rock, with less than 2 m over it, lies 0.2 mile NE of the islet. The south side of the islet is steep-to.

218   **Light.** — Major Islet light *(479.2)*, on the south end of the islet, is shown at an elevation of 31.1 m from a white tower with a red band at the top.

219   **Thulin Passage** separates **Copeland Islands**, which are known locally as Ragged Islands, from the mainland. The passage, not less than 137 m wide, is used by tugs with logbooms or scows. Logbooms are often secured to the east shore where there are a number of concrete abutments and dolphins. **Copeland Islands**

Marine Park encompasses the Copeland Islands, it has minimal development. A marina is in Sharpes Bay (local name) on the east side of Thulin Passage.

220   **Tidal streams** within Thulin Passage are weak.

221   **Lights.** — Lund light *(479)*, on the SE end of the south Copeland Island, is shown at an elevation of 6.4 m from a white tower.

222   Thulin Passage light *(479.5)* is on the north end of Copeland Islands.

223   **Bliss Landing** *(50°02'N, 124°49'W)* is at the head of **Turner Bay**. A marina, private floats and homes are located around the bay.

224   **Beacon.** — Bliss Landing daybeacon, on a rock near the north side of Turner Bay, has a starboard hand daymark.

225   **Powell Islets** *(50°02'N, 124°52'W)* and **Townley Islands** have a reef with less than 2 m over it between them, pass west of Powell Islets.

226   **Sarah Point**, the NW extremity of **Malaspina Peninsula**, is rounded and rocky. A hill rises a short distance within the point and from its summit the land on the NE side slopes gradually to the water's edge.

227   **Marine farm** facilities are 1 mile south of Sarah Point.

228   A **submarine cable area** crosses south of Sarah Point, to Tiber Bay on Cortes Island. A submarine cable is laid south of the cable area and extends from south of Sarah Point to NNW of Mary Point.

Manson Passage

229   **Manson Passage**, between **Savary Island** *(49°56'N, 124°50'W)* and **Hernando Island**, is only suitable for small craft, local knowledge is advised. A drying rock lies in mid-channel and a drying spit, with large boulders on it, extends 1.3 miles south from **Ashworth Point**. A drying ledge with large boulders on it extends 0.4 mile west from Savary Island. **Keefer Rock** lies 1.3 miles ENE of Ashworth Point.

230   **Tidal streams** attain 2 kn at times. A strong wind opposing the tide creates rough, steep seas in the shallow waters of Manson Passage.

231   **Keefer Bay**, on the north side and at the east end of Savary Island, has a drying spit on its west side that extends 0.6 mile north from the island. It is reported that the soft sand bottom off Savary Island affords a poor holding ground. The public wharf in Keefer Bay has a wharfhead length of 12 m and is equipped with a 3 tonne crane. A float for small craft is secured to the south side of the wharfhead. There is a store and water taxi service to and from Lund.

232   **Light.** — Savary Island wharf light *(478.5)*, on the wharf on the N side of the island, is shown at an elevation of 6.4 m from the top of a shed on the public wharf.

Baker Passage

233   **Baker Passage**, between Hernando Island and **Twin Islands**, is deep and about 0.7 mile wide at its narrowest part. **Spilsbury Point** *(50°00'N, 124°57'W)* is low, sandy and covered with trees.

Lund (1990)

Bliss Landing (1990)

Thulin Passage from south (1990)

Thulin Passage from Turner Bay (1990)

Chart 3538

234   **Tides**. — Tidal differences for Twin Islands (Index No. 7892), referenced on Point Atkinson, are in *Tide Tables, Volume 5*.

235   **Tidal streams** in Baker Passage attain 2 kn at times.

236   **Light**. — Spilsbury Point light *(481.5)*, on the N tip of Hernado Island, is shown at an elevation of 6.1 m from a white tower.

237   **Local magnetic disturbances** have been experienced in the vicinity of Spilsbury Point.

238   **Stag Bay**, between Spilsbury and Hidalgo Points, has a conspicuous white boulder on its shore about 0.7 mile west of **Hidalgo Point**. Private wharves are in Stag Bay. **Dog Bay**, SE of Hidalgo Point, has **Dog Rock** in its north part and drying rocks in its centre. **Iron Point** is the SE extremity of Twin Islands and **Echo Bay** lies close west of it.

239   **Little Rock**, in the west entrance to the channel between Twin Islands and Cortes Island, is 4 m high. **Central Rock** is a drying rock midway between the north end of Twin Islands and Cortes Island. Drying ledges and reefs extend from the SE coast of Cortes Island between Little Rock and Sutil Point.

240   **Marine farm** facilities are off the NW shore of the north Twin Island.

241   **Three Islets** *(50°03'N, 124°55'W)*, in the approach to Cortes Bay, are white, bare and rocky.

242   **Cortes Bay** has a narrow entrance encumbered with a drying rock with a light on it. When entering Cortes Bay pass to the south of the light. A rock with 2.7 m over it lies in the centre of the bay.

243   **Sewage disposal** in the waters of Cortes Bay is prohibited under the *Pleasure/Non-Pleasure Craft Sewage Pollution Prevention Regulations*.

244   The **public float**, on the SW side of the bay, is 87 m long with a depth of 9 m alongside. Yacht club floats are on the north and south shores.

245   **Light**. — Cortes Bay light *(481)* is on a drying rock in the entrance.

246   **Anchorage** can be obtained in Cortes Bay in 9 to 15 m, soft mud bottom, but holding ground is poor. NW winds funnel in from the head of the bay and with strong SE winds a confused sea can be encountered.

Baynes Sound

Chart 3527

247   **Baynes Sound** *(49°30'N, 124°47'W)* separates **Denman Island** from Vancouver Island. It is entered from the south between Chrome Island and Mapleguard Point. From the north, it is entered by way of Comox Bar. Generally, the sound is about 1 mile wide, broadening to about 2 miles at its north end. The fairway is reduced in several places by extensive drying sand and mud flats, its narrowest part, between Mapleguard and Repulse Points, is 0.3 mile wide. Many drying flats are leased for commercial oyster production. The E&N Railway and a road run along the west shore of the sound.

248   **Marine farming**. — Baynes Sound is one of the largest oyster producing regions on the British Columbia coast. Tidelands are leased for commercial production of oysters and harvesting oysters in these areas is a criminal offence. Some facilities are marked by buoys.

249   **Tides**. — Tidal differences in Baynes Sound, referenced on Point Atkinson, for Denman Island (Index No. 7955) and Comox (Index No. 7965) are in *Tide Tables, Volume 5*.

250   **Tidal streams** in Baynes Sound attain 2 or 3 kn in the south entrance, but within the sound the rate is considerably less, decreasing as the channel widens. When tide flows against an opposing wind a nasty chop can be raised that can be uncomfortable for small craft. For further details see *Current Atlas, Juan de Fuca Strait to Strait of Georgia*.

251   **Ferry**. — Regular ferry service crosses Baynes Sound connecting Denman Island to Buckley Bay on Vancouver Island.

Chrome Island to Comox Bar

252   **Chrome Island** *(49°28'N, 124°41'W)*, known locally as Yellow Island, is bare and yellow. White buildings with red roofs make a conspicuous landmark. **Boyle Point**, the south extremity of Denman Island, is steep sided and flanked on its east side by massive yellow sandstone pillars streaked with guano.

253   **Overhead cables**, with a vertical clearance of 15 m, cross between Chrome Island and Boyle Point; they are marked by red and white air obstruction balls.

254   **Light range**. — Chrome (Yellow) Island Range lights *(495, 496)*, in line bearing 098°, lead through the channel south of Repulse Point. The front light shown at an elevation of 14 m from a mast, visible in line of the range only, is fitted with a red daymark with a white vertical stripe. The rear light shown at an elevation of 22 m from a white tower, 7.6 m high, is on the east end of the island.

255   **Mapleguard Point** is low, few maple trees remain and there are houses all along the point. Exercise caution when rounding Mapleguard Point because of shoal water extending 0.5 mile east and drying sand flats extending 0.3 mile north from it.

Baynes Sound south entrance (1991)

Cortes Bay (1985)

Cortes Bay public float (1985)

Chart 3527

256   **Repulse Point** is a cliff of red earth. A drying reef extends about 0.3 mile south from the point.

257   **Buoys. — Light buoys**. — Starboard hand buoy "P40" marks the extremity of the reef extending from Repulse Point. Port hand buoy "P41" marks the west extremity of the drying sand flats extending from Mapleguard Point.

258   Maple Spit light buoy "P39" *(497.5)*, marking the north extremity of the drying flats extending from Mapleguard Point, is a port hand buoy.

259   Repulse Point light buoy "P42" *(498)*, 0.7 mile WSW of Repulse Point, is a starboard hand buoy.

260   **Light**. — Deep Bay light *(497)*, on the SW extremity of Mapleguard Point, is shown at an elevation of 9.1 m from a white tower with a green band at the top.

261   **Deep Bay** *(49°28′N, 124°44′W)* has a marina and public floats near its SE end. Public floats, 18 to 146 m long, have a common connection to a pier and are protected by a floating breakwater. A 3 tonne crane, public telephone, garbage and used oil disposal facilities are on the pier. A sewage pumpout facility is located on the main off-loading float. Washroom and shower facilities are located near the office at the pier entrance and near the parking lot. Tidal grids lie on both sides of the pier. Power and fresh water are available on the floats, groceries are obtainable nearby. Several private floats and mooring buoys are in the bay. The wreck of a 14 m fishing vessel, sunk in 2003, is 0.1 mile WNW of the public floats. It is reported to lie in 18 m of water.

262   **Marine farm** facilities, in Deep and Mud Bays, consist of longline oyster culture rafts and buoys.

263   **Anchorage** can be obtained in Deep Bay in a depth of about 30 m, mud bottom.

264   **Mud Bay** is encumbered with mud flats with numerous boulders, and fronted by steep-to drying reefs. A rock awash is in the centre of the south entrance. The bay has a booming ground and a marina, which is protected by a breakwater. The channel leading to the marina dries.

265   **Ship Peninsula** *(49°30′N, 124°48′W)* is fringed with reefs extending 0.15 mile from shore. A housing development on its east side and dark trees make the peninsula conspicuous. Land west of it is low and partially cleared of trees. **Base Flat**, 1.5 miles NW of Ship Peninsula, is encircled by a steep-to drying mud flat, its outer extremity is marked by port hand **buoy** "P43".

266   **Fanny Bay** is bounded on its south side by a drying mud flat and on its NW side by the drying flat off Base Flat. When entering from the south, give **Ship Point** a berth of not less than 0.3 mile. Marine farm facilities and a booming ground are in the bay.

267   The settlement of Fanny Bay has a store, hotel and restaurant, the post office is 1.6 km north.

268   A **conspicuous white tower**, close SW of the public wharf, is 39 m high.

269   **Wharf**. — The public wharf in Fanny Bay has a depth of 4.6 m at its head. A float is attached to the NW end of the public wharf.

270   **Anchorage** in Fanny Bay can be obtained in 13 to 15 m, mud bottom, with the extremity of Ship Point in line with the SW extremity of Denman Island bearing 117° and Denman Island light structure bearing 345°.

271   **Submarine cables** cross Baynes Sound between Base Flat and Denman Island settlement.

272   **Buckley Bay** is the site of a ferry landing from which regular service operates to Denman Island. The south part of the bay has a booming ground and barge loading berth.

273   **Light. — Fog signal**. — Buckley Bay Ferry Landing light *(496.2)*, on a dolphin, is private. Radar reflectors are shown from the ferry landing. The fog signal is operated by ferry personnel when required for ferry movements.

274   **Denman Island** village, on the east side of Baynes Sound opposite Buckley Bay, is the site of a ferry landing that provides regular service to Buckley Bay. A post office and store are within walking distance of the public wharf. There is road connection to the ferry landing at Gravelly Bay, then by ferry to Hornby Island.

275   **Tides**. — Tidal differences for Denman Island (Index No. 7955), referenced on Point Atkinson, are in *Tide Tables, Volume 5*.

276   **Berths**. — The public wharf, close south of the ferry landing, has a berthing length of 34 m with a depth of 5.5 m alongside. A float, attached to the inner side of the wharfhead, is 24 m long.

277   A **boat harbour**, close south of the public wharf, is protected by a pile and timber breakwater.

278   **Lights. — Fog signal**. — Denman Island Ferry Landing light *(496.1)*, on the W side of island, on a dolphin, is private. Radar reflectors are shown from the ferry landing. The fog signal is operated by ferry personnel when required for ferry movements.

279   Denman Island light *(499)*, on a reef 0.3 mile NW of the ferry landing, is shown at an elevation of 6.1 m from a white tower with a red band at the top.

280   **Denman Point**, 1.5 miles NW of the ferry landing, is low. Good anchorage can be obtained 0.35 mile NNW from Denman Point and about 0.25 mile offshore. The anchorage may be restricted by marine farm facilities. Starboard hand **buoy** "P44" marks a drying ledge off Denman Point.

281   **Marine farm** facilities are in several locations along the Denman Island shore.

282   **Union Bay** *(49°35′N, 124°53′W)* was a bunkering and shipping port for coal, facilities and mines closed in 1959. The settlement of Union Bay is connected to the Island Highway and the E&N Railway, it has a hotel, post office and a store. A log dump and booming ground are in the bay. A rockfill breakwater protects a launching ramp.

283   **Anchorage** can be obtained close offshore in the vicinity of Union Bay.

284   **Union Point**, north of Union Bay, is fronted by an extensive drying flat, marked at its outer end by port hand **buoy** "P45".

285   An A-frame and **booming ground** are 0.5 mile NNW of Union Point.

286   **Henry Bay** *(49°36′N, 124°50′W)* is the site of commercial oyster beds. A sand and mud drying spit extends 2.5 miles NNW from **Longbeak Point**, the north extremity of Denman Island, and terminates at **White Spit**. **Sandy Island**, known locally as Tree Island, and **Seal Islets** lie on the above-mentioned drying spit and comprise **Sandy Island Marine Park**. **Palliser Rock** lies close-off its east edge.

287   **Anchorages**. — Safe and convenient anchorage can be obtained in Henry Bay in about 16 m. Good temporary anchorage for small craft is available to the west of Sandy Island where the sand spit drops off sharply, or south of the island with good

Chrome Island

Deep Bay (1991)

Fanny Bay (1991)

Chart 3527

protection from the NW. The sand spit between Sandy Island and Longbeak Point protects this anchorage from SE seas but not from SE winds.

Comox Bar

288   **Comox Bar** extends NNW from White Spit to the beach fronting **Willemar Bluff** *(49°40'N, 124°54'W)*. The passage across the bar is marked by range lights and the least depth on this range, cleared by a wire drag, was 2.4 m in 1969. Several vessels have reported grounding while crossing the shallowest part of the bar. Tide, sea state, and vessel draught must be carefully considered before a decision is made to cross the bar.

289   **Caution. — To assure clearing the shallow spit extending SE from Cape Lazo, when approaching Comox Bar from the north, do not haul in for the leading line until Willemar Bluff bears more than 250°. When departing Comox note the range is obscured by houses and trees until about 0.1 mile from the leading line.**

290   **Light range**. — Comox Bar range lights *(501, 502)*, on the west shore of Baynes Sound about 2 miles west of Sandy Island, when in line bearing 222° indicate the track across Comox Bar.

291   **Light buoy. — Buoys**. — Comox Bar light and bell buoy "P54" *(500)*, at the east edge of Comox Bar and close north of the leading line, is a starboard hand buoy.

292   Starboard hand buoys "P50" and "P52" are on Comox Bar SW of the light buoy; buoy "P50" has a radar reflector.

Comox Harbour

293   **Gartley Point** *(49°39'N, 124°55'W)*, the south entrance point to Comox Harbour, is low and swampy. Port hand buoy "P47" marks the east edge of the drying flats around the point.

294   **Goose Spit**, on the north side of the entrance to Comox Harbour, is a narrow tongue of land extending SW and west from Willemar Bluff. It is mainly grassy, with some sandy hillocks and clumps of trees. A Canadian Forces Base (HMCS Quadra) is on the middle section of the spit. An Indian Reserve is on the north side and a regional park is on the narrow section of land at the east end of the spit. A drying sand flat extends south from the south side of Goose Spit for about 0.25 mile in places, the west side of this flat is steep-to. A booming ground with mooring buoys is north of the spit.

295   **Lights**. — Goose Spit light *(503)* is on the west extremity of the spit.

296   Comox Harbour breakwater light *(504)* is 0.6 mile NNW of Goose Spit light on the seaward end of the west breakwater.

297   Comox Harbour East breakwater light *(504.1)* is on the outer end of the east breakwater, 0.5 mile north of Goose Spit light.

298   **Comox Harbour**, entered between Gartley Point and Goose Spit, is a well-protected anchorage available to all but very large vessels. Depths range from 20 to 26 m and drying mud flats extend a considerable distance from its shores.

299   **Approach**. — The approach to Comox Harbour through Baynes Sound is deep.

300   **Local magnetic disturbance**, 2° in excess of the normal variation, has been reported but it does not appear to extend beyond the confines of the harbour.

301   **Tides and Currents**. — Tidal differences for Comox (Index No. 7965), referenced on Point Atkinson, are in *Tide Tables, Volume 5*.

302   Tidal streams in Comox Harbour are complicated by eddies due to fresh water discharged by the Courtenay River, which causes surface currents to flow in directions different from those of the salt water underneath. In addition these latter are complicated by configuration of the mud banks.

303   **Meteorological information** for Comox is in the Appendices.

304   A **submarine pipeline** (sewer outfall) crosses the drying flats north of Goose Spit and extends 0.5 mile SE of the spit.

305   **Anchorage** in 20 to 26 m can be obtained almost anywhere as convenient. Small craft can obtain anchorage off Royston. It is partially protected from southeasterlies by the mud flats of the **Trent River** off Gartley Point.

306   **Royston**, about 1 mile west of Gartley Point on the south side of Comox Harbour, is a settlement connected to the Island Highway and on the E&N Railway. It has a store, hotel, boat launching ramp and post office.

307   A **breakwater of derelict ships**, close west of Royston at the outer end of the Courtenay River mud flats, provides protection for a booming ground.

308   **Comox**, on the north side of the harbour, is a town and the centre of an agricultural district. It is the site of a Canadian Forces Base (airfield). Facilities include accommodation, stores, marinas and boat launching sites, a hospital and post office.

309   **Breakwaters. — Fishing Pier**. — Rockfill breakwaters, protecting the boat basins, extend ESE and WNW from the outer end of the causeway that leads to the public wharf. A public recreation and fishing pier is on the western breakwater. A rockfill breakwater that protects a marina is west of the fishing pier.

310   **Marine farm** facilities are close south of the east breakwater.

311   **Berths**. — An oil wharf on the south side of the harbour at Royston is connected to shore by a pier, 366 m long. Its outer berthing face is 30 m long with depths of 3 to 4.2 m alongside. It is for unloading petroleum products only.

312   A **Department of National Defence (DND) wharf** is at the east end of the harbour, on the north side of Goose Spit. A DND wharf on the north shore of the harbour extends south from the outer end of the causeway leading to the public wharf.

313   The **west boat basin**, entered between the fishing pier and the breakwater west of it, has the public wharf extending WNW from the causeway. Extensive public floats are attached to the public wharf. Water and power are laid on the floats.

314   The **east boat basin**, entered east of the eastern breakwater, has extensive public floats extending ESE from the causeway. Power and water are laid on the floats.

315   **Marinas** are close north and west of the public floats in the west boat basin.

316   **Supplies**. — Provisions, diesel fuel and gasoline are obtainable from the marinas.

317   **Harbour services**. — The harbour has several launching ramps for small craft. It also has a marine railway, small craft can obtain hull and engine repairs.

318   **Communications**. — Highway transportation services are available. The E&N Railway operates between Courtenay and Victoria. Scheduled air services are available at Comox Airport. Ferry service to Powell River operates from Little River, 5 miles north of Comox.

319   **Courtenay River** has an estuary filled with drying mud flats. The channel across these drying flats is marked by daybeacons and ranges and was dredged (1982) to a width of 35 m and to a depth that dries 1 m. The river is fed partly by tributaries leading

Comox (1990)

Comox boat basin (1990)

Courtenay River (1990)

Courtenay River (1990)

Chart 3527

from glaciers and snow-fields on **Forbidden Plateau**. Even in late summer, when most other island rivers are almost dry, there is usually 1.8 m of water right up to the Courtenay Bridge south of Lewis Park.

320 **Water levels** in the estuary are affected by tidal and weather conditions along with fresh water runoff that is controlled by a B.C. Hydro dam upstream. It is essential that mariners check local water level conditions before attempting to navigate the river.

321 **Water aerodrome**. — The mouth of the Courtenay River is a water aerodrome.

322 **Caution. — Aids to navigation. — Because of changing conditions in the estuary aids to navigation are moved to mark the best channel. Local knowledge and familiarity with local conditions are advised before attempting to navigate the river. Numerous deadheads can be encountered in the channel.**

323 **Light**. — Courtenay River beacon #1 light *(504.3)*, on mud flats in the river entrance, is shown from a dolphin with two port hand daymarks.

324 **Light range**. — Courtenay River range lights *(505, 506)*, on the north bank of the river, form a leading line across the mud flats.

325 **Beacon ranges**. — Range beacons, each with a diamond-shaped daymark, form leading lines through the channel from Courtenay River range lights into the Courtenay River.

326 **Speed limit** of 8 km/h (4 kn) is prescribed by the *Boating Restriction Regulations* for Courtenay River.

327 A **highway bridge** with a lift span, operated by the Ministry of Transportation and Highways, crosses Courtenay River. The bridge has a vertical clearance of 2.1 m and maximum width of the channel is 13.7 m. To request an opening of the bridge telephone (250) 336-8897 at least 24 hours in advance. A float, on the west shore downstream of the bridge, can be used for temporary mooring while waiting for the bridge to open.

328 **Overhead cables** (power), upstream from the bridge, have a vertical clearance of 18 m.

329 **Submarine pipelines** cross the Courtenay River.

330 A fixed span **highway bridge**, upstream from the overhead cables, crosses the Courtenay River.

331 **Courtenay** is the terminus of the E&N Railway from Victoria. It has a post office, banks, comprehensive shopping facilities, doctors, dentists and pharmacies. Bus service operates to Nanaimo and Campbell River. An aircraft landing strip with an asphalt runway 549 m long is operated by the city.

332 **Facilities**. — Two sets of marine railways, which can handle vessels up to 21 m, are located in Courtenay River. Engine repairs can be made, diesel fuel and gasoline are obtainable. A public float is in the basin between the overhead cables and the fixed span highway bridge. There are several small wharves with berthing lengths of 37 m and depths alongside up to 1.8 m at river LW.

Welcome Passage

Chart 3535

333 **Welcome Passage** *(49°30′N, 123°56′W)*, at the SE end of Malaspina Strait, separates **Thormanby Islands** from the British Columbia mainland. The fairway is deep but has several dangers on either side, it has a minimum width of 0.2 mile.

334 **Magnetic anomaly**. — A local magnetic disturbance has been reported in Welcome Passage.

335 **Tidal streams** are strongest in the narrow portion of Welcome Passage where 2 to 3 kn can be expected, the flood sets NW and the ebb SE. At the south end of the passage streams decrease in strength and seldom attain more than 2 kn.

336 In the south entrance, the flood stream has a tendency to set toward dangers off Lemberg Point. The ebb stream generally sets fairly through the channel and its south approach.

337 **Submarine cables**. — A cable crosses the channel between Merry Island and Sechelt Peninsula. An abandoned cable is laid across Welcome Passage close NW of Jeddah Point. A cable commences at the head of Halfmoon Bay and passes along the centre of the passage, landing in Buccaneer Bay at Oaks Point.

338 The south entrance to Welcome Passage is between **Reception Point**, on the mainland, and **Dennis Head**, the SE extremity of **South Thormanby Island**. **Bertha Island** lies 0.3 mile SW and **Pirate Rock** lies 0.2 mile SE of Dennis Head. **Merry Island** and **Franklin Island** lie in the centre of the south entrance. A shoal, with 9.1 m over it, lies in mid-channel east of Merry Island and a 10.1 m shoal lies 0.2 mile north of Merry Island. Foul ground, with an islet and drying rocks, extends 0.2 mile south of Merry Island. The channel west of Merry Island is deep.

339 **Lights**. — Reception Point light *(448.8)*, on a drying spit extending south from the point, is shown at an elevation of 7.3 m from a white tower with a red band at the top.

340 Merry Island light *(449)*, on the SE extremity of island at the SE entrance to Welcome Passage, is shown at an elevation of 18.3 m from a white tower 8.2 m high. Conspicuous white buildings with red roofs stand nearby.

341 **Buoy**. — South cardinal buoy "QK" is 0.3 mile SE of Merry Island.

342 **Beacon**. — Pirate Rock daybeacon has a port hand daymark.

343 **Meteorological information** and a frequency of fog table for Merry Island are in the Appendices.

344 **Simson Marine Park** encompasses the south and east portion of South Thormanby Island and is undeveloped.

345 **Lemberg Point**, 1.5 miles north of Pirate Rock, has several rocks east and SE of it. **Fraser Rock**, 0.2 mile east, has 2.1 m over it. **Egerton Rock**, 0.4 mile SE, has 2.3 m over it.

346 **Jeddah Point**, 0.7 mile NNE of Lemberg Point, is the west entrance point to Halfmoon Bay. Islets and rocks extend SE from it. A rock, with less than 2 m over it, lies 0.4 mile SE of Jeddah Point.

347 **Grant Island**, 0.9 mile NW of Jeddah Point, is separated from **Wilbraham Point** by a narrow passage obstructed by drying reefs.

348 **Light**. — Wilbraham Point light *(450)* is shown at an elevation of 10.7 m from a white tower with a red band at the top on the west side of Grant Island.

349 **Derby Point** is the north extremity of South Thormanby Island. **Tattenham Ledge** is a narrow reef extending 0.5 mile NNW from Derby Point. The shoalest part of this reef dries 0.3 m.

350 **Light buoy**. — Tattenham Ledge light buoy "Q51" *(451)*, at the north extremity of the ledge, is a port hand buoy.

Chart 3535

Merry Island lighthouse from east

Halfmoon Bay

351   **Halfmoon Bay** *(49°30'N, 123°56'W)* is exposed to the south and during SE winds a heavy sea sets into it. **Priestland Cove**, at the head of Halfmoon Bay, has above-water and drying rocks in it. Numerous private floats are in the small coves along the north shore of Halfmoon Bay.

352   **Booming grounds** lie along the shores of Halfmoon Bay and Priestland Cove.

353   **Submarine pipelines**. — A sewer outfall extends almost 0.2 mile offshore from 0.4 mile WNW of the public wharf in Priestland Cove. Another pipeline in **Brooks Cove**, 0.3 mile NE of Jeddah Point, extends about 0.3 mile into Halfmoon Bay.

354   **Tides**. — Tidal differences for Halfmoon Bay (Index No. 7830), referenced on Point Atkinson, are in *Tide Tables, Volume 5*.

355   **Anchorage** in Halfmoon Bay is not recommended. In fine weather small craft can obtain anchorage in Priestland Cove.

356   **Halfmoon Bay** settlement, at the head of Priestland Cove, has a post office, a store and resorts. The road to Howe Sound passes through the settlement. **Redroofs**, on the east side of Priestland Cove, is a summer resort.

357   **Wharf**. — The public wharf at Halfmoon Bay has a berthing length of 12 m on the west side of its head, with depths of 3 m alongside. A float, on the west side of the wharf, is 27 m long with depths of 1 to 2.7 m alongside.

Buccaneer Bay

358   **Buccaneer Bay** *(49°30'N, 123°59'W)*, entered between Derby Point and **Oaks Point**, lies between the NW side of South Thormanby Island and the east side of North Thormanby Island. At the SW end of the bay, the two islands are joined by a drying flat. **Surrey Islands**, on the east side of the bay, are steep-to on their west sides but the channel east of them is foul. **Vaucroft Beach** is a summer resort on the west side of the bay.

359   **Caution must be exercised when entering Buccaneer Bay because of Tattenham Ledge and the shoal water extending north from the north end of North Thormanby Island**. The middle of **Gill Beach**, at the head of the bay, bearing 165°, leads in the fairway between these dangers and to the anchorage.

360   **Beacon**. — Buccaneer Bay daybeacon, on a drying rock in the entrance to **Water Bay**, has a port hand daymark.

361   **Anchorage** can be obtained between **Wolf Point** and **Grassy Point** in a depth of about 30 m, sand bottom. It is exposed to north winds.

362   **Wharf**. — The public wharf at Vaucroft Beach has a berthing length of 12 m. A float attached to the wharf is 18 m long, the wharf and float have a depth of 5.4 m alongside. These facilities are for loading only.

363   **Buccaneer Bay Park** at Grassy Point has limited on-shore development.

Smuggler Cove

364   **Smuggler Cove** *(49°31'N, 123°58'W)* is only suitable for small craft, **great care is required when entering the cove**. A provincial park sign with a dogwood emblem is on the north side of the entrance. It is entered by passing close south of **Isle Capri**. Two islets, 0.2 mile within the entrance, are connected to the south shore by drying ledges. **France Islet**, the higher of the two, has drying reefs extending north and east from it. A rock, with 0.9 m over it, lies in the middle of the cove NW of France Islet.

365   **Beacon**. — Smuggler Cove daybeacon, on the drying reef extending north from France Islet, has a starboard hand daymark.

366   **Sewage disposal** in the waters of Smuggler Cove is prohibited under the *Pleasure/Non-Pleasure Craft Sewage Pollution Prevention Regulations*.

367   **Anchorage** in Smuggler Cove is suitable for small craft and affords good protection with fairly good holding ground.

368   **Smuggler Cove Marine Park** has camping and sanitary facilities and is connected to the highway between Powell River and Howe Sound.

Secret Cove

369   **Secret Cove**, entered between the south end of **Turnagain Island** *(49°32'N, 123°58'W)* and **Jack Tolmie Island**, is only suitable for small craft. A drying rock lies in the entrance and a rock with 1.5 m over it lies about 0.15 mile NE of the drying rock. The cove consists of three arms and has several marinas. Fuel,

Priestland Cove (1990)

Halfmoon Bay public wharf (1990)

Smuggler Cove (1990)

Secret Cove entrance (1990)

Chart 3535

water and provisions are obtainable. Numerous private floats and moorings line the shores. Secret Cove is on the main highway between Powell River and Howe Sound.

370   **Speed limit**. — A yellow sign, on the SE end of Turnagain Island, reads "*Speed 5 MPH*".

371   **Light**. — Secret Cove Entrance light *(450.5)*, on the drying rock in the entrance to Secret Cove, has a starboard hand daymark.

372   **Beacon**. — Secret Cove daybeacon, on the north side of the entrance to the south arm of the cove, has a port hand daymark.

373   **Buoys**. — Buoys marked "Outfall" mark the submarine pipeline east of Turnagain Island, these are private.

374   **Submarine cables and pipelines** in Secret Cove are marked by signs. Sanitary outfalls commence on the north side of the cove and pass close east of Turnagain Island and down the entrance channel between Turnagain and Jack Tolmie Islands. A pipeline crosses the south arm and a cable crosses the entrance to the south and east arms. Cables are laid from the 50 m high island, known locally as Echo Island, to the shore north of it.

375   **Anchorage** for small craft can be obtained near the head of the north arm.

376   The **public float**, in the north arm of Secret Cove, is 44 m long with a depth of 4.6 m alongside. Power is available.

377   Ole's Cove (local name), 0.2 mile NW of the north extremity of Turnagain Island, has marina facilities.

Malaspina Strait

Charts 3512, 3513

378   **Malaspina Strait** *(49°30'N, 124°04'W)* separates the NE side of Texada Island from the mainland of British Columbia. It is entered from the south between Epsom and Upwood Points, or by way of Welcome Passage. The north entrance points are Grief Point and Grilse Point. Texada Island has a bold shoreline with narrow beaches of shingle or boulders. Agamemnon Channel, on the mainland side of Malaspina Strait, separates Nelson Island from Sechelt Peninsula. Jervis Inlet is entered along the north sides of Hardy and Nelson Islands. Malaspina Strait is 27 miles long with a least width of 2.5 miles and the fairway is deep.

379   **Sinclair Bank** *(49°42'N, 124°16'W)*, in mid-channel, has 33 m over it.

380   **Tides**. — Tidal differences along Malaspina Strait for Irvines Landing (Index No. 7836), Blind Bay (Index No. 7865), Blubber Bay (Index No. 7875) and Powell River (Index No. 7880), referenced on Point Atkinson, are in *Tide Tables, Volume 5*.

381   **Tidal streams** in the strait are generally weak, and seldom exceed 1 kn, see *Current Atlas, Juan de Fuca Strait to Strait of Georgia*.

382   **Weather**. — Sea and wind conditions east of Upwood Point are often completely different from conditions to the west. With strong west or NW winds the razor back ridge of Texada Island acts as a wind break and calm conditions often prevail as far north as Pender Harbour.

383   **Submarine pipelines** (gas) cross Malaspina Strait from south of Wood Bay on the mainland to north of Anderson Bay on Texada Island.

384   **Submarine cables** cross Malaspina Strait from Cape Cockburn, on Nelson Island, to Texada Island *(49°38'N, 124°17'W)*.

They are marked by flashing yellow lights on both shores. Another cable area crosses the north end of the strait from Grief Point, on the mainland, to Van Anda Cove on Texada Island.

385   **Spoil ground**. — An ocean dump site, under permit through the *Ocean Dumping Control Act*, is in *49°45'N, 124°27'W*.

Upwood Point to Northeast Point

Chart 3512

386   **Anderson Bay**, 1.5 miles north of Upwood Point, offers very good protection from all except SE winds. An island lies across the entrance. The passage north of this island has a drying rock close-off the north entrance point, pass south of this rock. A log dump and booming ground are in the bay.

387   The **submarine pipelines** (gas) that crosses Malaspina Strait lands on the Texada Island shore 0.7 mile north of Anderson Bay.

388   **Mount Grant** *(49°37'N, 124°18'W)* has power cables on it's north slope ascending from the shoreline.

389   **Light**. — A flashing yellow light, 5.5 miles SE of Northeast Point, is maintained by B.C. Hydro to mark the landing site of the submarine cable area.

390   **Northeast Point** *(49°42'N, 124°21'W)* has a radio tower with red air obstruction lights 3 miles west of it on **Mount Pocahontas**. **Northeast Bay**, 1 mile NW of the point, has McQuarry Island (local name) near its centre and affords some shelter for small craft from west and SE winds.

391   **Light**. — Northeast Point light *(467)* is shown at an elevation of 9.4 m from a white tower with a green band at the top. A windmill generator is near the light.

Epsom Point to Black (Albion) Point

392   **North Thormanby Island** *(49°30'N, 124°00'W)* is flat topped and wooded. A conspicuous white cliff on the north end of the island has boulders at its foot. **Epsom Point** forms the west extremity of the island.

393   **Light**. — Epsom Point light *(452)* is shown at an elevation of 6.5 m from a mast, 8.7 m high, close-off the point.

394   **Wood Bay** *(49°33'N, 123°59'W)* has marine farm facilities, marked by cautionary buoys close north and 0.5 mile SE of it. **Bjerre Shoal**, 1.2 miles NW of **McNaughton Point**, has 5.2 m over it.

395   **Submarine pipelines** (gas) cross Malaspina Strait from 0.4 mile SE of Wood Bay.

396   **Anchorage** for small craft, with fair shelter, can be obtained inside **Harness Island**. A marina, protected by a breakwater, and marine farm facilities are on the mainland east of the island.

397   The approaches to Bargain Bay, Pender Harbour and Agamemnon Channel lie between Harness Island and Fearney Point, 4.5 miles NW.

398   **Nelson Island** *(49°40'N, 124°10'W)* is indented by several bays on its south and west sides. This coast should be given a berth of at least 1 mile to ensure clearing several shoals and rocks. **Nelson Rock**, 1 mile west of Fearney Point and about 0.5 mile offshore, is steep-to. **Acland Rock**, 1.3 miles WNW of Nelson Rock, has 7.9 m over it.

Chart 3512

Anderson Bay (1985)

399   **Light**. — Nelson Rock light *(456)* is shown at an elevation of 5.2 m from a white tower with a red band at the top. A large rectangular base of a former light structure is beside the light.

400   **Submarine cables** run parallel to the south and west coasts of Nelson Island.

401   **Mermaid Point**, 0.6 mile NW of Nelson Rock, is the east entrance point to Quarry Bay. **Flat Rock Bay**, the second small bay NW of Mermaid Point, has a private float.

402   **Quarry Bay** has submarine cables along its centre, do not anchor here. Small craft can find anchorage close to shore. Numerous above and below-water rocks are at the head of the bay. Private floats, a floating log breakwater and private mooring buoys are near the head of the bay.

403   **Wharf**. — A pier, on the south coast of Nelson Island about 2 miles west of Quarry Bay and 1 mile east of Cape Cockburn, is 110 m long and has a float 137 m long at its outer end. It is used by barges for loading gravel and has a conveyor on it.

404   **Cape Cockburn** *(49°40'N, 124°12'W)* is composed of white granite and has a few stunted trees on its summit. A drying rock lies 0.1 mile south of the cape. A B.C. Hydro terminal for submarine cables is on the cape, the cable towers are conspicuous.

405   **Lights**. — Cape Cockburn light *(455)*, on the cape on the W side of Nelson Island, is shown at an elevation of 15.2 m from a white tower with a red band at the top.

406   A flashing yellow light, about 0.2 mile north of Cape Cockburn light, maintained by B.C. Hydro marks the landing site of the submarine cables.

407   **Submarine cables and pipelines**. — A cable area crosses Malaspina Strait from the vicinity of Cape Cockburn. A water intake pipe and an outfall pipe enter Malaspina Strait in the vicinity of the cape.

408   **Cockburn Bay** has an entrance less than 90 m wide and is almost completely obstructed by drying rocks. It can be entered by small craft at or near HW, local knowledge is advised. A submarine cable passes through the entrance and lands on the south shore of the bay. Marine farm facilities, private floats and a B.C. Hydro float are in the bay.

409   **Strawberry Islet** and several unnamed islets lie close offshore between Cockburn and Billings Bays.

410   **Billings Bay**, SE of **Maynard Head**, has a rock that dries 2.4 m, 30 m off its NE shore. A submarine cable passes along the centre of the bay.

411   **Hidden Basin** has an islet 30 m high in the centre of its entrance. The channel north of the islet dries and is encumbered with boulders that dry 3.4 m. The entrance channel south of the islet has boulders that dry 3 m. There are strong tidal streams in the entrance. The south passage is preferred and should be entered only at or near HW slack, local knowledge is advised. A drying spit, 0.2 mile east of the islet, extends from the north shore and considerably narrows the entrance channel. Several drying rocks lie close-off the south and east shores of the basin inside the 10 m contour line. Private floats are located around the shores.

412   **Anchorage** can be obtained in 10 to 15 m at the NE end of Hidden Basin. The maximum depth in the basin is 38 m.

413   **Blind Bay**, between the NW side of Nelson Island and the SE side of **Hardy Island**, has a number of islands and islets on either side of its entrance, with a deep channel between them. **Fox Island**, **Oyster Island**, **Kelly Island**, **Nocturne Island** and **Clio Island** are named islands in the bay. Marine farm facilities may be found along both shores of Blind Bay and numerous private floats line the shores.

414   **Musket Island Marine Park** encompasses the islet between Hardy and Fox Islands.

415   **Ballet Bay**, on the SE shore of Blind Bay, is sheltered by numerous islands. Some reefs in the entrance are marked by private daybeacons. Mariners without local knowledge are advised to approach with caution and at LW when reefs are more likely to be visible.

Quarry Bay (1985)

Cockburn Bay (1985)

Entrance to Hidden Basin (1985)

Ballet Bay from SW (1985)

Chart 3512

Stillwater Bay (1990)

416   **Submarine cables** cross the entrance of Blind Bay and run along its south and east sides. Submarine cables are laid in Ballet Bay.

417   **Booming grounds** lie along the south shore of Hardy Island.

418   **Tides**. — Tidal differences for Blind Bay (Index No. 7865), referenced on Point Atkinson, are in *Tide Tables, Volume 5*.

419   **Anchorage** in Blind Bay is reported to be good north of Fox Island, or in Ballet Bay clear of the submarine cables.

420   **Alexander Point** *(49°43'N, 124°14'W)* is the SW extremity of Hardy Island. **Scotch Fir Point**, 2 miles NW of Alexander Point, is rocky and rises to a thickly wooded hill. Another hill, 0.8 mile NW of the first hill, has a bare summit. Jervis Inlet is entered between these two points.

421   **Neville Rock**, 0.4 mile SSW of Scotch Fir Point, has 7.3 m over it. **Western Rock**, 0.8 mile WNW of Neville Rock, has 3 m over it. **McRae Islet**, 0.2 mile north of Western Rock, has foul ground in its vicinity and should be given a wide berth.

422   **McRae Cove**, NW of Scotch Fir Point, has several islets and drying rocks in its entrance and offers some shelter for small craft, local knowledge is advised. **Frolander Bay** is NW of McRae Cove.

423   **Stillwater Bay**, 2.5 miles NW of Scotch Fir Point, is almost filled with booming grounds and an A-frame and log dump

are at the head of the bay. **Stillwater** settlement, at the head of the bay, is connected to the main highway.

424   **Landmarks**. — A hydroelectric power plant, on the north shore of Stillwater Bay, and a light coloured water tank a short distance inland from the power plant, are conspicuous landmarks.

425   **Overhead cables**, with a vertical clearance of 15 m, cross Stillwater Bay from a logging wharf close east of the power plant to a spar tree on the south shore.

426   **Anchorage**. — Small craft can obtain temporary anchorage in a depth of about 30 m with the west end of the power plant bearing about 037°, distant 0.35 mile.

427   **Lang Bay**, 1.3 miles WNW of Stillwater Bay, has a rock, with 4 m over it, in its entrance. The public wharf has a depth of 3.4 m alongside. A store is near the wharf. A boulder breakwater at the west end of the bay protects a booming ground.

428   **Black Point** *(49°46'N, 124°24'W)*, formerly known as Albion Point, is composed of earth cliffs. A shoal spit extends 0.3 mile south from the point.

Malaspina Strait — West End

Chart 3513

429   **Pocahontas Bay** *(49°44'N, 124°26'W)* is small but affords emergency shelter for small craft during SE winds. Some

Chart 3513

buildings and dolphins are at the head of the bay. **Raven Bay** has a limestone quarry and loading facilities. **Spratt Bay**, close south of **Butterfly Point**, has a limestone quarry and wharf for loading limestone.

430   **Van Anda Point**, 1.7 miles WNW of Butterfly Point, is a high, steep-to point. A conspicuous quarry is 0.6 mile ESE of it.

431   **Eagle Cove**, 1.3 miles NW of Van Anda Point, provides limited shelter to small craft from west and SE winds.

432   A **microwave tower** is on Texada Island in *49°07'N, 124°36'W*.

433   **Myrtle Rocks** *(49°47'N, 124°28'W)* are a group of rocky islets connected to the mouth of **Myrtle Creek** by drying flats. A reef that dries 4 m lies 0.2 mile SE of Myrtle Rocks; the south extremity of the reef has 2.1 m over it. Booming grounds lie between the rocks and creek.

434   A **marina** belonging to a resort hotel, 1.7 miles WNW of Myrtle Rocks and 0.3 mile SE of Grief Point, is protected by a rock breakwater.

435   **Grief Point** *(49°48'N, 124°31'W)* is low, grassy and fringed with a sandy beach.

436   **Lights**. — Grief Point light *(469)*, on the west extremity of the point, is shown at an elevation of 10.7 m from a white tower with a red band at the top.

437   Grief Point East light *(468.5)* is on the SW end of the breakwater protecting the marina.

438   **Submarine cables** cross Malaspina Strait from the vicinity of Grief Point to Van Anda Point.

Sturt Bay and Van Anda Cove

Chart 3536

439   **Sturt Bay** *(49°46'N, 124°34'W)*, known locally as Marble Bay, is entered between **Marble Bluff** and **Hodgson Point**. **Scott Rock** has 2.1 m over it. **Ursula Rock** is 1 m high and has a drying ledge extending north from it.

440   **Beacons**. — Hodgson Point daybeacon has a starboard hand daymark.

441   Ursula Rock daybeacon, NE of Ursula Rock on the extremity of the drying ledge, has a port hand daymark.

442   **Booming grounds** lie between Marble Bluff and Ursula Rock and at the NW end of Sturt Bay.

443   **Boat basin**. — A rockfill breakwater, extending NW from the shore to Ursula Rock, protects a small boat basin and floats belonging to the Texada Boating Club.

444   **Caesar Cove**, west of **Grant Bluff**, has a quarry and ruins of conveyors and mooring ramps on its west side.

445   **Anchorage** can be obtained by small vessels in 25 m in the middle of Sturt Bay, west of Ursula Rock. Small craft can find shelter in Caesar Cove.

446   **Van Anda Cove** offers no protection from the north. A drying spit and shoal water extend NW from its east entrance point. Conspicuous white cylindrical fuel storage tanks are on the SE side of the cove.

447   **Wharf**. — The public wharf, on the SE side of Van Anda Cove, has 2.4 m alongside the NE side of its wharfhead. A moveable ramp lies off the end of the wharf and a float 16 m long is on the NE side of the wharf. The wharf is exposed to north winds.

448   **Van Anda** has a post office, store, hotel and restaurant. Fuel and fresh supplies are obtainable. Water taxi service operates to Westview and the community is on the Texada Island road system.

Pender Harbour and Approaches

Chart 3535

449   **Francis Peninsula** *(49°37'N, 124°03'W)*, formerly known as **Beaver Island**, is connected to Sechelt Peninsula by a bridge and drying flats at Bargain Narrows. **Francis Point** is its SW extremity and **Moore Point** its west extremity.

450   **Light**. — Francis Point light *(453)* is shown at an elevation of 10.4 m from a white tower.

451   **Pearson Island** and **Martin Island**, NW of Francis Peninsula, lie in the approach to Pender Harbour. **Temple Rock**, 0.6 mile WSW of Pearson Island, has 5.3 m over it. **Jacob Rock**, 0.3 mile west of Pearson Island, has 7.7 m over it. **Nares Rock**, 0.3 mile north of Martin Island, dries 0.6 m.

452   **Beacon**. — Nares Rock daybeacon has a bifurcation/junction daymark, preferred channel to the right.

453   **Pender Harbour** is the only completely sheltered anchorage on this part of the coast. The main entrance is between **Henry Point** and **Williams Island**. The channel between Williams Island and **Charles Island** has a drying reef in the centre of its fairway at the east end. **The Gap**, south of Charles Island, is obstructed by an islet and some drying reefs, it should not be attempted.

454   **Light**. — Pender Harbour light *(454)* is on a reef north of Williams Island.

455   **Beacons**. — Charles Island daybeacon, on a drying reef between Charles and Williams Islands, has a starboard hand daymark.

456   Pender Harbour daybeacon, 1 mile east of Williams Island, is on a drying rock in the entrance of **Hospital Bay** and has a bifurcation/junction daymark, preferred channel to the right.

457   **Tides**. — Tidal differences for Pender Harbour (Index No. 7837) and Irvines Landing (Index No. 7836), referenced on Point Atkinson, are in *Tide Tables, Volume 5*.

458   **Water aerodrome**. — Pender Harbour is a water aerodrome.

459   **Skardon Islands**, 0.2 mile east of Williams Island, consist of four islands, the three eastern ones are joined by drying ledges. A rock, with less than 2 m over it, lies about 90 m ESE from the south extremity of the east Skardon Island and is marked by port hand buoy "Q39". The fairway north of Skardon Islands has a depth of 8.3 m through it and the fairway south of the group has a depth of 6.2 m through it. A rock that dries 1.4 m lies close offshore about 0.3 mile east of Pope Landing. A rock, with less than 2 m over it, lies on the south side of the fairway, north of **Donnely Landing** and is marked by starboard hand buoy "Q40".

460   **Submarine cables**. — A submarine cable passes along the centre of the entrance channel between Henry Point and Williams Island and lands on the west side of **Joe Bay**, close east of Henry Point. Submarine cables (telephone/power) are laid from Pearson Island to the mainland, close south of Fisher Island. Submarine cables cross Pender Harbour from Donnely Landing to the west side of **Duncan Cove** and from **Madeira Park** to the south side of **Garden Peninsula**. A submarine cable is laid across Gunboat Bay 0.2 mile east of the overhead cable.

Chart 3535

Pender Harbour (1990)

Pender Harbour (1990)

461 **Gunboat Bay**, at the head of Pender Harbour, is entered through a narrow channel that has a least depth of 0.7 m. A rock that dries 1.1 m lies in the entrance close to the north shore.

462 An **overhead cable** with a vertical clearance of 32 m crosses the entrance to Gunboat Bay.

463 **Anchorage** can be obtained west of Garden Peninsula in 15 to 20 m, mud bottom, or off **Welbourn Cove** in 11 to 15 m, mud bottom. Small vessels can obtain anchorage in 6 to 11 m in Gerrans Bay, or in about 9 m in **Garden Bay** though swinging space is limited. Small craft can obtain good anchorage with mud bottom in Gunboat Bay.

464 **Caution**. — During SE gales passages in Pender Harbour are subject to strong squalls.

465 **Gerrans Bay**, the south arm of Pender Harbour, is suitable for small craft but has a number of dangers within it. A narrow, tortuous passage, in the SE part of the bay leads to Bargain Narrows. **Griffin Ledge** in the entrance of the bay and east of **Mary Islet** has 2.2 m over it.

466 **Beacons**. — Gerrans Bay daybeacon No. 1, on a drying rock close south of Mary Islet, has a port hand daymark.

467 Three daybeacons with port hand daymarks are on drying rocks in the approach to Bargain Narrows.

468 **Overhead cables**, with a vertical clearance of 14 m, cross the channels between **Calder Island**, **Dusenbury Island** and Francis Peninsula.

Chart 3535

469   **Submarine cables** cross the channel between Mary Islet and Calder Island.

470   **Bargain Narrows**, known locally as Canoe Pass, leads from the SE end of Gerrans Bay to Bargain Bay. A rock that dries 1.1 m lies in the north approach and is marked by a daybeacon with a starboard hand daymark. The passage, about 25 m wide at its narrowest part, dries 2.1 m and is navigable only at or near HW, local knowledge is advised.

471   A **bridge** with a vertical clearance of 4 m crosses Bargain Narrows at its narrowest part.

472   **Wharves. — Floats. — Public floats** with a common connection to shore are on the east side of Hospital Bay. Each float is 37 m long and depths alongside are 3 to 6 m. Power and garbage and used oil disposal facilities are available.

473   The **public wharf**, in Madeira Park at the head of Welbourn Cove, has a depth of 4.8 m alongside, a 3 tonne derrick is on the wharf. Floats attached to the west side of the wharf have a combined length of 104 m with depths of 4 to 8.4 m alongside. Power is available on the floats, water, garbage and used oil disposal facilities are available on the wharfhead.

474   The **public float**, at the south end of Gerrans Bay in **Whiskey Slough**, has a berthing length of 93 m. Power and garbage and used oil disposal facilities are available.

475   Private floats are in **Bill Bay, Dingman Bay, Farrington Cove** and numerous private floats line the shores throughout the harbour.

476   **Marinas** are in **Irvines Landing**, Duncan Cove, Hospital Bay, Garden Bay, Gerrans Bay, Madeira Park and in the cove 0.3 mile east of Madeira Park. A pier with a fuel float at its outer end is at **Pope Landing**.

477   **Garden Bay Marine Park**, on the north shore of Garden Bay, has a dinghy float, picnic and sanitary facilities.

478   **Repair** facilities for small craft, with boat hoists or marine ways, are available in Hospital Bay, Garden Bay, Madeira Park and Gerrans Bay.

479   **Facilities.** — Post offices are at Garden Bay and Madeira Park. A pharmacy, medical clinic and stores are in Madeira Park. Gasoline, diesel fuel and provisions can be obtained at or near most of the marinas. Several motels, resorts and a hotel are in the area.

480   **Communications.** — Pender Harbour is connected by road to Langdale where it connects with a ferry to Horseshoe Bay and then by road to Vancouver. Scheduled bus service operates to Vancouver and Powell River.

481   **Whitestone Islands** (*49°36'N, 124°03'W*), south of Francis Peninsula, and Edgecombe Island, 0.5 mile NE, lie in the approach to Bargain Bay. The channel east of **Edgecombe Island** is foul and should not be attempted.

482   A **submarine cable** is laid across the channel east of Edgecombe Island. A submarine cable crosses the channel east of the 27 m high island that lies 0.2 mile SE of Edgecombe Island.

483   **Bargain Bay** is best approached west of Edgecombe Island but local knowledge is advised. A shoal with 2.2 m over it lies on the east side of the fairway, about 0.1 mile west of Edgecombe Island. Two rocks, 0.2 mile NW of Edgecombe Island, have less than 2 m over them, the fairway between these two rocks is about 100 m. The head of the bay affords sheltered anchorage for small craft in a depth of about 7 m.

Approach to Agamemnon Channel

484   **Fearney Point** (*49°39'N, 124°05'W*), the SW entrance point of Agamemnon Channel, is bold and has cliffs on its east side.

485   **Hodgson Islands**, 0.4 mile south of Fearney Point, lie in the centre of the SW approach to Agamemnon Channel and have foul ground around and between them. Jacob and Temple Rocks, both described with the approach to Pender Harbour, lie to the south of Hodgson Islands. Shoals lie to the NW, SE and east of Hodgson Islands.

486   **Daniel Point**, formerly known as Norman Point, lies 1 mile SE of Fearney Point. A shoal with 2.5 m over it, and a rock with less than 2 m over it lie within 0.2 mile NW of Daniel Point. **The rock should be given a wide berth as it is frequently struck by small craft. Lee Bay** lies between Daniel Point and **Fisher Island**.

487   **Submarine cables** cross the south approach to Agamemnon Channel.

Agamemnon Channel

Charts 3512, 3514

488   **Agamemnon Channel** (*49°40'N, 124°05'W*), about 9 miles long, separates Nelson Island from Sechelt Peninsula; it leads north then NE from Malaspina Strait to Sechelt and Jervis Inlets. The channel is about 0.5 mile wide with fairway depths from 35 to 260 m.

489   **Tidal streams** in Agamemnon Channel attain 1 to 2 kn and follow the general direction of the channel. The flood sets NE and the ebb SW.

490   **Booming grounds** and log dumps are in several locations along the shores of Agamemnon Channel.

491   **Marine farm** facilities may be found in several locations in Agamemnon Channel. Reduce speed when passing marine farms to avoid damage.

492   **Overhead cables** (power), 3 and 6.5 miles north of Fearney Point, cross Agamemnon Channel and have vertical clearances of 38 and 34 m. Red spheres are attached to the cables to make them more visible. Red and white chequered boards located at the HW line to mark the crossings are visible from all directions of approach.

493   A **submarine cable** crosses Agamemnon Channel 0.5 mile north of Fearney Point.

494   **Ferry.** — A scheduled ferry operates between Earls Cove, at the NE end of Agamemnon Channel, and Saltery Bay in Jervis Inlet.

495   The east shore of Agamemnon Channel SE of Caldwell Island is an **Ecological Reserve**.

Chart 3512

496   **Green Bay** (*49°42'N, 124°04'W*) has rocks close-off its east shore and a drying rock near the head of the bay. Several houses, a log dump and booming ground are at the NW end of the bay.

497   **Anchorage** with limited swinging room for small craft can be obtained in 10 to 30 m in Green Bay.

Chart 3512

Green Bay (1985)

Earls Cove (1985)

Chart 3514

498　**Caldwell Island** *(49°44′N, 124°03′W)* is steep-to and has a drying rock close-off its south side.

499　**Annis Bay**, 1.5 miles NE of Caldwell Island, has a booming ground in its north part and a marine farm in its SW part.

500　**Agamemnon Bay** is near the north end of Sechelt Peninsula. **Earls Cove**, a small indentation near the west entrance point of Agamemnon Bay, is the site of a ferry landing from which regular service for passengers and vehicles is maintained to Saltery Bay. The ferry landing is connected by road to Pender Harbour and Howe Sound.

501　**Lights. — Fog signal**. — Private fixed red and green lights are shown from the ferry berth. Radar reflectors are on the floating leads at the landing.

502　Earls Cove Fog Signal *(460.3)* is operated by ferry personnel when required for ferry movements.

503　**Nile Point**, at the NE extremity of Nelson Island, is the NW entrance point to Agamemnon Channel.

504　**Agnew Passage** separates Captain Island from Nelson Island, it is about 0.3 mile wide and deep.

505　**Light**. — Agnew Passage light *(460)* is on the north side of an islet, at the SE end of the passage.

Sechelt Inlet

Charts 3512, 3514

506　**Sechelt Inlet** *(49°45′N, 123°56′W)* commences at the junction of Agamemnon Channel and Jervis Inlet and leads 20 miles SSE between **Sechelt Peninsula** and the mainland, terminating in Porpoise Bay. Narrows and Salmon Inlets lead NE from its east side. Apart from Skookumchuck Narrows and Sechelt Rapids in the entrance, the inlet and its branches are deep. Extensive logging operations are carried out in Sechelt, Narrows and Salmon Inlets. Gravel quarrying operations, logging, and marine farm facilities for salmon and oysters are located in Sechelt

Charts 3512, 3514

Inlet. Numerous private floats line the shores of Sechelt and Narrows Inlets.

507   Entry to Sechelt Inlet is governed entirely by tidal conditions at Sechelt Rapids, and in general can be effected only at slack water.

508   **Tides**. — Tidal differences in Sechelt Inlet, referenced on Point Atkinson, for Egmont (Index No. 7842), Storm Bay (Index No. 7847) and Porpoise Bay (Index No. 7852) are in *Tide Tables, Volume 5*.

509   **Marine farm** facilities are located in several locations along the shores of Sechelt Inlet, some are marked by buoys. Reduce speed when passing to avoid damaging these facilities.

510   **Caution**. — **Because of the tortuous nature of the fairway and strong tidal streams in Sechelt Rapids, it is recommended that no vessel more than 40 m long and 3.4 m draught should attempt to enter.**

511   **Sechelt Inlets Marine Recreation Area** consists of eight sites, Tzoonie Narrows, Kunechin Point, Thornhill Creek, Nine Mile Point, Tuwanek Point, Piper Point, Skaiakos Point and Halfway Islet. Most are marked by park signs and have primitive camping and sanitary facilities.

Skookumchuck Narrows

Chart 3514

512   **Skookumchuck Narrows** *(49°45'N, 123°56'W)* forms the entrance to Sechelt Inlet and is about 3 miles long. **Sutton Islets**, 0.7 mile south of **Egmont Point**, consist of three islets lying in mid-channel, a rock that dries 4.6 m lies 0.1 mile SE of the SE islet. A safe passage through the narrows is on either side of these islets.

513   **Water aerodrome**. — The entrance to Sechelt Inlet is a water aerodrome known as Egmont.

514   **Light**. — Skookumchuck Narrows light *(461)* is on the drying rock SE of Sutton Islets.

515   **Beacon**. — Skookumchuck Narrows daybeacon, on Sechelt Peninsula 0.3 mile SW of light, has a starboard hand daymark.

516   A **marina** is close west of the daybeacon.

517   A **submarine cable area** (power) crosses Skookumchuck Narrows 0.4 mile SSE of Skookumchuck Narrows light. Another cable crosses the narrows 0.8 mile SSE of the light.

518   **Secret Bay** *(49°45'N, 123°56'W)* has an islet, 2 m high, in the centre of its entrance and offers very limited anchorage out of the tidal stream to small craft. The settlement of **Egmont** has a post office, stores, air service, and is connected by road to the main highway at Earls Cove. A marina is close south of the public wharf. Private wharves and mooring buoys lie around the bay.

519   **Beacons**. — A private daybeacon with a starboard hand daymark is on the SE extremity of the islet in the approach to Egmont. Secret Bay daybeacon, on the NW side of a drying rock, in the approach to the marina, has a port hand daymark.

520   A daybeacon with a starboard hand daymark, close SE of Secret Bay daybeacon, marks the SE side of the drying rock. **Do not pass between these daybeacons.**

521   A yellow diamond-shaped daybeacon, marked "Danger" is on the centre of the drying rock.

522   **Tides**. — Tidal differences for Egmont (Index No. 7842), referenced on Point Atkinson, are in *Tide Tables, Volume 5*.

523   **Wharf. — Floats**. — The public wharf at Egmont has a wharfhead width of 15 m with a depth of 3 m alongside its north face. It is equipped with a 3 tonne derrick. A float 9 m long is attached to the north side of the wharfhead. Floats attached to the south side of the wharfhead have lengths of 62 and 49 m. The south float is reserved for seaplanes. Garbage and used oil disposal facilities are available at the wharfhead.

524   A **conspicuous quarry**, 1.3 miles ESE of Secret Bay on the east side of the channel and close north of Sechelt Rapids, has a barge loading dock and barge ramp. A log dump and booming ground are close south of the barge dock.

525   **Sechelt Rapids**, known locally as Skookumchuck Rapids, is at the south end of Skookumchuck Narrows. It is formed by **Boom Islet**, **Sechelt Islets** and numerous rocks and shoals. The roar from the rapids can be heard for several miles. Several shoals lie in the centre of the fairway through the rapids and the least depth over them, 4.6 m, is about 0.1 mile SSE of Sechelt Islets light.

526   **Light**. — Sechelt Islets light *(462)* is on the south end of the centre islet.

527   **Tidal streams** attain 16½ kn on the flood and 16 kn on the ebb during large tides. The turn to flood occurs earliest off **Roland Point**, approximately 0.15 mile south of Sechelt Islets light. Flood streams of 5 kn can be experienced as little as 15 minutes after LW slack off Roland Point.

528   Daily predictions for times of slack water, and times and rates of maximum flood and ebb, are tabulated for current station Sechelt Rapids (Index No. 4200) in *Tide Tables, Volume 5*.

529   **Flood stream**. — Strongest flow occurs off Roland Point and to the SE, where an extremely hazardous rip forms shortly after slack water. West of Sechelt Islets light the flood stream attains a maximum of approximately 8 kn. A back eddy forms east of the light that might be used as a haven in an extreme emergency.

530   **Ebb stream**. — Strongest ebb stream occurs just west of Sechelt Islets light with a strong cross-channel set toward the WNW. A large back eddy occurs to the north of the light and whirlpools form close to the light, they break away and are carried downstream. During large tides ebb streams of 5 kn can be encountered as far as 0.4 mile SE of Sechelt Islets light.

531   **Caution. — It is hazardous for any vessel to attempt to navigate Sechelt Rapids except at or near slack water.**

532   Tugs towing logbooms or gravel barges can be encountered in vicinity of the rapids near time of slack water.

533   **Directions**. — The preferred time for transit of Sechelt Rapids is at HW slack. The best route through is west of Boom Islet and Sechelt Islets light, give Roland Point a wide berth on the flood to avoid dangerous rips and heavy overfalls.

534   When the ebb is running it is recommended that larger vessels avoid the passage between Sechelt Islets light and the small island 0.2 mile NW. The main ebb stream runs approximately WNW from the light toward the opposite shore. Low powered vessels, or those that answer the helm sluggishly, can find themselves being spun about or set upon the west shore if attempting to abort passage through the rapids.

Skookum Island to Porpoise Bay

Chart 3512

535   **Skookum Island** *(49°43'N, 123°52'W)* has a drying rock about 0.1 mile west of its west end. A logging camp, with a float,

Marina SW of Sutton Islets (1985)

Egmont (1985)

Sechelt Rapids (1985)

Sechelt Rapids (1985)

Chart 3512

is 0.5 mile NNW of Skookum Island light, buildings are prominent.

536   **Light**. — Skookum Island light *(463)*, on the NW end of the island, is shown at an elevation of 7 m from a white tower.

537   **Booming grounds** and a log dump are close north of **Doriston** *(49°43'N, 123°53'W)*, on the west side of the inlet.

538   **Storm Bay** *(49°40'N, 123°50'W)*, east of **Cawley Point**, provides good anchorage for small vessels near its head. Small craft can find good shelter south of the islets on the west side of the entrance. Marine farm facilities are located at Sockeye Point.

539   **Tides**. — Tidal differences for Storm Bay (Index No. 7847), referenced on Point Atkinson, are in *Tide Tables, Volume 5.*

540   **Overhead cables**, vertical clearance of 39 m, cross Sechelt Inlet about 1 mile south of Cawley Point. Red and white spheres are attached to the cables to increase visibility and large billboard daybeacons are on both shores.

541   **Artificial reef. — Buoys**. — HMCS Chaudiere has been sunk in the bay NW of Kunechin Point as an artificial reef for divers. It is marked by cautionary buoys.

542   **Kunechin Islets** *(49°37'N, 123°48'W)* and **Kunechin Point** form the north entrance point to Salmon Inlet.

543   **Light**. — Kunechin Islets light *(464)* is on the south tip of the largest islet.

544   A **telephone relay tower** is on the west side of Sechelt Inlet, about 1.3 miles NW of **Halfway Islet**.

545   A **measured distance** of 1,853 m is close NW of **Piper Point**, marked by a pair of beacons at each end. It is laid out for courses 151° and 331°.

546   **Lamb Islets** *(49°33'N, 123°46'W)* lie 0.7 mile SSE of **Tuwanek Point**. A drying rock lies close NE of the north islet. A submarine cable connects the islets to the mainland.

547   **Booming grounds** and a log dump are in a bay 0.2 mile SE of Lamb Islets and in the bay NW of **Carlson Point**.

548   **Tillicum Bay**, close south of **Gray Creek**, is the site of a marina, protected by a rock breakwater.

549   A **submarine pipeline** (outfall/intake) is laid about 0.15 mile north of the marina.

550   **Four Mile Point** lies 1 mile SW of Tillicum Bay. **Four Mile Shoal**, 0.2 mile west of the point, has 4.9 m over it.

551   **Angus Creek** is 1.2 miles SE of Four Mile Point. A bay, close north of Angus Creek, has dolphins offshore and conveyors from a large quarrying operation. A private mooring buoy is in the bay.

552   **Porpoise Bay Park**, SE of Angus Creek, has mooring buoys close offshore.

553   **Porpoise Bay** is the head of Sechelt Inlet. A narrow isthmus, connecting Sechelt Peninsula to the mainland, separates the bay from the Strait of Georgia. **Poise Island** has a shoal with 2.7 m over it lying 0.2 mile NNE of it and another shoal with 5.8 m over it lies 0.2 mile NW of the island. Drying flats fill the head of the bay. Residential development stretches along the east side of the bay as far north as Tillicum Bay.

554   **Water aerodrome**. — Porpoise Bay is a water aerodrome known as Sechelt.

555   A log dump and **booming ground** are about 0.5 mile ESE of Poise Island.

556   A **marina**, protected by rockfill breakwaters, lies west of Poise Island.

557   **Anchorage** with good holding ground can be obtained west of Poise Island in about 15 m and off the public wharf in 12 m.

558   **Tides**. — Tidal differences for Porpoise Bay (Index No. 7852), referenced on Point Atkinson, are in *Tide Tables, Volume 5.*

559   **Wharf**. — The public wharf, at the head of Porpoise Bay and close west of the drying flats, has floats attached to its head. Power and water are available and a 3 tonne crane is on the wharf.

560   **Marinas** are close east and 0.2 mile west of the public wharf.

561   **Facilities**. — Numerous retail stores offering most provisions are available. The public wharf is connected by road to the village of Sechelt, centered on the south side of the isthmus. A tidal grid is west of the public wharf and a launching ramp is on its east side.

Narrows Inlet

562   **Narrows Inlet**, entered between **Highland Point** *(49°41'N, 123°50'W)* and **Sockeye Point**, extends 8 miles NE from Sechelt Inlet. A drying rock lies 0.1 mile west of Highland Point. Depths within the inlet are too great for anchorage.

563   **Marine farm** facilities are east of Highland Point and WSW of Tzoonie Point.

564   **Booming grounds** are 0.6 mile east and 1.7 miles NE of Sockeye Point.

565   **Tzoonie Point**, 2.2 miles NE of Sockeye Point, has above and below-water rocks NE of it.

566   **Tzoonie Narrows**, 0.7 mile NE of Tzoonie Point, is about 90 m wide and free of turbulence. A depth of 11 m can be carried through the narrows but is so constricted it is only suitable for small vessels.

567   **Tidal streams** in Tzoonie Narrows attain 3 to 4 kn. Secondary current station Tzoonie Narrows (Index No. 4210), referenced on Sechelt Rapids, is in *Tide Tables, Volume 5.*

568   Rocks, with less than 2 m over them, lie on the east side of the inlet 2.5 miles above Tzoonie Narrows.

569   **Booming grounds** are on both shores and near the mud flats of the **Tzoonie River** at the head of the inlet, there are numerous piles and a logging camp on the east shore.

Salmon Inlet

570   **Salmon Inlet**, entered between Kunechin Islets *(49°37'N, 123°48'W)* and **Nine Mile Point**, extends 12 miles ENE from Sechelt Inlet.

571   **Overhead cables** traverse the south shore of Salmon Inlet. At a number of points they pass over navigable water with a vertical clearance of 7.6 m. Caution should be exercised when approaching the south shore. **Overhead cables** (power), with a vertical clearance of 30 m, cross Salmon Inlet near the mouth of Sechelt Creek. This power line cuts a conspicuous swath along the north shore of the inlet.

572   **Marine farm** facilities are in several locations along the north shore between Kunechin Islets and **Mid Point** and along the south shore from SW of **Black Bear Bluff** to Chum Point.

573   **Booming grounds** are 3 miles east of **Chum Point**, in Misery Bay and at the head of the inlet.

Tzoonie Narrows (1985)

Head of Narrows Inlet (1985)

Chart 3512

574   **Sechelt Creek**, 10 miles ENE of Nine Mile Point, enters the south side of the inlet. A drying spit extends 0.1 mile north from the mouth of the creek, give it a wide berth.

575   **Clowhom River** flows into the head of Salmon Inlet. A dam and power generating plant are in the entrance of the river. A water-tower, 60 m high, makes a conspicuous landmark. A wharf, near the entrance of the river, is protected from the power station runoff by a rockfill breakwater.

576   **Anchorage** can be obtained in 20 to 40 m near the head of Salmon Inlet. Small craft can obtain good anchorage in **Misery Bay**, about 0.5 mile west of Sechelt Creek, in 10 to 20 m.

Jervis Inlet

Chart 3514

577   **Jervis Inlet**, entered from Malaspina Strait, is 46 miles long with a general width of 1 to 1.5 miles. The main entrance is between Alexander Point *(49°43′N, 124°14′W)* and Scotch Fir Point, 2 miles NW. It can also be entered by way of Telescope Passage, which separates the east end of Hardy Island from Nelson Island, or by way of Agamemnon Channel, along the east side of Nelson Island.

578   Depths in Jervis Inlet range from 300 m at the entrance to over 600 m in the inlet and high rugged mountains rise steeply from its steep-to shores. The slopes in most places are thickly wooded, but there are bare strips caused by logging, winter storms, or avalanches during spring thaws. Several rivers entering the inlet have flat deltas at their mouths, other rivers or creeks plunge as waterfalls off the mountain sides.

579   Numerous logging camps in the inlet are served by tug and barge services from Vancouver. The more permanent ones are usually sited on beaches at the head of bays. Temporary ones are usually on floats moored to shore and are moved according to requirements.

580   **Tides**. — Tidal differences in Jervis Inlet, referenced on Point Atkinson, are given for Saltery Bay (Index No. 7868) in *Tide Tables, Volume 5*.

581   **Tidal streams** in Jervis Inlet are weak, irregular and influenced by winds. In the entrances of Princess Louisa and Sechelt Inlets they are strong.

582   A **submarine cable** crosses the entrance of Jervis Inlet between Alexander and Scotch Fir Points.

583   **Overhead cables** cross Jervis Inlet from a position on Nelson Island about 3.5 miles east of Ball Point to the mainland at Ahlstrom Point. They have a vertical clearance of 49 m and orange spheres are attached to make them more visible. Red and white chequered boards, conspicuous from all directions of marine approach, are located at the HW line to mark the crossing.

584   **Ferry**. — A scheduled ferry crosses the entrance of Jervis Inlet running between Saltery Bay and Earls Cove in the north end of Agamemnon Channel.

585   **Marine farms** are in several locations in Jervis Inlet. Reduce speed when passing to avoid damage.

Ball Point to Captain Island

586   **Ball Point** *(49°45′N, 124°13′W)* is the NW extremity of Hardy Island. Several islets and rocks lie close offshore between 1 and 1.5 miles east of Ball Point.

587   **Marine farm** facilities lie along the north shores of Hardy and Nelson Islands.

588   **Telescope Passage** *(49°45′N, 124°09′W)* separates the islands NE of Hardy Island from Nelson Island and connects the head of Blind Bay with Jervis Inlet. It is very narrow and has drying rocks in mid-channel and on its west side. Favour the Nelson Island shore. The least depth through the fairway is 7.2 m. Mariners not familiar with Telescope Passage are advised to navigate it at LW when dangers are visible.

589   **Marine farm** facilities are along the Nelson Island shore of Telescope Passage.

590   **Thunder Bay** *(49°46′N, 124°16′W)* is one of the few places in Jervis Inlet where anchorage can be obtained. Depths in the bay range from 20 to 50 m, beyond the 50 m line there is a sudden drop to greater depths. A sandy beach is at the head of the bay.

591   **Saltery Bay**, 4 miles east of **Thunder Point**, has depths of 14 m and provides limited anchorage to small craft. A log dump and booming ground occupy the east part of the bay. There is highway connection with Powell River and Vancouver via the ferry. A ferry landing is in the bay, service is maintained with Earls Cove in Agamemnon Channel.

592   **Tides**. — Tidal differences for Saltery Bay (Index No. 7868), referenced on Point Atkinson, are in *Tide Tables, Volume 5*.

593   **Light**. — A private light and radar reflector are on an outer dolphin at the ferry landing.

594   **Fog signal**. — Saltery Bay Fog Signal *(456.6)* is operated by ferry personnel when required for ferry movements.

595   **Wharf**. — The public wharf, east of the ferry landing, has a float for small craft with a berthing length of 127 m.

596   **Ahlstrom Point** lies 1 mile east of Saltery Bay. Overhead cables crossing Jervis Inlet here are described at the beginning of the section.

597   **Light**. — Ahlstrom Point light *(457)* is on the N shore of Jervis Inlet.

598   **Vanguard Bay**, 2 miles SE of Ahlstrom Point, is too deep for anchorage but small craft can find limited anchorage close inshore north of the islets off its east shore. A private mooring buoy is on the east side of the bay. Marine farm facilities are in several locations in the southern portion of the bay.

599   **Booming grounds** are 1 mile east of Vanguard Bay.

600   **St. Vincent Bay** *(49°50′N, 124°05′W)*, entered between **Culloden Point** and **Elephant Point**, is too deep for anchoring. Extensive booming grounds lie between its west shore and **Sykes Island**. Several houses with floats lie on the north shore of the bay. Marine farm facilities are on the south side of Sykes Island and near the head of St. Vincent Bay. A private daybeacon marks a drying rock at the head of the bay.

601   **Junction Island**, close SW of Elephant Point, is connected to the north shore by drying and above-water rocks. Marine farm facilities lie north of Junction Island.

602   **Captain Island** *(49°47′N, 123°59′W)* is bold, steep-to and thickly wooded. It is separated from Nelson Island by Agnew Passage.

603   **Light**. — Captain Island light *(458)*, on the NW shore of the island, is shown at an elevation of 8.2 m from a white tower.

604   **Military exercise area**. — The area between St. Vincent Bay, Captain Island and the entrance of Hotham Sound is a

Telescope Passage from south (1985)

Saltery Bay (1985)

Sykes Island from south (1985)

Junction Island from east (1985)

Chart 3514

Harmony Islands (1985)

Canadian Forces exercise area. For details see *Notices to Mariners 1 to 46 Annual Edition.*

Hotham Sound

605   **Hotham Sound**, entered east of Elephant Point, extends 6 miles north and is too deep for anchorage, except for small craft. Mountains rise steeply from its steep-to shores.

606   **Granville Bay** *(49°50'N, 124°00'W)* has a conspicuous waterfall at its north end. Marine farm facilities are at the head of the bay and in the small bay 0.6 mile south of Granville Bay.

607   **Harmony Islands** lie close-off the east side of the sound, midway between Granville Bay and **Syren Point**. **Harmony Islands Marine Park** includes north and south islands, and the passage between the islands and the mainland. It is undeveloped.

608   **Anchorage** for small craft can be obtained east of Harmony Islands or in the basin formed by the three north islands. Most craft anchor with a stern line to shore. A rock with less than 2 m over it lies in the entrance to the basin.

609   **Mooring buoys**, WSW of Syren Point, are marked "NAVY" and have radar reflectors. They are maintained by DND, for use by Navy vessels.

610   **Landmark**. — A conspicuous landslide is on the west side of the sound, 1.5 miles NW of Syren Point.

611   **Baker Bay**, at the head of Hotham Sound, has a conspicuous peak on its west side.

612   **Marine farm** facilities are in several locations NNW of Elephant Point and at the head of the sound in **Lena Bay**. A booming ground is 1 mile south of Lena Bay.

Prince of Wales Reach

613   **Prince of Wales Reach**, entered between **Foley Head** *(49°48'N, 123°58'W)* and Egmont Point, trends 6 miles NNE to **Saumarez Bluff** then about 7 miles NW to **Moorsam Bluff**.

614   **Miller Islet**, 0.7 mile north of Egmont Point, is steep-to on its west side and bare except for a topknot of trees. A drying rock lies 140 m SE of the islet.

615   **Killam Bay**, 1 mile east of Miller Islet, is deep but can afford anchorage to small craft close inshore. A small breakwater is at the head of the bay.

616   **Dark Cove**, north of Foley Head, affords anchorage to small vessels west of **Sydney Island** in 30 m, but holding ground is reported to be poor. A wrecked barge is on the north shore of Sydney Island. Marine farm facilities are west and NE of Sydney Island. Private moorings and several houses are located around the cove.

617   **Goliath Bay**, north of Dark Cove and west of **Dacres Point**, is deep and affords no anchorage. Marine farm facilities are in the SW part of the bay.

618   **Treat Creek**, 2.2 miles ENE of Dacres Point, has a pier with float attached, conveyor belt loading facilities, and oil tanks near its entrance. A small quarrying operation is 1 mile south. A prominent bare gravel hillside is near the creek entrance.

619   **Marine farm** facilities are 0.5 mile south of Saumarez Bluff.

620   **Vancouver Bay** *(49°55'N, 123°52'W)* is too deep for anchorage. Sides of the bay are precipitous but the head is low with steep-to drying flats formed by sediments from **Vancouver River**

Malibu Rapids (1985)

Princess Louisa Inlet (1985)

Chart 3514

and **High Creek**. A house is on the south side of Vancouver River entrance.

621 **Brittain River**, at the junction of Prince of Wales Reach and Princess Royal Reach, flows into the inlet through a prominent U-shaped valley. Sand and gravel drying flats front its entrance.

Princess Royal and Queens Reaches

622 **Princess Royal Reach** extends 10 miles NE from Brittain River to **Patrick Point**.

623 **Marine farm** facilities are at **Osgood Creek**.

624 **Deserted Bay**, at the NE end of Princess Royal Reach, affords indifferent anchorage, in its SE part, in a depth of about 30 m, it is only suitable for small vessels. A large valley containing the **Deserted River** trends NE from the head of the bay.

625 **Queens Reach** extends 10 miles NW from Patrick Point to the head of Jervis Inlet. **Hill Rock**, 2.5 miles NW of Patrick Point and about 0.4 mile offshore, has 3.2 m over it.

626 **Booming grounds** are at the head of the inlet.

627 **Skwawka River** enters the head of Jervis Inlet across low swampy ground. Some buildings are at the head of the inlet. Anchorage for small craft is available close to shore or near the mud flats. Water is often discoloured by glacial runoff.

Princess Louisa Inlet

628 **Malibu Rapids** *(50°10'N, 123°51'W)* flows through a narrow gorge that forms the entrance to Princess Louisa Inlet. It is suitable for small vessels and should be negotiated at or near slack water. **Malibu Islet** and several other islets lie in its south entrance. Keep in mid-channel between the light and Malibu Islet. The channel east of Malibu Islet is not recommended.

629 **Light**. — Malibu Rapids light *(459)* is on a rock on the west side of the entrance to the rapids.

630 **Tidal streams** in Malibu Rapids attain 9 kn on the flood and ebb on large tides. Times of turn to flood and ebb in Malibu Rapids can be obtained from secondary current station Malibu Rapids (Index No. 4375) in *Tide Tables, Volume 5*.

631 **Malibu**, on the peninsula forming the NW side of Malibu Rapids, is the site of a summer camp. A float, on the north shore of the peninsula, is 62 m long and owned by the camp. Overnight moorage is not permitted.

632 A **submarine pipeline** is laid close east of the float.

633 **Princess Louisa Inlet** extends 4 miles NE from Malibu Rapids and is hemmed in by high mountains. Depths in the inlet are great. **Chatterbox Falls** at the head of the inlet can be heard from a considerable distance when running strongly.

634 **Princess Louisa Marine Park** which includes Chatterbox Falls and **Macdonald Island** has picnic, camping and sanitary facilities. Garbage disposal facilities and fresh water are available.

635 **Floats** close south of Chatterbox Falls have 274 m of berthing space.

636 **Anchorage** with good shelter can be obtained by small craft inside Macdonald Island, and there are mooring buoys. In settled weather small vessels can find anchorage in the narrow belt of depths under 20 m off Chatterbox Falls. If there is significant up-inlet winds be prepared to move.

CHAPTER 6

Discovery Passage, Johnstone and Broughton Straits

General

Chart 3001

1   This chapter covers the main shipping route between the Strait of Georgia and Queen Charlotte Strait. This route passes through Discovery Passage, Johnstone Strait and Broughton Strait. Blackney Passage and Blackfish Sound, which connect the west end of Johnstone Strait to the east end of Queen Charlotte Strait, are described as an alternate route to Broughton Strait. Traffic Separation Schemes in Johnstone Strait and Broughton Strait are recommended for use by all ships.

Discovery Passage

Charts 3539, 3540

2   **Discovery Passage** *(50°00′N, 125°12′W)*, separating Quadra and Sonora Islands from Vancouver Island, is the main shipping channel leading NW from the north end of the Strait of Georgia. It is entered from the south between Cape Mudge and Willow Point. The north limit of Discovery Passage is Chatham Point. South of Seymour Narrows shores are relatively low lying. North of the narrows they become steep and mountainous, especially on the west side. **Mount Menzies**, NW of Menzies Bay, attains an elevation of 1,239 m and snow often remains on its summit until late June.

3   **Vessel Traffic Services (VTS).** — Discovery Passage is in *Sector Four* of the *Vancouver Traffic Zone* and is administered by *Comox Traffic.* Assigned frequency is 156.575 MHz, Channel 71.

4   A brief description of this VTS is in *PAC 200*. Details are in *Radio Aids to Marine Navigation (Pacific and Western Arctic)*. Calling-in points in Discovery Passage are:

5   *Calling-in Point No. 26, Cape Mudge,* is a line running 090°–270° through Cape Mudge Sector light *(511)*. Northbound mariners shall report their ETA for Steep Island and Maud Island light.

6   *Calling-in Point No. 27, Steep Island,* is a line running 050°–230° through Steep Island light *(514)*. Northbound mariners shall report their ETA for Separation Head and update Maud Island light ETA if any change.

7   *Calling-in Point No. 28, Separation Head,* is a line running 090°–270° through Separation Head light *(516.6)*. Southbound mariners shall report their ETA for Steep Island and update Maud Island light ETA if any change.

8   *Calling-in Point No. 29, Cinque Island,* is a line running 090°–270° through Cinque Islands light *(517.5)*. Southbound mariners shall report their ETA for Separation Head and Maud Island lights.

9   **Ferry.** — Regular ferry service crosses Discovery Passage from Campbell River on Vancouver Island, to Quathiaski Cove on Quadra Island. The charted route is a general indication of the route followed.

10   **Tides.** — Tidal predictions in Discovery Passage are given for Campbell River (Index No. 8074).

11   Tidal differences in Discovery Passage, referenced on Campbell River, are given for Quathiaski Cove (Index No. 8079), Gowlland Harbour (Index No. 8082) and Duncan Bay (Index No. 8087). Tidal differences, referenced on Owen Bay (Index No. 8120), are given for Bloedel (Index No. 8095), Seymour Narrows (Index No. 8105), Brown Bay (Index No. 8110) and Chatham Point (Index No. 8180). These tidal predictions and differences are in *Tide Tables, Volume 6.*

12   **Tidal streams** through Discovery Passage are particularly troublesome off Cape Mudge, in Menzies Bay, and in Seymour Narrows where they attain 16 kn. The flood tidal stream sets south and the ebb north through Discovery Passage.

13   Predictions of times and rates of maximum current and times of slack water are given for Seymour Narrows (Index No. 5000) in *Tide Tables, Volume 6.*

14   **Navigation of Discovery Passage** is very simple except in Seymour Narrows. Here tidal streams, which at some stages of the tide attain 16 kn, make it advisable for low powered vessels and small craft to await slack water. Elsewhere in Discovery Passage it is only necessary to steer in mid-channel.

15   Mariners navigating Seymour Narrows against the tidal stream and meeting another vessel proceeding in the opposite direction, should pay due regard to the fact that such vessel may not be in full control. Give that vessel as much clearance as possible.

16   Vessels of low power, vessels with tows, small craft and strangers particularly, are strongly advised to navigate Seymour Narrows at or near slack water maintaining a mid-channel course. Even at slack water pay attention to the caution given with the description of Seymour Narrows.

17   Duncan and Menzies Bays on the south, and Plumper Bay on the north side of Seymour Narrows, afford convenient anchorage for awaiting slack water.

18   **To proceed against the tidal stream during spring tides**, and to ensure maximum control, a speed of 13 kn is necessary during the first and last hours of the tidal stream, 15-16 kn during the second and fourth hours, and 17 kn to drive through at full strength of the tide. The vessel should be quick and handy to answer the helm to achieve full control.

19   **During neap tides** when velocity of tidal stream is weaker, less power is required to proceed through the narrows at the full of the stream. A speed 3-4 kn more than the maximum velocity as predicted in *Tide Tables* for any particular tide should be adequate. Mariners proceeding through the narrows with the tidal stream should adjust their speed as necessary for maximum control.

20   **North bound with ebb stream**. — Pass Race Point at a distance of about 0.4 mile and steer to pass Maud Island light at about 0.1 mile distance. When the light bears 000°, haul round gradually to starboard to pass it at a distance of about 0.1 mile taking care to keep out of the eddy in the vicinity of Maud Island, north of the light. Then keeping in the tongue of the stream, a

Charts 3539, 3540

course should be steered for a point about mid-channel off North Bluff, where eddies from both sides of the channel meet. This point is clearly defined and easily visible. Thereafter a mid-channel course can be steered.

21 **North bound against the flood stream**. — After passing Gowlland Harbour, keep well to the east of mid-channel to avoid heavy swirls off Race Point. Round Race Point at a distance of about 0.4 mile, and head for Stephenson Point bearing 285°. Take care to avoid being set into the violent rips that extend about 0.4 mile south of Maud Island. This course should be maintained until the apex of the flood stream is seen, when course should be altered to enter the main stream at the apex, and to pass Maud Island light at a distance of about 0.1 mile. After passing Maud Island light, course should be set to pass North Bluff in about mid-channel. Thereafter a mid-channel course can be maintained.

22 **South bound with the flood stream**. — Mariners should keep in mid-channel until North Bluff is abeam, then steer to pass Maud Island light at a distance of about 0.2 mile. Hold this course, keeping in the tongue of the stream, until clear of the violent rips that extend about 0.4 mile south of Maud Island light, when course should be altered to about 105°. This course should be maintained until Cape Mudge is well open of Orange Point, the latter bearing about 153°, after which, course should be altered to the south, favouring the east shore to obtain full benefit of the tidal stream.

23 **South bound against the ebb stream**. — A mid-channel course should be steered until nearly abeam North Bluff, where the tongue of the main stream should be entered and a course set to pass Maud Island light at a distance of 0.2 mile. Care should be taken to avoid being set into the eddy. A course should then be steered to pass Race Point at a distance of about 0.1 mile. A notable feature on the ebb is that 1 hour after times of maximum rates, turbulence on both sides of the channel diminishes greatly. This change is so remarkable that mariners approaching the narrows about the time of maximum velocity will find that by waiting an hour they will find passage much easier provided adequate power is available.

24 **Meteorological information** for Campbell River, at the south end of Discovery Passage, and for Chatham Point at the north end, and a frequency of fog table for Campbell River are in the Appendices.

25 **Speed**. — To avoid damage to tows, logbooms and shore installations mariners are requested to proceed at moderate speed and minimize wash while proceeding through Discovery Passage.

26 **Towing**. — Vessels engaged in towing operations are reminded of the requirement to prevent damage to submarine cables. Where there is a possibility of the tow line scouring, vessels are to shorten lines and reduce the catenary.

Discovery Passage — South Entrance

27 **Mariners approaching the south entrance of Discovery Passage** should experience no difficulty in identifying Cape Mudge, and should then steer to pass midway between it and Willow Point, keeping Orange Point bearing more than 325°, and open west of the cape.

28 **If the south-going tidal stream is running**, care must be taken to avoid being set over toward the reef extending south from the cape (Wilby Shoals).

29 **If the north-going tidal stream is running**, care must be taken to avoid being carried into Sutil Channel. This should be especially guarded against in thick or foggy weather, when the west shore of the passage should be kept well aboard. After rounding Cape Mudge in mid-channel, a course of 000° should be steered until Yaculta village is abeam, after which a mid-channel course should be steered.

30 A **microwave tower**, 2.3 miles north of Cape Mudge, is 197 m high and shows red air obstruction lights at night and white lights during daylight. Visible for considerable distance, the tower is a valuable aid when approaching Discovery Passage from the south.

31 A **radio tower**, with red obstruction lights, is located near Cape Mudge light.

32 **Cape Mudge** (50°00'N, 125°11'W) is flat, wooded, and ends in a conspicuous whitish yellow earth cliff covered with scattered vegetation, the cliff faces SE. During summer months, numerous small pleasure craft will be encountered here. There are several resorts located at Cape Mudge.

33 **Light**. — Cape Mudge Sector light (511) is shown at an elevation of 17.7 m from a white tower, 12.2 m high. The fog signal consists of one blast every 30 seconds.

34 **Tidal streams** in the vicinity of Cape Mudge attain 7 to 9 kn, the flood flowing south and the ebb north. On a strong flood there is a strong counter current along the edge of Wilby Shoals as far as the lighthouse, small craft take full advantage when proceeding north. On the ebb, a similar backeddy is evident along the shore between Cape Mudge lighthouse and Yaculta village.

35 **Caution. — Between Cape Mudge and Willow Point there is a heavy race on south-going streams. When opposed by strong SE winds short steep swells and a rough sea form that can be very dangerous. Under such conditions small vessels are advised to pass through the area at or after HW slack.**

36 **Wilby Shoals**, with a least depth of 3.2 m, are steep-to and extend 2.5 miles ESE of Cape Mudge. In summer they are marked by kelp.

37 **Buoy**. — Wilby Shoals light buoy "P60" (510), off the south edge of the shoals, is a starboard hand buoy.

38 Port hand buoy "P61" marks the east extremity of Wilby Shoals.

39 **Willow Point** (49°58'N, 125°12'W) is low and covered with willows. A rocky ledge extends about 0.3 mile east from it (Chart 3538). A large boulder, 1.3 miles NW of Willow Point, is 7 m high and conspicuous. Boat launching ramps are north of the boulder.

Chart 3540

40 **Yaculta Bank** (50°01'N, 125°13'W) extends about 0.6 mile from the west shore of Discovery Passage and has a least depth of 5.2 m approximately at its centre. Kelp grows on the shallowest part during summer but is visible only at or near slack water.

41 **Clearing marks**. — The west extremity of Gowlland Island, in line with the extremity of the land north of Quathiaski Cove, bearing 339°, leads about 0.2 mile east of the bank.

42 The First Nations village of **Yaculta**, on Quadra Island opposite Yaculta Bank, has a public wharf, with a berthing length of 86 m, protected on its south side by a pile and timber breakwater. A museum, lodge and boatworks with haul out are located in Yaculta. Mooring overnight at the public wharf is not recommended because of cruise ship wakes.

Chart 3540

43　　A **submarine pipeline** (sewer outfall), 0.5 mile south of the public wharf, extends 0.1 mile offshore.

Campbell River to Duncan Bay

44　　**Campbell River** municipality *(50°01'N, 125°15'W)* is a logging, mining, commercial fishing centre, and resort area noted for sport fishing. Accommodation, banks, restaurants, numerous stores, and complete postal service are available. An RCMP detachment is based here with a patrol vessel. Physicians, surgeons and a modern hospital are available. Several marinas and launching ramps are available.

45　　**A Coast Guard rescue vessel is based at Campbell River.**

46　　**Arrival information**. — Campbell River is a port of entry with resident Customs officials, office hours are 0830 to 1630, Monday to Friday.

47　　**Hidden Harbour**, a private marina with a breakwater, is 1 mile south of the public boat basin.

48　　A **public fishing and recreation pier** extends east then north from the south end of the south breakwater at the boat basin. It is lighted at night and not designed for berthing.

49　　The **approach** to Campbell River from the south is encumbered with Yaculta Bank. A large neon sign on the Discovery Inn, just north of the boat basin, is conspicuous.

50　　**Lights. — Beacon**. — Campbell River breakwater light *(512)* is on the north extremity of the south breakwater.

51　　Campbell River North light *(512.2)*, close north of the ferry landing breakwater, is shown at an elevation of 6.1 m from a dolphin with a port hand daymark.

52　　Campbell River Ferry Terminal Dolphins Nos. 2 and 3 lights *(512.3, 512.4)*, NE of Campbell River North light, are on dolphins. The north light has starboard hand daymarks and the south light has port hand daymarks.

53　　Private lights and radar reflectors are at the ferry landing.

54　　A port hand daybeacon is on the breakwater 0.3 mile north of the ferry landing.

55　　Tyee Spit South breakwater light *(511.3)* marks the marina entrance and has a port hand daymark.

56　　Tyee Spit North breakwater light *(511.5)* is on a dolphin at the north end of the north breakwater.

57　　**Light range**. — Private range lights lead north of the ferry landing breakwater.

58　　**Anchorage**. — As tidal streams are strong and holding ground poor, only temporary anchorage during calm weather should be considered in the vicinity of Campbell River. During rough weather Duncan Bay provides the only safe anchorage for large vessels. Small craft can obtain shelter within the boat harbours, in Quathiaski Cove or Gowlland Harbour.

59　　A **submarine cable area** crosses Discovery Passage from north of the ferry landing in Campbell River to Quathiaski Cove.

60　　**Submarine pipelines** extend from the west side of Discovery Passage in three locations. The first extends from the south end of the breakwater that protects the boat basin. A sewer outfall extends NE from shore 0.5 mile NW of Tyee Spit. A sewer outfall extends from the east side of the point that forms Duncan Bay.

61　　**Meteorological information** and a frequency of fog table for Campbell River are in the Appendices.

62　　**Tides**. — Tidal predictions for Campbell River (Index No. 8074) are in *Tide Tables, Volume 6*.

63　　**Berths**. — Fisherman's Wharf (Campbell River Harbour Authority), 1.7 miles south of Tyee Spit, is protected by a rock breakwater, 0.25 mile long. It is approached around the north end of the breakwater and has depths of 1.8 m in its entrance and at the north floats. Public wharves are in this boat basin. The north wharf is 88 m long and has public floats on its north face and a fish company float on its south face. The south wharf is 37 m long and has public floats extending from it. Water, power, washrooms, showers, tidal grids and pay phones are available.

64　　A **ferry landing** and a marina, 0.2 mile north of the boat basin, are protected on their east side by a rock breakwater. Power, pumpout, washrooms, showers and laundry are available. This is the closest marina to downtown and is part of the Coast Discovery Inn hotel.

65　　A **marina** and fuel float are in the large dredged basin protected by two rock breakwaters. Gas, diesel, washrooms, showers, laundry, garbage drop, power and internet access are available. A shopping plaza and restaurant are adjacent. Commercial vessel moorage and limited pleasure craft moorage is available at the Campbell River Public Wharf at north end of the basin. Washrooms, showers, tidal grid, waste oil disposal and telephone are available.

66　　**Discovery Terminal** (Boliden/Westmin Resources), on the east side and south end of Tyee Spit, is 122 m long with a depth of 10.3 m alongside (1980). Mooring dolphins 21 m NNW and SSE of the wharf are connected to it by catwalks. It is used to load ore concentrates by conveyors and ship loaders into deep-sea vessels and barges. The largest vessel to use the facility was 179 m long with a draught of 11.6 m, silting has occurred since.

67　　**Communications**. — Regular daily bus service north to Port Hardy and south to Victoria is available. The airport, about 8 km south of the town, has an asphalt runway 1,524 m long. There are daily scheduled flights to and from Vancouver and other centres. Frequent ferry service for passengers and vehicles operates to and from Quathiaski Cove on Quadra Island.

68　　**Campbell River** enters Discovery Passage at the north end of Campbell River municipality. Its entrance is blocked by drying sand bars and an extensive booming ground. **Tyee Spit** is a low neck of land extending NNW from the east side of the river entrance. Floats for aircraft, a marina and a heliport are on the west side of Tyee Spit. Several marinas and repair ramps for aircraft are located just inside the river entrance on its west side.

69　　The entrance to Campbell River, west of Tyee Spit, and the area in Discovery Passage NE of Tyee Spit, is a **water aerodrome**.

70　　**Light**. — A flashing aeronautical light, on a red mast at the north end of Tyee Spit, is activated by the aircraft pilot when intending to land or take off.

71　　**Speed limit**. — A sign at the north end of Tyee Spit reads *"Danger Area Vessels Proceed Slowly 5 Knots or Less Watch For Seaplanes By Order Department of Transport"*.

72　　**Light range**. — Tyee Spit range lights *(512.6, 512.7)*, on the middle ground between the spit and the west shore, when in line bearing 205½° lead into the entrance of Campbell River.

73　　**Caution. — Silting is reported in the entrance channel to Campbell River and along the Tyee Spit range leading line.**

Campbell River boat basin (1990)

Campbell River ferry landing & marina (1990)

Tyee Spit (1990)

Campbell River entrance (1990)

Chart 3540

Duncan Bay (1987)

74   **Orange Point** *(50°04'N, 125°16'W)* is low and faced with earthy cliffs of a reddish colour.

75   **Duncan Bay** *(50°04'N, 125°17'W)* is the site of a large pulp and paper mill. Main exports are pulp and newsprint, main incoming cargo is fuel oil. The port is used by bulk carriers, cargo vessels and tugs and barges. Considerable silting occurs alongside the berths.

76   **Middle Point**, on the west side of Duncan Bay 1.2 miles NW of the mill, is low and shelving. **Warspite Rock**, 0.1 mile east of Middle Point, has less than 2 m over it. Kelp, run underwater when tidal streams are strong, grows on the rock during summer months.

77   **Approach**. — No dangers lie in the approach to Duncan Bay. Conspicuous chimneys at the mill are good navigation marks.

78   **Lights**. — Lights, on dolphins off the west shore of the bay, are private.

79   **Booming grounds** and private mooring buoys line the west shore of Duncan Bay.

80   A **submarine pipeline** (sewer outfall) extends 0.2 mile offshore from 0.5 mile south of Middle Point.

81   **Good anchorage** can be obtained in the bay in 30 m, sand. It is well out of the tidal stream and provides shelter from all but NW winds.

82   **Tides**. — Tidal differences for Duncan Bay (Index No. 8087), reference on Campbell River, are in *Tide Tables, Volume 6*.

83   **Wharves**. — **Pulp Wharf**, west berth, is 152 m long and has a least depth of 9.6 m alongside. The east berth has a least depth of 3.8 m alongside. Depths alongside were taken in 1981. There are no shore cranes, vessels use their own loading gear. Fresh water, power, and a telephone are available.

84   **Paper Shipping Wharf**, close south of the pulp wharf, has a berthing length of 152 m with a least depth of 4.6 m at the shore end on its north face. The south face has a least depth of

3.2 m alongside. Depths alongside were taken in 1981. Fresh water is available at 9 tonnes/hour. Power, telephone and a 6 m shore gangway are available at the berth.

85   **Barge loading facilities** are south of the Paper Shipping Wharf.

86   **Floats** connected to shore by a pier and mooring buoys are 0.4 mile south of Middle Point.

87   A **marine terminal** for barges, 0.1 mile south of Middle Point, is 145 m long and has a deck elevation of 1.5 m. Red and white radio masts, one each end of the terminal, have red air obstruction lights.

88   **Harbour services**. — Tugs are available on request.

Quathiaski Cove

89   **Quathiaski Cove** *(50°03'N, 125°13'W)* affords shelter for small vessels. Much of the bottom is rocky and at times a strong current sets through the cove. It can be entered north or south of **Grouse Island**, but the south entrance is generally used. Two rocks with 0.2 m over them lie close near the SE corner of the cove. A net store is in the SE corner and a launching ramp and public floats, each 91 m long, are immediately north of the ferry wharf. Garbage disposal and a barge grid are available.

90   **Lights**. — Quathiaski Cove light *(512.5)* is on the drying reef extending SE from Grouse Island.

91   **Ferry landing**. — In the south part of the cove provides regular service to Campbell River. A private light and radar reflector are at the ferry landing. **Give the ferry a wide berth.**

92   A **submarine pipeline** (sewer outfall) extends from the SE corner into the S entrance of the cove.

93   A **submarine cable area** passes through the south entrance.

94   **Tides**. — Tidal differences for Quathiaski Cove (Index No. 8079), referenced on Campbell River, are in *Tide Tables, Volume 6*.

Chart 3540

95   **Quathiaski Cove** settlement has stores, lodging, gas station, and a post office approximately 500 m inland

96   **Communications**. — The settlement is connected by road with Gowlland Harbour, Heriot Bay, Drew Harbour, Hyacinthe Bay, Granite Bay, Bold Point and Surge Narrows. Ferry service provides transportation for passengers and vehicles to Campbell River on an hourly schedule.

Gowlland Harbour

97   **Gowlland Harbour** *(50°05′N, 125°14′W)*, entered between **Vigilant Islets** off the north end of **Gowlland Island**, and **Entrance Rock** is encumbered with several islets and rocks. The south end is a fine land-locked anchorage. **Spoil Rock**, 0.1 mile east of Vigilant Islets, has 6.4 m over it and like Entrance Rock is marked by kelp. **Entrance Bank**, between Entrance Rock and **May Island**, has 0.2 m over it, sand bottom. **Wren Islet, Crow Islet, Mouse Islets, Fawn Islet, Stag Island** and **Doe Islet** are on the north and east sides of the harbour and are Provincial Park Reserves.

98   **Steep Island** *(50°05′N, 125°15′W)* is steep sided with cliffs on its SW side. A boat passage between the SW extremity of Gowlland Island and **April Point** is encumbered with drying and below-water rocks but gives access to the south part of Gowlland Harbour.

99   **Aids to Navigation**. — Starboard hand buoy "N2" marks rocks extending NE from April Point.

100   Steep Island light *(514)* is on the west side of the island.

101   A daybeacon, on the NW point of Steep Island, has a starboard hand daymark.

102   **Tides**. — Tidal differences for Gowlland Harbour (Index No. 8082), referenced on Campbell River, are in *Tide Tables, Volume 6*.

103   A **submarine cable** crosses from the south end of Gowlland Island to 0.2 mile east of April Point.

104   **Facilities**. — A resort is NW of Fawn Islet, limited moorage with power, water, laundry and telephones are available. Numerous private floats line east and north shores. A sport fishing resort with floats is at April Point and a marina is 0.3 mile SE. Moorage, launching ramp, power, water, showers, laundry, garbage disposal and a free shuttle to April Point Resort and Painter's Lodge are available.

105   **Anchorage** can be obtained in Gowlland Harbour south of Doe Islet in 15 m, mud.

106   **Booming grounds** on the east side of Gowlland Island reduce the fairway to about 0.1 mile wide in vicinity of Wren and Mouse Islets. Booming grounds are also located NE of Entrance Rock, east and SE of Stag Island, at the south end of the harbour and in the bay north of May Island.

Menzies Bay and Approach

Chart 3539

107   **Race Point** *(50°07′N, 125°19′W)* is a bold, rocky bluff that is steep-to.

108   **Light**. — Race Point light *(515)* is on the east extremity of the point.

109   **Menzies Bay**, on the west side of the approach to Seymour Narrows, has a ruined pier on **Josephine Flat** near the entrance to **Mohun Creek**. Booming grounds with numerous dolphins, a mooring buoy and barge loading ramp are close-off **Huntingford Point**. **Bloedel**, on the south side of Menzies Bay, is fronted by booming grounds and has a log dump and conveyor for loading barges.

110   **Tides**. — Tidal differences for Bloedel (Index No. 8095), referenced on Owen Bay, are in *Tide Tables, Volume 6*.

111   **Tidal streams**. — When the flood, or south-going, tidal stream is running at strength through Seymour Narrows, it strikes the shore about midway between Race and Huntingford Points. Part flows east past Race Point, and the other turns west to Huntingford Point, where it is deflected NW and lost in the middle of Menzies Bay.

112   The flood stream attains 11 kn off Race Point causing overfalls and eddies extending some distance east. **With fresh east or SE winds this race becomes very dangerous to small**

Menzies Bay and Seymour Narrows (1987)

craft. Between Middle and Race Points there is a strong counter current along the shore when the south-going stream is strong.

113 When the ebb stream is running at strength toward Seymour Narrows its west part impinges on Stephenson Point but without much force and the portion of it that flows west is lost almost immediately. There is very little swirl west of a line joining Stephenson Point and a position about midway between Race and Huntingford Points.

114 **Defender Shoal**, in the middle of Menzies Bay, is composed of sand, steep-to on its east side, and dries 1.5 m near its middle. A 1.5 m shoal is off the NE end of Defender Shoal. A narrow channel, NE of the shoal, has a navigable width of about 130 m.

115 **Buoy.** — A private lighted port hand buoy marks the NE end of Defender Shoal.

116 **Booming grounds** with numerous dolphins lie between Defender Shoal and the west shore of Menzies Bay. A log dump is about 60 m from shore in the form of an oval turnabout. A line of dolphins lies along the mud flats fronting **Menzies Creek**.

117 **Anchorage.** — The bottom of Menzies Bay is littered with bark and debris from years of log booming.

118 **Temporary anchorage**, convenient when waiting the turn of the tidal stream in Seymour Narrows, can be obtained in the south part of Menzies Bay, in 9-11 m, with no inconvenience from tidal streams or eddies. Care must be taken to avoid the 4.9 m shoal near Bloedel. Vessels should on no account get into depths less than 10 m.

119 **Secure anchorage** is NW of Defender Shoal in 11-12 m, mud and sand, entirely out of the tidal streams. When approaching, give Stephenson Point a wide berth. If the tidal stream is running strongly get into slack water in the middle of the SE part of the bay. The NE shore, which is steep, should then be closed and kept at a distance of not more than 90 m until the mouth of a conspicuous green ravine with a large grey boulder in it is abeam. When this ravine has been passed, the vessel will be inside Defender Shoal, anchorage can be obtained as convenient. Leaving Menzies Bay and proceeding north on a strong ebb stream, proceed to the east about 0.2 mile off the south shore until abeam Race Point, before turning to shape a course through Seymour Narrows.

120 **Nymphe Cove** *(50°08′N, 125°22′W)*, east of **Stephenson Point**, does not offer good anchorage, it is exposed to the SE and holding ground is poor. The bottom south of the drying mud flats at its head is bare rock. An overhead cable, vertical clearance 21 m, crosses mud flats at the head of the cove.

Seymour Narrows

121 **Seymour Narrows** *(50°08′N, 125°21′W)*, the narrowest portion of Discovery Passage, begins about 1 mile NW of Race Point, it is nearly 2 miles long and not less than 0.4 mile wide. Shores on either side are high, rugged and steep-to. Ripple Rock, almost in the middle of the channel, causes considerable turbulence when tidal streams are running at strength.

122 **Caution.** — **Mariners are advised to navigate Seymour Narrows only at or near slack water if their vessel is of low power, towing other vessels, or is a small vessel under about 20 m long. Fatal accidents have occurred to small vessels when attempting to navigate this narrows when the tidal stream is running at full strength.**

123 **Small vessels have been capsized with loss of life while navigating Seymour Narrows even near slack water and in reasonable weather conditions. They were in light condition with considerable top weight. Precautions should be taken to maintain adequate stability and trim even when planning to transit at slack water. All crew members should be alert and ready to cope with any emergency.**

124 If one must go through on the flood stream the west side of the narrows should be avoided.

125 **Maud Island** *(50°08′N, 125°21′W)* lies on the east side at the south end of Seymour Narrows. A narrow passage north of the island is blocked by a dam and an overhead cable close west of the dam has a vertical clearance of 42 m. **Yellow Island**, 0.4 mile east of Maud Island, is rocky, bare and easily identified.

126 **Artificial reef.** — HMCS Columbia was sunk east of Maud Island as an artificial reef for divers. It is marked by buoys.

127 **Marine farm** facilities and booming grounds are NW of Yellow Island.

128 **Lights.** — Maud Island South light *(515.5)* is shown at an elevation of 6.8 m from a white tower with a red band at the top on the south extremity of the island.

129 Maud Island light *(516)* is shown at an elevation of 8.5 m from a white tower with a red band at the top on a rock on the west side of the island.

130 **Wilfred Point**, on the west side and at the south end of Seymour Narrows, is bare on its east side and has prominent hydroelectric towers.

131 **Light.** — Wilfred Point light *(516.3)* is shown at an elevation of 6.7 m from a white tower with a green band at the top.

132 **Overhead cables** (power), vertical clearance 58 m, cross Seymour Narrows between towers. One tower is about 0.13 mile north of Wilfred Point, and the other about the same distance north of Maud Island light. The cables are fitted with orange and white spheres.

133 **Ripple Rock**, which has two heads with 13.7 and 15.2 m over them, is about 0.2 mile in extent and slightly to the west of mid-channel, with the south and shallowest head about 0.25 mile west of Maud Island light. Channels on either side of the rock have depths in excess of 50 m.

134 **North Bluff** is a prominent headland on the east shore, about 0.6 mile north of Maud Island light. **Puget Bluff**, also on the east side of the narrows, is nearly 1 mile north of North Bluff. Between them about 0.3 mile inland is **Mount Lolo**.

135 **Tides.** — Tidal differences for Seymour Narrows (Index No. 8105), referenced on Owen Bay, are in *Tide Tables, Volume 6*.

136 **Tidal steams** in Seymour Narrows attain 16 kn, the flood sets south and the ebb north. **When either stream is running at strength, eddies and swirls are extremely heavy, and when these are opposed by a strong wind, the races become very dangerous to small vessels.** In the vicinity of Ripple Rock near the shallowest parts there are up-wellings that vary in strength with the velocity of the stream. These up-wellings occur about every 5 seconds, increase in size and are swept away in the current causing eddies and whirlpools.

137 Daily predictions of times of slack water, and times and rates of maximum flood and ebb streams, are tabulated for current station Seymour Narrows (Index No. 5000) in *Tide Tables, Volume 6*. Duration of slack water can be as much as 12 or 15 minutes, but when there is a large range of tide the interval of

Chart 3539

Seymour Narrows on the flood (1987)

Seymour Narrows on the ebb (1986)

change can be considerably less. Local weather conditions particularly when severe, can affect the duration of slack water considerably.

138   **Flood stream**. — On the flood along the west shore eddies and rips start about opposite North Bluff, and further south under the power cables they extend out about 0.1 mile. Upwellings over Ripple Rock start under the power cables, and from there to the west shore water is very turbulent. Rips and up-

wellings then curve gently to mid-channel south of Maud Island light. In the centre and east part of the channel, current is straight and true to abeam Maud Island light and to the south to where rips on both sides meet. Along the east shore, rips and eddies start north of North Bluff and extend in an almost straight line down to Maud Island light. Rips extend due south of the light to about the middle of the channel where they meet rips and eddies from the west shore and culminate in large whirls and eddies. This area of maximum

Chart 3539

turbulence extends beyond Race Point and gradually diminishes toward the entrance to Gowlland Harbour. Maximum strength of the stream can be expected in the vicinity of Maud Island.

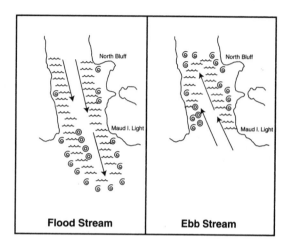

Flood Stream   **Ebb Stream**

139   **Ebb stream**. — On the ebb smooth water is present in the tongue of the stream to the north as far as North Bluff, about 0.6 mile north of Maud Island light. At this point rips from both east and west sides meet and culminate in large smooth whirls and eddies. Due to the course of the main stream through the narrows, up-wellings over Ripple Rock are much further over toward the west shore. Therefore on the ebb no turbulence is met until abeam North Bluff. From this point to Puget Bluff, the channel is all whirls and eddies that diminish gradually farther north and disappear almost entirely abreast Separation Head. Maximum strength of the stream is encountered in the vicinity of Maud Island light.

Discovery Passage — North Part

140   From Seymour Narrows, the north part of Discovery Passage trends about 12 miles north to its junction with Johnstone Strait. North of Seymour Narrows navigation is simple and a mid-channel course should be maintained.

141   **Tidal streams** in this portion of the passage are comparatively weak and do not exceed 3 kn.

142   **Plumper Bay** *(50°10'N, 125°20'W)* is a convenient stopping place for vessels waiting the turn of the tidal stream in Seymour Narrows. Most of the east slope is bare. Booming grounds are at the NE corner and the head of the bay. A detached rocky patch, with 11 m over it, lies in the middle of the bay about 0.3 mile ENE of **Plumper Point**, it must be avoided when anchoring. Good anchorage, well-sheltered and out of the tidal stream, can be obtained in Plumper Bay, in 15 to 18 m, mud and sand, about 0.5 mile ENE of Plumper Point. Vessels anchored in depths over 20 m can at times experience strong tidal streams and eddies, which might cause them to surge on the cables.

143   An **RV park**, with float, fishing pier and launching ramp, is in the small bay south of Brown Bay.

144   **Brown Bay**, on the west shore of Discovery Passage, is the site of a marina, but too deep for anchorage. A floating breakwater, consisting of former tank cars, protects the marina, enter to the north of the breakwater. Gas, diesel, propane, moorage, power, washrooms, showers and laundry are available. Strong tidal streams set through the bay on large tides.

145   **Light**. — Brown Bay light *(516.5)*, on an islet close north of the bay, is shown at an elevation of 7.2 m from a white tower with a green band at the top.

146   **Tides**. — Tidal differences for Brown Bay (Index No. 8110), referenced on Owen Bay, are in *Tide Tables, Volume 6*.

147   **Separation Head** *(50°11'N, 125°21'W)* is cliffy in places and steep-to. Fishing boundary markers are on Separation Head and the north entrance point to Deepwater Bay.

148   **Light**. — Separation Head light *(516.6)* is on the point.

149   **Deepwater Bay**, NE of Separation Head, has depths in excess of 40 m with sand and mud bottom. A small vessel can anchor in 20 m close inshore in the south corner of the bay. Dolphins are on the west side of the bay. A logging camp (1986) is on the east shore, 1.7 miles north of Separation Head.

150   **McMullen Point** *(50°15'N, 125°24'W)* is a steep-to headland. A private float and fishing pier are in Eagle Cove (local name), close north of the point.

151   **Light**. — McMullen Point light *(517)* is shown at an elevation of 8.5 m from a white tower with a green band at the top.

152   **Kanish Bay** *(50°15'N, 125°20'W)*, entered between **Bodega Point** and **Granite Point**, has the **Chained Islands** along its south shore. Several drying rocks lie in the passage between Bodega Point and the west Chained Island, great care is needed in this part of the passage. **Nixon Island** is 1 mile SE of Granite Point. **Nixon Rock**, south of Nixon Island, has less than 2 m over it. Booming grounds and mooring buoys are south of Chained Islands.

153   **Marine farm** facilities are in the bay between Granite Bay and Small Inlet, at the SE end of Chained Islands, and along the north shore between Small Inlet and Granite Point.

154   **Granite Bay**, in the SE part of Kanish Bay, has a rock with less than 2 m over it in its approach and its entrance fairway is less than 90 m wide. A booming ground and float are at the head of the bay.

155   **Small Inlet**, in the NE part of Kanish Bay, has a narrow entrance with depths of 2.4 m.

156   **Anchorage** for small craft can be obtained 0.7 mile east of Bodega Point, south of Chained Islands, in 26 m, mud. Good sheltered anchorage can also be obtained in Granite Bay in 7 to 13 m, mud bottom, or in Small Inlet.

157   **Islet Point** *(50°18'N, 125°24'W)* is the north entrance point at the west end of Okisollo Channel. **Cinque Islands**, close west of Islet Point, are fringed with foul ground.

158   **Light**. — Cinque Islands light *(517.5)*, on the west shore of the largest island, is shown at an elevation of 6 m from a mast fitted with a starboard hand daymark.

159   A rock, which dries 1.2 m, lies 0.1 mile off the east shore 0.4 mile north of Cinque Islands. A logging camp and log dump (1986) are in Green Sea Bay (local name), 1.3 miles north of the Cinque Islands.

160   **Elk Bay** *(50°17'N, 125°26'W)*, between **Moriarty Point** and **Elk Point**, has numerous dolphins along its south shore and a drying sand bank extends nearly 0.2 mile from the west shore. A logging camp and private float (1986) are in the bay.

161   **Fair anchorage**, open to north and east but out of the strength of tidal streams, can be obtained in Elk Bay in a depth of about 26 m, mud and sand. The anchorage is often used when awaiting slack water at Seymour Narrows.

Chart 3539

162   **Rock Bay Marine Provincial Park** includes the foreshore and waters from close south of Slab Point (Discovery Passage) to 0.4 mile west of Rock Bay. Anchorage and a boat launching area are available.

163   **Otter Cove**, 2.5 miles north of Elk Bay, offers sheltered anchorage to small craft near its head. Approach should be made between Rocky Islets and Limestone Island. The passage south of Limestone Island is encumbered with foul ground. **Limestone Island** lies 0.2 mile NW of **Slab Point**. **Snag Rock**, 0.1 mile east of Limestone Island, has 4.9 m over it. **Rocky Islets**, close-off the north shore of Otter Cove, consist of two islets connected by a drying rock ledge.

164   **Chatham Point** *(50°20'N, 125°26'W)*, at the junction of Discovery Passage and Johnstone Strait, is low, wooded and rocky. White buildings with red roofs on the point are prominent. Foul ground, in which there are drying and sunken rocks, extends from the shore north of the point. When rounding Chatham Point it should be given a berth of about 0.5 mile.

165   **Beaver Rock**, with less than 2 m over it, lies close NNE of Chatham Point light. **Small craft are warned against attempting passage inside Chatham Point light. It can be very rough off Chatham Point when the prevailing west wind blows against an ebb tide.**

166   **Light**. — Chatham Point light *(518)*, on a drying rock 0.2 mile north of the point, is shown at an elevation of 6.4 m from a white tower with a green band at the top. The fog signal consists of one blast every 20 seconds.

167   A **submarine cable** (power) is laid from Vancouver Island to Chatham Point light.

168   A **radio tower** with red air obstruction lights is 0.3 mile NW of Chatham Point.

169   **Meteorological information** for Chatham Point is in the Appendices.

Johnstone Strait

Charts 3543, 3544, 3545, 3546

170   **Johnstone Strait** *(50°20'N, 125°28'W)* extends along the NE coast of Vancouver Island from Chatham Point at its east end, to Blinkhorn Peninsula at its west end, a distance of about 54 miles. Mountain ranges separated by valleys through which flow streams of considerable size, rise abruptly from the water's edge along the south shore. Some of the highest peaks are snow covered year round.

171   **Thurlow Islands**, Hardwicke Island, a portion of the mainland, West Cracroft and Hanson Islands form the north shore of Johnstone Strait. Mountains on the north shore are not so rugged nor do they attain such great elevations. The north shore is broken by several channels and inlets.

172   **Vessel Traffic Services (VTS)**. — Johnstone Strait is in *Sector Four* of the *Vancouver Traffic Zone* and is administered by *Comox Traffic*. Assigned frequency is 156.575 MHz, Channel 71. Calling-in points in are:

173   *Calling-in Point No. 30*, *Ripple Point*, is a line running 000°–180° through Ripple Point light *(521)*.

174   *Calling-in Point No. 31*, *Vansittart Point*, is a line running 000°–180° through Vansittart Point light *(522)*.

175   *Calling-in Point No. 32*, *Fanny Island*, is a line running 045°–225° through Fanny Island light *(542.8)*.

176   *Calling-in Point No. 33*, *Boat Bay*, is a line running 000°–180° through Boat Bay light *(544)*.

177   A brief description of this VTS is in *PAC 200*. Details are in *Radio Aids to Marine Navigation (Pacific and Western Arctic)*.

178   **Tides**. — Tidal differences in Johnstone Strait, referenced on Owen Bay, for Chatham Point (Index No. 8180) and Knox Bay (Index No. 8195) and tidal differences, referenced on Alert Bay, for Billygoat Bay (Index No. 8210), Kelsey Bay (Index No. 8215), Yorke Island (Index No. 8233), Port Neville (Index No. 8245) and Port Harvey (Index No. 8250) are in *Tide Tables, Volume 6*.

179   **Tidal streams** in Johnstone and Broughton Straits are predominantly semi-diurnal with the flood setting east and the ebb west. There is also a large residual westerly current at the surface where the strongest average currents are on the mainland side of the channel. This residual current results in much stronger ebbs than floods. In fact, many days can pass before there is any appreciable surface flood current in Johnstone Strait. In winter, prevailing SE winds tend to increase the ebb and reduce duration of the flood current. In summer prevailing NW winds have the opposite effect.

180   **At the junction of Discovery Passage and Johnstone Strait** maximum flood occurs 30 minutes later than at Johnstone Strait – Central, and maximum ebb 50 minutes later. Times of slack water are very close to those at Seymour Narrows. At Bear Point, about 9 miles west, maximum flood and ebb occur 30 and 20 minutes later respectively, than at Johnstone Strait – Central, but times of slack water are quite different. Turn to flood occurs 35 minutes earlier and turn to ebb 1 h 35 later than at Johnstone Strait – Central. In this stretch of Johnstone Strait during spring tides both daily ebbs have the same velocity of 2½ kn. The current appears to level off at this speed, and to maintain it for 2½–3 hours. When the range of tide is less than 1 m there is diurnal inequality in the ebbs and the maximum speed drops to 1½ kn. The flood stream has a large diurnal inequality with a maximum just over 2 kn. When the range of tide is less than 1 m there will be no flood current for that period.

181   **In Race and Current Passages**, 8 miles west of Bear Point, maximum flood and ebb occur at the same time as those for Bear Point. Slack water times however are greatly affected by the difference in the residual current between the surface and the bottom in Johnstone Strait. The turn to flood in both Race and Current Passages occurs at the same time, but the turn to ebb in Current Passage occurs 1 h 15 earlier than that in Race Passage.

182   **In Sunderland Channel**, north of Yorke Island, about 5 miles west of Current Passage, times of slack water and maximum ebb are 1 h 40 earlier, while maximum flood is 1 h 10 earlier than that at Johnstone Strait – Central.

183   **In the main body of Johnstone Strait** west of Yorke Island the surface current quickly rises after slack water to 75% or more of maximum current and holds this speed for 3½ hours or more. When the prediction for lower HW at Alert Bay is less than 3.7 m, there generally will be no flood current for that period. At Forward Bay, about 11 miles west of Johnstone Strait – Central, maximum currents and turn to flood occur 10 minutes earlier than, and the turn to ebb occurs at the same time as, those for Johnstone Strait – Central.

184   **At the west end of Johnstone Strait**, in Blackney Passage and Broughton Strait, times of maximum current are the same, or nearly the same as Johnstone Strait – Central. Times of

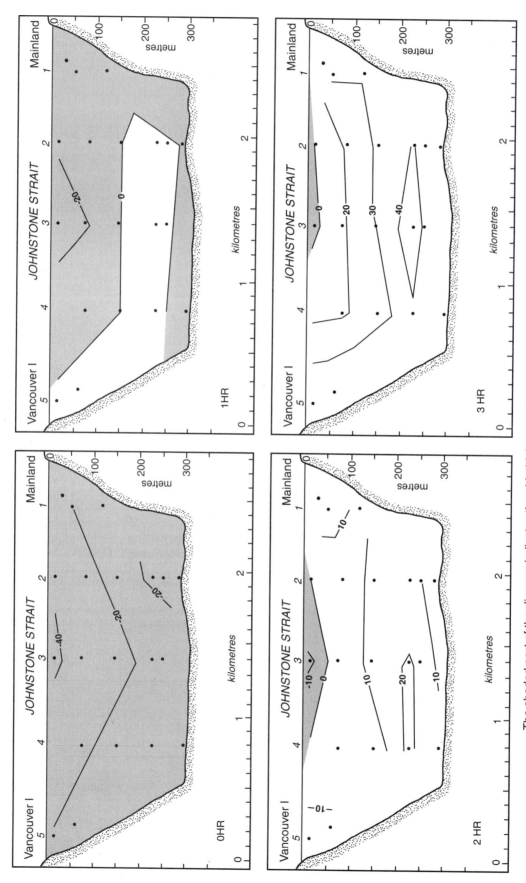

The shaded part of the diagram indicates the ebb tidal stream (west going); the white area indicates the flood tidal stream (east going). The figures within the profile denote cm/sec (51.5 cm/sec equals 1 kn).

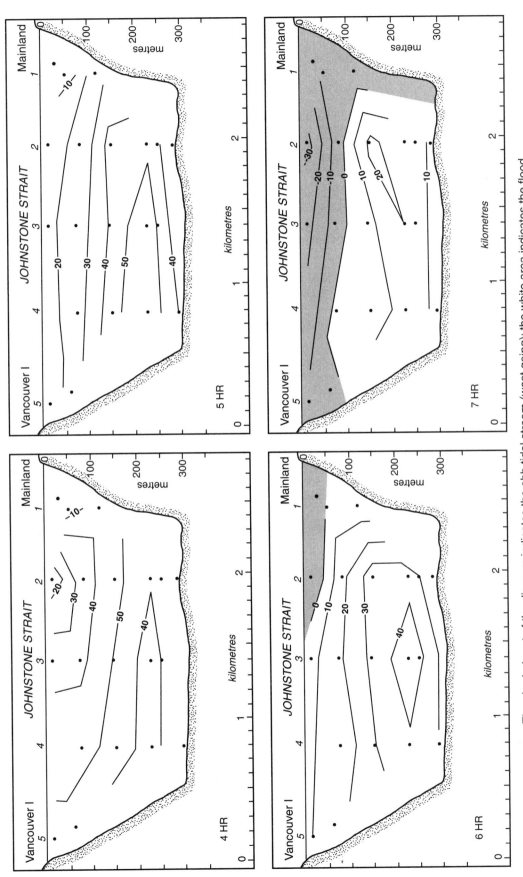

The shaded part of the diagram indicates the ebb tidal stream (west going); the white area indicates the flood tidal stream (east going). The figures within the profile denote cm/sec (51.5 cm/sec equals 1 kn).

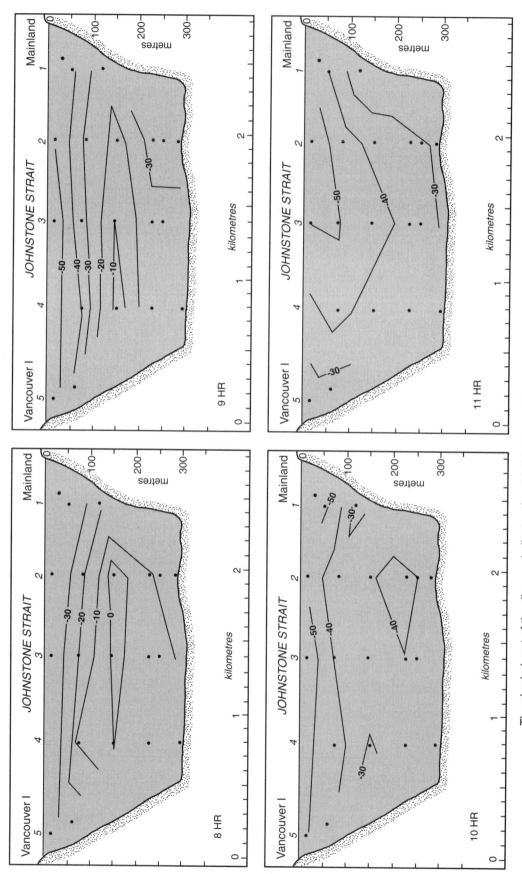

The shaded part of the diagram indicates the ebb tidal stream (west going); the white area indicates the flood tidal stream (east going). The figures within the profile denote cm/sec (51.5 cm/sec equals 1 kn).

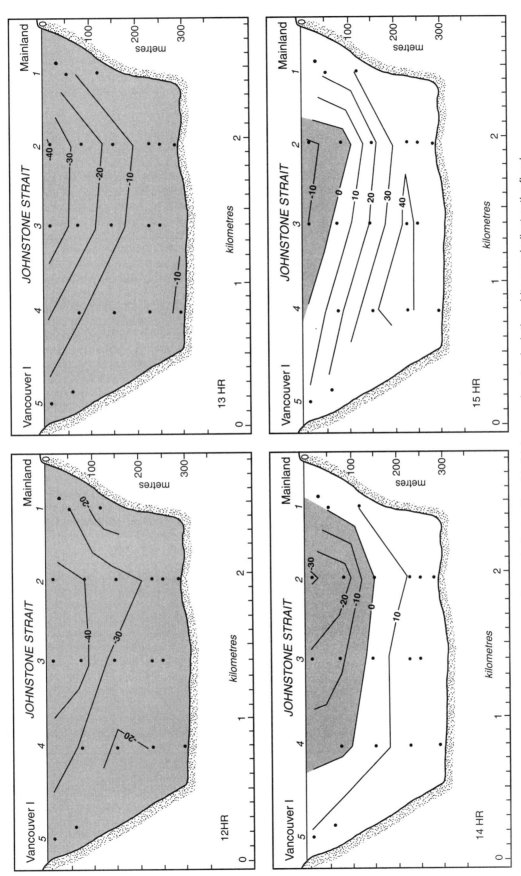

The shaded part of the diagram indicates the ebb tidal stream (west going); the white area indicates the flood tidal stream (east going). The figures within the profile denote cm/sec (51.5 cm/sec equals 1 kn).

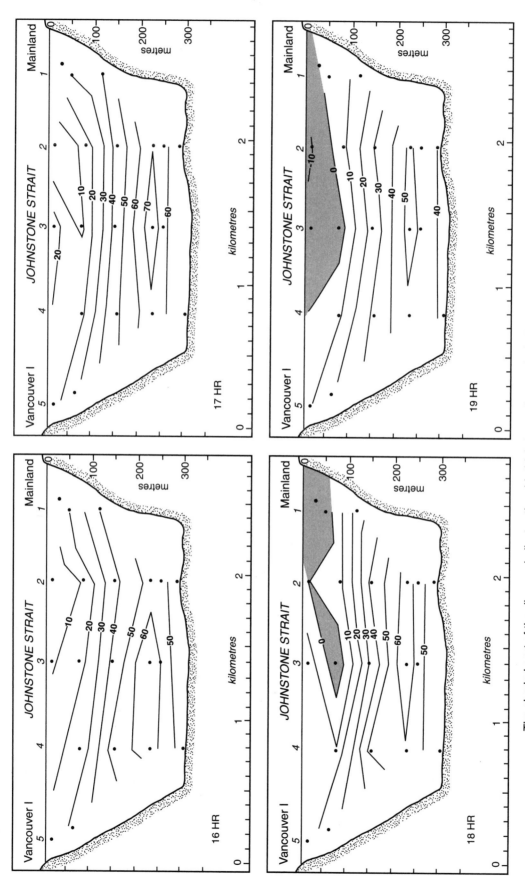

The shaded part of the diagram indicates the ebb tidal stream (west going); the white area indicates the flood tidal stream (east going). The figures within the profile denote cm/sec (51.5 cm/sec equals 1 kn).

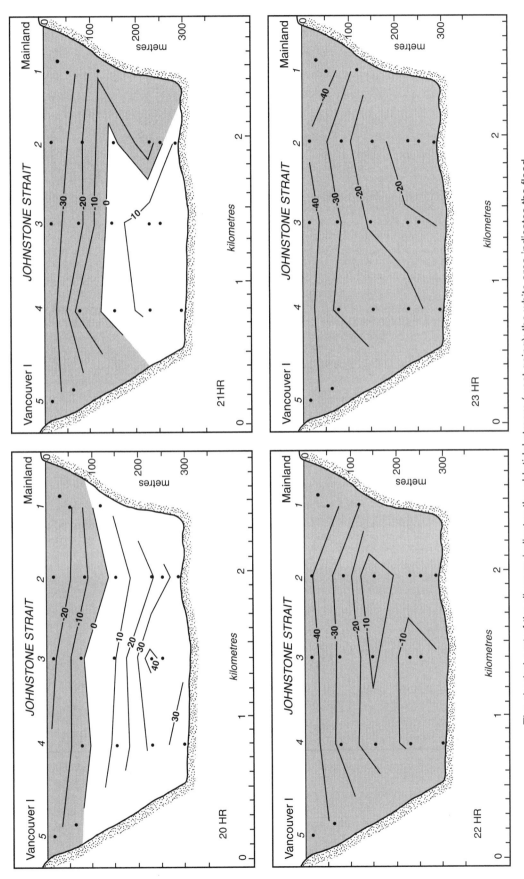

The shaded part of the diagram indicates the ebb tidal stream (west going); the white area indicates the flood tidal stream (east going). The figures within the profile denote cm/sec (51.5 cm/sec equals 1 kn).

slack water differ considerably and are best referenced to slack water times at Seymour Narrows, see secondary current stations Blackney Passage (Index No. 6035), Alert Bay (Index No. 6040) and Pulteney Point (Index No. 6046) in *Tide Tables, Volume 6.*

185   **A cross section of Johnstone Strait** about 1.5 miles west of Port Neville is shown during a time of average tide heights on the accompanying diagram. Large differences from one side to the other in both speeds and times of turn are evident on the surface. The flood current starts at depths around 200 m and builds up to speeds greater than ¾ kn while there is still an ebb current running on the surface. On the surface the flood current starts along the Vancouver Island shore at about the same time as it starts at depth, but takes over 2 hours to cover the strait completely from one side to the other. Current along the Vancouver Island shore is much stronger than elsewhere across the strait. However, as soon as the flood current covers the entire strait the speed drops off dramatically, to about one-third of its maximum speed. In less than 2 hours after the flood current covers the entire surface, the ebb current is starting to run along the mainland shore and within the hour the whole strait on the surface is ebbing. The flood current still continues to run at depth for about 2 hours after the start of the ebb on the surface. At the time of maximum ebb, current speed is the same across the strait then falls off quickly on the Vancouver Island shore prior to the start of the next flood current. The ebb current runs strongest on the surface with speed decreasing with depth.

186   At a cross section of Johnstone Strait about 1.5 miles east of Port Neville the start of the flood current is similar to the cross section west of Port Neville, but the ebb current starts in the centre of the channel rather than along the mainland shore. When running at its maximum the ebb is much stronger along the mainland shore. On a large flood the flood current runs for 6 hours on the surface, longer at depth. Change to ebb on the surface is much quicker, within the hour, than on the change to flood.

187   **Tide-rips, dangerous to small craft, are encountered off Ripple Point, in Race and Current Passages and between Kelsey Bay and Port Neville.**

188   Times and rates of the maximum current and time of slack water are predicted and tabulated as daily tables for current station Johnstone Strait – Central (Index No. 6000), which is about 1.5 miles to the west of Port Neville. These predictions are in *Tide Tables, Volume 6.*

189   Secondary current stations in Johnstone Strait, referenced on Johnstone Strait – Central, are given for Bear Point (Index No. 6008), Camp Point (Index No. 6012), Current Passage (Index No. 6014), Sunderland Channel (Index No. 6018) and Forward Bay (Index No. 6028) in *Tide Tables, Volume 6.*

190   **Meteorological information** in Johnstone and Broughton Straits is given for Chatham Point and Alert Bay and a frequency of fog table for Alert Bay are in the Appendices.

Chatham Point to Tyee Point

Chart 3543

191   **Rock Bay** *(50°20′N, 125°28′W)*, between Chatham Point and **Rock Point**, has a launching ramp and float, protected by a floating breakwater, on its west side. A road from the bay connects with the main highway system.

192   **Light.** — Rock Point light *(519)* is shown at an elevation of 5.8 m from a white tower with a green band at the top.

193   **Little Bear Bay**, west of Rock Point, is almost completely filled with a moderately steep-to drying bank. Booming grounds with dolphins are in the bay, and blue tanks of a salmon hatchery are on shore west of the drying flats. A submarine pipeline extends into the bay from the hatchery.

194   **Turn Island** *(50°21′N, 125°28′W)* is wooded and about 0.1 mile off the south extremity of **East Thurlow Island**.

195   **Siwash Rock**, 0.1 mile south of the west end of Turn Island, has less than 2 m over it.

196   **Light.** — Turn Island light *(518.5)*, on the south side of the island, is shown at an elevation of 11.9 m from a mast fitted with a starboard hand daymark and a prominent solar panel.

197   **Anchorage** for small vessels can be obtained in 13 to 15 m in the middle of **Turn Bay**, north of Turn Island. The bay is protected from seas but exposed to winds. A considerable tidal stream sets through Turn Bay.

198   **Walkem Islands** *(50°22′N, 125°31′W)* lie on the north side of the strait. A log dump is on the east side of the largest Walkem Island.

199   **Caution.** — **Tidal streams are strong in vicinity of Walkem Islands. These islands should not be approached within a distance of 0.2 mile. Anchorage in the channel north of the largest island is not recommended.**

200   **Light.** — Walkem Islands light *(520)* is on a drying rock close south of the islands.

201   **Edith Point** *(50°23′N, 125°33′W)* is the SW extremity of East Thurlow Island. **Ivanhoe Rock**, 0.4 mile SSE of Edith Point, is awash.

202   **Ripple Point** *(50°22′N, 125°35′W)* rises steeply to the mountains of **Halifax Range**.

203   **Light.** — Ripple Point light *(521)* is shown at an elevation of 6.1 m from a white tower with a green band at the top.

204   **Tidal streams.** — Off Ripple Point the ebb or west-going stream attains 2-4 kn, the flood stream 2-3 kn. **At times there is a race dangerous to small craft in vicinity of the point.**

205   **Knox Bay**, an indentation in the shore of **West Thurlow Island**, has a log dump and booming ground on the west shore. Depths in the bay are too great for anchorage. It is reported that small craft can obtain anchorage in 15 m close to shore in the NW corner. **Heavy tide-rips are often formed off Needham Point.** A drying rock lies about 0.1 mile off the west entrance point of the bay.

206   **Tides.** — Tidal differences for Knox Bay (Index No. 8195), referenced on Owen Bay, are in Tide *Tables, Volume 6.*

207   **Bear Bight** *(50°22′N, 125°39′W)* affords shelter to small craft east or west of the islet connected to shore. A fishing boundary marker is on the north side of the islet. The bay is a booming ground and white buildings of a logging camp (1995) are conspicuous from NW.

Chart 3544

208   **Humpback Bay** *(50°22′N, 125°41′W)*, 0.8 mile west of **Bear Point**, forms the mouth of **Amor De Cosmos Creek**. A drying flat extends 0.1 mile out from the mouth of the creek and a house is in the cove west of the bay. **Palmer Bay** is 1.2 miles west of Humpback Bay.

209   **Light.** — Bear Point light *(521.6)* is on the point.

210   **Vansittart Point** *(50°23′N, 125°45′W)* is on the south shore of West Thurlow Island, at the foot of **Mount Vansittart**.

Okisollo Channel from Discovery Passage (1986)

Nodales Channel from south of Turn Island light (1986)

Walkem Islands and Chatham Point from Ripple Point (1986)

Mayne Passage from south of Knox Bay (1986)

Chart 3544

211   **Light**. — Vansittart Point light *(522)* is on the point.

212   **Vere Cove**, entered between **Tyee Point** and **Eden Point** at the west end of West Thurlow Island, has steep wooded shores and affords anchorage to small vessels in 20 to 30 m, well out of the tidal streams, it is exposed to the west. **Dorothy Rock**, off the south shore, dries 4 m.

213   **Light**. — Tyee Point light *(522.2)* is on a point close south of Tyee Point.

Race and Current Passages

214   **Current Passage** lies to the north of Helmcken Island and **Race Passage** lies to the south. Chancellor Channel, to the east of these passages, leads north of West Thurlow Island.

215   **Johnstone Strait Traffic Separation Scheme**. — Commences close west of Vansittart Point and extends to the west end of Hardwicke Island. It is recommended for use by all vessels. Separation of traffic is achieved by using Helmcken Island and Ripple Shoal as natural obstacles to divide east from westbound traffic and by introducing separation zones to the east and west of the natural obstacles at the junctions of Race and Current Passages. No inshore traffic zones are provided.

216   It is recommended that eastbound traffic pass to the south of the separation zones and obstacles by using Race Passage, and that westbound traffic pass to the north of the separation zones and obstacles by using Current Passage.

217   **Caution**. — **In some instances a large vessel or a towboat with rafts proceeding westbound on an ebb tide may have difficulty in making the turn to starboard into Current Passage and clearing Ripple Shoal. Under such circumstances the Master may decide to proceed against the traffic flow through Race Passage and should make every effort to warn traffic in the area.**

218   **Radio communications**. — Mariners should follow procedures set out for Vessel Traffic Services *Sector Four* of the *Vancouver Traffic Zone* administered by *Comox Traffic*. Assigned frequency is 156.575 MHz, Channel 71. Calling-in points east and west of the Traffic Separation Scheme are off Vansittart Point light and off Fanny Island light.

219   **Tides**. — Tidal differences, referenced on Alert Bay, are given for Billygoat Bay (Index No. 8210), Kelsey Bay (Index No. 8215) and Yorke Island (Index No. 8233) in *Tide Tables, Volume 6*.

220   **Tidal streams** in the vicinity of Camp Point and Ripple Shoal attain 6 kn with heavy tide-rips at times. Tidal streams are also very strong off Tyee Point, and there are often heavy tide-rips usually with the flood stream when it is opposed by a strong SE wind.

221   Tidal streams run strongly through Current and Race Passages. They attain 5 kn on the ebb and flood in Current Passage and 6 kn on the ebb and flood in Race Passage. **Eddies and swirls in these passages are numerous and frequently strong. When wind opposes the tidal stream they can become dangerous to small vessels.**

222   **Over and around Earl Ledge heavy tide-rips and swirls are sometimes formed. The west approach to Race and Current Passages can be extremely dangerous to small craft when winds oppose the ebb tidal stream.**

223   Secondary current stations, referenced on Johnstone Strait – Central, are given for Camp Point (Index No. 6012), at the east end of Race Passage, and Current Passage (Index No. 6014) in *Tide Tables, Volume 6*.

224   **Caution**. — **On a strong ebb (westbound) tidal stream, care should be taken to avoid being set on Ripple Shoal when altering course to pass north of it. After rounding Helmcken Island care should be taken to avoid being set toward Earl Ledge.**

225   **Camp Point** *(50°23'N, 125°50'W)* is a rounded projection fronted by rock ledges. The coast is fringed with drying rocks, rock ledges, boulders and gravel beaches for 1 mile ESE of the point. To the west it is steep and cliffy with mountains rising abruptly from the water's edge.

226   **Lights**. — Race Passage East light *(522.5)* is on a 1 m high rock about 0.6 mile ESE of Camp Point.

227   Camp Point light *(523)* is on the point.

228   **Ripple Shoal**, in the fairway between Camp and Eden Points, is about 1 mile long with several heads, least depth is 2.8 m. The fairway between the shoal and Camp Point has a minimum width of about 0.3 mile. Kelp grows on the shoal during summer months but is drawn under by tidal streams.

229   **Helmcken Island** *(50°24'N, 125°52'W)*, in the middle of Johnstone Strait, is a natural obstacle used to divide east from westbound traffic. Coasts are rugged and indented, especially on its north side, off which there are several islets and rocks close to shore. **Speaker Rock**, 0.3 mile east of Helmcken Island, dries 2.6 m.

230   **Anchorage** for small craft sheltered from west winds can be found on the north side of Helmcken Island, east of the north peninsula. **Billygoat Bay** offers anchorage with mud bottom but holding ground is poor, running mooring lines to shore is recommended.

231   A **prominent white storage tank** and a red and white radio mast are (1986) on the east end of the 42 m high island close NE of Billygoat Bay.

232   **Beacon range. — Lights**. — Helmcken Island Sector light *(525)*, on a drying rock at the east end and on the north side of the island, is shown at an elevation of 4.7 m from a white tower. The white sector indicates the preferred channel south of Ripple Shoal.

233   A daybeacon, on the east end of the 43 m high island about 0.4 mile WNW of the light, is a white tower with a white rear range daymark with a red vertical stripe. The daybeacon is clearly visible from abreast Tyee Point. Light structure and daybeacon in line bearing 296½° lead south of Ripple Shoal.

234   Helmcken Island South Sector light *(533)* is on the south side of the island.

235   Peterson Islet light *(534)* is on the north extremity of the islet.

236   Current Passage Sector light *(524)*, on the south side of Hardwicke Island about 1 mile NW of Eden Point, is shown at an elevation of 5.6 m from a white tower. The white sector indicates preferred channel east of Ripple Shoal.

237   Helmcken Island North light *(526)* is on the north extremity of the island.

238   Earl Ledge light *(534.3)* is on the south extremity of the ledge.

Helmcken Island from south of Ripple Shoal (1984)

Helmcken Island from Kelsey Bay (1984)

Chancellor Channel from Current Passage (1985)

Sunderland Channel from Johnstone Strait (1984)

Chart 3544

239   **Hardwicke Island**, on the north side of the strait, is mountainous and toward its centre is the conspicuous summit of **Mount Royston**.

240   **Earl Ledge** *(50°25'N, 125°55'W)* extends 0.25 mile south from the south shore of Hardwicke Island and is steep-to on its west side with shoal ground, over which there is extensive kelp, extending 0.3 mile from its east side. The ledge is covered by the red sector of Helmcken Island South Sector light. **Hardwicke Island** locality is close NE of Earl Ledge. A float and fishing boundary marker are west of the ledge.

241   A **booming ground** is on the east side of Earl Ledge.

242   **Peterson Islet** *(50°23'N, 125°55'W)*, 1.1 miles SW of the west extremity of Helmcken Island, has drying rock ledges extending from its SW and east sides and a fishing boundary marker is close west of the light structure.

243   **Hkusam Bay**, 0.5 mile west of Peterson Islet, is only suitable for small craft. Three rocks, with less than 2 m over them, lie about 0.15 mile offshore between Peterson Islet and Hkusam Bay. Remains of the Indian village **Hkusam** lie on the west shore of Hkusam Bay.

244   **Salmon Bay** *(50°23'N, 125°57'W)*, the estuary of **Salmon River**, is filled with drying mud flats that are steep-to along their outer edge. **Graveyard Point** is on the east side of the entrance to the bay. Small craft frequently use the estuary. The river is of considerable size and flows through a valley that separates **Prince of Wales Range** from **Newcastle Ridge**.

245   A **speed limit** of 10 km/h (5 kn) is prescribed by *Boating Restriction Regulations* for the Salmon River estuary.

246   **Kelsey Bay** *(50°24'N, 125°58'W)* is a small indentation on the west entrance point to Salmon Bay. **Kelsey Bay** settlement, along the west side of Salmon Bay, is a logging settlement with a few stores and an RCMP detachment. A loading ramp, derrick and marine gas are reported to be available. **Sayward**, on the west bank of Salmon River about 5 km south of Kelsey Bay, is a village with a post office, hotel, restaurant, store and camp grounds. The settlements are connected by road to the main highway. Logging and tourism are the primary industries for both settlements.

247   **Tides**. — Tidal differences for Kelsey Bay (Index No. 8215), referenced on Alert Bay, are in *Tide Tables, Volume 6*.

248   **Berths**. — The public wharf has a berthing length of 55 m on its east side and a depth of about 8 m alongside. A float attached to and parallel with the west side of the wharf is 31 m long and suitable for small craft. It is protected by a timber breakwater built on the west side of the wharf. During strong SE winds a considerable sea sets on to the wharf. Westerly winds also cause a sea to curl around the breakwater into the wharf area.

249   **Floats** south of the public wharf provide berthing for small craft and are given moderate protection by the former ferry landing breakwater. Power, water and garbage disposal facilities are available.

250   The **former ferry landing**, south of the floats, consists of a breakwater, several dolphins, connected by a catwalk, and a landing complex.

251   **Booming ground**. — Five grounded hulks, SE of the former ferry landing, form breakwaters for an extensive booming area to the south. The hulks were formerly the Cardena (Union Steamship), HMCS Runnymede, Lasalle and Longueil (World War 2 frigates), and one unknown.

252   **Brasseau Bay**, 0.4 mile NW of Kelsey Bay, has a float and dolphins at its head.

253   **Yorke Island** *(50°27'N, 125°59'W)* lies in the entrance to Sunderland Channel. Two buildings, halfway up the slope on the SW side of Yorke Island, are remains of a World War 2 gun battery. Two drying rocks lie about 0.1 mile off the NW extremity of the island. A ledge of drying boulders extends south for nearly 0.1 mile from the south extremity of the island. A rock, which dries 1.2 m, lies close east of the boulder ledge. Close east of the above ledge are the bases of a few piles, remains of an old jetty.

254   **Tides**. — Tidal differences for Yorke Island (Index No. 8233), referenced on Alert Bay, are in *Tide Tables, Volume 6*.

255   **Artillery Islets**, 0.2 mile south of the south extremity of Yorke Island, are surrounded by drying ledges. A fishing boundary marker is on **Hardwicke Point** and **Nichols Bay** is 0.4 mile SE of the point. **Clarence Island** is wooded and **Fanny Island** is bare. They lie about 0.4 and 0.6 mile, respectively, NW of Yorke Island. Navigation between the islands is inadvisable because of shallow depths.

256   **Light**. — Fanny Island light *(542.8)* is shown at an elevation of 6.2 m from a mast.

Blenkinsop Bay and Port Neville

Chart 3564

257   **Tuna Point** *(50°29'N, 126°00'W)* has foul ground extending 0.1 mile SW from it. **Mary Island**, 0.4 mile SE of Tuna Point, has white cliffs on its south side. The bay north of Mary Island and **McLeod Bay**, 0.5 mile east of Mary Island, are reported to afford shelter from west winds.

258   **Light**. — Tuna Point light *(543)* is on the west side of the point.

259   **Blenkinsop Bay** *(50°29'N, 126°00'W)* has extensive drying flats at its head, north of **Black Island**. **Tuna River** flows across these flats. The west shore rises steeply from **White Bluff** to **Hardy Peak**, the east shore is of moderate height. **Blink Rock** and **Elf Shoal** lie off the east shore, north of Tuna Point. **Datum Boulder** lies close east and **Jesse Island** 0.5 mile SW of **Point George**.

260   **Anchorage** in Blenkinsop Bay is well protected with good holding ground. Enter in mid-channel, passing west of Blink Rock and Elf Shoal, anchor in the west part of the bay in 11 to 18 m, mud bottom. The small bay west of Point George also affords good anchorage with shelter from west winds.

261   **Port Neville**, entered between **Ransom Point** *(50°29'N, 126°05'W)* and **Neville Point**, affords secure anchorage for small craft. It is often used by fish boats. **Milly Island**, close south of Neville Point, is wooded. The entrance channel, between Ransom Point and **July Point** 1.4 miles north, is 0.3 mile wide. During summer months kelp grows across it. **Channel Rock**, 0.3 mile SW of July Point, and three other rocks with less than 2 m over them, lie on the sill that crosses the entrance channel.

262   **Tides**. — Tidal differences for Port Neville (Index No. 8245), referenced on Alert Bay, are in *Tide Tables, Volume 6*.

263   **Tidal streams** in the entrance to Port Neville attain 3 kn at times.

264   **Piles and dolphins**, some submerged, lie close-off the east shore of the entrance channel.

265   **Port Neville** settlement, 0.5 mile north of Ransom Point and on the east side of the entrance, has a post office, there is no store.

Chart 3564

266 **Berths**. — A public float, attached to two dolphins, is 17 m long at its outer end and has a depth of about 6 m alongside. A float for small craft attached to the north end of the main float is 18 m long. It has been reported that tidal streams are strong at the public wharf.

267 A private wharf with a float 30 m long lies close south of the public float.

268 **Robbers Nob**, 1.2 miles NE of July Point, is a conspicuous mass of scrub covered rock at the extremity of a low grassy point. Booming grounds line the shore west of Robbers Nob and a private float is on the SE end of Robbers Nob.

269 **Submerged piles** extend from the south side of **Baresides Bay**.

270 The channel between **Hanatsa Point** and **Collingwood Point** is less than 0.1 mile wide and a depth of about 2.1 m can be carried through it. **Cuthbert Rock**, SW of Collingwood Point, dries 2.7 m. East of Collingwood Point Port Neville deepens to about 17 m then terminates in drying flats over which the **Fulmore River** drains.

271 **Booming grounds** lie along the north shore west of Fulmore River.

Blenkinsop Bay to Swaine Point

Chart 3545

272 The Vancouver Island shore, west of Kelsey Bay, rises abruptly to high mountain ranges except near the mouths of a few river valleys.

273 **Light**. — **Hickey Point** light *(535)* is shown at an elevation of 8.8 m from a skeleton tower.

274 **Windy Point** *(50°28'N, 126°10'W)* is high and steep-to with some above-water rocks close NW. **St. Vincent Bight**, east of Windy Point, offers shelter from west winds for small craft close inshore at its west end. A logging camp with a booming ground and A-frame are in the bay 1 mile west of Windy Point (1995).

275 **Danger**. — A detached rock, with less than 2 m over it, lies about 0.1 mile offshore 1 mile west of Windy Point.

276 **Adam River** *(50°28'N, 126°17'W)* flows into the south side of the strait across steep-to drying mud flats. A logging camp, breakwater and booming ground are at the mouth of the river (1995).

277 **Danger**. — A detached rock, with 1.2 m over it, lies about 91 m offshore about 0.7 mile WNW of Adam River.

278 A log dump and float are 0.5 mile west of **Cederstedt Creek**.

279 **Naka Creek** *(50°29'N, 126°25'W)* has conspicuous white buildings, a rock breakwater, booming grounds and a logging camp near its entrance (1995).

280 **Robson Bight** *(50°29'N, 126°35'W)* has drying flats at its south end formed by the sediments of **Tsitika River**.

281 **Robson Bight Ecological Reserve** has been established to protect core habitat of the *Orcinus orca* (killer whale). The reserve includes a 1,248 hectare marine portion and 505 hectares of forested shoreline. Because killer whales (See http://www-comm.pac.dfo-mpo.gc.ca/publications/WhaleBook_e.pdf) are easily observed anywhere in northern Johnstone Strait, recreational viewing of whales should take place outside the reserve. Vessels should not enter the waters of the reserve which are patrolled. The upland portion of the reserve is closed to all entry except by permit.

282 **Mount Nelson** *(50°30'N, 126°10'W)* is a prominent summit that dominates the rugged shore on the north side of the strait.

283 **Stimpson Reef** *(50°30'N, 126°12'W)*, 0.6 mile ESE of **Stimpson Point**, is a drying reef, steep-to on its south side. A fishing boundary marker is on Stimpson Point.

284 **Beacon**. — A starboard hand daybeacon is on Stimpson Reef.

285 **Broken Islands**, 3 miles WNW of Stimpson Point, are steep-to on the south and west sides. Foul ground lies between the islands and between them and **Domville Point**.

286 **Light**. — Broken Islands light *(536)*, on the SW extremity of the island, is shown at an elevation of 9.7 m from a white tower.

287 **West Cracroft Island** has Johnstone Strait on its south side, Port Harvey and Cracroft Inlet on its east side and Clio Channel and Baronet Passage on its north and west sides. **Mount Thomas** near the east end has a rounded summit.

288 **Escape Reef** *(50°31'N, 126°21'W)* is about 0.25 mile long and has three heads with less than 2 m over them. Kelp grows on the reef during summer months.

289 **Clearing marks**. — When entering Havannah Channel keep Bockett Point *(50°32'N, 126°15'W)* in line with Domville Point, bearing 065°, which will lead about 0.2 mile SE of Escape Reef.

290 **Forward Bay** *(50°31'N, 126°23'W)* affords fair anchorage in 27 to 29 m near its north end. Small craft can find shelter from strong westerly winds north of **Bush Islets**, in the west part of the bay.

291 Between Forward Bay and Boat Bay, about 6 miles west, a number of rocks and shoals, marked by kelp in summer, lie within 0.2 mile of the north shore of Johnstone Strait.

292 **Boat Bay** *(50°31'N, 126°34'W)* affords good shelter for small craft north of the islet lying about 0.15 mile offshore. A drying rock lies about 0.15 mile south of the west extremity of the islet. A rock, with less than 2 m over it, lies 0.2 mile ENE of the islet.

293 **Swaine Point** is 0.6 mile west of the islet in Boat Bay.

294 **Light**. — Boat Bay light *(544)*, on Swaine Point, is shown at an elevation of 10.7 m from a white tower with a red band at the top and is obscured by high land northward of 102°.

Swaine Point to Blinkhorn Peninsula

Chart 3546

295 **Sophia Islands** *(50°32'N, 126°38'W)* consist of two large and several smaller islands with numerous drying and sunken rocks around them. They form two groups. Small craft can navigate between the two groups, and between the islets and the north shore. **Baron Reef** lies 0.8 mile NW of the west Sophia Island.

296 **Growler Cove**, known locally as Pig Ranch Cove, is entered between Sophia Islands and Baron Reef. It is a narrow inlet that dries at the head and has several rocks close to both shores. Small craft can obtain sheltered anchorage in 9 to 13 m in the cove which is also used by commercial fishermen. Kelp is reported to grow off the south entrance point.

297 **Cracroft Point** *(50°33'N, 126°41'W)* is the east entrance point at the south end of Blackney Passage. Heavy tide races are formed off the point on both flood and ebb tidal streams.

Chart 3546

298   **Light**. — Cracroft Point light *(544.4)* is on the west end of the point. It is obscured on WNW bearings.

299   **Hanson Island** lies on the north side of the west end of Johnstone Strait; its south coast is fairly straight and moderately steep-to.

300   **Blinkhorn Peninsula**, on the south shore opposite the west end of Hanson Island, has drying and sunken rocks close offshore at its west end.

301   **Light**. — Blinkhorn Peninsula light *(545)*, on the north extremity of the peninsula, is shown at an elevation of 9.5 m from a white tower with a green band at the top.

Blackney Passage and Blackfish Sound

302   **Blackney Passage**, entered west of Cracroft Point, leads north between Hanson and Parson Islands into Blackfish Sound. Baronet Passage, north of Cracroft Point, leads east from Blackney Passage.

303   **Tidal streams** in Blackney Passage attain 5 kn with heavy races off Cracroft Point on both flood and ebb. The flood flows south through Blackney Passage. At the south end of the passage there is a strong tidal race where this flow meets the east-going flood stream in Johnstone Strait.

304   Secondary current station Blackney Passage (Index No. 6035), referenced on Johnstone Strait – Central, is in *Tide Tables, Volume 6*.

305   **Licka Point** *(50°34'N, 126°41'W)* is the east extremity of Hanson Island. **Alexander Rock**, 0.4 mile NNW of Licka Point, has 6.7 m over it. Houses are in the bay NW of Licka Point.

306   **Light**. — Hanson Island East Sector light *(544.5)* is on Licka Point.

307   **Parson Island** lies on the east side and at the north end of Blackney Passage. Two drying rocks lie about 0.2 mile north of Parson Island.

308   **Light**. — Parson Island light *(544.6)* is on a drying rock north of the island.

309   **Parson Bay**, entered between Parson Island and **Red Point**, indents the west end of **Harbledown Island**. **Harris Shoals** lie in the middle of its entrance.

310   **Whitebeach Passage**, entered between Red Point and **Fire Point**, leads from Blackfish Sound into Indian Channel and Farewell Harbour; it is only suitable for small craft.

311   **West Passage**, between **Compton Island** and Swanson Island, is entered between **Slate Point** and **Fresh Rock**. Two drying reefs, **Punt Rock** and **Star Islets**, lie on the south side of the fairway. **Apples Islet**, on the north side of the fairway, is connected to Swanson Island by a drying ledge and a drying reef extends 0.1 mile WSW from the islet. **Stoker Point** is the SE extremity of Swanson Island.

312   **Farewell Harbour**, south of **Kamux Island**, affords secure anchorage for small vessels. A sport fishing lodge with float and a submarine pipeline (sewer outfall) are on the west side of **Berry Island**. Visitors may be able to use dining facilities.

313   **Freshwater Bay**, at the SW corner of Swanson Island, is entered between **Flower Island** and Fresh Rock. It is too open for good anchorage.

314   **Blackfish Sound** *(50°35'N, 126°42'W)* leads from Blackney Passage to the SE part of Queen Charlotte Strait. Hanson Island and Plumper Islands form its south side and **Swanson Island** forms its north side.

315   **Tidal streams** in the main part of Blackfish Sound attain 1 to 3 kn. Near **Donegal Head**, the east extremity of Malcolm Island, they attain 4 kn and in the vicinity of Egeria Shoal there are often tide-rips.

316   **Booming grounds** are in the bay 0.6 mile west of **Burnt Point** *(50°35'N, 126°42'W)*.

317   **Spout Islet** *(50°35'N, 126°45'W)* lies close-off the north coast of Hanson Island. The bay south of Spout Islet offers good anchorage and shelter in 5 to 10 m.

318   **Double Bay**, west of Spout Islet, is used by commercial fishermen and congested during the fishing season. A fishing resort with transient moorage is in the bay.

319   **Bold Head**, the NW extremity of Swanson Island, has drying reefs extending 0.2 mile west.

320   **Egeria Shoal** *(50°38'N, 126°46'W)* has a rocky head with 29 m over it.

Broughton Strait

321   **Broughton Strait** *(50°34'N, 126°52'W)*, a continuation of Johnstone Strait, leads into Queen Charlotte Strait at its west end. It is bounded on the south by Vancouver Island and on the north by the Pearse Islands, Cormorant Island and the west portion of Malcolm Island. At its east end Weynton Passage leads north into Cormorant Channel and Blackfish Sound, and Pearse Passage leads into the central part of Cormorant Channel.

322   **Vessel Traffic Services** (VTS). — Broughton Strait is in *Sector Four* of the *Vancouver Traffic Zone* and is administered by *Comox Traffic*. Assigned frequency is 156.575 MHz, Channel 71. Calling-in points in are:

323   *Calling-in Point No. 35*, *Lewis Point*, is a line running 000°–180° through Lewis Point light *(546)*.

324   *Calling-in Point No. 36*, *Pulteney Point*, is an arc with a 3-mile radius centred on Pulteney Point light *(553)*.

325   A brief description of this VTS is in *PAC 200*. Details are in *Radio Aids to Marine Navigation (Pacific and Western Arctic)*.

326   **The Broughton Strait/Haddington Island Traffic Separation Scheme** is recommended for use by all vessels. Separation of traffic is achieved by using Haddington Island to divide eastbound from westbound traffic and by separation zones to the SE and NW of Haddington Island. Eastbound traffic passes south of Haddington Island and westbound traffic passes north of Haddington Island using Haddington Passage. No inshore traffic zones are provided.

327   **Caution. — In some instances large vessels or tugs with long tows proceeding eastbound may have difficulty in making the turn to starboard to pass south of Haddington Island. The Master may decide to proceed against the traffic flow through Haddington Passage but should make every effort to warn other traffic in the area.**

328   **Ferry**. — A passenger and vehicle ferry crosses Broughton Strait between Port McNeill, Alert Bay and Sointula. Charted ferry routes are a general indication of the routes followed.

329   **Tides**. — Tidal predictions in Broughton Strait are given for Alert Bay (Index No. 8280). Tidal differences, referenced on Alert Bay, are given for Port McNeill (Index No. 8290) in *Tide Tables, Volume 6*.

Chart 3546

330   **Tidal streams** through the fairway of Broughton Strait attain 3 kn, but in Port McNeill they are not felt. The set is oblique across Neill Ledge, and on a strong flood tide there is often a strong counter current to the east of Alert Bay setting west along the north shores of the Pearse Islands. Two secondary current stations in Broughton Strait, referenced on Johnstone Strait – Central, are in *Tide Tables, Volume 6*; Alert Bay (Index No. 6040), which is the passage south of Cormorant Island, and Pulteney Point (Index No. 6046) at the west end of Broughton Strait.

Main Shipping Channel

331   The **main shipping channel** through Broughton Strait passes to the south of Cormorant Island, then through the Traffic Separation Scheme with westbound traffic passing to the north of Haddington Island through Haddington Passage, and eastbound traffic passing to the south of Haddington Island.

332   **Bauza Islet** *(50°33'N, 126°48'W)* is surrounded by foul ground. **Bauza Cove** can be entered on either side of Bauza Islet. It affords anchorage to small vessels in a depth of about 20 m.

333   **Wastell Islets** lie close north of **Wastell Point**, the west entrance point to Bauza Cove. **Ella Point** and **Lewis Point**, west of Wastell Islets, are the entrance points to Beaver Cove. A fishing boundary marker is on Lewis Point.

334   **Light**. — Lewis Point light *(546)* is obscured by trees when approaching from the west.

335   **Hidden Cove** (local name), 0.2 mile west of Lewis Point, has a resort. Moorage, accommodation and dining are available.

336   **Alder Bay** (local name) is 2.3 miles west of Lewis Bay. Resort facilities protected by a floating breakwater are in the bay. Moorage, boat launch, accommodation, showers and campground are available.

337   **Cormorant Island** *(50°35'N, 126°55'W)* is fringed with beaches of boulders and shingle extending nearly 0.1 mile offshore in places. **Gordon Bluff**, known locally as Pepper Point, is the SE extremity. **Yellow Bluff**, the south extremity of the west part of Cormorant Island, is an overgrown cliff. A beach of boulders and gravel, bordered by shallow depths marked by kelp, extends 0.1 mile south from the bluff.

338   **Light**. — Yellow Bluff Sector light *(549.2)*, on the drying ledge south of the bluff, is shown at an elevation of 8.5 m from a white tower with a red band at the top.

339   A **tower** with red air obstruction lights is 0.4 mile WNW of Gordon Bluff. Towers with red air obstruction lights are 0.5 mile WNW of Gordon Bluff, and towers with red air obstructions lights are in the village of Alert Bay about 1 mile NW of Gordon Bluff.

340   A **submarine cable** (power) and a submarine pipeline cross Broughton Strait between Vancouver Island and Gordon Bluff.

341   Waters of Broughton Strait fronting Alert Bay are a **water aerodrome**.

342   **Speed**. — Vessels passing Alert Bay should reduce speed to avoid damage to small craft and wharves.

343   **Nimpkish Bank** extends from the south shore across the mouth of the **Nimpkish River** and dries in places. **Green Islet**, on a drying part of Nimpkish Bank, is 1 m high and covered with coarse grass. **Kish Rock**, 0.4 mile NW of Green Islet, dries 0.9 m. **Alert Rock**, at the NW extremity of Nimpkish Bank and about 0.2 mile NNE of Kish Rock, has 4.9 m over it.

344   The Nimpkish River is barred by rapids, overhead power cables and a highway bridge. It can only be ascended by small craft for a short distance. Flats covered with boulders are on either side of the river mouth, between which the channel is narrow. **Flagstaff Islet** lies in the mouth of the river.

345   **Light**. — Nimpkish Bank light *(549)*, on a shoal near the NE extremity of the bank, is shown at an elevation of 6.4 m from a mast on a dolphin with a port hand daymark and a radar reflector.

346   **Light buoy**. — Alert Rock light buoy "N17" *(549.3)*, north of the rock, is a port hand buoy.

347   **Anchorage** can be obtained off the mouth of the Nimpkish River in 20 m, out of the tidal stream, with Green Islet bearing 110°, distant 0.5 mile.

348   **Haddington Island**, 2.3 miles west of Cormorant Island, is wooded and has some conspicuous stone quarries and an A-frame on its SE side.

349   **Haddington Passage**, to the north of Haddington Island, is the westbound traffic lane in the Broughton Strait/Haddington Island Traffic Separation Scheme.

350   **Dickenson Point** *(50°37'N, 127°01'W)* is prominent and has a gravel beach extending south.

351   **Haddington Reefs**, 0.8 mile SSE of Dickenson Point, has two drying rocks and several boulders, with less than 2 m over them, it is marked by kelp during summer.

352   **Lights. — Light buoy**. — Haddington Reefs Pier light *(550.2)*, on a drying rock on the reefs, is shown at an elevation of 7.7 m from a white tower with a red band at the top.

353   Haddington Island light *(550.5)*, on a drying ledge on the north side of the island, has a radar reflector.

354   Haddington Reefs light buoy "N20" *(550)*, at the west extremity of the reefs, is a starboard hand buoy.

355   **Broad Point** is on Vancouver Island about 1 mile SE of Haddington Island.

356   **Ledge Point** *(50°36'N, 127°05'W)* is the north entrance point of Port McNeill.

357   **Neill Ledge** extending east from Ledge Point to within 0.5 mile of Haddington Island has an uneven bottom, kelp is present during summer months.

358   **Neill Rock**, on the north side of Neill Ledge, has 9.8 m over it.

359   **Lights**. — Broad Point West (Hyde Creek) Sector light *(550.9)*, 0.8 mile west of Broad Point, is shown at an elevation of 6.4 m from a white tower fitted with a radar reflector. The white sector indicates the preferred channel west of Haddington Island.

360   Haddington Island South light *(550.8)* is on a drying ledge on the south side of the island.

361   **Beacon**. — Haddington Island West daybeacon, on the west extremity of the island, has a bifurcation/junction daymark, preferred channel to the right.

362   **Light buoys**. — Neill Ledge light buoy "NP" *(551)*, east of the ledge, is a port bifurcation buoy.

363   Neill Rock light buoy "N21" *(551.3)*, north of the rock, is a port hand buoy.

364   **Tidal streams** set obliquely over Neill Ledge at 1 to 3 kn. Times of slack water vary little from those in vicinity of Nimpkish Bank.

365   **Sointula** *(50°38'N, 127°01'W)*, on **Malcolm Island** between Dickenson Point and **Rough Bay**, is a farming and fishing settlement. Sointula Co-op has a food store near the head of the public wharf and a marine hardware store near the head of the

Chart 3546

small craft harbour. Telephone, museum, bank, hotel, restaurants, camping facilities, repair yards, postal service, water taxi, and charter aircraft are available. A passenger and vehicle ferry provides connection with Alert Bay and Port McNeill.

366   **Lights**. — Sointula breakwater light *(552.5)* is on the outer end of the floating breakwater at the small craft harbour.

367   A private light is on the ferry landing.

368   A **submarine pipeline** (sewer outfall), marked by a sign onshore, extends 0.35 mile west from Dickenson Point.

369   **Anchorage** suitable for small vessels can be obtained about 0.3 mile SW of the breakwater light in 13 to 18 m. Large vessels can anchor farther south in a depth of 30 m but it is exposed to the west.

370   **Berths**. — The small craft harbour, protected by a rock breakwater, is at the north end of Sointula in Rough Bay. Dredged to a depth of 3 m (1961), it has floats 60 to 116 m long with a common connection to a wharf, power is available. Washrooms, showers and laundry are available.

371   The **public wharf**, 1 mile SSE of the small craft harbour, has a berthing length of 15 m and depths of 8.5 to 10 m alongside its head. The north face is 46 m long with depths of 3 to 7.6 m alongside. The ferry landing, with berthing dolphins and a private float, are at the NE corner. The south face of the wharf is the same length with depths of 5.2 to 9.4 m alongside and has a large fisheries barge permanently moored alongside. The SE side has a float 18 m long extending from it. Telephone, garbage drop and waste oil disposal are nearby.

Chart 3548

372   **Pulteney Point** *(50°38′N, 127°09′W)* is at the SW extremity of Malcolm Island. **Graeme Point** is its west extremity.

373   **Light**. — Pulteney Point light *(553)* is shown at an elevation of 12.2 m from a white tower. The fog signal consists of three blasts every minute. White buildings with red roofs stand nearby.

374   **Tidal streams** attain 3 kn on the flood and ebb. Secondary current station Pulteney Point (Index No. 6046), referenced on Johnstone Strait – Central and Seymour Narrows, is in *Tide Tables, Volume 6*.

375   **Kelp Patch** *(50°39′N, 127°11′W)* has 5.2 m over it.

376   **Lady Ellen Point** *(50°37′N, 127°08′W)* is low, wooded and fringed with stone and shingle beaches. In the vicinity of **Cluxewe River** beaches extend up to 0.2 mile offshore.

377   **Single Tree Point** *(50°39′N, 127°15′W)* has a stone and gravel drying spit extending 0.3 mile off it.

378   **False Head** *(50°40′N, 127°17′W)*, at the NW end of Broughton Strait, is low.

Beaver Cove

Chart 3546

379   **Beaver Cove** *(50°32′N, 126°52′W)* is entered between Ella and Lewis Points.

380   **Telegraph Cove**, 0.3 mile SW of Ella Point and on the east side of Beaver Cove, has an entrance approximately 60 m wide. One of the wharf faces is 52 m long with depths of 5.2 to 6.7 m alongside and is currently used for whale watching tours. Another wharf face is 50 m long with depths of 0.37 to 2.4 m

alongside. There is a marina, two launching ramps, a camp ground, RV park, gift shops, general store and restaurants.

381   **Englewood** on the west arm of Beaver Cove has accommodation with free moorage. A marine farm with net pens, an outfall pipe and onshore processing plant, at the head of the arm, is marked by yellow spherical buoys.

382   **Beaver Cove** settlement, on the SE side of the cove, is a logging settlement with a wood chip plant. A log dump and barge loading ramp are in the SE corner of the cove. A seaplane float, inside of which the logging company secures boom boats, is adjacent to the log dump.

383   A **wharf** with a frontage of 61 m is on the east side of the bay. About 60 m north of this wharf is the old ferry slip. Ruins of the Nimpkish Iron Mines conveyor are farther north. Boathouses and a launching ramp are on the east shore.

384   **Extensive booming grounds** with numerous dolphins, piles and mooring buoys are in the south part of the cove, along the east shore and in the west arm of the cove. This area is served by the Canfor logging railroad.

385   Temporary **anchorage** can be obtained in about 55 m.

Alert Bay

386   **Alert Bay** *(50°35′N, 126°56′W)*, on the south side of Cormorant Island, is a commercial fishing port and distribution centre for logging communities in outlying districts. It is also a centre for First Nations culture.

387   **Facilities**. — Alert Bay has a post office, RCMP detachment, hospital, accomodation, campgrounds, several stores (including groceries and drug store), credit union and laundromats. Recreational facilities include museums, galleries, recreation centres, Visitor Information Centre and recreational charters. Mooring buoys are near the centre of the town and there are boat launching ramps. Alert Bay Shipyard has marine railways. The largest can handle vessel to 80 tonnes and 18.3 m long. Electronic repairs can be carried out on radios, radars and echo sounders. Diesel fuel, gasoline, lubricants, fresh water and provisions are obtainable. An asphalt airstrip 880 m long provides scheduled air service. A ferry for passengers and vehicles connects to Port McNeill and Sointula.

388   **Lights**. — Alert Bay breakwater light *(548)*, on the NW extremity of the breakwater, has a starboard hand daymark.

389   A privately operated light and radar reflector are on a dolphin at the ferry landing.

390   A **submarine pipeline** (sewer outfall), at the head of the bay, extends 0.25 mile offshore.

391   Good, well-protected **anchorage** can be obtained in Alert Bay, about 0.3 mile SW of the breakwater light, in depths of about 13 m sand bottom.

392   Waters of Alert Bay and Broughton Strait, fronting the bay, are a **water aerodrome**.

393   **Tides**. — Tidal predictions for Alert Bay (Index No. 8280) are in *Tide Tables, Volume 6*.

394   **Tidal streams** on the flood run strongly along the shoreline and the outer face of the wharves.

395   **Wharves**. — The main breakwater, with Alert Bay light on its NW extremity, extends 274 m from shore in a NW direction. This breakwater shelters a small craft harbour that has been dredged to 2.7 m in the outer section and 2.1 m in the inner section. Public finger floats are on the west side of a base float that is

Chart 3546

Alert Bay (1983)

Photo courtesy of W.T. McAthy

150 m long and extends north from the public wharf. A seaplane float is at the north end of these floats. Power and water are obtainable. A 3 tonne crane is on the public wharf.

396   A **ferry landing** is close south of the main breakwater.

397   A **fuel wharf** is between the ferry landing and public wharf, about 0.2 mile to the south.

398   The **public wharf**, 0.4 mile south of Alert Bay breakwater light, is 61 m long on the seaward side of its L-shaped head with depths of 8.2 to 9 m alongside. A freight shed and 3 tonne crane are on the wharf, and a float, 61 m long, for small craft is attached to the north end of the wharfhead. Mariners should be prepared to encounter a strong set onto the face of the public wharf. Ruins of the old ferry berth are close-off the south end of the wharf.

399   **Alert Bay Shipyard wharf** is south of the public wharf.

400   The former Shell Oil Dock, 0.2 mile SE of the public wharf, is a **marina** operated by the village. A privately owned fresh seafood retail facility is open six months of the year. Conspicuous totem poles are close north.

401   **At the head of the bay**, NW of Alert Bay breakwater light, is a log and pile breakwater protecting a wharf with floats attached to it. This wharf has a depth of 3.4 m alongside. There are also pilings and the remains of some old floats.

402   **Private mooring buoys** are north of the public wharf.

Port McNeill

403   **Port McNeill** *(50°36'N, 127°05'W)*, approached south of Neill Ledge, has generally low shores that are mostly fringed with beaches of boulders and shingle. The town of Port McNeill is on the south shore west of **Deer Bluff**. **Caution should be used as the harbour is becoming congested particularly with logboom and floatplane traffic.**

404   **Facilities**. — Port McNeill has a post office, an RCMP detachment, hospital with heliport, doctors, dentists, stores and accomodation. An asphalt airstrip is 732 m long. A daily bus service operates to Port Hardy and Campbell River. A passenger and vehicle ferry provides scheduled service to Sointula and Alert Bay. Gasoline and diesel fuel are obtainable.

405   **Eel Reef**, 0.4 mile WNW of Deer Bluff, dries 4 m and is connected to the south shore by a causeway. It is marked by a daybeacon with a port hand daymark.

406   **Anchorage**, sheltered from north and west winds, can be obtained 0.4 mile NE of Deer Bluff in 10 to 16 m. Anchorage can also be obtained farther east, south of Neill Ledge, in 16 to 38 m but there is less shelter from north winds.

407   **Lights**. — Port McNeill breakwater light *(551.5)* is on the outer end of the rock breakwater.

408   A private light and radar reflector are shown from the NE dolphin off the ferry landing.

409   The waters of Port McNeill are a **water aerodrome**.

410   **Tides**. — Tidal differences for Port McNeill (Index No. 8290), referenced on Alert Bay, are in *Tide Tables, Volume 6*.

411   **Wharves**. — A disused Oil Bulk Wharf, about 1.2 miles east of Deer Bluff, has a berthing length of 137 m with depths of 9.4 to 12.5 m alongside. It is a conspicuous landmark when approaching Port McNeill, but is scheduled for demolition.

Chart 3546

412 The **small craft harbour** consists of an L-shaped rock breakwater with public floats on its west side. The municipal floats have 1,500 m of moorage and the commercial vessel floats 700 m of moorage. The float area was dredged to 3 m (2003). Water and power are laid on the floats. Showers, washrooms, garbage and used oil disposal, and sewage pump-out facilities are available. A tidal grid with vehicle access is available.

413 The **public wharf**, which extends north from the breakwater, has berthing faces of 38 and 21 m on its north and west sides, respectively, and a depth of about 7.6 m alongside. A 3 tonne crane and a storage shed are on the wharf.

414 The **ferry landing** extends from the east side of the public wharf.

415 A **wharf**, with a fuel float and an aircraft float at its outer end, is west of the boat launching ramp.

416 A **causeway**, 0.3 mile west of the public wharf, is part of a booming ground enclosure. A rock breakwater extends north from this causeway to the west of Eel Reef.

417 A long **jetty**, 0.5 mile west of the causeway, is for unloading logs. Numerous piles and dolphins for mooring logbooms lie along the shore. Tugs use this area for shelter during SE gales.

Cormorant Channel

418 **Cormorant Channel** (*50°36'N, 126°52'W*) parallels the east end of Broughton Strait to which it is connected by Weynton and Pearse Passages. Its north side, formed by Malcolm Island, is comparatively low and undulating with densely wooded rounded hills. However, behind the settlement of Sointula the trees have been cleared and the land cultivated.

419 **Cormorant Channel Marine Provincial Park** includes the eastern portion of the Pearse Islands, the Plumper Islands, Stephenson Islet and Stubbs Island; it is undeveloped.

420 **Submarine cables** cross Cormorant Channel between Leonard and Meynell Points.

421 A **submarine pipeline** (sewer outfall), 0.5 mile ESE of Leonard Point, extends 0.2 mile offshore.

422 **Weynton Passage** (*50°35'N, 126°49'W*) leads NW from the junction of Johnstone and Broughton Straits into Blackfish Sound and the east end of Cormorant Channel. The fairway, which is deep, has a minimum width of 0.7 mile.

423 **Tidal streams** in Weynton Passage attain 6 kn at times and set over and across shoals extending from Stephenson Islet. The flood sets south and the ebb north through Weynton Passage. There are heavy tide-rips at times near both shores and in the vicinity of Stubbs Island. Times and rates of maximum current and times of slack water are predicted and tabulated as daily tables for current station Weynton Passage (Index No. 6500) in *Tide Tables, Volume 6*.

424 **Weynton Island**, on the east side of the passage, has drying rocks close west and 0.4 mile SE of it. The narrow passage between Weynton and Hanson Islands is foul. **Plumper Islands** extend NW from the NW extremity of Hanson Island. **Ksuiladas Island**, the western island of the group, is an Indian Reserve. Channels through this group are tortuous and have numerous islets, rocks and shoals.

425 **Stubbs Island** (*50°36'N, 126°49'W*) lies in the centre of the east entrance to Cormorant Channel and north of Weynton Passage.

426 **Stephenson Islet**, at the south end and on the west side of Weynton Passage, has two smaller islets close SE and foul ground on which there are drying rocks extending 0.4 mile ESE of it. **Pearse Islands** are a group of ten thickly wooded islands. It is not advised to pass between these islands and Stephenson Islet without the aid of local knowledge. A reef runs parallel to and about 0.1 mile south of the south shore of the main island.

427 **Pearse Reefs**, north of **Kuldekduma Island**, consist of drying and sunken rocks. A detached drying rock lies 0.4 mile WNW of the west end of Pearse Reefs.

428 **Pearse Passage** separates Pearse Islands from Cormorant Island and is about 0.7 mile wide. **Gordon Rock**, in the middle of Pearse Passage, has two drying heads. The passage is narrowed by drying and above-water rocks lying off the east side and by shallow depths off the west shore. The best channel is to the west of Gordon Rock, **but neither is recommended**.

429 **Tidal streams** set obliquely through Pearse Passage and attain 4 kn at times.

430 **Leonard Point**, the north extremity of Cormorant Island, is fronted by a sand and gravel spit extending 0.1 mile NW. **Leonard Rock**, 1.2 miles west of Leonard Point in the west entrance to Cormorant Channel, has 3 m over it and is marked by kelp during summer. The channel between Leonard Rock and Cormorant Island is deep.

431 **Meynell Point** (*50°37'N, 126°55'W*) is faced with conspicuous brown cliffs. A private wharf is on the west side of the point.

432 **Mitchell Bay** (*50°38'N, 126°51'W*) is deep but shallows gradually toward a shingle beach at its head. The bay is free of offlying dangers and sheltered from all but south winds. The public float, on the east side of the bay, is 12 m long with a depth of about 5.8 m alongside. During the fishing season, a fish camp supplies some facilities.

CHAPTER 7

Mainland Inlets — Strait of Georgia to Queen Charlotte Strait

General

Chart 3001

1   This chapter describes inlets, channels and passages along the mainland shore of British Columbia between Cape Mudge *(50°00'N, 125°11'W)*, at the north end of the Strait of Georgia, and Queen Charlotte Strait.

2   Waters described in this chapter are generally narrow and very deep with few anchorages. Terrain is mountainous and heavily wooded. Industries are fishing, marine farming, logging and tourism. There are a number of small settlements and a few transient camps in support of them. Of the many Indian Reserves charted few are permanently occupied, these being mentioned in the text. Whether occupied or not, an Indian Reserve should not be landed on without permission. Marine traffic consists mainly of fish boats, tugs with barges or logbooms and mainly in summer, pleasure craft.

3   **Sheltered route**. — A series of channels and passages, known locally as the **Inside Passage**, is used by low powered or small vessels, and by tugs with barges or logbooms to avoid strong tides and winds that funnel through Johnstone Strait. This route leads NW from Powell River *(49°52'N, 124°33'W)* through Desolation Sound and Lewis Channel, or through Sutil Channel to Calm Channel, then through Yuculta Rapids, Cordero Channel and Chancellor Channel to join Johnstone Strait near Race Passage. An alternative route from Chancellor Channel leads NW and WSW through Wellbore and Sunderland Channels to join Johnstone Strait NW of Hardwicke Island.

Sutil Channel

Charts 3538, 3541

4   **Sutil Channel** *(50°06'N, 125°05'W)* leads 17 miles north and NNE along the west side of **Cortes Island**, and connects the Strait of Georgia to the junction of Calm Channel, Lewis Channel and Deer Passage.

5   **Tides**. — Tidal differences for Gorge Harbour (Index No. 8037) and Whaletown Bay (Index No. 8038), referenced on Point Atkinson (Index No. 7795), are in *Tide Tables, Volume 5*.

6   **Tidal streams** in Sutil Channel are weak, rarely exceeding 2 kn. The flood stream flows north in the south portion, south in the north portion, meeting about Penn Islands.

7   **Ferry**. — A passenger and vehicle ferry crosses Sutil Channel between Heriot Bay and Whaletown. Charted ferry route is a general indication of the route followed.

Francisco Point to Hyacinthe Point

Chart 3538

8   **Francisco Point** *(50°01'N, 125°09'W)* is high and cliffy with drying rocks extending almost 0.3 mile off it. **Wilby Shoals**, with a least depth of 3.2 m, are steep-to and extend 2.5 miles off the south end of **Quadra Island**. In summer shoals are marked by kelp.

9   **Light buoy. — Buoy**. — Wilby Shoals light buoy "P60" *(510)*, off the south edge of Wilby Shoals, is a starboard hand buoy.

10   Port hand buoy "P61" marks the east extremity of Wilby Shoals.

11   **Drew Harbour** *(50°06'N, 125°12'W)*, sheltered by **Rebecca Spit**, affords good anchorage but the bottom is hard, small craft may have difficulty in getting an anchor to hold. The harbour is subject to strong squalls during south or SE gales. The best shelter for small craft is close south of the north tip of Rebecca Spit. The harbour is surrounded by a white sandy beach and **Rebecca Spit Marine Provincial Park** has picnic and sanitary facilities, a launching ramp and fresh water. A resort with marine facilities is in the harbour.

12   **Light**. — Drew Harbour light *(485)* is at the tip of Rebecca Spit.

Charts 3538, 3539

13   **Heriot Bay** *(50°06'N, 125°13'W)* is entered between a rock with 1.8 m over it close SE of **Heriot Island** and a shoal spit marked by port hand buoy "N3" projecting from the east entrance point. The bay affords fair anchorage in its west part, away from the ferry route. The ferry landing, providing service to Cortes Island, is on the east side of the bay. The settlement has a general store with post office and bakery. The Heriot Bay Inn and Marina has gas, diesel, propane, ice, moorage with power, washrooms, showers, laundry, campground, dining and accommodation. A road connects the settlement to Quathiaski Cove where a ferry operates to Campbell River.

14   **Light**. — A private light is shown from the ferry landing.

15   **Wharf**. — The public wharf, at the head of Heriot Bay, has a berthing length of 12 m with floats at the outer end providing 397 m of berthing. A 3 tonne crane is on the wharf. Power, water, garbage disposal facilities, and a launching ramp are available.

16   **Hyacinthe Bay** and **Open Bay**, separated by **Hyacinthe Point**, are open with scattered rocks and shoals and not suitable as anchorages. A rock breakwater and piles are at the head of Open Bay.

Cortes Island — SW Shore

Chart 3538

17   **Sutil Point** *(50°01'N, 124°59'W)* has extensive drying banks studded with numerous boulders extending 0.9 mile SE from it.

18   **Light buoy**. — Sutil Point light and bell buoy "Q20" *(482)*, near the SW extremity of the banks, is a starboard hand buoy.

19   **Smelt Bay**, 1.5 miles north of Sutil Point, is lined with houses. **Smelt Bay Provincial Park** is in the south part of the bay. Campsites, picnic facilities, water, pit toilets and a boat launching ramp are available. Temporary anchorage for small craft can be found close to shore.

Chart 3538

20   **Marina Island** *(50°04'N, 125°03'W)* is fringed by sandy beaches strewn with boulders. **Marina Reef** is a drying spit, studded with boulders, extending 1 mile south from the island. It is marked at its south end by starboard hand **buoy** "Q16".

21   **Clearing marks**. — Cliffs on the SW side of Savary Island, bearing less than 125° and open south of Hernando Island, leads SW of Marina Reef. The east extremity of Subtle Islands *(50°07'N, 125°05'W)*, bearing more than 000° and open west of Marina Island, leads west of Marina Reef.

22   **Submarine cables** (abandoned) run from Marina Island to Quadra and Cortes Islands.

23   **Manson Bay** *(50°04'N, 124°59'W)* is exposed to SW winds but affords temporary anchorage for small craft, some shelter is available behind the islets off its west entrance point. A private float and piles are at the head of the bay.

24   **Mansons Landing Provincial Park**, with beaches fronting on Sutil Channel and **Hague Lake**, has picnic and sanitary facilities.

25   **Sewage disposal** in the waters of Mansons Bay and Mansons Landing Provincial Park is prohibited under the *Pleasure/Non-Pleasure Craft Sewage Pollution Prevention Regulations.*

26   **Mansons Landing** is on a spit fronting a drying lagoon along the east side of Manson Bay.

27   **Wharf**. — The public wharf at Mansons Landing has a berthing length along its T-shaped head of 22 m and a least depth of 5.2 m alongside. Floats with a berthing length of 110 m are attached to the north side of the wharf. The end float is reserved for seaplanes. A telephone is near the wharf.

28   The area between Marina and Cortes Islands is a **water aerodrome** called Mansons Landing.

29   **Deadman Island**, 0.7 mile east of Manson Bay, is joined to shore by a drying sand bar.

30   **Guide Islets** *(50°05'N, 125°01'W)*, in the approach to The Gorge, are two bare, yellow-topped islets that are conspicuous from the south, being identifiable from abreast Mitlenatch Island. A windmill on a trestle tower is on the point 0.3 mile NW of Guide Islets.

31   **The Gorge**, north of Guide Islets, is the narrow entrance to Gorge Harbour. It is about 0.5 mile long and less than 61 m wide in places. Least depth in the fairway is 11 m. On the west side of The Gorge are Indian rock paintings on flat patches of rock, and on the east side there are huge boulders that formed burial caverns.

32   **Tidal streams** attain 4 kn at the entrance to The Gorge.

33   **Tides**. — Tidal differences for Gorge Harbour (Index No. 8037), referenced on Point Atkinson, are in *Tide Tables, Volume 5.*

34   **Tide Islet** lies in mid-channel at the north end of The Gorge. A rock, dries 3.4 m, lies close east of Tide Islet. Preferred channel is west of Tide Islet.

35   **Gorge Harbour** affords good anchorage for vessels of moderate size and is a popular small craft anchorage although squalls sweep down from the surrounding hills. The best anchorage is south of the public wharf in 18 to 22 m. **Tan Island**, **Ring Island**, **Neck Islet**, **Pill Islets**, **Stove Islets**, **Bee Islets** and numerous drying and below-water rocks lie in Gorge Harbour. Private floats and mooring buoys are in the harbour. Marine farm facilities are west and north of Stove and Pill Islets, in the bay at the east extremity of the harbour, and close north of Bee Islets.

36   **Sewage disposal** in the waters of the approach to and within Gorge Harbour is prohibited under the *Pleasure/Non-Pleasure Craft Sewage Pollution Prevention Regulations.*

37   A **submarine cable** (power) is laid along the south shore of Gorge Harbour, it is marked by signs.

38   **Gorge Harbour** settlement, in the NW part of the harbour, has a marina where overnight moorage, provisions, fresh water, fuel and a restaurant are available.

39   **Wharf**. — The public wharf and float with depths of 2.4 to 3 m alongside and 33 m of berthing space are in the NW part of Gorge Harbour. Commercial vessels have priority.

40   **Uganda Passage** *(50°06'N, 125°02'W)*, which leads around the end of **Shark Spit**, at the north end of Marina Island turns through more than 90°. It is encumbered with rocks and shoals and its least depth is 11 m. **Heather Islets** lie in the south approach.

41   **Light**. — Uganda Passage light *(483)* is on a rock in the passage.

42   **Buoys**. — Uganda Passage is marked by starboard hand buoy "Q14" and port hand buoys "Q13" and "Q11". Upstream direction for buoys is proceeding north through the passage.

43   **Tidal streams** in Uganda Passage are reported to be 2 to 3 kn.

44   **Whaletown Bay** *(50°07'N, 125°03'W)* has a drying rock marked by starboard hand buoy "Q10" in the middle of its approach. A drying rock in the bay is marked by a daybeacon with a port hand daymark. The ferry landing, with service to Quadra Island, is on the north shore of the bay. **Whaletown**, on the south shore, has a post office and store.

45   **Lights**. — Whaletown Bay Entrance light *(483.3)* is on a drying rock off the west entrance point.

46   A private light is shown from the ferry landing.

47   **Wharf**. — The public wharf is 15 m long, along its north face, with a least depth of 3.4 m alongside. Floats, with 96 m of berthing space, extend NE from the SE corner of the wharf, the outer float is reserved for seaplanes. A 3 tonne crane and garbage disposal facilities are on the wharf.

48   **Tides**. — Tidal differences for Whaletown Bay (Index No. 8038), referenced on Point Atkinson, are in *Tide Tables, Volume 5.*

49   Waters off Whaletown Bay are a **water aerodrome**.

Read Island — East Shore

50   **Viner Point** *(50°08'N, 125°08'W)*, the south extremity of **Read Island**, is bare and steep-to. **Lake Bay** and **Twin Bay** are deep and offer limited anchorage.

51   **Burdwood Bay** has several islets and rocks in it. An islet in the south part of the bay has a drying rock close north of it marked by a **daybeacon** with a port hand daymark.

52   **Marine farm** facilities are on the NW side of the island with the daybeacon and north and west of the islets known locally as Wild Flower Islands.

53   **Anchorage** for small vessels is available west of the Wild Flower Islands but is exposed to southerly winds and seas. Unsheltered anchorage can be obtained in the north part of Burdwood Bay.

54   **Hill Island** *(50°10'N, 125°04'W)* has a private lodge with floats, protected by a floating breakwater in **Totem Bay** on its north shore. Large barrel buoys marking the entrance are at the ends of the breakwater.

Mansons Landing (1985)

Gorge Harbour entrance (1985)

Uganda Passage from Marina Island (1985)

Whaletown Bay (1985)

Charts 3538, 3541

55 **Evans Bay** *(50°11'N, 125°05'W)* is entered SW of **Frederic Point**, which is bold. The bay does not afford suitable anchorage for large vessels. Small craft can find anchorage, open to southerly winds, in **Bird Cove** and in the NE arm of the bay that has booming grounds and a log dump at its head (1995). It is reported that the NE arm, which can be recognized by its logged off hillside, affords the best all-weather shelter.

56 **Marine farm** facilities are in the bay close NW of Frederic Point and off the east shore 1.4 miles NW of Frederic Point.

57 **Read Island** settlement has a public float providing 37 m of berthing. The float is reported to be well protected from all winds although strong SE winds sometimes raise an uncomfortable sea. A drying rock, east of the float, is marked by port hand buoy "Q3". There is a store and post office.

58 **Whale Passage** separates **Penn Islands** from Read Island. A 3.7 m shoal lies midway between the two west Penn Islands. Marine farm facilities are south of the north Penn Island.

59 The east coast of Read Island north of Penn Islands is rocky and steep-to but fringed in places by shoals and rocks.

Cortes Island — NW and West Shores

Chart 3538

60 **Subtle Islands** *(50°07'N, 125°05'W)*, connected by a causeway, are separated from the west extremity of Cortes Island by **Plunger Passage**. The passage between Subtle Islands and **Centre Islet**, which is treeless, is restricted by a drying spit projecting from Subtle Islands. Both passages are suitable for small craft.

61 **Submarine cables** (power and telephone) are laid across Plunger Passage from Cortes Island to the south Subtle Island.

62 A **private float** is east of the causeway on the south Subtle Island.

63 **Coulter Bay** is reported to afford good anchorage for small craft, with fair protection from westerly winds being found close to **Coulter Island**.

64 **Carrington Bay** has **Jane Islet** and drying and below-water rocks near its centre and **Carrington Lagoon** at its head. It is reported that the bottom is rocky and holding ground poor.

65 **Sewage disposal** in the waters of Carrington Bay and Carrington Lagoon is prohibited under the *Pleasure/Non-Pleasure Craft Sewage Pollution Prevention Regulations.*

66 **Quartz Bay** is reported to provide limited anchorage for small craft. Marine farm facilities are located throughout Quartz Bay and in the bay 1.1 miles NE.

67 **Von Donop Inlet** *(50°10'N, 124°57'W)* is a good anchorage for small craft, the most popular berths being at the head, with good holding reported. In the narrowest part of the inlet, about 50 m wide, a rock with less than 2 m over it lies in mid-channel. It is usually marked by kelp and only visible at LW. The preferred route leads west of this rock. A rock that dries 2.8 m is at the head of the inlet.

68 **Ha'thayim (Von Donop) Marine Provincial Park** includes Von Donop Inlet, **Robertson Lake** and **Wiley Lake**. It is an undeveloped marine wilderness park.

Chart 3541

69 The coast from Von Donop Inlet *(50°10'N, 124°57'W)* to **Bullock Bluff** is fringed by rocks and reefs for about 0.1 mile offshore. Robertson Cove (local name) lies at the outlet to Robertson Lake. The bottom of the cove is reported to be undependable for holding.

70 **Marine farm** facilities are in Robertson Cove and in the cove 0.5 mile NW.

Deer Passage

71 **Deer Passage** leads between **Raza Island**, which rises steeply to a peak, and **West Redonda Island**.

Chart 3555

72 **Redonda Bay** *(50°16'N, 124°57'W)* has **Deceit Rock** near its centre and a shoal projecting from its south shore. It is too exposed for comfortable anchorage as seas form with almost any wind. The old public wharf and cannery wharf have been demolished, only a few piles remain. Marine farm facilities are in the east part of the bay. Booming grounds are in the bay, SSE of Deceit Rock.

73 **Tides**. — Tidal differences for Redonda Bay (Index No. 8025), referenced on Point Atkinson, are in *Tide Tables, Volume 5.*

Calm Channel

Chart 3541

74 **Calm Channel** *(50°18'N, 125°04'W)*, entered SW of Raza Island, leads about 8 miles NW from Sutil and Lewis Channels, joining Bute Inlet and Cordero Channel at Stuart Island.

75 **Tidal streams** are weak in Calm Channel but strong in the adjoining section of Cordero Channel leading west of Stuart Island.

76 **Drew Passage**, which leads west of **Rendezvous Islands**, is clear of dangers. The passage between the middle and south Rendezvous Islands is foul but small craft can carry 8 m through it, local knowledge is advised. A logging camp and log dump are in the bay on Maurelle Island 1 mile NW of the north Rendezvous Island (1995).

77 **Church House** *(50°20'N, 125°05'W)* is a First Nations settlement with a conspicuous church and a public wharf with floats.

78 **Raza Passage** *(50°19'N, 125°01'W)*, entered north of **Raza Point**, connects Calm Channel to Ramsay Arm and Pryce Channel.

79 **Frances Bay** *(50°21'N, 125°02'W)*, locally known as Fanny Bay, affords anchorage for small craft at its head with protection from all but SE winds.

80 **Marine farm** facilities are in the bay 1.8 miles NE of Raza Point.

Bute Inlet

Charts 3541, 3542

81 **Bute Inlet**, entered WNW of **Johnstone Bluff** *(50°21'N, 125°05'W)*, has mountains on both sides rising abruptly to high peaks. Several large rivers empty into the inlet and water is often milky.

82 **Henrietta Point**, the east extremity of Stuart Island, lies on the west side of Bute Inlet 2 miles within the entrance. A log dump and booming ground are SW of the point.

83 **Tidal streams**. — Due to land drainage, a definite overlay of fresh water flows almost constantly out of the inlet at 1 to 2 kn, being strongest during spring runoff and weakest during a dry summer. This overlay, augmented by runoff along the way, increases in volume and rate as it flows from the head toward the foot of the inlet.

84 **Tides**. — Tidal differences for Orford Bay (Index No. 8065) and Waddington Harbour (Index No. 8069) at the head of the inlet, referenced on Point Atkinson, are in *Tide Tables, Volume 5*.

Chart 3542

85 **Lawrence Point** *(50°27′N, 125°06′W)*, **Amor Point**, **Alpha Bluff**, **Boyd Point**, **Mellersh Point**, **Bear Bay** and **Littleton Point** are on the west side of Bute Inlet. On the east side are **Fawn Bluff**, **Clipper Point**, **Orford Bay**, **Hovel Bay**, **Purcell Point** and **Ward Point**.

86 **Waddington Harbour** *(50°55′N, 124°50′W)* has **Southgate River** flowing into its SE part through **Pigeon Valley**, and **Homathko River** flowing into its NW corner. **Hamilton Point** and **Potato Point** are on the west side of the harbour. Booming grounds are north of Hamilton Point. Water is pale green due to mineral content of runoff from **Homathko Icefield**, 5 miles NE. A float with 4.3 m alongside and protected by a breakwater lies abreast a logging camp on the north side of Southgate River.

87 **Indifferent anchorage**, unsafe in strong SW winds, can be obtained close to the edge of the drying flats. As the bottom shoals rapidly and the flats are subject to change pay close attention to depths.

88 **Booming grounds** and logging camps are near the entrance to **Moh Creek**, in Orford Bay, SE of Boyd Point and east of Littleton Point. A breakwater is SW of Mellersh Point. A booming ground with mooring buoys is off the west shore 1.5 miles north of Littleton Point.

89 An **aircraft landing strip** owned by a logging company is at Homathko River.

Cordero Channel

Chart 3543

90 **Cordero Channel**, whose east end is entered either SW or north of **Stuart Island** *(50°23′N, 125°07′W)*, leads about 20 miles NW and west to join Chancellor Channel north of West Thurlow Island. The route between the Strait of Georgia and Johnstone Strait leading through Calm and Cordero Channels is more protected and has less traffic than that through Discovery Passage.

91 **Tides**. — Tidal differences for Big Bay (Index No. 8060), referenced on Campbell River, and for Mermaid Bay (Index No. 8135), Shoal Bay (Index No. 8145), Cordero Islands (Index No. 8150), use Blind Channel in Mayne Passage (Index No. 8155), and Sidney Bay in Loughborough Inlet (Index No. 8162), referenced on Owen Bay, are in *Tide Tables, Volume 6*.

92 **Tidal rapids**. — Strong tidal streams with overfalls and at times violent eddies and whirlpools exist in parts of Cordero Channel. During large tides these tidal streams reach maximum velocities of 10 kn in Yuculta Rapids, 12½ kn in Barber and Gillard Passages, 14 kn in Arran Rapids, 11 kn in Dent Rapids and 7 kn in Greene Point Rapids.

93 Predictions for times of turn to flood and ebb, and maximum rates in Gillard Passage (Index No. 5500) and Arran Rapids (Index No. 5600), and time differences and maximum rates for secondary current stations Yuculta Rapids (Index No. 5505) and Dent Rapids (Index No. 5530), referenced on Gillard Passage, and for Greene Point Rapids (Index No. 5045), referenced on Seymour Narrows, are in *Tide Tables, Volume 6*.

94 **Duration of slack water at all places is very brief**, usually not more than 5 minutes. Local weather and the amount of land drainage can affect the turn of the stream, which at times can be abrupt with no period of dead slack water.

95 **Directions**. — Due to the strength of tidal streams and turbulence that develops in various areas, navigation of Yuculta, Arran, Dent and Greene Point Rapids, and Gillard and Barber Passages, should not be attempted other than at or near slack water, at which time they can be taken without difficulty.

96 **Small craft** with low power bound westward are advised to approach Yuculta Rapids about 1 hour before turn to ebb, taking advantage of a back eddy along the Stuart Island shore until off **Kellsey Point** *(50°22′N, 125°09′W)*, then to cross to the Sonora Island shore where there is a prevailing northerly current. This should allow time to transit Gillard and Dent Rapids before the ebb current reaches full force. If late for slack water and unsure of Dent Rapids, small craft are advised to wait in Big Bay for the next slack water.

Yuculta Rapids to Dent Rapids

97 **Yuculta Rapids** is entered west of **Harbott Point** *(50°22′N, 125°08′W)*. The Yucultas is a local name used to cover the Yuculta Rapids proper, Gillard and Barber Passages and Dent Rapids.

98 **Light**. — Harbott Point light *(529)* is on the SW end of Stuart Island.

99 **Shoals**, with 3.7 and 4.9 m over them, lie on the west and east sides respectively of the rapids close south of **Sea Lion Rock** and **Whirlpool Point**.

100 **Private floats** and a fishing resort are on Sonora Island south and east of Sea Lion Rock.

101 **Big Bay** *(50°24′N, 125°08′W)* has a detached shoal with 4 m over it, marked by kelp, in its central part. Big Bay settlement has the Stuart Island Post Office, general store, restaurant, accommodation, bakery, and numerous private floats. The marina has gas, oil, diesel, showers, laundry and limited water and power. Water taxi service is available from Campbell River and daily flights from Seattle, Vancouver and Campbell River. Reduce speed to avoid excessive wake before entering the bay.

102 **Wharf**. — The public wharf in Big Bay, protected by a breakwater, has floats with 213 m of berthing. The outer end of the eastern float is reserved for seaplanes.

103 Big Bay is a **water aerodrome**.

104 **Tides**. — Tidal differences for Big Bay (Index No. 8060), referenced on Campbell River, are in *Tide Tables, Volume 6*.

105 **Currents**. — A southerly current is felt close to the public floats on both ebb and flood tides.

Chart 3543

106   **Innes Passage**, which leads south of the largest of the **Gillard Islands**, is narrow, shallow and suitable only for small craft, local knowledge is advised. A log dump is at the west end of the passage.

107   **Gillard Passage** *(50°24'N, 125°10'W)*, between the large Gillard Island and **Jimmy Judd Island**, is used by vessels bound east or west. Shoal depths, including **Jimmy Judd Reef**, fringe the south shore of Jimmy Judd Island.

108   **Light**. — Gillard Islands light *(530)* is on the NE extremity of the large island.

109   **Dangerous whirlpools** form east of Gillard Islands, between 2 hours after turn to flood and 1 hour before turn to ebb.

110   **Barber Passage** leads between Jimmy Judd Island and Stuart Island. A drying rock and shoal depths fringe the east side of the passage near **Hesler Point**. Private floats protected by a breakwater between two private light buoys are in **Bells Bay**, private floats are also on the north side of **Asman Point** and 0.7 mile NNE of Asman Point.

111   **Arran Rapids** *(50°25'N, 125°08'W)*, which join Cordero Channel to Bute Inlet, have **Arran Point** and **Turnback Point** on the south side.

112   **Vancouver Bay**, 0.6 mile ENE of Arran Point, is an Indian Reserve with private floats.

113   **Dent Island** *(50°24'N, 125°11'W)* is joined to the north shore by drying ledges. A fishing lodge and floats with marina facilities are on the islet NNE of Dent Island. Moorage, water, power, showers and a restaurant are available.

114   **Engels Rock**, with 3.7 m over it, lies close-off the SE shore of Dent Island. **Mermaid Bay**, on the south side of the island, is a mooring ground for tugs with logbooms awaiting slack water to navigate the rapids.

115   **Tides**. — Tidal differences for Mermaid Bay (Index No. 8135), referenced on Owen Bay, are in *Tide Tables, Volume 6.*

116   **Tugboat Passage**, between Dent Island and **Little Dent Island**, is not recommended because of islets, shoals and confused currents, but is used extensively by tugs, local knowledge is advised. A private float is on the SE side of Little Dent Island.

117   **Light**. — Dent Islands light *(531)*, on the west extremity of Little Dent Island, is shown at an elevation of 7.3 m from a white tower with a red band at the top.

118   **Dent Rapids**, between Little Dent and Sonora Islands, are swift and turbulent with **dangerous overfalls and eddies**. In **Devils Hole**, violent eddies and whirlpools form between 2 hours after turn to flood and 1 hour before turn to ebb. Favour the Sonora Island shore of Dent Rapids.

Dent Rapids to Frederick Arm

119   **Caution. — A shoal, with 6.4 m over it, 0.5 mile NW of Dent Islands light, creates dangerous turbulence and a large overfall on ebb tides.**

120   Tugs towing logbooms will frequently be found moving with the last of the ebb from **Horn Point** *(50°25'N, 125°13'W)* to **Burnt Bluff** and from there through Tugboat Passage to Mermaid Bay, or from Mermaid Bay through Gillard Passage. Tugs with booms can also be encountered at Dent Rapids on the turn of the flood. The bay north of Horn Point is used as a mooring ground for tugs with log booms.

121   **Dangers**. — **Secord Rock**, a drying rock NNW of Horn Point, and **Denham Rock**, ESE of **Denham Islet** *(50°26'N,* 125°15'W)*, sometimes marked by kelp, are isolated dangers. A shoal with 3.7 m over it lies 0.1 mile offshore, 0.5 mile north of Horn Point.

Frederick Arm

122   **Frederick Arm**, entered west of **Gomer Island** *(50°27'N, 125°16'W)*, has no dangers beyond 0.15 mile from shore. Depths under 30 m extend 0.5 mile from the head of the arm, appearing to afford better anchorage than is found in most mainland inlets. Booming grounds are 0.5 mile NE of Gomer Island and at the head of the arm. Marine farm facilities are in several locations within Frederick Arm (1995). A floating restaurant is located on the east side near the entrance.

123   **Estero Basin** flows into the head of Frederick Arm over a drying flat. It is unsurveyed.

Nodales Channel

124   **Nodales Channel**, which joins Cordero Channel to Discovery Passage, is entered between **Hall Point** *(50°27'N, 125°17'W)* and **Johns Point**, on East Thurlow Island.

125   **Tidal streams** in Nodales Channel attain 3 kn, the flood stream flowing northward with turbulence off Johns Point where the flood streams meet.

126   A booming ground and log dump are close north of **Sonora Point** and marine farm facilities are south of Sonora Point, 0.8 mile SSW of **Thurlow Point** and in the bay north of **Brougham Point**.

127   **Hemming Bay** *(50°24'N, 125°22'W)* is entered SW of **Lee Islands** which are fringed with shoal water. The channel between Lee Islands and **Jackson Point** is obstructed by a rock with less than 2 m over it. **Menace Rock**, with less than 2 m over it, lies near the centre of Hemming Bay ESE of **Pinhorn Islet**. The NW part of the bay is shoal with numerous islets and reefs. Marine farm facilities are in the coves on the north shore. A loading ramp and booming ground, and the ruins of a house are at the head of the bay.

128   **Anchorage** for small vessels can be obtained in the NE part of the head of Hemming Bay. Small craft can find anchorage close north of the islet 44 m high near the head, also SW of this islet in an enclosed nook.

129   **Thurston Bay** *(50°22'N, 125°19'W)*, entered between **Davis Point** and **Wilson Point**, has **Block Island** in its north part. A detached drying and above-water reef lies close-off the south shore of the bay.

130   **Thurston Bay Marine Provincial Park** includes Thurston Bay, Handfield Bay and Cameleon Harbour. It is undeveloped, though camping is allowed.

131   It is reported that reasonably sheltered **anchorage** can be obtained behind Block Island, and by small craft in the lagoon on the south shore of the bay. The lagoon has a depth of 0.6 m in its entrance channel.

132   **Cameleon Harbour** can be approached either side of **Hardinge Island** through **Burgess Passage** or **Young Passage**, and is entered between **Bruce Point** and **Greetham Point**.

133   **Dangers**. — **Maycock Rock** and **Entry Ledge** lie on the south side of the inner approach. **Douglas Rock** lies close SW of Bruce Point. Drying rocks lie SE of **Edward Point** and off the south side of Young Passage.

Arran Rapids from SW (1985)

Gillard Passage from Big Bay (1985)

Dent Rapids from SE (1985)

Dent Rapids from NW (1985)

Chart 3543

134 **Marine farm** facilities are on the south side of the inner approach, close west of Maycock Rock.

135 **Handfield Bay**, entered from **Binnington Bay**, has drying rocks and **Tully Island** in its entrance.

136 **Piddell Bay** is on the east side of Cameleon Harbour.

137 **Anchorage** sheltered from all winds can be obtained by small vessels near the SE end of Cameleon Harbour. Larger vessels can obtain good anchorage in Young Passage SE of the south extremity of Hardinge Island. Small craft can find anchorage in Handfield Bay and at the head of Cameleon Harbour.

138 **Howe Island** *(50°20'N, 125°24'W)* and **Suffolk Point**, 1.2 miles NW, mark the south limit of Nodales Channel.

Frederick Arm to Mayne Passage

139 **Channe Passage**, which leads SE of **Channe Island** *(50°27'N, 125°20'W)*, has rocks and shoal water projecting from its SW shore to mid-channel and shoal water fringing its NE shore for 90 m off.

140 **Shoal Bay** is entered 1 mile WNW of Channe Island. **Thurlow**, at the head of the bay, has a public wharf and floats with 200 m of berthing space. Gold was mined in this area and by 1898 there were over 200 mineral claims and a substantial settlement. It remained a very active community well into the 1950s, but gradually declined. The original Lodge burnt down in 2000 but has been rebuilt. It has accommodation and restaurant facilities, and offers fishing and adventure tours. Laundry and shower facilities are being built adjacent to the public wharf, camping is available during summer months.

141 **Tides**. — Tidal differences for Shoal Bay (Index No. 8145), referenced on Owen Bay, are in *Tide Tables, Volume 6.*

142 **Godwin Point** is on the south side of Cordero Channel, 0.3 mile WNW of Shoal Bay. **Picton Point**, on the north side, has a large conspicuous aluminum sided building in a logging camp close west of it. Booming grounds are in the bay SW of the point.

143 **Phillips Arm** *(50°29'N, 125°22'W)* affords anchorage close to the drying flat at its head and, for small vessels, in **Fanny Bay**. Extensive logging operations with booming grounds are carried out at the head of the arm and in Fanny Bay. Marine farm facilities are off the east shore, 0.5 mile south of **Richard Point**. **Bullveke Point**, **Hewitt Point** and **Dyer Point** are named features in Phillips Arm. It is reported that the bottom in the vicinity of Dyer Point is fouled with sunken logs.

144 **Bickley Bay** *(50°27'N, 125°24'W)* has **Noel Islet**, **Peel Rocks** and a rock, with 4.9 m over it, close SE of Peel Rocks, on its west side and in its approach. Marine farm facilities are along the east shore of Bickley Bay. Anchorage for vessels awaiting slack water in Greene Point Rapids, 4 miles west, can be obtained in the inner part of the bay and for small craft close to its head, mud bottom. Poor holding has been reported.

145 A log dump and booming ground are in Brooks Bay (local name), 1 mile west of Bickley Bay.

146 **Lorte Island** lies on the north side of Cordero Channel, 2 miles west of Bickley Bay. Cordero Lodge, in the bay NE of the island, has a floating restaurant and floats for vessels and aircraft. Small craft can find temporary anchorage north of the island.

147 **Light**. — Lorte Island light *(531.5)* is on the south side of the island.

148 Cordero Channel fronting Lorte Island is a **water aerodrome** known as Camp Cordero.

149 **Tallac Bay** has a reef with three heads with less than 2 m over them lying close SE of its entrance.

150 **Crawford Anchorage** *(50°26'N, 125°28'W)*, sheltered by **Erasmus Island** and **Mink Island**, is suitable for small vessels but reported to afford poor anchorage for small craft. Approach this anchorage from west. Rocks with less than 2 m over them lie close SE of Mink Island, 0.25 mile WSW of **Parrott Point**, and 0.25 mile east of **Rowland Island**.

Mayne Passage

151 **Mayne Passage**, known locally as Blind Channel, connects Cordero Channel to Johnstone Strait. **Edsall Islets** *(50°26'N, 125°30'W)* lie on a shoal spit projecting from the west side of the north entrance to the passage.

152 **Charles Bay**, entered south of **Shell Point**, is shallow. **Eclipse Islet** stands on a boulder bank near the centre of the bay.

153 **Blind Channel** settlement, on the west side of the passage, has a resort with a well stocked store, restaurant and post office. The public wharf and float provide 37 m of berthing. Part of the float is reserved for aircraft and marina floats extend north from the public wharf. Gas, diesel, oil, propane and fresh water are obtainable. Power, water, washrooms, showers and laundry are available. Currents in the area are reported to be tricky.

154 Mayne Passage fronting Blind Channel is a **water aerodrome**.

155 **Tides**. — Tidal differences for Blind Channel (Index No. 8155), referenced on Owen Bay, are in *Tide Tables, Volume 6.*

156 **Tidal streams** flow north on the flood and attain 5 kn. Secondary current station Blind Channel (Index No. 5048), referenced on Seymour Narrows, is given in *Tide Tables, Volume 6.* Whirlpools and overfalls occur in the north part of the passage.

157 **Mayne Point** projects from the south side of Mayne Passage opposite **Butterfly Bay**, on the north side. Logging operations with booming grounds are in the bay 2 miles ENE of Mayne Point and in Butterfly Bay (1995).

158 **Anchorage** is available in mid-channel south of Butterfly Bay.

Greene Point Rapids

159 **Greene Point Rapids** *(50°26'N, 125°31'W)* leads between **Cordero Islands**, to the NE, and **West Thurlow Island**, to the SW, stretching from Edsall Islets to **Greene Point**.

160 **Light**. — **Griffiths Islet** light *(532)* is on the west end of the islet.

161 **Tides**. — Tidal differences for Cordero Islands (Index No. 8150), referenced on Owen Bay, are in *Tide Tables, Volume 6.*

162 **Tidal streams** in the rapids reach 7 kn with considerable overfalls, whirlpools and eddies, particularly with large tides. Passage at slack water is recommended. Secondary current station Greene Point Rapids (Index No. 5045), referenced on Seymour Narrows, is in *Tide Tables, Volume 6.*

163 **Caution. — Low powered vessels and vessels towing, when eastbound through the rapids with the flood current, should take care not to be set on Erasmus Island.**

Chart 3543

164   **Anchorage** with fair shelter is available to small vessels between Cordero Islands and the north shore.

165   **Lyall Island** *(50°27'N, 125°36'W)*, with reefs close south and NE of it, marks the junction of Cordero Channel with Chancellor Channel and Loughborough Inlet.

166   **Light**. — Lyall Island light *(532.2)* is on the SW end of the island.

Loughborough Inlet

167   **Loughborough Inlet** entered between **Grismond Point** *(50°27'N, 125°36'W)* and **Styles Point**, lies between high wooded mountains rising abruptly from its shores. There is a considerable amount of logging in the inlet. Because of deep water and steep-to shores anchorages are scarce, the only good ones being in Beaver Inlet.

168   **Tidal streams** in Loughborough Inlet seldom exceed 2 kn. Due to land drainage, an overlay of fresh water flows almost constantly out of the inlet at 1 to 2 kn, being strongest during spring runoff and weakest during a dry summer. This overlay, augmented by runoff along the way, increases in volume and rate as it flows from the head toward the foot of the inlet.

169   **Tides**. — Tidal differences for Sidney Bay (Index No. 8162), referenced on Owen Bay, are in *Tide Tables, Volume 6.*

Chart 3555

170   **Beaver Inlet** *(50°30'N, 125°35'W)*, on the west side of Loughborough Inlet 2 miles within the entrance, is entered between **William Point** and **Mary Point**. Private floats are NE of **Goat Islets** and NE of **Dickson Point**. Anchorage for small craft is obtainable south of **Hales Point** in **Edith Cove**. Small vessels can find anchorage with good holding in mud near the head of the inlet. It is reported that logging debris litters the bottom west of **Barry Point** and **Margaret Point**.

Chart 3543

171   **Sidney Bay** *(50°31'N, 125°36'W)* has booming grounds, private floats and affords anchorage for small vessels near its head. Marine farm facilities lie close-off its north shore.

172   **Roy** (locality), east of Sidney Bay, has booming grounds and a reef of drying and below-water rocks north of it.

173   **Statham Point** has a log dump and booming grounds 0.5 mile NE of it.

174   **Cosby Point** *(50°33'N, 125°33'W)* has drying and below-water rocks extending 0.8 mile SW from it. **Wignell Point** is 0.9 mile NE.

175   **Heydon Bay**, partially filled by a drying mud flat with a steep-to edge, is an Indian Reserve and a booming ground. A float with a fresh water pipe is 1 mile north of Heydon Bay.

176   **Mitchell Point**, on the west side of Loughborough Inlet, and **Campbell Point**, on the opposite shore, are 1 mile north of Heydon Bay.

177   **Towry Head**, at the south end of **Cooper Reach**, is prominent and cliffy on its south side. A logging camp and a float are at **Latelle Creek**, 2 miles east.

178   **Frazer Bay**, between **Pym Point** and **Pan Point**, is a booming ground.

179   **McBride Bay**, east of Pan Point, has a shoal with 3.7 m over it in its central part and drying reefs close south of **Heard Point**.

Chancellor Channel

Charts 3543, 3544

180   **Chancellor Channel** *(50°26'N, 125°37'W)* leads 8 miles WSW from its junction with Loughborough Inlet and Cordero Channel, joining Johnstone Strait east of Current and Race Passages. **Tucker Point** projects from the north shore of West Thurlow Island, opposite the mouth of Loughborough Inlet. **Fittleton Point** is on the mainland shore 2 miles west. Marine farm facilities are off the south shore opposite Fittleton Point.

181   **Tidal streams** in Chancellor Channel seldom exceed 2 kn, are free of turbulence and run parallel to shore throughout its length.

182   **Dickson Shoal**, SE of **D'Arcy Point**, has 9.5 m over it. A booming ground is east of D'Arcy Point.

183   It is reported that the bay east of **Shorter Point** affords anchorage for vessels waiting for the tide to turn. Marine farm facilities are in the east part of the bay.

Wellbore Channel

Chart 3544

184   **Wellbore Channel** *(50°27'N, 125°45'W)*, which separates Hardwicke Island from the mainland to the east, joins Chancellor and Sunderland Channels. It provides a route to Johnstone Strait that by-passes Current and Race Passages, where wind against current can cause heavy tide-rips, see Chapter 6.

185   **Bulkely Island** lies in the south entrance to Wellbore Channel.

186   **Whirlpool Rapids** is in the narrowest part of the channel, abreast **Carterer Point**.

187   **Tidal streams** in Whirlpool Rapids create strong whirlpools, upwellings and backeddies. The turbulence occurs south of Carterer Point with the flood tide and north of the point with the ebb. The flood sets SE and the ebb NW. Secondary current station Whirlpool Rapids (Index No. 5050), referenced on Seymour Narrows, is in *Tide Tables, Volume 6.*

188   **Light**. — Carterer Point light *(542)*, on the NE end of an islet close NE of the point, is shown at an elevation of 5.6 m from a white tower with a green band at the top.

189   **Forward Harbour** is entered between **Horace Point** and **Louisa Point** *(50°28'N, 125°46'W)*. When entering the harbour, take care to avoid the shoal rock south of **Midgham Islets**. Anchorage can be obtained anywhere in the harbour, the best location being off **Douglas Bay** where there is shelter from west winds. Booming grounds are along the south shore of the harbour.

190   **Robson Point**, **Maud Point** and **Blanche Point** are named features on the north shore. **Florence Point** and **Cust Point** are on the south shore.

Sunderland Channel

191   **Sunderland Channel**, entered from SE between **Althorp Point** and **Thynne Point**, leads 8 miles WSW to Johnstone Strait.

Chart 3544

192   **Tidal streams** of 4 kn with heavy tide-rips sometimes occur in the west entrance of Sunderland Channel, but farther east rates seldom exceed 1½ kn. Secondary current station Sunderland Channel (Index No. 6018), referenced on Johnstone Strait – Central, is in *Tide Tables, Volume 6.*

193   **Bessborough Bay** *(50°29'N, 125°47'W)*, at the east end of the channel, affords anchorage for small vessels in its SE part, with no protection from west winds.

194   West winds cause a confused sea around **Termagant Point** *(50°29'N, 125°29'W)*.

195   **Topaze Harbour** is entered between **Geneste Point** *(50°30'N, 125°51'W)* and **Murray Island**. **Jackson Bay**, on the north side of the harbour between **Neale Point** and **Molesworth Point**, has a logging camp and booming grounds.

196   **Jackson Bay** (landing), on the south side near **Hill Point**, is fronted by booming grounds and several private mooring buoys. On the north shore, **Read Bay** is filled with a drying flat. A breakwater and float are 0.2 mile east of **Haswell Point**.

197   **Anchorage** can be obtained almost anywhere in Topaze Harbour or in Jackson Bay, but there is little shelter for small craft.

198   **Poyntz Island** and **Seymour Island**, which has a drying reef close east of it, lie near mid-channel 1 mile west of Termagant Point.

199   **Light**. — Seymour Island light *(542.5)*, on the south side of the island, is shown at an elevation of 5.5 m from a mast. The light is not visible from northward.

200   **Marine farm** facilities are on the north shore of Hardwicke Island, about 0.9 mile SSW of Seymour Island.

201   **Shaw Point**, 1.5 miles west of Seymour Island, has a submarine cable extending north from it. Booming grounds are north of the point.

202   **Gunner Point** *(50°28'N, 125°58'W)* is at the west entrance to Sunderland Channel. It is reported that temporary shelter from westerlies can be obtained in the bay east of Gunner Point.

Hoskyn Channel

Chart 3539

203   **Hoskyn Channel** *(50°10'N, 125°09'W)* leads north between Quadra Island and Read Island to Surge Narrows and Whiterock Passage. Several cabins lie along the shores of the channel.

204   **Tides**. — Tidal differences for Surge Narrows (Index No. 8045), referenced on Point Atkinson, are in *Tide Tables, Volume 5.*

205   **Tidal streams** ebb north and flood south at 1-2 kn.

206   **Breton Islands** *(50°08'N, 125°11'W)* have reefs extending from them. **Moulds Bay**, 0.5 mile NNW of Breton Islands, is reported to offer good anchorage to small craft in 7 to 10 m. Marine farm facilities are on the west side of Breton Islands.

207   **Shoals**. — A detached shoal with a least depth of 3.7 m lies close-off the SW extremity of Read Island, midway between **Read Point** and **Hoskyn Rock**. An isolated 7.9 m shoal lies almost midway between **Dunsterville Islet** and **King Islets**.

208   **Marine farm** facilities are in the bays south and north of Dunsterville Point and in the channel east of King Islets.

209   **Village Bay**, in the SE part of Quadra Island, is open to SE but affords temporary anchorage for small vessels in its centre part and in the SW corner near the head, for small craft. Several cottages lie around the shores of the bay. Marine farm facilities are in the south part of the bay.

210   **Crescent Channel** *(50°10'N, 125°10'W)* is entered west of **Bold Point**, a prominent point at the south end of **Bold Island**. **Marine farm** facilities are in Crescent Channel. Well protected anchorage for small craft is available in the channel. Take care to avoid drying rocks and rocks with less than 2 m over them.

211   **Marine farm** facilities front **Bold Point** settlement.

212   **Conville Bay** and **Conville Point** lie on the west side of Hoskyn Channel. An isolated 5.8 m shoal lies 0.3 mile south of Conville Point. Marine farm facilities are in Conville Bay and close south of Conville Point.

213   **Anchorage** for small craft can be obtained in **Hjorth Bay**, on the east side of Hoskyn Channel, or farther north on the east side of **Sheer Point**, in a bay known locally as **Boulton Bay**.

Chart 3537

214   **Surge Narrows** settlement, NE of **Surge Point** *(50°13'N, 125°07'W)*, on the east side of Hoskyn Channel, has a general store and post office on the public wharf.

215   **Wharves**. — The public wharf and floats provide 55 m of berthing space; the outer float is reserved for seaplanes. A private wharf and float are south of the public wharf.

216   **Buoy**. — A rock that dries 0.3 m, NW of the public wharf, is marked by port hand buoy "Q1".

217   A **submarine pipeline** (sewer outfall) is laid close north of the public wharf.

218   Waters off the settlement are a **water aerodrome**.

Whiterock Passage

219   **Whiterock Passage** *(50°15'N, 125°06'W)* leads NE from Hoskyn Channel to Calm Channel, providing a route to avoid strong currents in Surge Narrows and Hole in the Wall. The passage has drying banks on both sides and is obstructed at the south end by an islet and several drying rocks. A channel with a least depth of 1.5 m has been dredged through the bank. Several cabins lie along the shores of the passage.

220   **Tidal streams** in Whiterock Passage are weak, usually less than 2 kn. The flood stream sets north.

221   **Light**. — Whiterock Passage light *(484)*, on the islet in the SW entrance to the passage, is shown at an elevation of 5.1 m from a white tower.

222   Whiterock Passage 1 range lights *(484.1, 484.2)*, bearing 065½°, lead through the south part of the dredged channel.

223   Whiterock Passage 2 range lights *(484.3, 484.4)*, bearing 211½°, lead through the north part of the dredged channel.

Okisollo Channel

224   **Okisollo Channel** leads from Surge Narrows to Discovery Passage, separating Quadra Island from **Maurelle Island** and **Sonora Island**. Hole in the Wall connects the NE part of Okisollo Channel to Calm Channel. Because of currents and shoal rocks in Surge Narrows, Upper and Lower Rapids and Hole in the Wall, the route through Okisollo Channel is suitable only for small vessels and small craft.

Chart 3537

225   **Tides**. — Tidal predictions for Owen Bay (Index No. 8120), and tidal differences for Octopus Islands (Index No. 8050), and Florence Cove in Hole in the Wall (Index No. 8055), referenced on Campbell River, are in *Tide Tables, Volume 6.*

226   **Tidal streams** reach 12 kn in Surge Narrows and in the west entrance to Hole in the Wall, and 11 kn in the Upper Rapids in Okisollo Channel. Times of turn in the Lower Rapids are almost the same as those at Upper Rapids, and maximum rates are about 6 kn. **Overfalls and eddies in Upper Rapids are extremely dangerous.**

227   Predictions of times and rates of maximum current and times of slack water for Hole in the Wall (Index No. 5100) and Beazley Passage (Index No. 5200), and secondary current station Okisollo Channel (Upper Rapids) (Index No. 5030), referenced on Seymour Narrows, are in *Tide Tables, Volume 6.*

Surge Narrows

228   **Surge Narrows** *(50°14'N, 125°09'W)* joins Hoskyn Channel to Okisollo Channel leading SW of **Antonio Point**. It is obstructed at its SE end by the **Welsford Islands** and the **Settlers Group**. The name Surge Narrows is applied locally to the entire route, from Hoskyn Channel through Beazley Passage, described below, to Okisollo Channel. **This route should be navigated only at or near slack water.**

229   **Beazley Passage**, between **Sturt Island** and **Peck Island**, is the only navigable passage through or around Settlers Group into Okisollo Channel. It has a minimum width of 60 m. **Tusko Rock**, which dries 1.6 m, lies at the west end of the passage.

230   **Anchorage** in the vicinity of Settlers Group is not recommended because of strong tidal streams and poor holding.

231   **Tides**. — Tidal differences for Surge Narrows (Index No. 8045), referenced on Point Atkinson, are in *Tide Tables, Volume 5.*

232   **Tidal streams**. — The strongest tidal streams in the Surge Narrows area occur in Beazley Passage, where at large tides they reach 11½ kn on the flood and 9½ kn on the ebb. Duration of slack water throughout Surge Narrows varies from 5 to 11 minutes. Daily predictions for times of slack water, and times and rates of maximum flood and ebb streams, are tabulated for current station Beazley Passage (Index No. 5200) in *Tide Tables, Volume 6.*

Surge Narrows to Hole in the Wall

233   **Anchorage** for vessels awaiting slack water in Surge Narrows can be obtained in **Yeatman Bay** *(50°14'N, 125°11'W)*. Bottom near shore is rock and holding ground indifferent.

234   **Dangers**. — **Cyrus Rocks** lie on the west side of the channel 1.5 miles NNW of Yeatman Bay. **Barnsley Shoal** is an isolated reef near mid-channel east of Waiatt Bay.

235   **Marine farm** facilities are ENE of Cyrus Rocks.

236   **Waiatt Bay** affords well-protected anchorage for small vessels in its centre and for small craft near its head or in small bays in the marine park. Bottom is mud with some sand and shale near shore. Marine farm facilities are on the north side of the bay.

237   The entrance to Waiatt Bay south of **Octopus Islands** has several islets, shoals and drying reefs in it. Local knowledge is advised as there are no natural leading marks for clearing these reefs. The narrow passage from Bodega Anchorage to Waiatt Bay, leading west of Octopus Islands, is clear of dangers except for a drying reef and a rock with 0.2 m over it at the south entrance to this passage. These reefs are reported to be easy to see in the clear water of the bay.

238   **Octopus Islands Provincial Park**, on the north side of Waiatt Bay, is undeveloped.

239   **Tides**. — Tidal differences for Octopus Islands (Index No. 8050), referenced on Campbell River, are in *Tide Tables, Volume 6.*

240   **Bodega Anchorage**, north of Octopus Islands, is useful for craft awaiting slack water for passage through Hole in the Wall or Upper Rapids. Holding is reported to be good. **Chasina Island** is in the entrance to the anchorage.

241   **Francisco Island** has a 4.4 m shoal 0.1 mile SE of it and a rock that dries 3.2 m 0.1 mile NW of it.

Hole in the Wall

242   **Hole in the Wall** *(50°19'N, 125°11'W)*, entered between **Springer Point** and **Etta Point**, leads from Okisollo Channel to Calm Channel. It is normally used by commercial traffic in preference to Surge Narrows as the channel is wider. Hole in the Wall should only be navigated at or near slack water.

243   **Light**. — Hole in the Wall West light *(528)* is on the south shore at the west end of the channel.

244   **Dangers**. — Two shoals lie in the west entrance to Hole in the Wall. Midway through the passage a drying rock lies close-off the north shore, and a rock with less than 2 m over it lies close-off the south shore.

245   **Anchorage** for small vessels can be obtained in **Florence Cove**, which indents the south shore of Hole in the Wall.

246   **Tides**. — Tidal differences for Florence Cove (Index No. 8055), referenced on Campbell River, are in *Tide Tables, Volume 6.*

247   **Tidal streams** in Hole in the Wall reach 12 kn on the flood and 9½ kn on the ebb in the narrows, at the west entrance of the channel. The flood sets NE, and the duration of slack on average is 4 minutes. The stream in the east entrance, between **Bernard Point** and **Bassett Point**, is about 2 kn. Times and rates of maximum flood and ebb streams are tabulated for current station Hole in the Wall (Index No. 5100) in *Tide Tables, Volume 6.*

Hole in the Wall to Discovery Passage

248   **Upper Rapids** *(50°18'N, 125°14'W)*, between **Cooper Point** and islands off the east shore, has a maximum rate of 11 kn. **Overfalls and eddies are extremely dangerous. Upper Rapids should be navigated only at or near slack water.** Secondary current station Okisollo Channel (Upper Rapids) (Index No. 5030), referenced on Seymour Narrows, is in *Tide Tables, Volume 6.*

249   **Dangers**. — Bentley Rock, which dries 0.1 m, and a reef with 3.4 m over it close SE, lie near mid-channel at the SE end of Upper Rapids. A rock that dries 0.1 m lies close offshore SE of Cooper Point.

250   **Diamond Bay** and the bay close north have private floats in them.

251   **Owen Bay** *(50°19'N, 125°14'W)* is entered through a channel less than 0.1 mile wide between a drying reef close-off the

Hole in the Wall from Okisollo Channel (1985)

Beazley Passage from Hoskyn Channel (1985)

Whiterock Passage from Hoskyn Channel (1985)

Chart 3537

SE side of **Walters Point** and **Grant Island**. A drying reef lies 0.1 mile SW of Grant Island. Take care not to be set by the currents and eddies into the reefs.

252   **Owen Bay** settlement, on the SE shore, has no supplies or services. The public wharf has a float providing 17 m of berthing.

253   **Good anchorage** is available in Owen Bay over mud bottom. It is reported that the islands SW of the wharf should be avoided as the tidal currents rush between them with remarkable force.

254   **Tides**. — Tidal predictions for Owen Bay (Index No. 8120) are in *Tide Tables, Volume 6.*

255   A private float and **mooring buoy** are in the bay 0.4 mile NNW of Walters Point.

256   **Lower Rapids**, which lead south of **Okis Islands**, are obstructed by **Gypsy Shoal**, which has two heads. The SW rock dries 0.4 m and the NE rock has 0.2 m over it. The fairway passes south of Gypsy Shoal, **it should be navigated only at or near slack water**. Lower Rapids can be avoided by passing north of Okis Islands where the channel is free of dangers although the currents are still strong.

257   **Barnes Bay** *(50°19'N, 125°16'W)* affords anchorage for vessels in its east part. The bottom is reported to be rock. Marine farm facilities are in the east part of the bay.

258   **Nutcracker Bay**, close west of **Haro Island**, has booming grounds. **Woods Bay**, west of Nutcracker Bay, has an extensive drying reef near its head.

259   **Pulton Bay**, south of Barnes Bay, has a drying reef close-off its SE shore and a house with a boathouse and private floats on its SW shore.

260   Booming grounds line the south shore west of **Pulton Point** and are in the bay 1.2 miles west of Pulton Point.

261   **Bjerre Rock** is an isolated drying rock lying near mid-channel NNW of **Chonat Point** *(50°18'N, 125°19'W)*.

262   **Beacon**. — Bjerre Rock daybeacon has a bifurcation/junction daymark, preferred channel to the right.

263   **Marine farm** facilities lie off the north shore of the channel 0.7 mile NNE of Bjerre Rock.

264   **Chonat Bay**, which is used for storing logbooms, has a conspicuous cliff on the south side of its entrance. Anchorage is available in the middle of the bay, but note the 5.8 m shoal in the middle of the entrance.

265   **Venture Point** is a bold point on the north side of the channel. **Brent Island**, to the south, is wooded. **Metcalf Islands**

lie close to the south shore, near the west entrance of Okisollo Channel.

266   **Fresh water** is reported to be obtainable from a waterfall on the Sonora Island shore, north of Metcalf Islands.

267   **Min Rock** *(50°17'N, 125°23'W)* is a detached rock with 0.6 m over it. It is usually marked by kelp in summer.

Redonda Islands and Surrounding Waterways

Chart 3538

268   **Desolation Sound** *(50°06'N, 124°49'W)*, named by Captain Vancouver in 1792, because of the rugged countryside and gloomy, silent, forests lies south of West Redonda Island. It is entered from south between **Sarah Point** and **Mary Point**, which is high and cliffy. The sound joins Lewis Channel at Junction Point on Cortes Island and joins Homfray Channel south of Horace Head on East Redonda Island.

269   **Tidal streams**. — Because this is the region where the flood stream from Queen Charlotte Sound through Johnstone Strait meets the flood stream from Juan de Fuca Strait, via the Strait of Georgia, tidal streams are inconsistent and weak, seldom exceeding 2 kn, and are strongly affected by winds. The flood stream flows north up the west side of Kinghorn Island, E along the north side of the island then NE through Desolation Sound. The boundary between the flood streams from north and south can be abreast Squirrel Cove in settled weather, or as far north as the north entrance of Lewis Channel in sustained SE winds.

270   **Desolation Sound Marine Provincial Park**, on the south shore of the sound, includes Gifford Peninsula, Prideaux Haven, Tenedos Bay and Grace Harbour. There are no floats or mooring buoys.

271   **Sewage disposal** in the waters of Desolation Sound Marine Park is prohibited under the *Pleasure/Non-Pleasure Craft Sewage Pollution Prevention Regulations*.

272   **Submarine cables** cross the entrance to Desolation Sound, from south of Sarah Point to the SE corner of Cortes Island. A submarine cable area is laid south of Sarah Point to Tiber Bay.

273   **Kinghorn Island** *(50°05'N, 124°51'W)* has **Station Island**, **Kinghorn Rocks** and several shoal and drying rocks lying off its north part. **Martin Islands** lie close-off the south extremity of West Redonda Island. Marine farm facilities lie off the West Redonda Island shore, north of Martin Islands.

Desolation Sound from SSW (1974)

Chart 3538

South Approach to Lewis Channel

274   **Tiber Bay** *(50°04'N, 124°53'W)* has a logging company ramp and float in its south part.

275   **Seaford**, 1.2 miles NNW, is the site of a former settlement.

Chart 3555

276   **Squirrel Cove** *(50°07'N, 124°54'W)* is a popular small craft anchorage. **Boulder Point**, on the north side of the entrance, is low with a drying reef projecting south from it and a conspicuous above-water boulder lying on its south shore.

277   **Beacon**. — A daybeacon, with two starboard hand daymarks, is on the above-mentioned drying reef.

278   **Sewage disposal** in the waters of Squirrel Cove is prohibited under the *Pleasure/Non-Pleasure Craft Sewage Pollution Prevention Regulations.*

279   **Squirrel Cove** settlement, on the south shore, has a general store, restaurant and laundromat. Fuel is obtainable in small quantities at the store but must be carried by hand to the wharf. An Indian village is NW of the public wharf. The church spire is a conspicuous landmark.

280   **Wharf**. — The public wharf on the south shore of Squirrel Cove just within the entrance has a depth of 16 feet (4.9 m) at its outer end. A 3 tonne crane and garbage disposal facilities are on the wharf. Floats attached to the wharf provide about 400 feet (122 m) of berthing space.

281   **Marine farm** facilities are in several locations throughout Squirrel Cove.

282   **Anchorage** for small vessels is available off the wharf or in the inner part of the cove, entered SW of **Protection Island** through a channel with a least depth of 15 feet (4.6 m) in the fairway. A wreck (position approximate) is close north of Protection Island and a drying rock is close offshore in the NW part of the cove. There is risk of anchors being fouled by numerous sunken logs and logging cables on the bottom of the inner cove. Holding is good in mud.

283   **Refuge Cove** *(50°07'N, 124°51'W)*, in the SW part of West Redonda Island, is a popular supply centre for small craft. Marine farm facilities extend from the north side of the island, in the central part of the cove. A barge for garbage drop off moors near the mouth of Refuge Cove from mid June.

284   **Light**. — Refuge Cove light *(479.8)* is on the south entrance point.

285   **Refuge Cove** settlement has a fuel dock and general store, shops, laundromat and post office. Gas, diesel, lubricants, propane and fresh water are obtainable. Washrooms, showers and guest moorage are available. There is also float plane service.

286   **Wharf**. — Public floats with 850 feet (259 m) of berthing space and private floats with about 150 feet (46 m) are on the east side of Refuge Cove. Depths of 8 to 16 feet (2.4 to 4.9 m) exist alongside.

Lewis Channel and Teakerne Arm

Charts 3538, 3541

287   **Lewis Channel** leads about 7 miles NNW from **Junction Point** *(50°08'N, 124°54'W)*, joining Sutil Channel abreast Bullock Bluff.

288   **Light**. — Junction Point light *(480)* is shown at an elevation of 8.8 m from a white tower with a green band at the top.

289   **Marine farm** facilities are on West Redonda Island 1.2 miles NW of Refuge Cove.

290   **Booming grounds** are on the west shore 2.8 miles NW of Joyce Point.

291   **Teakerne Arm**, entered north of **Joyce Point**, is not recommended for anchorage because it is exposed to the NW. Booming grounds and marine farm facilities are in several locations throughout the arm. **Talbot Cove** has **Talbot Islet**, a 3.7 m shoal and a drying reef in its west part. It is not recommended for anchorage because holding is reported to be poor.

292   **Teakerne Arm Provincial Park**, at the head of the inlet, is undeveloped except for a dinghy float. A waterfall cascades down from the outlet of **Cassel Lake**.

293   **Cliff Peak** *(50°11'N, 124°57'W)*, on the west side of Lewis Channel, is conspicuous.

294   **Light**. — West Redonda Island light *(527)*, on the east shore at the north entrance to Lewis Channel, is shown at an elevation of 6.6 m from a white tower with a red band at the top.

Malaspina and Adjacent Inlets

Chart 3559

295   **Malaspina Inlet**, entered from Desolation Sound between **Myrmidon Point** *(50°04'N, 124°48'W)* and **Zephine Head**, is a popular small craft cruising area. **Stacey Rock**, a drying rock, lies close offshore west of Myrmidon Point. Several logging camps are in the inlet.

296   **Marine farm** facilities, vulnerable to damage from vessels wash, are in several locations along the shores of Malaspina Inlet. Reduce speed when passing these facilities.

297   **Tidal streams** in the entrance attain 2 to 4 kn, but within the inlet are weak.

298   **Galley Bay** *(50°04'N, 124°47'W)* is a popular small craft anchorage, the best berths being in the westernmost cove and behind the island in the east part of the bay. Drying reefs lie in the central portion of the bay and a rock with 1.3 m over it lies south of the island in its east part. Private floats are in several locations and marine farm facilities are at the south end of the bay.

299   **Hare Point**, on the NE side of the inlet, is steep-to. A rock, with 1.2 m over it, lies 0.25 mile NW.

300   **Beulah Island** and the large island close SE are joined together and to the mainland by drying ridges. The coves north and south of these drying ridges are known locally as Parker Harbour. Temporary anchorage can be obtained in the north part of the harbour. The float on the mainland shore is private. It is reported that more protected anchorage can be found in the south part of Parker Harbour, which is entered north of the drying reefs lying north of **Thorp Island**. Marine farm facilities are south of Thorp Island.

301   **Josephine Islands**, east of Beulah Island, lie in the middle of the inlet. **Cavendish Rock** and a rock close west of it lie east of the south extremity of Josephine Islands.

302   **Cross Islet** has a drying rock and unnamed islets between it and the mainland shore to the east. **Rosetta Rock** dries 2.8 m and lies in the middle of the fairway, SW of Cross Islet.

303   **Cochrane Islands**, joined by a drying ledge with several rocks and islets on it, have several detached drying rocks north and

Squirrel Cove public wharf (1985)

Squirrel Cove (1985)

Refuge Cove (1985)

Malaspina Inlet entrance (1985)

Chart 3559

Grace Harbour (1985)

west of them. Marine farm facilities lie along the shore behind Cochrane Islands. Good anchorage can be found SW of the islands.

304   **Neville Islet**, close-off the NE shore, is surrounded by drying ledges.

305   **Kakaekae Point**, on the NE side of the inlet, is bold and steep-to. Temporary anchorage can be obtained in the bight on the east side of the point.

306   **Grace Harbour**, entered between **Scott Point** and **Moss Point**, affords anchorage for small vessels NE of **Jean Island** in about 25 m. The inner part of the harbour provides completely protected anchorage for small craft.

307   **Coode Island** and **Coode Peninsula** form the east side of **Trevenen Bay**. **Marine farm** facilities, some marked by buoys, are in Trevenen Bay, in the channel between Coode and Isbister Islands and along the east side of Coode Peninsula. The north island of **Isbister Islands** has a detached rock with 3.8 m over it close NE of it. Drying rocks lie farther NE and east, on the east side of the fairway. Anchorage, sheltered from SE winds, can be obtained in Trevenen Bay.

308   **Lion Rock** lies near mid-channel SSE of **Selina Point**.

309   **Marine farm** facilities are in **Salubrious Bay**, which is between Selina Point and **Edith Island**.

310   **Okeover Inlet** is entered between the north end of Coode Peninsula and **Hillingdon Point** *(50°02'N, 124°43'W)*, a bold headland.

311   **Tides**. — Tidal differences for Okeover Inlet (Index No. 8006), referenced on Point Atkinson, are in *Tide Tables, Volume 5.*

312   **Boundary Rock** lies close SE of the south extremity of Coode Peninsula. **Penrose Bay**, on the SW side of Coode Peninsula, has a marina on its west shore. Small craft can obtain anchorage in 7.4 m at the head of the bay.

313   **Marine farm** facilities are in several locations along the shores of Okeover Inlet.

314   **Wharf**. — A public wharf with a 3 tonne derrick and floats, with 73 m of berthing space, are on the west side of Okeover Inlet, 1 mile south of Penrose Bay. Newly established floating breakwaters protect both NE and NW sides of the wharf. A launching ramp is close SE of the wharf. A resort above the wharf has a restaurant, small store and public telephone. A road leads from here to Lund and the main highway leading south.

315   **Light**. — Okeover Inlet light *(479.7)* is on the seaward end of the floating breakwater NW of the public wharf.

316   **Beacon**. — Okeover Inlet Daybeacon, on the seaward end of the floating breakwater NE of the public wharf, has a port hand daymark.

317   **Okeover Arm Provincial Park**, close north of the public wharf, has camping and picnic facilities and a launching ramp.

318   A **submarine cable** crosses the inlet close north of the public wharf, it is marked by signs on both shores. Booming grounds, a log slip and spar pole are close south of the cable on the east shore.

319   Buildings and a causeway, ramp and float of Sliammon Indian Seafoods Company lie 1.3 miles SE of the public wharf. A rock, 1 m high, lies close to shore on the north side of the causeway. A submarine pipeline (water) is laid across **Freke Anchorage** from the Seafoods company.

Penrose Bay (1985)

Public wharf south of Penrose Bay (1985)

Chart 3559

Isabel Bay (1985)

320   **Marine farm** facilities are along the west shore of Freke Anchorage.

321   **Lancelot Inlet**, east of **Gifford Peninsula**, is entered between Hillingdon Point and Edith Island *(50°02'N, 124°44'W)*. **Stopford Point** is 0.65 mile NE of Edith Island.

322   **Marine farm** facilities, protected by booms and marked by buoys, line the shore between Hillingdon Point and **Bunster Point**.

323   **Isabel Bay** *(50°03'N, 124°44'W)* is entered between **Polly Island** and **Madge Island**. A rock, which dries 0.4 m, lies 90 m NE of Polly Island and drying ledges extend north and NE from Madge Island. Isabel Bay is a popular anchorage for small craft in its south extremity or west of Madge Island.

324   **Thors Cove**, although open to west winds which are reported to exist even when a SE wind is blowing up Okeover Inlet, provides anchorage for small vessels in its centre in 30 m, mud. A good anchorage for small craft is behind the islet close-off the south shore. Marine farm facilities are on the north and south sides of the cove. **Theodosia Arm**, at the head of the cove, dries.

325   **Thynne Island** lies close-off **Bastion Point**. A drying rock lies in the passage east of the island.

326   **Theodosia Inlet**, entered SE of **Galahad Point**, provides good anchorage for small craft. The narrow entrance channel has a rock awash on its north side, 0.2 mile SE of Galahad Point, and a least depth in the fairway of 2.4 m. Booming grounds are in several locations.

327   The smaller of **Susan Islets**, SE of **Grail Point**, has a prominent pointed rock on its summit. Small craft can find good anchorage behind the islets, mud bottom. Marine farm facilities are off the south shore, south of Susan Islets.

328   **Wootton Bay**, at the head of Lancelot Inlet, affords anchorage for small vessels.

Desolation Sound — East Part

Chart 3538

329   **Mink Island** *(50°07'N, 124°46'W)* affords anchorage for small craft in the bay on its SE coast, a float is at the head of the cove. **Curme Islands** and several drying rocks lie close-off the NE end of Mink Island. **Portage Cove**, on the mainland SE of Mink Island, has drying rocks on its east side.

330   **Tenedos Bay**, on the mainland east of Mink Island, has several drying rocks in it but affords good **anchorage** for small vessels in its north extremity in 12 m. Small craft can find good anchorage in several coves within the bay. When approaching Tenedos Bay from the NW, do not pass between **Ray Rock** and **Bold Head** and give Bold Head a wide berth when entering to avoid a submerged rock.

331   **Otter Island** *(50°08'N, 124°44'W)* has a very small protected anchorage, suitable for small craft, in the passage on its east side. When approaching this anchorage from the north take care to avoid **Sky Pilot Rock**, which dries 2.1 m.

332   **Morgan Island** and **Melville Island** lie off the south shore at the entrance to Homfray Channel. **Pringle Rock**, which dries 4.9 m, lies west of Morgan Island.

Prideaux Haven

Chart 3555

333   **Prideaux Haven** *(50°09'N, 124°41'W)* has many well-protected anchorages, used extensively by small craft.

Theodosia Inlet entrance (1985)

Theodosia Inlet (1985)

Chart 3555

Prideaux Haven entrance (1985)

334 **Sewage disposal** in the waters of Prideaux Haven is prohibited under the *Pleasure/Non-Pleasure Craft Sewage Pollution Prevention Regulations.*

335 **Tidal streams** in the north approach to Prideaux Haven anchorages are weak, influenced by winds, and seldom exceed 1.5 kn.

336 **Tides**. — Tidal differences for Prideaux Haven (Index No. 8008), referenced on Point Atkinson, are in *Tide Tables, Volume 5.*

337 **Mary Islands**, with **Grass Islet** at their east end, lie in the west approach to Prideaux Haven.

338 **Eveleigh Anchorage**, entered SW of **Eveleigh Island**, affords anchorage for small vessels in 13 fathoms (23.8 m), sand.

339 **Prideaux Haven** is entered east of **Lucy Point** and west of **Scobell Island** and **William Islands**. The fairway has a least depth of 8 feet (2.4 m) and narrows to about 100 feet (30 m) between a ledge with 2 feet (0.6 m) over it projecting from Eveleigh Island and a ledge with 5 feet (1.5 m) over it projecting from **Oriel Rocks**.

340 When entering **Melanie Cove**, note the drying ledge projecting from the south shore SW of **Melanie Point**.

341 **Paige Islets** lie off the east end of Scobell Island, in the west approach to Laura Cove.

342 **Laura Cove**, entered between **Copplestone Island** and **Copplestone Point**, affords sheltered anchorage. The entrance channel, which leads east of a rock that dries 1 foot (0.3 m), has a least depth of 11 feet (3.4 m) in the fairway and a width of about 135 feet (41 m). The land at the head of the cove is an Ecological Reserve belonging to the University of British Columbia.

343 **Roffey Island** lies in the NE approach to the cove.

Waddington Channel and Pendrell Sound

Charts 3538, 3541

344 **Waddington Channel**, entered from south between **Marylebone Point** *(50°10'N, 124°45'W)* and **Horace Head**, separates East and West Redonda Islands and connects Desolation Sound to Pryce Channel.

345 **Tidal streams** in Waddington Channel flood north and seldom exceed 1 kn.

346 **Roscoe Bay**, entered north of Marylebone Point, is a popular small craft anchorage. Access to the head of the bay is restricted by a drying bar 0.4 mile inside the entrance. The inner bay, which offers a sheltered anchorage, should be entered on a rising tide at or near HW. **Roscoe Bay Provincial Park** has camping and sanitary facilities.

347 **Sewage disposal** in the waters of Roscoe Bay is prohibited under the *Pleasure/Non-Pleasure Craft Sewage Pollution Prevention Regulations.*

348 **Elworthy Island**, 1 mile NW of **Church Point**, has marine farm facilities off its SW shore. Anchorage for small vessels can be obtained behind the island clear of the marine farms.

Chart 3541

349 **Pendrell Sound** is entered between **Durham Point** *(50°12'N, 124°45'W)* and **Walter Point**. The waters of Pendrell Sound, being warmer than most in this region, allow the production and collection of oyster spat, usually in July. Marine farm facilities are 2.5 miles north of Durham Point and near the head of the sound.

Chart 3541

Roscoe Bay (1985)

350   The east shore of Pendrell Sound is an **Ecological Reserve**.

351   **Speed limit**. — A speed limit of 6 km/h (4 kn) is prescribed by the *Boating Restriction Regulations* in Pendrell Sound.

352   **Warning**. — A floating sign, 0.3 mile NW of Durham Point, reads *"Provincial Shellfish Reserve. Vessels with TBT (Tributyltin) anti-fouling paint on hull please do not enter beyond this point"*.

353   A **submarine cable** has been reported off the NW shore of the large island near the head of the sound. The cable is considered a hazard to vessels anchoring in the area.

354   **Anchorage** for small craft can be obtained off the mouth of a drying lagoon on the west side or behind the islets at the head of the sound. There is no good anchorage for larger craft.

355   **Allies Island** *(50°13'N, 124°49'W)* has marine farm facilities and booming grounds NNW of it.

356   **Light**. — Waddington Channel light *(527.7)* is on the west side of the channel abreast **Shirley Point** *(50°14'N, 124°49'W)*.

357   **Doctor Bay**, west of **Bishop Point** *(50°15'N, 124°49'W)*, has marine farm facilities in it.

358   **Walsh Cove** affords sheltered anchorage for small vessels. **False Passage** leads north of the **Gorges Island**. **Walsh Cove Provincial Park** is undeveloped. Recommended approach to Walsh Cove is from the south, west of **Bluff Point**.

359   **Marine farm** facilities are on the east shore of Waddington Channel, 0.4 mile SE of **Butler Point**.

360   The channel close south of **Dean Point** is fringed on both sides by shoals. **Dean Rock**, 0.2 mile south of the point, lies in mid-channel and has 2.4 m over it.

361   **Light**. — Dean Point light *(527.9)* is on the NE extremity of West Redonda Island.

Homfray Channel

Charts 3538, 3541

362   **Homfray Channel** entered south of Horace Head *(50°10'N, 124°44'W)* separates **East Redonda Island** from the mainland. The channel is very deep with no off-lying dangers.

363   **Tidal streams** in Homfray Channel seldom exceed 1½ kn, the flood stream flowing south throughout most of the channel but north in the south part. Rates and boundary between north and south flowing flood streams are greatly influenced by winds.

364   The east arm of East Redonda Island is an **Ecological Reserve**. **Mount Addenbroke** is dome shaped.

365   **Price Point** *(50°09'N, 124°39'W)* and **Lloyd Point** are on the east side of the channel.

Chart 3541

366   **Forbes Bay** *(50°14'N, 124°36'W)*, north of **Bohn Point**, is too deep for anchorage, except for small vessels near shore, and offers little shelter. **Booker Point** is west of Bohn Point.

367   **Foster Point** and **Homfray Creek** are north of Forbes Bay. Marine farm facilities are at Homfray Creek.

368   **Attwood Bay** *(50°19'N, 124°40'W)* has a private float and a log dump in its NE corner. Anchorage with good shelter can be obtained by small vessels.

Chart 3541

369   **Hepburn Point** is the north extremity of East Redonda Island.

Toba Inlet

370   **Toba Inlet** entered west of **Brettell Point** *(50°20'N, 124°44'W)*, between **Channel Island** and **Double Island**, leads 20 miles NE to the sand and mud flat estuary of the **Toba River** at its head.

371   **Tides.** — Tidal differences for Channel Island (Index No. 8015), referenced on Point Atkinson, are in *Tide Tables, Volume 5.*

372   A **conspicuous waterfall** is on the west side of the inlet 2.8 miles NNE of Brettell Point.

373   A **log dump and booming ground** are in Higgins Bay (local name), 3.5 miles NE of Brettell Point.

374   **Brem Bay** *(50°26'N, 124°40'W)* is the site of an abandoned logging camp and is used as a log dump. The bay is reported to be full of logging debris. An old stone breakwater is reported to provide indifferent shelter for small craft.

375   **Snout Point**, on the south shore, is prominent. A conspicuous waterfall is about 3.5 miles east of the point. A log dump and booming grounds are on the east shore, 0.8 mile south of **Chusan Creek**. A log dump with booming grounds and conspicuous oil tanks are on the west side, at the head of Toba Inlet.

376   **Anchorage** can be obtained in 35 m at the head of the inlet. Caution is advised because depths shoal rapidly and the bottom is not visible through milky water.

Pryce Channel and Ramsay Arm

377   **Pryce Channel** leads 7 miles along the north shore of Redonda Islands, joining Homfray Channel to Deer and Raza Passages, which lead to Calm Channel.

378   **Light.** — Pryce Channel light *(527.2)* is on the north side of the channel, opposite **Gloucester Point** *(50°17'N, 124°49'W)*.

379   **Elizabeth Island** is 1 mile west of the above-mentioned light. A rock which dries at 1.5 m is on the south side of the island.

380   **Anchorage** for small vessels is available in the bay east of Gloucester Point.

381   **Connis Point** is the NE and **Tibbs Point**, on Raza Island, the NW entrance points of Deer Passage.

382   **Ramsay Arm**, entered west of **George Head** *(50°21'N, 124°58'W)*, is deep with no good anchorages. **Quatam Bay** is the site of a logging camp located on the north side of **Quatam River**. A log dump is at the head of Ramsay Arm.

Havannah Channel

Chart 3564

383   **Havannah Channel** *(50°32'N, 126°14'W)*, entered west of Broken Islands leads to Port Harvey, Call Inlet and Chatham Channel. Chatham Channel leads to Knight Inlet and is suitable for small vessels.

384   The area between Broken Islands and **Domville Point** is filled with reefs. **Hull Rock** is a detached rock, with 2.1 m over it, lying west of mid-channel abreast Domville Point.

385   **Lily Islet**, **Havannah Islets** and **Bockett Islets** lie east of Domville Point. A shoal with 4 m over it lies in the passage between Havannah and Bockett Islets.

386   **Beacon. — Light.** — Lily Islet daybeacon has a starboard hand daymark.

387   Havannah Islets light *(537)* is on the south extremity of the islets.

388   **Marine farm** facilities are located 0.8 mile east of Domville Point and off the west side of Havannah Islets.

389   **Booming grounds** are in the bay west of **Bockett Point** and SW of **Whitebeach Point**. A conspicuous white sandy beach is at Whitebeach Point.

390   **Boughey Shoal**, an isolated rock with 5.8 m over it, lies in the entrance to **Boughey Bay**. Anchorage can be obtained in the middle of the bay. Booming grounds are at the head.

391   **Mistake Island** and **Hull Island** *(50°33'N, 126°12'W)* lie in mid-channel abreast **Malone Point**, which is bold. A marine farm is located on the north side of Mistake Island.

392   **Triangle Island**, **Tom Islet** and **Browning Rock**, with less than 2 m over it, lie north of Hull Island.

393   **Round Island**, NW of Hull Island, separates **Soderman Cove** and **Burial Cove**. Private floats are in the bay north of Malone Point, known locally as Cookson Cove, and in Soderman and Burial Coves. Burial Cove affords good anchorage for small craft.

394   **Indian Islands** lie off the abandoned Indian village **Matilpi**, only the ruins of one house remain. Small craft can find good anchorage behind the islands.

Port Harvey

395   **Port Harvey** *(50°33'N, 126°17'W)* is an inlet entered west of **Transit Point**. **Open Cove**, on the north side of **Harvey Point**, affords good anchorage for small craft except in westerly winds, which raise a considerable sea. Good anchorage for small vessels can be obtained NNW of **Mist Islets** and excellent anchorage for small craft north of **Range Island**.

396   **Tides.** — Tidal differences for Port Harvey (Index No. 8250), referenced on Alert Bay, are in *Tide Tables, Volume 6.*

397   A log dump is 0.6 mile WSW of Transit Point and **booming grounds** are NE of Transit Point and at the head of the port. A pier is on the south side of the SW Mist Islet. A row of dolphins extends south from **Tide Pole Islet**. Two houses and the ruins of a public wharf are at the head of the port.

Call Inlet

Charts 3545, 3564

398   **Call Inlet**, entered north of **Turn Point** *(50°34'N, 126°11'W)*, extends 10 miles ENE between unusually steep shores. The inlet is free of mid-channel dangers except for **Call Shoal**, with 10.7 m over it, lying 2 miles within the entrance. **Squire Point**, ENE of **Grogan Island**, is bold.

399   Depths in most places are too deep for good anchorage and east winds are reported to funnel strongly down the inlet. **Warren Islands** are reported to provide inadequate shelter for small craft.

Chatham Channel

Chart 3564

400 **Chatham Channel**, entered between **Root Point** *(50°35'N, 126°12'W)* and **Ray Point**, leads along the north coast of **East Cracroft Island** and connects Havannah Channel to Knight Inlet. The channel is narrow and shallow at the east end, south of **Bowers Islands**. A rock, with 1.5 m over it, lies in the east entrance and kelp grows almost across the channel in summer and autumn.

401 **Tidal streams** flood to the east and have a rate at springs of 5 kn, being strongest in the first mile west of Root Point. Secondary current station Chatham Channel (Index No. 5075), referenced on Seymour Narrows, is in *Tide Tables, Volume 6*.

402 **Beacons**. — A daybeacon with a port hand daymark is on Root Point. Two daybeacons with port hand daymarks are on the south side of the channel, between Root Point and Bowers Islands. A daybeacon with a starboard hand daymark is on the SW Bowers Island.

403 **Light ranges**. — The fairway through the east part of the channel is marked at both ends by light ranges.

404 Ray Point range lights *(538, 539)*, on the point, in line bear 088°.

405 East Cracroft Island range lights *(540, 541)*, WSW of Bowers Islands, in line bear 271°.

406 **Hadley Bay**, NE of **Atchison Island**, has private berthing facilities and a conspicuous orange house (1981). The islet south of Atchison Island has a cliff with a white patch on it.

407 A private float is on the east side of the channel 1.2 miles WNW of Bowers Islands.

408 **Slide**. — Stay outside the 5 m line to avoid a slide area extending from East Cracroft Island 1.5 miles NW of Bowers Islands.

409 **Amyes Island** lies in the south approach and **Cutter Islet** in the entrance to **Cutter Cove** *(50°37'N, 126°16'W)*. Anchorage is obtainable for small vessels with good holding in mud.

410 **Minstrel Island** is separated from East Cracroft Island by **The Blow Hole**, which is suitable only for small craft. It is narrow, shallow and has kelp growing almost across it in summer and autumn. However, it is reported to be easily navigated. A submarine pipeline (water) crosses The Blow Hole.

411 Chatham Channel off Minstrel Island settlement is a **water aerodrome**.

412 **Minstrel Island** settlement has a postal drop, public wharf with a 3 tonne crane, floats for small craft and seaplanes, and a resort with marina facilities. Gas, diesel, moorage, washrooms, showers, laundry, café, internet access and charts are available. Haulouts to 40 feet are possible. Scheduled float plane service operates to Campbell River, Vancouver, Port McNeil and Seattle. Charter service is available.

Lagoon Cove

413 **Lagoon Cove** *(50°36'N, 126°19'W)*, entered SW of **Perley Island** from Clio Channel, affords sheltered anchorage, mud bottom, for small vessels. Care should be taken when anchoring as logging cables are reported to foul both east and west sides.

A marina is on the east shore of the cove. Gas, diesel, propane, washroom and showers are available. There is power to the floats and small stores.

414 **Tides**. — Tidal differences for Lagoon Cove (Index No. 8258), referenced on Alert Bay, are in *Tide Tables, Volume 6*.

Baronet Passage

Charts 3546, 3545

415 **Baronet Passage** *(50°33'N, 126°35'W)*, between **West Cracroft Island** and **Harbledown Island**, is partially obstructed by reefs near Walden Island and should be navigated with caution. The route through Baronet Passage and Clio Channel to Knight Inlet is sometimes used by small vessels.

416 **Tidal streams** off Walden Island flood to the west at a maximum of about 3 kn. Secondary current station Baronet Passage (Index No. 5085) (for a location 1.5 miles west of Walden Island), referenced on Seymour Narrows, is in *Tide Tables, Volume 6*.

417 **Bell Rocks** lie on the north side, at the west entrance to the passage. The flood current flowing west through Baronet Passage meets that flowing south through Blackney Passage near Bell Rocks, resulting in a counter-clockwise circulation.

Chart 3545

418 **Walden Island** *(50°33'N, 126°33'W)* has rocks and shoals west, east and close north of it. The channel north of the island, being deeper, is preferred. A floating fishing resort is in the bay 1 mile WSW of the island and a float house is in the bay 0.7 mile east of the island.

419 **Wilson Passage** has rocks on both sides of its south part and a drying reef on the east side near its north end. A drying reef lies 0.2 mile NNE of **Jamieson Island**. The channel NW of Jamieson Island is useful for smaller vessels.

Beware Passage

420 **Beware Passage** *(50°35'N, 126°32'W)* is obstructed by numerous islands, rocks and shoal areas. Local knowledge is advised and it is prudent to navigate at LW on a rising tide when underwater dangers are visible. Close attention should be paid to drift from tidal streams.

421 **Kamano Island** lies in the SE entrance and **Care Rock** and **Beware Rock** are named mid-channel dangers.

422 **Karlukwees**, at the SW end of **Turnour Island**, NW of **Nicholas Point**, is the site of an occasionally occupied Indian village. The wharf and float are in disrepair.

423 **Caution Cove**, north of **Care Island**, has **Caution Rock** in the middle of its entrance. The cove provides anchorage for small craft with reported good holding over mud but is open to prevailing winds. A logging camp with float is on the north side of the cove, and booming grounds are at the head.

424 **Beware Cove**, entered north of **Cook Island**, offers protection from NW winds but is exposed to those from SE and NE.

425 A detached shoal, with 4.9 m over it, lies 0.4 mile south of **Mink Point**, and a shoal with 8.8 m over it lies midway between Mink Point and **Dead Point**.

Chart 3545

Clio Channel

426   **Clio Channel** *(50°35'N, 126°25'W)*, between West Cracroft and Turnour Islands, connects Baronet and Beware Passages to Knight Inlet.

427   A rock, with less than 2 m over it, lies midway between **Klaoitsis Island** *(50°34'N, 126°29'W)* and **Joliffe Island**. **Turnour Rock** lies in the approach to **Turnour Bay**. A log dump is close NW of **Air Point** (1998).

428   **Tidal streams** in Clio Channel flood to the west at about 1 kn.

429   **Potts Lagoon**, on the south side of the channel, and a cove at the entrance to the lagoon, offer good all-weather anchorage for small craft. Float homes are moored in the inner bay.

430   **Bend Island** is on the south side of the channel. It is reported that anchorage for small craft can be obtained at either end of the island. A log dump and booming ground are in the cove 1.2 miles ENE of Bend Island.

431   **Beacon**. — A daybeacon with a bifurcation/junction daymark, preferred channel to the left, is on **Negro Rock**.

432   **Bones Bay** *(50°35'N, 126°21'W)* has a conspicuous abandoned cannery near its head. The jetty is in disrepair. A sport fishing camp and float are SW of the abandoned cannery.

433   **Cracroft Inlet**, entered east of **Sambo Point**, with **Dorman Island** and **Farquharson Island** on its NE side, is a drying gorge leading to Port Harvey *(Chart 3564)*.

434   Clio Channel enters Knight Inlet 1 mile north of **Bennett Point**.

Knight Inlet and Approaches

Charts 3546, 3545, 3515

435   **Knight Inlet** *(50°38'N, 126°34'W)*, the longest inlet on the British Columbia coast, leads for much of its length between mountains with summits more than 1,500 m, many snow-clad throughout the year. Depths are great with few off-lying dangers. Anchorages are few and widely separated. Winds are frequently strong, funneled by the steep sides. Large quantities of logs are shipped from the inlet. There are several logging camps but no settlements.

436   **Tides**. — Tidal differences for Glendale Cove (Index No. 8310), 33 miles inside the entrance, referenced on Alert Bay, are in *Tide Tables, Volume 6*.

437   **Tidal streams** between the entrance and Steep Head, 15 miles east, reach 3 kn on the ebb but considerably less on the flood. Heavy tide-rips occur in places. The turn of current occurs 1 to 2 hours after HW and LW, time being considerably affected by the amount of land drainage runoff.

438   Wind also has a considerable affect on the rate of the tidal currents. An increase of 2 kn can be expected when strong winds are blowing up or down the channel with the current.

439   During summer months, when there is a large land runoff, the flood stream in the upper reaches disappears entirely and there is a marked increase in the strength of the ebb stream. At this time of year there is an overlay of fresher water for a considerable distance from the head.

West and North Approaches

Chart 3546

440   The main approach channel to Knight Inlet lies between Swanson Island and **Wedge Island** *(50°38'N, 126°43'W)*.

441   **Light**. — Wedge Island light *(556)*, on the south side of the island, is shown at an elevation of 10.4 m from a white tower.

442   **Surge Islands**, **Whale Rock**, **Round Islet** and **White Cliff Islets** *(50°39'N, 126°44'W)*, which are light coloured and conspicuous, are among the islets and rocks extending north from Wedge Island. **Passage Islet** and **Fire Shoal** lie in the middle of the passage east of this group.

443   **Providence Passage**, 1 mile east of White Cliff Islets, leads between **Fire Island** and **Owl Island**, to SW, and **Cedar Island** and **Midsummer Island**, to NE. This passage is suitable for small craft. **Tree Point** is the west extremity of Midsummer Island.

444   **Spring Passage**, entered between **Sedge Islands** *(50°41'N, 126°42'W)* and **Canoe Islets**, provides an alternative route into Knight Inlet for small vessels. Local knowledge is advised because of numerous unmarked dangers between Midsummer and Gilford Islands.

445   **House Islet** *(50°40'N, 126°42'W)* has an elevation of 37 m and shoals lie east and west of it. **Green Rock** with other isolated rocks lie 1 mile east. **Wolf Island** and **Morning Islets** lie north of Midsummer Island. **Henrietta Island** lies off the west end of Gilford Island. **Bare Hill**, at the SW extremity of Gilford Island, is heavily wooded.

446   **Marine farm** facilities are off the NW shore of Midsummer Island.

447   **Potts Bay**, in the NE part of Midsummer Island, has a house and float in it (1979).

448   **Ridge Islets** and **Ridge Rock**, which dries 2.7 m, lie in the south entrance to Spring Passage. **Caution. — Numerous rocks and shoals are in this area and no aids to navigation.**

449   **Gull Rock**, **Puzzle Island** *(50°38'N, 126°43'W)*, **Mist Island**, a rock with 7.6 m over it NNW of **Twist Island**, **Chick Reef**, drying and below-water rocks north of **Whirl Island** and **Twilight Rock** lie on the south side of the main approach to Knight Inlet. Marine farm facilities lie off Swanson Island, west of **Western Islets** and between Twist and Whirl Island.

450   **Night Islet**, **Jumble Island** and **Pering Islets** lie in the middle of the approach.

451   **Swanson Passage**, west of **Crease Island**, leads to Farewell Harbour, described in Chapter 6. **Boundary Rock**, **Dot Islet**, **Lone Tree Islet** and **Point Reef** extending from **Charles Point** lie in the north approach to the passage. **Tuft Rock** and **Rough Islets** lie at the south end of the passage. A floating fish camp is south of **Maggy Point**.

452   **Village Channel** leads south of Crease Island, **Goat Islands**, **Fern Island** and **Maud Island** of the **Indian Group**. It is reported that anchorage for small craft can be obtained in the bay at the SE end of Crease Island, enter north of Goat Islands.

453   **Indian Channel**, entered through Whitebeach Passage, leads south of **Sarah Islets**, **Berry Island** and the **Carey Group** (**Leone Island**, **Madrona Island**, **Larsen Island**, **Alder Island** and **Ralph Island**). Marine farm facilities are NW of Larsen Island. It is reported that good anchorage can be obtained by small craft south of **Mound Island** and in the bay between Leone and Madrona Islands.

Chart 3546

454   An Indian Reserve, on the north end of Harbledown Island, has the ruins of a jetty and several houses of the occasionally occupied Indian village.

Chart 3545

455   **Native Anchorage** *(50°37′N, 126°34′W)* has **Cecil Islet** and **Hail Islets** in its west approach. The anchorage offers little protection from westerly winds, and east winds are reported to funnel down **Canoe Passage** with considerable force.

456   **Eliot Passage** *(50°37′N, 126°36′W)* leads north between **Pearl Island** and **Village Island**. **Chart Islet**, **Grave Island**, **Scrub Islet** and numerous rocks and unnamed islets extend from the SW extremity of Village Island. **Mamalilaculla**, an Indian village on the west side of Village Island, is in ruins. **Clock Rock** *(50°38′N, 126°36′W)* lies in the NW approach to Eliot Passage.

457   **Anchorage** for small craft, with fair shelter and good holding but limited swinging room, can be found NE of the jetty ruins at Mamalilaculla. Tour floats, mooring buoys, water taxi service and a float house store are in the bay north of the village.

458   **Village and Indian Channels, and Eliot Passage, sprinkled with unmarked rocks and shoals, are suitable only for small craft and should be navigated with caution.**

Knight Inlet

459   The entrance to Knight Inlet lies between **Warr Bluff** *(50°38′N, 126°35′W)* and **Slope Point**.

460   **Chop Bay**, 2 miles east of Slope Point, has above and below-water rocks in it.

461   **Island Cone** *(50°38′N, 126°33′W)* and **Tribune Point**, the south extremity of Gilford Island, are cone-shaped and symmetrical. **Ripple Bluff** and **Dinner Point** are the NE and east extremities of Village Island.

462   **Lady Islands** *(50°39′N, 126°25′W)*, with **Lord Islet** at their west end, lie in the approach to Port Elizabeth.

463   A **booming ground**, with a private buoy, is at **Gilford Point**.

464   **Port Elizabeth**, entered east of Gilford Point, affords good anchorage in **Duck Cove** at its west end for small vessels and small craft, and in **Maple Cove** for small vessels. Logging operations are underway on the east side of the port. Marine farm facilities, on the south shore, are 1.7 miles NW of Gilford Point.

465   **Gilford Bay**, NE of Lady Islands, has a log dump and booming grounds in it.

466   **Batt Bluff** *(50°38′N, 126°21′W)*, **White Nob Point** and **Littleton Point** mark the north entrances to Clio and Chatham Channels.

467   **Stormy Bluff** is on Gilford Island, opposite White Nob Point. **Doctor Islets**, **Shewell Island**, **Martin Islets**, **Clapp Passage** and **Nickoll Passage** lie in the south approach to Tribune Channel. **Steep Head** is the SE entrance point of Sargeaunt Passage.

468   **Montagu Point** is on the south shore, opposite Viscount Island. **Tsakonu Cove**, south of **Protection Point** *(50°39′N, 126°10′W)*, affords anchorage but is exposed to east winds. It is reported that the bottom is hard and rocky and that some dragging is possible. **Shelterless Point** is on the north shore 1.4 miles NE of Protection Point.

Chart 3515

469   **Hoeya Sound** *(50°42′N, 125°58′W)*, entered north of **Hoeya Head**, a relatively low headland, is too deep for anchorage. A logging camp is at the head of the sound. **Lull Bay** has piles on its west shore.

470   **Rest Islets**, **Prominent Point** *(50°40′N, 126°01′W)*, **Rough Point**, 4 miles east, and **Tomakstum Island** are on the south shore.

471   **Matsiu Creek** *(50°42′N, 125°50′W)* enters Knight Inlet through **Matsiu Valley**. **Siwash Bay** is on the south side of the inlet, 2 miles SE. Anchorage is possible along the east shore.

472   **Glendale Cove** *(50°41′N, 125°44′W)*, entered between **Macdonald Point** and **Duncan Point**, affords anchorage open to northerly winds off the edge of the drying flat at its head, depths shoal rapidly. The former logging settlement of Glendale Cove is now the Knight Inlet Lodge offering fishing and eco-tours. No services are available for visiting boats.

473   **Tides**. — Tidal differences for Glendale Cove (Index No. 8310), referenced on Alert Bay, are in *Tide Tables, Volume 6*.

474   **Duncan Bight** is east of Glendale Cove. The area is being actively logged and buoys are reported in the bight.

475   The bay between **Sallie Point** and **Naena Point** *(50°43′N, 125°43′W)* is the site of a logging camp. Named features in the next 5 miles are **Adeane Point**, **Kwalate Point**, **Herries Point**, **Tsukola Point** and **Escape Point**. A waterfall at **Cascade Point** is conspicuous from north. **Glacier Bay** *(50°52′N, 125°34′W)* has a log dump.

476   **Ahnuhati River** flowing through the **Ahnuhati Valley** enters the inlet south of **Ahnuhati Point**.

477   Named features to the head of the inlet are **Transit Head**, **Axe Point**, **Wahkash Point**, **Rubble Point** and **Hatchet Point**.

478   **Wahshihlas Bay** *(51°01′N, 125°36′W)*, at the mouth of the **Sim River**, is a booming ground.

479   **Klinaklini River** and **Franklin River** flow into the head of Knight Inlet across drying flats. Booming grounds lie off **Dutchman Head**.

480   **Anchorage** is available close inshore in the bay north of Ahnuhati Point *(50°53′N, 125°38′W)*, in Wahshihlas Bay near its head and at the head of Knight Inlet, close to the drying flat. **Use these anchorages with caution, depths shoal rapidly and are unsafe in strong north winds common during winter months.**

Tribune Channel

481   **Tribune Channel** *(50°40′N, 126°14′W)* leads around east and north sides of **Gilford Island** and joins Fife Sound SE of Broughton Island.

482   **Tidal streams** in Tribune Channel are less than 2 kn with no turbulence.

483   **Light**. — **Bamber Point** light *(557)* is on the west side of **Viscount Island** *(50°42′N, 126°14′W)*.

484   A drying rock and **Braza Island** lie close-off the west shore. **Humphrey Rock**, with less than 2 m over it, and a rock with 4.6 m over it lie in mid-channel WSW of the light.

485   **Sargeaunt Passage**, which has a least charted depth of 6.7 m in its narrowest part, is frequently used by fishing vessels. It runs between steep-sided mountains. Favour the west side of the

Chart 3515

passage to avoid the shoal extending from the east shore in the narrowest part. It is reported that secure anchorage for small craft is available either north or south of the narrows depending upon the wind direction. **Pumish Point** is at the north entrance to the passage. Marine farm facilities are on the north side of Steep Head.

486   **Kumlah Island**, south of **Trafford Point**, is near where tides from Knight Inlet and Tribune Channel meet. It is reported that driftwood is usually in this vicinity. Booming grounds are on the east shore SW of **Cleve Point**.

487   **Thompson Sound** *(50°47'N, 126°04'W)* is entered south of **London Point**. North of Sackville Island, indifferent anchorage with limited swinging room can be obtained between mud flats at its head. A logging camp, at the entrance to **McAlister Creek**, has a sewage lagoon with a submarine pipeline extending from it.

488   **Bond Sound** *(50°51'N, 126°11'W)*, entered north of **Loaf Point**, has no sheltered anchorage.

489   **Beacon**. — A daybeacon with a port hand daymark is on **Irvine Point** *(50°49'N, 126°14'W)*.

490   **Anchorage** with good shelter for small vessels and small craft can be obtained in **Wahkana Bay**. A shoal lies close-off **Clam Point**. It is reported that there has been a rockslide on the NW side of the head of the bay resulting in depths less than charted.

491   **Kwatsi Bay**, north of **Miller Point** and **Kwatsi Point**, affords less sheltered anchorage for small vessels. However, the inner cove at the head of Kwatsi Bay is reported to afford excellent anchorage for small craft on the SE side. The marina offers secure moorage, gift shop and showers.

492   **Watson Cove**, entered NNW of **Gormely Point**, provides sheltered anchorage for small craft. A rock with less than 2 m over it lies in the entrance.

493   **Booming grounds** line the south shore east of **Rainy Point**.

494   **Deep Sea Bluff** *(50°49'N, 126°30'W)* and **Raleigh Point**, of the Burdwood Group, form the west entrance points of Tribune Channel.

West and SW Approaches to Tribune Channel

495   West and SW approaches to Tribune Channel *(50°49'N, 126°28'W)* are almost filled by a large group of islands and rocks. Fife Sound, on the north side of this group, is the main access route to Tribune Channel, Arrow and Retreat Passages afford alternative though intricate routes.

496   **Broughton Archipelago Marine Provincial Park** encompasses numerous islands, islets and adjacent foreshore west of Gilford Island. The park is undeveloped.

Fife Sound

Chart 3547

497   **Fife Sound**, entered between **Duff Islet** *(50°45'N, 126°43'W)* and **Gordon Point**, is deep and free of mid-channel dangers. A rock, with less than 2 m over it, lies 0.25 mile NW of **Screen Island** close-off the west end of **Eden Island**. **Gore Rock**, which is 2 m high, and a 4.3 m shoal 0.4 mile west of it, are the outermost dangers on the north side of the entrance.

498   **Light**. — Duff Islet light *(558)* is shown at an elevation of 8.8 m from a white tower on the north side of the islet.

499   **Tidal streams** in Fife Sound are negligible.

500   **Marine farm** facilities may be encountered in several locations along the shores of Fife Sound.

501   **Cullen Harbour** *(50°46'N, 126°44'W)* is entered between Gordon Point and **Nelly Islet**. **Ben Rock**, which dries 1.8 m, and **Ogden Island** are on the west side of the entrance. Well-protected anchorage for small vessels and small craft is obtainable, the bottom is reported to be mud.

502   **Booker Lagoon** is entered through **Booker Passage**, a narrow passage with a least mid-channel depth of 6.4 m, which leads around the north end of **Long Island**. Tidal streams run swiftly through the passage, enter near slack water. Marine farm facilities are reported in all four arms of the lagoon.

503   Small vessels and small craft can find **anchorage**, clear of the marine farms, in the four arms of the lagoon, depending upon winds. Holding is reported to be good in mud.

504   **Anchorage**, protected from west winds, is reported to be obtainable on the north side of **Wicklow Point** *(50°47'N, 126°42'W)*.

505   The entrance to **Twin Lagoon** *(50°47'N, 126°40'W)* dries. **Duff Point** and **Arthur Point** are on the north shore of Eden Island.

Charts 3547, 3515

506   **Indian Passage** *(50°46'N, 126°38'W)* leads south of **Rees Island, John Island, Davis Island** and **Fife Rock**, which comprise the **Benjamin Group**. It is used by small vessels.

507   It is reported that the bay SW of **Fly Island** affords excellent anchorage for small craft.

Chart 3515

508   **Deep Harbour** *(50°48'N, 126°35'W)*, in the SE part of **Broughton Island**, forms the east extremity of a bay entered between **Pemberton Point** and **Sharp Point**. **Jumper Island** lies north of Sharp Point. Marine farm facilities lie in the centre of the harbour. Small vessels can obtain limited anchorage in 40 m near the head of the harbour, clear of the booming ground.

509   **Sharp Shoal** lies off **Pearse Peninsula** in the east approach to Deep Harbour.

510   **Notice Point** and **Ragged Island**, with **Pym Rocks** close east, mark the east entrance of Fife Sound. **Care should be taken to give Pym Rocks a wide berth as groundings have been reported.**

Passages South of Eden Island

Chart 3547

511   **Monday Anchorage** *(50°44'N, 126°39'W)* on the north side of **Mars Island**, east of **Marsden Islands**, affords anchorage for small vessels in about 12 m with little shelter from west winds. The entrance from Queen Charlotte Strait, through either **Trainer Passage** or **Philips Passage**, is obstructed by rocks particularly in the latter. Local knowledge is advised.

512   **Joe Cove** *(50°45'N, 126°40'W)*, in the south part of Eden Island, is reported to provide completely protected anchorage for small craft in the SE arm of its head, mud bottom.

Chart 3547

513 **Misty Passage** leads between Eden Island and **Tracey Island**. **Old Passage** entered north of **George Point**, separates **Insect Island** from **Baker Island**. **Blunden Passage**, with **Innis Island** in its south entrance, leads between Tracey and Baker Islands. **These passages are narrow and shoal in places, caution is advised.**

Chart 3546

514 **Sunday Harbour** *(50°43'N, 126°42'W)*, south of **Crib Island**, affords anchorage for small vessels with little protection from west winds.

515 **Tides**. — Tidal differences for Sunday Harbour (Index No. 8340), referenced on Alert Bay, are in *Tide Tables, Volume 6*.

516 **Directions**. — To enter **Crib Passage** pass midway between **Liska Islet** and **Huston Islet**, taking care to avoid the rock with 4.3 m over it 0.1 mile west of Huston Islet, then steer a mid-channel course.

517 To enter east of **Narrows Islet** via **Sunday Passage** steer for the south extremity of **Angular Island**, bearing 098°, to pass between 90 m and 0.1 mile south of **Kate Islet**. When Sunday Passage opens, steer a mid-channel course through it. When approaching from SW note the rock, with 6.7 m over it, 0.3 mile WNW of **Coach Islets**.

Arrow Passage and SW Approach

518 **Arrow Passage** is entered from the west between **Horse Rock** *(50°42'N, 126°42'W)* and **Evening Rocks**. A rock, with 7.3 m over it, lies 0.3 mile east of Horse Rock.

519 **Sedge Islands** *(50°41'N, 126°42'W)*, **High Island**, **Start Island** and **Ledge Rock** are the outermost named features among the numerous islands and rocks extending 1.5 miles off the west coast of **Bonwick Island**. It is not advised to enter this area without local knowledge. Shoal rocks lie up to 0.3 mile west of Sedge Islands and Start Island.

520 **Dusky Cove**, on the west side of Bonwick Island, affords anchorage for small vessels but provides little shelter from west winds, local knowledge is advised. The cove is approached between **Loon Rock**, **Cove Islet** and **Leading Islet**, to the north, and **Trap Rock** and **South Islet** to the south. An isolated rock, with 5.5 m over it, lies WSW of Loon Rock. **Purves Cove**, to the NW, lies east of **Fog Islets**.

521 **Spiller Passage** leads north from Arrow Passage between **Hudson Island** and **Morrow Island** on the west, and Mars Island to the east.

522 **Marine farm** facilities, on the south side of Arrow Passage, are in the west part of **Sedgley Cove** and a private float is in **Betty Cove**.

Retreat and Cramer Passages

523 **Retreat Passage** is entered from Spring Passage, between **Success Point** and **Seabreeze Island** *(50°41'N, 126°38'W)*.

524 **Magnetic anomaly**. — Compass errors up to 18° have been reported in Retreat Passage, particularly in the vicinity of **Meade Bay**.

525 Retreat Passage is a **water aerodrome** called Gilford Island (Health Bay).

526 **Marine farm** facilities are located at the north entrance to **Carrie Bay** and may be encountered in other locations throughout Retreat Passage.

527 **Gilford Rock**, 0.4 mile NE of Seabreeze Island, is light coloured showing white in the sun. **Yellow Rock**, 0.9 mile NE of Seabreeze Island, appears yellow in summer, from the colour of its vegetation.

528 **Health Bay** (locality), NE of **Sail Island**, is fronted by rocks and shoals and has a wharf and float.

529 A **submarine pipeline** (sewer outfall) at Health Bay extends into Retreat Passage.

530 **Anchorages**. — **Health Bay** *(50°41'N, 126°35'W)* affords anchorage for small vessels in its mouth and for small craft farther in. A detached shoal, with 7 m over it, lies in mid-bay. **Health Lagoon** dries except for the rock strewn entrance channel.

531 Small craft can find anchorage, open to the SE, in **Carrie Bay**. Anchorage can be obtained off Meade Bay.

532 **Grebe Cove** provides anchorage for small vessels and small craft but east and west winds are reported to blow strongly through it.

533 **Waddington Bay**, in the NE part of Bonwick Island, is reported to provide sheltered anchorage for small craft with good holding in sticky mud.

534 **Fox Group** *(50°44'N, 126°36'W)* lies at the junction of Retreat, Arrow, Blunden and Cramer Passages.

535 **Dangers**. — **Solitary Islet** lies in mid-channel east of Fox Group. **Browne Rock**, an isolated rock that dries 0.6 m and usually marked by kelp in summer, lies SW of **Isle Point**, in the approach to Cramer Passage. Detached shoals lie 0.3 and 0.5 mile to the east. A rock that dries 2.7 m lies close-off the south extremity of Baker Island, NNE of **Steep Islet**. A rock that dries 5.2 m and a rock with less than 2 m over it lie 0.2 mile east of Steep Islet.

Chart 3515

536 **False Cove** *(50°44'N, 126°33'W)* provides good anchorage, but is open to west winds.

537 **Cramer Passage** *(50°45'N, 126°32'W)* has rocks extending more than 0.1 mile from the SW entrance point. **Baxter Shoal** and a reef off **Powell Point**, the NE entrance point, are the only other dangers more than 0.1 mile offshore. **Evans Point** and **Horsford Point** are the SE and NE extremities of Baker Island.

538 **Shoal Harbour** provides anchorage for small craft, mud bottom. The best berth is reported to be south of the islet SSW of the entrance, where there is adequate protection from west winds but not much from east winds. A wharf with floats, a booming ground and logging camp are in the harbour.

539 Between Shoal Harbour and Echo Bay is a small bay with a dock, home, sawmill and marine railway haulout. A museum houses a fascinating collection of local artifacts.

540 **Echo Bay** *(50°45'N, 126°30'W)* is a popular destination for small craft. There are marinas, hotel, cabins, gallery, well equipped store and the Simoom Sound Post Office. Gasoline, diesel, propane, lubricants, charts, and groceries are obtainable. Moorage with power, water, internet access, washrooms, showers, laundry, garbage disposal and haulout are available. There is scheduled float plane service to Seattle, Campbell River and Port McNeill.

541 **Echo Bay Marine Provincial Park**, on the NE side of the bay, is undeveloped except for a small public float.

Chart 3515

542   Waters fronting this area are a **water aerodrome** called Gilford Island (Echo Bay).

543   **Simoom Sound** settlement, 0.6 mile north, is abandoned.

544   **Scott Cove** *(50°46'N, 126°28'W)* has a logging camp and booming grounds. Shoals lie close-off **Evangeline Point and Powell Pt**, and **Evangeline Rock** lies in the mouth of the cove. A submarine pipeline outfall extends into the cove from the logging camp. A marina with laundry and shower facilities, limited water, internet access, accommodation, dining room and bakery is located on the west shore.

Approach to Kingcome Inlet

545   **Hornet Passage** entered between Evangeline Point and **Denham Island** leads east of the **Burdwood Group**. It connects with Tribune Channel between **Walker Islet** and **Smith Rock**.

546   **Viner Sound** *(50°47'N, 125°25'W)* has **King Point** and **Penn Islet** at its north entrance. Anchorage is obtainable for small vessels near its head, just clear of the drying flats, and in the cove, on the north side of its head. It has been reported that there is little shelter from east and west winds.

547   **Raleigh Passage**, west of the Burdwood Group, is entered west of **Village Point**. **Bermingham Island** lies on the NE side of the passage.

548   **Hayle Bay** *(50°49'N, 126°34'W)* is too deep and exposed for anchorage. **Laura Bay**, north of **Hayle Point**, offers anchorage with reasonable protection for small craft north of the islet in its north part. A rock awash lies 90 m ENE of the islet.

549   **Simoom Sound** *(50°51'N, 126°29'W)* is entered south of **Pollard Point** and west of **Louisa Islet**. Booming grounds are NNW and ENE of Louisa Islet. **Esther Shoal** lies in mid-channel 0.5 mile NE of Louisa Islet and detached rocks lie west of **Hannant Point**.

550   **Anchorage** is obtainable NW of **Esther Point**, in **McIntosh Bay** and in **O'Brien Bay**, entered NW of **Curtis Point**.

551   **Penphrase Passage** *(50°50'N, 126°35'W)* is bounded to SE by **Trivett Island, Sir Edmund Head, Nicholls Island** and **Hayes Point** and to NE by **Steep Point** and **Vigis Point** of **Wishart Peninsula**. **Trivett Rock** is an isolated rock in the south entrance of the passage.

552   **Sir Edmund Bay**, where there are ruins of an abandoned logging operation, has an isolated shoal near its centre. Numerous reefs lie between Nicholls Island and Hayes Point *(Chart 3547)*, enter the bay east of Nicholls Island. Anchorage for small craft is obtainable at the head of the west arm and behind the drying rock in the south arm. It has been reported a fish farm is located on the east side of the bay.

553   **Shawl Bay** *(50°51'N, 126°34'W)* is used as an anchorage by fishing vessels in its south part, the north part is not recommended for anchorage. Float houses and a floating marina are in the bay. Moorage, power, water, internet access, washrooms, showers, laundry and convenience store are available. There is regular float plane service to Campbell River and Port McNeill and a water taxi to Port McNeill. A logging camp and booming ground are on the south side of the bay. The passage east of Gregory Island is reported to be frequently used by fish boats.

Kingcome Inlet

554   **Kingcome Inlet**, entered between **Bradley Point** *(50°52'N, 126°36'W)* and **Magin Islets**, has no off-lying dangers and is deep to about 1.5 miles from its head, where it shoals gradually and then abruptly to a drying mud flat. High snow-clad mountains on the north shore are conspicuous from Queen Charlotte Strait.

555   **Reid Bay** *(50°53'N, 126°39'W)* has an isolated shoal near its centre. It is not recommended for anchorage because of depths and limited swinging room. The unnamed bay to the south is reported to afford anchorage for small craft with good protection from west winds *(Chart 3547)*.

556   **Moore Bay** *(50°53'N, 126°33'W)*, between **Gregory Island** and **Thomas Bluff**, is generally too deep for satisfactory anchorage. **Thief Rocks**, in the centre of the bay, dry 2.7 m. It is reported that small craft can find anchorage sheltered to the west in the bay SW of **Thief Island**. Anchorage sheltered to the east can be found in the bay east of the easternmost island in Moore Bay. A B.C. Forest Service float is in the NE part of the bay. Fresh water is available. A mooring buoy is in the SE part of the bay.

557   **McKenzie Cove**, north of **Olivia Point**, is on the west side of the inlet. **Ellen Point** is 1.2 miles ENE and **Ellen Cove** has a log dump and booming grounds.

558   **Wakeman Sound**, entered east of **Upton Point** *(50°56'N, 126°31'W)*, does not offer good anchorage and terminates in the estuary of **Wakeman River**. Runoff from snow-clad mountains makes water quite fresh near the head at LW and gives it a dull, milky appearance.

559   A conspicuous landslide (reported 1978) on the west side of **Mount Plowden** reaches the sound 1 mile NNW of **Philadelphia Point** *(50°57'N, 126°28'W)*.

560   **Frances Point** and **Galway Point** are on the south shore opposite Wakeman Sound.

561   **Belleisle Sound**, on the south side of Kingcome Inlet, is generally too deep to afford satisfactory anchorage except in a few places near shore for small craft, and is reported to provide little protection from west winds. A reef extends east of **Edmond Islet** in the entrance to the sound.

562   **Terease Point** *(50°56'N, 126°23'W)* is on the north shore of Kingcome Inlet. **Charles Creek** has ruins of a logging camp and it was reported (1976) that a white monument stands near the water's edge. **Sybilla Point** and **Halliday Point** are on the south shore.

563   The estuary of **Kingcome River** is low, marshy and dotted with scrub and stunted trees. **Petley Point**, on the north shore near the head, has public floats secured to shore accessible only by water. Float plane service operates to Port Hardy. A logging camp, the Indian village **Kingcome**, and the Kingcome Inlet Post Office are about 1 mile up the Kingcome River. The river is navigable only by small craft.

564   **Anchorage Cove**, on the south side at the head of the inlet, affords anchorage near shore for small vessels but is open to north and west winds.

SW Coast of Broughton Island

Chart 3547

565   **Dobbin Bay** *(50°47'N, 126°49'W)* and **Cockatrice Bay**, which has rocks extending from its south shore, are too exposed

Chart 3547

for anchorage. **Gawler Point** and **Card Point**, 1.9 miles NW, are named features on Broughton Island.

566   **Polkinghorne Islands**, 1 mile off the coast, have a relatively shoal spit extending SE from them. A rock with 5.5 m over it lies on this spit 1 mile SE of **Fantome Point**. **Brig Rock** lies close east of Fantome Point.

567   **Vincent Island**, **Percy Island**, **Drew Islet** and **Dickson Island** have numerous reefs between them and Broughton Island, local knowledge is advised for this area. **Aimee Bay** and **Ralph Bay** are east of Drew Islet.

Wells Passage

568   **Wells Passage**, entered east of **Boyles Point** *(50°49′N, 127°01′W)*, leads 6.5 miles NE to Sutlej Channel, Drury Inlet and Grappler Sound. The passage is generally deep but has occasional depths of 27 to 37 m near mid-channel. **Compton Point** and **Providence Point** form its north end.

569   **Tidal streams** in Wells Passage attain up to 3 kn.

570   **Light**. — **James Point** light *(559)* is shown at an elevation of 9.1 m from a white tower.

571   **Dangers**. — Drying rocks extend 0.4 mile SSW of Boyles Point. Lewis Rocks, described in Chapter 8, and several rocks south of them lie 1 mile farther SW. A rock with 3.4 m over it lies near mid-channel 0.6 mile south of James Point. Rocks extend more than 0.1 mile into the channel from **Ommaney Islet**, and the area SE and eastward of this islet is filled with numerous rocks and shoals. A rock, with 7.9 m over it, lies 0.15 mile south of **Popplewell Point**. A 7.3 m shoal lies 0.2 mile off Providence Point.

572   **Wehlis Bay**, on the west side of Wells Passage, is not recommended for anchorage.

573   **Booming grounds** and a log dump are in the cove 0.5 mile west of **Cane Point** *(50°51′N, 126°53′W)*.

Tracey Harbour

574   **Tracey Harbour** *(50°51′N, 126°52′W)*, entered south of **Lambert Island**, has shoal water and rocks fringing its shores. **Wolf Cove** leads NE between **Wolf Point** and **Baronet Point**. **Mauve Islet** is close-off the south shore. A drying rock, a wreck, and **Star Rock** lie close-off the north shore between **Wood Point** and **Bath Point**. **Freshwater Cove** is on the south shore opposite Bath Point. **Napier Bay**, entered between **Griffith Point** and **Preston Point**, affords good anchorage for small vessels, mud bottom. Stay well clear of the submarine pipeline crossing the bay. Left over buildings from a former logging operation are on **Carter Point**.

Carter Passage

575   **Carter Passage** *(50°50′N, 126°54′W)*, between the west ends of Broughton and North Broughton Islands, connects Wells Passage to Greenway Sound. The fairway dries about 2.5 miles east of the west entrance and has boulders in it that dry 3.7 m. It can only be navigated by small craft at HW, local knowledge is advised.

576   **Tidal streams** attain 7 kn in the west entrance which should be navigated only near HW slack.

577   From Wells Passage, it is approached south of **Bourmaster Point** and a group of rocks lies close west of the entrance. The west entrance has a least depth of 3 m and narrows to about 15 m north of rocks on the south side. The east entrance has a rock and drying ledge extending south of **Broughton Point**.

578   **Anchorage** for small craft with good protection is reported to be obtainable in either end of Carter Passage.

Sutlej Channel

579   **Sutlej Channel**, entered from west through **Patrick Passage** *(50°54′N, 126°51′W)*, connects Wells Passage to Kingcome Inlet. **Surgeon Islets**, in the west approach to the passage, have shoals lying up to 0.2 mile east of them.

580   **Light**. — Surgeon Islets light *(560)* is on the north side of the north islet. The light is obscured by trees (1982) on north to NW bearings.

581   **Sullivan Bay** *(50°53′N, 126°50′W)* has a well stocked store, post office, float homes, and lodge built on floats secured to shore. Moorage, gas, diesel, supplies, water, power, internet access, washrooms, shower, laundry and boat sitting are available. There is daily air service to Seattle and other destinations. On entering the bay note the rocks fringing **Atkinson Island**, and shoal patches off the east entrance point.

582   Sullivan Bay is a **water aerodrome**.

583   **Tides**. — Tidal differences for Sullivan Bay (Index No. 8364), referenced on Alert Bay, are in *Tide Tables, Volume 6*.

584   A shoal, with 10.4 m over it, lies in mid-channel between **Sullivan Point** and **Codrington Point** *(50°54′N, 126°49′W)*. **Connolly Point**, 0.9 mile east, is prominent and has rocks and shoals off both sides. Booming grounds are in the bay east of the point.

585   **Cartwright Bay** affords anchorage for small craft but provides protection from south and west winds only.

586   **Greenway Sound**, entered between **Cardale Head** and **Walker Point** *(50°52′N, 126°42′W)*, is connected by Carter Passage on its west side to Wells Passage. Marine farm facilities are on the north shore, 0.6 mile WNW of **Maude Islet**.

587   **Broughton Lagoon** enters the sound through tidal rapids east of **Cecil Island**.

588   **Greenway Sound Marine Resort**, on the east side of the bay east of Greenway Point, has marina facilities. Moorage is available late May to mid September, and restaurant available mid June to end of August. Washrooms, laundry, garbage drop, power, convenience store and boat sitting services are available. Float plane service can be arranged. A dingy dock, at the south end of the bay, allows access to a BC Forest Service Picnic area and hiking trails to Broughton Lake.

589   **Dangers. — A rock that dries 0.3 m lies in mid-sound west of Greenway Point, and 8.2 and 6.1 m shoals lie off the north and west sides of the point.**

590   **Anchorage** is reported to be obtainable behind Cecil Island and south of Simpson Island, near the head of the sound.

Chart 3547

Several drying rocks lie off the east shore and south of Simpson Island.

591   **Pasley Passage** and **Sharp Passage** *(50°51'N, 126°39'W)*, separated by **Stackhouse Island**, lead from Sutlej Channel into Kingcome Inlet. **Pasley Rock**, 0.2 mile SW of **Philip Point**, lies in the middle of Pasley Passage. **Harry Bay** and **Moore Point** are on the south shore of Sharp Passage.

592   **Cypress Harbour** *(50°50'N, 126°40'W)* is entered between **Donald Head** and **Fox Rock**, a drying reef extending from **Woods Point**. A B.C. Forest Service campsite is on the south shore.

593   Sheltered anchorage for small vessels in 26 m, mud, is available off **Harbour Point** and **Blount Point**, and for small craft in **Miller Bay** or **Berry Cove**, depending upon wind direction. Note the 5.8 m shoal in the entrance to Miller Bay. Anchorage is also available in **Stopford Bay**. A rock with less than 2 m over it lies close south of **Roffey Point**. The bay entered between **Talbot Point** and **Cawston Point** dries.

Grappler Sound and Adjacent Channels

594   **Grappler Sound** *(50°55'N, 126°53'W)*, entered from Wells Passage between **Pandora Head** and **Kinnaird Island**, has **Kinnaird Rock** in the middle of its entrance.

595   **Carriden Bay**, south of **Linlithgow Point**, offers good anchorage for small vessels, and in good weather for small craft, but is exposed to easterly winds and seas. **Claydon Bay**, entered between **Morton Point** and the rocks in its entrance, affords good anchorage for small vessels in its south part and for small craft in its north arm.

596   **Woods Bay** is on the east side of the sound. **Embley Lagoon** *(50°57'N, 126°52'W)* and **Overflow Basin**, approached north of **Watson Point**, are in the north part of Grappler Sound.

597   **Dunsany Passage** *(50°54'N, 126°50'W)* separates Kinnaird Island from **Cunning Point** and connects Sutlej Channel to Hopetown Passage.

598   **Hopetown Passage**, with **Buckingham Island** in its west entrance, leads east from Grappler Sound. The east end of the passage is obstructed by a drying reef and can be navigated only by shallow draught craft at HW. Anchorage with mud bottom and good shelter is available in **Hoy Bay**, on the south side of **Watson Island** east of **Hopetown Point**. The Indian village in Hoy Bay is occupied (1985) and booming grounds and a barge ramp are on the west side of the bay.

Kenneth Passage

599   **Kenneth Passage** is obstructed by an island and reefs abreast **Kenneth Point** *(50°57'N, 126°49'W)*, the channel leads SW of **Jessie Point** which has a shoal rock close south of it. **Caution is advised.**

600   **Tides.** — Tidal differences for Jessie Point (Index No. 8371), referenced on Alert Bay, are in *Tide Tables, Volume 6.*

601   **Tidal streams** near Kenneth Point are fairly strong.

602   **Turnbull Cove** *(50°58'N, 126°50'W)* affords anchorage for small vessels. It is reported that the holding is excellent in mud, but winds in a SE gale circle the cove at full force. Booming grounds and float houses of a logging operation are in the cove.

603   **Nepah Lagoon** *(50°58'N, 126°47'W)* is entered through **Roaringhole Rapids**, navigation of this rapid should be attempted only at HW slack. **Yuki Bay** is on the SE side of the lagoon.

604   **Steamboat Bay**, on the south side of Kenneth Passage, affords anchorage for small craft.

Mackenzie Sound

605   **Mackenzie Sound** *(50°56'N, 126°45'W)* is free of offshore dangers except for shoal areas between **Turner Island** and **Stirling Point** and NE of **Nimmo Islet**. The entrance to **Nimmo Bay** at **Nimmo Point** is obstructed by drying ledges and below-water rocks, local knowledge is advised. A fishing lodge is on the north shore of **Little Nimmo Bay**.

606   **Burly Bay**, entered SW of **Claypole Point**, affords anchorage for small vessels south of **Blair Islet** near its head in about 20 m, but is reported to offer little protection from strong SE winds. Small craft can obtain anchorage nearer the head of Burly Bay, and with local knowledge in Little Nimmo Bay 4 miles ENE, but shelter from west winds in the latter is not good.

607   **Booming grounds** and a log dump are on the north shore near the head of the sound.

Drury Inlet

608   **Drury Inlet**, entered between Compton Point *(50°53'N, 126°54'W)* and Pandora Head, leads 12 miles west between low hills. Depths through most of the inlet and connecting waters are less than 40 m and there are numerous rocks and shoals. **Caution is advised.**

609   **Stuart Narrows** *(50°54'N, 126°54'W)*, at the entrance of Drury Inlet, is obstructed by **Morris Islet** and several rocks in its entrance, by **Welde Rock** in its central part, and by **Leche Islet** and some isolated shoals near its west end.

610   **Tides.** — Tidal differences for Stuart Narrows (Entrance) (Index No. 8379), referenced on Alert Bay, are in *Tide Tables, Volume 6.*

611   **Tidal streams** in Stuart Narrows attain 7 kn on the ebb and 6 kn on the flood. Secondary current station Stuart Narrows, Drury Inlet (Index No. 6240), referenced on Alert Bay, is in *Tide Tables, Volume 6.*

612   **Helen Bay** *(50°54'N, 126°56'W)* affords anchorage, gravel bottom. **Restless Bay** is south of Welde Rock. **Richmond Bay** is reported to afford anchorage south and SE of the islets and shoals in the centre of the bay. **Bughouse Bay** is on the north shore of Stuart Narrows.

613   **Ligar Islet** *(50°54'N, 127°00'W)*, with shoal areas east and south of it, and **Voak Rock** lie on opposite sides of the fairway west of **Cumming Point**.

614   **Tancred Bay**, south of Ligar Islet, has shoals in its centre part and is open to NW winds. **Davis Bay**, with **Davis Islet** in its entrance, is reported to have limited anchorage close-off the north shore.

615   **Booming grounds** *(50°53'N, 127°03'W)* line the south shore between **Everard Islets** and **Blount Rock**.

616   **Jennis Bay** *(50°55'N, 127°02'W)*, on the north side of Drury Inlet, can be entered either side of **Hooper Island**. Booming grounds are north of **Byron Point**. A resort with a wharf and float is on the north shore of Jennis Bay. It is reported that good anchorage can be obtained in the NW part of the bay.

Chart 3547

617 **Tides**. — Tidal differences for Jennis Bay (Index No. 8384), referenced on Alert Bay, are in *Tide Tables, Volume 6*.

618 **Centre Rock** *(50°54'N, 127°04'W)* lies in the middle of Drury Inlet, between **Bedwell Point** and **O'Keefe Point**. **Shuckburgh Point** is on the south shore and **Collinson Bay** and **Blackney Point** are on the north shore.

619 The channel leading north of **Wilson Island**, **Keith Islets** and **Muirhead Islands**, near the west end of the inlet, has several detached shoals in mid-channel.

620 **Macgowan Bay**, south of **Cunningham Point**, is filled with islets and shoals extending south from Muirhead Islands. A log sorting area and booming grounds lie off its south shore.

621 **Sutherland Bay**, at the west end of Drury Inlet, is entered north of **Jenkins Islet**. It is reported to afford good anchorage over mud for small craft sheltered from all but strong easterly winds.

Actaeon Sound

622 **Dove Island**, west of **Charlotte Point** *(50°56'N, 127°08'W)*, lies in the entrance of **Actress Passage**, which leads to **Actaeon Sound** *(50°57'N, 127°05'W)*. This sound, encumbered with islets and rocks, is suitable only for small craft and local knowledge is advised. There is a slight tidal stream in the entrance to the sound but not much current in it.

623 The section of the channel leading from **Charters Point** around **Bond Peninsula**, known locally as Snake Pass, **requires extra caution**, particularly through the shoals off **Skeene Point**.

624 **Anchorages**. — **Bond Lagoon** is reported to afford good anchorage, however the entrance dries 0.9 m. Anchorage is also reported to be obtainable in **Hand Bay**, Creasy Bay and behind the islet south of **England Point**.

625 **Creasy Bay** has booming grounds and an abandoned logging camp with a jetty on its west shore.

626 **Booming grounds** and a scow grid are close south of the entrance to Tsibass Lagoon.

627 **Tsibass Lagoon** *(51°00'N, 127°03'W)*, entered through a very narrow channel with tidal rapids and a least depth of 0.6 m, is accessible only by small craft at HW slack, which occurs about 2 h 20 after HW at Alert Bay. A large logging operation is reported to be active at the head.

CHAPTER 8

Queen Charlotte Strait, Seymour and Belize Inlets

General

Chart 3001

1   This chapter covers Queen Charlotte Strait, Goletas Channel, Seymour and Belize Inlets, at the west end of Queen Charlotte Strait. Seymour Inlet, Nugent Sound and Belize Inlet, approached by way of Slingsby or Schooner Channels, have Nakwakto Rapids as their common entrance.

2   The east end of Queen Charlotte Strait is fronted by numerous islands and rocks through which several channels lead into Knight Inlet, Kingcome Inlet, Wakeman Sound and Drury Inlet.

Queen Charlotte Strait

Charts 3546, 3547, 3548, 3549, 3550, 3598

3   **Queen Charlotte Strait** *(50°45'N, 127°15'W)* separates the NE side of Vancouver Island from the mainland and connects Johnstone and Broughton Straits to Queen Charlotte Sound. The seaward entrance of the strait is between Cape Sutil *(50°52'N, 128°03'W)* on Vancouver Island and Cape Caution *(51°10'N, 127°47'W)* on the mainland. With the exception of Goletas Channel the west part of Queen Charlotte Strait is open to the Pacific Ocean and there is frequently a heavy swell.

4   **The deepest route from Johnstone Strait into Queen Charlotte Strait** is through Blackney Passage and Blackfish Sound entering the east end of Queen Charlotte Strait through George Passage. The most direct route from Johnstone Strait is through Broughton Strait entering Queen Charlotte Strait along the west side of Malcolm Island.

5   Gordon Channel is the usual route followed through Queen Charlotte Strait into Queen Charlotte Sound. An alternative is to follow Goletas Channel as far as Noble Islets, then through Christie Passage and Gordon Channel into Queen Charlotte Sound. The route through Goletas Channel has Nahwitti Bar across its west end. In west gales heavy seas break across this bar.

6   **Anchorages** along the south side of Queen Charlotte Strait suitable for vessels of moderate size are in Beaver Harbour, Hardy Bay, Port Alexander and Bull Harbour. Along the north side of the strait anchorages are in Blunden Harbour, Allison Harbour and east of Knight Island.

7   **Vessel Traffic Services** (VTS). — Queen Charlotte Strait and the portion of Queen Charlotte Sound south of a line joining Cape Caution with Triangle Island and north of a line joining Triangle Island with Cape Scott are in *Sector Four* of the *Vancouver Traffic Zone* and is administered by *Comox Traffic*. Assigned frequency is 156.575 MHz, Channel 71. Calling-in points in Queen Charlotte Strait are:

8   *Calling-in Point No. 34*, *Lizard Point*, a line running 045°–225° through Lizard Point light *(555.8)*.

9   *Calling-in Point No. 37*, *Doyle Island*, a line running 045°–225° through Doyle Island light *(568)*.

10   *Calling-in Point No. 38*, *Pine Island*, a line running 045°–225° through Pine Island light *(576)*.

11   Change point for entering *Prince Rupert Traffic Zone* is **Calling-in Point No. 39**, *Cape Caution/Triangle Island*, a line joining Cape Caution light *(578)* with Triangle Island.

12   Change point for entering *Tofino Traffic Zone* is **Calling-in Point No. 40**, *Cape Scott*, a line joining Cape Scott light *(66)* with Triangle Island.

13   A brief description of this VTS is in *PAC 200*. Details are in *Radio Aids to Marine Navigation (Pacific and Western Arctic)*.

14   **Tides**. — Tidal differences in Queen Charlotte Strait, referenced on Alert Bay (Index No. 8280), are given for Raynor Group (Index No. 8394), Port Hardy (Index No. 8408), Shushartie Bay (Index No. 8416) and Sunday Harbour (Index No. 8340) in *Tide Tables, Volume 6*.

15   **Tidal streams** in Queen Charlotte Strait set ESE on the flood and WNW on the ebb. A WNW current prevalent along the north shore is strengthened during snow-melt period in early summer. This results in strong ebbs and weak floods along the north shore. Along the south shore flood and ebb are of about equal strength except during summer months. During summer months prevailing NW winds tend to enhance the flood. In winter the prevailing SE winds enhance the ebb.

16   Secondary current stations in Queen Charlotte Strait, referenced on Johnstone Strait (Central) (Index No. 6000), are given for a position 2 miles ENE of Masterman Islands (Index No. 6058) and for a position about 3 miles south of Browning Islands (Index No. 6062) in *Tide Tables, Volume 6*.

17   **Winds** in Queen Charlotte Strait are predominantly from NW in summer and SE in winter months. During summer months on clear sunny days a sea breeze usually starts in late morning, and combined with the prevailing wind can lead to wind speeds of 30 kn by late afternoon. This sea breeze dies out just before dusk and is replaced by a weaker land breeze. During winter months, when very cold air accumulates on the interior plateau of British Columbia, strong winds periodically blow down mainland inlets such as Kingcome and Knight Inlets. These can lead to gale force winds over limited areas of Queen Charlotte Strait and are of particular importance because of their suddenness. Further information on weather systems is given in *PAC 200*.

18   **Meteorological information** and frequency of fog tables for Bull Harbour and Port Hardy are in the Appendices.

Blackfish Sound to Gordon Channel

Chart 3546

19   **Malcolm Island** separates Cormorant Channel and Broughton Strait from the east part of Queen Charlotte Strait. The north side of the island is fringed with sand and gravel beaches, and during summer months kelp grows up to 0.2 mile offshore. **Lizard Point** *(50°40'N, 126°54'W)* is the NE extremity of Malcolm Island and **Malcolm Point** its NW extremity.

20   **Light**. — Lizard Point light *(555.8)* is shown at an elevation of 5.5 m from a white tower with a green band at the top.

Chart 3546

21 **Foster Island** *(50°42'N, 126°51'W)* is high and level except for a conical hill on its south extremity. **Penfold Islet** is 1.5 miles SE and **Twin Islets** lie 0.2 mile south of Foster Island.

22 **Foster Rock**, 0.7 mile west of Foster Island, has 5.5 m over it. Several detached shoals and drying rocks surround Foster Island and Twin Islets.

23 **George Passage** separates the NE side of Malcolm Island from Foster Island and is deep.

24 **Tidal streams** in George Passage attain 3 kn.

25 **Trinity Bay**, between Lizard Point and **Bowlder Point**, has a sand and gravel bottom and is exposed to all but south winds. Anchorage can be obtained off Trinity Bay in depths of about 18 m.

Chart 3548

26 **Staples Islet** *(50°46'N, 127°07'W)* is 0.3 mile SW of Numas Islands.

27 **Morgan Shoal** *(50°47'N, 127°15'W)*, 5.2 miles west of Numas Islands, has 18.3 m over it. **Taylor Bank**, 2.5 miles north of Morgan Shoal, has a least depth of 59 m over it.

28 The south shore of the strait, between False Head *(50°40'N, 127°17'W)* and **Thomas Point**, 4.5 miles NW, is low. **Keogh Shoals**, midway between False Head and Thomas Point, is an extensive area of foul ground extending 1 mile offshore. Kelp grows in profusion on this area during summer months.

29 **Light**. — Port Hardy Aeronautical Beacon light *(554)*, 1 mile SSE of Thomas Point, is visible from seaward and shown from a tower at Port Hardy Airport. A large white hangar on the airfield is conspicuous.

30 **Conspicuous black rectangular microwave towers**, with red air obstruction lights, are on the highest summit of **The Seven Hills**, which are on the peninsula separating Beaver Harbour from Hardy Bay.

31 **Round Island** *(50°44'N, 127°22'W)* is the outermost of the group of islands fronting Beaver Harbour. Several drying reefs and below-water rocks surround the island.

32 **Light**. — Round Island light *(555)*, on the north extremity of the island, is shown at an elevation of 12 m from a white tower.

33 **Masterman Islands**, close north of the peninsula separating Beaver Harbour from Hardy Bay, are four wooded islands. The passage between them and Vancouver Island is encumbered with rocks and usable only by small craft.

34 **Light**. — Masterman Islands light *(563)*, on the NE extremity of the NE island, is shown at an elevation of 10.1 m from a white tower with a green band at the top.

35 **Tidal streams**. — Secondary current station Masterman Islands (Index No. 6058), referenced on Johnstone Strait (Central), is about 2 miles ENE of Masterman Islands. It is in *Tide Tables, Volume 6*.

36 **Doyle Island** *(50°48'N, 127°28'W)*, in the east approach to Goletas and Gordon Channels, is the largest of the Gordon Islands. **Miles Cone**, its SW summit, is a conspicuous conical hill. Above-water and drying rocks extend 0.25 mile SE of the island.

37 **Light**. — Doyle Island light *(568)*, on an islet SE of Doyle Island, is shown at an elevation of 14.1 m from a white tower with a green band at the top.

Beaver Harbour and Hardy Bay

38 **Beaver Harbour**, between Thomas Point and **Dillon Point** *(50°45'N, 127°25'W)*, is protected by several islands in its entrance and affords good anchorage. Its shores are low and lined with houses. The south and SW shores are fronted by extensive drying flats. On the SW side these are composed of sand and shingle and on the south side, in front of **Fort Rupert**, are composed of white shells and shingle.

39 **Daedalus Passage**, along the west side of Beaver Harbour, has **Charlie Islands**, which are bare, and **Peel Island**, which is wooded, on its east side. **Herald Rock**, on the west side of the passage, has 2.4 m over it with drying rocks between it and the shore. A detached shoal, with 4.6 m over it, lies on the east side of the passage 0.1 mile SW of the west extremity of Peel Island.

40 **Patrician Cove**, 0.5 mile SSW of Herald Rock, has a drying rock in its centre.

41 **Cattle Islands**, south of Peel Island, are connected to one another by drying reefs and have three drying reefs close-off their NW side. **Shell Island**, SW of Cattle Islands, is surrounded by a conspicuous white shell beach and has drying reefs close south and NE of it. **Cormorant Rock**, 0.4 mile WNW of Shell Island, dries 4.3 m.

42 **Beacon**. — Cormorant Rock daybeacon has a bifurcation/junction daymark, preferred channel to the right.

43 **Marine farm** facilities lie off the west shore of Cattle Islands.

44 **Anchorage** west of Cattle Islands in Beaver Harbour is well protected in 20 to 25 m, mud. Small craft can anchor closer to Cattle Islands in 5 to 10 m.

45 **Deer Island** lies 0.6 mile north of Thomas Point. Deer Island is a native reserve, permission is required before camping. **Eagle Island** is close-off Deer Island's SE side. Depths in the passage between the point and the islands are irregular with a shoal and drying reef close north of Thomas Point and above-water rocks close south of Eagle Island.

46 The passage between Deer and Peel Islands has a drying spit of boulders extending 0.25 mile NW from the NW side of Deer Island. **Twin Rocks**, in the centre of this passage, have foul ground extending 0.15 mile east from them and a rock with less than 2 m over it 0.2 mile to the SE.

47 **Directions**. — Two channels are recommended for entering Beaver Harbour. Daedalus Passage is deep throughout if a mid-channel course is maintained with care being taken to avoid Herald Rock and the 4.6 m shoal 0.1 mile SW of the west extremity of Peel Island.

48 The second entrance channel is between Thomas Point and Eagle Island. Pass about 0.1 mile south of rocks on the south side of Eagle Island in order to avoid the shoal water extending north from Thomas Point. Pass 0.2 mile south of Shell Island to avoid the drying rock off its south side, then pass close west of Cormorant Rock and proceed to the anchorage.

49 **Hardy Bay**, entered between **Duval Point** *(50°46'N, 127°29'W)* and **Daphne Point** 2 miles SE, has a drying ledge extending 0.4 mile from its west side and a drying mud flat at its south end. **Quatse River** flows into its south end and **Glenlion River** into its SW side. Marine farm facilities are in the cove 0.6 mile south of Daphne Point.

50 A **speed limit** of 5 km/h (3 kn) is prescribed by *Boating Restriction Regulations* for Hardy Bay (Inner Harbour).

Chart 3548

51   Hardy Bay is a **water aerodrome**. An aeronautical strobe light, east of the boat basin, is activated by aircraft when intending to land or take off.

52   **Lights**. — Hardy Bay light *(564)* is on the outer edge of the drying ledge 2.3 miles south of Duval Point.

53   Hardy Bay Inner light *(565)*, 0.7 mile south of Hardy Bay light, has a starboard hand daymark.

54   Port Hardy Boat Basin North and South lights *(566, 566.1)* are shown from the outer ends of the breakwaters at the boat basin.

55   **Buoys**. — Yellow cautionary buoys, "ND", "NE" and "NF", NW of Hardy Bay Inner light, mark the outer edge of a drying ledge. **Caution. — Many vessels have run aground on the drying ledge when taking a direct course from Hardy Bay to the boat basin and Seafood Products wharf. Charts must be consulted to ensure a safe route is taken east of the rocks, cautionary buoys, and Hardy Bay Inner light.**

56   A **submarine pipeline** crosses the drying flats on the west side of Hardy Bay, close north of Port Hardy.

57   A **submarine cable** crosses Hardy Bay close south of the boat basin.

58   **Anchorage** for vessels of moderate size can be obtained between Hardy Bay light and Hardy Bay Inner light, NE of the public wharf.

59   **Bear Cove**, on the east side of Hardy Bay, has the BC Ferries terminal for scheduled service to Prince Rupert in its NE corner. A boat launching ramp protected by a breakwater is on the east shore, south of the ferry terminal.

60   **Berths**. — A fishing company wharf and fuel float protected by a floating barge breakwater are on the south side of Bear Cove. Gas, diesel, kerosene, propane, washrooms, showers, tackle, bait, ice and waste oil disposal are available. Towing and repairs can be arranged.

61   Close east mooring dolphins, connected to shore by a catwalk, are designed for berthing an oil tanker barge 80 m long with a draught of 5 m. Oil storage tanks are close south of the berth.

62   **Beacon**. — A daybeacon with a port hand daymark is on the outer end of the breakwater.

63   **Lights**. — A private light and radar reflectors are at the west end of the ferry terminal.

64   Private lights are shown from a breakwater in the south part of the cove.

65   **Buoy**. — Port hand buoy "N25" marks a drying ledge on the east side of Bear Cove.

66   **Port Hardy**, on the west side of Hardy Bay, is a community with all amenities and offers recreational facilities and a visitor centre. It is a commercial fishing centre and most boat problems can be repaired. Medical services, including a hospital with heliport, are available. Port Hardy Airport is about 8 km SE of the community.

67   **Coast Guard has a year-round rescue unit based in Port Hardy.**

68   **Tides**. — Tidal differences for Port Hardy (Index No. 8408), referenced on Alert Bay, are in *Tide Tables, Volume 6.*

69   **Meteorological information** and a frequency of fog table for Port Hardy are in the Appendices.

70   **Booming grounds** are NE of **Jensen Cove** and along the edge of the drying flats at the south end of Hardy Bay where there are numerous dolphins.

71   **Berths**. — The public wharf, 0.5 mile SSW of Hardy Bay light, is 61 m long. During summer months a T-shaped float attached to its north side has a least depth of 3.4 m alongside. Floats on the south side of the wharf are for Coast Guard vessels. A 2 tonne crane is on the wharf, fresh water is obtainable and power is laid on. Mooring buoys for pleasure craft use are reported to be adjacent to the public wharf.

72   **Seafood Products wharf**, S of the public wharf, has floats, a net repair barge and fuel dock. Gas, diesel, stove oil, kerosene, naptha, waste oil disposal, washrooms, charts and fishing supplies are available.

73   **Public floats**, close south of Seafood Products wharf, are 94 m long and used mainly by large fishing vessels.

74   The **boat basin**, 0.3 mile SW of Hardy Bay Inner light, with a depth of 3 m in the entrance, is protected by breakwaters extending from its north and south sides. Mainly used by commercial fishing vessels, there is room for pleasure craft. Public floats have depths of 3.2 m alongside. Power and water are laid on, garbage and used oil disposal facilities are available. There is a launching ramp, tidal grid and holding tank pumpout.

75   A **marina**, resort and fuel dock is at the south end of the boat basin. Gas, diesel, propane, moorage, power, washrooms, showers, laundry and Internet access are available. Engine and hull repairs for small craft and electronic maintenance can be undertaken. The only travel lift between Nanaimo and Shearwater is 6.7 m wide and has a 60 ton capacity. There is hotel accommodation and a store.

76   **Seaplane floats** are close SE of Glenlion River.

77   **Transportation**. — Scheduled bus service operates between Port Hardy and Victoria. Scheduled air services operate from Port Hardy Airport, which has asphalt runways the longest being 1,524 m. BC Ferries operates a scheduled ferry service between Port Hardy and Prince Rupert. Information can be obtained from Victoria (250) 386-3431, reservations are recommended.

Queen Charlotte Strait — NE Part

Charts 3546, 3547

78   The NE side of Queen Charlotte Strait is fronted by numerous islands and rocks through which several channels lead into mainland inlets. The most direct route to Knight Inlet is entered between Swanson Island *(50°37'N, 126°43'W)* and Wedge Island. Fife Sound, entered between Eden Island *(50°45'N, 126°42'W)* and Broughton Island, leads into Tribune Channel and then to Knight Inlet or NW through Penphrase Passage to Kingcome Inlet. Wells Passage entered between Boyles Point *(50°49'N, 127°01'W)* and Percy Island, leads NE to Drury Inlet, Grappler Sound or through Sutlej Channel into Kingcome Inlet.

79   **Holford Islets** *(50°44'N, 126°48'W)* are two islands midway between Broughton and Foster Islands.

80   **Holford Rocks**, 0.25 mile west of the north Holford Islet, consist of two drying rocks and several heads with less than 2 m over them.

81   **Salmon Channel** separates Foster Island from Holford Islets and is 1.9 miles wide. Shoals lie off the NE side of Foster Island and close south of Holford Islets, otherwise the channel is deep.

Charts 3546, 3547

82   **Nowell Channel** separates Holford Islets from Broughton Island. Several shoals lie within 0.5 mile of the Broughton Island shore, otherwise the channel is deep.

83   **Tidal streams** in Salmon and Nowell Channels attain 3 kn.

Chart 3547

84   **Nowell Bank** *(50°45'N, 126°51'W)* has 35 m over it. A rock, with 5.5 m over it, lies 2 miles NW of Nowell Bank and about 1.2 miles SE of Polkinghorne Islands.

85   **George Bank** *(50°44'N, 126°58'W)* has 22 m over it. **Numas Bank**, 2.7 miles WNW, has 20.1 m over it.

86   **Labouchere Passage** separates **Numas Islands** *(50°46'N, 127°04'W)* from Lewis Rocks. Vessels using this passage should favour the Numas Islands side.

87   **Light**. — Numas Island light *(559.5)*, on the north side of the east island, is shown at an elevation of 6.3 m from a white tower.

88   **Lewis Rocks** *(50°48'N, 127°03'W)*, on the north side of Labouchere Passage and off the west side of the entrance to Wells Passage, are an extensive group of drying, above and below-water rocks. The highest of these rocks has an elevation of 7 m. They should be given a wide berth. **Lewis Cove** has several drying rocks in it.

89   **Howcraft Point**, 2.2 miles NW of Lewis Rocks, has a chain of drying and below-water rocks SE of it.

90   **Taylor Point**, 2 miles NW of Howcraft Point, is backed by white cliffs. **Aylmer Point** is 2 miles NW.

Chart 3548

91   **Raynor Group** *(50°53'N, 127°14'W)* is a group of islands and rocks lying close offshore between **Akam Point** and **Cohoe Bay**. **Gillot Rock**, 0.2 mile south of the SE island in the group, dries 5.5 m. **Brandon Rock**, 0.1 mile west of the westernmost island, is 2 m high.

92   **Marine farm** facilities lie off the west shore of the northernmost island of the Raynor Group.

93   **Tides**. — Tidal differences for Raynor Group (Index No. 8394), referenced on Alert Bay, are in *Tide Tables, Volume 6*.

94   **Browning Islands** *(50°54'N, 127°20'W)* lie within 0.5 mile of shore. A rock, which dries 2.7 m, lies 0.2 mile SE of the south island. **Snell Islet**, 0.5 mile east of Browning Islands, is bare and light coloured.

95   **Tidal streams**. — Secondary current station Browning Islands (Index No. 6062), referenced on Johnstone Strait Central, is about 3 miles south of Browning Islands, see *Tide Tables, Volume 6*.

96   **Stuart Rock**, 0.8 mile NW of Browning Islands, has 3.4 m over it.

97   **Marsh Bay**, 1.5 miles NW of the Browning Islands, does not afford anchorage as it is exposed SE and encumbered with drying rocks on its east side.

Blunden Harbour and Approach

98   **Robinson Island** *(50°54'N, 127°17'W)* lying across the entrance to Blunden Harbour is densely wooded. **Nankivell Islands**, 0.4 mile west of Robinson Island, have foul ground extending SE from them and should be given a wide berth. The largest island is wooded but others are bare and rocky. **Shelf Head** is the east extremity of Robinson Island.

99   **Burgess Island**, 0.3 mile SW of Shelf Head, is a rock surmounted by a clump of trees, it is easily identified from westward. **Siwiti Rock**, 0.3 mile SE of Shelf Head, has less than 2 m over it and is marked by kelp. **Barren Rock**, 0.3 mile east of Shelf Head, has an elevation of 2 m with a drying ledge extending north and rocks, with less than 2 m over them, to the west of it. Drying and below-water rocks extend south from **Tomlinson Point**.

100   **Blunden Harbour**, entered between Shelf Head and **Edgell Island**, is separated into two arms by **Augustine Islands**, which are connected to one another and joined to the north shore by a drying mud flat with many boulders on it.

101   **Directions**. — When approaching Blunden Harbour difficulty may be experienced in identifying the entrance. Burgess Island and Barren Rock can usually be clearly identified at a distance of about 1 mile. Care must be taken to avoid Siwiti Rock in the approaches to the harbour entrance, made easier when swells are breaking on it.

102   If proceeding to the inner anchorage, care must be taken to avoid the rock with less than 2 m over it NW of **Brandon Point**, drying reefs and rocks with less than 2 m extending south from Augustine Islands, and a drying reef close north of **Bartlett Point**.

103   **Anchorage** in the outer part of Blunden Harbour can be obtained south of the north Augustine Island in a depth of about 13 m, mud bottom. In the inner part a good anchorage is between Moore Rock and **Grave Islet** in 6 m, mud bottom. The bight immediately east of Bartlett Point is also used. These anchorages afford good shelter.

104   A rock with 3.7 m over it lies 0.1 mile NW of **Edgell Point**. The site of an Indian village is on the north shore, NW of Augustine Islands. Little can be seen apart from fallen posts protruding from the grassy bank above the shell midden. **Moore Rock**, 0.1 mile west of Augustine Islands, dries 2.1 m and has a cairn on it. **Byrnes Island** is an abandoned Indian burial ground, trespassing is prohibited. **Gregory Islet** lies at the west end of the harbour.

105   **Jula Island** and **Frost Islands**, at the north end of the east arm, have several drying reefs to the south. **Deer Cove**, north of the islands, dries. A narrow channel suitable for small craft lies NW and leads to rapids at the entrance to **Bradley Lagoon**. These rapids can only be passed at HW slack.

Gordon Channel

Charts 3549

106   **Gordon Channel** *(50°51'N, 127°29'W)* is entered at its SE end between Gordon Islands and the Deserters Group, its NW entrance lies between Hope and Pine Islands. A sill crosses the channel between Bell Island, on its south side, and Staples Island on its north side; the fairway across this sill is deep. Dangers lie on both sides of the channel but the fairway is not less than 0.8 mile wide.

107   Islands on both sides of Gordon Channel provide good radar presentation.

108   **Gordon Islands** *(50°49'N, 127°29'W)*, **Heard Island**, **Bell Island** and **Hurst Island** lie along the south side and at the east end of Gordon Channel. Marine farm facilities lie among the

Chart 3549

islands off the NW shore of Doyle Island. **Meeson Cone**, near the middle of Hurst Island, is a well-defined conical hill.

109 **Anchorage** for small craft with good protection is reported to be obtainable in the passage between Bell Island and the two islands south of it.

110 There is a passage between the Gordon Islands. The passage between the north end of Gordon Islands and Heard Island has drying and below-water rocks about 0.1 mile east of Heard Island. The passage between Heard and Bell Islands is encumbered with rocks and has marine farm facilities in it. The passage between Bell and Hurst Islands is 0.1 mile wide but has rocks and shoals in its north and south entrances.

111 **Harlequin Bay**, on the NE side of Hurst Island, is very shallow and its approach is encumbered with islets and rocks.

112 **Crane Islands** are three small bare islets, 0.3 mile north of the east end of Bell Island. A rock, with 1.1 m over it, lies 0.1 mile north of the islands.

113 **Light**. — Crane Islands light *(569)*, on the summit of the west and highest islet, is shown at an elevation of 14.2 m from a white tower with a green band at the top.

114 **Boyle Island**, 1.5 miles WNW of Crane Islands, has a rock with 1.5 m over it, 0.3 mile WSW of it, and several drying and below-water rocks extend 0.5 mile from its NW side. **Tribune Rock** is 0.3 m high.

115 **Light**. — Tribune Rock light *(569.3)* is on the rock.

116 **God's Pocket Marine Provincial Park** encompasses Bell, Hurst, Crane and Boyle Islands and adjacent waters. The park is undeveloped but offers some of the best scuba diving on the Pacific Coast.

117 **Deserters Group** *(50°53'N, 127°28'W)* consists of **Wishart Island, Deserters Island, McLeod Island** and several smaller islands and rocks. The passage between Wishart and Deserters Islands has a rock, with 0.2 m over it, near its south entrance and is only suitable for small craft. The passage between Deserters and McLeod Islands has shoals, islets and drying rocks in its SE entrance and a shoal with 1.9 m over it at its NW end. **Castle Point**, the SE extremity of Deserters Island, is steep-to.

118 **Shelter Passage** separates Deserters Group from **Walker Group** and is entered west of **Bleach Rock** and **Race Island**. It leads north from Gordon Channel to Ripple Passage and, although 0.2 mile wide and relatively deep, is not recommended except for small vessels. **Staples Island**, the south island of Walker Group, is densely wooded and hilly.

119 **Marine farm** facilities lie off the NW shore of Wishart Island.

120 **Anchorage** for small vessels with shelter from SE winds can be obtained in 16 m, sand and shell, between the west side of Wishart Island and the unnamed 40 m high island close SW.

121 **Davey Rock**, 1 mile south of Staples Island, lies on the NE side of the fairway through Gordon Channel and has 8 m over it. **Roach Rock**, 0.5 mile NNW of Davey Rock, has 8.7 m over it. **Alex Rock**, 0.5 mile NNW of Roach Rock, dries 0.8 m. **Nye Rock**, 1.1 miles NW of Alex Rock, dries 4 m.

122 **Light buoy**. — Davey Rock light buoy "N32" *(569.2)*, close SE of the rock, is a starboard hand buoy.

123 **Redfern Island** *(50°54'N, 127°35'W)* lies on the NE side of the fairway through Gordon Channel and **Sussex Reefs** extend SE from it. **Barge Rock**, on the SW side of Sussex Reefs, is 2 m high. The passage between Sussex Reefs and Nye Rock is encum-

bered with several shoals and a rock with 0.2 m over it and is not recommended.

124 **Bolivar Passage** separates Walker Group from **Hedley Islands** and the fairway is 0.5 mile wide at its narrowest part. Drying reefs lie 0.3 mile SE of Hedley Islands but the passage can be safely taken in clear weather during daylight hours by favouring the Walker Group side of the channel.

125 **Torrance Islet**, at the NW end of Walker Group, is grass covered and steep-to on its west and north sides. A reef, on which there is a drying rock, extends SE from the islet.

126 **Malpas Rock**, 1 mile west of Torrance Islet, dries 5.3 m and has shoals NW of it.

127 **Anchorage** for small craft is reported to be good in the shallow, 2.1 m, basin between the north side of Staples Island and the SE end of Kent Island. Kelp usually grows in both entrances and a rock, with 4.2 m over it, lies in the west entrance.

128 **Jane Rock** *(50°55'N, 127°35'W)* is the outermost of a chain of islands extending 0.3 mile north of the NW extremity of Redfern Island. **Scylla Rock**, 0.15 mile NW of Jane Rock, has 2.2 m over it. **Alleviation Rock**, 0.5 mile west of Jane Rock, has 0.7 m over it.

129 **Balaklava Island** *(50°51'N, 127°37'W)*, on the south side of Gordon Channel, separates Christie Passage from Browning Passage. **Scarlett Point** is the NE point of the island. **Croker Rock**, 0.5 mile north of the NW point of the island, dries 1.4 m. The north coast of Balaklava Island is fronted by extensive drying ledges and below-water rocks.

130 **Light**. — Scarlett Point light *(570)* is shown at an elevation of 23.8 m from a white tower, 8.4 m high and operates only at night. Conspicuous white buildings with red roofs stand nearby.

131 **Clam Cove** *(50°52'N, 127°40'W)* (local name) is entered between two groups of wooded islets 0.7 mile SSE of **Hougestal Point**. A rock, with less than 2 m over it, lies in mid-channel 0.2 mile south of the entrance. Anchorage for small craft can be obtained near the head of the cove but there are snags and deadheads. A log dump and logging camp (1988) with floats are on the west shore.

132 **Hunt Rock**, 0.9 mile north of Hougestal Point and 0.7 mile off the coast of Nigei Island, has 2.5 m over it.

133 **Light buoy**. — Hunt Rock light buoy "N35" *(570.5)* is a port hand buoy.

134 **Greeting Point**, with drying reefs extending NW from it, and **Cholberg Point**, 0.4 mile west, are at the north extremity of Nigei Island.

135 **Light**. — Cholberg Point light *(571)* is shown at an elevation of 11.3 m from a white tower.

136 **Cascade Harbour** *(50°55'N, 127°44'W)* usually has a heavy swell entering it, particularly during summer when NW winds prevail. It is reported that small craft can obtain protection from the swell by anchoring close to the south part of the island, on the west side of the harbour. The harbour is used by fishing vessels.

137 **Thornton Reef**, 1.8 miles WNW of Greeting Point, lies in the north entrance to Bate Passage and has 4 m over it.

138 **Hope Island** *(50°55'N, 127°55'W)* lies on the south side and at the west end of Gordon Channel, and separates it from Goletas Channel. **Cape James, Secretary Point** and **Ashby Point** are on the north side of the island. **Roller Bay**, between Ashby Point and **Rason Island**, is separated from Bull Harbour by a

Chart 3549

narrow isthmus. **Plover Island** and numerous drying rocks lie off the NW side of Hope Island.

139   A **radio tower** with red air obstruction lights is on the above-mentioned isthmus.

140   **Buckle Group** *(50°56'N, 127°39'W)* consists of a number of islands, rocks and shoals on the NE side of Gordon Channel. **Bright Island** is bare except for a clump of trees on the west side of its summit. A fishing boundary marker is on its south side. **Herbert Island** has a few scattered trees and one prominent tall dead tree with no branches. A white tripod survey marker is on the east side. **Prosser Rock**, 0.6 mile SSW of Herbert Island, is 2 m high, bare and surrounded by shoals.

141   **Sunken Rock**, 1.6 miles NW of Bright Island, dries 2 m. Several shoals lie between Buckle Group and Pine Island.

142   **Pine Island** *(50°59'N, 127°44'W)* lies on the north side and at the west end of Gordon Channel. It is heavily wooded, level topped and the south and west sides are steep-to.

143   **Light**. — Pine Island light *(576)*, on the SW point of the island, is shown at an elevation of 28.3 m from a white tower. The light is obscured by high land on its east side. White buildings with red roofs stand nearby.

144   The Buckle Group and Pine Island are an **Ecological Reserve**.

Ripple Passage and Richards Channel

Charts 3548, 3549

145   **Ripple Passage** *(50°53'N, 127°26'W)* is separated from Gordon Channel by Deserters and Walker Groups. Mary Rock, Millar Group, David Rock and Wentworth Rock separate it from Richards Channel. Several islets and sunken rocks lie in Ripple Passage.

146   **Tidal streams** in Ripple Passage attain 4 kn at times with heavy tide-rips and eddies in places. They set SE on the flood and NW on the ebb.

Chart 3548

147   **Barry Islet** *(50°53'N, 127°26'W)*, 9 m high and bare, and a rock with 1.3 m over it on its east side, are at the SE end of Ripple Passage.

148   **Echo Islands** are wooded. A rock, with 1.8 m over it, is steep-to and lies in the fairway about 0.4 mile east of Echo Islands. A rock with 1.3 m over it lies 0.2 mile east of the NW Echo Island.

149   **Echo Rock**, 0.25 mile NW of Echo Islands, dries 5.3 m and has two rocks that dry 2.8 m 0.1 mile SE of it.

150   **Willoughby Rocks**, 1.2 miles NW of Echo Islands, consist of two above-water rocks. **Ellinor Rock**, 1 mile NW of Willoughby Rocks, has 3.2 m over it and is steep-to.

151   **Mary Rock**, at the SE end of Ripple Passage, is 1 m high and has drying rocks close NW and 0.2 mile east of it.

152   **Richard Islets**, 1.4 miles NW of Mary Rock, consist of two bare islets 5 m high. Two rocks, with 0.4 m over them, lie 0.3 mile SE of Richard Islets.

153   **Millar Group** forms the NE side of Ripple Passage. A small craft passage leads between the islands but local knowledge is advised. The passage is entered at its SW end between two groups of wooded islets, then between the two largest islands of the Millar Group into Richards Channel, 0.5 mile west of Ghost Island. **David Rock**, 0.4 mile NW of Millar Group, dries 0.3 m.

Chart 3549

154   **Kent Island** *(50°55'N, 127°33'W)* is densely wooded and the hill at its north end, near **Tommy Point**, shows up distinctly as a rounded peak from some directions. **Philcox Island** is the NW island of a chain lying off the NE side of Kent Island. **Ragged Rock**, 0.4 mile north of Philcox Island, has two heads 2 m high. A rock, with 0.8 m over it, lies 0.2 mile SSW of Ragged Rock. **Joan Island**, 0.3 mile WSW of Ragged Rock, is bare. Several drying and below-water rocks lie within 0.5 mile west of Joan Island.

155   **Anchorage** for small craft can be obtained between Kent and Philcox Islands but care is necessary to avoid dangers in the approach. Another anchorage for small craft, at the SE end of Kent Island, is described with Bolivar Passage.

156   **Wentworth Rock** *(50°57'N, 127°30'W)*, at the north end of Ripple Passage and Richards Channel, is 4 m high and bare.

157   **Light buoy**. — Wentworth Rock light and whistle buoy "N31" *(561.4)*, NE of the rock, is a port hand buoy.

Chart 3548

158   **Richards Channel** *(50°56'N, 127°27'W)* is entered at its SE end between **Stuart Point** and Mary Rock, its NW entrance is between Wentworth Rock and Wallace Islands. **Leading Hill** lies 1.5 miles NW of Stuart Point and the mainland coast is rugged.

159   **Tidal streams** in the narrowest part of Richards Channel attain 3 kn, elsewhere velocity is much less. They set SE on the flood and NW on the ebb. **Heavy overfalls dangerous to small craft frequently occur between Jeannette Islands and Ghost Island when tidal streams are opposed by strong winds.**

160   **Jeannette Islands** *(50°55'N, 127°25'W)* are two thickly wooded islands. **Robertson Island** is separated from the NW Jeannette Island by a passage that is foul.

161   **Light**. — Jeannette Islands light *(561)*, on the SW side of the south island, is shown at an elevation of 9.5 m from a white tower with a red band at the top. A large wind-powered generator is close south.

162   **Anchorage** for small craft can be obtained in the bay between Robertson Island and Leading Hill. Reefs lie in its approach and the anchorage is foul in places; local knowledge is advised.

163   **Ghost Island**, on the SW side of the fairway through Richards Channel, is conspicuous and has a rounded appearance when viewed from SE or NW. Drying reefs lie about 0.1 mile NE of Ghost Island. The passage between Ghost Island and Millar Group is narrow, with a 1 m high rock on the south side and a rock with 4.5 m over it on the north side.

164   **Directions**. — Approaching Richards Channel from SE keep Jeannette Islands light structure bearing less than 323° in order to avoid Mary Rock. Pass between Jeannette Islands and Ghost Island, favouring the Jeannette Islands side in order to avoid the drying reefs and shoals close-off Ghost Island. After passing Jeannette Islands set a course to pass 0.5 mile NE of Wentworth Rock.

Charts 3548, 3549

165   **Shelter Bay** *(50°58'N, 127°27'W)*, at the NE end of Richards Channel, is entered between **Wallace Islands** and **Westcott Point**. **Annie Rocks** and detached shoals, 1 mile WNW of Westcott Point, lie in the approach to Shelter Bay. The bay is

Charts 3548, 3549

about 0.5 mile wide at the entrance and its inner end is divided into two arms. Marine farm facilities are on the south shore at the entrance to Shelter Bay. **Lower Lagoon** enters the north side of the bay. In its most sheltered parts, the bay is encumbered with rocks and local knowledge is advised.

Europa Passage and Approaches

Charts 3549, 3550

166   **Farquhar Bank** *(50°59'N, 127°37'W)* has a least depth of 11.8 m.

167   **Tree Islets** *(50°59'N, 127°43'W)* consist of five islands. The two SW islands are wooded and the NE islet at one time had a solitary tree on it. Shoals extend 0.3 mile south of the islets, otherwise the passage between these islets and Pine Island is clear.

168   **Sealed Reef**, 1 mile north of Tree Islets, has 2.2 m over it and is usually marked by breakers. A second head, with a depth of 5.9 m, lies 0.3 mile NW from the first.

169   **Storm Islands** *(51°02'N, 127°44'W)* are wooded but none have any conspicuous features. **Reid Islets**, 0.5 mile SE of Storm Islands, consist of five islets, the highest has some trees on its summit and the east one is bare with a peaked summit. A chain of reefs, usually marked by breakers, extends 2.3 miles SE from Reid Islets. Named ones are **Ta-aack Rock**, **Dominis Rocks** and **Lama Shoal**.

170   The Buckle Group, Pine Island, Tree Islets, Storm Islands, Reid Islets and Naiad Islets are an **Ecological Reserve**.

171   **Europa Passage**, between Sealed Reef and Storm Islands, is clear and deep.

Shelter Bay to Cape Caution

172   **Coast Hill** *(51°00'N, 127°30'W)* is the north summit of a flat topped hill with an elevation of 244 m, the highest in the vicinity. **Allison Cone**, 1.5 miles NNW of Coast Hill, is a conspicuous conical hill that rises to an elevation of 184 m.

173   **Southgate Group** is a group of islands west of Coast Hill. **Arm Islands** and **Tinson Islands** form the south end of the group. The anchorage between Knight and Southgate Islands is described later with the approach to Allison Harbour.

174   **Simpson Rock**, 0.2 mile south of Tinson Islands, is 2 m high. A rock that dries 1.4 m and one with 1.9 m over it lie 0.2 mile south and SE, respectively, of Simpson Rock.

175   The passage between Arm Islands and Knight Island, to the NW, is encumbered with islets and rocks and only suitable for small craft; local knowledge is advised.

176   **Harris Island** *(51°00'N, 127°34'W)* is light coloured and bare.

177   **Light.** — Harris Island light *(562)*, on the SW corner of the island, is shown at an elevation of 13.8 m from a mast. The mast is often difficult to distinguish against the light coloured rock of the island.

178   **Dickenson Rock** and **Rogers Islands**, NNW of Harris Island, are bare. Shoals extend SE from both Dickenson Rock and Rogers Islands. **Allan Rocks**, 1.8 miles WNW of Rogers Islands, dry 4.8 m. **Middle Rocks**, 0.7 mile WSW of Allan Rocks, dry 3.4 m. **Naiad Islets** *(51°02'N, 127°41'N)* are bare and rocky.

179   **Light buoy.** — Allan Rocks light and whistle buoy "N33" *(576.4)*, NE of the rocks, is a port hand buoy.

Chart 3550

180   **Emily Group** *(50°02'N, 127°34'W)* consists of wooded islands.

181   **Bramham Island** *(51°04'N, 127°35'W)* separates Schooner Channel from Slingsby Channel, these channels are described later in this chapter. **Mayor Island**, 0.4 mile SW of Bramham Island, has trees on it that impart a wall-like appearance and render it rather conspicuous. Drying and below-water rocks lie to the north and east of Mayor Island and local knowledge is advisable for the passage between Mayor and Bramham Islands.

182   **Miles Inlet**, entered between **Bramham Point** and **McEwan Point**, penetrates the west coast of Bramham Island and divides into two arms at its head. **Morphy Rock**, which dries 4 m, and several drying and below-water rocks lie west of McEwan Point. A rock that dries 2.7 m lies 0.1 mile NNW of Bramham Point.

183   **Anchorage** for small craft can be obtained at the head of Miles Inlet, where it branches.

184   **McEwan Rock** *(51°04'N, 127°38'W)* is light coloured and has drying reefs extending 0.1 mile ESE from it. A rock with 4.6 m over it lies 0.6 mile ESE of McEwan Rock.

185   **Light.** — McEwan Rock light *(577)* is shown at an elevation of 12.6 m from a mast. The mast is often difficult to distinguish against the light colour of McEwan Rock.

186   **Dalkeith Point**, 1.3 miles NNW of McEwan Rock, is bold and prominent. A rock awash lies 0.4 mile SE of Dalkeith Point. **Lascelles Point** lies 0.6 mile NW of Dalkeith Point; these two points form the entrance to Slingsby Channel.

187   **Buccleugh Point** *(51°06'N, 127°40'W)* is bold and steep-to. **Bremner Islet** lies 0.8 mile WNW from it.

188   **Burnett Bay**, between **Bremner Point** and **Wilkie Point**, is fringed with a sandy shelving beach. **Hayes Rock**, with 0.8 m over it, lies 1 mile NW of Bremner Point and several detached shoals lie in Burnett Bay.

189   **Silvester Bay**, between **Raynor Point** and Cape Caution, has shoals and drying rocks at its north end.

190   **Cape Caution** *(51°10'N, 127°47'W)* is moderately high and level. The coast in this vicinity is granite and appears white.

191   **Light.** — Cape Caution light *(578)* is shown at an elevation of 21.3 m from a skeleton tower.

Goletas Channel

Chart 3549

192   **Goletas Channel** *(50°47'N, 127°30'W)* is the SW of four channels connecting Queen Charlotte Strait with Queen Charlotte Sound. Entered from the east between Duval Point and Doyle Island, it extends 23 miles WNW between Vancouver Island on the south and a chain of islands on the north side. Several navigable channels between islands on the north side connect Goletas Channel to Gordon Channel. Except at the west end shores of Goletas Channel are high, rugged and steep-to. Nahwitti Bar at the west end generally prevents high seas rising in Goletas Channel during west gales. **Tide-rips and overfalls on Nahwitti Bar can be dangerous to small craft.**

193   **Tides.** — Tidal differences in Goletas Channel, referenced on Alert Bay, are given for Port Hardy (Index No. 8408) and Shushartie Bay (Index No. 8416) in *Tide Tables, Volume 6.*

Chart 3549

194 **Tidal streams** in Goletas Channel and across Nahwitti Bar set east on the flood and west on the ebb. In the east part of Goletas Channel, tidal streams do not exceed 3 kn but at the west end, in vicinity of Nahwitti Bar, they sometimes attain 5½ kn.

195 **Anchorage** for vessels of moderate size can be obtained in Port Alexander. Small vessels can also obtain anchorage between Heard and Bell Islands, in Shushartie Bay and Bull Harbour.

Duval Point to Christie Passage

196 **Anchorage** for small vessels can be obtained between the islets south of Bell Island and the west side of Heard Island clear of marine farm facilities. The anchorage is secure in 21 to 26 m but the north entrance, leading to Gordon Channel, is encumbered with rocks.

197 **Duncan Island** *(50°49'N, 127°33'W)* is steep-to on its south side and fringed with drying ledges on the other shores. **Blyth Islands** are two islands and rocks on the west side of Duncan Island. **Mouat Rock**, midway between Blyth Islands and Hurst Island, has 0.8 m over it.

198 **Marine farm** facilities lie off the NW shore of Duncan Island.

199 **Noble Islets**, 0.7 mile west of Blyth Islands, are two islands 21 and 23 m high with a few stunted bushes and some coarse vegetation.

200 **Light**. — Noble Islets light *(567)*, on the west extremity of the NW islet, is obscured from the vicinity of Duncan Island by the elevation of the islets.

201 **Christie Passage**, entered between Noble Islets and **Nolan Point**, leads north from Goletas Channel to Gordon Channel, it separates Hurst Island from Balaklava Island. The fairway is deep but several shoals lie on each side of it. **George Rock**, on the west side of the passage, dries 0.8 m. The west side of the passage is within the limits of God's Pocket Marine Park.

202 **Tidal streams** through Christie Passage set south with the flood and north with the ebb; they attain 3 kn at times.

203 **God's Pocket**, a local name for the small cove on the west side of Hurst Island, provides good shelter to small craft from all winds. It is used extensively by fish boats. A scuba diving resort is in the cove.

204 An **overhead cable**, across the entrance of the cove south of Scarlett Point, has a vertical clearance of 0.5 m.

Port Alexander and Browning Passage

205 **Jerome Island** and **Lucan Islands** *(50°50'N, 127°38'W)* lie close-off the SW side of Balaklava Island. Port Alexander and Browning Passage are approached from Goletas Channel between Lucan Islands and the islet close-off **Boxer Point**.

206 **Port Alexander** penetrates the SE side of **Nigei Island** and is entered between Boxer Point and **Hussar Point**. It is easy of access and affords good anchorage sheltered from all but SE winds. **Fraser Island**, about 0.5 mile within the entrance, lies in the fairway.

207 **Anchorage** in Port Alexander can be obtained north of Fraser Island in 20 to 22 m. However there are no objects to take bearings of when anchoring as hills on either side are high and densely wooded.

208 **Browning Passage**, between Balaklava and Nigei Islands, provides an alternative route from Goletas Channel to Gordon Channel and is convenient for vessels leaving Port Alexander. The fairway is 0.2 mile wide but, because of drying rocks on both sides, the passage should be navigated during daylight hours.

209 **Tidal streams** in Browning Passage set south on the flood and north on the ebb. Maximum rate is 3 kn.

210 **Booming grounds** lie east of the islets and drying reefs off the east shore.

211 **Raglan Point**, several drying rocks and **Cardigan Rocks** are at the NE entrance to Browning Passage.

Browning Passage to Bull Harbour

212 **Mount Lemon** *(50°53'N, 127°47'W)* is a conspicuous conical peak on Nigei Island. **Magin Saddle**, 1.5 miles west of Mount Lemon, has two peaks. The south side of Nigei Island is in most places steep-to and cliffy.

213 **Loquillilla Cove**, on the south side of Nigei Island, affords shelter to small craft during west winds. **Lemon Point** and **Gorotisa Point**, west of Loquillilla Cove, are on the north and south sides respectively, of Goletas Channel.

214 **Willes Island** is separated from the west extremity of Nigei Island by a narrow channel, encumbered with rocks. **Slave Island**, 3 m high, is 0.3 mile south of Willes Island.

215 **Shushartie Bay** *(50°51'N, 127°52'W)* is fairly sheltered and offers anchorage, with limited space in the centre of the bay SW of Dillon Rock light in 43 to 49 m. **Halsted Islet** is connected to its east entrance point by a drying reef. **Dillon Rock** lies in the entrance to Shushartie Bay. A house in ruins on the shore south of Halsted Islet is conspicuous from NW.

216 **Light**. — Dillon Rock light *(572)* is on the rock.

217 **Tides**. — Tidal differences for Shushartie Bay (Index No. 8416), referenced on Alert Bay, are in *Tide Tables, Volume 6*.

218 **Heath Point**, the south extremity of Hope Island, is bold and steep-to. The cove west of Heath Point affords anchorage for small craft seeking shelter from west winds.

219 **Jepther Point**, 1.5 miles SW of Heath Point, is a low projection fringed with a beach. Landing west of the point is difficult except in calm weather.

220 **Godkin Point** *(50°54'N, 127°56'W)* and **Jones Point**, 0.6 mile WNW, are high, steep, cliffy bluffs; they are the entrance points to Bull Harbour.

221 **Light**. — Godkin Point light *(573)* is shown at an elevation of 17.2 m from a white tower with a red band at the top. A wind-powered generator on a skeleton tower is nearby.

Bull Harbour

222 **Bull Harbour**, entered between Jones and Godkin Points, is an indentation on the south side of Hope Island. The island belongs to the Tlatalsikwala First Nation and should not be landed on without permission. The harbour is often crowded with commercial fishing vessels during fishing season. During SE gales winds gust through the harbour, when Pine Island *(50°58'N, 127°43'W)* was reporting SE winds at 70 kn, measured gusts in Bull Harbour were 55 kn. West gales are generally of lower velocity in the harbour but they can blow quite strongly. **Norman Island**, 0.8 mile north of Jones Point, is close to the west shore, the fairway passes east of it. A drying mud and sand flat fills the head of the harbour.

Chart 3549

223   **Lights**. — Bull Harbour Entrance light *(573.6)*, 0.1 mile NE of Norman Island, is shown at an elevation of 4 m from a dolphin.

224   A **radio tower** on the isthmus at the north end of the harbour has red air obstruction lights.

225   **Speed**. — No vessel shall navigate in Bull Harbour at a speed exceeding 3 kn.

226   **Anchorage**, with good holding ground in heavy mud, can be obtained by small vessels in Bull Harbour. Above Norman Island anchorage is secure but with limited scope. The south part of the bay is reported to be fouled with old chain and cable, the bottom is reported to be less foul toward the head of the bay. When strong winds are forecast ensure the anchor has adequate scope.

227   **Wharves**. — A wharf, on the east shore about 0.2 mile north of Norman Island, has a berthing face of 15 m and a depth of 6 m alongside. A float is attached to the north side of the wharf. A 3 tonne crane is on the wharfhead and the wharf is floodlit. A dolphin close south is connected to the wharf by a catwalk.

228   A **public float**, not connected to shore, is 0.2 mile SE near the entrance light.

229   **Meteorological information** and a frequency of fog table for Bull Harbour are in the Appendices.

Bate and Shadwell Passages

230   **Bate Passage** *(50°53'N, 127°51'W)* leads NE from Goletas Channel to Gordon Channel, it lies between Nigei Island on the SE and Hope and Vansittart Islands on the NW. The fairway is straight, not less than 0.5 mile wide, and can be taken with safety.

231   **Tidal streams** set SW on the flood and NE on the ebb. In both Bate and Shadwell Passages they are strong, attaining 5 kn at times. Strong tide-rips form off the SW side of Vansittart Island and in the vicinity of Centre Islet.

232   **Quoin Island** and **Kalect Island** *(50°54'N, 127°51'W)* lie close-off the coast of Hope Island at the south end of Bate Passage. The bay north of Kalect Island is mainly foul. The site of the Indian village on the east entrance point of the bay can be identified by a conspicuous clearing.

233   **Vansittart Island** *(50°55'N, 127°48'W)* and **Nicholas Islands** separate the north end of Bate Passage from Shadwell Passage. **Stick Island** lies close south and **Flat Island** and a rock that dries 0.9 m lie close east of Vansittart Island. **Magicienne Point** is the SE extremity of Vansittart Island.

234   **Roller Reef**, 0.3 mile NNE of Flat Island, has 4 m over it. Thornton Reef, 0.8 mile NE of Roller Reef, lies in the north approach to Bate Passage and is described with Gordon Channel.

235   **Shadwell Passage**, entered from Bate Passage between **Pivot Point** and Vansittart Island, leads north to Gordon Channel. The passage is not recommended because of numerous islets, rocks and shoals. A heavy swell is usually present at the north end of the passage.

236   **Centre Islet** is 0.4 mile NE of Pivot Point. **Suwanee Rock**, 0.1 mile WNW of Centre Islet, dries 1.4 m. **Onetree Islet**, 0.5 mile NNE of Centre Islet, has a dead snag on its summit and is conspicuous from north. **Breaker Reef**, 0.4 mile north of Onetree Islet, has 1.4 m over it. Numerous drying, above and below-water rocks extend from the NW shore of Vansittart Island.

237   **Anchorage** sheltered from all but north winds can be obtained in Shadwell Passage about 0.2 or 0.3 mile NNW of Centre Islet.

Nahwitti Bar

238   **Nahwitti Point** *(50°54'N, 127°59'W)* is 2 miles west of Bull Harbour. **Mexicana Point**, 0.7 mile NW, is the west extremity of Hope Island.

239   **Light**. — Nahwitti Point light *(574)* is shown at an elevation of 15.3 m from a white tower, 6.1 m high.

240   **Nahwitti Bar** extends from the west end of Hope Island, across the west entrance to Goletas Channel. **Tatnall Reefs**, on the south part of Nahwitti Bar, extend NW from Vancouver Island. The fairway north of Tatnall Reefs is about 0.8 mile wide with depths of 11 m. Depths on the seaward side of the bar increase very gradually but on the inside they increase suddenly to about 72 m. **A swell is nearly always present on the bar. In bad weather with a west wind opposing a strong west-going tidal stream, there is a very heavy sea on it that breaks and is dangerous to small vessels. In strong west gales, the sea breaks across the bar and it is dangerous to attempt crossing the bar.**

241   **Tidal streams** set fairly across Nahwitti Bar in the direction of the channel and attain 5½ kn. The flood sets east and the ebb west. Secondary current station Nahwitti Bar (Index No. 6220), referenced on Alert Bay, is in *Tide Tables, Volume 6*. The duration of HW and LW slack is about 12 and 17 minutes, respectively. **Heavy rips and overfalls are formed when the tidal stream is opposed by strong winds, these rips and overfalls can be dangerous to small craft. The best time to cross the bar is at or near slack water.**

242   It is reported that small craft can avoid crossing Nahwitti Bar by passing south of Tatnall Reefs and following the Vancouver Island shore. Weser Island can be then passed on either north or south side. Shelter can be found in the bay on the east side of Cape Sutil if required.

243   **Light buoy**. — Nahwitti Bar light and whistle buoy "MA" *(575)*, 2.2 miles west of Nahwitti Point, is a fairway buoy.

244   **Cape Sutil** *(50°52'N, 128°03'W)*, the north tip of Vancouver Island, is a low promontory. **Northwest Nipple** *(Chart 3598)*, 1.5 miles SW of Cape Sutil, has an elevation of 229 m and is a prominent landmark. **Weser Island** lies 1 mile ESE and **Edmund Rock** 0.2 mile north of Cape Sutil.

Slingsby Channel

Chart 3550

245   **Slingsby Channel** *(51°05'N, 127°39'W)* is the main channel leading from Queen Charlotte Strait to Seymour Inlet. It lies along the north sides of **Fox Islands** and Bramham Island. The fairway through Slingsby Channel is about 0.1 mile wide in its narrowest parts but depths are in excess of 37 m. Channels between Fox Islands are not navigable. The channel between the east Fox Island and Bramham Island is only suitable for small craft, local knowledge is advised.

246   **Outer Narrows**, at the west end of Slingsby Channel south of **Vigilance Point**, is about 0.1 mile wide with depths of 35 m. The narrows should be navigated only at or near slack water; small vessels should also await fine weather.

247   **Tides**. — Tidal differences in Slingsby Channel, referenced on Alert Bay, are given for Treadwell Bay (Index No. 8440) in *Tide Tables, Volume 6*.

Chart 3550

248   **Tidal streams** in Slingsby Channel flow east on the flood and west on the ebb. In Outer Narrows the flood attains 7 kn and the ebb 9 kn. Secondary current station Slingsby Channel (Outer Narrows) (Index No. 6770), referenced on Nakwakto Rapids, is in *Tide Tables, Volume 6*. Slack water lasts about 15 minutes.

249   **Caution. — At the entrance to Outer Narrows, a west wind against a strong ebb tide forms a steep short swell that can be dangerous to small craft. With a strong ebb during these conditions, mariners should be careful not to be carried into the narrows, as it is very difficult to reverse or turn in Outer Narrows.**

250   **Vigilance Cove**, on the north side of Outer Narrows, is too exposed to be used as an anchorage.

251   A rock that dries 2.7 m lies close-off the north shore, 0.6 mile east of Vigilance Point and a rock with less than 2 m over it lies 0.1 mile west of **Digby Point** *(51°05'N, 127°35'W)*. The bay between **Town Point** *(51°06'N, 127°35'W)* and **Boot Point** is almost filled by foul ground.

252   Drying and above-water rocks lie off the north shore of the middle Fox Island. **Stream Point**, on the north side of Bramham Island, is 0.25 mile SE of Boot Point.

Chart 3921

253   **Slingsby Rock**, close south of **Anchor Islands** *(51°06'N, 127°32'W)*, dries 2.4 m. It restricts the fairway south of it to a width of about 0.1 mile.

254   **Treadwell Bay** is approached between a rock awash, close east of the SE Anchor Island, and **Kitching Point**. It is entered between **Quiet Point** and the east side of Anchor Islands. The bay lies north of the larger Anchor Island and is well-sheltered from tidal streams. Two rocks, with less than 2 m over them, lie about 0.1 mile offshore on the south side of Treadwell Bay. There is a lodge located at Treadwell Bay.

255   **Anchorage** for small vessels, with good holding ground, can be obtained in Treadwell Bay. It is used by vessels awaiting slack water at Nakwakto Rapids or Outer Narrows. Because of lack of swinging space, mooring is recommended.

256   **Tides.** — Tidal differences for Treadwell Bay (Index No. 8440), referenced on Alert Bay, are in *Tide Tables, Volume 6*.

Allison Harbour, Schooner Channel and Approach

257   **Knight Island** *(51°00'N, 127°32'W)* and **Southgate Island** are the two largest islands in Southgate Group.

258   **Anchorage** can be obtained between Knight Island and the mainland, it is completely sheltered but suitable only for small vessels owing to dangers within the entrance. Approach the anchorage between **Stevens Island** and Knight Island. The best position in which to anchor is with **Guard Rock** bearing 250°, distant 0.1 mile, in 26 m, mud and sand. **New Island** lies 0.2 mile NNE of Guard Rock.

259   **Tidal streams** in the anchorage do not exceed 1 kn, the turn occurs at HW and LW.

260   Dangers in the approach to Allison Harbour lying between Southgate and Emily Groups are **Elizabeth Rocks**, with shoals extending 0.35 mile SW, **Woods Rock** and **Slater Rocks**.

Shoal areas, with less than 2 m over them, lie 0.5 mile WNW and 0.4 mile SE of Slater Rocks.

261   **Frederick Islands**, 0.5 mile NNE of Slater Rocks, are wooded. **Town Rock**, 0.5 mile east of Frederick Islands, is 2 m high. **Allison Reefs**, south and SW of Town Rock, have less than 2 m over them.

262   **Beacons.** — **Eno Island** daybeacon, on the SW extremity of the island, has a starboard hand daymark.

263   **City Point** daybeacon has a starboard hand daymark.

264   **Allison Harbour**, entered north of City Point and east of **Ray Island** and **Roy Islet**, extends nearly 2 miles NNE. A cove on the east side of the fairway and 0.6 mile within the entrance is the site of an abandoned settlement. A rock, with less than 2 m over it, and drying rocks lie close-off the east shore and numerous drying and below-water rocks are at the head of the harbour.

265   **Anchorage**, mud bottom, can be obtained in 13.7 m 0.8 mile north of City Point, or in 12.8 m about 0.1 mile north of the 2.4 m drying rock, or in 7 m near the head of the harbour.

Charts 3550, 3921

266   **Directions.** — From SE the most direct approach to Allison Harbour or Schooner Channel is between Harris Island and Southgate Group, taking care to avoid the shoals SW of Tinson Islands. Approaching from NW give Dickenson Rock a wide berth and set a course to pass about 0.15 mile north of Harris Island. Pass about 0.1 mile off the NW coast of Southgate Group taking care to avoid Elizabeth Rocks and the shoals SW of them. Favour the Southgate Island shore until the drying reef 0.3 mile NE of Elizabeth Rocks is cleared then set a course with City Point daybeacon ahead bearing 021° to pass between Eno Island and the east danger of Allison Reefs. Favour the west shore of Allison Harbour.

Chart 3921

267   **Eliza Islands** *(51°02'N, 127°33'W)* are two densely wooded islands. Cliffs on the NW side of the larger island have some conspicuous white marks on them. **Deloraine Islands** lie NE of Eliza Islands. An extensive area of foul ground, with numerous above-water and drying rocks, extends NW from Deloraine Islands. **Murray Labyrinth**, NE of Deloraine Islands, consists of numerous islands and islets. The passage between Deloraine Islands and Murray Labyrinth and the passage along the north side of Murray Labyrinth are suitable for small craft.

268   **Skull Cove**, NW of Deloraine Islands, is entered NE of the island lying in the entrance. It affords good shelter for small craft. Two drying rocks lie in the middle of the cove.

269   **Schooner Channel** entered from the south between Ray Island and the rocks off the south extremity of Murray Labyrinth, leads north into the east end of Slingsby Channel. Murray Labyrinth and Bramham Island form its west side and the mainland its east side. The fairway through Schooner Channel is narrow with several dangers and is reduced to 61 m wide west of a reef with 1.8 m over it and some islets 1.8 miles north of Ray Island. Two drying rocks lie in mid-channel, SE of **Goose Point**, at the north end of the passage. It is not advisable to attempt this channel without local knowledge.

270   **Tidal streams** through Schooner Channel attain 5 kn on the flood and 6 kn on the ebb. Secondary current station Schooner Channel (Index No. 6750), referenced on Nakwakto Rapids, is in *Tide Tables, Volume 6*.

Chart 3921

271   **Anchorage** for small craft is reported to be excellent in the bay at the NE end of the channel, SE of Goose Point.

272   **Butress Island**, with a smaller island close south of it, lies in the north approach to Schooner Channel. Passages east and west of Butress Island are encumbered with rocks and tidal streams are strong, they should be navigated with caution and local knowledge is advised. **Cougar Inlet** *(51°05′N, 127°30′W)*, entered south of **Barrow Point**, has a narrow entrance with a least depth of 0.6 m, and is suitable only for small craft.

Nakwakto Rapids

273   **Nakwakto Rapids** *(51°06′N, 127°30′W)*, between **Harvell Point** and an island 0.2 mile south of **Johnson Point**, connects Slingsby and Schooner Channels to Seymour Inlet. **Turret Rock**, known locally as Tremble Island, lies in the middle of the rapids and has dangerous reefs extending up to 0.1 mile SSW of it. Turret Rock can be passed on either side but the west channel is preferred.

274   **Caution. — Mariners are strongly advised to navigate Nakwakto Rapids only at slack water. At no other time is it possible to navigate this rapid safely.**

275   **Tides.** — Tidal differences for Johnson Point (Index No. 8470), referenced on Alert Bay, are in *Tide Tables, Volume 6.*

276   **Tidal streams** in Nakwakto Rapids attain a maximum of 11½ kn on the flood and 14½ kn on the ebb, one of the highest rates in the world, their main strength impinging on Turret Rock. Duration of slack is about 6 minutes.

277   Daily predictions for times of slack water, and times and rates of maximum flood and ebb streams, are tabulated for current station Nakwakto Rapids (Index No. 6700) in *Tides Tables, Volume 6.*

Seymour Inlet

Chart 3552

278   **Seymour Inlet** *(51°06′N, 127°30′W)* is entered through Nakwakto Rapids, which lies 5 miles from its west end and 38 miles from its east end. Sides of the inlet are steep and mountainous and an ice field, on a plateau at the east end of the inlet, can be a source of Squamish winds during winter months. Belize Inlet is entered 2.5 miles WNW of Nakwakto Rapids. Nugent and Frederick Sounds are entered 1.5 and 29 miles east, respectively, of Nakwakto Rapids.

279   **Tides.** — Tidal differences in Seymour Inlet, referenced on Alert Bay, are given for Johnson Point (Index No. 8470) in *Tide Tables, Volume 6.*

Seymour Inlet — East Part

280   **Harvell Islet** *(51°06′N, 127°29′W)* and **Holmes Islets**, 0.3 mile east, lie in the entrance to the east part of Seymour Inlet. Drying, above and below-water rocks lie about 0.1 mile north of Harvell Islet and NE of Holmes Islets. A rock with 6.2 m over it lies 0.1 mile SSE of Harvell Islet and a rock with 2.1 m over it lies about 0.1 mile west of Holmes Islets. The fairway lies to the south of Harvell Islet and Holmes Islets.

281   **Nugent Point** *(51°05′N, 127°28′W)* is the south entrance point to Nugent Sound. Two islets lie 0.1 mile SSE of Nugent Point; drying rocks and shoals lie NW and SE of them.

282   **Nugent Sound**, entered between **Holmes Point** and Nugent Point, extends 10.5 miles east from Seymour Inlet.

283   **Tides.** — Tidal differences for Nugent Sound (Index No. 8464), referenced on Alert Bay, are in *Tide Tables, Volume 6.*

284   A **fishing boundary marker** is 1 mile east of Holmes Point on the north side of the sound.

285   **Rock.** — A rock awash *(51°05′N, 127°15′W)* lies in mid-channel about 2.5 miles from the inner end of Nugent Sound.

286   **Anchorage** for small vessels can be obtained in the bay NW of the island in mid-channel 3 miles inside the entrance, depths are about 15 m, sand. Anchorage can also be obtained in the bay at the head of Nugent Sound on the north side in a depth of about 23 m, mud and sand.

287   **Schwartzenberg Lagoon**, at the head of Nugent Sound, has a very narrow entrance with depths of less than 1 m and several drying rocks. Inside depths range from 50 to 75 m.

288   **Tidal streams** in the narrow entrance of Schwartzenberg Lagoon attain over 5 kn on the ebb.

289   **Charlotte Bay** *(51°04′N, 127°23′W)* is entered south of a group of islands that front its north entrance point. Several islets lie close-off the north shore east of the islands. A drying flat with boulders forms the head of the bay. Rocks marked by kelp during summer months lie off the south entrance point of the bay.

290   **Anchorage** for small vessels can be obtained in Charlotte Bay in 8 m, mud.

291   **Ellis Bay**, SW of Charlotte Bay, is entered south of **Isabella Point**. Several islands and drying rocks lie in its approach. Its narrow entrance, with a rock awash and numerous drying rocks, has a twisting channel through which depths of 0.2 m can be maintained. Local knowledge is advised. Depths inside the bay are about 6 m.

292   **Harriet Point** *(51°02′N, 127°19′W)* lies at a sharp S-bend in Seymour Inlet.

293   **Wawatle Bay**, entered south of Harriet Point, has depths of about 50 m, mud bottom. A rock awash lies close-off the north shore, about 0.5 mile inside its entrance.

294   An unnamed inlet extends 2.5 miles SE from the south entrance point of Wawatle Bay and is separated from Seymour Inlet by **Florence Range**. A log dump and booming ground are adjacent to the entrance to Woods Lagoon. **Woods Lagoon** enters the south side of this inlet about 1.3 miles inside the entrance. The entrance to Woods Lagoon dries and has several boulders in it, inside depths are about 8 m. The narrows at the head of the unnamed inlet has depths of less than 1 m and several obstructions in it. It is not suitable for navigation.

295   **Tidal streams** through the narrows are 6 kn on the ebb and 5½ kn on the flood. Secondary current station Nenahlmai Lagoon Entrance (Index No. 6710), referenced on Nakwakto Rapids, is in *Tide Tables, Volume 6.*

296   **Nenahlmai Lagoon** is entered through the narrows. **McKinnon Lagoon** extends NE and **Bamford Lagoon** extends west from it. A wreck is at the head of Bamford Lagoon. **Whelakis Lagoon**, at the south end of Nenahlmai Lagoon, is entered through a narrows with a depth of 0.8 m.

297   East of Harriet Point Seymour Inlet widens and depths in excess of 200 m are about 0.1 mile offshore.

Nakwakto Rapids on the ebb

Nakwakto Rapids on the ebb

Chart 3552

298   **Fishing boundary markers** are on Harriet Point and on the opposite shore west of the point. Fishing boundary markers, on the north and south shores, are 1.4 miles west of Harriet Point.

299   A group of islands north of Harriet Point lies in the entrance to a bay to the NW. A rock that dries 0.5 m lies north of the largest island and about 0.1 mile off the north shore. Ruins of a barge and a cabin are at the head of the bay.

300   An unnamed bay, 1.2 miles NE of Harriet Point, has a large island in its centre and two islets close-off its west entrance point. A rock that dries 1.1 m lies in the west part of the bay, about 0.1 mile north of the islets. Depths north of the large island are about 16 m.

301   **Frederick Bay** *(51°02′N, 127°14′W)*, entered between **Henry Point** and **Nea Point**, is too deep for anchorage. A small cove on its west side has depths of about 30 m and offers shelter for small craft.

302   **Warner Bay**, 5 miles east of Frederick Bay, has a low islet and some drying rocks close-off its east entrance point. A rock that dries 1.2 m lies in the centre of the bay about 0.2 mile from its head. Booming grounds with a large shed and float are at the head of the bay. A fishing boundary marker is on the west entrance point of Warner Bay and another is 0.6 mile east of it.

303   **Hibbard Point**, 2 miles ENE of Warner Bay, has a hooked peninsula on its west side with a small island close SW. Depths between the island and shore are 25 m. A waterfall is halfway between Hibbard Point and **Poison Point**.

304   **Conical Range** extends along the north side of Seymour Inlet, from **Mensdorff Point** to **Stripe Bluff**. The bays west of **Shaffer Point** and east of Stripe Bluff are too deep for anchoring.

305   **Safe Cove**, NE of **Howard Point**, can offer temporary anchorage to small vessels in depths of about 27 m within 0.1 mile of shore; outside this distance depths drop off steeply.

306   **Jesus Pocket** *(51°05′N, 126°54′W)* is the local name for the small cove midway between Safe Cove and Maunsell Bay. The cove is entered to the east of the islet lying in its entrance.

307   **Anchorage** for small vessels can be obtained in Jesus Pocket in 7 m, sand.

308   **Towry Point** is a hook shaped point south of Jesus Pocket. The small cove west of the point has depths of 6 m in it and offers shelter for small craft. The cove on the east side of the point has a treed islet near its head, close-off its north shore. Depths south of the islet are about 5 m, outside the islet depths drop off steeply.

309   A **conspicuous waterfall** is on the south shore of Seymour Inlet about 1 mile east of Towry Point.

310   **Maunsell Bay**, entered between **Dine Point** and **Martin Point**, has a bottom of sand, mud and shells but is too deep for satisfactory anchorage. The inlet at its NE end has a narrow entrance with depths in excess of 20 m. A conspicuous waterfall is near the south entrance point to the inlet. Anchorage for small vessels can be obtained near the head of the inlet in 24 m, mud and gravel.

311   A **fishing boundary marker** is on the south side of **Brew Peninsula** about 2 miles east of Martin Point. Another marker is on the south shore of Seymour Inlet about 2.5 miles east of **Miles Point**.

312   **Eclipse Narrows** *(51°04′N, 126°46′W)*, the entrance to Frederick Sound, is about 90 m wide with a fairway depth of 11 m. An old log dump is 0.2 mile SW of its south entrance point.

313   **Tidal streams** in Eclipse Narrows attain 5 kn. Secondary current station Eclipse Narrows (Index No. 6730), referenced on Nakwakto Rapids, is in *Tide Tables, Volume 6*.

314   **Tides**. — Tidal differences for Frederick Sound (Index No. 8458), referenced on Alert Bay, are given in *Tide Tables, Volume 6*.

315   **Frederick Sound** extends east and then south for about 5.5 miles from Eclipse Narrows. About 1 mile east of Eclipse Narrows the sound curves south and depths increase to more than 200 m. Several waterfalls and slide areas are on both sides of the sound. The head of Frederick Sound curves sharp west then opens into a basin, with depths of 50 to 60 m, mud bottom.

316   **Salmon Arm**, entered between **Nose Point** and **Taaltz Point**, extends about 2.5 miles east from Frederick Sound and has waterfalls and slide areas on both sides. **Green Point** is on the north shore near the head of the arm. Depths gradually decrease up the arm and the bottom is mud.

317   **Haig Bay** *(51°07′N, 126°45′W)*, on the east shore of Seymour Inlet 3 miles NE of Eclipse Narrows, is deep and its slopes are steep. **Wigwam Bay**, 1 mile NE of Haig Bay, is also deep with steep slopes, **Rainbow Creek** flows into its head.

318   **Seymour River** flows into the head of Seymour Inlet across a steep-to drying flat composed of stones and boulders. A logging camp with extensive booming grounds is on the east side of the river entrance.

Seymour Inlet — West Part

319   A **fishing boundary marker** is on the north shore of Seymour Inlet, 0.5 mile north of Johnson Point *(50°06′N, 127°30′W)*.

320   **Mignon Point** *(51°08′N, 127°33′W)* should be given a wide berth because of drying rocks lying 0.1 mile off it.

321   **Helm Island**, 1.5 miles WNW of Mignon Point, has drying above and below-water rocks extending west of it to the mainland. **Rowley Bay**, entered south of Helm Island, has a mud bottom.

322   **Lassiter Bay**, NW of Helm Island, has a mud bottom and forms the NW end of Seymour Inlet. **Jezzard Rock** lies 0.5 mile NW of Helm Island and about 0.1 mile off the south shore of the bay.

Belize Inlet

323   **Belize Inlet** *(51°08′N, 127°33′W)* is entered north of Mignon Point and extends 25 miles east. The sides of the inlet are steep and mountainous. **Fraser Range**, **Nicholl Range** and **Tottenham Range** are on its south side. The head of the inlet reaches within 1 mile of Maunsell Bay in Seymour Inlet.

324   **Anchorage** can be found in Westerman Bay, Mereworth Sound and Alison Sound.

325   **Tides**. — Tidal differences for Belize Inlet (Index No. 8482), Mereworth Sound (Index No. 8476) and Alison Sound (Index No. 8488), all referenced on Alert Bay, are in *Tide Tables, Volume 6*.

326   A **conspicuous white cliff** is on the north shore 0.7 mile NE of Mignon Point.

327   **Westerman Bay** *(51°08′N, 127°28′W)*, on the north side of Belize Inlet, is entered west of **Charles Point** and has depths of

Chart 3552

42 m, sand bottom. Depths shoal rapidly near its head. Small craft can find anchorage at the head of the bay in about 4 m.

328   **Mereworth Sound**, 2 miles east of Westerman Bay, extends 4.5 miles north then 6.5 miles east. Islets and drying rocks lie off the west entrance point.

329   **Strachan Bay**, on the west side of Mereworth Sound, affords anchorage in its SW part, mud bottom. A narrow channel that dries at its NE end leads into **Pack Lake**. A small cove at the SW end of Strachan Bay has a narrow entrance with depths of 3 m, it offers shelter and anchorage for small craft.

330   **Village Cove**, on the east side of Mereworth Sound, offers anchorage that is well sheltered by two wooded islands in its entrance. A drying reef and a rock, with less than 2 m over it, lie off the west shore NW of Village Cove.

331   **Rock Island** lies on the south side of the fairway about 2.3 miles east of the point where Mereworth Sound makes its abrupt turn east. A shoal, with 2.9 m over it, lies 0.1 mile off the north shore of Mereworth Sound, 1 mile WNW of Rock Island. A shoal with 4.8 m over it lies midway between Rock Island and an islet west of it. A rock with 0.5 m over it lies 0.1 mile off the south shore of Mereworth Sound, about 1 mile east of Rock Island.

332   **Alison Sound** *(51°08'N, 127°07'W)* leads 3.5 miles NNE from Belize Inlet then 8 miles in an easterly direction. A sill, about 0.5 mile inside its entrance, has 21.4 m over it. A shoal with 3.4 m over it lies about 0.1 mile off the west shore, close south of the sill.

333   **Obstruction Islet** (local name), 1.4 miles inside Alison Sound, is 30 m high and conspicuous. A rock ledge that dries 0.6 m extends 10 m in a westerly direction from the west side of the islet. The channel west of the islet is about 80 m wide with a depth of 9.9 m. East of the islet the channel is narrower with a depth of 7 m.

334   **Tidal streams** through the narrows at Obstruction Islet have a maximum rate of 3 kn.

335   A bay on the north side of a peninsula, 0.7 mile north of Obstruction Islet, offers sheltered **anchorage** in depths of 42 m, mud and sand. A creek flowing into the head of this bay is a good source of fresh water.

336   The point on the east side of Alison Sound, 0.4 mile north of the above-mentioned bay, has a shoal spit, with 1.7 m over it, extending NW from it and should be given a wide berth. The sound curves east around this point.

337   **Chief Nollis Bay**, 2 miles north of Obstruction Islet, has a steep-to drying flat at its head. Depths in the bay are 60 to 70 m, mud bottom. A shoal with 2.2 m over it lies in its entrance, 0.2 mile off its east entrance point.

338   **Peet Bay**, on the south shore of Alison Sound, has depths of 7 m near its head. Small craft can find sheltered anchorage in this bay.

339   **Summers Bay**, on the north shore of Alison Sound, has quite steep slopes that level out at a depth of 70 m, mud and sand bottom. A conspicuous waterfall is at the head of the bay. Small craft can find anchorage close to shore.

340   **Waump Creek** flows into the head of Alison Sound across steep-to drying flats.

CHAPTER 9

West Coast Vancouver Island, Cape Sutil to Cape Beale

General

Chart 3001

1   This chapter covers NW and W coasts of Vancouver Island from Cape Sutil *(50°52'N, 128°03'W)* to Cape Beale *(48°47'N, 125°13'W)*.

2   **Vessel Traffic Services (VTS)**. — The area north and east of a line joining Triangle Island and Cape Scott is in *Sector Four* of the *Vancouver Traffic Zone* and is administered by *Comox Traffic*. Assigned frequency is 156.575 MHz, Channel 71. Calling-in Points are:

3   *Calling-in Point No. 40*, *Cape Scott*, is a line joining Cape Scott light *(66)* with Triangle Island. It is for changing from *Vancouver Traffic Zone* to *Tofino Traffic Zone*.

4   The area south of the line is in the *Tofino Traffic Zone*. Assigned frequency is 156.725 MHz, Channel 74. Calling-in Points are:

5   *Calling-in Point No. 12*, *Cape Scott/Triangle Island*, a line extending 281° from Cape Scott light *(66)* passing through Cox and Lanz Islands to Triangle Island.

6   *Calling-in Point No. 13*, *Zone Limit*, a line extending 220° from Triangle Island to the limit of the Territorial Sea.

7   *Calling-in Point No. 10*, *Solander Island*, a line extending 220° from Solander Island light *(77)* to the limit of the Territorial Sea.

8   *Calling-in Point No. 7*, *Estevan Point*, a line extending 220° from Estevan Point light *(114)* to the limit of the Territorial Sea.

9   *Calling-in Point No. 6*, *Amphitrite Point*, a line extending 220° from Amphitrite Point light *(135)* to the limit of the Territorial Sea.

10   A brief description of this VTS is in *PAC 200*. Details are in *Radio Aids to Marine Navigation (Pacific and Western Arctic)*.

11   **Fishing vessels**. — From April 15 to September 30 numerous fishing vessels can be encountered inside the 100 m line on La Pérouse Bank, in the approach to Juan de Fuca Strait. These vessels may be trolling, towing nets or particularly at night, they may be at anchor. Because of the prevalence of fog and low visibility, mariners approaching the area from any direction are advised to pass to the south and clear of the bank. Mariners obliged to cross the bank should navigate with extreme caution in order to avoid risk of collision with fishing vessels. Information concerning locations of concentrations of fishing vessels can be obtained from the Marine Communications and Traffic Services Centre *Tofino Traffic*. For further details see *Notices to Mariners 1 to 46 Annual Edition*.

12   **A Pacific Pilotage Authority boarding station** is off Cape Beale *(48°47'N, 125°13'W)* at the entrance to Trevor Channel in Barkley Sound. For details on how to obtain a Pilot see *PAC 200*.

13   **Military exercise areas** are offshore to the south and west of Solander Island *(50°07'N, 127°56'W)*. Area designations are WP, WCFA North, and WCFA South. These areas are used for anti-aircraft firing, air to sea firing and anti-submarine exercises.

For information on military exercise areas see *Notices to Mariners 1 to 46 Annual Edition* and monitor *NOTSHIP* broadcasts.

14   **A local magnetic anomaly**, differing as much as 7° from normal, was reported (1964) 75 miles SW of Cape Scott.

15   **Anomalous sounding**. — A depth of 20 fathoms (37 m), position doubtful, lies about 37 miles WSW of Cape Scott in *50°38'N, 129°22'W*.

16   **Tides**. — Tidal predictions along the west coast of Vancouver Island are given for Tofino (Index No. 8615). Tidal differences along the outer part of the west coast of Vancouver Island, referenced on Tofino, are given for Cape Scott (Index No. 8790), Kyuquot (Index No. 8710), and Ucluelet (Index No. 8595) in *Tide Tables, Volume 6*.

17   **Tidal streams and currents**. — Tidal streams along the west coast of Vancouver Island between Cape Scott and Cape Beale are significant over the continental shelf where they are modified by shelf waves which produce currents with comparable diurnal and semi-diurnal components. This makes it difficult to predict currents based on tide heights at Tofino or other coastal locations.

18   **Tidal streams in the open ocean** are rotary and rarely exceed 0.1 kn. Along the continental shelf tidal streams are more aligned with the coastline and appreciably stronger, up to ½ kn at times. The flood stream sets NW and accentuates the prevailing NW current in winter and reduces the SE current in summer. West of Tofino maximum flood occurs 3 h 50 before HW at Tofino. Caution should be exercised because tidal streams on the continental shelf are not always large enough to reverse direction of flow associated with non-tidal currents.

19   **Non-tidal currents between Cape Scott and Cape Beale** generally set to the NW in winter at 0.1 to 0.5 kn, although strong flows as large as 2 kn have been reported. Over the continental shelf currents are stronger and respond more quickly to changes in wind. In summer non-tidal currents within 10 miles of the coast continue to set NW at 0.3 kn. Farther offshore the current sets SE at 0.4 kn. In both cases they can be strengthened or reversed with strong winds.

20   **In shallow depths around Scott Islands** tidal streams are stronger than non-tidal currents and attain 2 to 3 kn. NW of Scott Islands, in the entrance of Queen Charlotte Sound, tidal streams are rotary turning clockwise. Maximum flood occurs 3 hours before HW at Tofino and sets 025° at 2 kn. The last of the flood sets 110° at about 1 kn. Maximum ebb occurs 3 hours before LW at Tofino and sets 230° at about 1½ kn. The last of the ebb sets 280° at about 1½ kn.

21   **To the NNE of Scott Islands on Cook Bank** *(51°00'N, 128°42'W)*, the tidal stream is rotary with the maximum flood running at 2 kn in a 040° direction, and the maximum ebb running in a 235° direction at 1¾ kn.

22   **Meteorological information** for Estevan Point and Tofino and frequency of fog tables for Cape Scott, Spring Island, Estevan Point and Tofino, and a wind table for Cape Beale are in the Appendices.

Chart 3001

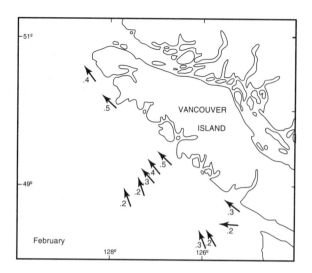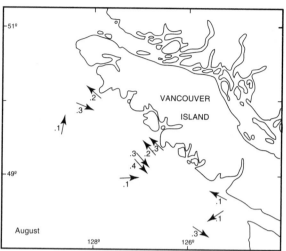

Non - tidal currents, summer and winter (rates in knots)

23   **Navigation**. — Loran-C coverage in open waters off the west and NW coasts of Vancouver Island is good. It is not reliable close to shore or in confined waters of inlets. For details regarding best signal strength and position fixing geometry see *PAC 200*.

24   A radiobeacon is located SE of Green Point in Tofino.

Cape Sutil to Scott Islands

Charts 3598, 3624

25   The coast from Cape Sutil to Cape Scott, 15 miles SW, is fringed with rocks and shoals to nearly 1 mile offshore and should be given a wide berth. **Thomsen Rock** lies 1.3 miles west of Cape Sutil. Strong in-draughts can be encountered.

26   A wreck, not dangerous to surface navigation, was reported (1989) to lie approximately 1.8 miles NNE of **Christensen Point**.

27   **Anchorage** for small craft can be obtained at the SW end of **Nissen Bight**, in **Fisherman Bay**. It is used by fishing vessels during south winds. A rock awash lies close north of the east entrance point to Fisherman Bay.

28   **Cape Scott Provincial Park** extends west from Shushartie Bay *(50°51'N, 127°52'W)* along the north shore of Vancouver Island to Cape Scott, then south to include San Josef Bay. The park is a wilderness area without supplies or equipment. Facilities are limited but include camp sites, pit toilets and launching for canoes and kayaks.

Charts 3625, 3624

29   **Cape Scott** *(50°47'N, 128°26'W)* is connected to the NW end of Vancouver Island by a low sandy isthmus.

30   **Light**. — Cape Scott light *(66)* is shown at an elevation of 229 feet (69.9 m) from a skeleton tower. Three white buildings are nearby.

31   A **frequency of fog table** for Cape Scott is in the Appendices.

32   **Nels Bight**, south of **Frederiksen Point**, is open to the west.

33   **Anchorage** for small craft can be obtained in **Experiment Bight**, on the north side of Cape Scott. A rock with less than 6 feet (1.8 m) over it lies about 0.2 mile off the west side of the bight and a drying rock lies close-off its south shore. **Guise Bay**, on the south side of Cape Scott, affords anchorage but has rocks in its approach and it is not advised to be entered without local knowledge. **Strange Rock**, 12 feet (3.7 m) high, lies in the south approach to Guise Bay.

34   **Scott Channel**, between Cape Scott and Scott Islands is a safe navigable channel in which the only dangers are rocks extending 0.5 mile off Cape Scott, and strong tidal streams. Small craft should try to navigate the channel at slack water and avoid conditions of wind against the tidal stream.

35   **Tides**. — Tidal differences for Cape Scott (Index No. 8790), referenced on Tofino, are in *Tide Tables, Volume 6*.

36   **Tidal streams** in Scott Channel set NE on the flood and SW on the ebb attaining 3 kn. After passing Cape Scott, the flood tidal stream divides, part turning east and flowing into Goletas Channel while the main stream continues NNE into Queen Charlotte Sound.

37   Predictions of times and rates of maximum current and time of slack water are given for Scott Channel (Index No. 8500) in *Tide Tables, Volume 6*.

38   **Heavy tide-rips and overfalls occur on both sides of Scott Channel. In conditions of wind against current, tide-rips and overfalls can be dangerous to small craft.**

Chart 3625

39   **Scott Islands** *(50°48'N, 128°50'W)* extend nearly 26 miles west from Cape Scott and consist of five named islands and several smaller unnamed islets and reefs. **Cox Island, Lanz Island** and **Beresford Island** are wooded. **Sartine Island** is grassy with islets and rocks extending west from it. **Triangle Island** *(50°52'N, 129°05'W)* is precipitous and bare.

40   **Ecological Reserves**. — Scott Islands Provincial Park consists of four Ecological Reserves. A permit is required to land on any of the Scott Islands.

41   **Caution. — When navigating near Scott Islands it is recommended they be given a good offing as tidal streams set**

Chart 3625

strongly through passages between them. **During the strength of the stream there are heavy tide-rips that are particularly dangerous to small craft.**

42   **Anchorage** can be obtained on the NW side of Cox Island and off the NE side of Lanz Island. Fair temporary anchorage during SW winds can be obtained about 0.3 mile from the head of the bight, on the NE side of Triangle Island.

43   **Cook Bank** extends up to 20 miles north of Scott Islands and the north coast of Vancouver Island and has depths less than 50 fathoms (91 m). It is used by commercial fishing vessels.

Cape Scott to Kwakiutl Point

Chart 3624

44   **Coast.** — The west coast of Vancouver Island from Cape Scott *(50°47'N, 128°26'W)* to Lawn Point *(50°20'N, 127°58'W)* is rocky and indented and should not be approached within the 20 fathom (37 m) line.

45   **Hansen Bay** and **Lowrie Bay** between Cape Scott and Cape Russell afford no shelter. Hansen Bay was the site of a Danish settlement in the early 1900's and is reported to be used by commercial fish boats.

46   **Cape Russell** *(50°41'N, 128°22'W)* is a conspicuous headland on which the sea breaks heavily.

47   **Sea Otter Cove**, east of Cape Russell, has mooring buoys and offers indifferent shelter. It is used by fish boats and small craft during summer months. **Winifred Islands**, bare and yellow topped, are conspicuous from NW. **Helen Islands**, in the entrance of the cove, are sparsely wooded. The most commonly used entrance to Sea Otter Cove lies between **Hanna Point** and Helen Islands. A landslide on **Mount St. Patrick** is a conspicuous landmark.

48   **Light.** — Sea Otter Cove light *(67)*, on the east side of the entrance channel to the cove, is shown at an elevation of 18 feet (5.5 m) from a mast.

49   **Beacon.** — Sea Otter Cove daybeacon, on an island in the middle of the cove, has a starboard hand daymark.

50   **San Josef Bay**, entered south of Hanna Point, affords no shelter except from north winds. Shores are high and fringed by drying reefs. **San Josef River**, at the head of the bay, can be entered at HW and small craft can obtain shelter.

51   **Anchorage** can be obtained 2 miles ESE or close NE of Hanna Point.

52   A **conspicuous tower** 6 miles east of San Josef Bay is on the summit of a hill.

53   **Cape Palmerston** *(50°36'N, 128°18'W)* is bold, rocky and rises steeply. **Raft Cove**, between Cape Palmerston and **Commerell Point**, affords no shelter. **Macjack River** enters the south part of the cove. **Raft Cove Provincial Park** is undeveloped.

54   **Bushby Rock**, 1.5 miles SW of Commerell Point, has 23 feet (7 m) over it. **Topknot Point** *(50°32'N, 128°13'W)* is low and takes its name from the shape of a hill close east.

Chart 3679

55   **Grant Bay** *(50°28'N, 128°05'W)* is exposed to all winds but anchorage in fine weather can be obtained near the middle of the bay in 11 m, sand bottom. **Quinn Rock**, 0.8 mile SE of **Lippy Point** and in the approach to Grant Bay, has 0.4 m over it.

56   **Cape Parkins** *(50°27'N, 128°03'W)* is precipitous and fringed with foul ground. **Parkins Rock**, 0.4 mile WSW of Cape Parkins, a drying rock and a rock awash, 0.4 mile NW, are marked by tide-rips. **Kwakiutl Point**, 6 miles SSE of Cape Parkins, is low and rocky.

57   **Vessel Traffic Services** (VTS). — *Calling-in Point No. 11* of the *Tofino Traffic Zone, Kains Island (Quatsino Sound)*, is a line joining Kwakiutl Point to Cape Parkins. When entering or leaving Quatsino Sound, a report should be made to *Tofino Traffic*. Assigned frequency is 156.725 MHz, Channel 74.

Brooks Bay

Chart 3680

58   **Brooks Bay**, entered between Lawn Point and Cape Cook *(50°08'N, 127°55'W)*, is open. Numerous shoals and rocks lie in the approaches to two inlets, at the head of the bay.

59   **Caution.** — Brooks Bay should not be entered east of a line joining its entrance points until leading marks for the inlets have been identified. When approaching from the north Lawn Point should be given a berth of at least 2 miles.

Klaskino Inlet and Approach

60   **Lawn Point** *(50°20'N, 127°58'W)* is low and grassy. **Restless Mountain**, 1.5 miles ENE of Lawn Point, has an elevation of 2,240 feet (683 m). **Sieward Hill**, 4.5 miles ENE of Lawn Point, is a useful leading mark when approaching from seaward. **Red Stripe Mountain**, 5 miles east of Lawn Point, has been logged along its SE slope.

61   **Scarf Reef**, 1 mile SW of Lawn Point, has 15 feet (4.6 m) over it and breaks in heavy weather. Several shoals extend 1.5 miles SE from the reef.

62   **Rugged Islands** *(50°19'N, 127°55'W)* have foul ground and shoals extending 1.5 miles SW and south of them.

63   **Light.** — Rugged Islands light *(75)*, on the north point of the north island, is shown at an elevation of 33 feet (10 m) from a mast. The light is obscured from 318° through north to 050°.

64   **Newton Entrance**, between the shoals extending SE from Scarf Reef and those SW of Rugged Islands, is the approach channel to Klaskino Inlet.

65   **Leading marks.** — The NW extremity of Rugged Islands in line with Sieward Hill, bearing 045°, leads through Newton Entrance.

66   **Side Bay**, with **Keefe Island**, **Mayday Island**, **Half Moon Islets** and **Keith River** on its west side, is too exposed for satisfactory anchorage.

67   **Heater Point** *(50°17'N, 127°52'W)* has **Morris Rocks** and **Steele Reefs** extending 1.8 miles NW from it. **Martin Rock**, 0.4 mile NNE from the north extremity of Steele Reefs, dries 3 feet (0.9 m). Drying and above-water rocks extend NE from Martin Rock to Half Moon Islets.

68   **Buoys. — Caution.** — Port hand buoy "M17" is SW of Martin Rock and starboard hand buoy "M18" is off the north extremity of Steele Reefs. These buoys, being in an exposed location, are particularly liable to be dragged off position during severe weather.

69   **Klaskino Inlet**, entered north of Heater Point between the buoys, offers two sheltered anchorages. Its shores are steep and

Chart 3680

mountainous. A logging road follows the north shore from Red Stripe Mountain to its head.

Chart 3651, 3680

70   **Klaskino Anchorage** *(50°18'N, 127°49'W)* is well-sheltered with depths of 15 to 18 m. Its entrance is slightly less than 0.1 mile wide between islets and rocks off the south extremity of **Anchorage Island** and the drying flat extending from the south shore of the inlet. A rock 1 m high and several drying rocks lie 0.3 mile west of the entrance and slightly more than 0.1 mile off the south shore. Public mooring buoys are in Klaskino Anchorage.

71   **Directions**. — Give Lawn Point *(50°20'N, 127°58'W)* a berth of at least 2 miles. Enter Newton Entrance with Sieward Hill in line with the NW extremity of Rugged Islands, bearing 045°. When Lawn Point bears 315°, alter course to pass midway between Rugged Islands and the mainland to the west and north. Round the north end of Rugged Islands and pass midway between Rugged Islands and Martin Rock. Pass midway between the buoys marking Martin Rock and the north end of Steele Reefs by keeping the south extremity of Anchorage Island ahead bearing 105°, proceed to the anchorage.

72   **Scouler Entrance**, north of Anchorage Island, leads NE to the inner part of Klaskino Inlet. Islets and shoals extend 0.15 mile south from **Mocino Point**. Drying reefs extend NW from the NW side of Anchorage Island, their west extremity is marked by starboard hand buoy "M22".

73   **Scouler Pass** leads through the chain of islands and reefs obstructing Klaskino Inlet NE of Anchorage Island. The north passage is about 76 m wide with a least depth of 10.7 m. The south passage is about 122 m wide with a least depth of 2.5 m.

74   **Beacons. — Buoy**. — Scouler Pass North daybeacon, on a drying reef on the south side of the north passage, has a starboard hand daymark.

75   Port hand buoy "M23" is on the north side of the north passage.

76   Scouler Pass South daybeacon, on a drying reef on the south side of the south passage, has a starboard hand daymark.

77   **Anchorage** is obtainable east of the chain of islands in Scouler Passage SW of **Langsdorff Point**, in about 37 m, mud. It is reported that small craft may anchor to the east of small island near the head of the inlet

Klaskish Inlet and Approach

Chart 3651, 3680

78   **Harris Peak** *(50°13'N, 127°44'W)* is easily identified by its sharp summit. **Shields Cone**, 1.5 miles north of Harris Peak, is a useful leading mark when approaching Klaskish Inlet.

79   **Hughes Rock** *(50°15'N, 127°53'W)* dries 5 feet (1.5 m) and breaks heavily. **Clerke Reefs**, 2.3 miles south of Hughes Rock, consist of two groups of drying reefs. A rock, 11 feet (3.4 m) high, is in the south group. Recommended approach to Klaskish Inlet is between Hughes Rock and Clerke Reefs.

80   **Directions**. — Shields Cone in line with Bonner Islet, bearing 084°, leads between Hughes Rock and Clerke Reefs, and between dangers on both sides of the entrance. When the NW Donald Islet bears 154°, alter course to pass midway between Bonner Islet and McDougal Island.

81   No attempt should be made to pass between Clerke Reefs, **Hackett Island**, **Guilliams Island**, **Clerke Islet** and Brooks Peninsula without local knowledge.

82   **Gould Rock** *(50°15'N, 127°50'W)* is surrounded by rocks awash and shoals. **Donald Islets**, on the south side of the entrance to Klaskish Inlet, have several drying and below-water rocks in their vicinity.

83   **Light**. — Donald Islets light *(76)*, on the north side of the north islet, is shown at an elevation of 90 feet (27.4 m) from a mast with a starboard hand daymark.

84   **Klaskish Inlet**, entered between **Orchard Point** and **Sapir Point**, offers anchorage SE of McDougal Island and in the basin at its head.

85   **McDougal Island** is wooded and fringed with shoals. **Bonner Islet**, 0.4 mile north of McDougal Island, is 75 feet (23 m) high and has a few stunted trees, the north shore of the inlet in its vicinity is fringed by reefs.

86   **Klaskish Anchorage**, SE of McDougal Island, offers small craft anchorage in 10 to 13 fathoms (18 to 24 m) but the bottom is irregular. A low swell is reported to be encountered in this anchorage even in calm days.

87   **Beacon**. — Klaskish Anchorage daybeacon, on a rock off the NE entrance point to the anchorage, has a port hand daymark.

88   **Klaskish Basin**, at the head of Klaskish Inlet, has a very narrow entrance, less than 300 feet (91 m) wide, but the least depth is 7 fathoms (13 m). The basin provides protection from all seas but strong winds blow down the mountains and through the **Klaskish River** valley. Public mooring buoys are in the basin.

89   Drying flats at the head of Klaskish Basin and the Klaskish River are an **Ecological Reserve**.

Brooks Peninsula

Charts 3680, 3623, 3604

90   **Brooks Peninsula** *(50°09'N, 127°50'W)* separates Brooks Bay from Checleset Bay. Shores are rocky and mountains rise abruptly to elevations in excess of 2,000 feet (600 m). The shelf edge lies only 4 miles SW of Brooks Peninsula where depths increase steeply into **Ououkinsh Canyon**. Waters off the peninsula are some of the most hostile on the West Coast. Caution and respect for weather and sea conditions is required when rounding the peninsula.

91   **Brooks Peninsula Provincial Park** encompasses the shoreline of Brooks Peninsula from Klaskish Inlet to Clerke Point. Also included are Nasparti Inlet, Johnson Lagoon and the west shore of Ououkinsh Inlet. The park is undeveloped.

92   **Cape Cook** *(50°08'N, 127°55'W)* is a conspicuous wooded bluff. Waters in this area can be very dangerous when conflicting currents meet accelerating winds. **Solander Island**, 1.3 miles SW of Cape Cook, is cone shaped. It is an Ecological Reserve, landing is prohibited without permit.

93   **Light**. — Solander Island light *(77)*, on the summit of the island, is shown at an elevation of 309 feet (94.2 m) from a white tower.

94   **Clerke Point**, the south extremity of Brooks Peninsula, lies 5 miles SE of Cape Cook. The coast between is foul and should be given a wide berth. **Banks Reef** dries 13 feet (4 m). **Eldridge**

Newton Entrance, leading marks (1988)

Shields Cone in line with Bonner Islet, bearing 084°   McDougal Island   Donald Islets

Klaskish Inlet, leading marks

(Original dated prior to 1866)

Solander Island light bearing 020° (1988)

Cutler Rock   Scarf Island, 019°   Nasparti Inlet   492m summit   O'Leary Islets

Leading marks for entering Nasparti Inlet

(Original dated 1862)

Charts 3680, 3623, 3604

Rock has 13 feet (4 m) over it and breakers are nearly always present.

Checleset Bay

Chart 3683

95   **Checleset Bay** (50°05'N, 127°40'W), between Clerke Point and the Mission Group 15 miles SE, has numerous islets and reefs that are a continuation of the Barrier Islands. Most of the sunken dangers are identifiable by breakers caused by heavy swell usually present in the bay. Nasparti Inlet, Ououkinsh Inlet and Malksope Inlet are approached through this chain of islets and reefs.

96   **Caution. — Recent surveys have determined that depths are shoaler than charted in Checleset Bay and in vicinity of Barrier Islands.**

97   Checleset Bay is an **Ecological Reserve**.

98   The coast along the SE side of Brooks Peninsula, NE of Clerke Point, known locally as Shelter Shed, is used as an anchorage by fishing vessels during NW winds.

99   **Caution. — To avoid approaching too close to Barrier Islands and their associated reefs, keep Solander Island bearing not less than 292° and open SW of Brooks Peninsula until marks and leading lines have been identified.**

Nasparti Inlet and Approach

100   **Directions.** — Approach Nasparti Inlet with Scarf Island in line with the 1,615 foot (492 m) summit close west of the head of the inlet, bearing 019°. This will lead between Baker Rock and Sulivan Reefs. When Yule Rock is nearly abeam, alter course to bring Lorenz Point ahead bearing 030° and just open west of another point 1 mile SSW, this course leads between the dangers SE of Scarf Island and a rock that dries 13 feet (4 m), 0.4 mile ESE of Scarf Island. When Scarf Island bears 270°, follow a midchannel course up the inlet.

101   **Sulivan Reefs** (50°04'N, 127°40'W) have less than 6 feet (1.8 m) over them. **Baker Rock**, 1.6 miles NW of Sulivan Reefs, is awash. **Cutler Rock**, 0.8 mile NNE of Baker Rock, is 13 feet (4 m) high. A 4 fathom (4.9 m) shoal lies 0.8 mile NNE of Cutler Rock. **Quineex Reef**, 1.6 miles west of Baker Rock, dries 8 feet (2.4 m). The leading marks for entering Nasparti Inlet pass between Sulivan Reefs and Baker Rock.

102   **O'Leary Islets** (50°06'N, 127°39'W) are sharp topped and steep sided. **Yule Rock**, 0.6 mile north of O'Leary Islets, is 19 feet (5.8 m) high. **Ferey Rock**, 0.7 mile NNW of Yule Rock, dries 10 feet (3 m).

103   **Jackobson Point**, the west entrance point of Nasparti Inlet, is low and a drying rock spit extends south from it. A rock with 16 feet (4.9 m) over it lies 0.2 mile east of Jackobson Point and **Boit Rock**, 0.3 mile NE of the point, has less than 6 feet (1.8 m) over it.

104   **Columbia Cove**, known locally as Peddlers Cove, is on the north side of Jackobson Point. The cove affords sheltered anchorage to small craft and has public mooring buoys.

105   **Nasparti Inlet** has high shores and a drying flat at its head. Booming grounds line the west shore, 1 mile north of **Lorenz Point**.

106   **Scarf Island**, in the middle of the entrance to Nasparti Inlet, is prominent from seaward. Steep-to reefs extend 0.2 mile west and north from the island. A rock, with less than 6 feet (1.8 m) over it, lies 0.1 mile ESE and a 4 fathom (5 m) shoal is 0.2 mile SE of the island.

107   **Anchorage** can be obtained in about 22 fathoms (40 m), 0.4 mile WSW of Lorenz Point or in 15 fathoms (27 m), mud bottom, about 0.8 mile from the head of the inlet.

108   **Johnson Lagoon**, on the west side of Nasparti Inlet, has a very narrow rock encumbered entrance. There are tidal rapids in the narrows and entry by small craft can be made only at HW slack. At spring tides slack water is 2 hours after HW and 2 h 30 after LW.

Ououkinsh Inlet and Approach

109   **Byers Cone** (50°07'N, 127°36'W), at the SW end of **Acous Peninsula**, is well defined. **Cuttle Islets** with numerous drying reefs and shoals extend 1 mile south of Acous Peninsula.

110   **McKiel Rock**, 3 miles south of Byers Cone, dries 3 feet (0.9 m). **Clara Islet**, 1 mile NE of McKiel Rock, is 26 feet (7.9 m) high, bare and surrounded by drying reefs. Two detached shoals lie in the fairway NNW of Clara Islet. Recommended approach to Ououkinsh Inlet is between McKiel Rock and Sulivan Reefs.

111   **Ououkinsh Inlet**, entered between Cuttle Islets and **Mahope Point**, is deep and shores in its inner part are high. **Cautious Point**, **Checkaklis Island** and **Green Head** are named features SSE of Mahope Point.

112   **Directions.** — Approaching Ououkinsh Inlet from the south bring the west islet of O'Leary Islets into line with Scarf Island, bearing 350°. Keep on this leading line until Mahope Point bears 046° and is well open eastward of Izard Point. Steer for Mahope Point on this bearing. When the south Cuttle Islet bears 316° alter course into the inlet favouring the SE side of the fairway.

113   **Tides.** — Tidal differences in Ououkinsh Inlet, referenced on Tofino, are given for Bunsby Island (Index No. 8720) in Tide Tables, Volume 6.

114   **Battle Bay** with **Skirmish Islets** in its centre is encumbered with rocks and not recommended as an anchorage. However, it is reported small craft, using caution, can find anchorage in the vicinity of the Indian Reserve. **Longback Rocks**, SW of **Theodore Point**, lie east of the north entrance point of the bay.

115   **Gay Passage**, between the two largest **Bunsby Islands**, has a number of rocks in it but can be used by small craft, local knowledge is advised. It is reported anchorages suitable for small craft lie in Gay Passage, in the small bay on the east side of the south Bunsby Island, or the slightly larger bay on the west side of the north island. Careful navigation is required to avoid numerous rocks in this area.

116   **Izard Point** is bold. **Hisnit Islands**, on the NW side of the fairway, are steep-to on their south side. **Power River** flows into the inlet north of these islands.

117   **Ououkinsh River** flows into the head of the inlet across an extensive drying flat. A float with a hut on it is attached to the south shore near the outer end of the drying flat (1988). A logging road leads to the float from the valley to the south.

118   **Anchorage** can be obtained about 0.3 mile off the drying flats at the head of Ououkinsh Inlet, in 16 fathoms (29 m), mud.

Chart 3683

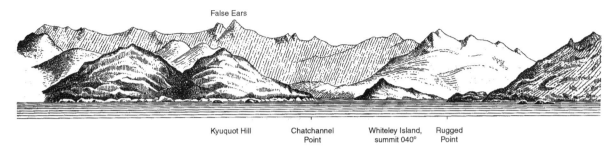

Leading marks for entering Kyuquot Sound
(Original dated 1862)

Malksope Inlet and Approach

119   **Malksope Inlet**, entered between **Upsowis Point** and **Malksope Point**, affords anchorage in 11 to 18 fathoms (20 to 33 m), mud. Several islets and rocks, 1.5 miles north of Malksope Point, obstruct the fairway. Pass NW of these islets to enter the inner part of the inlet.

120   **Mount Paxton** *(50°06'N, 127°28'W)* is conspicuous. **Thomas Island**, 2.4 miles SW of Mount Paxton, is cliffy and prominent.

121   **Caution. — Because of numerous dangers in the approach to Malksope Inlet no attempt should be made to approach the inlet except in clear weather, with the aid of local knowledge. Buoys marking the route are in an exposed location and are liable to be dragged off position during severe weather.**

122   **Buoyed route**. — Pass 0.5 mile west of the 15 foot (4.6 m) high rock 1.3 miles WNW of Lookout Island. Steer to pass east of the shoal marked by port hand buoy "M27", then pass west of the dangers NW of Thomas Island marked by starboard hand buoy "M28".

Approaches to Kyuquot Sound

Charts 3682, 3683, 3623

123   **Kyuquot Sound Approaches**. — **Barrier Islands** are a chain of islets and reefs extending 20 miles NW from **Jurassic Point** *(49°53'N, 127°11'W)* to the entrance of Ououkinsh Inlet.

124   Brown Channel is the most direct and safest approach for Clanninick Cove anchorage and Kyuquot. Kyuquot Channel is the safest and most direct approach for Kyuquot Sound.

125   **Caution. — During poor visibility keep in depths not less than 35 fathoms (64 m) when in the vicinity of Barrier Islands. Recent surveys have determined that depths are shoaler than charted in the vicinity of the Barrier Islands.**

126   **Mission Group** *(50°00'N, 127°25'W)*, part of the Barrier Islands, is an extensive group of islands and islets surrounded by reefs. **Spring Island**, **Aktis Island** and **Kamils Island**, locally known as Cemetery Island, are the largest islands in the group. **Sobry Island** is NE of Kamils Island. An occupied Indian settlement is on the east shore of Aktis Island.

127   A **frequency of fog table** for Spring Island is in the Appendices.

Chart 3683

128   **Kamils Anchorage** *(50°00'N, 127°24'W)*, in the middle of Mission Group, is approached from the south by **Favourite Entrance**. The anchorage is only suitable for small craft, local knowledge is advised. A narrow passage leads NE to **Barter Cove** which is shallow.

Brown Channel to Kyuquot

129   **Brown Channel**, entered between Spring Island and **Lookout Island**, leads north and NE to join the west end of Nicolaye Channel abreast **Ahmacinnit Island**, locally known as Deadman Island. Numerous islets and drying reefs fringe the south and west sides of Spring Island. **Trapp Bluff** is steep and prominent.

130   **Light**. — Lookout Island light *(78)*, on the east side of the island, is shown at an elevation of 48 feet (14.6 m) from a white tower with a green band at the top, on a white building.

131   An **abandoned submarine cable** crosses Brown Channel from Lookout Island to the south end of Spring Island.

132   **Cole Rock** *(50°01'N, 127°27'W)*, 19 feet (5.8 m) high, lies on the north end of a drying reef. **McLean Point** is the south extremity of **McLean Island**.

133   **Chief Rock**, 0.3 mile SE of McLean Island, dries 5 feet (1.5 m) and is marked by port hand buoy "M29".

134   **Clanninick Cove**, east of McLean Island, affords anchorage for small vessels in 9 fathoms (16 m). **Yakats Rock**, 0.3 mile north of Chief Rock, lies in the entrance of the cove and has less than 6 feet (1.8 m) over it. A rock, 2 feet (0.6 m) high, lies 0.2 mile east of Yakats Rock.

Chart 3651

135   **Gayward Rock** *(50°01'N, 127°23'W)* lies on the south side of the west end of Nicolaye Channel.

136   **Light**. — Gayward Rock light *(81)* is shown at an elevation of 8.2 m from a white tower 5.2 m high.

137   **Anchorage** can be obtained in mid-channel, 0.5 mile east of Gayward Rock, in a depth of 33 m.

138   **Walters Cove**, north of **Walters Island**, is approached from either the east or west sides of **Rolston Island**. Preferred approach is west of Rolston Island.

139   **Light**. — Rolston Island light *(81.5)*, on the west end of the island, is shown from a mast with a starboard hand daymark.

Chart 3651

140   **Beacons. — Buoys**. — The channel west of Rolston Island is marked by Rolston Island light, port hand buoy "M31" and starboard hand buoy "M32".

141   The channel east of Rolston Island is marked by two daybeacons; one has a starboard hand daymark and the other has a port hand daymark.

142   The fairway SW of **Kon Tiki Island** is marked by port hand buoys "M33" and "M35" and starboard hand buoy "M34".

143   Walters Island daybeacon, on the extremity of a breakwater extending from the NE end of the island, has a port hand daymark. A private daybeacon, on the island north of Walters Island daybeacon, has a white triangular slatwork daymark.

144   **Dredged channel**. — The channel between Walters Island daybeacon and the private daybeacon close north has been dredged to a width of 24 m and a depth of 4.6 m.

145   **Submarine cables and pipelines** cross the entrance channel and Walters Cove in several locations. Some are marked by signs and mariners should avoid anchoring in their vicinity.

146   An **overhead cable**, vertical clearance unknown, crosses between Kon Tiki Island and **Okime Island**.

147   Walters Cove and Nicolaye Channel SW of Walters Island is a **water aerodrome** known as Kyuquot.

148   **Tides**. — Tidal differences for Kyuquot (Index No. 8710), referenced on Tofino, are in *Tide Tables, Volume 6*.

149   **Kyuquot**, a settlement on the north shore of Walters Island, has about 300 full time residents. It has a post office, a store, accommodation, seasonal restaurant, sport fishing lodge, and a Red Cross Outpost Hospital under the charge of a resident nurse. A doctor makes scheduled visits. Fresh water is obtainable. A lift for boats up to 9 m and telephones are available. Air and water taxi services, daily from Artlish and Fair Harbour, are available. Scheduled freight service is provided by the Nootka Sound Service Ltd ferry (Uchuck III) operating from Gold River.

150   **Berths**. — The public wharf has berthing lengths of 31 m on its north and south faces and 15 m on its east face with a depth of 4.3 m alongside. A storage shed and a 3 tonne crane are on the wharf. Floats, attached to the north and south sides, are each 52 m long and for the use of small craft. Attention is drawn to submarine pipelines adjacent to the wharf. Numerous private floats are in the cove.

151   **McKay Cove**, about 0.5 mile north of Rolston Island, has an entrance almost completely blocked by rocks and islets. The approach channel, to the north of Okime Island, has a tidal fall. The channel east of the islands lying east of Kon Tiki Island is obstructed by a dam.

152   A **submarine pipeline** is laid from the east entrance point of the cove to Kon Tiki Island.

153   **Marine farm** facilities are located at the NE extremity of Kon Tiki Island.

Nicolaye Channel

Chart 3682

154   **Nicolaye Channel** *(50°00'N, 127°20'W)* leads between Barrier Islands and the SW coasts of Walters, Amos and Union Islands. It connects Brown Channel to Kyuquot Channel. An approach channel from the SW, between **Thornton Islands** *(49°58'N, 127°21'W)* and **Minx Rocks**, 0.2 mile NW, is not advised to be attempted without local knowledge as there are several dangers in it and no aids to navigation. Crowther Channel leads NE from Nicolaye Channel into Kyuquot Sound.

155   **Amos Island** *(50°01'N, 127°21'W)* has a chain of islets and rocks extending 0.6 mile SE from it. A drying rock, at the SE extremity of this chain, has a white concrete pyramid, 5 feet (1.5 m) high, on it. The pyramid is the remains of a daybeacon. A rock, with less than 6 feet (1.8 m) over it, lies about 0.1 mile SSE of the pyramid. The fairway SW of Amos Island is narrowed to 0.1 mile wide by above-water, drying and sunken rocks extending from the Mission Group.

156   **Light**. — Amos Island light *(82)*, on the SW extremity of the island, is shown at an elevation of 23 feet (7.1 m) from a white tower.

157   **Kate Rocks** *(49°59'N, 127°19'W)* are two bare rocks on the south side of Nicolaye Channel. A rock, with less than 6 feet (1.8 m) over it, lies in the fairway 0.8 mile NW of Kate Rocks. **Moos Islet** is the largest of a group of islets SW of Kate Rocks.

158   **Kyuquot Bay**, on the SW side of Union Island, is entered south of **Racoon Point**. The SE part of the bay is encumbered with islets and rocks and the bay is open SW.

Crowther Channel

159   **Crowther Channel** *(50°02'N, 127°19'W)* connects Nicolaye Channel to Kyuquot Sound. It is not recommended without local knowledge as the south entrance is encumbered with islets and rocks and the NE end is narrowed to about 300 feet (91 m) wide by **Surprise Island**.

160   A **sport fishing lodge** is in a cove on the southeast side of the channel.

161   **Traill Creek** flows into a bay 0.4 mile west of Surprise Island and has the site of a former wharf and cannery near its entrance.

162   **Fishing boundary markers** are on north and south shores abreast the east end of Surprise Island.

163   **Anchorage** for small craft can be obtained in 10 to 15 fathoms (18 to 27 m) in a bay north of Surprise Island.

Kyuquot Channel

164   **Union Island** *(50°00'N, 127°16'W)* lies in the entrance to Kyuquot Sound. **Kyuquot Hill**, on the south end of the island, is lower than hills on the north end but is prominent from seaward. **White Cliff Head** is the south extremity of the island.

165   **Remarkable Cone** *(49°58'N, 127°12'W)* and **Eliza Dome**, 6 miles SE, are prominent from seaward.

166   **Kyuquot Channel**, SE of Union Island, has a deep fairway not less than 0.7 mile wide and is almost straight.

167   **West Entrance Rock** *(49°57'N, 127°19'W)*, with less than 6 feet (1.8 m) over it, and **Munsie Rocks**, a group of above- and below-water rocks 0.8 mile NE, are on the west side of the approach to Kyuquot Channel.

168   **East Entrance Reef**, 2 miles ESE of West Entrance Rock, is 14 feet (4.3 m) high. A group of above-water and drying reefs lie 0.5 mile north of the reef. **Volcanic Islets** and **Nipple Rocks** lie north of the reef.

169   **Light buoy**. — Kyuquot Channel light and whistle buoy "M38" *(84)*, 0.7 mile west of East Entrance Reef, on the east side of the approach to Kyuquot Channel, is a starboard hand buoy.

170   **Rugged Point** *(49°58'N, 127°15'W)* is the SE entrance point to Kyuquot Channel.

171   **Light**. — Rugged Point light *(83)*, on the north end of the point, is shown at an elevation of 46 feet (14.1 m) from a mast with a starboard hand daymark.

Chart 3682

172   **Rugged Point Provincial Park** encompasses the area west of **Robin Point** and south to **Gross Point**. There is limited onshore development and bears are often encountered. **Anchorage** is obtainable between Rugged and Robin Points.

173   **McLean Cove** and **Volcanic Cove** are NE of Rugged Point.

174   **Chatchannel Point**, the east extremity of Union Island, is low and rocky with a well-defined knob close to its extremity. A rock, which dries 7 feet (2.1 m), lies 0.1 mile east of the point.

Clear Passage

175   **Clear Passage** is entered from north between **Grogan Rock** *(49°57'N, 127°15'W)* with shoals close NNW and a rock that dries 4 feet (1.2 m) 0.3 mile to the east. The passage leads SE inside the Barrier Islands to its south entrance between **McQuarrie Islets** and **Tatchu Rocks** and is only suitable for small craft. Local knowledge is advised. Drying reefs and below-water rocks, among which are **Kapoose Rocks**, extend up to 0.4 mile off the Vancouver Island shore. **Grassy Island**, **Diver Islet** and **Clark Island** are the central group of Barrier Islands in this vicinity; several drying reefs lie along this side of Clear Passage. **Kapoose Point**, **Brecciated Point**, **Mushroom Point** and **Gregoire Point** are named features on the mainland shore.

Tatchu Point to Estevan Point

Charts 3604, 3603

176   The coast between **Tatchu Point** *(49°51'N, 127°09'W)* and Estevan Point, 37 miles SE, is indented by Esperanza Inlet, Nuchatlitz Inlet and Nootka Sound.

177   **Caution. — Mariners are warned that there is likely to be an in-draught into these large inlets, especially during strong winds from SE to SW. This part of the coast should be given a wide berth.**

178   **Nootka Island** *(49°45'N, 126°50'W)* separates Esperanza Inlet from Nootka Sound. Its SW coast is low with sandy beaches in places, and the sea usually breaks heavily on it.

179   **Vessel Traffic Services**. — *Calling-in Point No. 9* of *Tofino Traffic Zone*, *Esperanza Inlet*, is a line joining Tatchu Point and Ferrer Point. When entering or leaving Esperanza Inlet report to *Tofino Traffic*. Assigned frequency is 156.725 MHz, Channel 74.

180   **Bajo Point** *(49°37'N, 126°50'W)*, the SW extremity of Nootka Island, is low and rocky. **Bajo Reef**, with depths of less than 2 m in places, and **Inner Bajo Reef**, which has several drying heads, extend 3 miles offshore.

181   **Light buoy**. — Bajo Reef light and whistle buoy "M56" *(106)*, south of the reef, is a starboard hand buoy.

182   **Vessel Traffic Services**. — *Calling-in Point No. 8* of the *Tofino Traffic Zone*, *Nootka Sound*, is a line joining Bajo Point and Estevan Point light *(114)*. When entering or leaving Nootka Sound report to *Tofino Traffic*.

Charts 3603, 3674

183   **Estevan Point** *(49°23'N, 126°33'W)*, the SW extremity of **Hesquiat Peninsula**, is low, wooded and fringed with drying and below-water rocks and a sand and boulder beach. **Perez Rocks**, 3 miles NW of Estevan Point, are a group of drying and below-water rocks.

184   **Hesquiat Peninsula Provincial Park** encompasses the peninsula south of Escalante Point *(49°32'N, 126°34'W)*. This park is a significant tourism corridor for coastal hiking, boating and sea kayaking and is home to the heritage attraction known as Cougar Annie's Garden. This undeveloped wilderness park has no facilities but camping is allowed.

185   **Meteorological information** and a frequency of fog table are given for Estevan Point in the Appendices.

186   **Light**. — Estevan Point light *(114)* is shown at an elevation of 37.5 m from a white tower.

Hesquiat Harbour

Chart 3674

187   **Hesquiat Harbour** is entered between **Matlahaw Point** *(49°23'N, 126°29'W)* and **Hesquiat Point**. **Hesquiat Bar**, across its entrance, protects the harbour to a great extent from the ocean swell. Kelp grows in patches on the bar. A drying reef lies 0.6 mile SW of Hesquiat Point. **Antons Spit**, on the west side and at the north end of the bar, has a rock that dries 3 m near its extremity. When covered the spit can usually be identified by breakers. At the head of the harbour a cabin is 0.5 mile west of Rae Basin and a wreck is on the beach close south of Rae Basin.

188   **Hesquiat**, on the west side of the harbour entrance, is an Indian village. The church near the north end of the village is prominent. A concrete breakwater at the south end of the village provides limited shelter.

189   **Anchorage** in Hesquiat Harbour is good. During strong south or SW gales the sea breaks heavily on Hesquiat Bar but the anchorage is safe and landing can always be made in Rae Basin. Anchor either 0.7 mile south of **Le Claire Point** in 16 m, mud, or 1 mile north of **Rondeault Point** in 14 m, mud.

190   **Rae Basin**, at the head of Hesquiat Harbour, has two above-water rocks, one drying rock and a mud bottom, it is suitable only for small craft. A stream from **Hesquiat Lake** flows into its north end. A cabin is on the east shore near the stream entrance. A bridge for a restricted logging road crosses the stream.

Approaches to Clayoquot Sound

Charts 3674, 3673

191   **Clayoquot Sound Approaches**. — The entrance channels to Clayoquot Sound *(49°12'N, 126°06'W)* are Sydney Inlet, Russell, Brabant, Father Charles and Templar Channels. Numerous islets and reefs encumber the channels and approaches to all except Sydney Inlet. **Navigating the area requires great caution.**

192   **Wreck**. — Fishing vessel *Klekane* anchored and sank (1984) at *49°08'N, 126°12'W*.

193   **Flores Island**, in the NW part of the sound, is low on its south and west sides but mountains in its interior rise steeply to high elevations. **Mount Flores** *(49°19'N, 126°10'W)* is its summit. **Rafael Cone**, 2 miles SW of Mount Flores, is prominent from NW.

Charts 3674, 3673

194   **Flores Island Provincial Park** encompasses the west and south portions of the island and islands off the south shore. It is one of the most popular destinations in Clayoquot Sound and offers a 10 km hiking trail from the village of Ahousat to the top of Mount Flores. Wolves are known to frequent camping areas.

Chart 3673

195   **Vargas Island** *(49°11'N, 126°00'W)*, SE of Flores Island, is low and undulating but its south coast is rugged with numerous off-lying rocks.

196   **Vargas Island Provincial Park** encompasses the west and south portions of the island and the offshore islands. It is a very popular paddling and wilderness camping destination. Wolves frequent the area.

197   **Catface Range**, north of Vargas Island, is flat topped with conspicuous cliffs and patches of bare white rock near the middle of its south side.

198   **Meares Island**, in the SE part of the sound, is mountainous. **Mount Colnett** is its summit. **Lone Cone**, on the west side of the island, is conspicuous.

Sydney Inlet Approach

Chart 3674

199   **Sydney Inlet Approach.** — **Rafael Point** *(49°17'N, 126°14'W)* and **Dragger Point** are low and wooded. Several shoals, drying rocks and islets lie close-off the west coast of Flores Island north of Rafael Point.

200   **Barney Rocks** *(49°21'N, 126°17'W)* consist of one 4 m high rock and several drying and below-water rocks.

201   **Openit Peninsula** separates Hot Springs Cove from Sydney Inlet. **Sharp Point**, the south extremity of Openit Peninsula, has a rock 1 m high close SE of it and a rock with 2.5 m over it lies 0.2 mile SSE of the point.

202   **Light.** — Sharp Point light *(117.5)* is shown at an elevation of 26.7 m from a white tower 1.5 m high. The fog signal consists of one blast on a horn every 30 seconds.

203   **Maquinna Marine Provincial Park** encompasses the south portion of Openit Peninsula and foreshore from Sydney Inlet west to Estevan Point, including Hesquiat Harbour. The park has picnic and sanitary facilities but water is not safe to drink without treatment. Geothermal hot springs cascade down a waterfall into half a dozen rocky pools.

Hot Springs Cove

204   **Hot Springs Cove** *(49°21'N, 126°16'W)* is entered between Sharp Point and **Mate Islands**. A rock with 0.5 m over it lies on the east side of the fairway about 0.3 mile north of Sharp Point. Drying rocks off the west shore, close north of Mate Islands, narrow the fairway in this vicinity to barely 0.1 mile wide.

205   A trail from the public wharf leads through Maquinna Marine Provincial Park to **Ramsay Hot Spring**, about 1 mile south. An Indian village is on the west side of the cove. Fresh water and fuel may be obtainable at the village floats, but availability should be confirmed with the Hesquiat Band.

206   **Light.** — Mate Island light *(117)*, on the west side of the entrance to Hot Springs Cove, is shown from a white tower with a green band at the top and is fitted with a radar reflector.

207   **Submarine pipelines.** — A water pipeline crosses from the Indian village to Freddy's Cove (local name) on the east shore. A sewer outfall extends 61 m off the west shore in the vicinity of the Indian Reserve. A water pipeline is laid from the Indian village, on the west shore, to the head of the cove.

208   **Anchorage**, well-sheltered from all winds, can be obtained about 0.2 mile north of the public wharf in the middle of Hot Springs Cove, in a depth of about 7 m.

209   **Wharf.** — The public wharf is on the east side of the cove about 0.8 mile inside the entrance. It consists of a pier 73 m long, and a 67 m float with depths of 4.7 m alongside.

210   **Public mooring buoys** lie north of the public floats.

211   **Private floats** and a breakwater are at the Indian Reserve on the west side of the cove.

Russell and Brabant Channels

Chart 3673

212   **Russell Channel** *(49°14'N, 126°06'W)* leads into Clayoquot Sound through a fairway not less than 0.5 mile wide. **Siwash Cove** and **Cow Bay** are on the south shore of Flores Island.

213   **Garrard Group**, on the north side of the entrance to Russell Channel, has several drying and below-water rocks in the vicinity. An isolated rock east of the group dries 0.7 m. **Kutcous Point, Kutcous Islets, McKinn Islets** and **Whitesand Cove** lie on the north side of the fairway.

214   **Tibbs Islet**, the NW extremity of islets and reefs extending west from **Bartlett Island**, is bare.

215   **Light.** — Tibbs Islet light *(122)* is shown at an elevation of 11.1 m from a mast 1.5 m high.

216   **Whaler Islets, Shag Islet** and **Shot Islets** extend ENE from Bartlett Island and form the south side of Russell Channel.

217   **Brabant Channel** *(49°12'N, 126°05'W)* affords a good entry into Clayoquot Sound for mariners with local knowledge. During strong SW gales the sea is reported to break right across the channel between Lawrence and Hobbs Islets.

218   The NW side of the channel is formed by **Sea Otter Rock, Hagen Reef, Lawrence Islets, Edwin Reef** and **Leeke Islets**.

219   On the SE side of the channel **Cleland Island** is bare and prominent, **Blunden Island, Hobbs Islet** and **Burgess Islet** are wooded. **Plover Reefs**, west of Blunden Island, consist of several above-water and drying rocks.

220   Cleland Island is an **Ecological Reserve**, a permit is required to land.

221   **Ahous Bay**, east of Blunden Island, has **Foam Reefs** and **Ahous Point** on its south side.

222   **Leading marks.** — Approaching Brabant Channel from seaward bring the SE side of Lawrence Islets in line with the gap between Leeke Islets and the north summit of Catface Range bearing 047°. These marks lead between the reefs east of Sea Otter Rock and Plover Reefs.

223   A **submarine cable** is laid across the east ends of Russell and Brabant Channels.

Tofino and Approaches

Charts 3685, 3673

224   **Tofino Approaches.** — The most direct approach to Tofino is by way of Templar Channel. Father Charles Channel is

Charts 3685, 3673

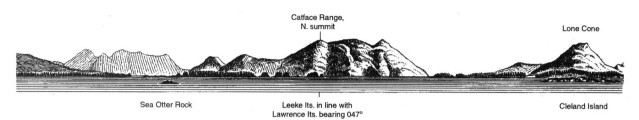

Clayoquot Sound, entrance to Brabant Channel
(Original dated prior to 1863)

not recommended without local knowledge. It can also be approached from seaward by any of the other approach channels to Clayoquot Sound.

225   **LaCroix Group** *(49°09'N, 126°00'W)*, south of Vargas Island, lies on the west side of the approach to Father Charles Channel. **Wilf Rock** is the SE rock of the group.

226   **Light**. — Wilf Rock light *(126.5)*, shown at an elevation of 12.1 m from a mast, is a seasonal light.

227   **Lennard Island** *(49°07'N, 125°55'W)* lies at the south end and in the centre of the approach to Father Charles and Templar Channels. **Nob Rock** and **Surprise Reef**, together with several drying reefs, extend NW from the island.

228   **McKay Reef**, 0.7 mile NW of Surprise Reef, lies on the east side of the south approach to Father Charles Channel and consists of two above-water rocks and several drying rocks.

229   **Light**. — Lennard Island light *(134)*, on the SW side of the island, is shown at an elevation of 35.1 m from a white tower, with a red band at the top. A white structure with a red roof is SE.

230   **Cox Bay** *(49°06'N, 125°53'W)*, entered between **Frank Island** and **Cox Point**, has low sandy shores and is unfit for anchorage. **Vargas Cone**, 1 mile ESE of Cox Point, is prominent from the west.

231   **Towers**, with red air obstruction lights, are 1.4 miles ESE of Cox Point and a conspicuous tower is on the summit of **Radar Hill**, about 2 miles ESE of Cox Point.

Father Charles Channel

Chart 3685

232   **Father Charles Channel** *(49°09'N, 125°57'W)*, between Vargas Island on the west and Wickaninnish and Stubbs Islands on the east, has a least navigable width of 0.2 mile. Numerous rocks lie in the entrance and on either side of the fairway. **This channel should not be attempted if the ship's position cannot be known with certainty at all times. Local knowledge is advised.**

233   **Tidal streams** in the channel rarely exceed about 2 kn. The flood sets north.

234   **Jensen Rock**, 0.7 mile NNE of McKay Reef, is 1 m high.

235   **Moser Point** *(49°09'N, 125°58'W)* is low and rocky. A rock 1 m high lies 0.15 mile NE of the point. **Father Charles Rock**, 0.3 mile east of the point, is 1 m high.

236   An abandoned **submarine cable**, 0.9 mile north of Moser Point, crosses the channel to Stubbs Island.

237   **Yarksis**, at the head of a bay with a sandy beach 1.5 miles north of Moser Point, is the ruins of an Indian village. **Mud Bay**, 2 miles north of Moser Point, is filled with drying flats.

238   **Anchorage** can be obtained 0.2 to 0.4 mile SE of Yarksis in 3 to 5 m.

Templar Channel

239   **Templar Channel**, the SE channel leading into Clayoquot Sound, is entered between Lennard Island and Frank Island *(49°06'N, 125°54'W)*. Seas break across the entrance in heavy weather.

240   **Caution. — Templar Channel is shallow in its north part. Vessels drawing more than 4 m should not attempt it without local knowledge.**

241   **Tidal streams** in Templar Channel attain 1 to 2 kn, the flood setting north.

242   **Abandoned submarine cables** cross Templar Channel from Lennard Island. One passes close north of Frank Island and terminates at **Chesterman Beach**, the other leads NE across the channel terminating at **MacKenzie Beach**.

243   **Tonquin Island**, 0.5 mile north of Lennard Island, is on the west side of the fairway.

244   **Thorn Reef** extends north from Tonquin Island, its east extremity is marked by port hand buoy "Y1". An Indian village, on the east shore of **Echachis Island**, is usually inhabited during the summer fishing season.

245   Two rocks, with 1.6 and 2.2 m over them, lie on the west side of the fairway about 0.2 mile off the south end of **Wickaninnish Island** and two drying rocks lie NNW of them about 0.1 mile offshore.

246   **Light buoys**. — Templar Channel light buoy "Y2" *(133)*, 0.6 mile north of Tonquin Island, is a starboard hand buoy.

247   Felice Island light buoy "Y3" *(132)*, 0.3 mile south of Felice Island, is a port hand buoy.

248   **Beacon**. — Wickaninnish Island daybeacon, on a drying spit extending from the NE part of the island, has a port hand daymark.

249   **Directions**. — Pass 0.2 mile east of Lennard and Tonquin Islands then pass about 0.1 mile east of Thorn Reef, which is marked by port hand buoy "Y1". When the SE extremity of Echachis Island is bearing 244°, and seen north of the rock 0.2 mile north of Tonquin Island, alter course NW until the NW extremity of Stubbs Island is just open east of the NE extremity of Wickaninnish Island, bearing 341°. On no account close these two

Chart 3685

points, because of the dangers on the west side of the fairway, but keep them just open to pass close west of light buoy "Y2". When Lennard Island light structure appears west of the summit of Tonquin Island, bearing 171°, steer up the fairway. If bound for Duffin Passage and Tofino pass south and east of light buoy "Y3", SSW of Felice Island. If bound for Van Nevel Channel and Clayoquot pass west of light buoy "Y3".

Duffin Passage and Tofino

250   **Duffin Passage**, entered between **Felice Island** and **Grice Point**, leads round the north end of **Esowista Peninsula** to join Browning Passage at Usatzes Point. A rock with 1.8 m over it lies on the east side of the approach, about 0.6 mile SSW of Grice Point. A reef that dries 3.8 m lies in the centre of the fairway, about 0.1 mile SW of **Arnet Island**.

251   **Tidal streams** in Duffin Passage attain 2 to 3 kn. The flood sets north and in the vicinity of Grice Point sets NE.

252   Duffin Passage, north of Tofino, is a **water aerodrome**.

253   **Submarine cables**. — An abandoned cable crosses the passage between Grice Point and Felice Island. Cables cross the channel from the north side of Grice Point to Stubbs and Meares Islands, and also cross the east end of the passage north of Tofino.

254   **Submarine pipelines**. — A sewage outfall commences from the north side of Grice Point and goes around its north and west sides, terminating in mid-channel west of Felice Island. Another pipeline, 0.25 mile east of Grice Point, extends 0.1 mile offshore.

255   **Lights**. — Tofino breakwater light *(129.9)*, about 0.5 mile east of Grice Point on the outer end of the breakwater, is shown at an elevation of 5.7 m from a mast fitted with two starboard hand daymarks.

256   Tofino East breakwater light *(130)*, on the north end of the east breakwater, is shown from a mast with a starboard hand daymark.

257   **Beacon. — Buoys**. — A narrow channel, between Tofino East breakwater light and Usatzes Point 0.5 mile ESE, lies between Esowista Peninsula and two drying banks to the north. It has a least depth of 0.5 m.

258   The west end of the channel is entered between Tofino East breakwater light and port hand buoy "Y29".

259   Browning Passage daybeacon, 0.2 mile SE of Tofino East breakwater light on the south side of the channel, has a starboard hand daymark.

260   The east entrance of the channel is marked by port hand buoy "Y33" and starboard hand buoy "Y34".

261   **Usatzes Point** *(49°09'N, 125°53'W)* has drying rocks close north of it. Two drying reefs and **Thompson Rock** lie in mid-channel between Usatzes Point and Riley Island. **Strawberry Island**, 0.2 mile NW of Usatzes Point, has unmarked drying and below-water reefs extending 0.2 mile north from it.

262   **Beacon**. — Thompson Rock daybeacon has a bifurcation/junction daymark, preferred channel to the right.

263   **Tofino**, on the north end of Esowista Peninsula, is a municipality with a hospital and heliport, post office, and RCMP detachment. There are also stores, including groceries and a drug store, laundromat, accommodation, tourist attractions and restaurants. It has a Coast Guard base with a search and rescue craft and heliport. Waters off Tofino are busy especially during summer months. A mixture of traffic, including kayaks, pleasure craft, whale watching excursions, tour boats, water taxis and float planes, requires caution particularly when transiting the area from First Street Dock to Fourth Street Dock.

264   **Marina** and resort facilities are available. Gas, diesel, stove oil, propane, charts and supplies are available.

265   **Supplies**. — Diesel fuel, gasoline, stove oil, fresh water, fresh and frozen meat, groceries and hardware can be obtained.

266   **Transportation**. — Tofino is connected by road to Ucluelet, Port Alberni and to the main highway along the east side of Vancouver Island. Scheduled bus service operates between Tofino and Port Alberni. Scheduled air service operates to local destinations such as Ahousaht, Hot Springs Cove, Stewardson and Mooyah Bay, and to Vancouver, air charter service is available.

267   Tofino Airport *(49°05'N, 125°46'W)*, at the SE end of Esowista Peninsula, has paved runways 1,524 m long.

268   **Tides**. — Tidal predictions for Tofino (Index No. 8615) are in *Tide Tables, Volume 6.*

269   **Meteorological information** and a frequency of fog table for Tofino are in the Appendices.

270   **Municipal Wharf (First Street Dock)**, 0.1 mile east of Grice Point, has a berthing face of 37 m with 4 m alongside. It has a 3 tonne crane. A float at the west end of the wharf is 31 m long. Two seaplane floats are at the east end of the wharf. Public berths in Tofino are heavily utilized and berthing space may not be available.

271   The **Coast Guard wharf** and heliport are close east of the Municipal Wharf.

272   The **public float**, a short distance east of the Coast Guard wharf, is 43 m long and projects north from an approach structure, 25 m long. The float is in an area that has been dredged to a depth of 1.5 m.

273   The **small craft harbour (Fourth Street Dock)**, 0.5 mile east of Grice Point, is protected on its NW side by a pile and timber breakwater, in 1985 there were depths of 1.8 m. It has floats, 60 to 70 m long, with a common connection to a wharf. Water and a 3 tonne crane are available on the wharf and power is laid on the floats. It has a public telephone, used oil disposal facilities and a launching ramp. A tidal grid on the north side of the wharf is exposed to west winds.

274   The **public float (Crab Dock)**, close west of Usatzes Point, has 122 m of berthing space with depths of about 3.6 m alongside.

275   A **fuel float** and private wharves lie between Grice Point and the small craft harbour.

Templar Channel to Amphitrite Point

Chart 3603

276   **Between the entrance to Templar Channel *(49°05'N, 125°55'W)* and Amphitrite Point, 18 miles SE, the coast should not be approached closer than 2 miles because of off-lying dangers.**

277   **Gowlland Rocks** *(49°04'N, 125°51'W)* are a group of above-water, drying, and sunken rocks.

278   **Schooner Cove**, between **Portland Point** and **Box Island**, affords some shelter from west winds for small craft.

279   **Wickaninnish Bay** *(49°02'N, 125°45'W)*, between Box Island and **Quisitis Point**, is not suitable for anchorage. It is

Chart 3603

fronted by **Long Beach**. A rock awash lies about 1.5 miles offshore in the centre of the bay.

280   **Light buoy**. — An ODAS light buoy is moored 2 miles south of Wya Point.

281   **Tofino radiobeacon** is on the shore of Wickaninnish Bay, 3 miles SE of the airport. See *Radio Aids to Marine Navigation (Pacific and Western Arctic)*.

282   **Florencia Bay**, between Quisitis Point and **Wya Point**, is shallow, foul and so exposed as to be unfit for anchorage. **Florencia Islet** lies in the middle of its entrance.

Chart 3671

283   **Amphitrite Point** *(48°55'N, 125°32'W)*, the NW entrance point to Barkley Sound, is the SW extremity of **Ucluth Peninsula** and the site of Tofino MCTS Centre.

284   **Light**. — Amphitrite Point light *(135)* is shown at an elevation of 15.2 m from a white tower. The fog signal consists of one blast on a horn every 20 seconds.

Ucluelet Inlet and Approaches

285   **Ucluelet Inlet Approaches**. — Ucluelet Inlet can be approached from seaward by way of Felice Channel, Alpha Passage or Carolina Channel. The best approach route from Barkley Sound is by Newcombe Channel.

286   **Spoil ground**. — An ocean dump site, under permit through the *Ocean Dumping Control Act*, is in the approach to Ucluelet Inlet in *48°53.6'N, 123°32.5'W*.

Felice and Newcombe Channels

287   **Felice Channel** *(48°54'N, 125°30'W)* is the best channel for approaching Ucluelet Inlet from seaward. It also gives access to Loudoun Channel through Newcombe Channel, or by way of a passage SW of Sargison Bank. The fairway has a minimum width of 0.4 mile.

288   The NW side of the channel is bounded by **Humphries Reef**, some reefs extending 0.4 mile east from **Janson Island**, and a detached reef 0.5 mile east of **George Fraser Islands**.

289   **Starlight Reef**, **Heddington Reef**, **Sykes Reef** and **Chrow Islands** lie on the SE side of the channel. A rock that dries 3.5 m lies 0.3 mile WNW of Starlight Reef and a rock that dries 2.6 m lies 0.3 mile west of Heddington Reef.

290   **Light**. — Chrow Islands light *(139)*, on the NW extremity of the north island, is shown at an elevation of 9.6 m from a grey mast.

291   **Spoil ground**. — An ocean dump site, under permit through the *Ocean Dumping Control Act*, is at the junction of Felice and Newcombe Channels in *48°54.7'N, 123°29.3'W*.

292   **Newcombe Channel** leads from Ucluelet Inlet into Loudoun Channel NW of Chrow Islands and **Sargison Bank**. A rock that dries 0.3 m lies 0.2 mile SSW of **Food Islets**. The sea sometimes breaks on the NE and SW parts of Sargison Bank.

293   **Forbes Island** lies 3.3 miles NE of Food Islets.

294   **Light**. — Forbes Island light *(141)*, on the south side of the island, is shown from a white tower with a red band at the top.

295   **Directions**. — Entering Felice Channel, keep Chrow Islands light ahead bearing 043° until Francis Island light bears

309° and is open NE of the two islets 0.5 mile east of the larger of the George Fraser Islands. At this position, alter course to 340° to clear the rock patches west of Chrow Islands. When Chrow Islands light bears 081°, alter course to bring Francis Island light ahead bearing 300°. Maintain this course until the north islet of the George Fraser Islands group is abeam where the course should be altered to enter Ucluelet Inlet.

296   **If entering Barkley Sound by way of Felice and Newcombe Channels**, proceed as directed above for Felice Channel until Chrow Islands light bears 081°. At this position alter course to pass Chrow Islands light at a distance of about 0.2 mile. When Chrow Islands light is abeam alter course to bring Forbes Island light ahead bearing 051°, then when Page Island bears 100°, alter course to pass about 0.2 mile south of Curwen Island daybeacon. From the position 0.2 mile south of Curwen Island daybeacon follow directions given for Loudoun Channel.

297   The channel between Chrow Islands and Sargison Bank can be entered from Felice Channel by bringing Sail Rock into line with the SW side of Alley Rock, bearing 123°, and keeping it so until Great Bear Rock is abeam. When Great Bear Rock is abeam alter course to pass about 0.1 mile SW of Alley Rock.

298   **Caution. — In heavy weather care should be taken to avoid being set NE when inside the islands.**

Alpha Passage and Carolina Channel

Chart 3646

299   **Jenny Reef** *(48°55'N, 125°31'W)* separates Alpha Passage from Carolina Channel. It consists of several drying rocks and some above-water rocks that have a maximum elevation of 2 m.

300   **Alpha Passage**, between Jenny Reef and George Fraser Islands, is only suitable for small craft in calm weather during daylight hours.

301   **Carolina Channel**, close SE of Amphitrite Point, is the channel most frequently used by vessels of shallow draught in calm weather approaching Ucluelet Inlet from seaward. In bad weather, when a long swell rolls in from seaward, it becomes dangerous as several rocks and shoal patches lie in the fairway. **Francis Island**, also known as **Round Island**, is joined to the SE end of Ucluth Peninsula by a drying bank.

302   **Light**. — Francis Island light *(137)*, on the SE side of the island, is shown at an elevation of 8 m from a mast.

303   **Light buoys**. — Carolina Channel light and whistle buoy "Y42" *(136)*, 0.5 mile south of Amphitrite Point, is a starboard hand buoy.

304   Carolina Passage Inner light and bell buoy "Y43" *(136.5)*, 0.3 mile WSW of Francis Island light, is a port hand buoy.

305   **Directions**. — Enter Carolina Channel with Francis Island light structure ahead, bearing 058°, passing close north of light buoy "Y42" and close south of light buoy "Y43". When the summit of the south Beg Island bears 097°, steer for it on that bearing until the east extremity of Francis Island is abeam then round that island at a distance of 0.2 mile and enter Ucluelet Inlet.

Ucluelet Inlet

306   **Ucluelet Inlet** is entered between Francis Island and the **Beg Islands**, about 1 mile ESE. The NE shore of the inlet, for about 1 mile within the entrance, has a number of above-water, drying

Courtesy of B.C.Government

Lyche Island

Native Rock

Ucluelet Inlet from Stuart Bay (1980)

Lyche Island

Ucluelet Inlet (1988)

Ucluelet Small Craft Harbour (1988)

Chart 3646

and below-water rocks lying off it. The fairway in this vicinity is marked by buoys and beacons.

307 **Speed limit**. — Speed signs, on the east extremity of Hyphocus Island and on Native Island daybeacon, read "*Maximum Speed 7 kn*".

308 **Submarine pipelines**. — A water pipeline crosses the inlet from the camp in Spring Cove to the south end of Stuart Bay. Another pipeline crosses the inlet about 0.1 mile NW of Lyche Island. An abandoned pipeline crosses the inlet about 0.8 mile NW of Lyche Island. Sewage outfalls, marked by signs, extend east from the SE shore of Hyphocus Island, SW from the north end of Stuart Bay and from the west side of Ucluelet Inlet, 0.2 mile north of Hyphocus Island.

309 **Submarine cables** cross the inlet immediately NW of Lyche Island.

310 **Radio towers** on Hyphocus Island have red air obstruction lights.

311 Ucluelet Inlet is a **water aerodrome**.

312 **Beacon. — Buoys**. — Ucluelet Inlet daybeacon, 0.1 mile north of Francis Island, has a port hand daymark.

313 Starboard hand buoy "Y46", 0.2 mile NE of the daybeacon, is close west of a rock with 0.8 m over it.

314 Starboard bifurcation buoy "YG", 0.3 mile north of the daybeacon, is close SW of a mid-channel shoal.

315 **Spring Cove** is entered south of **Hyphocus Island** *(48°56'N, 125°32'W)*. The public float, in the SE corner of the cove, is 49 m long with a least depth of 1.7 m alongside. Several private floats and a closed fish camp and floats are in the NW corner of the cove.

316 A rock, with 1.2 m over it, lies close NE of the south entrance point of the cove.

317 **Light buoy**. — Spring Cove light buoy "Y45" *(137.3)*, on the north side of the rock is a port hand buoy.

318 **Stuart Bay**, on the NE side of the inlet and east of Hyphocus Island, affords anchorage to small craft. Several rocks, awash and drying, lie in a chain extending SE from the NW entrance point of Stuart Bay.

319 **Beacons**. — A private daybeacon with a white diamond-shaped daymark marks a danger 0.1 mile NE of the south entrance point of Stuart Bay.

320 Stuart Bay daybeacon, 0.15 mile NW, has a starboard hand daymark.

321 Native Island daybeacon, about 0.1 mile west of **Native Rock**, has a starboard hand daymark.

322 **Light. — Beacon**. — Indian Reserve light *(137.5)*, on a rock 0.1 mile west of the north entrance to Stuart Bay, is shown from a white tower with a red band at the top.

323 Indian Village daybeacon, 0.15 mile farther NNW, has a starboard hand daymark.

324 **Sutton Rock**, with 1.2 m over it, lies in mid-channel 0.35 mile NW of Indian Village daybeacon.

325 **Light buoy**. — Sutton Rock light buoy "Y44" *(138)*, close south of the rock, is a starboard hand buoy.

326 **Lyche Island** lies in the middle of the inlet north of Ucluelet village. A least depth of 8.3 m lies in the passage NE of the island. The passage SW of Lyche Island is narrowed considerably by foul ground and has a depth of 3.9 m. An islet, steep-to on its west side, lies 0.2 mile NNW of Lyche Island.

327 **Beacons**. — Lyche Island daybeacon, close NW of Lyche Island, has a starboard hand daymark.

328 Boat Basin East daybeacon, 0.1 mile WNW of Lyche Island daybeacon, has two port hand daymarks on a dolphin.

329 Port Albion daybeacon, 0.15 mile NE of Lyche Island, has a starboard hand daymark.

330 **Port Albion**, on the NE shore of the inlet above Lyche Island, has a fishing company wharf. A store is near the wharf, diesel fuel, gasoline and fresh water are obtainable.

331 The north end of Ucluelet Inlet, from 0.7 mile NW of Lyche Island, is a **booming ground** and has numerous dolphins in it.

332 **Mooring buoys**. — Private mooring buoys are close SW of Lyche Island daybeacon, 0.6 mile NW of Lyche Island daybeacon and 0.1 mile north of **Kvarno Island**. Public mooring buoys lie SE of Lyche Island and north of the small boat harbour.

333 **Anchorage** can be obtained in 15 to 25 m about midway between the rocky area NW of Sutton Rock and Lyche Island. Small craft can obtain anchorage in Stuart Bay and Spring Cove, and in other areas where depths are suitable, taking care to avoid the submarine pipelines and cables.

334 **Directions**. — Commencing from about 0.2 mile east of Francis Island, keep the NE extremity of Hyphocus Island in line with the SW side of Lyche Island until the south entrance point of Spring Cove is abeam. Then bring Native Island daybeacon ahead and keep it so until Stuart Bay daybeacon is abeam. From here a mid-channel course can be steered.

335 Keep Sutton Rock light buoy to starboard, taking care to avoid Sutton Rock and the 4 m rock close NW of it. If proceeding past Lyche Island the channel to the NE of Lyche Island is recommended.

336 The islet 0.2 mile NNW of Lyche Island can be passed on either side, but care must be observed to avoid the rocky ledges extending SE and NW from it.

Ucluelet

337 **Ucluelet** *(48°56'N, 125°32'W)* is a village on the west side of Ucluelet Inlet. Principal industries are tourism, fishing and shipping logs. There are several stores, restaurants, a laundromat, post office, bank, tourist information centre, RCMP detachment, and accommodation. A medical clinic is operated in conjunction with the hospital at Tofino. The inlet is frequented by pleasure craft and commercial fish boats.

338 **Harbour services**. — There are two slips capable of docking small craft and two machine shops that can carry out repairs and metal fabrication. Electronic repairs can be attended to.

339 **Communications**. — Ucluelet is on the main highway system of Vancouver Island and bus transportation is scheduled to Port Alberni, with connections to major points on the island. There are scheduled flights to Vancouver through Tofino Airport and aircraft charters are available locally. The Alberni Marine Transportation Company (Lady Rose Marine Services) provides a scheduled summer ferry service to Port Alberni.

340 **Arrival information**. — Ucluelet is the only customs reporting station on the West Coast of Vancouver Island. Telephone 1-888-CANPASS or 250-754-0341.

341 **Tides**. — Tidal differences for Ucluelet (Index No. 8595), referenced on Tofino, are in *Tide Tables, Volume 6*.

Chart 3646

Cape Beale light (1985)

Cape Beale light bearing 040° - 1 mile (1985)

342   **Berthing**. — On the west side of the harbour the fuel dock, 0.5 mile SE of Lyche Island, lies near the south end of the village. The pier is about 100 m long and its outer face is 30 m wide with 8.2 m alongside.

343   **Wholley Seafoods** close NW has a 6.7 m alongside.

344   **Neptune Packers** wharf and building and two small private wharves lie NW of the Fisherman's Co-op wharf.

345   The **public float**, close NW of the private wharves and west of Sutton Rock, is 140 m long with depths along its outer side varying from 3 m at the SE end to 12.8 m at the NW end, piles are on the inside of the float and the depth is 3.6 m near the outer end. A rock that dries 0.6 m lies about 3 m off the south end of this float.

346   **Pioneer Boatworks** wharves and marine railway are NW of the public float.

Chart 3646

347 The **public wharf**, close NW of the West Coast Machine Works and abreast the SE end of Lyche Island, has a length of 43 m along its outer face and depths of 6 to 7 m. Floats attached to the inner side of the wharfhead on the south side, are 37 m long. A seaplane float, 13 m long, is attached to the outer float.

348 **Ucluelet Seafood Processors** wharf has a least depth of 3.2 m at its north end.

349 **Ostergaard and Sons** fish wharf has a depth of 3.4 m along its outer end.

350 **Ucluelet Seafood** wharf and float, close NW of Ostergaard and Sons, has depths of less than 2 m on the inner side of the float.

351 A **marina and fishing resort**, protected by rock breakwaters on its north and south sides, has a dredged boat basin and floats. Limited power, washrooms, showers, laundry, sanitary facilities, launching ramp, charts and marine supplies are available.

352 **Ucluelet Small Craft Harbour**, entered 0.2 mile west of the north end of Lyche Island, was dredged to a depth of 3 m (1968); in 1976 there was a least depth of 2.6 m in the entrance. A breakwaters lies off the entrance, and public floats with about 245 m of berthing are inside the basin. Power, water and washrooms are available. Docks A and B are for commercial boats only.

353 The **Canadian Princess**, a floating hotel, charter service and restaurant, is moored in the dredged basin SW of the public floats. A float 64 m long and 2.4 m wide with a depth of 1.8 m is alongside. This ship, formerly the William J Stewart, served the Canadian Hydrographic Service and spent many years surveying the coast of B.C. prior to retirement.

354 **Trans Pacific Fish wharf**, 0.5 mile WNW of the north end of Lyche Island, has a depth of 7 m along the outer face. A boat launching ramp is close west. It has been reported this facility is closed.

355 A **public float**, 50 m long with depths of 3.9 to 4.8 m along its outer face, is on the east side of the harbour, 0.1 mile east of the SE side of Lyche Island.

356 A **public wharf** within an Indian Reserve is 0.8 mile SE of Lyche Island, close east of Indian Village daybeacon.

Approaches to Barkley Sound

Chart 3671

357 **Barkley Sound Approaches**. — Barkley Sound is entered between Amphitrite Point *(48°55'N, 125°32'W)* and Cape Beale *(48°47'N, 125°13'W)*, 16 miles SE. It is encumbered with numerous islands, islets and sunken rocks, especially in the approaches. The three main entrance channels are Trevor, Imperial Eagle and Loudoun Channels.

358 **Caution**. — **Mariners are advised to give the entrance to Barkley Sound a wide berth when passing. There are several off-lying dangers, and the set of the tidal stream toward land is likely to be accentuated by in-draught into the sound, especially during strong winds from SE to SW.**

359 **Mount Ozzard** *(48°58'N, 125°29'W)* is conspicuous, especially from the south as it is the SW summit of a mountain range on the NW shore of the sound. A large white radar dome, on the summit of Mount Ozzard, is the radar scanner for MCTS on Amphitrite Point. The dome has red air obstruction lights.

360 **Broughton Peaks** *(49°00'N, 125°14'W)* dominate the sound from every angle.

361 **Vessel Traffic Services** (VTS). — *Calling-in Point No. 2 Tofino Traffic Zone, Cape Beale*, is a line joining Cape Beale light *(176)* with Amphitrite Point light *(135)*. Mariners shall indicate whether their course is through Trevor Channel, Imperial Eagle Channel or Loudoun Channel. Assigned frequency is 156.725 MHz, Channel 74.

362 **Cape Beale** *(48°47'N, 125°13'W)* is a bold, rocky point covered with trees. It is reported to give a poor radar response at 20 miles under normal conditions. Reefs fringe the promontory to a distance of 0.5 mile and it is strongly advised to give the cape a wide berth.

363 **Light**. — Cape Beale Sector light *(176)* is shown at an elevation of 50.8 m from a skeleton tower with white slatwork daymarks on three sides. It is fitted with an emergency light.

364 A **wind frequency table** for Cape Beale is given in the Appendices.

365 **Pilot boarding station**. — A boarding station for the Pacific Pilotage Authority is off Cape Beale at the entrance to Trevor Channel. For details on how to obtain a Pilot see *PAC 200*.

CHAPTER 10

West Coast Vancouver Island, Coastal Inlets

General

Chart 3001

1   This chapter covers Quatsino Sound, Kyuquot Sound, Esperanza Inlet, Nootka Sound, Clayoquot Sound and Barkley Sound.

Quatsino Sound and Approach

Chart 3679

2   **Quatsino Sound** is the most NW of the larger inlets on the west coast of Vancouver Island. It is approached between Cape Parkins *(50°27'N, 128°03'W)* and Kwakiutl Point *(50°21'N, 127°59'W)* and entered north of Cliffe Point *(50°28'N, 127°56'W)*. Forward Inlet is on the north side of the approach. The sound leads 13 miles ENE to Drake Island, where it divides, branching SE into Neroutsos Inlet or north through Quatsino Narrows into Holberg and Rupert Inlets.

3   **Caution. — Dangers on each side and in the fairway of the approach are marked by breakers only in heavy weather.**

4   **Aspect**. — The entrance to Quatsino Sound is easily identified. On the SE side of the approach there are several inshore islets. **Mount Kains** and **Flat Top Mountain** lie on the north side, west of Forward Inlet. East of Forward Inlet **Plumper Hill** has steep cliffs on its SW side and **Nose Peak** is easily identified by its sharp rocky summit. **Mount Bury** lies 1.7 miles SSE of Cliffe Point.

5   **Vessel Traffic Services (VTS)**. — *Calling-in Point No. 11* of the *Tofino Traffic Zone, Kains Island (Quatsino Sound)*, is a line joining Kwakiutl Point and Cape Parkins. When entering or leaving Quatsino Sound report to *Tofino Traffic*. Assigned frequency is 156.725 MHz, Channel 74.

6   A brief description of this VTS is in *PAC 200*. Details are in *Radio Aids to Marine Navigation (Pacific and Western Arctic)*.

7   **Tides**. — Tidal predictions in Quatsino Sound are given for Winter Harbour (Index No. 8735). Tidal differences referenced on Winter Harbour are given for Berg Cove (Index No. 8754). These predictions and differences are in *Tide Tables, Volume 6*.

8   **Tidal streams** in the approach to Quatsino Sound, west of Gillam Islands, set north and south and attain 3 kn at springs.

9   North of Drake Island *(50°31'N, 127°39'W)* the east-going tidal stream divides about midway between Bergh Cove and the NE coast of Drake Island, one part flowing SE into Neroutsos Inlet and the other ENE toward Quatsino Narrows, each attaining about 3 kn at springs. The junction of the west-going parts of the tidal stream takes place in about the same position. Tidal streams turn about 1 hour after HW and LW.

10   In Buchholz Channel tidal streams set east and west. At its west end the east-going stream sets strongly toward Farmer Islets and the foul ground in their vicinity.

11   **Anchorage** can be obtained NE of Kains Island, or in North Harbour, Winter Harbour, Koskimo Bay or Koprino Harbour.

Approach to Quatsino Sound

12   **Rowley Reefs** *(50°24'N, 127°59'W)* extend 1.3 miles offshore. **Pilling Rock**, which dries 0.9 m, is their outermost drying rock. **Restless Bight** south of Rowley Reefs affords no shelter and is encumbered with rocks.

Chart 3686

13   **Kains Island** *(50°27'N, 128°02'W)* can be easily identified by the lighthouse. The boat passage between the island and Vancouver Island NW is only suitable for small craft in fine weather.

14   **Anchorage** with shelter from west winds can be found NE of Kains Island.

15   **Light**. — Quatsino light *(68)*, on the SE end of Kains Island, is shown at an elevation of 28.4 m from a white tower.

16   **South Danger Rock** *(50°26'N, 128°00'W)* is awash. **Robson Rock**, 0.6 mile NNW of South Danger Rock, dries 0.3 m. A rock with 1.8 m over it lies between the two. These rocks lie in the middle of the fairway and are not always marked by breakers.

17   **Heron Rock**, 0.2 mile south of Kains Island, has 7 m over it. **Pinnacle Island**, 0.6 mile NNE of Kains Island, is a jagged rock with a few low bushes.

18   **Leading marks**. — Cliffe Point, seen through the widest gap in the Gillam Islands and bearing 041°, leads NW of Rowley Reefs and SE of South Danger Rock. The east side of Hunt Islets in line with Pinnacle Island, bearing 353°, leads between South Danger and Robson Rocks on the east and Kains Island on the west.

19   **Gillam Islands** *(50°27'N, 127°58'W)* are bare and grassy except for one at the north end, which is wooded.

20   **Billard Rock**, 0.4 mile south of Gillam Islands, has 7.9 m over it. **Brown Rock**, 0.8 mile NW of Gillam Islands, has 4.9 m over it. **Pilley Shoal**, 1.1 miles NNE of Gillam Islands and about 0.2 mile off the north shore, has 5.5 m over it and is steep-to. **McAllister Islet**, about 0.5 mile north of Brown Rock, lies 0.1 mile offshore.

21   **Light buoy**. — Billard Rock light and whistle buoy "M3" *(68.2)*, south of the rock, is a port hand buoy fitted with a Racon (— —•).

22   Brown Rock buoy "M6", NW of the rock, is a starboard hand buoy.

23   **Cliffe Point** *(50°28'N, 127°56'W)* is a steep-to precipitous bluff from which the land rises to a mountain summit.

24   **Light**. — Cliffe Point light *(68.3)* is shown at an elevation of 10.5 m from a white tower with a red band at the top, 3.6 m high.

25   **Gooding Cove** *(50°24'N, 127°57'W)* affords anchorage for small craft in fine weather, in a depth of about 10 m, sand bottom.

26   **Harvey Cove** *(50°26'N, 127°56'W)* is exposed to the west and not recommended as an anchorage.

Forward Inlet

27   **Forward Inlet**, entered between **Kains Point** *(50°28'N, 128°02'W)* and **Montgomery Point**, affords sheltered anchorage in North Harbour and Winter Harbour. **Hunt Islets** and **Matthews Island** lie on the SW side of the fairway.

Chart 3686

28   **Tides**. — Tidal differences for Hunt Islets (Index No. 8736), referenced on Winter Harbour, are in *Tide Tables, Volume 6.*

29   **Hall Bank**, south of **Hazard Point**, extends nearly 0.5 mile from the east shore.

30   **North Harbour**, NW of Matthews Island, affords sheltered anchorage midway between the island and **Flint Rock** in a depth of 16 m.

31   A drying rock and a rock with 1.2 m over it, off the west side of Matthews Island, are marked by starboard hand buoys "M12" and "M8".

32   **Browning Inlet** leads NW from North Harbour into a basin completely filled by a drying flat.

33   **Winter Harbour**, entered east of **Greenwood Point**, has low shores fringed with sandy beaches. It affords secure, well-sheltered anchorage in a depth of about 15 m, mud bottom, 0.6 mile NNE of Greenwood Point.

34   **Light**. — Greenwood Point light *(67.8)* is shown from a white tower with a green band at the top.

35   A **submarine pipeline** crosses the harbour close north of Greenwood Point, it is marked by signs.

36   **Tides**. — Tidal predictions for Winter Harbour (Index No. 8735), are in *Tide Tables, Volume 6.*

37   **Winter Harbour** settlement, on the west shore north of Greenwood Point, has a post office, restaurant, and general store where fresh and frozen produce, hardware, charts and fishing gear are obtainable. Fuel, petroleum products and fresh water are available year round. Showers, laundry (summer only) and garbage drop are available. Emergency repairs only can be arranged from Port Hardy and there is a boat launching ramp for small craft. A water taxi service operates to Holberg and charter aircraft are obtainable. A dirt road connects Winter Harbour to Holberg, then by gravel road to the main highway system. Camping facilities with fresh water and a launching ramp are north of the settlement.

38   **Wharves**. — The public wharf has a berthing face of 27 m. A float 74 m long is attached to its north side, and a float 34 m long is attached to the south side. A shed and 3 tonne crane are on the wharf, fresh water is obtainable.

39   A private wharf close south has floats each 37 m long attached to its south side.

40   Further south is a privately operated fuel float selling Chevron products.

41   **Marine farm** facilities are on the north side of the peninsula 1 mile NNE of Greenwood Point.

42   **Booming grounds** are on the east shore 0.7 mile NE of Greenwood Point, 0.3 mile west of Wedel Island where the point has a log dump and sorting area on it, and north of Wedel Island.

43   **Wedel Island**, with several other islets and drying flats, encumber the head of Winter Harbour. **Ahwhichaolto Inlet**, at the head of Winter Harbour, is entered through a narrow, shallow, passage. The inlet extends 3.5 miles east *(Chart 3679)* and is unsurveyed.

44   **Marine farm** facilities are in the centre of Ahwhichaolto Inlet, 2 miles inside the entrance.

Cliffe Point to Quatsino Narrows

45   **Nordstrom Cove** *(50°29'N, 127°55'W)*, with drying and below-water rocks in it, affords anchorage suitable only for small craft.

Chart 3679

46   **Bedwell Islands** *(50°29'N, 127°54'W)* are separated from the north shore by a narrow boat passage. A small pointed rock, at the south extremity of the group, is only 2 m high but somewhat prominent. **Monday Rocks**, 0.5 mile ENE of Bedwell Islands, are steep-to.

47   **Light. — Buoy**. — Bedwell Islands light *(68.5)* is on the south end of the islands.

48   Port hand buoy "M7" marks the south end of Monday Rocks.

49   **Koskimo Bay** is a broad bight south of Bedwell Islands. A narrow boat passage separates **Mabbott Island** from shore and the ruins of a concrete wharf and former cannery are at its SE end. **Chapman Islet**, 0.8 mile east, lies close west of the drying flats fronting **Mahatta Creek**.

50   **Anchorage**, in 25 m sand and mud bottom, is obtainable 0.4 mile NE of Chapman Islet. It is reported that small craft can anchor south of the east end of Mabbott Island and east of the drying flats off Mahatta Creek.

51   **Marine farm** facilities, protected by a floating breakwater, are SSE of Mabbott Island, north of the former cannery.

52   **May Point** *(50°29'N, 127°51'W)*, the NW extremity of Koskimo Islands, is steep-to. The narrow boat channel between **Koskimo Islands** and Vancouver Island has a rock that dries 3.7 m in the centre of it. Depths of 2.1 m lie to the north of the drying rock and depths of less than 0.7 m lie to the south.

53   **Light**. — Koskimo Island light *(68.6)* is on the north extremity of the largest island.

54   **Koprino Harbour**, entered between Monday Rocks and **Prideaux Point**, is only suitable for small vessels. **Jones Rock**, **Diggs Islet**, **Skedin Islet** and **Linthlop Islet** lie on the outer edge of the drying flat from the **Koprino River** that fills the north end of the harbour. **Spencer Cove** has a camp ground, boat ramp and the concrete abutments of a former wharf near its east entrance point. **Robson Cove**, with **Dockyard Islet** in its entrance, has an A-frame and booming ground along its west side. **East Cove**, with **Botel Islet** in its entrance, has a cabin in ruins at its head.

55   **Anchorage** for small vessels can be obtained in Koprino Harbour, west of **Schloss Island**, in 22 m, mud, or 0.1 mile NNW of **Ives Islet** in 15 m, but vessels using the latter anchorage should moor as swinging room is limited and **Allan Bank** lies to the west. It is reported that East Cove affords well-sheltered anchorage for small craft.

56   **Quatsino Provincial Park** encompasses the drying flats of Koprino River, the east side of Koprino Harbour and extends east including **Shapland Cove**. This is a wilderness park with no facilities and is not regularly patrolled.

57   **Spoil ground**. — An ocean dumping site, under permit through the *Ocean Dumping Control Act*, is about 0.5 mile east of Koskimo Islands in about 150 m *(50°28.5'N, 127°50'W)*.

58   **Mahatta River** *(50°27'N, 127°48'W)*, south of **Salmon Islands**, is the site of a former logging community. It has an A-frame and a wharf with a depth of 9 m alongside. Booming grounds line the shore.

59   **Brockton Island** *(50°29'N, 127°46'W)*, covered with low bushes, is steep-to on its east and SW sides. **Lind Islet**, 1 mile west of Brockton Island, is 1 m high and bare.

60   **Light**. — Brockton Island light *(68.8)* is on the NW end of the island.

Chart 3679

61   **Fishing boundary markers** are on Vancouver Island south of Brockton Island, and on the east entrance point of a bay 0.8 mile east of Brockton Island.

62   **Booming grounds** with a float, a logging camp, log breakwater and ramp are in the bay fronting **Cleagh Creek**, SE of Brockton Island.

63   **Bish Creek**, 2 miles NE of Brockton Island, and **Kewquodie Creek**, 2 miles east of Brockton Island, are fronted by drying flats.

64   **Drake Island** *(50°31'N, 127°40'W)* has gently wooded slopes and a considerable portion of the south part of the island is under cultivation. The fairway north of Drake Island is entered between **Newcomb Rocks** and **Ildstad Islands**. **Percy Ledge** extends 0.6 mile west from Ildstad Islands.

65   **Light**. — Ildstad Islands light *(69)*, on the SW extremity of the east island, is shown at an elevation of 5.7 m from a mast.

66   **Pamphlet Cove** locally known as Quiet Cove, on the north side of Drake Island, affords sheltered anchorage for small craft. Keep in the middle when entering to avoid drying rocks on either side. A tidal grid and remains of old docks are along the shore. The area is part of a Provincial recreation reserve.

67   **Sherberg Island** and **Akre Rocks**, 1 mile NE of Pamphlet Cove, lie close-off the north shore. Ruins of a wharf are north of the island and a float on the north shore is close east of Sherberg Island. Submarine pipelines (sewage) extend from the Vancouver Island shore north of and 0.2 mile east of Sherberg Island. A submarine cable crosses the channel from the float to Sherberg Island.

68   **Buchholz Channel**, on the south side of Drake Island, is entered at its west end between **Holloway Point** and **Bland Island**. **Noot Rock**, **Farmer Islets**, **Norgar Islet**, and several drying and below-water rocks, lie in the middle of the west entrance. **Lakken Point**, at the east end of the channel, is the SE extremity of Drake Island and has shoal water extending 0.1 mile from it.

69   **Buchholz Channel is not recommended to be used at night** or without the aid of local knowledge. The best time to enter is stemming the ebb stream. It should be noted that the flood stream sets strongly toward Farmer Islets and the dangers in their vicinity.

70   **Klootchlimmis Creek**, south of Bland Island and Noot Rock, has an extensive drying flat extending from its mouth; the passage between is only suitable for small craft. The west side of the drying flat is a booming ground and dry land sorting area (1988). A fishing boundary marker is on the east side.

71   **Kultus Cove** *(50°29'N, 127°37'W)* has irregular depths and affords no anchorage except to small craft. North cardinal buoy "MB" marks a shoal in the cove. A wooded islet and some drying rocks lie near its head. The east and south shores are booming grounds (1988). The cove is used by deep-sea freighters and tugs with log barges for loading logs, they moor to log rafts extending from shore.

72   **Julian Cove**, SE of **Banter Point**, has depths of 10 to 15 m, mud, and limited swinging room but is a useful anchorage for small craft. The west side is a booming ground (1988).

73   **Smith Cove**, 0.5 mile east of Julian Cove, has a rock that dries 1.3 m in the middle of the cove and drying rock ledge extending from the east shore. Anchorage is available only to small craft.

Neroutsos Inlet

74   **Neroutsos Inlet** extends 13 miles SSE from Drake Island and terminates in an extensive mud flat. The narrowest part of the fairway, in the vicinity of Port Alice, is 0.2 mile wide. Depths in the fairway are in excess of 100 m except in the approach to Port Alice where they decrease to about 40 m. Shores are high, rugged and backed by mountains. Winds are reported to blow strongly down the inlet during most afternoons.

75   **Ice** forms occasionally but does not interfere with ocean-going vessels.

76   **Tides**. — Tidal differences in Neroutsos Inlet, referenced on Winter Harbour, are given for Port Alice (Index No. 8750) in *Tide Tables, Volume 6.*

Chart 3681

77   **Cross Island** *(50°31'N, 127°37'W)*, on the west side of the fairway, has drying reefs extending 0.2 mile south of it. **McNiffe Rock**, 0.3 mile ENE of Cross Island, is a drying rock on the east side of the fairway.

78   **Light**. — McNiffe Rock light *(73.4)* is shown at an elevation of 4.7 m from a white tower with a green band at the top.

Chart 3679

79   **Atkins Cove** *(50°31'N, 127°35'W)* has drying flats with boulders extending from its east shore and is exposed to the south. A narrow passage, with a depth of 1.1 m, leads into a small lagoon at its head, known locally as Early Bird Cove. A log dump is on the west shore of the lagoon.

80   **Pender Point** *(50°29'N, 127°35'W)* has a fishing boundary marker on it. **Buchholz Rock**, 0.5 mile ESE of Pender Point, has 2 m over it.

81   **Light buoy**. — Buchholz Rock light buoy "M14" *(73.5)*, east of the rock, is a starboard hand buoy.

82   **Yreka**, on the west shore 2 miles SE of Pender Point, is the site of an abandoned mine with the ruins of a wharf and barge landing.

83   **Spoil ground**. — An ocean dump site, under permit through the *Ocean Dumping Control Act*, is east of Yreka in about 187 m *(50°27.7'N, 127°32.1'W)*.

84   **Lyons Point**, on the east shore 3 miles SE of Pender Point, has a log sorting area on it and a booming ground on its north side.

85   **Jeune Landing**, 1.5 miles SE of Lyons Point, is a small settlement on the road between Port Alice and the main island highway. A drying spit, close north of the public wharf, extends 0.1 mile from the mouth of **Nequiltpaalis Creek**. Approach the public wharf from the south to avoid this drying spit.

86   **Wharf**. — The public wharf has a berthing face of 27 m with 4.6 to 8.5 m alongside. A float, 30 m long, is secured to the outer end of the wharfhead, the outer end is reserved for seaplanes. The wharf has a 3 tonne crane, fresh water and power. A log breakwater and boat launching ramp are south of the public wharf.

Chart 3681

87   **Mist Rock** *(50°26'N, 127°30'W)* is a drying rock with shoals extending 0.1 mile NNW and SSE from it.

88   **Light**. — Mist Rock light *(74.5)* is on the rock.

89   **Port Alice Water aerodrome** includes waters between Jeune Landing and Port Alice.

90   **Rumble Beach**, east of Mist Rock, is the residential town site for Port Alice. It has a floating breakwater, a boat launching ramp and berthing facilities of Port Alice Yacht Club. There is a post office, shopping centre, stores, restaurants, hotel, hospital

Chart 3681

with a heliport, and an RCMP detatchment. A paved road connects it to the main island highway near Port Hardy.

91 A **submarine pipeline** and booming ground are north of the town site. Booming grounds lie to the south, in the passage east of **Frigon Islets**; the passage is only suitable for small craft.

92 **Light**. — Frigon Islets light *(74)*, on the west islet, is shown at an elevation of 5.1 m from a mast.

93 **Thurburn Bay** *(50°23'N, 127°29'W)* affords no anchorage. The west side of the bay is steep-to. A log dump, booming ground, boat ramp and float are close south of the west entrance point.

94 **Ker Point**, the east side of Thurburn Bay, has **Muir Rocks** extending 0.1 mile NE from it.

95 **Cayuse Creek**, 0.5 mile SE of Ker Point, is fronted by an extensive drying flat.

96 **Ketchen Island** is separated from Cayuse Creek drying flat by a narrow channel with two drying reefs close-off the Ketchen Island shore. The area SW of Ketchen Island is well-sheltered and used as a log storage area. The SE entrance to this area is very narrow and encumbered with a drying rock.

97 **Port Alice** *(50°23'N, 127°27'W)* is the site of a large pulp mill owned by Western Pulp Limited. The port is used mainly for shipping pulp. The future of the mill is uncertain and extensive shut downs have occurred.

98 **Tides**. — Tidal differences for Port Alice (Index No. 8750), referenced on Winter Harbour, are in *Tide Tables, Volume 6*.

99 **Anchorage** for vessels waiting for a berth at Port Alice can be obtained NW of Ker Point in 50 to 80 m, mud bottom.

100 **Berths**. — Pulp mill wharf has a straight face of 126 m at its NW end, then angles outward at 30° for 18 m, then trends in the same direction as the main face for another 45 m. Berthing piers and dolphins are 53 and 100 m NW of the NW end. The SE end is used by waiting vessels and barges. The largest vessel to use the wharf had a length of 183 m with a draught of about 11 m. Depths alongside the wharf shown on the inset of the chart were taken in 2000 and tend to shoal due to deposits of waste pulp. Wide fenders or pontoons are used to keep large vessels off the wharf in deep water while loading. Fresh water is obtainable. There is 1,393 m² of open storage and a 4,515 m² storage shed.

101 A **wharf**, used by barges for discharging rail tank cars, is 0.1 mile east of the south end of the pulp mill wharf. Three dolphins lie on the NW side of the approach to this wharf. A depth of 2.9 m, rock bottom, lies 25 m SW from the face of this wharf.

102 The **public wharf**, in a small cove 0.3 mile NW of the pulp mill wharf, has a float for small craft.

103 A **submarine pipeline** (sewer outfall) marked by a sign, 0.1 mile NW of the pulp mill wharf, extends 244 m offshore.

104 **Facilities**. — Tugs for berthing at the pulp mill wharf are obtainable from Western Pulp Limited (250) 284-3331. Minor repairs can be obtained at the mill. Arrangements can be made for divers from Port Hardy for inspection and underwater repairs. Air services and road transportation are available.

105 **Spoil ground**. — An ocean dump site, under permit through the *Ocean Dumping Control Act*, is SE of Port Alice in *50°22.7'N, 127°26.6'W*.

106 **Cayeghle Creek** and **Colonial Creek** flow into the head of Neroutsos Inlet across an extensive drying flat. The head of the inlet south of Port Alice is lined with booming grounds.

Quatsino Narrows and Approach

107 **Quatsino Narrows** connects Quatsino Sound to Rupert and Holberg Inlets. It is approached from Quatsino Sound between **Jesdal Islet** *(50°32'N, 127°37'W)* and **Evenson Point**. The fairway has a minimum width of 0.1 mile with a least depth at its north end of 8.1 m. A rocky shoal spit, 0.3 mile south of Sorenson Point, has a depth of 4.2 m and extends almost to mid-channel from the west shore. A submarine cable crosses the south approach between Evenson Point and Quatsino.

108 **Tides**. — Tidal differences in Quatsino Narrows, referenced on Winter Harbour, for Bergh Cove (Index No. 8754), Kwokwesta Creek (Index No. 8755) and Makwazniht Island (Index No. 8756) are in *Tide Tables, Volume 6*.

109 **Tidal streams** attain 9 kn on the flood and 8 kn on the ebb in the vicinity of Makwazniht Island. North of Quattische Island and east of Ohlsen Point maximum rates are approximately 5 kn and run past the entrance to Hecate Cove *(50°33'N, 127°36'W)* at 1 to 3 kn. Strong turbulence is encountered throughout the main channel. Predictions of times and rate of maximum current, and time of slack water, are given for current station Quatsino Narrows (Index No. 9200) in *Tide Tables, Volume 6*.

110 **Flood currents** tend to set toward the east shore with the strongest velocities experienced at the north end of the narrows, just west of Makwazniht Island. A large tide-rip occurs NW of Makwazniht Island and a rip forms off Ohlsen Point. A large backeddy occurs east of Quattische Island.

111 **Ebb currents** tend to set toward the west shore of the narrows, with the strongest velocities occurring SW of Makwazniht Island. A large tide-rip forms NW of Makwazniht Island and a rip occurs off Ohlsen Point. A large backeddy occurs east of Quattische Island.

112 **Slack water** there is only a brief period, and the time of turn may not be the same at the surface as below the surface. On small tides the turn may be later by as much as 1 hour. According to local information the turn to ebb at the south end of the narrows occurs approximately 30 minutes later than the ebb at the north end.

113 **Caution. — At or near slack water logbooms under tow can be encountered at the north end of the narrows.**

114 **Bergh Cove** *(50°32'N, 127°37'W)* is entered east of **Leeson Point**. **Leeson Rock**, 0.1 mile SE of Leeson Point light, is marked by starboard hand buoy "M10".

115 **Light**. — Leeson Point light *(70)* is on a drying reef south of the point.

116 **Quatsino** settlement, east of Bergh Cove, has a post office, hotel, historic church and store. A short length of road leads west along the shore from the Indian village, SE of **Hecate Cove**, to about 1 mile west of Leeson Point. Transportation is by seaplane or sea. Water taxi service to Coal Harbour is available.

117 **Wharves**. — The public wharf in Bergh Cove has a berthing face of 31 m with a depth of 6 m alongside. A float 31 m long is secured to the west side of the wharfhead and a seaplane float is at its outer end. The wharf has a 3 tonne crane, a storage shed and power, but no fresh water.

118 Private floats are on the west side of Bergh Cove, NW and NNE of Jesdal Islet, and in Hecate Cove.

119 **Facilities**. — A boatyard and machine shop, on the SW side of Hecate Cove, has a slipway capable of handling vessels up

Port Alice from east of Ker Point (1988)

Port Alice pulp mill (1988)

QUATSINO NARROWS

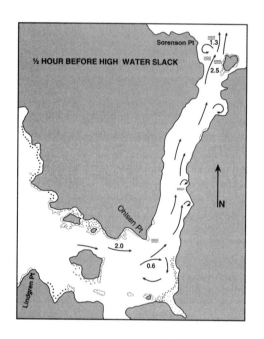

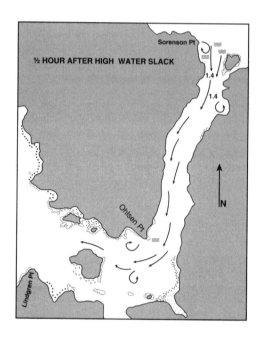

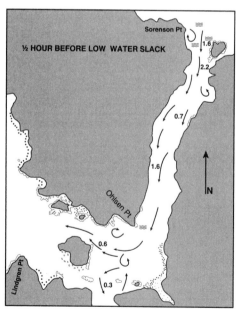

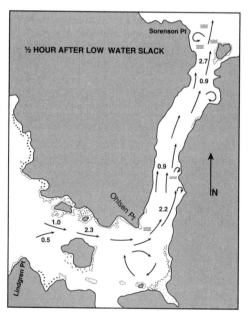

(rates in knots)

Chart 3681

to 27 tonnes. Repairs, moorage, water taxi and towing are available.

120   **Anchorage** for small vessels can be obtained in Hecate Cove, NW of **Kitten Islet**. **Caution should be exercised when entering Hecate Cove as there are strong tidal streams in the entrance**. A fishing boundary marker is on Kitten Islet.

121   **Meteorological information** for Quatsino is in the Appendices.

122   **Quattische Island** *(50°32'N, 127°35'W)* lies in midchannel with the fairway on its north side. **Lindgren Point** is 0.3 mile west of Quattische Island and **Ohlsen Point**, 0.4 mile ENE of the island, is bold and rocky. **Kwokwesta Creek** is 0.5 mile SSE of Ohlsen Point.

123   **Light**. — Ohlsen Point light *(71)* is on a drying ledge extending from the point.

124   **Beacons**. — Quatsino Narrows Entrance daybeacon, on a drying ledge on the north side of the channel NW of Quattische Island, has a port hand daymark.

125   Kwokwesta Creek daybeacon, close north of the creek entrance, has a starboard hand daymark.

126   A private daybeacon, on the east side of Quattische Island, has a white rectangular daymark.

127   **Kokwina Cove**, SE of Quattische Island, has drying reefs and strong tidal streams in its approach. It is only suitable as a small craft anchorage.

128   **Marine farm** facilities are in Kokwina Cove.

129   **Makwazniht Island** lies at the north end, and on the east side, of Quatsino Narrows; drying ledges extend from its SW side. **Kultah Point** lies SE of the island. **Sorenson Point** is the NW entrance point to Quatsino Narrows.

130   **Light**. — Makwazniht Island light *(72)*, on the NW end of the island, is shown at an elevation of 3 m from a mast.

131   **Beacon**. — Kultah Point daybeacon, on a drying ledge about 0.2 mile south of Makwazniht Island, has a starboard hand daymark.

132   **Beacon range**. — Quatsino Narrows daybeacon range, on the east shore 0.5 mile SSW of Makwazniht Island, when in line bearing 193° leads through the north end of the narrows.

Rupert Inlet

Chart 3679

133   **Rupert Inlet** *(50°34'N, 127°33'W)*, entered between **Hankin Point** and **Kenny Point**, extends 5 miles ENE from Quatsino Narrows and terminates in an extensive drying flat. A fishing boundary marker is on Kenny Point. A logging camp and A-frame are on the south shore 2 miles NE of Hankin Point.

134   **Marble River Provincial Park** includes the waters and shores of Quatsino Narrows, Varney Bay and about 3 miles up the Marble River.

135   **Varney Bay** *(50°33'N, 127°32'W)* is only useful as an anchorage for small vessels. It has drying and below-water rocks in it and the **Marble River** flows into its head across an extensive drying flat.

136   **Island Copper Mine** *(50°36'N, 127°30'W)* was on the north shore of Rupert Inlet, about 2.5 miles NE of Hankin Point. The mine is closed, the last shipment of copper concentrate was in January 1996. The operations area of the mine site may be used for future industrial development, while the open pit has been flooded and the immediate surrounding area returned to a natural state.

137   **Wharf**. — The former Island Copper Mine bulk ore loading wharf consists of a pier extending 61 m offshore with four dolphins at its outer end connected by a catwalk that form a berthing face about 213 m long.

138   A **barge ramp** formerly used for handling railcars is in a bay close west of the mine wharf.

139   **Submarine pipelines**, 0.3 mile east of the wharf, are marked by a sign onshore.

140   **Fishing boundary markers** are on the north and south sides of Rupert Inlet, just west of the drying flat at its head.

141   **Washlawlis Creek** flows into the drying flats, on the north side at the head of the inlet. Logging road bridges cross the entrance to the creek and a log dump and booming ground are in this vicinity.

Holberg Inlet

142   **Holberg Inlet**, entered between Sorenson and Hankin Points, extends 18 miles west from Quatsino Narrows and terminates in an extensive drying flat.

143   A **submarine cable area** crosses the inlet WNW of Sorenson Point and is marked by signs.

144   **Spoil grounds**. — Inactive ocean dumping sites are in *50°35'N, 127°35'W*, 70 m, and in *50°38.7'N, 127°59'W*, 55 m.

145   **Tides**. — Tidal differences in Holberg Inlet, referenced on Winter Harbour, are given for Coal Harbour (Index No. 8765) in *Tide Tables, Volume 6*.

Chart 3681

146   **Coal Harbour** *(50°36'N, 127°35'W)* is fringed with sand, gravel and mud beaches. A shoal spit extends NW from **Stewart Point** and **Stephens Creek** flows into its north end over a drying mud flat. The east side of the harbour is a booming ground.

147   **Coal Harbour** settlement, the site of the last whaling station on the West Coast (closed 1967) and an RCAF seaplane base during World War 2, has a post office, store and coffee shop. It is connected by a paved road to the main highway at Port Hardy. There is a boatyard where engine and hull repairs can be undertaken. A marine railway can haul craft up to 15 m long. Gasoline, diesel fuel and used oil disposal facilities are available at the fuel dock.

148   **Wharf**. — The public wharf has a berthing length of 31 m on its outer face and a depth of 6.4 m alongside, it has a 3 tonne crane and shed. Floats attached to the east and west sides are 58 and 37 m long with depths of about 3.6 m alongside. Power and water are available, and there is a paved boat launching ramp.

149   A **wharf**, 0.3 mile SW of the public wharf, was used for loading ammunition but is in disrepair.

150   **Submarine cables**, west of the public wharf, commence on the north shore and cross the entrance of the harbour to the south side of Holberg Inlet.

151   A **submarine pipeline** (sewer outfall), marked by a sign, extends about 300 m from the north shore 0.5 mile WNW of Stewart Point.

152   **Anchorage** in Coal Harbour can be obtained 0.3 mile NNE of Stewart Point in 22 m, mud bottom. Do not anchor west of a line drawn south from the public wharf.

Chart 3681

153   Coal Harbour is a **water aerodrome**.

154   **Fishing boundary markers** are close south of Stewart Point and about 0.5 mile WSW of the public wharf.

Chart 3679

155   **Thorp Point** *(50°35'N, 127°37'W)* is cliffy and steep-to. Marine farm facilities are close east and west of Thorp Point.

156   **Pot Rock**, 0.6 mile NW of Thorp Point, has three drying heads. The bay, 0.4 mile NE of Pot Rock, has drying reefs in its entrance and a conspicuous white cliff on its west side.

157   **Apple Bay** is filled with drying flats of gravel and boulders. A fishing boundary marker is on the west end of **Orr Island** and an abandoned log dump and concrete remains of a barge ramp are 1 mile west.

158   **Glerup Rock** is a drying rock at the east extremity of **Straggling Islands**.

159   **Light**. — Straggling Islands light *(73)*, on the west extremity of the largest island, is shown at an elevation of 5.6 m from a white tower with a red band at the top.

160   **Henriksen Point** is low, swampy, fringed with a stony drying flat and has a fishing boundary marker on it. **Michelsen Point**, on the south shore, has a drying shingle ledge extending from it.

161   **Jules Bay**, SE of **Dahlstrom Point**, is filled with a gravel drying flat. A log dump, A-frame and booming ground are close NW of **Norton Point**. The bay on the south shore 4 miles WNW of Dahlstrom Point is filled with a gravel drying flat.

162   **Caution. — The section of Holberg Inlet, 4.5 miles west of Dahlstrom Point, is known locally as Holberg Narrows. The fairway, with depths in excess of 10 m, is narrowed to about 100 m by a drying reef and shoal off the south shore and a shoal spit extending from the north shore.**

163   **Beacon**. — A private daybeacon, on the south shore at the west end of Holberg Narrows, is a white tripod in disrepair (1988).

164   **Clesklagh Creek**, 4.5 miles from the head of Holberg Inlet, flows into the north side of the inlet across a gravel drying flat. A rock with 1.5 m over it lies near mid-channel south.

165   **Fishing boundary markers** are on the north and south sides of the inlet, about 3 miles from its head.

166   **Holberg** is a logging community. There is a coffee shop, store and post office. A gravel road connects it to the main island highway at Port Hardy and a dirt road leads south to Winter Harbour.

167   **Floats**. — A pier extends across the drying flat at the head of the inlet; it has berthing floats at its outer end and on its north side. The outer end of the pier has three sheds on it. A floating breakwater extends south from the north shore and protects floats on the north side of the pier. The floats have power but no fresh water. A boat launching ramp is on the north side.

168   **Booming grounds** line the north and south sides of the inlet in the vicinity of Holberg.

Kyuquot Sound

Chart 3682

169   **Kyuquot Sound** *(50°00'N, 127°13'W)*, surrounded by high mountains, has two main branches and a number of smaller ones. Several islands lie within the sound. Union Island lies in the entrance and separates Kyuquot Channel from Crowther Channel.

170   **Whiteley Island** *(50°01'N, 127°12'W)* lies at the NE end of Kyuquot Channel. Except for some drying rocks close east of its south extremity it is steep-to. **Balcom Point** is its east extremity. Marine farm facilities are in **Centre Cove**, on the NE shore.

171   **Cachalot Inlet** *(50°00'N, 127°09'W)*, entered south of **Machta Point**, has the remains of a whaling station and cannery fronted by ruined piles 0.5 mile WSW of Machta Point. Little is visible except the concrete statue of a whale partially hidden in the bushes. Remains of disused log dumps are on the south entrance point and on the north shore, close east of the Indian Reserve on Machta Point. It is reported that during strong SE gales heavy squalls funnel through the valley at the head of the inlet.

172   **Amai Inlet** *(50°01'N, 127°09'W)* has a high precipice close east of its north entrance point. **Amai Point**, its south entrance point, has drying and below-water rocks on its north side. Marine farm facilities are 0.6 mile NE of Amai Point. A few broken piles are all that remain of an old wharf at the head of the inlet.

173   **Anchorage** can be obtained near the head of Amai Inlet in 14 fathoms (26 m), mud bottom. During south gales heavy squalls from the valley make this anchorage unsafe.

174   **Pinnace Channel** separates **Hohoae Island** from the east shore of the sound; **Markale Point** is at the north entrance. The channel is deep but several dangers lie within 0.1 mile of both shores. Marine farm facilities are in the cove 1.25 miles ESE of Hohoae Point.

175   **Tides**. — Tidal differences in Pinnace Channel, referenced on Tofino, are given for Copp Island (Index No. 8714) in *Tide Tables, Volume 6*.

176   **Dixie Cove**, on the west side of Pinnace Channel, is protected by **Copp Island** and provides sheltered **anchorage** in 8 fathoms (15 m). A narrow passage leads to a secluded inner cove with rock cliffs on one side. **Dixie Cove Marine Park** includes all of Copp Island and surrounding waters and portions of Hohoae Island surrounding Dixie Cove, there are no facilities.

177   **Unsworth Point** *(50°01'N, 127°14'W)* has a rock awash and several drying reefs close-off its south side. **Hohoae Point** is the west extremity of Hohoae Island. **Chutsis Island** is separated from the north extremity of Union Island by a passage fouled with rocks. A fishing boundary marker is on **Guillod Point** *(50°03.5'N, 127°16'W)*.

178   **Chamiss Bay** *(50°04'N, 127°17'W)* is entered between Guillod Point and **Chamiss Point**. A rock, with less than 6 feet (1.8 m) over it, 0.2 mile off the south shore is marked by port hand buoy "M37". The settlement has a large logging camp with an oil storage tank and float.

179   **Jansen Bay**, north of Chamiss Point, is the site of a former logging camp. The small cove at the north end of Jansen Bay has drying rocks in its entrance but affords sheltered anchorage for small craft.

180   **Markale Passage** separates Hohoae Island from **Moketas Island**. **Warren Rocks**, the highest of which is 1 foot (0.3 m) high, lie on the north side of the fairway and are steep-to.

181   **Eelstow Passage**, between Moketas Island and the north shore of the sound, has a drying rock off the south side of the passage, midway along the north shore of Moketas Island. A rock that dries 15 feet (4.6 m) and a rock with less than 6 feet (1.8 m) over it lie in the middle of the east entrance, about 0.5 mile north of **McGrath Point**.

182   **Tahsish Inlet** extends 6 miles NE from Moketas Island and has steep, rugged shores. **Werner Bay** *(50°06'N, 127°10'W)*

Chart 3682

has the remains of a log dump and an abandoned barge at its head, and is fronted by a booming ground. **Yaku Bay**, north of **Christine Island**, is too deep for satisfactory anchorage. **Artlish River** is fronted by a drying flat with a booming ground, barge grid and float at its south end. A boat launch and parking area are available, and well maintained gravel roads provide the shortest access from Kyuquot Sound to Highway 19. Slopes on the south side of Artlish River have been logged and a logging road follows the slope to the barge grid. **Tahsish River**, at the head of the inlet, is fronted by an extensive drying flat.

183 **Tides**. — Tidal differences in Tahsish Inlet, referenced on Tofino, are given for Fair Harbour (Index No. 8715) in *Tide Tables, Volume 6*.

184 The estuary of the Tahsish River is an **Ecological Reserve**.

185 The head of Tahsish Inlet is within the boundary of **Tahsish-Kwois Provincial Park**.

186 **Fair Harbour**, on the south side of the entrance to Tahsish Inlet, is entered between **Markale Peninsula** and **Karouk Island**. An area of drying rocks extends 0.1 mile north from Markale Peninsula and rocks and shoals extend south from Karouk Island. The channel east of Karouk Island is not recommended because of shoal areas and rocks NE and SE of the island.

187 **Lights**. — Karouk Island light *(85)*, on the west side of the island, is shown at an elevation of 7.2 m from a white tower.

188 Fair Harbour Approach light *(86)* is on a drying rock close south of Karouk Island.

189 Fair Harbour light *(87)* is 0.7 mile SE of Karouk Island and shown at an elevation of 10.6 m from a white tower.

190 Shores of Fair Harbour are high and steep, except at the west end where a low isthmus separates it from Pinnace Channel, and at the east end where **Kaouk River** flows into the harbour. An extensive drying flat with boulders extends 0.8 mile from the east end of the harbour. A causeway, part of a restricted logging road that connects the harbour to Zeballos, crosses the drying flat.

191 **Anchorage** with mud bottom and good holding ground can be obtained near the east end of Fair Harbour in 16 fathoms (29 m) or near the west end in a depth of 19 fathoms (35 m). During north gales the wind funnels through the east reach making the anchorage uncomfortable.

192 **Wharf**. — The public wharf, on the south side near the drying flats at the east end of Fair Harbour, has a berthing length of 80 feet (24 m) on its NE side. A float 94 feet (29 m) long is attached to it, and the wharf has a 3 tonne crane. It is reported (2004) that a store and fuel facility are operating near the public wharf. Gas, diesel, propane and provisions are available.

193 The ruins of a large timber wharf are close north. There is a boat launching ramp, a barge crib and a large parking lot. A forestry service campsite with outhouses is close east.

194 **Directions**. — Approaching Fair Harbour give a wide berth to drying rocks extending north from Markale Peninsula and pass midway between Markale Peninsula and Karouk Island. Care must be taken when passing Fair Harbour Approach light because of shoals extending south of the light and north from the south shore. When the south part of the entrance channel is well open steer a mid-channel course into the harbour.

195 **Kashutl Inlet**, entered between **Expedition Islets** *(50°06′N, 127°14′W)* and a group of islets and drying rocks 0.8 mile west, extends 6 miles NW and terminates in the drying mud flat formed by **Kashutl River**.

196 **Anchorage** can be obtained at the head of Kashutl Inlet, about 0.2 mile from the edge of the drying flat, in 15 to 20 fathoms (27 to 37 m).

197 **Hankin Cove**, east of Expedition Islets, affords sheltered anchorage to small craft in 7 to 9 fathoms (13 to 16 m), mud. The bay north of Hankin Cove has a log dump, floats and booming ground (1988).

198 **Monteith Bay**, 2.3 miles NW of Expedition Islets, has several rocks near its south entrance point. A booming ground and ruined wharf are in the SE corner (1988). A barge loading ramp and conveyor serving a silica mine are in the NW corner.

199 **Easy Inlet** *(50°08′N, 127°18′W)* provides anchorage in 16 fathoms (29 m), 0.5 mile south of **Kayouk Bluff**. A drying reef lies close north of Kayouk Bluff. The east shore of the inlet should be favoured because two drying flats, at the mouths of rivers, extend up to 0.2 mile off the west side. The site of a cannery and a barge loading wharf are on the west shore and booming grounds line the east and west shores (1988).

200 **Kauwinch River**, on the NE side of Kashutl Inlet, has an extensive steep-to drying flat at its entrance. Fuel tanks and a private float are on the point to the south of the river.

201 **Wood Cove** *(50°09′N, 127°19′W)* is reported to provide anchorage for small craft. Booming grounds are on the east shore 0.4 mile NE of Wood Cove (1991) and at the head of the inlet.

Esperanza Inlet

Chart 3676

202 **Esperanza Inlet** *(49°50′N, 127°00′W)* separates the north side of Nootka Island from Vancouver Island. Hecate Channel and Tahsis Narrows, at its east end, connect Esperanza Inlet to Tahsis Inlet. Port Eliza, Espinosa and Zeballos Inlets, are on its north side. It connects with Nootka Sound forming a sheltered "inside passage" for this portion of the West Coast.

203 The entrance is encumbered with many dangers but the fairway through the inlet, with the exception of Tahsis Narrows at its east end, has a least width of 0.5 mile. Shores are rugged and backed by high mountains.

204 **Anchorage** can be obtained in Rolling Roadstead, Port Eliza or in the bay east of Garden Point.

205 **Aspect**. — **Leading Hill** *(49°52′N, 127°01′W)*, conical in shape, is conspicuous from seaward. **Eliza Dome** *(49°53′N, 127°06′W)* and **Mount Rosa** *(49°48′N, 126°54′W)* are prominent from seaward.

206 **Tides**. — Tidal differences in Esperanza Inlet, referenced on Tofino, are given for Ceepeecee (Index No. 8664) in *Tide Tables, Volume 6*.

207 **Vessel Traffic Services** (VTS). — *Calling-in Point No. 9* of the *Tofino Traffic Zone, Esperanza Inlet*, is a line joining Tatchu Point *(49°51′N, 127°09′W)* to Ferrer Point *(49°45′N, 126°59′W)*. When entering or leaving Esperanza Inlet, a report should be made to *Tofino Traffic*, 156.725 MHz Channel 74.

208 A brief description of this VTS is given in *PAC 200*. Full details are in *Radio Aids to Marine Navigation (Pacific and Western Arctic)*.

Chart 3676

Esperanza Inlet — Entrance

209   Three channels lead through the dangers in the entrance to Esperanza Inlet. **Catala Island** *(49°50'N, 127°03'W)*, **Double Island** *(49°51'N, 127°00'W)* and **Rosa Island** *(49°50'N, 126°58'W)* are wooded. **Flower Islet**, close NW of Rosa Island, is bare.

210   **Catala Island Marine Park** encompasses the island and surrounding waters including White Rock, Halftide Reef, Twin Islands and Mid Rock. There are no facilities.

211   **Gillam Channel** leads between **Blind Reef** and **Middle Reef** and has a fairway 0.6 mile wide. It is the widest and best approach to Esperanza Inlet. The highest part of Blind Reef is 1.2 m and Middle Reef is 1 m high at its SW extremity. Breakers are usually present on both reefs and kelp is present during summer and autumn months.

212   **Buoys.** — Esperanza Inlet light and whistle buoy "MD" *(88)*, about 1 mile SSE of Middle Reef in the seaward approach to Gillam Channel, is a fairway buoy with a Racon (— • —).

213   Middle Reef light buoy "M41" *(89)*, east of the reef, is a port hand buoy.

214   Blind Reef starboard hand buoy "M42" lies west of the reef.

215   **Lights.** — Double Island light *(91)* is shown at an elevation of 10.2 m from a white tower with a green band at the top, 3.8 m high.

216   Nuchatlitz light *(90)*, on an unnamed island 0.5 mile SW of Rosa Island, is shown at an elevation of 11.2 m from a white tower, 4.5 m high.

217   **North Channel**, separated from Gillam Channel by Middle Reef, is not recommended. It is encumbered with shoals and rocks with 2.1 and 1.3 m over them. **Low Rock, Outer Black Rock, Twin Islands, Mid Rock** and **Black Rock** lie on its NW side.

218   **Leading marks.** — Black Rock in line with the east Double Island, bearing 044°, leads between the dangers SE of Low Rock and those north of Middle Reef.

219   **Halftide Reef** *(49°50'N, 127°05'W)*, **Obstruction Reef, High Rocks, White Rock** and many unnamed reefs and rocks lie west of Catala Island in the west approach to Rolling Roadstead. The channels between these dangers are narrow, intricate and local knowledge is advised. **Yellow Bluff Bay**, between **Yellow Bluff** and **Peculiar Point**, has white buildings of a logging camp on its east shore (1998).

220   **Rolling Roadstead** separates the north coast of Catala Island from Vancouver Island. Drying and below-water rocks fringe the north shore of the passage.

221   **Entrance Reef**, which dries 2 m, and **Arnold Rock**, which is 1 m high, lie in the east entrance to Rolling Roadstead. A rock with 2.7 m over it lies 0.4 mile north of Entrance Reef.

222   **Buoy.** — Entrance Reef buoy "MJ" is a port bifurcation buoy.

223   **Anchorage** for small vessels can be obtained in Rolling Roadstead in fair wather about 0.5 mile NW of Entrance Reef in about 7 m, sand and shell, or between Entrance Reef and Double Island in about 14 m, sand. A swell is usually present. Careful navigation is required to avoid dangers in the entrances.

224   **Directions.** — Enter Rolling Roadstead from the east by bringing White Rock in line with the north point of Catala Island, which is low and grassy. These two marks in line bearing 285° lead between Entrance Reef and the rock with 2.7 m over it.

225   **Nuchatlitz** *(49°49'N, 126°58'W)* is an Indian community on the island 0.9 mile SE of Nuchatlitz light. Buildings are abandoned and in ruins. Several houses are in the surrounding area. Nuchatlitz is approached from the south side of Esperanza Inlet through a narrow and tortuous channel entered between Rosa Island and Nuchatlitz light. Drying reefs lie in the entrance and within the channel. Starboard hand buoys "M46" and "M48" mark dangers in the channel. Local knowledge is advised. Marine farm facilities, marked by buoys, are east of the community.

226   **Rosa Harbour** (local name), on the east side of Rosa Island, affords good anchorage with little swell and protection from most winds.

Esperanza Inlet — Inner Reach

227   **Centre Island** *(49°51'N, 126°56'W)* is wooded. **Graveyard Bay** lies on the north side of the inlet, 2.5 miles ENE of Centre Island. **Ehatisaht**, 0.7 mile east of Graveyard Bay, is an abandoned, overgrown Indian village with no visible remains.

228   **Lights.** — Centre Island light *(92)* is on the NW side of the island.

229   Ehatisaht light *(93)* is on a point 1.3 miles east of Ehatisaht.

230   **Cliff Cove** (local name), 0.7 mile NE of Ehatisaht light, has a fishing boundary marker on the south entrance point and marine farm facilities on its north side.

231   **Anchorage** for small vessels can be obtained in the bay east of **Garden Point** *(49°51'N, 126°54'W)* in 30 m with good holding, mud bottom.

232   **Saltery Bay**, SW of **Steamer Point** *(49°53'N, 126°48'W)*, is too deep for anchorage. Marine farm facilities are off the south shore of Saltery Bay, in the bay SE of Steamer Point and 0.8 mile NW of Steamer Point.

233   **Light.** — Steamer Point light *(94)* is on the point.

234   A **booming ground** with a barge loading ramp is on the south side of Esperanza Inlet 1.1 miles east of Garden Point. A logging camp, barge ramp, A-frame and float are at the head of Cliff Cove (1988).

Hecate Channel and Tahsis Narrows

235   **Hecate Channel** connects the east end of Esperanza Inlet to Tahsis Narrows. The fairway is deep and free of dangers.

236   **Lord Waterfall** *(49°53.5'N, 126°26'W)*, at the mouth of **Lutes Creek**, is conspicuous.

237   **Marine farm** facilities are about 0.4 mile south of the waterfall and 1.1 miles SE of Haven Cove.

238   **Haven Cove** *(49°53'N, 126°47'W)*, known locally as **God's Pocket**, provides limited anchorage for small craft. A rock, with 1.1 m over it, lies off the entrance to the cove and a rock, with 1.4 m over it, lies off the south entrance point.

239   **Esperanza** on the north shore of Hecate Channel has the Nootka Mission, which operates year-round. It is not connected by road to other settlements. The Nootka Sound Ferry calls at frequent intervals.

240   **Beacon.** — Esperanza daybeacon, 0.1 mile WNW of the public wharf on a dolphin, has a port hand daymark. It marks the edge of a drying bank.

241   **Wharf.** — An L-shaped public wharf has a berthing length along its seaward side of 29 m and depths of 4.9 to 5.8 m alongside. A fuel float, attached to the east side of the wharfhead, is 15 m long with a depth of 5.8 m alongside. Gas, diesel, water, moorage, water, laundry, and showers are available.

Chart 3676

Nuchatlitz (1988)

242   A wharf, 0.1 mile NW of the public wharf, has floats with a combined length of 43 m.

243   **Ceepeecee**, 1 mile east of Esperanza, is abandoned. Steamer Point Lodge and float are 0.4 mile south of Ceepeecee.

244   **Light**. — McBride Bay light *(97.8)* is on the west extremity of the peninsula separating McBride Bay from Tahsis Narrows.

245   **McBride Bay** *(49°51′N, 126°43′W)* has two large concrete pier footings on the south shore, close east of a small islet and a wreck is south of the islet. A rock that dries 0.8 m lies between the islet and shore. **Hecate** on the west entrance point is abandoned. Concrete pier footings and two buildings are all that remain of the former logging camp. Fuel tanks are 0.4 mile NW of Hecate.

246   **Tahsis Narrows** connects Hecate Channel to Tahsis Inlet and has a minimum width of 0.1 mile in its fairway. Two shoals lie in the middle of the fairway; the least depth over them is 9.6 m.

247   **Tides**. — Tidal differences for Ceepeecee (Index No. 8664), referenced on Tofino, are in *Tide Tables, Volume 6.*

248   **Tidal streams** in Tahsis Narrows are weak.

249   **Lights**. — Tahsis Narrows North light *(98)* is on the north side of the narrows about 0.6 mile SSE of Ceepeecee.

250   Tahsis Narrows South light *(98.3)* is on the south side of the narrows 0.7 mile ESE of the north light.

251   Tahsis Narrows light *(99)* is on **Mozino Point**.

252   **Beacon**. — Tahsis Narrows North daybeacon, on the north side of the narrows 0.3 mile NE of Tahsis Narrows South light, has a starboard hand daymark.

Port Eliza

253   **Harbour Island** *(49°51′N, 126°59′W)* is wooded and lies in the entrance to Port Eliza. **Fairway Island**, 0.3 mile east of Harbour Island, is covered with stunted trees.

254   **False Channel**, west of Harbour Island, is encumbered with drying and below-water rocks. Local knowledge is advised.

255   **Birthday Channel**, east of Harbour Island, is obstructed by Fairway Island and rocks surrounding it. Several drying reefs, 0.3 mile north of Fairway Island, extend from the Vancouver Island shore.

256   **Channel Reef**, 0.5 mile north of Harbour Island, dries 2.1 m in its north part and lies in mid-channel.

257   **Beacon**. — Channel Reef daybeacon, on the south end of the reef, has a bifurcation/junction daymark, preferred channel to the left.

258   **Directions**. — Enter Port Eliza by way of Birthday Channel passing either west or NE of Fairway Island. If passing NE of Fairway Island give drying reefs close-off the Vancouver Island shore a wide berth and pass slightly less than 0.1 mile east of Harbour Island. **Caution is required in these passages.**

259   If proceeding to Queen Cove pass east of Channel Reef daybeacon and west of the islands in the entrance to the cove.

260   When proceeding to the head of Port Eliza pass to the west of Channel Reef daybeacon and then maintain a mid-channel course.

Chart 3676

261   **Queen Cove**, NNE of Channel Reef, has a narrow entrance with a least depth of 5 m; it is almost land-locked but easy of access. Concrete ruins of a cannery lie close south of **Saddle Point**. **Queens Cove**, an Indian village on the east entrance point, has a conspicuous church spire at its east end. Anchorage for small vessels can be obtained in 10 to 12 m, mud bottom.

262   **Port Eliza** has high shores and its fairway is narrowed in places by drying and below-water rocks. The cove, 0.4 mile SSW of **Eliza Island**, has a floating logging camp, an A-frame, booming ground (1996) and a short length of logging road leading through the valley north of Leading Hill terminating near Yellow Bluff. **Eliza Creek**, at the head of the inlet, is fronted by a drying flat. A logging camp, dry land sorting area, oil storage tanks and a booming ground are on the east side near the drying flats (1996). Anchorage can be obtained about 0.5 mile from the head of Port Eliza, in 20 to 30 m, mud bottom.

Espinosa Inlet

263   **Espinosa Inlet** has no dangers beyond 0.1 mile offshore and is too deep for satisfactory anchorage. A drying flat, at the head of the inlet, forms the mouth of **Espinosa Creek**. A float is on the east shore at the edge of the drying flat.

264   **Otter Islands** *(49°52'N, 126°56'W)* lie off the west entrance point to Espinosa Inlet with a rock, which dries 3.8 m, 0.1 mile SW of the south island. The passage west of these islands is only suitable for small craft; local knowledge is advised. A fishing boundary marker is on the east entrance point to the inlet.

265   **Newton Cove**, 0.5 mile NW of Otter Islands, is small and free of dangers. A floating fishing lodge on the south side of the cove offers moorage, accommodation and limited mechanical repairs. A pipeline (fresh water) runs from the creek at the head of the cove to the lodge. A pipeline (sewage discharge) runs from the lodge down the centre of the cove to its entrance. The cove affords temporary anchorage for small craft taking care to avoid the pipelines.

266   **Booming grounds** are on the east shore of the inlet 1.5 miles NNE of Otter Islands and on the west side of the inlet, opposite the entrance to Little Espinosa Inlet.

267   **Marine farm** facilities are on the east shore in the cove 0.5 mile north of the entrance to Little Espinosa Inlet.

268   **Little Espinosa Inlet**, on the east side of Espinosa Inlet, has a narrow entrance obstructed with rocks and a drying flat fronting **Nuchatlitz Creek**. It is usable by small craft at or near HW, local knowledge is advised. A bank that dries 2.1 m, 1.7 miles within the entrance, extends across the inlet. A bridge, with a vertical clearance of 0.7 m, crosses the inlet at this drying bank. The restricted logging road on the south side of this bridge leads around the head of the inlet then north to Zeballos. The restricted logging road on the north side of the bridge leads to the head of Espinosa Inlet then NW to Fair Harbour.

269   **Marine farm** facilities are on the west side of the inlet SW of the bridge.

Zeballos Inlet

270   **Zeballos Inlet** *(49°54'N, 126°47'W)* leads north from the east end of Esperanza Inlet. Its shores are rocky and steep-to. Depths are too great for anchorage.

271   **Lights**. — Zeballos Inlet South light *(95)* is on the west shore 1.3 miles north of Steamer Point light.

272   Zeballos Inlet light *(96)*, 2.5 miles north of the south light, is on the east of two islets close-off the west shore.

273   Zeballos Inlet North light *(97)* is 1.5 miles NW of Zeballos Inlet light.

274   **Little Zeballos River**, 0.5 mile north of Zeballos Inlet light, has a drying bank extending from its entrance and a small float is on its west entrance point.

275   **Resolution Park** (Provincial Ministry of Forests), with a float, picnic and camping facilities, is on the south shore 1.5 miles west of Zeballos Inlet light.

276   A **breakwater** and a floating logging camp are 0.3 mile north of Zeballos Inlet North light.

277   **Spoil ground**. — A non-active ocean dumping site is near the head of Zeballos Inlet in *49°58'N, 126°51'W*.

278   **Booming grounds** are on the west shore at the head of the inlet.

279   The head of Zeballos Inlet is a **water aerodrome**.

280   **Zeballos**, at the head of the inlet, is a village with a post office, accommodation, restaurants, store, laundromat, museum, and library. The medical clinic has a doctor in attendance two days a week. Iron ore and gold mines are long closed, and the village is now a centre for logging operations. A gravel road connects the village to the main island highway between Sayward and Port McNeill. Nootka Sound Service Ltd (Uchuck III) operates a scheduled service to Tahsis, Gold River and other settlements in the connecting inlets. Water taxi service is available.

281   **Tides**. — Tidal differences for Zeballos (Index No. 8670), referenced on Tofino, are in *Tide Tables, Volume 6.*

282   **Floats**. — Public floats, on the east side of the causeway, are 91 m long with a depth of 2 m alongside. Power and fresh water are available. A boat launching ramp is close north. **Caution. — A rock with 1.2 m over it lies in the approach to the floats.**

283   A seaplane float and fuel float are located next to the ice plant. Gas, diesel and propane are available.

284   The Village of Zeballos Dock is for loading commercial vessels only, an adjoining small float can be used for temporary tie-up.

285   A line of charred piles extending across the drying flat west of the causeway is all that remains of a wharf used for loading iron ore.

286   **Overhead cables** (power), with a vertical clearance of 14.7 m, close north of the public floats, cross from the east shore to the causeway.

Nuchatlitz Inlet

287   **Nuchatlitz Inlet** indents the west coast of Nootka Island for 10 miles. Both sides of the inlet are mountainous. **Northwest Cone** *(49°45'N, 126°58'W)* is prominent from the SW.

288   **Nuchatlitz Reef** *(49°46'N, 126°59'W)* lies in the middle of the entrance to the inlet. **Pin Rock**, 0.6 mile north, dries 3.3 m. Numerous detached rocks, with a least depth of 0.1 m and that break in heavy weather, lie between Nuchatlitz Reef and Pin Rock. Drying and below-water rocks and **Ensanada Islet** lie off the north shore.

289   **Danger Rock**, 0.4 mile south of Nuchatlitz Reef and 1 mile NNW of **Ferrer Point**, has 0.8 m over it and breaks in heavy weather. Isolated rocks with 8.3 and 4.5 m over them, 0.3 mile NW

Chart 3676

Nuchatlitz Inlet leading marks (1988)

and 0.8 mile NE of Ferrer Point, **South Reef** and **Frank Rocks** are dangers off the south shore.

290   **Justice Rock** *(49°46'N, 126°56'W)* is 8 m high and bare. **Fitz Island**, 0.7 mile ENE, is wooded. **Cameron Rocks**, 0.6 mile NE, consist of a group of drying and above-water rocks.

291   **Leading marks**. — The NW extremity of Fitz Island in line with **Mark Hill** *(49°47'N, 126°49'W)*, bearing 076°, leads about 0.2 mile south of Danger Rock and 0.2 mile north of the 4.5 m rock lying west of South Reef (see photograph).

292   **Louie Bay**, entered between **Tongue Point** *(49°45'N, 126°56'W)* and **Florence Point**, has drying reefs off both entrance points. It is only suitable for small craft and local knowledge is advised. A large steel wreck, broken into three parts, lies on the drying flat in Louie Bay. Tongue Point is densely wooded.

293   **Port Langford** is entered between **Colwood Rocks** *(49°47'N, 126°56'W)* and **Belmont Point**. A rock, 0.3 mile SE of Colwood Rocks, has 3.3 m over it. Port Langford is not recommended as an anchorage as it is exposed to SW and holding ground is poor.

294   **Hixson Bluff**, with **Sara Islet** and drying rocks close west of it, are on the south shore of Nuchatlitz Inlet. **Benson Point**, on the north shore, has islets and drying rocks east and west of it.

295   **Mary Basin**, between **Lord Island** and **Narrows Island**, provides anchorage in about 7 m, mud.

296   **Inner Basin**, at the head of Nuchatlitz Inlet, is entered through a narrow passage only suitable for small craft. Local knowledge is advised. Tidal streams run with strength through the passage. Fishing boundary markers are on the north and south shores at the entrance to Inner Basin.

Nootka Sound

Chart 3675

297   **Nootka Sound**, on the east side of Nootka Island, is entered between **Maquinna Point** *(49°35'N, 126°40'W)* and

Escalante Point, 5 miles SE. Shores at the entrance are low, but within the sound they become high, rugged and precipitous.

298   Tahsis Inlet, at the NW end, is connected to Esperanza Inlet, on the west side of Nootka Island, by Tahsis Narrows. The narrows are deep, free of dangers, and have little current running through them. Tlupana Inlet leads north and Muchalat Inlet leads east from the sound.

299   **Aspect**. — From seaward a number of features in fine weather readily aid identifying Nootka Sound. **Nootka Cone** *(49°37'N, 126°39'W)* is conspicuous. **Conuma Peak** *(49°50'N, 126°19'W)* is a remarkable steeple-shaped mountain *(Chart 3001)*. Land on both sides of the entrance is low with breakers off it.

300   **Anchorage** in Nootka Sound can be obtained in the Spanish Pilot Group or Plumper Harbour. Small craft can obtain anchorage in Friendly Cove.

301   **Tides**. — Tidal differences in Nootka Sound, referenced on Tofino, are given for Saavedra Islands (Index No. 8645) in *Tide Tables, Volume 6*.

302   **Vessel Traffic Services** (VTS). — *Calling-in Point No. 8* of the *Tofino Traffic Zone, Nootka Sound*, is a line joining Bajo Point *(49°37'N, 126°50'W)* to Estevan Point light *(114)*. When entering or leaving Nootka Sound, a report should be made to *Tofino Traffic*, 156.725 MHz, Channel 74.

303   A brief description of this VTS is in *PAC 200*. Details are in *Radio Aids to Marine Navigation (Pacific and Western Arctic)*.

Nootka Sound — Entrance

304   **Escalante Rocks** *(49°32'N, 126°35'W)* consist of a group of above-water and drying rocks, the highest has an elevation of 4 m. **Escalante Island** is wooded. Reefs extend up to 1 mile offshore between Escalante Rocks and **Burdwood Point**, 3 miles north.

305   A **submarine cable** (abandoned) crosses the entrance of Nootka Sound from a bay close north of Burdwood Point to Santa Gertrudis Cove.

306   **Yuquot Point** *(49°35'N, 126°37'W)*, 2 miles ENE of Maquinna Point, together with **San Miguel Islands** and **San Rafael Island**, form the south side of Friendly Cove. Shoals and

Chart 3675

Nootka light bearing 230° (1988)

reefs extend up to 0.7 mile offshore between Maquinna and Yuquot Points.

307   **Light**. — Nootka light *(105)*, on the summit of San Rafael Island, is shown at an elevation of 30.9 m from a skeleton tower.

308   **Friendly Cove**, NW of San Rafael Island, affords limited anchorage to small craft. Captain Vancouver and Captain Quadra negotiated the Nootka convention here in 1790 giving control of the Pacific Northwest to England. Shores are rocky and the church in the village is prominent. **Yuquot** is an Indian village at the head of the cove. Most of the surrounding land belongs to the Mowachaht First Nation and a fee is charged for landing. There are cabins for rent, water taxi service and charter float planes. The Uchuck III provides regularly scheduled summer ferry service.

309   **Rock breakwaters** connect the west side of San Rafael Island to Nootka Island and the north side of the same island to a small islet close north.

310   The **public wharf**, in the SW corner of Friendly Cove, has a long trestle approach and a berthing face of 15 m with a depth of 2.1 m alongside. A seasonal float is moored between the dolphins on the NW side of the public wharf (1998). The wharf has a storage shed on it. A private float is north of the public wharf. A mooring buoy close north of the NE end of the public wharf is for Coast Guard use only for re-supplying the Nootka light station.

311   **Santa Gertrudis Cove**, 0.5 mile north of Friendly Cove, is encumbered in its entrance by an islet, above-water rocks and a drying rock. Inside it offers sheltered anchorage for small craft.

312   **Bligh Island Marine Park** encompasses the south portion of Bligh Island, the Spanish Pilot Group and Villaverde Islands.

313   **Bligh Island**, the largest island in the centre of Nootka Sound, has mountains with elevations in excess of 305 m. **Ewin Inlet** penetrates the south side of Bligh Island.

314   **Spanish Pilot Group**, off the SW end of Bligh Island, consists of several islands, numerous islets, rocks and reefs. Those channels encumbered with drying and below-water rocks should not be used. The named islands are **Pantoja Islands**, **Spouter Island**, **Clotchman Island**, **Narvaez Island**, **Vernaci Island** and **Verdia Island**.

315   **Anchorage** with limited swinging room can be obtained midway between Narvaez and Vernaci Islands in 44 m, mud bottom. Care should be taken to avoid rocks, covered 3 and 3.2 m that lie off the SW and SE extremities, respectively, of Vernaci Island. Another rock, covered 2.6 m, lies off the north extremity of Narvaez Island.

Cook Channel and Eliza Passage

316   **Cook Channel** leads north between Nootka Island and the Spanish Pilot Group to the inlets in the north and NW parts of Nootka Sound.

317   **Boston Point** *(49°40'N, 126°37'W)* forms the east side of **Marvinas Bay**. Several rocks lie in the bay and a large cabin with a float is at the NW end.

318   **Lights**. — Vernaci Island light *(104.8)*, on a drying rock off the west side of the island, is shown at an elevation of 7.9 m from a mast 6 m high.

319   Boston Point light *(104)* is on the east side of the point.

320   **McKay Passage**, between **Saavedra Islands** *(49°37'N, 126°37'W)* and Nootka Island, is narrow but provides a convenient route for small craft bound for Nootka. A rock, with 0.1 m over it, lies off the west shore midway through the passage. A private resort, with a float protected by a floating breakwater, and oil storage tanks and cabins lie on the west side of the central Saavedra Island.

321   A **submarine pipeline** (water), marked by signs, crosses McKay Passage at the central part of the middle Saavedra Island.

322   **Nootka**, 0.3 mile west of the north Saavedra Island, is the site of a sport fishing resort. Several large cabins and private floats are in the cove on the south side of the peninsula. Ruins of a large wharf with a shed on it extend north from the north side of the isthmus. Large concrete blocks at the SE end of the peninsula are all that remain of a cannery.

323   **Boca del Infierno Bay**, close south of Nootka, has a narrow entrance. A rock that dries 1.3 m lies at the west end of the narrows. A submarine cable sign is on its south entrance point. Tidal streams in the entrance are so strong it can only be entered by small craft at slack water.

324   **Fidalgo Passage**, between **Villaverde Islands** *(49°40'N, 126°35'W)* and Bligh Island, is encumbered with drying, above and below water rocks. The fairway is deep and not less than 0.25 mile wide. Booming grounds and a log dump are in the bay on the west shore of Bligh Island 0.7 mile SW of San Carlos Point.

325   **Eliza Passage**, between Villaverde Islands and Strange Island, provides the best approach to the south entrances of Tahsis and Tlupana Inlets.

326   **Salter Point** *(49°41'N, 126°35'W)* is the SE extremity of Strange Island. **San Carlos Point**, 2.5 miles east, is the north extremity of Bligh Island.

327   **Lights**. — Salter Point light *(103.5)* is on the point.

328   San Carlos Point light *(108)* is shown at an elevation of 6 m from a white tower, 5.6 m high.

Chart 3675

329 **Spoil ground**. — An ocean dump site, under permit through the *Ocean Dumping Control Act*, is in the east part of Eliza Passage in *49°40.8'N, 126°34.3'W*.

Zuciarte and Hanna Channels

330 **Zuciarte Channel**, entered north of **Discovery Point** *(49°35'N, 126°33'W)*, leads north along the east side of **Clerke Peninsula** to Hanna Channel and the entrance of Muchalat Inlet. Its fairway is deep and free of dangers.

331 **Resolution Cove**, on the east side of Clerke Peninsula, is inconvenient as an anchorage. It is of historical interest where Captain Cook refitted his ships in April 1778.

332 **Anderson Point** *(49°39'N, 126°28'W)* is the north extremity of a high rounded projection; it is steep-to.

333 **Lights**. — Clerke Peninsula light *(107)*, on the south extremity of the peninsula, is shown at an elevation of 12.2 m from a mast.

334 Zuciarte Channel South light *(108.5)* is 0.8 mile SE of Clerke Peninsula light.

335 Zuciarte Channel light *(109.5)* is on the east side of Bligh Island at the north end of Zuciarte Channel.

336 Anderson Point light *(109.8)* is on the point.

337 **Spoil ground**. — A non-active ocean dump site is at the north end of Zuciarte Channel *(49°39'N, 126°29'W)*.

338 **Hanna Channel**, entered NE of **Concepcion Point** *(49°40'N, 126°29'W)*, connects Zuciarte Channel to the entrance of Tlupana Inlet and Eliza Passage.

339 The small bay, SW of Concepcion Point, is too deep and confined for satisfactory anchorage. The south entrance point to the bay is a prominent cliffy projection.

340 **Light**. — Hanna Channel light *(109)* is on the NE shore of Bligh Island 1 mile NW of Concepcion Point.

341 **Buoy**. — Hanna Channel starboard hand buoy "M52" is 0.5 mile NE of Concepcion Point, SW of a rock with 1 m over it. Upstream direction for buoyage purposes is proceeding NW through Hanna Channel.

342 A **marina**, protected by a floating breakwater, is in the cove 0.9 mile NE of Concepcion Point. A breakwater is on the north side of the north entrance point to the marina (1998). The marina offers moorage, boat launching, gas, oil, store, bait and showers.

Kendrick Inlet and Princesa Channel

343 **Kendrick Inlet** *(49°42'N, 126°38'W)* is formed by Nootka Island on its west and Strange and Bodega Islands on its east side. **James Cone** on **Strange Island** is prominent.

344 **Plumper Harbour**, on the west side of the inlet, is protected by **Funter Island** and **Matute Island**. It is used extensively as a booming ground and has a logging camp with an A-frame on its west shore.

345 **Beacon**. — Matute Island daybeacon, on the SW point of the island, has a starboard hand daymark.

346 **Anchorage** with good shelter can be obtained in 22 m in the middle of Plumper Harbour. The anchorage can be approached between Funter and Matute Islands, avoiding the rocks east of Funter Island, or north of Matute Island rounding it at a distance of not more than 0.1 mile to avoid the rock with 2.5 m over it lying 0.2 mile NNW of Matute Island.

347 A chain of islets *(49°43'N, 126°39'W)* lie close-off the west shore 1.2 miles NNE of Matute Island.

348 **Light**. — Kendrick Inlet light *(102)* is on a rock at the north end of the islets.

349 **Kendrick Camp**, 0.5 mile NW of Kendrick Inlet light, is a logging camp that has some prominent buildings and an A-frame.

350 **Princesa Channel** leads between Strange and Bodega Islands into Tahsis Inlet. It is very narrow, encumbered with rocks, and only suitable for small craft. Local knowledge is advised.

351 **Beacon**. — Princesa daybeacon, on the south extremity of an unnamed island 0.1 mile south of Bodega Island, has a starboard hand daymark. Upstream direction is proceeding from Tahsis Inlet toward Kendrick Inlet.

352 **Light**. — Princesa Channel light *(101)* is on a reef on the south side of the east entrance of the channel.

Tahsis Inlet

Charts 3675, 3676

353 **Tahsis Inlet**, entered from Nootka Sound between Salter Point *(49°41'N, 126°35'W)* and **Coopte Point**, extends 15 miles in a north direction. Its shores are steep-to, rocky and mountainous. Depths in most places are too great for anchorage.

354 The fairway is narrowed to less than 0.15 mile wide at Tsowwin Narrows, 6 miles north of Salter Point. Tahsis Narrows, 11 miles north of Salter Point and on the west side of the inlet, connects the inlet to Hecate Channel and Esperanza Inlet.

355 **Tidal streams** in Tahsis Inlet attain 3 kn at times in Tsowwin Narrows. Elsewhere in the inlet they are considerably weaker. The flood sets north and the ebb south.

Chart 3675

356 **Canal Island** *(49°41'N, 126°35'W)* lies in the middle of the south entrance of Tahsis Inlet. The fairway on both sides of the island is not less than 0.15 mile wide.

357 **Jewitt Cove**, on the east side of Strange Island, affords anchorage to small vessels in 29 m, mud bottom. A rock with 3 m over it lies in the middle of the cove.

358 **Lights**. — Canal Island light *(103)* is on the west side of the island.

359 Jewitt Cove light *(102.5)*, on an island off the north entrance to the cove, is shown at an elevation of 6.4 m from a mast.

360 **Beacon**. — Canal Island daybeacon, on the north end of the island, has a port hand daymark.

361 **Bodega Island** *(49°44'N, 126°38'W)* lies north of Strange Island, on the west side of the fairway. The cove at the north end of Bodega Island, locally known as Heron Bay, is reported to afford anchorage with good protection from north and south. A camp with a float and road leading to it are in a small cove on the west side of the inlet 0.4 mile north of Bodega Island.

362 **Light**. — Bodega light *(100.8)* is on the east side of Tahsis Inlet opposite Bodega Island.

Chart 3676

363 **Tsowwin Narrows** *(49°47'N, 126°38'W)* is formed by a drying gravel bank off the mouth of **Tsowwin River** that reduces the fairway to about 0.13 mile wide. **Tidal streams** in the narrows attain 3 kn at times.

Chart 3676

Tahsis from east of Mozino Point (1988)

364   **Booming grounds** with a logging camp and dry land sorting area lie along the east shore close south of Tsowwin Narrows.

365   **Lights**. — Tsowwin Narrows West light *(100.2)* is on the west side of the narrows.

366   Tsowwin Narrows light *(100)*, on the east side of the narrows, is shown from a dolphin with two starboard hand daymarks.

367   Santiago light *(99.5)*, 1 mile NNW of Tsowwin Narrows West light, has two port hand daymarks.

368   **Blowhole Bay**, 3.5 miles north of Tsowwin Narrows, has a log dump, booming grounds, a logging camp with a jetty and float.

369   **Beacon**. — Mozino Point daybeacon, on the east side of the point, has a port hand daymark.

370   **Spoil ground**. — An ocean dump site, under permit through the *Ocean Dumping Control Act*, is in *49°51.6'N, 126°39.6'W*.

371   A **barge grid**, float and booming ground are in a small cove on the west shore 1 mile north of Mozino Point.

372   The head of Tahsis Inlet is a **water aerodrome**.

373   **Leiner River**, on the east side of the inlet, and **Tahsis River** at the head of the inlet are fronted by extensive drying mud flats.

374   A **fishing boundary marker** is on the east shore about 1 mile south of Leiner River.

375   **Booming grounds** line the east and west shores of the inlet in the approach to Tahsis.

376   **Submerged anchors and cables** extend south from the head of the inlet. The east cable is marked by a buoy.

377   **Overhead cables**, vertical clearances 9.1 and 7.2 m, cross the entrance of Tahsis River. A bridge, vertical clearance 2.1 m, crosses the river a short distance north of the cables.

378   **Tahsis**, on the west side of the entrance to Tahsis River, is a village with a post office, health centre, accommodation, retail stores, laundry and RCMP detachment. A well maintained gravel road connects the village to Gold River and from there by paved road to the main island highway at Campbell River. Nootka Sound Service Ltd (Uchuck III) operates a service to Gold River, Zeballos

and other settlements in the connecting inlets. Charter aircraft are available.

379   **Meteorological information** for Tahsis is in the Appendices.

380   **Caution. — A rock, with 7.9 m over it, lies 91 m off the Deep-sea Dock.**

381   **Berths**. — **Deep-sea Dock**, 0.1 mile SW at the head of the inlet, is 144 m long. The berth served the former saw mill which has been dismantled. All equipment has been removed and the major shipping facilities remain unused and in disrepair. It was designed for a vessel of dimensions; length 213 m, beam 30.5 m, draught at stern 12.5 m when berthed port side to, displacement 60,500 tonnes and dead-weight 48,720 tonnes. The fendering system is designed for such a vessel loaded to 75% capacity, approaching perpendicular to the wharf face at a velocity of 15 cm/sec. Fresh water is still obtainable at the wharf.

382   **Remanned Wharf**, on the west entrance point to Tahsis River, running at right angles to Deep-sea Dock is disused and in disrepair.

383   A disused **barge loading ramp** is between the Deep-sea Dock and Remanned Wharf.

384   Ruined piers are on the east side of the river mouth.

385   A **marina**, south of Deep-sea Dock, has floats and a marine service station protected by a floating breakwater. Gas, diesel, washroom, shower, laundry, power, a small store and a courtesy car are available.

386   The **municipal wharf**, on the south side of the entrance to **Ubedam Creek**, has a berthing length of 43 m with a least depth of 4.8 m alongside. A float 30 m long is attached to the north side of the wharfhead. A storage shed and 3 tonne crane are on the wharfhead.

387   A **seaplane float**, south of the municipal wharf, is protected from the south by a floating breakwater. The float is 37 m long and 18 m wide. A boat and aircraft launching ramp is between the seaplane float and municipal wharf.

388   **Supplies and Services**. — Fresh water is available. Light fuel oil, diesel fuel, gasoline, kerosene, lubricants and propane are obtainable. Underwater inspection and repair by divers are available.

Chart 3676

Above-water repairs such as cutting, welding and machinery repairs can be undertaken.

Tlupana Inlet

Chart 3675

389   **Tlupana Inlet** is entered between **Descubierta Point** *(49°41'N, 126°30'W)*, which is fringed by above-water and drying rocks, and **Hoiss Point**, 2 miles WNW. Depths are great and shores are steep and rocky.

390   **Anchorage** can be obtained in Galiano Bay, Hisnit Inlet, Nesook Bay, Moutcha Bay or Head Bay.

391   A float house is in the cove on the north side of Hoiss Point. **Three Bay Cove**, 0.4 mile NE of Descubierta Point, offers shelter for small craft and has float houses in it. Limiting depth into the inner basin is 2.1 m. Marine farm facilities are in the north arm of Three Bay Cove.

392   **Galiano Bay** *(49°43'N, 126°28'W)* can be entered either side of an island in its entrance. Passage south of the island is preferred to avoid dangers in the NE part of the bay. A rock, with less than 2 m over it and connected to the point on the east shore at LW, lies in the narrows leading to the anchorage. A float house is on the east shore of the bay (1998).

393   **Anchorage** in Galiano Bay can be obtained about 0.4 mile SSE of the island in 24 m, mud. Holding is good but swinging room limited.

394   **Cougar Creek Campground**, in an indentation on the SE shore, 0.5 mile NE of Galiano Bay, has a boat launching ramp and float connected to a logging road.

395   **Critter Cove** (local name), is 1.4 miles north of Descubierta Point. A marina and sportfishing resort with fuel float (summer only) protected by a floating breakwater are at the north entrance. There is a restaurant, small store and accomodation. The inner basin affords sheltered anchorage for small craft. Two rocks, one of which dries 1.5 m, lie in the narrow channel leading to the inner basin.

396   **Hisnit Inlet** has two rocks in its centre 1 mile NW of **Argonaut Point**, one dries 0.5 m and the other has less than 2 m over it. **Valdes Bay** lies NW of the north entrance point. Anchorage near the head of Hisnit Inlet can be obtained in 20 m, mud bottom.

397   **Princess Royal Point** *(49°45'N, 126°27'W)* is a bold, rounded point with a fishing boundary marker on it. **Perpendicular Bluff**, 0.8 mile north, has high steep cliffs. Booming grounds lie south of the islet off the west side of the inlet, 1.8 miles NW of Princess Royal Point.

398   **Nesook Bay** has a drying flat at its head over which flows the **Tlupana River**. Small vessels can obtain anchorage in 31 m, mud bottom, north of a rock with 8.4 m over it, 0.2 mile off the east shore. A private mooring buoy is 0.5 mile NE of **Santa Saturnina Point**. Marine farm facilities marked by buoys are on both shores at the head of the bay.

399   **Moutcha Bay**, north of **Quadra Saddle**, affords anchorage in 29 to 33 m SE of a rock that dries 2.6 m, off the north shore of the bay. **Conuma River** flows into the head of the bay across an extensive drying flat. Marine farm facilities lie off the north shore.

400   **Head Bay**, entered west of some islets and a drying bank extending from **Canton Creek**, affords anchorage in 23 m, mud. **Sucwoa River** flows into the head of the bay across a drying flat. A logging camp, conspicuous large shed, barge grid, A-frame and aircraft float, fronted by booming grounds are on the west shore close south of the drying flat.

Muchalat Inlet

401   **Muchalat Inlet**, entered between **Atrevida Point** *(49°39'N, 126°26'W)* and Anderson Point, extends about 14 miles east and then 3 miles SE. Depths are great and the fairway is 0.2 mile wide at its narrowest part. Marine farm facilities are on the east side of Atrevida Point.

402   **Tides**. — Tidal differences in Muchalat Inlet, referenced on Tofino, are given for Gold River (Index No. 8650) in *Tide Tables, Volume 6*.

403   **Mooyah Bay** *(49°38'N, 126°27'W)* has an extensive mud flat at its head and booming grounds with a logging camp on its west side.

Muchalat Inlet from north of Ous Point (1988)

Chart 3675

404 **Williamson Passage**, north of **Gore Island** *(49°39'N, 126°25'W)*, is deep and free of dangers. Booming grounds, a float and a dry land sorting area with fuel tanks lie off drying flats fronting **Kleeptee Creek**.

405 **Lights**. — Atrevida Point light *(110)* is on the point.

406 Gore Island West light *(110.3)* is on the west extremity of the island.

407 Gore Island light *(110.5)* is on the north side of the island 1.6 miles ENE of the west light.

408 Williamson Passage light *(110.7)* is on the north side of the passage 0.7 mile east of Gore Island light.

409 Muchalat Inlet light *(111)* is on the north side of the inlet 1 mile SE of Williamson Passage light.

410 **King Passage**, south of Gore Island, although deep is not recommended because of rocks on each side. Its east entrance is constricted by islets and rocks NW of **Ous Point**. A booming ground and log dump are SW of Ous Point.

411 **Houston River** *(49°38'N, 126°18'W)* has three islands close NE of it. A logging camp with a barge ramp, boat launching ramp and float are 0.7 mile east of the river and a booming ground and log dump are on the north shore NW of the river.

412 **Victor Island** *(49°40'N, 126°09'W)* is wooded. **Jacklah Bay**, south of Victor Island, has booming grounds, a wharf with a derrick and a dry land sort.

413 **McCurdy Creek**, NW of Victor Island, has booming grounds and a logging camp close east.

414 **Lights**. — Houston River light *(111.8)* is on the north side of an island NE of the river entrance.

415 Muchalat Inlet East light *(112)* is on the north shore 1.5 miles ENE of Houston River light.

416 Muchalat Inlet South Shore light *(112.2)* is on the south shore 2 miles east of Muchalat Inlet East light.

417 Victor Island light *(112.4)*, on the north side of the island, has a starboard hand daymark.

418 **Spoil ground**. — An ocean dump site, under permit through the *Ocean Dumping Control Act*, is in *49°39'N, 126°14.9'W*.

419 Muchalat Inlet, in the vicinity of Gold River, is a **water aerodrome**.

420 **Gold River** *(49°41'N, 126°07'W)* port facilities are on the west side of the entrance to Gold River. The pulp mill has been closed and equipment dismantled, though plans exist to redevelop the site. The Deep-Sea Dock, barge loading ramp and loading wharf are currently disused.

421 The village of Gold River, 13 km north, has a post office, hotel, shopping centre, and a RCMP detachment. The village has a medical clinic, resident doctors and a dentist.

422 A paved road connects the village to the main island highway at Campbell River and a gravel road connects it to Tahsis. Nootka Sound Service Ltd (Uchuck III) operates a ferry service to Tahsis, Zeballos and other settlements in connecting inlets. Charter aircraft are available.

423 **Tides**. — Tidal differences for Gold River (Index No. 8650), referenced on Tofino, are in *Tide Tables, Volume 6*.

424 **Lights**. — Gold River light *(113)* is on the west entrance point to Gold River.

425 Privately operated lights are on the outer ends of wharves and on dolphins extending from the former Newsprint Wharf.

426 **Berths**. — **Deep-sea Dock** is a finger pier extending SSE from the west part of the port. It is 213 m long with depths of 10.1 to 10.6 m alongside. Fresh water is available alongside on request.

Large dolphins are at the SE and SW corners of the pier. Log fenders protect the east and west sides of the pier.

427 A **barge loading ramp** is close west of the Deep-sea dock.

428 The **Former Newsprint loading wharf**, east of the Deep-sea Dock, has a berthing face on its west side of 61 m with a depth of 8.5 m alongside. Dolphins, joined by a catwalk, extend 33 m SSE from the wharf.

429 The **public wharf**, on the west entrance point of the river, is 56 m long with a depth of 5.2 m alongside. Public floats and a seaplane float are on the east side of the wharf. It is equipped with a 3-tonne derrick. A seaplane float is north of the public wharf.

430 Private wharves and floats line the harbour shores.

431 **Booming grounds** lie between the public wharf and the Deep-sea dock and to the west of the Deep-sea dock.

432 **Small craft facilities**. — Fuel can only be obtained at the town site 13 km away. A boat launching ramp is inside the river, north of the public wharf.

433 **Pierce Range** lies on the south side of Muchalat Inlet between **Guaquina Point** *(49°39'N, 126°06'W)* and its head. East and west shores south of Guaquina Point are lined with booming grounds.

434 **Matchlee Bay** is the head of Muchalat Inlet and **Burman River** flows into it over an extensive drying flat. A float cabin, overgrown log dump, and barge grid are on the north side of **Matchlee Creek**. A booming ground and wharf, with a road leading to it, are on the west side at the outer end of the drying flat fronting Burman River.

Clayoquot Sound

Charts 3673, 3674

435 **Clayoquot Sound** *(49°15'N, 126°10'W)* comprises a number of inlets and channels the main ones being Sydney, Shelter, Herbert and Tofino Inlets, Millar Channel and Bedwell Sound. In the entrance are three large islands, Flores, Vargas and Meares Islands, and several smaller ones.

436 **Numerous islets and rocks encumber the sound and its approaches. Navigation requires the greatest caution.**

Sydney and Shelter Inlets

Chart 3674

437 **Sydney Inlet**, entered east of Sharp Point *(49°21'N, 126°16'W)*, is the NW branch of Clayoquot Sound. Shores are high and rugged. Depths in the inlet increase from about 20 m in the entrance to 100 m near the head and the fairway is free of dangers. It is connected to Millar Channel, on the east side of Flores Island, by Shelter Inlet and Hayden Passage.

438 **Tides**. — Tidal differences in Sydney Inlet, referenced on Tofino, are given for Riley Cove (Index No. 8637) in *Tide Tables, Volume 6*.

439 A **submarine pipeline** extends from the west shore 1.2 miles north of Sharp Point and a submarine cable crosses the inlet close south of Starling Point.

440 **Anchorage** for small craft in Sydney Inlet can be obtained in Young Bay. Steamer Cove in Shelter Inlet affords good anchorage.

Chart 3674

441 **Hootla-Kootla Bay**, 2 miles NE of Sharp Point, has two above-water rocks in its entrance. Small craft can anchor here and also in the unnamed bay 0.6 mile S.

442 **Starling Point** *(49°24'N, 126°14'W)* is high and steep-to.

443 **Light**. — Starling Point light *(118)* is on the NW end of the point.

444 **Riley Cove**, east of Starling Point, affords some shelter for small craft, but does not offer particularly good anchorage. A rock, with 4.6 m over it, lies in the entrance to the cove. Two concrete columns are on the west shore at the head of the cove.

445 **Young Bay**, 2 miles north of Starling Point, affords secure anchorage for small craft. An islet near the north shore in the middle part of the bay has concrete footings of an old wharf on its south side.

446 **Beacon**. — Young Bay Entrance daybeacon, on a rock off the south entrance point to the bay, has a starboard hand daymark.

447 **Adventure Bay** (local name) is on the east side of the entrance to Holmes Inlet. **Bottleneck Cove**, at the head of Adventure Bay, has a very narrow entrance, with a least depth of 7.3 m. It is reported that the cove affords very sheltered anchorage.

448 **Holmes Inlet** is restricted to a width of 0.1 mile by two islands but is suitable for small vessels. Local knowledge is advised. Marine farm facilities are east of the two islands. **Pretty Girl Cove**, at the head of Holmes Inlet, dries.

449 **Sydney Inlet Provincial Park** encompasses the inlet north of Adventure Point. There are no facilities.

450 **Drying rocks** extend from the east side of Sydney Inlet, about 0.5 mile NW of **Adventure Point** *(49°26'N, 126°15'W)*. **Driver Point** is on the west side of the inlet, 1 mile NW of Adventure Point.

451 **Light**. — Driver Point light *(118.3)* is on a drying rock east of the point.

452 **Stewardson Inlet**, entered between Driver Point and **Darr Island**, is deep and free of dangers. A logging camp, at the head of the inlet, has a wharf with floats, booming grounds and barge grid. A restricted logging road leads from the head of the inlet to Hesquiat Harbour.

453 **Beacon**. — Stewardson Inlet daybeacon, 1 mile SW of Darr Island, has a port hand daymark.

454 **Sydney River** flows through a broad valley and over an extensive drying flat into the head of Sydney Inlet.

455 **Shelter Inlet**, entered north of Starling Point *(49°24'N, 126°14'W)*, leads east from Sydney Inlet along the north sides of Flores and Obstruction Islands. Hayden Passage connects it to Millar Channel.

456 **Clio Island** *(49°24'N, 126°11'W)* is steep-to on its south side.

457 **Light**. — Clio Island light *(118.5)*, on the summit of the island, is shown at an elevation of 17.7 m from a mast, fitted with a starboard hand daymark.

458 **Steamer Cove** can be entered on either side of **George Islands**; the west channel is the wider. It affords good anchorage in 31 to 35 m, mud bottom. Small craft can find good anchorage, mud, in a cove in its SW corner. A shed, barge ramp and float are on the SE shore and a float is on the south shore.

459 **Dixon Bay**, entered north of **Dixon Point** *(49°24'N, 126°09'W)*, is too deep for anchorage though small craft can anchor near the head.

460 **Marine farm** facilities are located NW of George Islands, on the south shore of Dixon Bay, just inside Dixon Point and on the north shore of Obstruction Island.

461 **Sulphur Passage Provincial Park** encompasses Shelter Inlet NW of Obstruction Island, Sulphur Passage, Obstruction Island and the east part of Hayden Passage. There are no facilities.

462 The west side of **Megin River** *(49°26'N, 126°05'W)* is an Ecological Reserve.

463 **Bacchante Bay** *(49°27'N, 126°02'W)* has a very narrow entrance encumbered with rocks on either side. The fairway is only about 91 m wide. It can be entered by small craft but local knowledge is advised. **Watta Creek** enters the head of the bay. Anchorage is reported to be well-sheltered with good holding, sand and mud bottom.

Hayden and Sulphur Passages

464 **Obstruction Island** *(49°25'N, 126°05'W)*, on the south side of Shelter Inlet, separates Sulphur Passage from Hayden Passage. Both passages lead south into Millar Channel.

465 **Hayden Passage** *(49°24'N, 126°07'W)* leads along the SW side of Obstruction Island and is used by coasting vessels. Shoals and drying rocks, at the NW end of the passage, extend up to 0.15 mile off the Obstruction Island shore. A group of above-water and drying rocks, at the SE end of the passage, extend about 0.1 mile off the Obstruction Island shore.

466 **Tidal streams** set SE on the flood and attain 4 kn in Hayden Passage. Duration of slack water is about 15 minutes. Secondary current station Hayden Passage (Index No. 9125), referenced on Tofino, is in *Tide Tables, Volume 6*.

467 **Light**. — Hayden Passage light *(119)* is on a rock in the middle of the passage.

468 **Beacons**. — Hayden Passage Entrance daybeacon, on the north extremity of Flores Island, has a port hand daymark.

469 Hayden Passage West daybeacon, on Flores Island about 0.5 mile ESE of the entrance daybeacon, has a port hand daymark.

470 Hayden Passage daybeacon at the SE end of the passage, on a group of rocks off Obstruction Island, has a starboard hand daymark.

471 Flores Island East daybeacon, on Flores Island at the SE end of the passage, has a port hand daymark. Upstream direction is proceeding from Millar Channel toward Shelter Inlet.

472 **Sulphur Passage**, entered west of **Belcher Point**, leads south along the east side of Obstruction Island to Millar Channel. It is encumbered with rocks but suitable for small craft. Local knowledge and careful navigation is advised.

473 **Marine farm** facilities are south of Belcher Point.

474 **Tides**. — Tidal differences for Sulphur Passage (Index No. 8634), referenced on Tofino, are in *Tide Tables, Volume 6*.

475 **Tidal streams** set south on the flood and attain 2 kn in Sulphur Passage.

476 **Anchorage** for small craft is reported to be obtainable at the head of the cove, at the SW end of Obstruction Island.

Millar Channel

477 **Millar Channel**, entered between **Kutcous Point** *(49°15'N, 126°05'W)* and an unnamed point 2.5 miles ESE, leads north along the east coast of Flores Island connecting to Hayden

Chart 3674

and Sulphur Passages at its north end. Herbert Inlet leads NE from its east side. Depths increase from 5.3 m, across the sill at its south end, to over 100 m in the north part. The fairway is 0.6 mile wide at its narrowest part.

478   **Submarine cables** (power) cross Millar Channel from 0.5 mile NNW of **Yates Point** to the Vancouver Island shore about 1.2 miles SE of Yates Point. A cable and anchorage prohibited sign is on the Vancouver Island shore.

479   A **submarine pipeline** (sewer outfall), marked by a sign at Marktosis, extends 0.8 mile NE into the channel. Another outfall sign is on the islet 0.2 mile NW of Clifford Point.

480   **Anchorage** can be obtained in Bawden Bay or Matilda Inlet.

481   **Bawden Bay** *(49°17'N, 126°01'W)*, entered north of **Clifford Point**, affords anchorage in its SE part in 17 to 25 m, mud. Allow sufficient space to clear shoals and rocks lying 0.1 mile offshore in this part of the bay.

482   **Ross Passage**, between **McKay Island** and Vancouver Island NE, is obstructed by islets and rocks. Marine farm facilities are in the passage.

483   **Light**. — McKay Island light *(119.4)* is on the west side of the island.

484   **Matilda Inlet** *(49°18'N, 126°04'W)* is sheltered by **McNeil Peninsula** and affords good anchorage about 0.6 mile south of Matilda Inlet light in 27 m, mud bottom. Numerous drying and below-water rocks encumber the inlet south of Ahousat.

485   **Lights**. — Matilda Inlet light *(120)*, on the outer edge of a reef at the west side of the entrance, is shown at an elevation of 5.3 m from a white tower with a red band at the top, 6 m high.

486   Marktosis light *(121)*, 1.6 miles SSE of Matilda Inlet light in the entrance of the bay leading to Marktosis, is shown at an elevation of 4.6 m from a white tower, 3.5 m high.

487   **Buoys**. — Port hand buoy "M57", 1 mile south of Matilda Inlet light, marks the outer end of a shoal spit extending off McNeil Peninsula.

488   Port hand buoy "M59", in the entrance of a bay 1.6 miles SSE of Matilda Inlet light, marks a rock with 1 m over it.

489   Two **submarine cables** cross Matilda Inlet from Ahousat to Marktosis. A submarine pipeline (water) crosses the inlet about 0.3 mile south of Ahousat.

490   **Ahousat**, on the west side of Matilda Inlet, is a settlement with a post office, general store and cafe. A marine slipway, close to the public wharf, can haul vessels up to 13 m long. A coastal freighter calls at intervals, and air service by charter float planes is obtainable. Gas and diesel are available at the fuel dock.

491   **Berths**. — The public wharf has a wharfhead 31 by 12 m with depths of 4.9 to 6.1 m alongside the outer face. It has a storage shed and 3 tonne crane.

492   Floats, close south of the public wharf, have two approach ramps and are connected in a line parallel to shore. Overall length is 115 m with depths of about 2.1 to 3 m alongside. The north float is for fuel.

493   **Marktosis**, at the head of a shallow bay on the east side of Matilda Inlet, is an Indian Reserve.

494   **Caution. — Local knowledge is advised to approach Marktosis from Matilda Inlet. The village can best be approached on its east side by small craft in fine weather.**

495   A **submarine cable** (telephone) and submarine pipeline (water) cross the entrance to Marktosis.

496   **Berths**. — A pier with a government type wharf and floats at its outer end extends across the drying flats from Marktosis. Another float is south of Marktosis light.

497   **Gibson Marine Provincial Park**, at the head of Matilda Inlet and extending south to Whitesand Cove, has a hot spring but no facilities.

Herbert Inlet

Charts 3674, 3673

498   **Herbert Inlet**, entered between **Bawden Point** *(49°18'N, 126°01'W)* and McKay Island, extends 8.5 miles NNE. Depths are considerable and shores in most places are steep.

499   **Tides**. — Tidal differences for Herbert Inlet (Index No. 8632), referenced on Tofino, are in *Tide Tables, Volume 6*.

500   **Marine farm** facilities are 0.3 mile east of Bawden Point.

501   **Anchorage** can be obtained in Whitepine Cove, in the unnamed cove SW of it, and in Gibson Cove.

502   **Whitepine Cove** *(49°18'N, 125°57'W)* affords anchorage to small vessels in 15 m near the edge of a drying bank at its head. Care must be taken to avoid **Sutlej Rock** and the two shoals, one with 4.5 m and the other with 8.5 m over it. Sheltered anchorage for small craft, in about 15 m mud, can be obtained south of the islets on the west side of the entrance to Whitepine Cove. Entry should be made south of the west islet. Local knowledge is advised. A mooring buoy with water hose is at the mouth of a bay on the sout side of the outer bay.

503   **Marine farm** facilities are 1 mile NE of Whitepine Cove and NE of Binns Island.

Chart 3674

504   **Bedingfield Bay** *(49°21'N, 125°59'W)* has foul ground and a booming ground at its head.

505   **Gibson Cove**, 3 miles NNE of **Binns Island** *(49°20'N, 125°58'W)*, has below-water rocks off both entrance points. Within the cove it is free of dangers and affords anchorage for small vessels.

506   **Moyeha Bay**, at the head of the inlet, is within the boundary of **Strathcona Provincial Park**. A waterfall drops over a steep cliff on the east side of the bay, north of **Cotter Creek**. There is comparatively deep water at the foot of the cliff making it a convenient place for watering a small vessel. Booming grounds line the shore south of the bay.

507   **Moyeha River** *(49°25'N, 125°45'W)* is fronted by a swamp and a steep-to drying flat extending 0.3 mile offshore.

Calmus Passage

Chart 3673

508   **Calmus Passage** separates Vargas Island from the Vancouver Island shore to the north. From the west it is entered between **Monks Islet** *(49°14'N, 126°01'W)* and **Eby Rock**, 0.8 mile south.

509   **Submarine cables** from the centre of Maurus Channel extend along Calmus Passage from the south end of Morfee Island to Vargas Island in *126°00'W*, and then NW passing west of Monks Islet. Cable and anchorage prohibited signs are posted on the south

Chart 3673

shore of Morfee Island and on Vargas Island 0.8 mile ESE of Eby Rock.

510　　**Tidal streams** set east on the flood and west on the ebb through Calmus Passage.

511　　**Buoyage.** — Upstream direction for buoyage in Calmus Passage is proceeding from west to east.

512　　**Light.** — Monks Islet light *(123)* is shown at an elevation of 14.2 m from a mast, 3.5 m high.

513　　**Beacon.** — Eby Rock daybeacon has a starboard hand daymark.

514　　**Coomes Bank** extends 1.5 miles WSW from the south point on the north shore and has a least depth of 2 m over it.

515　　**Light buoy.** — Coomes Bank light buoy "Y11" *(123.3)*, off the SW end of the bank, is a port hand buoy.

516　　**Morfee Island** *(49°13'N, 125°57'W)* lies at the east end of Calmus Passage. The fairway south of the island leads to Maurus Channel. **Eugvik Rock**, 0.2 mile south of Morfee Island, dries 0.4 m. A rock, with 2.4 m over it, lies 0.1 mile NW of Eugvik Rock and is marked by starboard hand buoy "Y10".

517　　**Light.** — Morfee Island light *(124)*, on the SE side of the island, is shown at an elevation of 8.1 m from a white tower with a green band at the top.

518　　**Epper Passage**, between the north side of Morfee Island and an unnamed island NW, provides the best entry from Calmus Passage toward the inner waters of Clayoquot Sound. **Note the rock with 9.8 m over it near mid-channel.**

519　　**Tidal streams** in Epper Passage set NE on the flood and attain 3 kn at times, but in the passage east of Dunlap Island the rate of flood is somewhat less.

520　　**Epper Passage Provincial Park** encompasses Morfee and Dunlap Islands and waters surrounding them. There are no facilities.

Maurus and Heynen Channels

521　　**Maurus Channel**, between Meares and Vargas Islands, leads north from Father Charles Channel to Calmus Passage or east of Dunlap Island to the approach to Bedwell Sound.

522　　**Tidal streams** in Maurus Channel attain 2 kn, with the flood setting north and the ebb south. North and south-going streams around Vargas Island meet in the vicinity of Elbow Bank.

523　　**Submarine cables**, commencing north of Kakawis on Meares Island, lead north along the centre of Maurus Channel then SW of Dunlap Island into Calmus Passage. A cable and prohibited anchorage sign is on Meares Island, 0.4 mile north of Kakawis.

524　　**Kakawis** *(49°11'N, 125°55'W)* is the site of several houses and a conspicuous cross. It has a wharf with a float and private mooring buoy *(Chart 3685)*.

525　　**Light.** — Maurus Channel light *(125)* is on the east side of the channel on a drying spit 1 mile NNW of Kakawis.

526　　**Elbow Bank**, on the west side of Maurus Channel, extends nearly 2 miles north of **Rassier Point**. **Dunlap Island**, about 0.2 mile north of the north end of Elbow Bank, is steep-to on its south and west sides.

Chart 3685

527　　**Heynen Channel**, entered south of **Meares Spit** *(49°10'N, 125°56'W)*, leads east from Father Charles Channel. Meares Island and **Stockham Island** are on its north side and its south side consists of drying flats extending from a group of islands.

528　　**Light buoys.** — Meares Spit light buoy "Y8" *(126)*, at the SW end of the spit, is a starboard hand buoy with the upstream direction for entering Maurus Channel. Entering Heynen Channel pass it on the port hand side.

529　　Stubbs Spit light buoy "Y25" *(128)*, on the NE extremity of the spit extending north from Stubbs Island, is a port hand buoy with the upstream direction for proceeding NE through Van Nevel Channel. In Heynen Channel, proceeding from Father Charles Channel, pass it on the starboard hand side.

530　　**Light.** — Stockham Island light *(127)* is on a drying spit off the west end of the island.

531　　**Beacon.** — Stockham Island daybeacon, on a drying rock about 0.1 mile south of the island, has a starboard hand daymark.

532　　**Submarine cables** cross Heynen Channel in several locations. A submarine pipeline (sewer) extends into the channel from close west of Opitsat.

533　　**Opitsat** is an Indian village on the north shore of Heynen Channel. Small craft can approach it through a narrow channel NW of Stockham Island. A marine slipway is capable of handling vessels up to 12 m long.

534　　**Public floats** in Opitsat, attached to a pier, provide 167 m of berthing space with depths of 2 to 5 m alongside. A crane is on the pier.

Charts 3685, 3673

535　　**Lemmens Inlet** *(49°12'N, 125°52'W)*, entered east of Stockham Island, penetrates Meares Island and is shallow in its south part. **Sloman Island**, **Arakun Islands** and **Sharp Island** are on the drying bank on the east side of the entrance. The entrance is reported to be filled with cab trap floats, many shrouded in kelp. The inlet is only suitable for small craft, local knowledge is advised.

Chart 3673

536　　**Monas Island** *(49°11'N, 125°53'W)* and **Lagoon Island** lie on the west side of the entrance.

537　　**God's Pocket** (local name), NW of Lagoon Island, affords anchorage for small craft. A shoal with 4 m over it lies in the entrance. Oyster growing facilities are in the entrance and float homes are at the head.

538　　**Adventure Cove**, entered north of **Columbia Islet**, is the historic site of **Fort Defiance**. Built by American Captain Robert Gray, commander of the Columbia Rediviva, who built a sloop named Adventure in the cove in 1791. It is reported that the cove affords well-protected anchorage for small craft. It is also reported that heavy ropes criss-cross the cove and anchor a float home on the east shore. Enter the Cove north of Columbia Islet only.

539　　**Hansen Island**, with drying rocks extending SE and NE from it, lies NW of Adventure Cove.

540　　The NW arm at the head of the inlet is reported to afford anchorage for small craft. A float home and oyster growing facility are at the north end.

541　　**Marine farm** facilities are WNW of Monas Island, north of Lagoon Island and in several coves around the inlet.

Chart 3685

542　　**Van Nevel Channel** *(49°09'N, 125°56'W)*, between **Stubbs Island** and **Felice Island**, connects Templar Channel to

Chart 3685

Heynen Channel and the west end of the approach to Browning Passage. The deepest channel for approaching Browning Passage, south of Stockham Island, is between the islet 0.1 mile SE of Stockham Island daybeacon and Stone Island.

543 **Tidal streams** in Van Nevel Channel attain 3 kn, the flood setting NE. About 2 kn can be expected at the junction of Van Nevel and Heynen Channels.

544 **Beacons. — Buoy**. — Van Nevel Channel daybeacon No. 1, NE of Clayoquot on the outer edge of a drying bank extending from Stubbs Island, has a port hand daymark.

545 Starboard hand buoy "Y6" is in mid-channel about 0.2 mile NE of Clayoquot.

546 Van Nevel Channel daybeacon No. 3, 0.6 mile NE of Felice Island on the outer end of the drying bank extending NE from the island, has a starboard hand daymark.

547 **Submarine cables** cross Van Nevel Channel at its south and north ends.

548 **Clayoquot**, on the east side of Stubbs Island, is the site of a resort with hotel facilities. The resort has a wharf with a depth of 4.5 m alongside.

549 **Deadman Passage** separates **Deadman Islets** from the drying bank extending NE from Felice Island. The fairway is about 90 m wide and carries a least depth of 3.3 m.

550 **Light**. — Deadman Islets light *(129)* is on the SW islet.

551 **Buoys**. — Starboard hand buoys "Y18" and "Y22" and port hand buoys "Y19" and "Y21" mark the fairway. Upstream direction is when proceeding north.

552 A **submarine cable** extends along Deadman Passage.

553 The passage between **Beck Island** and **Stone Island** has drying reefs in its south end and a submarine cable down its centre. Local knowledge is advised.

Bedwell Sound and Approaches

Chart 3673

554 The approach to Bedwell Sound from either Maurus Channel or Epper Passage is made between **Kraan Head** *(49°15'N, 125°56'W)* and **Robert Point**, 1.2 miles SSE.

555 **Anchorage** can be obtained in Ritchie Bay, Hecate Bay and Cypress Bay. Small vessels can obtain anchorage in two locations in Bedwell Sound.

556 **Yellow Bank**, between Robert Point and **Saranac Island**, has a least depth of 0.9 m. The passage between Saranac Island and **Welcome Island**, 0.7 mile NE, is deep and free of dangers. Marine farm facilities are off the east and west shores of Saranac Island and north of Welcome Island. A private mooring buoy is 0.2 mile NW of Welcome Island.

557 **Ritchie Bay**, ESE of Yellow Bank, has rocky shores and affords good anchorage in 10 to 20 m. Rocks off the north entrance point are usually marked by kelp and a rock with 2.4 m over it lies 0.8 mile ENE of Robert Point.

558 **Hecate Bay**, between Kraan Head and **Knocker Islet**, is easy of access, well-sheltered, free of dangers and one of the best anchorages in Clayoquot Sound, with depths of 13 to 18 m. Booming grounds are west of Kraan Head. A wharf with a float attached and white buildings of a fish farming camp are 0.3 mile NW of Kraan Head. Marine farm facilities are close north of Knocker Islet.

559 **Cypress Bay** is entered between **Rhodes Island**, on the west, and **McLeod Island** and the islets and rocks off the east entrance point. The bay affords good anchorage in 22 m, about 0.5 mile off its NW shore. It is open SW but no sea rises. Entering the bay take care to avoid shoals close north of Welcome Island, a rock with 1 m over it, and **Mussel Rock** in the east part of the bay. East and west shores of the bay are low and the north side is high. Marine farm facilities occupy the channel between the north shore and two islets 0.5 mile ENE of **River Island** and in several locations among the islets off the east entrance point.

560 **Tides**. — Tidal differences for Cypress Bay (Index No. 8630), referenced on Tofino, are in *Tide Tables, Volume 6*.

561 **Quait Bay**, on the NE side of Cypress Bay, has a narrow entrance with a least depth of 4 m, obstructed by an islet. It is only suitable for small craft and local knowledge is advised. Anchorage is reported to be good, mud bottom. The Clayoquot Wilderness Resort in the NW part of the bay has accommodation and dining facilities. The 100 year old restored tug Ivanhoe is ancored off this floating resort and serves as staff accommodation.

562 **Bedwell Sound**, entered east of **Rant Point** *(49°16'N, 125°50'W)*, has high rugged shores and is inconveniently deep for anchorage. Small vessels can obtain anchorage 2 miles north of Rant Point, about 0.2 mile off the west shore, in 30 to 40 m, or 0.7 mile SW of **Bare Bluff** in 30 m, about 0.1 mile SE of a conspicuous bare 4 m high islet. Marine farm facilities are close south of Bare Bluff, 0.5 mile WSW, 1 mile NE, 0.9 mile N and 2.2 miles NNE of Rant Point.

563 **Bedwell River**, at the head of the sound, has a swamp and drying flats in its entrance.

564 **Matlset Narrows**, 1.5 miles SE of Rant Point, leads from the south end of Bedwell Sound into the north end of Fortune Channel. The fairway has a minimum width of 0.15 mile. Foul ground, usually marked by kelp, extends from the south shore west of an islet off the end of a small peninsula. **Maltby Islets** lie almost in mid-channel off the east end of the narrows; the south islet is covered with bushes.

565 **Tidal streams** of 4 kn can be expected at spring tides in Matlset Narrows. Strong tide-rips occur at times in vicinity of Maltby Islets. The flood sets east and the ebb west through the narrows.

Browning Passage

Chart 3685

566 **Browning Passage** *(49°09'N, 125°53'W)* leads south of Meares Island connecting to Tofino Inlet and Fortune Channel at its east end. The fairway is barely 0.1 mile wide at its SE end. Local knowledge is advisable because of strong currents and numerous dangers.

567 The deepest and safest route leading to the north end of Browning Passage is between Stockham and Stone Islands. This channel leads SE through the narrows between **Morpheus Island** *(49°10'N, 125°53'W)* and **Calf Island**, on the east, and **Neilson Island** and **Riley Island** on the west.

568 **Dangers**. — A reef that dries 4.1 m lies between the south end of Neilson Island and Morpheus Island. A rock with 0.8 m over it lies 0.1 mile east of the south extremity of Riley Island and is marked by port hand buoy "Y35".

Chart 3685

569　　**Tidal streams** in the channel between Riley and Morpheus Islands attain 3 to 5 kn, farther SE where the fairway is wider velocities are considerably less. The flood sets south and the ebb north.

570　　A **submarine pipeline** (water) crosses Browning Passage 0.2 mile south of Usatzes Point and then north along the channel between Morpheus and Meares Islands into Lemmens Inlet. Notice boards on both sides of the passage warn of its presence. Another water pipeline marked by signs crosses between **Laddie Island** and **Ginnard Creek**.

571　　**Buoys**. — The fairway, between the rocks east of **Mikes Island** and **Ducking Island**, is marked by port hand buoy "Y37" and starboard hand buoy "Y38".

572　　**Ginnard Point** *(49°08′N, 125°51′W)*, on the NE side of the channel, is prominent.

573　　**Tsapee Narrows** *(49°07′N, 125°49′W)* is divided at its west end by **Eik Islets**. The fairway lies south of these islets. The passage north of the islets is foul. **McBey Islets** lie on a drying ledge on the south side of the narrows.

574　　**Tidal streams** in Tsapee Narrows attain 4 kn at springs. The flood sets east and begins shortly after LW and the ebb sets west beginning shortly after HW at Tofino.

575　　**Auseth Point**, on the north side of the east entrance to Browning Passage, is steep-to. **Indian Island**, 0.5 mile east of Auseth Point, has a drying bank west of it that reduces the fairway to 0.2 mile wide.

576　　**Beacon**. — A private daybeacon, on a point 0.2 mile NE of Auseth Point, is a white mast.

577　　**Grice Bay**, SE of Indian Island *(Chart 3673)*, is almost filled with a drying flat. A boat launching ramp is on the west entrance point, south of the west end of Indian Island.

Fortune Channel

Charts 3685, 3673

578　　**Fortune Channel** *(49°08′N, 125°47′W)*, between the east coast of Meares Island and Vancouver Island, connects the east end of Browning Passage to Matlset Narrows. From Browning Passage it is entered between Auseth Point and **Baxter Islet**, 0.8 mile NE.

579　　**Anchorage** can be obtained in Mosquito Harbour and Warn Bay.

Chart 3685

580　　**Windy Bay** *(49°08′N, 125°48′W)* is 1 mile NW of Baxter Islet. It is reported that anchorage can be found here, mud bottom. However it should be used with caution as winds can funnel from the mountain tops between the bay's steep sides.

581　　**Dawley Passage** *(49°09′N, 125°47′W)* is a winding passage and the fairway is 0.1 mile wide at its narrowest part. **Lane Islet** lies in the south end of the passage.

582　　**Tidal streams** in Dawley Passage attain 3 kn on the flood and ebb on large tides. The flood sets SE and the ebb NW.

583　　**Dawley Passage Provincial Park** encompasses Lane Islet, the passage and the SE shore.

584　　**Heelboom Bay**, at the north end on the west side of Dawley Passage, has drying rocks extending from its west entrance point. It is exposed to NE winds, but is reported to be a good anchorage for small craft.

Chart 3673

585　　**Dark Island** *(49°11′N, 125°46′W)*, **Kirshaw Islets** and **Wood Islets**, together with other small islets and rocks, lie on the west side of Fortune Channel, in the approach to Mosquito Harbour. Marine farm facilities lie between the Wood Islets and SE of Kirshaw Islets.

586　　**Hankin Rock**, with 1.4 m over it, and a rock 0.1 mile north, with 2.9 m over it, are in the approach between Wood Islets and **Plover Point**. Foul ground fringes the point and a rock with 3.4 m over it lies 0.2 mile SE of the point.

587　　**Mosquito Harbour**, north of Wood Islets, affords anchorage in 11 m about 0.4 mile south of **Blackberry Islets**. Small craft can anchor in 4 to 6 m north of Blackberry Islets. The entrance is narrow and shallow with drying mud flats on both sides.

588　　**Directions**. — Approaching Mosquito Harbour from north give Plover Point a berth of about 0.3 mile then steer to pass south of Hankin Rock and north of the islets north of Dark Island. Alter course to pass west of Hankin Rock and the shoal north of it, but note the 6.7 m shoal off Wood Islets. After passing these dangers steer a mid-channel course.

589　　Entering Mosquito Harbour from south vessels can pass west of Kirshaw Islets and the Wood Islets keeping midway between their west sides and the shore west of them. Note the 3.3 m shoal on the west side of the passage abreast the north end of the north Wood Islet.

590　　**Marine farm** facilities are on the east shore of Fortune Channel 0.6 mile ESE of Maltby Islets.

591　　**Warn Bay**, at the north end of Fortune Channel, affords anchorage near its head in 30 m, mud bottom. **Bulson Creek** flows into the head of Warn Bay across a drying flat. Note shoals with 3.8, 6.7, 3.4 and 5.8 m over them.

592　　**Tides**. — Tidal differences for Warn Bay (Index No. 8626), referenced on Tofino, are in *Tide Tables, Volume 6*.

Tofino Inlet

593　　**Tofino Inlet** *(49°09′N, 125°40′W)* extends 10 miles NE from the junction of Browning Passage and Fortune Channel.

594　　**Tides**. — Tidal differences in Tofino Inlet, referenced on Tofino, are given for Kennedy Cove (Index No. 8623) in *Tide Tables, Volume 6*.

595　　**Anchorage** can be obtained in Gunner Inlet, Island Cove or NW of the mouth of Kennedy River. Tofino Inlet lacks good anchorages, depths in most places are too great.

596　　**Warne Island** *(49°08′N, 125°44′W)*, with **Almond Islet** close south of it, lie on the north side of the fairway.

597　　**Island Cove**, NW of Warne Island, provides good anchorage. The entrance south of **Ocayu Island** has drying rocks close-off the SW shore and a shoal with 5.6 m over it in the south approach.

598　　**Gunner Inlet**, north of Warne Island, affords good anchorage to a small vessel in 16 m east of the rock that dries 0.7 m and to the SSE of the 1 m high rock. The approach is difficult and requires careful navigation to avoid charted dangers.

599　　**Marine farm** facilities are in the north part of **Indian Bay**, in the small bay 0.7 mile NE of Indian Bay and SW of **McCall Island**.

600　　**Cannery Bay**, close north of the mouth of **Kennedy River**, has extensive drying flats in it. **Kennedy Cove** forms the

Chart 3673

mouth of Kennedy River and has ruined piles on its north shore. A logging road is on its south shore. A sunken float house is reported to be in the east part of the cove.

601 **Anchorage** in 15 to 18 m can be obtained in Kennedy Cove.

602 **Berryman Point**, north of Kennedy River, has above-water and drying rocks off its extremity, its SW side is cliffy.

603 **Light**. — Berryman Point light *(131.5)*, on a rock NW of the point is shown at an elevation of 4.9 m from a mast 3.7 m high fitted with a starboard hand daymark.

604 **Berryman Cove**, SE of Berryman Point, has a log loading facility with a float and an A-frame on its east side. A logging road follows the east shore north to Irving Cove.

605 **Rankin Cove**, NW of Berryman Point, has booming grounds, a logging camp, A-frame, float and launching ramp. A private mooring buoy is in the entrance.

606 **Tranquil Inlet**, entered between **Rankin Rocks** and **Wingen Islets**, has high, rocky shores. A rock, with 0.6 m over it, lies in the fairway about 1 mile north of Wingen Islets. Drying flats from **Tranquil Creek** form the head of the inlet. Marine farm facilities are south west of **Mugford Island**. Anchorage for small craft is reported to be good in the small un-named cove on the NW side.

607 **Wollan Islets** lie off the SE extremity of **McCaw Peninsula**.

608 **Auseth Islet** *(49°11'N, 125°39'W)* lies in mid-channel with deep clear passages on either side.

609 **Corning Point**, the NW entrance point to **Irving Cove**, has several islets off it. An islet, 0.1 mile west of the point, has a prominent bare rock close west of it. Marine farm facilities line the shore of Corning Point.

610 **Woman Island** and **Similar Island** lie in the approach to Deer Bay.

611 **Deer Bay**, at the head of Tofino Inlet, has a very narrow entrance encumbered with islets and rocks. Local knowledge is advised.

Barkley Sound

Chart 3671

612 **Barkley Sound** is entered between Amphitrite Point *(48°55'N, 125°32'W)* and Cape Beale *(48°47'N, 125°13'W)*, 16 miles to the SE. It is encumbered with numerous islands, islets and submerged rocks, especially in the approaches and NW part. **Exercise of great caution and vigilance is necessary to avoid them.**

613 Shores of Barkley Sound are low and backed by rugged mountains. In the north part and among the inlets, mountains rise steeply from shore. Outer islands have shorelines of shattered rock.

614 Alberni Inlet is the main inlet at the head of the sound. Ucluelet Inlet, near the NW entrance point, and Bamfield Inlet, 4.5 miles NE of Cape Beale, offer shelter and supplies to small craft.

615 Trevor, Imperial Eagle and Loudoun Channels are the main entrance channels. Trevor Channel is the route usually followed by vessels bound for Port Alberni.

616 **Heavy swells. — Barkley Sound is exposed to the full sweep of the Pacific Ocean. Rough seas and heavy swells can be**

expected during passage of any weather system. Even during calm weather outer islands often experience large swells. Only in inner sheltered reaches can one expect a quiet safe anchorage.

617 **Tides**. — Tidal differences in Barkley Sound, referenced on Tofino, are given for Ucluelet (Index No. 8595), Stopper Islands (Index No. 8588), Effingham Bay (Index No. 8585), Mutine Point (Index No. 8556) and Bamfield (Index No. 8545) in *Tide Tables, Volume 6*.

618 **Pilotage**. — The Pilot boarding station for the Barkley Sound area is off Cape Beale, at the entrance to Trevor Channel. For details see *PAC 200* and *Notices to Mariners 1 to 46 Annual Edition*.

619 **Vessel Traffic Services (VTS)**. — Barkley Sound and Alberni Inlet are in the *Tofino Traffic Zone*. Assigned frequency is 156.725 MHz, Channel 74.

620 **Calling-in Point No. 2**, *Cape Beale*, is a line joining Cape Beale light *(176)* with Amphitrite Point light *(135)*. Mariners shall indicate whether their course is through Trevor Channel, Imperial Eagle Channel or Loudoun Channel.

621 A brief description of this VTS is in *PAC 200*. Details are in *Radio Aids to Marine Navigation (Pacific and Western Arctic)*.

Loudoun Channel

622 **Loudoun Channel**, entered between **Mara Rock** *(48°52'N, 125°29'W)* and Sail Rock, 3.25 miles east, leads into Barkley Sound NW of Broken Group. A rock that dries 1.4 m lies 0.2 mile SE of Mara Rock. David Channel is at the north end of Loudoun Channel. Sechart Channel, the lighted channel between Hand and Brabant Islands, Peacock Channel, Thiepval Channel, the lighted channel between Clarke and Benson Islands, and Coaster Channel, all lead east into the Broken Group.

623 **Great Bear Rock**, **Alley Rock** and Sargison Bank, NE of Mara Rock, form the NW side of Loudoun Channel.

Chart 3670

624 **Sail Rock** *(48°53'N, 125°24'W)* is sail-shaped and easily identified. Rocks, with 3.2 and 2.3 m over them, lie 1.1 miles SSW of Sail Rock. A rock with 1.6 m over it, 0.4 mile WNW of Sail Rock, lies on the east side of the fairway.

625 **Pigot Islets** and **Drum Rocks** together with numerous drying rocks and reefs extend west from Benson and Clarke Islands.

626 **Hankin Island** *(48°55'N, 125°22'W)* has a 5.1 m shoal 0.1 mile WSW of its west extremity and drying rocks off its NE end. **Single Rock** lies 0.4 mile NE and **Pinder Rock** 0.4 mile NW of Hankin Island. The passage between Pinder Rock and **Page Island**, 0.3 mile NNW, has a rock with 1.5 m over it in its west approach.

627 **Bryant Islands** *(48°57'N, 125°22'W)*, **Castle Islet**, **Curwen Island** and a number of drying rocks and shoals in the vicinity, form a group on the NW side of Loudoun Channel.

628 **Beacon**. — Curwen Island daybeacon, on a drying rock 0.1 mile SE of the island, has a port hand daymark.

629 **Warner Rock**, midway between Bryant Islands and **St. Ines Island**, has less than 2 m over it and is marked by kelp during summer months.

Charts 3670, 3671

630 **Directions**. — Castle Islet bearing 023°, and open west of Page Island, leads clear of dangers in the south half of Loudoun Channel. When Sail Rock is abeam, alter course to pass between

Charts 3670, 3671

Sail Rock and Benson Island from west of Drum Rocks (1985)

Hand and Brabant Islands from Loudoun Channel (1985)

Pinder Rock and Hankin Island, taking care to avoid the shoal 0.1 mile WSW of Hankin Island that can create a confused sea in heavy weather. Pass midway between shoals east of Curwen and Bryant Islands on the west and Wilkins Islet on the east.

Macoah Passage

Chart 3670

631 **Macoah Passage** *(48°58′N, 125°23′W)*, on the NW side of Barkley Sound, leads from Newcombe Channel to Toquart Bay. From Newcombe Channel it is entered west of Forbes Island. Local knowledge is advised because of drying and shallow depths off the Vancouver Island shore, foul ground in vicinity of the islands and shoals in mid-channel. **David Island**, **Ottaway Islet**, **Rowlands Islet**, **Spilling Islet**, **Staff Islet** and **Larkins Island** lie on its SE side. The Barkley Sound Kayak Centre is located on the W side of the S entrance to Macoah Passage.

David Channel and Toquart Bay

632 **David Channel**, at the north end of Loudoun Channel, leads north to Toquart Bay and Pipestem Inlet. **Lyall Point** *(48°58′N, 125°19′W)*, **Shears Islands** and **Harris Point** are on its east side. **Richard Rock** and the reefs between it and **Stopper Islands**, together with **Hermit Islet** and the reef 0.2 mile north of it, are on the west side of David Channel.

633 **Tides.** — Tidal differences for Stopper Islands (Index No. 8588), referenced on Tofino, are in *Tide Tables, Volume 6.*

634 **Lights.** — Lyall Point light *(146)* is on the west extremity of the point.

635 Richard Rock light *(144)* is on the rock.

636 Shears Islands light *(143)* is on a rock west of the islands.

637 Toquart Bay light *(142)* is on a reef 0.2 mile north of Hermit Islet.

638 **Mayne Bay**, between Lyall Point and Shears Islands, affords good anchorage in its SE part in 30 m, mud. An orange and white mooring buoy, in the NE part of the bay, is for Department of National Defence (DND) vessels only. A booming ground lines the south shore, 0.9 mile ENE of Lyall Point.

639 **Entrance Inlet** *(49°00′N, 125°18′W)* has a rock awash off its east shore, 0.4 mile inside its entrance. **Cigarette Cove**, at the head of the inlet, is reported to provide sheltered anchorage, mud bottom, for small craft. A sport fishing resort, with several float cabins, is along the north shore.

640 **Toquart Bay**, north of David Channel, is well-sheltered and has low shores. **Pope Rocks**, 0.3 mile WNW of **Snowden Island**, have less than 2 m over them and a rock that dries 2.1 m lies 0.2 mile west of Pope Rocks.

641 **Dolphins** off the west shore, 0.6 mile SW of Pope Rocks, and ruins of a conspicuous pyramid-shaped shed and conveyor system are all that remain of a wharf and iron ore mine plant. A log dump, mooring buoys and booming grounds lie near the former mine plant site. A wharf with a float is at the south end of the booming grounds. A rock, 15 m SE of the float, dries 1.2 m and a rock awash is NE. A camp ground with a boat launching ramp protected by a rock breakwater lie south of the log dump and booming ground. A logging road connecting to the Port Alberni-Tofino Highway leads south and then west from the camp ground. Extensive drying flats, with a submarine pipeline across them, front the mouth of **Toquart River**.

642 **Anchorage** can be obtained in the outer part of Toquart Bay, in 25 m, with Hermit Islet bearing 153° and the south extremity of Snowden Island bearing 076°. Good anchorage can be obtained in 10 to 20 m about midway between the north extremity of Snowden Island and an islet close-off the north shore, north of it.

643 **Directions.** — After rounding Lyall Point pass east of Richard Rock. When Hermit Islet bears 323°, and is well open east of the northern Stopper Island, alter course to pass midway between Shears Islands and the northern Stopper Island then steer to pass east of Toquart Bay light.

Pipestem Inlet

644 **Pipestem Inlet** *(49°01′N, 125°18′W)*, on the east side of Toquart Bay, has steep rocky shores rising abruptly to high elevations on its north side, the south side is less steep. The inlet extends 4.5 miles ENE. Pipestem Inlet is used for commercial

Chart 3670

production and collection of oyster spat, usually in July. To avoid damage to spat collection gear, proceed with caution at reduced speed. **Hillier Island** and **Refuge Island** are on the north side of its entrance.

645 **Kirby Rock**, 0.1 mile SSW of Refuge Island, has 0.5 m over it.

646 **Lucky Creek**, 0.4 mile east of Refuge Island, has a drying gravel bank extending from its entrance. A cabin and float are in the cove 0.2 mile east of the creek.

647 **Armentières Rock**, close north of **Bazett Island**, dries 1.1 m.

648 **Marine farm** facilities are in the bay south of Bazett Island and east of Refuge Island.

649 **Anchorage** for small vessels can be obtained 0.1 mile SW of Bazett Island in 22 m, mud. Anchorage is also reported to be available for small craft SE of Bazett Island and E of Refuge Island. Private mooring buoys are off the north shore about 1.5 miles ENE of Bazett Island.

Broken Group

650 **Broken Group** is composed of a large number of comparatively low wooded islands, islets and rocks. Several channels lead through these islands. Sechart Channel, between Hand and Brabant Islands, Coaster Channel, and the channel between Clarke and Benson Islands, are the only channels marked by lights. With the exception of these, together with Peacock and Thiepval Channels, none of the other channels should be attempted without local knowledge.

651 **Anchorages** in the Broken Group are suitable for small vessels. Effingham Bay and an anchorage between Cooper and Batley Islands are approached from Coaster Channel. Island Harbour is approached from Imperial Eagle Channel by way of Harbour Entrance. Anchorage on the north side of Sechart Channel can be obtained between Pinkerton Islands and Canoe Island. Small craft can obtain anchorage north of Canoe Island. From Peacock Channel small craft can obtain anchorage between Dodd and Turtle Islands.

652 **National Park**. — Broken Group forms part of **Pacific Rim National Park**. Campsites are on Benson, Clarke, Turret, Willis, Dodd, Gilbert and Gibraltar Islands and on the islet NE of Hand Island. The park wardens float cabin is in the bay on the SW side of Nettle Island. **There is no source of safe, fresh drinking water in the Broken Group.** Visitors should ensure that they carry adequate supplies.

Sechart and Peacock Channels

653 **Sechart Channel**, at the north end of Broken Group, connects Loudoun Channel to Imperial Eagle Channel. It is entered from Loudoun Channel between Lyall Point light, and **Wilkins Islet** (*48°57'N, 125°20'W*) and **Hand Island**.

654 **Light**. — Hand Island light (*147*) is on an islet NE of Hand Island.

655 The channel between Hand Island and **Brabant Islands** and **Mence Island** leads from Loudoun Channel into Sechart Channel but has several rocks and shoals in its east approach.

656 **Light**. — Hand Island Passage light (*145*), on a rock off the NW point of Brabant Islands, is shown at an elevation of 8.5 m from a white tower with a green band at the top.

657 **Pinkerton Islands** extend 1 mile from the Vancouver Island shore; **Capstan Island** is the southernmost. Numerous drying and below-water rocks lie between the Pinkerton Islands.

658 A floating sport fishing camp is on the north side of the large island north of Williams Island.

659 Some ruined piles are near the entrance of a creek north of **Canoe Island** and a cabin is on the shore NE of Canoe Island. A breakwater encloses the bay east of Canoe Island. Sechart Lodge, a former whaling station, is now a centre for adventure tours. A water taxi is based at the lodge.

660 **Prideaux Island**, **Nettle Island**, **Glen Islet**, **Reeks Island** and **Swale Rock** form the SW side of Sechart Channel at its east end.

661 **Lights**. — Prideaux Island light (*149*) is on the north end of the island.

662 Swale Rock light (*150*) is on the east end of the rock.

663 Julia Passage, entered east of **Howard Point**, and Alma Russell Islands, on the north side of the east entrance to Sechart Channel, are described later with Imperial Eagle Channel. Foul ground extends west of **Mahk Rock** along the south shore of Alma Russell Islands.

664 **Anchorage** on the north side of Sechart Channel can be obtained between Pinkerton Islands and Canoe Island in a depth of about 35 m, or north of Canoe Island in 22 m.

665 **Peacock Channel** (*48°56'N, 125°19'W*) leads from Loudoun Channel into Sechart Channel, along the south and east sides of Brabant Islands. Foul ground fringes the north shores of **Dodd Island**, **Chalk Island** and the **Tiny Group**. **Galley Rock**, 0.3 mile NW of **Jarvis Island**, dries 1.5 m.

666 **Caution. — Extreme care must be taken when transiting the narrow channel between Dodd Island and Chalk Island. A large drying reef extending from the eastern most point of Dodd Island has resulted in a number of groundings. Drying pinnacle rocks NW of Chalk Island must also be avoided.**

667 **Anchorage** for small craft, in 8 m mud bottom, can be obtained in Turtle Bay (local name) between Turtle and Dodd Islands. It is approached from Peacock Channel but local knowledge and caution are advised. The entrance channel is narrowed by depths of 0.3 m extending from **Walsh Island** and 1.8 m extending from Dodd Island.

668 The passage leading south from Peacock Channel, between the Tiny Group and **Marchant Islet**, on the west, and Jarvis Island and **Jaques Island**, to the east, leads into Thiepval and Coaster Channels west of **Onion Island** (*48°54'N, 125°18'W*). It is suitable for small craft but has several detached reefs in mid-channel and foul ground extends west of Mullins Island. Local knowledge is advised.

669 **Treble Islands** lie in the west entrance to the passage north of Jarvis, Jaques and Gibraltar Islands. **Green Rocks**, between Treble Islands and **Denne Island**, **Erin Island** and numerous drying and below-water rocks lie in the passage. **Turner Islet** is at the NE entrance.

670 **Anchorage** can be obtained in the bay on the south side of Nettle Island. Do not tie up to the Park Ranger's float.

Coaster and Thiepval Channels

671 **Coaster Channel** leads through the south part of Broken Group and provides, with Thiepval Channel, a short route across Barkley Sound for small vessels. The SW entrance, between

Chart 3670

Raymond Island from south of Village Reef (1985)

Benson and Clarke Islands from Coaster Channel (1985)

Benson Island and **Combe Rock** (*48°52'N, 125°22'W*), is obstructed by **Verbeke Reef** and has several shoals in its approach.

672   A shallow but straight passage, between Benson Island and **Clarke Island**, is often used by small vessels but local knowledge is advised. A reef that dries 1 m lies in the east approach to this passage, about 0.6 mile east of Benson Island light. Campsites are on the north shores of Benson and Clarke Islands.

673   **Light**. — Benson Island light *(140)* is on an islet NE of the island.

674   **Camblain Island**, **Cooper Island** and **Moreton Island**, on the south side of Coaster Channel, lie on the north side of a shelter area.

675   **Anchorage**, well-sheltered, can be obtained in 33 m, mud, about 0.4 mile south of Cooper Island. It is approached west of Camblain Island by keeping the east end of Batley Island bearing 155° until the summit of Dicebox Island bears 133°. This bearing will lead between dangers on either side to the anchorage.

676   **Batley Island**, **Wouwer Island**, **Howell Island**, **Cree Island**, **Bauke Island**, **Austin Island** and **Pinnacle Rock** lie south and east of the anchorage. Local knowledge is advised to navigate passages between these islands as they are encumbered with numerous rocks and islets.

677   **Effingham Bay**, on the NW side of **Effingham Island** *(48°52'N, 125°18'W)*, affords sheltered anchorage with good holding ground, mud, in 14 m. The bay is approached from Coaster Channel between **Gilbert Island** and a rock awash, 0.2 mile north. It is entered south of an islet lying 0.3 mile south of **Raymond Island**, keeping slightly to the north of mid-channel to avoid a shoal spit extending north from Effingham Island.

678   **Tides**. — Tidal differences for Effingham Bay (Index No. 8585), referenced on Tofino, are in *Tide Tables, Volume 6*.

679   **Light**. — Coaster Channel light *(148)* is on the NW extremity of the islets extending west from Raymond Island.

680   **Thiepval Channel** entered north of **Lovett Island** leads SE from Loudoun Channel into Coaster Channel. Two rocks, 1 and

3 m high, in its west entrance, lie 0.3 mile north of **Trickett Island**. Shoals lie between the rocks and **Willis Island**. A group of above-water drying, and below-water rocks lie in mid-channel between Turret Island and **Turtle Island**. The navigable channel south of the rocks is 91 m wide and deep.

681   **Village Reef** *(48°53'N, 125°17'W)* lies on the north side of the east entrance to Coaster Channel. A detached, steep-to rock, with 7.4 m over it lies 0.3 mile SE of Village Reef. **Faber Islets**, 0.5 mile WNW, are surrounded by drying reefs. Drying and above-water rocks lie 0.5 mile west of Faber Islets. **Wiebe Island**, 0.5 mile north of Village Reef, has a bare moderately prominent rock close off its SE extremity.

682   **Meares Bluff**, the east extremity of Effingham Island, consists of cliffs about 30 m high that rise steeply to a hill with an elevation of 102 m.

683   **Directions**. — Entering Thiepval Channel from Loudoun Channel pass between the 3 m high rock that lies 0.3 mile north of Trickett Island and the rock with a depth of 2 m 0.15 mile ENE. After these dangers are cleared proceed along the NE coast of Turret Island at a distance of 90 m until dangers in mid-channel are passed, then give the NE end of Turret Island a good berth to avoid the shoal spit extending from it. Coaster Channel is approached between Faber Islets and a group of rocks extending 0.5 mile east from Turret Island, then proceed to Imperial Eagle Channel keeping about 0.2 mile off the NE coast of Effingham Island. Local vessels often use the passage leading to Imperial Eagle Channel between Wiebe Island and Village Reef.

Island Harbour and Approach

684   **Harbour Entrance**, between **Dempster Island** and **Gibraltar Island**, is the main channel leading from Imperial Eagle Channel to **Island Harbour** *(48°55'N, 125°17'W)*. **Eussen Rock**, in the centre of the fairway, has 3 m over it and is steep-to.

Chart 3670

Thiepval Channel from NW of Faber Islets (1985)

Thiepval Channel from Loudoun Channel (1985)

685 Island Harbour can also be entered by the passage south of Dempster Island. **Pinnace Rock**, **Elbow Rocks**, **Elbow Islet**, the unnamed islets between it and **Mullins Island** and the rocks and shoals SE of **Keith Island**, form the south and east sides of the passage.

686 Island Harbour affords well-sheltered **anchorage** for small vessels in 20 m, about 0.2 mile NE of the east extremity of Keith Island. Small craft can obtain anchorage in coves on the south shore of Jaques Island.

Imperial Eagle Channel

Chart 3671

687 **Imperial Eagle Channel** *(48°54'N, 125°12'W)* is bounded on its SE side by the Deer Group and on its NW side by the Broken Group and a short stretch of Vancouver Island. During south or SW gales there is a very heavy sea in this channel.

Entrance to Imperial Eagle Channel

688 **Miller Reef** *(48°50'N, 125°19'W)* consists of two drying rocks, about 0.2 mile apart. The reef is steep-to on its south side and breakers are usually present.

689 **Janit Reef**, 1.7 miles WNW of Miller Reef, dries 1.8 m.

690 Numerous dangers lie NE of a line joining Miller Reef, Janit Reef and a position about 2.5 miles NW.

691 **Caution. — Even in calm weather a large breaking wave can occur without warning in this area.**

692 **Hornby Rock**, 1.5 miles SE of Miller Reef, has 1.6 m over it and can usually be identified by breakers.

693 **Folger Island** *(48°50'N, 125°15'W)* is wooded and cliffy on its south and west sides.

694 **Bordelais Islets** lie at the SW extremity of the Deer Group. The largest islet is about 30 m high and has a cliffy appearance when seen from SW.

695 **Lights**. — Folger Island light *(175)* is shown at an elevation of 40.2 m from a white tower.

696 Bordelais Islets light *(174)* is shown at an elevation of 28.4 m from a white tower with a green band at the top.

697 **Folger Passage**, between Hornby Rock and Folger Island, affords the best entry to Imperial Eagle Channel in thick weather. **Hammond Passage**, between Folger Island and **Leach Islet** on the NW, and Bordelais Islets and Edward King Island on the SE, can be used in fine weather. Drying rocks extend 0.2 mile SE from Leach Islet.

698 **Directions. — Clearing marks**. — Approaching Imperial Eagle Channel from the NW, keep Cape Beale Lighthouse bearing less than 097° until the east extremity of Swiss Boy Island comes in line with Folger Island light bearing 043°. These clearing marks lead about 0.5 mile SE of Hornby Rock, but also over a rock with a depth of 17 m. When the lighthouse at Cape Beale bears 122°, course can be altered to pass in mid-channel through either Hammond Passage or Folger Passage. Folger Passage is the safer route.

699 Sail Rock, bearing more than 319° and open SW of Wouwer Island, leads SW of Hornby Rock and Miller Reef. It is possible to enter Imperial Eagle Channel between Hornby Rock and Miller Reef by keeping Nanat Islet *(48°53'N, 125°04'W)* bearing 068° and just open north of Ohiat Islet, until Folger Island is abeam, when course can be altered up channel as required. This passage leads over a 15.6 m shoal and is not recommended during SW gales or in poor visibility.

Imperial Eagle Channel — East Side

700 **Edward King Island** *(48°50'N, 125°12'W)* has many rocks and shoals extending from its NW shore.

701 **Dodger Channel** *(48°50'N, 125°12'W)* is entered between **Seppings Island** and **Kirby Point**. A rock that dries 1.2 m lies on the west side of the north entrance. The entrance from Trevor Channel is shallow and intricate, with rocks on both sides and an

Chart 3671

Dodger Channel from Imperial Eagle Channel (1985)

Dodger Channel from Trevor Channel (1985)

islet in the middle. The south part of the channel affords good shelter for small craft but local knowledge is advised.

702 The channel between **Diana Island** and **Helby Island** has a rock with 1.8 m over it in mid-channel. It is usable for small craft but local knowledge is advised.

703 **Satellite Passage** is the only navigable passage through **Deer Group**. It lies between Helby Island and **Sandford Island** about 0.6 mile north.

704 **Shoals.** — A shoal, with a least depth of 6.4 m, lies on the north side of the fairway about 0.2 mile SSW of the SW extremity of Sandford Island. A detached shoal with 9.8 m over it lies 0.3 mile NW of **Ohiat Islet** in the west approach.

705 **Prohibited anchorage.** — Because of submarine cables anchorage is prohibited in Satellite Passage.

706 **Clearing marks. — Directions.** — The middle of Dixon Island *(48°51'N, 125°07'W)* in line with the highest part of Wizard Islet bearing 101° leads midway between the dangers lying in the west end of the passage. Approaching Satellite Passage from Imperial Eagle Channel keep on this bearing until Foucault Bluff *(48°54'N, 125°05'W)*, bearing 058°, is well open SE of Sandford Island.

707 The passage between Helby Island and Ohiat Islet is foul, and should not be attempted.

708 **Adamson Rocks**, close-off the NW corner of **Fleming Island**, are usually marked by breakers in heavy weather and should not be approached within a distance of 0.3 mile.

709 A **rock**, with 8.8 m over it, lies near mid-channel 1.3 miles WNW of Adamson Rocks.

710 **Marble Cove**, at the SW end of Tzartus Island, is sheltered by **Fry Island** and has marine farm facilities at its north end.

711 Marble Cove is reported to afford good **anchorage** for small craft protected from westerlies. Tzartus Cove (local name), 0.7 mile north, is reported to offer shelter from SE winds.

712 **Swiss Boy Island**, 1 mile NNE of Adamson Rocks and at the SW end of the **Chain Group**, is cliffy. **Bull Rock**, 0.3 mile WNW

of Swiss Boy Island, breaks in bad weather. Drying rocks extend north and **Jupe Rock**, with 0.2 m over it, lies 0.3 mile NE from Swiss Boy Island.

713 **Meade Islets**, **Geer Islets** and **Diplock Island** are surrounded by numerous rocks and shoals.

714 **Holford Bay**, south of **Gattie Point**, is approached between **Stud Islets** and **Friend Island**. A rock with 6.8 m over it lies in the approach and a rock with 7 m over it is close south. It is reported that a swell rolls into the bay.

715 **Best Islet** and two drying rocks lie off the NW side of **Weld Island**. A rock that dries 3.8 m lies off the north extremity of Weld Island.

716 A passage leads north from Holford Bay along the NW coast of **Tzartus Island** and connects with Junction Passage at **Crosse Point**.

717 Ahmah Cove (local name), behind **Ahmah Island**, is reported to afford anchorage for small craft with good shelter and holding. The entrance is narrow and shallow and two float cabins are in the cove.

718 A **booming ground** is south of Crosse Point.

Imperial Eagle Channel — North End

719 **Baeria Rocks** *(48°57'N, 125°09'W)* are bare, rocky and conspicuous. Baeria Rocks are an Ecological Reserve and closed to the public.

720 **Light.** — Baeria Rocks light *(151)* is on the SE rock.

721 **Robinson Island** lies SW of **Kyen Point** on the east side of **Alma Russell Islands**. A rock that dries 1.8 m and **Harold Islet** lie in the approach to the north entrance of Julia Passage.

722 **Julia Passage**, NW of Alma Russell Islands, offers sheltered anchorage for small craft, local knowledge is advised. North and south entrances to Julia Passage are encumbered with rocks. Float houses are moored along both shores.

Charts 3671, 3668

723 **Effingham Inlet** *(48°59'N, 125°10'W)* is approached north of **Rutley Islands, George Islet** and **John Islet. Milhus Rock** lies about 0.3 mile SE and a rock that dries 0.6 m lies 0.1 mile south of **Palmer Point** at the north entrance to Effingham Inlet. The inlet is narrow and shores are high and rocky. Depths are too great for anchorage except off the drying flats at the head. Anchorage is reported to be available for small craft in the cove on the west side north of Webster Island. Booming grounds line both sides of the inlet.

724 **Marine farm** facilities are on both sides of the inlet close north of **Webster Island**.

Chart 3668

725 From **Coeur d'Alene Creek** *(49°03'N, 125°08'W)* a dry weather logging road leads through the valley along the north side of **Uchuck Lake** to Uchucklesit Inlet. Booming grounds and a log dump are on the west shore, opposite the creek.

726 **Marine farm** facilities are near the head of the inlet.

Charts 3671, 3668

727 **Vernon Bay** *(48°59'N, 125°09'W)* is entered between Palmer Point and **Allen Point**, about 1.5 miles ESE. Shores are high and rugged and depths are too great for anchorage. A group of drying rocks lie 0.5 mile NNW of Allen Point. **Jane Island**, at the head of Vernon Bay, lies in the entrance to a deep, sheltered basin known locally as Jane Bay. Entrance to the basin is only about 90 m wide in the fairway. Marine farm facilities lie off the west shore of the basin. A fishing lodge and floats are on the east side of the basin. Accomodation and dining are available, boaters are welcome.

Chart 3668

728 **Useless Inlet** *(48°59'N, 125°04'W)* entered 3 miles ESE from Palmer Point separates **Seddall Island** from Vancouver Island. It is accessible only to small craft because the entrance is foul.

Useless Inlet from west of Pill Point (1985)

Fatty Basin entrance from Useless Inlet (1985)

Chart 3668

Waters of Useless Inlet fall within the limits of Port Alberni Harbour. Marine farm facilities are in several locations.

Chart 3646

729 **Fatty Basin** *(48°59'N, 125°01'W)* leads SE from near the head of Useless Inlet. A narrow boat passage which almost dries connects it with the inlet. Trees hanging across this passage gave a low overhead clearance (1988). A sign reading *"No passage for boats beyond this point. Low overhanging cables."* is reported to be on the 42 m high islet. The south entrance, which dries 3.4 m, connects Fatty Basin to Rainy Bay. Marine farm facilities are located in the basin.

730 A **bridge**, with a vertical clearance of 4.2 m, crosses the north end of the channel between Rainy Bay and Fatty Basin. Trees hanging across this channel (1988) have a lower clearance than the bridge.

731 **Tidal streams** flood and ebb about 4 kn in both entrance channels to Fatty Basin.

Junction Passage

Charts 3671, 3668

732 **Junction Passage** *(48°58'N, 125°03'W)*, south of Seddall Island, is a deep channel leading from the NE part of Imperial Eagle Channel to the junction of Trevor Channel and Alberni Inlet. From the west it is entered between **Pill Point** and the islets lying off the NE side of **Link Island**. From the east it is entered between Chup Point and **Fullarton Point** *(48°57'N, 125°03'W)*, the NE extremity of Tzartus Island.

733 **Tyler Rock**, almost in the middle of the east approach, has 6.4 m over it. The fairway is nowhere less than 0.25 mile wide and Tyler Rock can be passed on either side.

734 **Harbour limits**. — The waters of Junction Passage and Rainy Bay fall within the limits of Port Alberni Harbour.

735 **Tidal streams** in Junction Passage attain 1 kn on the flood and ½ kn on the ebb, but are greatly influenced by the wind. The flood sets east and the ebb west.

736 **Light**. — Pill Point light *(152)* is on the south extremity of the point.

737 **Rainy Bay** lies on the north side of Junction Passage. Shores are rugged and depths are too great for anchorage. Numerous float cabins of a sport fishing lodge are in the narrow inlet 0.5 mile north of **Boyson Islands**. A house is on the east shore of Rainy Bay, east of Boyson Islands.

738 **Ecoole** is in a small bay on the SE side of Seddall Island, close within the entrance to Rainy Bay. The wharf and buildings are in ruins.

Trevor Channel

Chart 3671

739 **Trevor Channel** *(48°50'N, 125°10'W)* leads along the east side of Barkley Sound to Alberni Inlet. The fairway across a sill in its entrance, between Cape Beale and Seapool Rocks, is marked by two sectored lights and has about 25 m over it. Inside the fairway is deep and 0.4 mile wide at its narrowest part.

740 **Tidal streams** in Trevor Channel off Nanat Island *(48°53'N, 125°05'W)* attain ½ kn on the flood and ebb, but are greatly influenced by the wind.

741 **Prohibited anchorage**. — Because of submarine cables that extend along the fairway for the entire length of Trevor Channel, anchorage is prohibited in Trevor Channel in an area bounded on the SW by a line between Cape Beale and Bordelais Islets, and 6 miles NE by a line between Ellis Islet and the centre of Fleming Island.

742 **Anchorages**. — If it is necessary to anchor in Trevor Channel, Entrance Anchorage is recommended, as it is easy access from either Trevor or Imperial Eagle Channels. Mackenzie Anchorage, Roquefeuil Bay, Christie Bay and Sproat Bay also provide anchorage. Small craft can find shelter in Bamfield Inlet, Poett Nook, the inlet north of Congreve Island, or in the small bay NW of Clifton Point.

Cape Beale to Nanat Islet

743 **Cape Beale** *(48°47'N, 125°13'W)*, the SE entrance point of the channel, and Cape Beale Sector light are described in Chapter 9. Foul ground consisting of reefs and shoals, most of which are marked by kelp, surround Cape Beale. **It is strongly advised that the Cape be given a wide berth.**

744 A **wind frequency table** for Cape Beale is in the Appendices.

745 **Seapool Rocks**, 2 miles north of Cape Beale on the NW side of the fairway, consist of four drying rocks, the highest dries 2 m. A rocky area, with a least depth of 5.4 m over it, lies 0.2 mile south of Seapool Rocks. The sea generally breaks over the rocks and rocky area.

746 **Lawton Point** and **Whittlestone Point**, 1.8 miles NE of Cape Beale, are the entrance points to **Tapaltos Bay**. Several islets and rocks lie close-off Whittlestone Point. **Aguilar Point**, 2.5 miles NE of Whittlestone Point, is the west entrance point to Bamfield Inlet.

747 **Lights**. — Trevor Channel Entrance Sector light *(172.5)*, on an islet 0.3 mile NE of Whittlestone Point, is shown at an elevation of 13.3 m from a white tower. An additional light visible round 360° is shown at an elevation of 16.6 m.

748 Aguilar Point Sector light *(172)*, on the north extremity of the point, is shown at an elevation of 5 m from a white tower with a red band at the top.

749 White sectors of the lights indicate preferred channels.

750 **Light buoy**. — Seapool Rocks light and whistle buoy "Y49" *(173)*, south of the rocks, is a port hand buoy fitted with a Racon (— • —).

751 **Edward King Island**, on the NW side of the channel and 0.4 mile NE of Bordelais Islets, is joined by a drying ledge to **Haines Island**, close east.

752 The south entrance to Dodger Channel lies between **Taylor Islet** and **Voss Point**, the south extremity of Diana Island.

753 **Mackenzie Anchorage**, south of Helby Island, has depths of about 70 m but small vessels can anchor close to shore. **Cia Rock**, on the SW side of Mackenzie Anchorage and 0.5 mile NE of Voss Point, dries 3.2 m and is marked by a daybeacon with two port hand daymarks. **Self Point** is a small peninsula connected to Helby Island by a very low isthmus and has the appearance of an islet, it is sometimes conspicuous on a clear night.

Chart 3671

754 **Entrance Anchorage** (*48°51'N, 125°10'W*) is well sheltered with easy access from either Trevor Channel or Imperial Eagle Channel. The NE side of Helby Island should not be approached within a distance of about 0.15 mile. This anchorage is a convenient stopping place for vessels entering or leaving Barkley Sound.

755 **Wizard Islet**, on the north side of Entrance Anchorage, is 2.8 m high and bare with another islet close NE.

756 **Light**. — Wizard Islet light (*171*) is on the summit of the islet.

757 **Ross Islets**, 0.7 mile north of Wizard Islet, attain an elevation of 30 m and are surrounded by foul ground.

758 **Roquefeuil Bay** (*48°51'N, 125°07'W*) has low shores, an uneven bottom, and affords fairly sheltered anchorage in a depth of about 17 m. A rock that dries 2.4 m and another with 3.6 m over it are 0.1 and 0.2 mile north of **Dixon Island**. A rock with 0.1 m over it lies 0.1 mile south of **Ellis Islet**. Marine farm facilities line the east shore of Dixon Island and the cove 0.2 mile east of Dixon Island is boomed off with a float house in it.

759 **Danvers Islet**, 1.1 miles NE of Ellis Islet, is low with a drying rock close SW of it. Marine farm facilities are in the cove 0.1 mile east of the islet.

760 **Nanat Islet** (*48°53'N, 125°04'W*) is wooded and conspicuous from the entrance of Imperial Eagle Channel.

761 **Tidal streams** off Nanat Islet are ½ kn on the flood and ebb but are greatly influenced by wind.

Bamfield Inlet

Chart 3646

762 Bamfield and Grappler Inlets afford good shelter to small craft, but **anchorage is prohibited** in their common entrance because of submarine cables.

763 **Bamfield Inlet** (*48°50'N, 125°08'W*) lies on the east side of **Mills Peninsula**. **Burlo Island** and **Rance Island**, 1 mile south from the entrance, are connected at LW to the west and east sides of the inlet. The passage between them is about 30 m wide with a depth of 3.8 m but has a drying rock and a below-water rock off the Burlo Island shore. **Burts Island** lies on a drying flat SW of Burlo Island.

764 **Speed limit**. — A sign inside the entrance reads "*Maximum speed 7 kn*".

765 **Submarine cables**. — Abandoned cables are in the entrance to Bamfield Inlet. Cables cross the inlet 0.6 mile south of Aguilar Point and near the north ends of Burlo and Rance Islands.

766 **Submarine pipelines**. — A sewer outfall, marked by a sign, is close south of Aguilar Point. Pipelines, two of which are potable water intakes, extend into Bamfield Inlet from its east shore, about 0.3 mile SE of Aguilar Point. A water pipeline crosses the inlet about 0.6 mile south of Aguilar Point. Water pipelines cross from Rance Island to the east shore of the inlet and from Burlo Island to the west shore. Water pipelines cross from the south end of Rance Island to Burlo Island and from the south end of Burlo Island to the south shore.

767 **Overhead cables** (power), vertical clearances 5.2 and 17 m, cross the channels on the west and east sides of Burlo Island. A cable, vertical clearance 6.4 m, crosses from the east side of Rance Island.

768 **Beacons**. — Grappler Inlet Entrance daybeacon, 0.3 mile SE of Aguilar Point on the south entrance point to Grappler Inlet, has a starboard hand daymark.

769 Bamfield Creek daybeacon, on a reef on the west side of the inlet and about 0.6 mile south of Aguilar Point, has a starboard hand daymark.

770 **Buoys**. — Starboard hand buoy "Y54" marks a rock lying east of the reef near the public wharf.

771 Starboard hand buoy "Y56" marks the drying rock in the channel between Rance and Burlo Islands.

772 Public mooring buoys lie off the north end of Burlo Island.

773 **Storage tanks**. — Oil storage tanks and a water tank are on the west side of the inlet, 0.3 mile south of Aguilar Point. Oil storage tanks are on the east side of the inlet, close NE of Rance Island.

774 A **radio tower**, 59 m high and marked by red air obstruction lights, is on the east side of Bamfield Inlet about 0.7 mile SSE of Aguilar Point.

775 Bamfield Inlet is a **water aerodrome**.

776 **Bamfield**, a fishing settlement, has two separate sides that are not connected except by boat. On the west side is a Red Cross Outpost Hospital, post office, general store and the **Coast Guard year-round lifeboat station**. The east side has stores, accommodation, restaurants and fuel docks.

777 **Supplies and Services**. — Gasoline, diesel fuel and stove oil can be obtained from the marine service station. Fresh and frozen meat, groceries, propane and fresh water can be obtained at the settlement. Hull and engine repairs can be undertaken on small craft.

778 **Communication**. — The Alberni Marine Transportation Company (Lady Rose Marine Services) maintains a year-round, three days a week, ferry service to and from Port Alberni. A summer only bus servicing the West Coast Trail connects to destinations from Port Alberni to Victoria. Restricted logging roads connect the east side of Bamfield to Port Alberni, Cowichan Lake, Sarita Bay and Poett Nook.

779 **Anchorages**. — Small vessels can anchor 0.15 mile north of Rance Island, care must be taken to avoid submarine cables. Larger vessels can find anchorage in Entrance Anchorage on the west side of Trevor Channel.

780 **Tides**. — Tidal differences for Bamfield (Index No. 8545), referenced on Tofino, are in *Tide Tables, Volume 6*.

781 **Coast Guard Lifesaving Station float** is 0.2 mile SE of Aguilar Point on the west shore.

782 **Public wharf**, close south of the lifesaving station and immediately north of the post office, is 18 m long with a depth of 6.1 m alongside. A float 25 m long is attached to its south end. It has a 3 tonne crane.

783 **Public floats**, with a common connection to a shore approach structure, are 0.6 mile south of Aguilar Point and close WNW of Bamfield Creek daybeacon. These floats are 80 and 57 m long and have depths of about 4.3 m alongside.

784 **Public wharf** on the east shore, 0.8 mile SSE of Aguilar Point, has a berthing length of 18 m on its outer face. A crane and shed are on the wharf. It is approached from shore over a rockfill causeway. Floats with a common connection are attached to the south side.

785 **Western Canadian Universities Marine Biological Station**, on the east side of the inlet about 0.3 mile SE of Aguilar Point, is on the site of the former Trans Pacific Cable station. The main wharf is the south one, it is 35 m long with a depth of 6.4 m

Bamfield Inlet (1985)

Chart 3646

Bamfield Inlet entrance (1985)

Grappler Inlet and Port Désiré (1985)

alongside. Visitors are welcome, tours are offered on summer weekends.

786   **Grappler Inlet** is entered about 0.3 mile SE of Aguilar Point and to the north of Grappler Inlet Entrance daybeacon. It is surrounded by houses.

787   **Light**. — Grappler Inlet light *(171.5)*, on the north shore of **Port Désiré**, is shown at an elevation of 3.7 m from a mast.

788   **Submarine cables** cross the inlet about 0.1 mile east of Grappler Inlet Entrance daybeacon, and a telephone cable marked by signs is close east of Grappler Inlet light.

789   **Submarine pipelines**. — A water pipeline crosses the inlet 0.1 mile east of Grappler Inlet Entrance daybeacon. A water pipeline extends from close west of the public float, along the centre of Port Désiré and through the narrows to the entrance of **Sugsaw Creek**. Another pipeline crosses the inlet 0.2 mile east of the public wharf.

790   **Overhead cables**, vertical clearances 9 and 12 m, cross the bay on the north side of Port Désiré. Another cable, vertical clearance 23 m, crosses the inlet 0.2 mile east of the public wharf.

Overhead cables, vertical clearances unknown, cross the inlet entered south of Grappler Inlet No. 2 daybeacon.

791   **Wharf**. — A public wharf with a float and launching ramp are on the south side of Port Désiré. Many private floats are in Port Désiré.

792   **Buoys**. — Grappler Inlet buoy "Y47", a port hand buoy 0.2 mile ESE of Grappler Inlet light, marks a rock ledge extending south from the north shore.

793   Public mooring buoys in Port Désiré are reported to be in poor condition.

794   **Beacons**. — Grappler Inlet No. 2 daybeacon, on the south side of the narrows leading NE to the inner basin, has a starboard hand daymark.

795   Grappler Inlet No. 1 daybeacon, on the north side of the narrows, has a port hand daymark.

796   A bar that dries 0.2 m, 0.1 mile NNE of Grappler Inlet daybeacon No. 1, partially separates the inner basin of Port Désiré.

797   A **pipeline sign** is on the outer end of the drying flat at the head of the inner basin. A wharf and float are at the north entrance

Chart 3646

Robbers Passage from Trevor Channel (1985)

Robbers Passage from Imperial Eagle Channel (1985)

to Sugsaw Creek. Wrecks lie east of the island in the entrance to the inner basin.

Nanat Islet to Mutine Point

Chart 3668

798 **Robbers Passage** *(48°54'N, 125°07'W)* separates Fleming Island from Tzartus Island and connects Trevor Channel to Imperial Eagle Channel. It is only suitable for small craft because of numerous drying ledges and rocks in both entrances. Shoal depths of less than 2 m extend NE and E from Robbers Pass daybeacon to the shore of Tzartus Island, and a shoal with 2.6 m over it is 190 m SSE of the daybeacon. Port Alberni Yacht Club floats are on the Fleming Island shore, visitors are welcome. A sport fishing lodge is on the east side of the passage.

799 **Beacon**. — Robbers Pass daybeacon, on a drying rock in the SE entrance to Robbers Passage, has a starboard hand daymark. Upstream direction is proceeding from Trevor Channel toward Imperial Eagle Channel.

Charts 3668, 3671

800 **Foucault Bluff** *(48°54'N, 125°05'W)*, the SE extremity of Tzartus Island, is a steep point, conspicuous from the entrance of Trevor Channel.

801 **Sproat Bay** has islets and a shoal rock in its north part. Marine farm facilities are in the south part of the bay. Anchorage can be obtained in the south part.

802 **Kooh Rock**, with a depth of 2.8 m over it, is steep-to and lies about 0.1 mile ESE of the SE islet in Sproat Bay.

803 **Light buoy**. — Kooh Rock light buoy "Y51" *(169)*, east of the rock, is a port hand buoy.

804 **San Jose Islets**, on the SE side of the fairway about 1.3 miles NE of Nanat Islet, are low and surrounded by shoal water.

805 **Light**. — San Jose Islets light *(170)*, on the west side of the west islet, is shown at an elevation of 7.5 m from a white tower with a red band at the top.

806 **Hosie Islands**, about 1 mile NE of San Jose Islets, have a drying rocky ledge extending nearly 0.1 mile SW from the largest island. A rock with 0.8 m over it lies close-off the north islet.

807 **Numukamis Bay** *(48°54'N, 125°02'W)* has depths too great for anchorage in most places. Land in the vicinity of the bay rises gradually to mountains with elevations of 300 to 850 m a short distance inland.

808 **Poett Nook**, 1 mile east of Nanat Islet, is entered through a straight but narrow channel. A drying ledge, at the south end of the entrance channel where it opens into the basin, extends a short distance from the west shore into the channel and basin. The basin affords good anchorage and shelter to small craft. A camp ground is in the NE corner of the basin. A marina, adjacent to the camp ground, provides gas and supplies and has washrooms and showers. A restricted logging road provides access to Bamfield and Port Alberni. Marine farm facilites lie at the head of Poett Nook.

809 **Christie Bay** lies between Poett Nook and the SW extremity of **Santa Maria Island**. **Sarita Bay**, between the east entrance point of Poett Nook and the logging settlement **Sarita**, is a booming ground. A log dump, wharf and A-frame are visible from the bay. The settlement is connected by restricted logging roads to Bamfield and Port Alberni.

810 **Anchorage** in 10 to 20 m can be obtained in Christie Bay at a distance of about 0.2 mile offshore.

811 **Congreve Island** is separated from Vancouver Island by a drying channel. Between the north side of the island and Vancouver Island, is a bight with depths of 17 m, which offers anchorage and shelter for small craft. A sport fishing resort in the bight consists of a large floating lodge and several float houses.

812 **Clifton Point**, 1 mile west of Congreve Island, is steep-to. A rock that dries 0.2 m lies 0.1 mile SE of the point. The small cove,

Charts 3668, 3671

Poett Nook entrance (1985)   NOTE: reef on west side

Poett Nook (1989)

close NW of Clifton Point, provides sheltered anchorage for small craft. A large building and a private float are at the head of this cove.

813   **Chimmin Point**, 1.3 miles NNE of Clifton Point, is steep-to.

814   **Assits Island** *(48°56′N, 125°02′W)*, small and wooded, is separated from Vancouver Island by a narrow passage suitable only for small craft. A drying ledge extends east from the NE side of the island.

815   **Light**. — Assits Island light *(153)* is on the west extremity of the island.

816   **Crickitt Bay**, between Assits Island and **Mutine Point**, is encumbered with rocks. Mutine Point should be given a wide berth as rocks with 9 and 0.8 m over them lie up to 0.2 mile offshore.

817   **Port Alberni Harbour** is under the jurisdiction of the Port Alberni Port Authority. Harbour limits are defined as: "The areas covered by tidal waters of Trevor Channel and Alberni Inlet within the following limits:

818   **South Limit:** A line drawn on a bearing of 320° from the most northwesterly point of Congreve Island through **Tzartus** Island and Pill Point Light on Seddall Island and then across the entrance to Useless Inlet to the opposite shore;

819   **North Limit**: A line drawn south across Somass River from the southeast corner of the Ahahewinis Indian Reserve No. 1 to the opposite shore, including the waters of Junction Passage, Rainy Bay and all other bays and inlets within the said limits."

Charts 3668, 3671

820 **Regulations**. — Port Alberni Port Authority regulations are obtainable from:

Port Alberni Port Authority
2750 Harbour Road
Port Alberni, B.C. V9X 72X
Telephone (250) 723-5312.

821 Regulations require the Master, or Agent, to report to the Harbour Master. Regulations govern vessels manoeuvring or otherwise underway, at anchor, berthing or alongside a berth. No vessel shall move in the harbour at a rate of speed that may endanger or inconvenience any person or is in excess of any rate of speed authorized by the Port Authority. While alongside anchors are to be stowed, and a wire hawser of suitable size for towing is to be lowered from the bow and secured so that the bight of the hawser hangs just clear of the surface.

822 Vessels are regulated with respect to watch-keeping, bunkering, cargo handling operations and lighting. No oil or waste, including garbage or dunnage, shall be discharged into the harbour. Instructions for signalling in the event of fire are included. There are specific regulations for carrying and handling explosives and dangerous goods, as well as rules to be observed in the prevention of fire.

Alberni Inlet

Chart 3668

823 **Alberni Inlet** *(48°57'N, 125°01'W)*, a continuation of Trevor Channel, is entered between Chup and Mutine Points and continues 22 miles north to the mouth of the Somas River. Shores on either side are rocky and rugged, rising abruptly from the water's edge to summits of mountains. At the head of the inlet, in the vicinity of Port Alberni, land is low and fertile. An up-inlet wind develops to 25-30 kn during most summer afternoons producing a chop uncomfortable for small craft.

824 **Tides**. — *Tide Table, Volume 6*, give tidal predictions for Port Alberni (Index No. 8575), at the head of the inlet; tidal differences in Alberni Inlet, referenced on Tofino, are given for Mutine Point (Index No. 8556), Uchucklesit Inlet (Index No. 8559) and Franklin River (Index No. 8565).

825 **Tidal streams** in Alberni Inlet are typically about 1 kn on both flood and ebb, however surface currents are greatly influenced by wind. In Stamp Narrows outflow of Somass River influences currents so they are often stronger on the ebb than on the flood.

826 **Ferry**. — A ferry on a regular schedule from Port Alberni serves Bamfield and Ucluelet.

827 **Caution. — Marine farms**. — Fish farm holding pens are in San Mateo Bay *(48°57'N, 125°00'W)* and Macktush Creek *(49°07'N, 124°49'W)*. The pens are covered by galvanized sheds and several of them may be rafted together for various periods of time. Mariners should exercise caution and reduce speed when in vicinity of pens.

828 **Booming grounds** are in several locations on either side of the inlet.

829 **Submarine cables** extend along the centre of the inlet, from the entrance to Polly Point.

830 **Shelter** for small craft can be obtained close south of Bernard Point in San Mateo Bay, in Green Cove, Snug Basin, Limestone Bay and China Creek.

831 **Vessel Traffic Services (VTS)**. — Alberni Inlet is in the *Tofino Traffic Zone*. Assigned frequency is 156.725 MHz, Channel 74. Calling-in points in Alberni Inlet are:

832 *Calling-in Point No. 3*, *Chup Point*, is a line joining Chup Point light *(154)* with Mutine Point;

833 *Calling-in Point No. 4*, *Ten Mile Point*, is a line extending 256° from Ten Mile Point light *(158)* to the opposite shore of Alberni Inlet;

834 *Calling-in Point No. 5*, *Dunsmuir Point*, is a line extending 090° from Dunsmuir Point light *(162)* to the opposite shore of Alberni Inlet.

835 Vessel Masters must request clearance from *Tofino Traffic* before proceeding to or leaving any berth within Port Alberni Harbour limits.

836 A brief description of this VTS is in *PAC 200*. Details are in *Radio Aids to Marine Navigation (Pacific and Western Arctic)*.

Chup Point to Limestone Islet

837 **Chup Point** *(48°57'N, 125°02'W)* is a conspicuous cliffy projection.

838 **Light**. — Chup Point light *(154)* is on the east side of the point.

839 **Haggard Cove** has cabins of a sport fishing resort onshore and a marina protected by a rock breakwater across the entrance. The SW point of the bay, 1.3 miles NE of Chup Point, has a prominent abandoned house on it.

840 **San Mateo Bay**, on the south side of Alberni Inlet, is entered between **Bernard Point** and **Hissin Point**. **Chris Rock**, about 0.2 mile west of Hissin Point and in the entrance to San Mateo Bay, has 5.6 m over it. **Banton Island** lies nearly in the centre of the bay; between it and the head of the bay there is a rock that dries 1.6 m.

841 **Marine farm** facilities are SSW and east of Banton Island and at the head of the bay.

842 San Mateo Bay is mainly deep but **anchorage** for small vessels can be obtained close offshore and at the head of the bay, between Banton Island and the coast south of it, in 26 to 33 m. Care should be taken to avoid fish pens in this area.

843 **Float**. — A public float, on the south side of Bernard Point, has a depth of 11 m alongside and 46 m of berthing space. It is not connected to shore but provides sheltered mooring.

844 **Ritherdon Bay** entered between Hissin Point and **Blackstone Point** is clear of dangers, mainly deep and affords anchorage with good holding ground. A house close south of Blackstone Point is prominent from the approach. Ruins of a pier are on the south shore at the outer end of the drying flat. A restricted logging road leads east from the head of the bay. Marine farm facilites are east of Blackstone Point near the head of the bay.

845 **Limestone Islet** *(48°59'N, 124°58'W)*, close east of the entrance to Uchucklesit Inlet, is connected to shore by a drying flat at its north end.

846 **Light**. — Limestone Islet light *(154.8)*, on the south side of the islet, is shown at an elevation of 8.5 m from a white tower.

847 **Limestone Bay**, to the north of and sheltered by Limestone Islet, offers shelter and anchorage to small craft, especially from winds blowing down the channel.

Uchucklesit Inlet

Chart 3646

848 **Uchucklesit Inlet**, a branch of Alberni Inlet, is entered between **Burrough Point** *(48°59'N, 125°00'W)* and **Brooksby Point** 0.4 mile NE. High land rises gradually to the summits of mountains on its NE side, but the head of the inlet and its SW shore are low.

849 **Caution. — Numerous float houses and close to surface installations are moored in Uchucklesit Inlet. Mariners should reduce speed and proceed with caution.**

850 **Tides.** — Tidal differences for Uchucklesit Inlet (Index No. 8559), referenced on Tofino, are in *Tide Tables, Volume 6.*

851 **Chaputs Passage**, between **Cheeyah Island** and the peninsula SE, can be used by small vessels but care must be taken to avoid the rock that dries 3 m lying close-off the SE extremity of the island.

852 **Spoil ground.** — A non-active ocean dump site is located west of **Strawberry Point** *(49°59'N, 124°59'W)* in the entrance to Chaputs Passage.

853 **Green Cove**, east of Cheeyah Island, is a booming ground. A log dump is on the NE side of the cove. Well-sheltered anchorage in 10 to 20 m, mud and sand bottom, is obtainable clear of the logbooms.

854 **Seekah Passage**, which is wide and deep, lies between Cheeyah Island and the north shore of the inlet. A submarine pipeline (water) is laid across the passage.

855 **Kildonan**, once a fish cannery, is not connected by road and is inhabited by a small number of retired people. The post office is in a float house (1988). Ruins of the cannery and wharf, together with numerous piles and concrete piers, lie on the drying flats. Kildonan Cannery Lodge float is south of the ruins. The ferry operating between Port Alberni and Bamfield visits three days a week.

856 The SW shore of the inlet is fronted by **booming grounds** from **Setsup Bluff** to **Daller Point** 1.2 miles farther NW. A logging camp is on Daller Point.

857 **Blunden Rock**, 0.5 mile SE of Daller Point, dries 2.1 m, it is the SE extremity of foul ground.

858 **Snug Basin**, on the north side of the head of Uchucklesit Inlet, offers secure anchorage for small craft, mud bottom. **Caiger Point** has booming grounds, a float and dry land sorting area on its south side, the west entrance point has several houses and a float.

Limestone Islet to Polly Point

Chart 3668

859 **Lights. — Star Point** light *(155)*, about 1 mile ESE from Limestone Islet *(48°59'N, 124°57'W)*, is shown at an elevation of 5.3 m from a white tower with a red band at the top.

860 **Pocahontas Point** light *(156)* is 2.2 miles east of Limestone Islet.

861 **Spencer Creek** light *(156.5)*, 1.1 miles ENE of Pocahontas Point, has starboard hand daymarks on its SW and NE faces.

862 **Bilton Point** light *(157)*, 1.6 miles NE of Spencer Creek light, is shown at an elevation of 6.7 m from a white tower with a green band at the top.

863 **Ten Mile Point** light *(158)* is 3 miles NNE of Bilton Point light.

864 **Hocking Point** light *(159)* is 1.8 miles NNE of Ten Mile Point.

865 **Booming grounds** with conspicuous A-frames are 1.4 miles east of Star Point and 1 mile NE of Spencer Creek light.

866 Headquarters Bay (local name), 1 mile south of Ten Mile Point, forms the entrance to **Chesnucknuw Creek**. It has private berthing facilities for small craft protected by a breakwater. A private daybeacon with a port hand daymark is on the south end of the breakwater.

867 **Nahmint Bay**, opposite Ten Mile Point, has a grassy flat at the head that is fronted by a steep-to drying mud and gravel bank. Temporary anchorage can be obtained in the middle of the Bay in a depth of about 37 m. Ruined piles are on the south shore at the outer end of the drying flat.

868 **A public float** in Hook Bay, 0.5 mile NNE of Nahmint Bay, is 17 m long with a depth of 2 m alongside, it is not connected to shore. A rock with 5 m over it lies in the middle of the bay.

869 **Danger. — An isolated rock with 14.8 m over it lies about 0.4 mile NE of Hocking Point.**

Snug Basin from Uchucklesit Inlet (1985)

Chart 3668

870   **Sproat Narrows**, 1 mile NNE of Hocking Point, is reduced to a navigable width of 0.2 mile by drying banks extending from the mouth of the **Franklin River**, on the east side, and the mouth of **Macktush Creek**, on the west side. Silting from the river and creek is extending drying banks outside the lights. **Small craft sometime ground by passing too close to the lights.** A large shed is near the north end of the drying flat off Franklin River. A logging road connects Macktush Creek to Port Alberni.

871   **Tides**. — Tidal differences for Franklin River (Index No. 8565), referenced on Tofino, are in *Tide Tables, Volume 6*.

872   **Current**. — A flood current of about 1 kn and an ebb current of about 1½ kn can be encountered in the narrows.

873   **Lights**. — Franklin River light *(160)* is on a dolphin near the outer edge of the drying bank off the mouth of the Franklin River.

874   Macktush Creek light *(161)* is on a dolphin near the outer edge of the drying bank off the mouth of Macktush Creek.

875   Dunsmuir Point light *(162)*, 2.7 miles NNE of Macktush Creek light, is shown at an elevation of 6.8 m from a white tower with a green band at the top.

876   A privately operated light is shown from the breakwater at China Creek.

877   **Speed**. — Marine farm facilities in **Macktush Bay**, close north of Macktush Creek, are vulnerable. Reduce speed to prevent damage.

878   **Caution. — Particularly during summer months, wind surfers can be expected in the vicinity of China Creek to the upper reaches of Port Alberni Harbour. The Harbour Master requests that a prolonged blast be sounded when approaching China Creek to warn wind surfers to keep clear.**

879   **China Creek**, 0.5 mile east of **Dunsmuir Point**, enters Alberni Inlet through drying mud flats. **China Creek Park**, on the south side of the creek, has camping facilities, fresh water and a launching ramp. It is connected to Port Alberni by road.

880   **Marina**. — China Creek Marina, operated year round by the Port Alberni Port Authority provides berths with depths of 2 to 3 m alongside. Diesel, gas, laundry, showers and washrooms are available. Power and water are at the floats. Overnight moorage may be available but is usually limited in summer.

881   **Stamp Narrows** *(49°11'N, 124°49'W)*, between **Lone Tree Point** on the east and the drying bank off **Cous Creek** on the west shore, is deep and has a navigable width of about 0.15 mile.

882   **Current**. — Outflow from Somass River causes a current to flow south through Stamp Narrows, which sometimes attains more than 1 kn.

883   **Lights**. — Stamp Narrows light *(163)* is on a dolphin on the west side of the narrows.

884   Lone Tree Point light *(164)* is on the east side of the narrows.

885   **Spoil ground**. — An ocean dump site, under permit through *the Ocean Dumping Control Act*, is 0.1 mile north of the above-mentioned floats and marked by fluorescent orange daymarks onshore.

886   **Booming grounds** with A-frames are on both shores between Stamp Narrows and Polly Point.

Port Alberni

887   **Port Alberni** is a secure anchorage at the head of Alberni Inlet. It is entered between **Polly Point**, 2 miles north of Stamp Narrows, and **Stamp Point**, about 0.5 mile west. The west shore is high and rocky, on its east side is a plain and the city of Port Alberni.

888   **Vessel Traffic Services (VTS)**. — Port Alberni Harbour is in the *Tofino Traffic Zone*. Assigned frequency is 156.725 MHz, Channel 74.

889   A brief description of this VTS is in *PAC 200*. Details are in *Radio Aids to Marine Navigation (Pacific and Western Arctic)*.

890   **Light**. — Polly Point light *(165)*, on the west extremity of the point, is shown at an elevation of 4.3 m from a white tower with a red band at the top.

891   **Submarine cables**. — Polly Point is the landing site of several overseas cables. The Teleglobe building is on Polly Point.

892   **Spoil ground**. — A non-active ocean dump site is ENE of Stamp Point.

893   **Hohm Island**, 0.8 mile NNW of Polly Point, is bare, rocky and about 3 m high. A drying rock and a below-water rock lie up to 0.1 mile NE.

894   **Lights**. — Hohm Island light *(166)* is on the east side of the island.

895   **Boom mooring**. — A boom mooring extends 0.33 mile from the north side of Hohm Island, toward Hoik Island, with submerged anchors and cables. It is marked by private lights.

896   **Hoik Island** lies near the west shore, about 0.6 mile NNW of Hohm Island.

897   **Beacon**. — Hoik Island daybeacon has a port hand daymark.

898   **Lights** along the east side of Port Alberni Harbour are all private.

899   Port Alberni Terminals lights are on the south end of No. 1 Berth, and south and north ends of No. 3 Berth.

900   A light is shown from a dolphin 0.1 mile NNW of Berth 3.

901   Maritime Discovery Centre light *(167)* is on the pier close north of Berth 3. This light is not an aid to navigation and is privately operated between 1800 and 2300 daily.

902   Flood lights are on the outer wing of the floats at Fishermen's Harbour, the south light illuminates the entrance channel.

903   **Somass River**, at the head of Port Alberni Harbour, can be navigated by small craft for several miles. River discharge causes a continual current running south out of the harbour that frequently attains over 1 kn. The channel was dredged to a least depth of 3.3 m (1984) as far as the Paper Barge berth on the north side of **Lupsi Cupsi Point**, the depth is maintained by dredging.

904   **Lights**. — Alberni light *(168)*, at the west entrance point of Somass River, is on a dolphin with a port hand daymark.

905   Somass River light *(168.1)*, 0.4 mile NNW of Alberni light, is on a dolphin.

906   **Dolphins. — Beacons**. — Somass River entrance is marked by dolphins with radar reflectors.

907   **Buoys**. — Port hand buoys "Y53", "Y55", "Y57", "Y59" and "Y61" mark drying ledges in the river.

908   An **overhead cable** (power), vertical clearance 31 m, crosses the Somass River about 0.4 mile NE of Lupsi Cupsi Point. Towers from which the cable is suspended each have a red air obstruction light.

909   **Submarine cables and pipelines**. — A cable and a pipeline cross the river at the west extremity of Lupsi Cupsi Point. Pipelines cross the river in vicinity of the power cable.

Chart 3668

Port Alberni (1989)

Fishermen's Harbour (Argyle Street) (1989)

910   **Paper Barge Berth**, on the north side of Lupsi Cupsi Point, has mooring dolphins extending NW/SE from its outer end.

911   A **recreational fishing float** is at the mouth of **Rogers Creek**.

912   **Port Alberni Marina/Clutesi Boat Haven**, open year round, is on the east shore of Somass River about 0.5 mile upriver from the overhead cable. It provides berths for small craft, with

depths of 2 to 3 m alongside. Gas, power, water, garbage drop and a launching ramp are available.

913   **Port Alberni** city is on the east side of the harbour. Its principal exports are forest products. The largest vessels using the port are 213 m long with a draught of 12.2 m. Civic amenities include a hospital with heliport, stores (including marine supplies), accommodation, restaurants, entertainment and a post

Chart 3668

Port Alberni Terminals Berths 1 & 2 (1989)

Port Alberni Terminals Berth 3 (1989)

office. The port operates throughout the year as it is not affected by ice.

914   **Arrival information**. — Deratting is available in emergencies only. The port is under the jurisdiction of the Port Alberni Port Authority (250) 723-5312 and the Harbour Master's office is near Port Alberni Terminals Berth 3.

915   **Anchorage** in charted berths can be obtained by arrangement with the Harbour Master. Clearance from *Tofino Traffic* must be obtained before proceeding to or leaving any anchorage.

916   **Meteorological information** for Port Alberni is in the Appendices.

917   **Tsunami warning**. — Tsunami waves can on very rare occasions cause considerable damage in Port Alberni Harbour. For details on these waves and the warning systems in effect see *PAC 200*.

918   **Tides**. — Tidal predictions for Port Alberni (Index No. 8575) are in *Tide Tables, Volume 6*.

Chart 3668

Major Port Facilities — Port Alberni

Berth	Wharf Length (m)	Least Depth (m)	Elevation (m)	Remarks
Port Alberni Terminals Berths 1 & 2	320	11.4		Handles forest products – lumber, pulp and paper. Can handle Panamax size vessels. Loading by ships equipment supplemented by shore-based mobile cranes (120 tonnes) and forklifts. 4,650 m² covered storage 6.9 hectares open storage. Freshwater, power (110v/15 amps), telephones.
Port Alberni Terminals Berth 3	183	12.2		As above.

919   **Pilotage** is compulsory. For details regarding obtaining a Pilot see *PAC 200*.

920   **Berthing Caution**. — **When berthing at Port Alberni Terminals Berth 3, and using an anchor, note that deadman anchors, 100 m NNE of Berth 3, are used to moor a stiff-leg. Care should be taken not to foul these anchors.**

921   **Wharves**. — Details of wharves that can accommodate ocean-going vessels are given in the adjacent table.

922   The **Port Alberni Port Authority pier**, protected by a concrete breakwater, is close north of Port Alberni Terminal No. 3.

923   A **dock close SE of the Argyle Street Wharf** is used by small vessels for loading and discharging general cargo and for overnight tie-up. It has a berthing length of 54 m and a depth of 4.9 m alongside. Smaller vessels can berth along a 21 m float attached to the north face that has a depth of 3.4 m alongside decreasing to 0 m at the shore end. The wharf equipment consists of two 363 kg winches. No shore gangway or telephone are available, but fresh water and power are available.

924   **Argyle Street Wharf**, 0.1 mile south of the Somass Sawmill, is used by small coastal vessels. It has a berthing face of 33 m and a depth of 6 m alongside.

925   **Harbour Quay** is a new breakwater protected marina close to downtown. Power water and garbage drop are available and a public launching ramp is adjacent.

926   **Fishermen's Harbour**, in the basin close south of Somass Sawmill, consists of one long main float close south off, and parallel to, the south side of the mill. Several finger floats extend south from the main float. These floats are mainly used by commercial fishing vessels and are protected by a floating breakwater. The fairway along the south side of the finger floats was dredged to 5 m and berths at the finger floats to 3 m.

927   **Pulp and Paper Wharf**, on the east side of the mouth of the Somass River, is connected to Lupsi Cupsi Point by a long trestle. It is a staging facility for barges.

928   **Supplies**. — Ample supplies of provisions are obtainable. Diesel fuel, gasoline and other petroleum products can be obtained from marine service stations. There are no bunkering facilities for large vessels, but small quantities of diesel fuel and gasoline can be delivered by truck by arrangement.

929   **Harbour services**. — Dockside hull, machinery and electronic repairs can be undertaken and complete facilities exist for the construction and repair of wood or metal tugs, fish boats and pleasure craft. A marine railway capable of handling vessels up to 40 m long, 150 tonnes is available. Canadian Government Steamship Inspectors are based at Nanaimo. Mobile cranes, with capacities of 70 tonnes, are available. The harbour is equipped with a fireboat and fire fighting tugs. Tugs are available for berthing and unberthing.

930   **Communications**. — Road transportation to other centres on Vancouver Island is provided by various coach lines. The Alberni Marine Transportation Company provides marine transportation within Barkley Sound. Charter and scheduled air flights are available from an asphalt landing strip 1,219 m long.

SAIL PLAN

Step 1 – fill out for EACH VOYAGE.
Step 2 – leave with responsible person, or file with a Canadian Coast Guard Marine Communications and Traffic Service Centre (MCTS) by telephone, radio, or in person.
Step 3 – close Sail Plan on termination of voyage.

Owner's Name and Address_____

Telephone Number_____

Vessel Name and Licence Number_____ Sail_____ Power_____

Size and Type_____

Colour_____Hull_____Deck_____Cabin_____

Type of Engine_____Other Distinguishing Features_____

Radio Channels Monitored   HF_____VHF_____MF_____

Safety Equipment on Board

Life Rafts_____Dinghy or Small Boat (include colour)_____

Flares (number and type)_____Lifejackets or PFD's (Number)_____

Other_____

Search and Rescue Telephone Number_____

Trip Details (**include details every trip**)

Date of Departure_____   Time of Departure_____

Leaving From_____   Heading to_____

Proposed Route_____

Estimated Date of Arrival_____   Estimated Time of Arrival_____

Stop Over Points_____

_____

Number of Persons on Board_____

MARINE INFORMATION REPORT

Use this form to help keep Charts and Sailing Directions up to date

Name_____   Date Reported_____

Address (or Vessel)_____

City_____ Province/State_____ Postal Code_____

Phone_____ FAX_____

E-mail_____

Chart #_____ Edition Date_____ Last NOTMAR_____

Sailing Directions: ☐ Vol 1(South Portion) ☐ PAC200 ☐ PAC205 ☐ PAC 206

Page_____ Para_____ Lines_____

Observation Date_____ Time_____ ☐ PST ☐ PDT ☐ UCT

Location_____

Position: Latitude_____ Longitude_____

Position Method: ☐ DGPS ☐ GPS ☐ Radar Other_____

Estimated Position Accuracy_____

Horizontal Datum: ☐ NAD83 ☐ NAD27 Other_____

Description of Feature/Corrective action required_____

_____

_____

_____

_____

_____

_____

_____

_____

_____

_____

_____

_____

Forward to: Canadian Hydrographic Service
              9860 West Saanich Road, PO Box 6000
              Sidney, B.C. V8L 4B2

              Tel: (250) 363-6358
              Fax: (250) 363-6841
              E-Mail: chartsales@pac.dfo-mpo.gc.ca

DISTANCES: INSIDE PASSAGE BETWEEN VANCOUVER ISLAND AND THE MAINLAND

NOTES:

1. Distances from Victoria are via Sidney Channel and Active Pass. Via Boundary Pass *add 7* miles for New Westminster and Vancouver and 8 miles for remaining places.
2. For the head of Jervis Inlet and Porpoise Bay in Sechelt Inlet *add 46* miles and 30 miles, respectively.
3. Distances westward from Stuart Island are via Cordero and Chancellor Channels.
4. For Port Harvey *add 3* miles.

Blinkhorn Peninsula

	Blinkhorn Peninsula	Beaver Cove	Alert Bay	Port McNeill	Sointula
Beaver Cove	3				
Alert Bay	7	5			
Port McNeill	12	10	6		
Sointula	12	10	6	5	
Pulteney Point	15	14	9	8	5

Main distance chart (origins across the top; distances in nautical miles)

	Victoria (Ogden Point) (Note 1)	New Westminster	Vancouver (Brockton Point)	Nanaimo	Nanoose Bay (Richards Point)	Northwest Bay	Halfmoon Bay	Pender Harbour (entrance) (Note 2)	Blubber Bay	Powell River	Comox	Campbell River	Seymour Narrows	Stuart Island (settlement) (Note 3)	Kelsey Bay	Port Neville (entrance)	Broken Islands (Note 4)	Blinkhorn Peninsula	Pulteney Point	Blunden Harbour	Alison Harbour	Port Hardy	Bull Harbour (entrance)	Pine Island	Cape Scott
New Westminster	72																								
Vancouver (Brockton Point)	73	40																							
Nanaimo	76	46	34																						
Nanoose Bay (Richards Point)	81	53	40	13																					
Northwest Bay	88	59	46	20	12																				
Halfmoon Bay	85	54	35	21	18	18																			
Pender Harbour (entrance)	95	65	48	30	25	21	11																		
Blubber Bay	117	87	70	52	46	37	35	25																	
Powell River	118	88	70	52	46	41	35	26	5																
Comox	122	94	79	54	48	37	52	42	18	21															
Campbell River	143	114	99	75	69	58	53	29	31	33	33														
Seymour Narrows	151	122	107	83	77	66	61	37	39	41	41	8													
Stuart Island (settlement)	156	126	109	91	85	75	64	39	50	50	54	34	7												
Kelsey Bay	186	157	142	118	112	101	105	96	72	74	75	43	34	43											
Port Neville (entrance)	193	164	148	125	118	108	112	102	78	81	82	50	43	50	15										
Broken Islands	200	171	156	132	126	116	120	110	86	88	90	57	50	57	23	8									
Blinkhorn Peninsula	219	190	175	151	145	134	138	129	105	107	109	76	69	76	34	27	27								
Pulteney Point	234	205	190	166	160	150	154	144	120	123	124	91	85	91	49	42	34	19							
Blunden Harbour	252	223	208	184	178	168	172	162	138	141	142	109	103	109	67	60	52	33	15						
Alison Harbour	264	235	220	196	190	180	184	174	150	153	154	121	115	121	79	72	64	45	30	18					
Port Hardy	251	222	207	183	177	167	171	161	137	140	141	108	102	108	66	59	51	33	17	14	21				
Bull Harbour (entrance)	269	240	225	201	194	184	188	179	154	157	158	126	119	126	84	77	69	52	34	29	21	22			
Pine Island Lt.-050° 1 mile	265	236	221	197	191	180	184	174	151	153	155	122	115	122	80	73	65	46	31	20	9	20	11		
Cape Scott Lt.-150° 1.3 miles	289	260	245	221	215	204	208	199	175	177	179	146	139	146	104	97	89	73	55	39	49	55	43	30	
Cape Caution Lt.-078° 2.2 miles	277	248	232	208	202	192	196	186	162	165	167	133	127	133	91	85	76	58	42	27	16	42	39	12	32

The distances are approximate and expressed to the nearest even nautical mile.
They are based on the most frequently used tracks which may not be suitable for all vessels.

DISTANCES: THE GULF ISLANDS AND SAN JUAN ARCHIPELAGO

References:
- ***** via Dodd Narrows
- **•** via Active Pass
- **†** via Houstoun Passage
- **°** via Trincomali Channel
- **+** via Porlier Pass
- **‡** outside Gulf Islands

Column key (origins, left to right): Vic = Victoria (Ogden Point), Cad = Cadboro Bay (entrance), Sid = Sidney, Tse = Tsehum Harbour, Ful = Fulford Harbour, Fri = Friday Harbor (Wa.), Roc = Roche Harbor (Wa.), Rei = Reid Harbor (Wa.), Bed = Bedwell Harbour, Lya = Lyall Harbour, Gan = Ganges, Stu = Sturdies Bay, Mon = Montague Harbour, Cow = Cowichan Bay, Map = Maple Bay, Cro = Crofton, Che = Chemainus, Tel = Telegraph Harbour, Lad = Ladysmith, Por = Porlier Pass, Dod = Dodd Narrows, Gab = Gabriola Passage, Nan = Nanaimo, NW = New Westminster.

To \ From	Vic	Cad	Sid	Tse	Ful	Fri	Roc	Rei	Bed	Lya	Gan	Stu	Mon	Cow	Map	Cro	Che	Tel	Lad	Por	Dod	Gab	Nan	NW
Cadboro Bay (entrance)	8																							
Sidney	24	15																						
Tsehum Harbour	24	17	2																					
Fulford Harbour	32	23	9	9																				
Friday Harbor (Wa.)	27	25	19	17	24																			
Roche Harbor (Wa.)	23	15	10	14	17	11																		
Reid Harbor (Wa.)	23	16	10	10	14	11	3																	
Bedwell Harbour	28	20	10	10	10	16	9	9																
Lyall Harbour	35	27	17	18	14	20	16	14	9															
Ganges	39	30	16	16	12	28	20	18	14	13														
Sturdies Bay	39	31	19	17	13	28	20	18	15	11	7													
Montague Harbour	39	31	16	17	13	20	18	18	15	11	7	7												
Cowichan Bay	38	29	17	17	11	21	21	20	18	22	†18	21	21											
Maple Bay	42	33	15	15	9	25	25	22	22	25	†15	25	†17	8										
Crofton	46	37	19	19	14	29	29	26	25	26	†16	†20	†18	12	5									
Chemainus	51	42	28	28	24	34	33	33	29	33	†22	†22	†17	11	7	6								
Telegraph Harbour	51	42	28	28	24	34	33	33	29	33	†21	†21	†16	14	7	7	3							
Ladysmith	56	47	33	33	29	39	37	37	35	37	†27	†27	°21	22	15	11	10	6						
Porlier Pass	50	41	27	27	23	31	29	29	25	21	17	°17	°17	11	13	9	14	14	13					
Dodd Narrows	°60	°52	°38	°38	°34	°42	°40	°40	°36	32	28	°28	28	23	19	19	13	14	14	7				
Gabriola Passage	°58	°49	°35	°35	°32	°39	°38	°38	°33	30	26	‡23	20	22	18	14	14	14	14	9	7			
Nanaimo	°°65	°°57	°°43	°°43	°°39	°47	°45	°45	°41	°37	°33	°30	°30	°35	*28	*24	*19	*18	*19	*19	*24	5		
New Westminster	•72	•64	•50	•50	•46	•53	•52	•52	•47	•44	•44	•40	•40	•54	•43	•40	•41	•42	•45	+44	+31	+45	+35	
Vancouver (Brockton Point)	•73	•64	•50	•50	•46	•53	•52	•52	•47	•44	•44	•40	•40	•54	•41	•47	•42	•42	•42	+42	+36	+47	+28	40

The distances are approximate and expressed to the nearest even nautical mile. They are based on the most frequently used tracks which may not be suitable for all vessels.

DISTANCES: JUAN DE FUCA STRAIT, ADMIRALTY INLET, PUGET SOUND AND THE SE PART OF THE STRAIT OF GEORGIA

NOTES:
1. Distances from ports in Juan de Fuca Strait to New Westminster, Nanaimo and Vancouver are via Boundary Pass. For distances via Active Pass *deduct* 8 miles for Nanaimo and 7 miles for New Westminster and Vancouver.
2. Distances from ports in Admiralty Inlet and Puget Sound to ports in the SE part of the Strait of Georgia are via Rosario Strait and adjacent channels.
3. Distances from Everett to Anacortes, Bellingham and ports in the SE part of the Strait of Georgia are by way of Saratoga Passage and Deception Pass. For distances over route west of Whidbey Island and via Rosario Strait *add* 11 miles.

Column / port key:

1 Cape Flattery, Wa. (Tatoosh Is. Lt.-140° 3.5 miles) = CF
2 Neah Bay, Wa. = NB
3 Port Renfrew = PR
4 Sooke Harbour (entrance) = SH
5 Race Rocks Lt.-000° 1.5 miles = RR
6 Port Angeles, Wa. = PA
7 Victoria (Ogden Point) = VI
8 Point Wilson Lt.-225° 1 mile = PW
9 Port Townsend, Wa. = PT
10 Port Ludlow, Wa. = PL
11 Port Gamble, Wa. = PG
12 Everett, Wa. = EV
13 Eagle Harbor, Wa. = EH
14 Seattle, Wa. = SE
15 Bremerton, Wa. = BR
16 Tacoma, Wa. = TA
17 Olympia, Wa. = OL
18 Anacortes, Wa. = AN
19 Bellingham, Wa. = BE
20 Blaine, Wa. = BL
21 New Westminster = NW
22 Nanaimo = NA
23 Vancouver (Brockton Point) = VA

Port	CF	NB	PR	SH	RR	PA	VI	PW	PT	PL	PG	EV	EH	SE	BR	TA	OL	AN	BE	BL	NW	NA
Neah Bay	10																					
Port Renfrew	16	14																				
Sooke Harbour	43	35	36																			
Race Rocks	51	43	44	10																		
Port Angeles	61	54	54	21	12																	
Victoria	61	53	54	20	10	19																
Point Wilson	84	76	77	43	33	29	31															
Port Townsend	87	79	80	46	36	32	34	3														
Port Ludlow	100	92	93	59	49	45	47	16	16													
Port Gamble	105	97	98	64	54	50	52	21	21	10												
Everett	118	110	111	77	67	63	65	34	34	25	28											
Eagle Harbor	124	116	117	83	73	69	71	40	40	32	25	29										
Seattle	124	116	117	83	73	69	71	40	40	32	25	29	8									
Bremerton	133	125	126	92	82	78	80	49	49	41	13	38	13	14								
Tacoma	144	136	137	103	93	89	91	60	60	52	29	49	25	25	29							
Olympia	168	160	161	128	117	113	115	84	84	76	50	73	50	50	50	34						
Anacortes	92	84	85	51	41	42	35	29	26	42	66	49	66	66	75	86	110					
Bellingham	106	98	99	65	55	55	49	43	40	56	80	63	80	80	89	100	124	16				
Blaine	111	103	104	70	60	65	53	58	55	71	95	78	95	95	104	115	139	35	37			
New Westminster	138	130	131	97	87	91	79	91	88	104	128	111	128	128	137	148	172	69	70	47		
Nanaimo	143	135	136	102	92	100	85	97	94	110	134	116	134	134	143	154	178	74	74	53	46	
Vancouver	138	130	131	97	87	92	80	92	89	105	129	111	129	129	138	149	173	68	68	47	40	34

The distances are approximate and expressed to the nearest even nautical mile. They are based on the most frequently used tracks which may not be suitable for all vessels.

DISTANCES: WEST COAST OF VANCOUVER ISLAND

References:

- + via Felice Channel
- • via Cook Channel and Tahsis Inlet
- * via Tahsis Narrows

NOTE: The distances from Vancouver are by way of Boundary Pass and Haro Strait; for distance via Active Pass *deduct 7 miles.*

Places (with reference bearings where given):

1. Vancouver (Brockton Point)
2. Victoria (Ogden Point)
3. Race Rocks Lt-000°1.5 miles
4. Carmanah Point Lt-021°1.5 miles
5. Cape Beale Lt-075°1.5 miles
6. Bamfield
7. Port Alberni
8. Toquart Bay
9. Ucluelet Inlet (entrance)
10. Amphitrite Point Lt-031°3 miles
11. Tofino
12. Hot Springs Cove
13. Estevan Point Lt-036°3 miles
14. Gold River (Muchalat Inlet)
15. Tahsis
16. Zeballos
17. Fair Harbour (entrance)
18. Kyuquot
19. Solander Island Lt-040°2.5 miles
20. Kains Island Lt-000°1 mile
21. Winter Harbour
22. Port Alice
23. Coal Harbour
24. Holberg
25. Otter Cove
26. Cape Scott Lt-078°2 miles
27. Egg Island Lt-065°2 miles

Distance chart (nautical miles). Each row lists the distance from the named place to each of the following places, in the order given above.

From	2 Vic	3 RR	4 Carm	5 CB	6 Bam	7 PAlb	8 TB	9 Ucl	10 Amph	11 Tof	12 HSC	13 Est	14 GR	15 Tah	16 Zeb	17 FH	18 Kyu	19 Sol	20 Kai	21 WH	22 PAl	23 CH	24 Hol	25 OC	26 CS	27 Egg
1 Vancouver	80	87	140	163	169	198	182	178	177	200	218	226	262	263	278	283	279	296	317	323	346	342	357	335	342	378
2 Victoria		10	63	86	92	121	105	101	100	123	141	149	185	186	201	206	202	219	240	246	269	265	280	258	265	301
3 Race Rocks			53	76	82	111	95	91	90	113	131	139	175	176	191	196	192	209	230	236	259	255	270	248	255	291
4 Carmanah Pt				23	29	58	42	38	37	60	78	86	122	123	138	143	139	156	177	183	206	202	217	195	202	238
5 Cape Beale					6	35	19	15	14	37	55	63	99	100	115	120	116	133	154	160	183	179	194	172	179	215
6 Bamfield						30	17	19	20	43	61	69	105	106	121	126	122	139	160	166	189	185	200	178	185	221
7 Port Alberni							39	43	49	72	90	98	134	135	150	155	151	168	189	195	218	214	229	207	214	250
8 Toquart Bay								13	+16	39	57	65	101	102	117	122	118	135	156	162	185	181	196	174	181	217
9 Ucluelet Inlet									+6	29	47	55	91	92	107	112	108	125	146	152	175	171	186	164	171	207
10 Amphitrite Pt										23	41	49	85	86	101	106	102	119	140	146	169	165	180	158	165	201
11 Tofino											27	34	70	71	86	91	87	104	125	131	154	150	165	143	150	186
12 Hot Springs Cove												14	50	51	66	71	67	84	105	111	134	130	145	123	130	166
13 Estevan Point													36	37	52	57	53	70	91	97	120	116	131	109	116	152
14 Gold River														34	*42	*48	*43	•87	•108	•114	•137	•133	•148	•126	•133	169
15 Tahsis															16	48	44	62	83	89	112	108	123	101	108	144
16 Zeballos																44	40	58	79	85	108	104	119	97	104	140
17 Fair Harbour																	15	39	60	66	89	85	100	78	85	121
18 Kyuquot																		27	48	54	77	73	88	66	73	109
19 Solander Island																			21	27	50	46	61	39	46	82
20 Kains Island																				6	29	25	40	46	54	90
21 Winter Harbour																					31	27	42	21	27	65
22 Port Alice																						17	33	50	58	94
23 Coal Harbour																							17	46	54	90
24 Holberg																								61	69	105
25 Otter Cove																									10	46
26 Cape Scott																										36

The distances are approximate and expressed to the nearest even nautical mile.
They are based on the most frequently used tracks which may not be suitable for all vessels.

DISTANCES: PASSAGES AND INLETS ADJACENT TO THE NORTH END OF THE STRAIT OF GEORGIA

References:
+ via Homfray Channel
• via Sutil Channel and Deer Passage
* via Nodales Channel
° via Mayne Passage
† via Discovery Passage and Johnstone Strait

Powell River

11	Lund													
26	15	Manson Bay												
32	21	13	Heriot Bay											
31	20	13	16	Campbell River										
21	11	17	23	22	Refuge Cove									
+59	+49	+55	•45	•56	+41	Head of Toba Inlet								
32	22	22	16	27	11	30	Redonda Bay							
43	33	34	28	38	23	36	12	Head of Ramsay Arm						
37	27	26	20	31	16	34	7	13	Church House					
39	29	28	22	33	18	37	9	15	3	Stuart Island (settlement)				
75	65	67	61	72	57	75	48	54	41	41	Head of Bute Inlet			
51	41	40	34	*32	30	49	21	33	15	12	53	Shoal Bay		
78	68	68	62	°56	58	76	49	60	42	39	80	28	Head of Loughborough Inlet	
†74	66	64	58	†43	55	73	45	52	39	36	77	24	32	Kelsey Bay

The distances are approximate and expressed to the nearest even nautical mile.
They are based on the most frequently used tracks which may not be suitable for all vessels.

DISTANCES: PASSAGES ADJACENT TO JOHNSTONE AND QUEEN CHARLOTTE STRAITS

References:
+ via Knight Inlet
† via Fife Sound
• via Retreat and Cramer Passages
* via Johnstone Strait

NOTES:
1. For distance to the head of Knight Inlet *add* 28 miles.
2. For distance to the head of Kingcome Inlet *add* 6 miles.

Broken Islands

12	Minstrel Island (settlement)														
37	24	Glendale Cove (see Note 1)													
+29	17	39	Wedge Island												
29	18	32	32	Thompson Sound											
43	31	46	•13	24	Simoom Sound (settlement)										
†51	39	54	8	32	10	Duff Islet									
58	47	62	•33	39	20	27	Wakeman Sound								
58	46	61	•32	39	20	26	10	Charles Creek (see Note 2)							
48	37	51	•22	29	9	16	14	14	Cypress Harbour						
53	41	57	•27	34	15	21	19	18	6	Greenway Sound (logging camp)					
56	44	59	23	37	17	20	21	20	8	8	Sullivan Bay				
63	51	66	26	44	24	23	28	28	15	15	8	Jennis Bay (Drury Inlet)			
62	51	66	16	43	24	13	27	27	14	15	7	10	James Point		
19	+25	+47	8	+40	†23	14	†41	†40	†30	35	27	30	20	Blinkhorn Peninsula	
*51	+49	+71	32	+64	†40	31	49	49	36	37	29	32	22	*33	Port Hardy

The distances are approximate and expressed to the nearest even nautical mile.
They are based on the most frequently used tracks which may not be suitable for all vessels.

CANADIAN CLIMATE NORMALS

The meteorological data in the following tables is supplied by Environment Canada, Atmospheric Environment Service.

Starting and ending dates given with each station are the total period of observation. Values of the climate elements are averages for the period 1961-90, or for a portion of that period no shorter than 20 years. Extreme or maximum values are the highest or lowest occurrence for all years that data is available.

Alert Bay 50°35'N 126°56'W
1913 to 1990

Elevation 63 m (207 ft)

	Jan	Feb	Mar	Apr	May	June	July	Aug	Sept	Oct	Nov	Dec	Year
Temperature (°C)													
Daily average	3.3	4.6	5.7	7.5	10.0	12.2	13.9	14.3	12.4	9.1	5.5	3.6	8.5
Daily maximum	5.3	7.0	8.8	11.1	14.0	15.9	17.8	18.1	16.1	11.9	7.6	5.5	11.6
Daily minimum	1.4	2.1	2.5	3.8	6.0	8.4	10.0	10.4	8.6	6.2	3.4	1.6	5.4
Extreme maximum	13.9	16.7	18.7	23.5	35.2	30.0	29.4	33.3	27.9	23.9	17.8	15.6	
Extreme minimum	-11.1	-13.6	-7.8	-1.7	0.0	2.2	1.1	5.6	1.1	-3.9	-12.6	-13.3	
Precipitation													
Rainfall (mm)	187.1	134.3	115.7	93.3	67.4	68.8	54.1	62.6	110.7	220.4	222.6	202.8	1539.7
Extreme daily rainfall	105.2	94.0	69.6	56.6	41.9	59.2	55.4	49.3	90.2	102.4	116.1	100.3	
Days with rain	18	17	19	17	16	14	12	13	15	20	21	20	202
Snowfall (cm)	25.9	11.6	7.0	1.2	T	0.0	0.0	0.0	0.0	T	7.3	16.7	69.7
Extreme daily snowfall	45.7	61.0	37.6	10.9	0.0	0.0	0.0	0.0	0.0	1.8	27.9	30.5	
Days with snow	5	3	2	*	0	0	0	0	0	*	1	4	16
Days with precipitation	21	18	19	17	16	14	12	13	15	20	22	22	210

* = Average of less than one but greater than zero
T = Trace

Ballenas Islands Lightstation 49°21'N 124°10'W
1966 to 1990

Elevation 15 m (49 ft)

	Jan	Feb	Mar	Apr	May	June	July	Aug	Sept	Oct	Nov	Dec	Year
Precipitation													
Rainfall (mm)	86.7	70.3	63.7	41.2	36.8	35.5	21.6	24.8	44.0	70.7	114.1	109.6	719.0
Extreme daily rainfall	37.6	29.6	27.5	29.2	20.5	25.1	31.0	26.7	38.1	34.0	35.3	40.9	
Days with rain	17	15	15	13	12	10	7	7	9	14	18	18	155
Snowfall (cm)	13.3	5.1	0.8	0.2	0.0	0.0	0.0	0.0	0.0	0.3	3.2	6.7	29.5
Extreme daily snowfall	31.5	14.2	7.4	2.5	0.0	0.0	0.0	0.0	0.0	6.0	17.5	16.3	
Days with snow	3	1	*	*	0	0	0	0	0	*	*	2	7
Days with precipitation	19	15	15	13	12	10	7	7	9	14	18	19	158
Wind (knots)													
Speed	11	10	10	9	9	9	9	9	9	10	11	11	10
Most frequent direction	SE	SE	SE	W	W	W	W	W	W	SE	SE	SE	W
Maximum hourly speed	42	43	50	42	39	38	31	33	37	44	44	44	
Direction	E	E	W	E	E	E	E	NW	E	E	SE	E	

* = Average of less than one but greater than zero

Bull Harbour 50°55'N 127°57'W
1921 to 1988

Elevation 14 m (46 ft)

	Jan	Feb	Mar	Apr	May	June	July	Aug	Sept	Oct	Nov	Dec	Year
Temperature (°C)													
Daily average	3.6	4.8	5.4	6.7	8.9	11.2	13.0	13.4	11.9	9.2	5.8	3.9	8.1
Daily maximum	5.9	7.6	8.6	10.0	12.2	14.1	15.7	16.2	15.1	12.3	8.3	6.2	11.0
Daily minimum	1.3	2.0	2.2	3.4	5.6	8.2	10.2	10.5	8.7	6.1	3.3	1.5	5.2
Extreme maximum	16.7	20.0	22.2	22.5	30.4	37.8	25.6	30.0	28.9	26.3	23.9	15.6	
Extreme minimum	-12.8	-11.0	-10.6	-3.7	-2.2	1.1	4.4	1.2	0.0	-6.1	-13.8	-12.2	
Precipitation													
Rainfall (mm)	256.3	196.4	166.9	150.9	101.1	88.1	71.0	78.1	158.1	277.2	300.1	280.9	2125.2
Extreme daily rainfall	158.8	157.2	61.2	101.2	51.3	65.3	66.0	48.0	117.1	99.4	114.8	167.1	
Days with rain	20	19	21	19	18	15	14	15	16	22	23	22	223
Snowfall (cm)	21.8	10.8	8.0	3.0	T	T	0.0	0.0	T	0.3	5.0	13.9	62.9
Extreme daily snowfall	21.6	22.9	23.6	12.2	0.0	0.0	0.0	0.0	0.0	5.3	17.3	30.5	
Days with snow	5	2	2	1	0	0	0	0	0	*	1	3	16
Days with precipitation	22	20	21	19	18	15	14	15	16	22	23	23	228
Wind (knots)													
Speed	8	8	7	6	5	4	4	3	4	6	8	8	6
Most frequent direction	SE	SE	SE	SE	NW	NW	NW	NW	SE	SE	SE	SE	SE
Maximum hourly speed	65	70	52	52	39	55	43	28	48	61	61	61	
Direction	SE	SE	SE	SE	NW	E	SE	E	SE	SE	W	E	
Maximum gust speed	43	M	M	M	M	M	M	0	M	M	M	M	
Direction	W	M	M	M	M	M	M	C	M	M	M	M	

```
*  =  Average of less than one but greater than zero
M  =  No data available
T  =  Trace
```

Campbell River 49°57'N 125°16'W
1965 to 1990

Elevation 105 m (344 ft)

	Jan	Feb	Mar	Apr	May	June	July	Aug	Sept	Oct	Nov	Dec	Year
Temperature (°C)													
Daily average	0.9	2.7	4.5	7.2	10.8	14.2	16.7	16.7	13.0	8.1	4.1	1.5	8.4
Daily maximum	4.2	6.7	9.4	12.6	16.6	20.1	23.1	23.1	19.1	12.9	7.7	4.7	13.4
Daily minimum	-2.6	-1.3	-0.4	1.8	5.0	8.3	10.3	10.2	6.8	3.2	0.6	-1.7	3.4
Extreme maximum	16.1	15.8	20.6	27.2	33.2	36.9	37.2	37.8	31.6	23.2	17.8	13.3	
Extreme minimum	-23.9	-17.8	-12.8	-5.6	-2.2	-0.6	2.2	1.7	-2.8	-9.7	-20.4	-18.5	
Precipitation													
Rainfall (mm)	142.2	124.6	128.2	72.7	58.7	49.3	39.5	42.9	61.6	154.2	210.1	196.8	1281.0
Extreme daily rainfall	76.7	76.5	60.5	44.5	42.2	37.3	43.7	49.2	42.6	59.8	75.9	84.8	
Days with rain	18	14	17	14	12	11	8	8	10	17	20	17	163
Snowfall (cm)	43.5	19.9	8.4	1.8	T	0.0	0.0	0.0	0.0	1.2	16.0	37.1	127.9
Extreme daily snowfall	53.3	25.4	38.1	11.4	0.0	0.0	0.0	0.0	0.0	29.0	43.2	43.2	
Days with snow	5	3	2	*	0	0	0	0	0	*	2	5	17
Days with precipitation	19	16	17	14	12	11	8	8	10	17	20	20	173

```
*  =  Average of less than one but greater than zero
T  =  Trace
```

Cape Beale Light 48°47'N 125°13'W
1968 to 1990

Elevation: 27 m (89 ft)

	Jan	Feb	Mar	Apr	May	June	July	Aug	Sept	Oct	Nov	Dec	Year
Wind (knots)													
Speed	x	x	x	9	x	x	7	6	6	8	10	10	x
Most frequent direction	x	x	x	SE	x	x	x	SE	x	SE	SE	x	x
Maximum hourly speed	48	52	45	45	38	33	30	36	43	42	50	50	
Direction	W	SE	SE	SE	SE	SE	NW	W	SE	W	SW	SE	

X = Some data exists but not enough to derive a value

Cape Scott 50°47'N 128°26'W
1965 to 1990

Elevation 70 m (230 ft)

	Jan	Feb	Mar	Apr	May	June	July	Aug	Sept	Oct	Nov	Dec	Year
Temperature (°C)													
Daily average	4.5	5.1	5.9	7.0	9.2	11.3	13.1	13.7	12.5	9.8	6.9	4.8	8.6
Daily maximum	6.5	7.4	8.3	9.7	11.9	13.8	15.4	16.0	14.8	12.0	8.9	6.8	11.0
Daily minimum	2.4	2.8	3.4	4.4	6.5	8.8	10.7	11.3	10.2	7.6	4.6	2.8	6.3
Extreme maximum	17.9	17.2	15.4	18.3	27.0	21.7	20.6	23.9	26.7	20.4	21.1	13.3	
Extreme minimum	-8.3	-10.7	-2.8	-1.1	2.2	4.4	7.2	7.8	5.0	-3.2	-10.7	-11.1	
Precipitation													
Rainfall (mm)	327.3	242.8	248.7	206.5	154.4	120.6	82.6	100.2	187.2	334.0	356.1	323.0	2683.4
Extreme daily rainfall	145.8	82.2	77.5	80.8	69.0	123.0	44.6	46.2	130.7	109.4	129.0	94.5	
Days with rain	23	20	23	20	19	17	16	17	17	24	24	24	245
Snowfall (cm)	20.5	11.4	10.6	4.8	T	0.0	0.0	0.0	T	0.3	4.6	12.6	64.8
Extreme daily snowfall	25.9	23.0	16.0	24.4	0.4	0.0	0.0	0.0	0.0	3.6	18.3	25.0	
Days with snow	6	3	3	2	*	0	0	0	0	*	2	4	21
Days with precipitation	25	21	23	20	19	17	16	17	17	24	24	25	250
Wind (knots)													
Speed	10	10	9	9	8	7	6	6	8	10	10	10	9
Most frequent direction	SE	SE	SE	SE	S	NW	NW	N	S	SE	SE	SE	SE
Maximum hourly speed	52	42	42	36	33	42	28	31	43	45	48	45	
Direction	SE	S	S	SE	SE	SE	NE	S	SE	S	S	SE	
Maximum gust speed	81	72	69	66	60	68	50	49	70	76	79	78	
Direction	SE	SE	SE	SE	SE	SE	SE	S	SE	SE	SE	SE	

* = Average of less than one but greater than zero
T = Trace

Chatham Point 50°20'N 125°26'W
1958 to 1990

Elevation 23 m (75 ft)

	Jan	Feb	Mar	Apr	May	June	July	Aug	Sept	Oct	Nov	Dec	Year
Temperature (°C)													
Daily average	2.8	4.2	5.7	8.1	11.3	13.9	15.7	15.8	13.0	9.1	5.4	3.3	9.0
Daily maximum	4.4	6.2	8.3	11.3	15.1	17.7	19.8	19.6	16.1	11.3	7.0	4.8	11.8
Daily minimum	1.1	2.1	3.0	4.9	7.5	10.0	11.6	11.9	9.9	7.0	3.7	1.6	6.2
Extreme maximum	13.3	13.4	16.7	22.5	31.2	30.0	33.3	31.1	26.4	19.3	15.6	12.8	
Extreme minimum	-10.6	-11.5	-6.1	-0.6	0.0	4.4	6.7	7.2	1.7	-3.9	-13.0	-15.0	
Precipitation													
Rainfall (mm)	226.2	200.5	185.6	123.6	115.3	110.1	85.2	97.3	117.9	271.9	289.1	264.9	2087.6
Extreme daily rainfall	84.3	78.0	78.5	52.5	52.8	61.6	78.2	113.8	70.9	90.7	83.2	83.8	
Days with rain	19	17	18	16	14	12	9	9	12	19	21	19	187
Snowfall (cm)	32.8	12.9	6.7	3.1	0.0	0.0	0.0	0.0	0.0	0.4	10.2	31.5	97.7
Extreme daily snowfall	34.4	25.0	20.1	22.6	0.0	0.0	0.0	0.0	0.0	12.0	25.4	35.3	
Days with snow	6	3	1	*	0	0	0	0	0	*	2	5	17
Days with precipitation	22	18	19	16	14	12	9	9	12	19	21	22	195
Wind (knots)													
Speed	7	6	7	8	8	10	10	9	8	6	6	7	8
Most frequent direction	SE	SE	SE	W	W	W	W	W	W	SE	SE	SE	W
Maximum hourly speed	33	34	37	31	34	34	37	33	33	36	35	58	
Direction	SW	W	SE	W	W	W	SW	NW	W	SE	SE	E	

* = Average of less than one but greater than zero

Comox Airport 49°43'N 124°54'W
1944 to 1990

Elevation 24 m (79 ft)

	Jan	Feb	Mar	Apr	May	June	July	Aug	Sept	Oct	Nov	Dec	Year
Temperature (°C)													
Daily average	2.7	4.2	5.6	8.2	11.8	15.1	17.4	17.3	13.8	9.2	5.4	3.4	9.5
Daily maximum	5.4	7.3	9.4	12.5	16.5	19.8	22.5	22.4	18.5	12.9	8.4	6.0	13.4
Daily minimum	-0.1	1.0	1.8	3.9	7.0	10.4	12.3	12.3	9.1	5.5	2.4	0.7	5.5
Extreme maximum	16.7	16.3	18.9	23.9	31.7	34.4	34.4	33.6	30.6	22.2	17.8	16.0	
Extreme minimum	-21.1	-16.1	-13.9	-4.4	-2.8	0.5	5.0	4.4	-1.7	-4.8	-13.3	-15.0	
Precipitation													
Rainfall (mm)	135.2	110.8	104.7	57.4	43.3	36.2	30.6	36.1	48.5	129.8	187.4	171.3	1091.4
Extreme daily rainfall	77.0	80.2	56.6	40.9	29.2	30.5	37.3	69.1	42.2	59.4	69.9	113.0	
Days with rain	17	15	15	13	11	10	8	8	10	16	19	18	159
Snowfall (cm)	31.9	11.4	7.9	1.4	T	T	0.0	0.0	T	0.1	9.2	29.5	91.4
Extreme daily snowfall	60.2	27.7	37.3	15.2	0.3	0.0	0.0	0.0	0.0	3.3	35.8	59.7	
Days with snow	5	2	2	*	*	0	0	0	0	*	1	4	15
Days with precipitation	19	16	16	13	11	10	8	8	10	16	19	20	165
Wind (knots)													
Speed	6	7	8	7	6	6	6	5	5	6	7	8	6
Most frequent direction	C	SE	SE	SE	NW	NW	NW	NW	NW	SE	SE	SE	SE
Maximum hourly speed	42	45	44	36	34	35	30	26	35	37	50	44	
Direction	SE	E	SE	SE	SE	SE	SW	SE	SE	SE	SE	SE	
Maximum gust speed	61	62	72	57	49	50	52	42	52	86	70	65	
Direction	SE	E	SE	E	SE	SE	E	SE	E	SE	SE	SE	

* = Average of less than one but greater than zero
T = Trace

Cowichan Bay, Cherry Point 48°43'N 123°33'W
1913 to 1990

Elevation 1 m (3 ft)

	Jan	Feb	Mar	Apr	May	June	July	Aug	Sept	Oct	Nov	Dec	Year
Temperature (°C)													
Daily average	2.7	4.9	6.0	8.2	11.3	14.3	16.6	17.0	14.4	10.0	5.7	3.3	9.5
Daily maximum	5.2	8.0	10.0	12.6	16.0	19.0	21.7	22.1	19.2	14.0	8.5	5.5	13.5
Daily minimum	0.2	1.7	2.1	3.7	6.5	9.6	11.5	11.9	9.6	6.1	2.8	1.0	5.6
Extreme maximum	15.0	17.8	20.0	23.9	32.0	32.8	35.6	36.0	31.7	24.0	17.2	15.5	
Extreme minimum	-16.1	-11.7	-9.4	-3.9	-1.1	0.6	4.4	4.4	0.0	-4.4	-13.3	-15.0	
Precipitation													
Rainfall (mm)	130.5	105.7	87.0	49.2	39.1	33.8	23.9	28.4	42.7	87.4	154.7	161.3	943.8
Extreme daily rainfall	96.5	56.1	48.3	36.1	39.9	37.6	26.7	57.2	56.6	54.9	63.0	63.8	
Days with rain	17	16	16	13	12	10	7	8	9	15	19	18	158
Snowfall (cm)	23.3	8.9	4.4	0.2	0.0	0.0	0.0	0.0	0.0	0.0	2.6	20.4	59.7
Extreme daily snowfall	38.1	50.8	29.2	5.1	0.0	0.0	0.0	0.0	0.0	0.0	17.0	45.7	
Days with snow	4	2	*	*	0	0	0	0	0	0	*	4	11
Days with precipitation	19	17	16	13	12	10	7	8	9	15	19	20	164
Sunshine (hours)	45.3	76.0	133.0	162.5	225.0	221.9	273.9	251.2	184.6	119.5	55.4	37.3	1785.7

* = Average of less than one but greater than zero

Entrance Island 49°13'N 123°48'W
1969 to 1990

Elevation: 3 m (10 ft)

	Jan	Feb	Mar	Apr	May	June	July	Aug	Sept	Oct	Nov	Dec	Year
Wind (knots)													
Speed	x	x	x	x	x	x	x	x	x	x	11	x	x
Maximum hourly speed	42	37	40	39	37	34	40	42	35	39	40	43	
Direction	NW	NW	E	NW	NW	NW	N	N	NW	E	NW	E	

X = Some data exists but not enough to derive a value

Estevan Point 49°23'N 126°33'W
1908 to 1990

Elevation 7 m (23 ft)

	Jan	Feb	Mar	Apr	May	June	July	Aug	Sept	Oct	Nov	Dec	Year
Temperature (°C)													
Daily average	4.9	5.7	6.1	7.6	9.9	12.2	13.8	14.2	13.0	10.2	7.1	5.3	9.2
Daily maximum	7.4	8.3	9.1	10.6	12.8	14.7	16.4	16.8	16.0	12.9	9.8	7.7	11.9
Daily minimum	2.4	3.0	3.1	4.5	7.0	9.6	11.1	11.5	10.0	7.4	4.4	2.7	6.4
Extreme maximum	17.2	17.2	18.0	22.0	24.5	26.7	28.9	26.1	26.5	21.1	17.8	14.4	
Extreme minimum	-13.9	-10.6	-7.8	-3.3	0.0	2.8	4.4	5.0	-1.1	-4.4	-15.0	-11.7	
Precipitation													
Rainfall (mm)	386.4	339.0	319.8	246.9	154.1	133.5	81.3	97.7	167.8	368.6	432.6	402.9	3130.6
Extreme daily rainfall	218.9	126.5	120.1	108.4	81.3	94.4	95.3	72.1	120.7	131.8	191.0	145.8	
Days with rain	22	19	20	19	15	13	10	11	13	20	23	23	208
Snowfall (cm)	14.3	5.9	5.3	2.8	T	T	0.0	0.0	0.0	T	3.4	10.1	42.0
Extreme daily snowfall	25.9	51.8	30.7	14.0	1.0	0.0	0.0	0.0	0.0	0.7	15.7	25.9	
Days with snow	3	2	2	*	*	0	0	0	0	*	1	3	13
Days with precipitation	23	20	21	19	15	13	10	11	13	20	23	23	211
Sunshine (hours)	61.3	85.8	125.9	166.9	220.9	213.0	233.7	200.7	175.0	120.8	71.5	58.6	1734.0
Wind (knots)													
Speed	12	12	12	12	11	11	10	9	9	11	12	12	11
Most frequent direction	SE	SE	SE	SE	NW	NW	NW	NW	SE	SE	x	SE	x
Maximum hourly speed	63	63	62	57	53	54	40	44	45	50	60	71	
Direction	NW	S	NW	SE	S	SE	NW	SE	SE	SE	SE	NW	
Maximum gust speed	71	80	83	69	74	55	56	78	72	77	90	97	
Direction	W	SE	S	SE	E	SE	SE	SE	SE	SE	SE	W	

* = Average of less than one but greater than zero
T = Trace
X = Some data exists but not enough to derive a value

Gower Point 49°23'N 123°32'W
1961 to 1990

Elevation 34 m (112 ft)

	Jan	Feb	Mar	Apr	May	June	July	Aug	Sept	Oct	Nov	Dec	Year
Temperature (°C)													
Daily average	3.5	4.7	6.5	8.9	12.0	14.7	N	N	N	10.3	6.0	3.7	N
Daily maximum	5.8	7.3	9.8	12.6	15.8	18.2	N	21.2	N	13.2	8.4	5.9	N
Daily minimum	1.1	2.0	3.3	5.2	8.2	11.0	N	N	N	7.3	3.5	1.4	N
Extreme maximum	15.0	19.5	17.0	22.0	31.0	28.0	30.6	30.0	27.2	23.9	18.0	14.5	
Extreme minimum	-9.0	-12.0	-6.1	-1.1	1.7	5.0	7.2	7.2	2.8	-3.0	-11.0	-10.5	
Precipitation													
Rainfall (mm)	147.3	130.0	117.7	84.6	70.2	52.3	48.8	45.7	76.5	141.1	193.6	181.5	1289.4
Extreme daily rainfall	62.2	50.4	51.8	34.3	41.9	38.4	48.0	39.1	51.6	49.8	51.3	63.5	
Days with rain	17	15	16	14	12	10	7	8	10	16	19	18	162
Snowfall (cm)	17.4	10.0	4.2	0.5	0.0	0.0	0.0	0.0	0.0	0.4	3.0	21.2	56.7
Extreme daily snowfall	27.2	35.6	27.9	6.0	0.0	0.0	0.0	0.0	0.0	7.9	15.2	35.6	
Days with snow	3	2	*	*	0	0	0	0	0	*	*	3	9
Days with precipitation	19	16	16	14	12	10	7	8	10	16	19	20	168

* = Average of less than one but greater than zero
N = Some data exists but not enough to derive a value

Ioco 49°18'N 122°53'W
1916 to 1989

Elevation 53 m (174 ft)

	Jan	Feb	Mar	Apr	May	June	July	Aug	Sept	Oct	Nov	Dec	Year
Precipitation													
Rainfall (mm)	233.6	209.3	193.6	144.2	104.6	79.9	58.5	71.6	106.0	209.9	287.8	285.2	1984.2
Extreme daily rainfall	112.0	108.5	79.5	77.0	83.1	69.1	78.0	85.1	118.6	136.1	121.9	126.2	
Days with rain	15	14	15	14	12	10	7	7	9	14	19	17	153
Snowfall (cm)	17.1	7.7	1.3	T	0.0	0.0	0.0	0.0	0.0	T	3.0	16.7	45.8
Extreme daily snowfall	39.4	25.4	25.4	5.1	0.0	0.0	0.0	0.0	0.0	1.0	17.8	33.0	
Days with snow	3	1	*	*	0	0	0	0	0	*	*	3	8
Days with precipitation	17	15	15	14	12	10	7	7	9	14	19	19	158

* = Average of less than one but greater than zero
T = Trace

Merry Island 49°28'N 123°55'W
1954 to 1990

Elevation 8 m (26 ft)

	Jan	Feb	Mar	Apr	May	June	July	Aug	Sept	Oct	Nov	Dec	Year
Temperature (°C)													
Daily average	4.3	5.5	6.7	9.0	12.5	15.6	17.7	17.8	14.8	10.7	7.0	4.9	10.5
Daily maximum	6.0	7.5	9.2	11.8	15.6	18.7	21.0	21.0	17.6	12.8	8.8	6.5	13.0
Daily minimum	2.6	3.4	4.3	6.2	9.3	12.4	14.3	14.6	12.1	8.5	5.2	3.2	8.0
Extreme maximum	13.2	14.3	15.6	20.7	28.4	29.9	29.4	32.2	26.6	21.1	15.0	13.3	
Extreme minimum	-7.2	-10.1	-3.3	-1.1	3.3	5.6	9.0	8.9	3.9	-0.4	-7.3	-11.7	
Precipitation													
Rainfall (mm)	116.3	97.9	78.6	60.4	54.9	46.9	41.5	38.1	63.1	108.8	148.5	140.1	995.1
Extreme daily rainfall	78.2	49.0	44.7	31.8	28.7	41.9	37.1	42.4	69.4	62.2	50.0	66.0	
Days with rain	17	16	15	13	12	10	7	7	10	16	19	19	162
Snowfall (cm)	11.2	6.7	1.5	0.3	T	0.0	0.0	0.0	T	T	2.5	10.6	32.8
Extreme daily snowfall	22.9	22.9	8.9	5.1	1.0	0.0	0.0	0.0	0.0	0.2	9.6	40.6	
Days with snow	3	1	*	*	*	0	0	0	0	*	*	2	7
Days with precipitation	19	17	16	13	12	10	7	7	10	16	19	20	165
Wind (knots)													
Speed	11	11	11	10	9	9	8	8	8	10	11	12	10
Most frequent direction	E	E	E	NW	NW	SE	SE	NW	NW	E	E	E	E
Maximum hourly speed	52	43	46	48	48	38	35	38	43	48	54	54	
Direction	SE	SE	E	E	E	E	E	E	SE	E	SE	E	

* = Average of less than one but greater than zero
T = Trace

Mission 49°08'N 122°20'W
1953 to 1990

Elevation 60 m (197 ft)

	Jan	Feb	Mar	Apr	May	June	July	Aug	Sept	Oct	Nov	Dec	Year
Temperature (°C)													
Daily average	2.4	4.9	6.6	9.3	12.5	15.5	17.8	17.9	15.4	10.9	6.2	3.3	10.2
Daily maximum	4.9	8.1	10.5	13.8	17.4	20.3	23.2	23.3	20.4	14.8	9.0	5.8	14.3
Daily minimum	-0.2	1.7	2.7	4.7	7.6	10.6	12.3	12.4	10.4	6.9	3.4	0.8	6.1
Extreme maximum	15.6	20.6	21.7	28.0	36.5	36.0	37.8	36.5	36.0	27.0	18.9	17.5	
Extreme minimum	-14.4	-15.5	-12.2	-2.8	-2.2	2.2	4.4	5.0	0.6	-2.8	-13.3	-19.4	
Precipitation													
Rainfall (mm)	191.6	171.2	148.4	115.4	91.1	82.9	61.1	68.4	92.7	157.6	226.6	230.7	1637.8
Extreme daily rainfall	97.5	82.0	77.2	52.3	68.3	58.8	80.6	51.6	54.9	75.4	106.0	92.0	
Days with rain	17	16	17	16	14	12	9	10	10	17	20	19	177
Snowfall (cm)	24.1	9.5	3.8	0.4	0.0	0.0	0.0	0.0	0.0	T	3.7	22.2	63.7
Extreme daily snowfall	25.4	21.7	20.3	5.1	0.0	0.0	0.0	0.0	0.0	1.0	14.2	26.9	
Days with snow	5	2	*	*	0	0	0	0	0	*	1	4	13
Days with precipitation	20	17	17	16	14	12	9	10	10	17	20	22	184

* = Average of less than one but greater than zero
T = Trace

Nanaimo, Departure Bay 49°13'N 123°57'W
1913 to 1990

Elevation 8 m (26 ft)

	Jan	Feb	Mar	Apr	May	June	July	Aug	Sept	Oct	Nov	Dec	Year
Temperature (°C)													
Daily average	3.5	4.9	6.4	8.5	12.1	15.3	17.7	17.9	14.8	10.2	6.0	4.1	10.1
Daily maximum	5.9	7.8	10.0	12.4	16.2	19.4	22.0	22.0	18.8	13.5	8.7	6.2	13.6
Daily minimum	1.0	1.9	2.8	4.8	7.9	11.3	13.5	13.7	10.8	7.0	3.5	1.7	6.7
Extreme maximum	16.7	17.8	22.2	27.8	30.6	33.9	38.3	36.1	31.0	26.7	19.4	16.0	
Extreme minimum	-13.9	-12.0	-8.3	-6.7	-1.1	1.7	4.4	1.1	1.1	-4.4	-17.0	-14.0	
Precipitation													
Rainfall (mm)	120.1	94.9	88.4	51.8	45.8	35.3	26.1	30.4	45.6	87.3	130.4	150.2	906.2
Extreme daily rainfall	67.1	55.0	45.2	35.3	32.5	32.3	37.1	52.1	54.6	63.0	60.7	92.2	
Days with rain	16	14	14	12	11	9	7	6	9	13	16	16	142
Snowfall (cm)	15.8	9.3	1.5	T	0.0	0.0	T	0.0	0.0	0.2	3.6	10.7	41.2
Extreme daily snowfall	66.0	42.7	21.6	1.3	0.0	0.0	0.0	0.0	0.0	6.0	20.3	45.7	
Days with snow	2	2	*	*	0	0	0	0	0	*	*	2	7
Days with precipitation	18	14	14	12	11	9	7	6	9	13	16	18	146

* = Average of less than one but greater than zero
T = Trace

Pachena Point 48°43'N 125°06'W
1924 to 1990

Elevation 37 m (121 ft)

	Jan	Feb	Mar	Apr	May	June	July	Aug	Sept	Oct	Nov	Dec	Year
Temperature (°C)													
Daily average	4.7	5.7	6.1	7.6	9.9	11.9	13.5	13.7	12.6	9.8	7.0	5.1	9.0
Daily maximum	7.2	8.4	9.4	11.2	13.4	15.1	16.7	16.9	16.2	12.9	9.6	7.7	12.1
Daily minimum	2.2	2.8	2.8	4.1	6.4	8.8	10.2	10.5	9.0	6.7	4.3	2.6	5.9
Extreme maximum	14.5	16.1	20.0	22.8	27.0	31.7	31.7	29.0	27.2	22.2	18.9	15.0	
Extreme minimum	-15.6	-10.0	-6.7	-3.3	-1.7	1.1	3.9	4.0	-1.1	-5.0	-9.5	-10.0	
Precipitation													
Rainfall (mm)	372.9	346.7	338.3	212.5	150.4	110.9	83.1	99.3	145.5	355.9	430.2	418.7	3064.3
Extreme daily rainfall	143.5	139.7	117.1	97.8	82.6	115.6	167.6	120.7	104.9	145.3	148.8	124.0	
Days with rain	21	19	20	18	16	14	12	12	13	18	22	22	207
Snowfall (cm)	14.6	6.4	3.0	0.8	0.0	0.0	0.0	0.0	0.0	T	1.7	11.3	38.0
Extreme daily snowfall	27.9	25.7	36.8	16.5	0.0	0.0	0.0	0.0	0.0	1.6	16.5	40.4	
Days with snow	3	2	1	*	0	0	0	0	0	*	*	2	8
Days with precipitation	22	20	21	18	16	14	12	12	13	18	22	23	210

* = Average of less than one but greater than zero
T = Trace

Pitt River 49°18'N 122°38'W
1951 to 1990

Elevation 2 m (7 ft)

	Jan	Feb	Mar	Apr	May	June	July	Aug	Sept	Oct	Nov	Dec	Year
Temperature (°C)													
Daily average	2.1	4.1	5.9	8.6	12.1	15.2	17.3	17.3	14.3	9.9	5.4	2.6	9.6
Daily maximum	4.9	7.6	10.1	13.3	17.1	20.1	23.0	23.3	19.9	14.3	8.5	5.3	13.9
Daily minimum	-0.8	0.5	1.7	3.8	7.0	10.2	11.5	11.4	8.7	5.4	2.3	-0.1	5.1
Extreme maximum	15.0	18.3	21.0	29.0	35.0	33.9	36.1	35.0	35.5	28.0	19.4	17.0	
Extreme minimum	-23.3	-16.7	-11.7	-4.4	-2.2	1.7	4.4	2.8	-1.7	-6.0	-19.0	-18.0	
Precipitation													
Rainfall (mm)	277.5	250.3	207.5	167.7	117.5	95.3	77.6	74.5	123.5	239.0	328.1	311.5	2270.0
Extreme daily rainfall	134.1	131.0	67.1	98.0	57.5	55.0	109.6	56.1	119.6	111.3	143.8	126.0	
Days with rain	18	17	18	17	14	12	9	9	11	16	20	19	180
Snowfall (cm)	22.6	8.3	2.7	T	0.0	0.0	0.0	0.0	0.0	0.2	3.1	19.2	56.2
Extreme daily snowfall	45.0	36.0	11.7	0.0	0.0	0.0	0.0	0.0	0.0	5.0	18.8	33.0	
Days with snow	3	2	*	0	0	0	0	0	0	*	*	3	10
Days with precipitation	20	18	18	17	14	12	9	9	11	16	21	21	185

* = Average of less than one but greater than zero
T = Trace

Port Alberni 49°15'N 124°50'W
1969 to 1990

Elevation 2 m (7 ft)

	Jan	Feb	Mar	Apr	May	June	July	Aug	Sept	Oct	Nov	Dec	Year
Temperature (°C)													
Daily average	2.0	3.5	5.7	8.2	11.4	14.5	17.2	17.8	14.5	9.8	5.1	2.4	9.3
Daily maximum	4.5	7.0	10.6	13.9	17.4	20.5	24.2	25.2	21.4	14.7	7.9	4.7	14.3
Daily minimum	-0.6	-0.1	0.7	2.4	5.4	8.4	10.1	10.3	7.5	4.9	2.2	0.1	4.3
Extreme maximum	14.7	16.3	21.7	27.5	34.1	34.3	36.1	38.4	35.1	27.1	17.2	15.6	
Extreme minimum	-17.8	-15.1	-9.4	-6.1	-2.8	0.0	2.2	1.1	-3.3	-8.5	-16.8	-14.8	
Precipitation													
Rainfall (mm)	218.8	225.9	194.7	105.8	75.1	47.3	28.8	32.0	71.5	198.7	296.1	271.1	1765.8
Extreme daily rainfall	98.6	95.4	93.2	46.4	49.2	48.2	37.3	29.7	58.4	101.0	90.1	111.0	
Days with rain	17	16	18	16	15	11	7	7	11	16	20	18	172
Snowfall (cm)	36.8	28.6	12.6	1.6	T	0.0	0.0	0.0	0.0	0.7	11.3	29.0	120.5
Extreme daily snowfall	63.0	32.3	41.1	5.8	0.0	0.0	0.0	0.0	0.0	14.2	24.2	38.4	
Days with snow	6	5	3	*	0	0	0	0	0	*	2	5	21
Days with precipitation	20	18	18	16	15	11	7	7	11	16	21	21	181
Wind (knots)													
Speed	2	2	3	4	4	x	5	5	3	3	2	2	x
Most frequent direction	C	NW	NW	S	S	x	S	S	S	C	C	C	x
Maximum hourly speed	30	32	23	28	24	26	26	28	21	25	23	34	
Direction	S	S	S	S	S	S	S	S	S	SE	SE	S	

```
*  =  Average of less than one but greater than zero
T  =  Trace
X  =  Some data exists but not enough to derive a value
```

Port Hardy 50°41'N 127°22'W
1944 to 1990

Elevation 22 m (72 ft)

	Jan	Feb	Mar	Apr	May	June	July	Aug	Sept	Oct	Nov	Dec	Year
Temperature (°C)													
Daily average	3.0	4.1	5.1	6.8	9.4	11.8	13.7	13.9	11.8	8.6	5.2	3.3	8.1
Daily maximum	5.5	7.0	8.5	10.7	13.5	15.6	17.5	17.7	15.6	11.8	7.8	5.7	11.4
Daily minimum	0.5	1.2	1.5	2.8	5.2	8.0	9.9	10.1	7.9	5.4	2.5	0.9	4.7
Extreme maximum	13.7	16.7	18.3	23.3	33.4	31.7	26.7	28.3	25.6	25.6	18.9	14.8	
Extreme minimum	-14.4	-11.8	-12.8	-3.3	-1.1	1.7	2.8	3.3	-0.6	-5.4	-12.5	-12.2	
Precipitation													
Rainfall (mm)	221.8	160.9	134.0	118.5	75.4	78.1	56.1	62.9	131.5	258.8	261.2	243.5	1802.8
Extreme daily rainfall	98.3	66.9	58.4	74.8	37.8	42.2	35.8	54.6	96.3	113.7	86.6	153.8	
Days with rain	19	18	19	18	16	14	11	12	15	21	22	21	207
Snowfall (cm)	23.3	11.1	7.1	1.6	T	T	0.0	0.0	T	0.3	4.5	15.1	63.0
Extreme daily snowfall	29.2	25.8	21.1	5.3	1.5	0.0	0.0	0.0	0.0	3.8	14.0	21.1	
Days with snow	6	3	3	1	*	0	0	0	0	*	2	5	20
Days with precipitation	22	19	20	19	16	14	11	12	15	21	23	22	214
Sunshine (hours)	N	N	N	N	177.3	173.0	201.6	190.3	146.4	N	56.4	49.6	N
Wind (knots)													
Speed	9	8	7	6	6	5	5	4	4	6	8	9	6
Most frequent direction	SE	SE	SE	SE	C	C	C	C	C	SE	SE	SE	SE
Maximum hourly speed	57	43	41	45	37	30	29	25	31	38	41	40	
Direction	W	E	E	E	W	E	S	E	E	E	SE	E	
Maximum gust speed	61	64	60	56	45	42	39	45	42	55	60	61	
Direction	E	E	E	E	E	E	S	E	SE	E	SE	SW	

* = Average of less than one but greater than zero
N = Some data exists but not enough to derive a value
T = Trace

Port Mellon 49°31'N 123°29'W
1942 to 1989

Elevation 8 m (26 ft)

	Jan	Feb	Mar	Apr	May	June	July	Aug	Sept	Oct	Nov	Dec	Year
Precipitation													
Rainfall (mm)	367.9	361.9	328.7	204.4	164.8	102.5	100.1	88.9	172.6	393.3	474.4	453.9	3213.1
Extreme daily rainfall	167.6	133.2	153.2	104.9	106.7	106.7	156.0	86.0	121.9	224.3	327.6	159.8	
Days with rain	19	17	18	17	14	12	9	9	12	17	21	19	183
Snowfall (cm)	34.6	16.1	3.9	0.3	0.0	0.0	0.0	0.0	0.0	0.3	6.8	31.0	93.2
Extreme daily snowfall	38.1	48.3	25.4	4.2	0.0	0.0	0.0	0.0	0.0	9.0	20.3	38.1	
Days with snow	4	2	*	*	0	0	0	0	0	*	1	4	12
Days with precipitation	20	18	18	17	14	12	9	9	12	17	21	21	188

* = Average of less than one but greater than zero

Powell River 49°52'N 124°33'W
1924 to 1990

Elevation 52 m (171 ft)

	Jan	Feb	Mar	Apr	May	June	July	Aug	Sept	Oct	Nov	Dec	Year
Temperature (°C)													
Daily average	3.7	5.1	6.6	9.2	12.5	15.8	18.3	18.4	15.6	10.9	6.6	4.4	10.6
Daily maximum	6.1	8.0	10.3	13.2	17.0	20.3	22.9	22.7	19.4	13.8	9.0	6.6	14.1
Daily minimum	1.2	2.1	2.9	5.1	8.1	11.5	13.6	14.0	11.6	7.9	4.2	2.0	7.0
Extreme maximum	15.6	18.0	20.0	23.9	33.0	33.0	33.9	33.0	29.4	24.0	20.0	15.0	
Extreme minimum	-14.4	-12.0	-10.0	-1.7	-6.7	3.3	6.1	6.0	0.0	-4.0	-11.0	-12.8	
Precipitation													
Rainfall (mm)	119.7	97.8	96.0	61.4	63.0	53.2	44.6	48.5	60.1	127.5	155.8	146.9	1074.5
Extreme daily rainfall	64.8	49.0	56.1	27.7	50.3	58.9	48.3	46.5	57.2	49.0	58.0	68.3	
Days with rain	17	15	16	14	11	10	7	8	10	16	19	18	160
Snowfall (cm)	18.0	6.7	1.3	T	0.0	0.0	0.0	0.0	0.0	0.2	4.3	8.9	39.4
Extreme daily snowfall	50.8	31.8	21.6	3.0	0.0	0.0	0.0	0.0	0.0	5.0	20.0	29.2	
Days with snow	2	1	*	*	0	0	0	0	0	*	*	2	6
Days with precipitation	18	16	16	14	11	10	7	8	10	16	19	19	164

* = Average of less than one but greater than zero
T = Trace

Quatsino 50°32'N 127°39'W
1895 to 1990

Elevation 8 m (26 ft)

	Jan	Feb	Mar	Apr	May	June	July	Aug	Sept	Oct	Nov	Dec	Year
Temperature (°C)													
Daily average	3.4	4.5	5.7	7.6	10.3	12.8	14.9	15.3	13.4	9.7	5.7	3.6	8.9
Daily maximum	5.7	7.4	9.3	11.6	14.7	17.2	19.6	19.8	17.7	12.8	8.1	5.8	12.5
Daily minimum	0.9	1.5	2.0	3.5	5.8	8.4	10.3	10.7	9.1	6.5	3.2	1.4	5.3
Extreme maximum	17.5	16.1	20.0	26.0	30.0	32.2	33.9	32.2	29.5	22.5	20.6	15.0	
Extreme minimum	-16.7	-11.5	-10.0	-5.6	-2.8	-1.1	2.2	3.3	-0.6	-4.5	-12.0	-12.2	
Precipitation													
Rainfall (mm)	325.5	241.7	209.6	165.7	97.0	78.4	50.5	68.2	154.3	341.4	373.4	350.9	2456.5
Extreme daily rainfall	99.6	136.7	89.2	130.0	151.6	70.6	63.5	72.4	121.9	108.0	161.6	135.8	
Days with rain	22	20	22	20	17	15	11	13	14	22	24	22	222
Snowfall (cm)	19.8	8.4	7.4	0.7	0.0	0.0	0.0	0.0	0.0	0.2	3.6	12.5	52.6
Extreme daily snowfall	53.3	26.7	33.3	17.8	0.0	10.4	0.0	0.0	0.0	4.0	24.4	40.6	
Days with snow	4	2	2	*	0	0	0	0	0	*	1	3	14
Days with precipitation	23	20	22	20	17	15	11	13	14	22	24	24	226

* = Average of less than one but greater than zero

Race Rocks Lightstation 48°18'N 123°32'W
1969 to 1990

Elevation: 5 m (16 ft)

	Jan	Feb	Mar	Apr	May	June	July	Aug	Sept	Oct	Nov	Dec	Year
Wind (knots)													
Speed	x	11	x	x	x	14	x	12	x	x	11	12	x
Most frequent direction	x	NE	x	x	x	x	x	W	x	x	NE	NE	x
Maximum hourly speed	52	50	40	42	42	44	42	37	40	43	54	43	
Direction	W	W	SE	SW	W	N	W	W	N	SW	E	SW	

X = Some data exists but not enough to derive a value

Sand Heads 49°06'N 123°18'W
1967 to 1990

Elevation: 12 m (39 ft)

	Jan	Feb	Mar	Apr	May	June	July	Aug	Sept	Oct	Nov	Dec	Year
Wind (knots)													
Speed	11	11	11	10	9	9	9	9	9	10	11	12	10
Most frequent direction	E	E	E	E	SE	SE	SE	SE	NW	E	E	E	E
Maximum hourly speed	43	42	53	41	41	34	35	33	36	37	46	44	
Direction	SE	NW	NW	W	NW	NW	NW	SE	W	SE	SE	SE	

Saturna Island Light 48°47'N 123°03'W
1968 to 1990

Elevation: 25 m (82 ft)

	Jan	Feb	Mar	Apr	May	June	July	Aug	Sept	Oct	Nov	Dec	Year
Wind (knots)													
Speed	11	11	10	8	7	7	7	7	7	8	12	12	9
Most frequent direction	NW	NW	NW	SW	SW	SW	SW	SW	NW	NW	S	S	SW
Maximum hourly speed	45	51	52	43	43	28	29	34	39	48	47	50	
Direction	S	S	SE	SE	SE	SE	S	SE	SE	S	E	S	

Sooke 48°22'N 123°44'W
1970 to 1990

Elevation 27 m (89 ft)

	Jan	Feb	Mar	Apr	May	June	July	Aug	Sept	Oct	Nov	Dec	Year
Precipitation													
Rainfall (mm)	187.2	143.9	108.9	78.5	47.9	31.3	22.2	27.8	50.0	116.3	225.6	194.9	1234.6
Extreme daily rainfall	80.5	136.8	72.1	47.4	33.4	22.6	28.6	41.9	40.4	66.8	102.6	93.7	
Days with rain	17	16	16	13	11	8	5	5	9	14	19	18	151
Snowfall (cm)	9.5	5.9	2.2	T	T	0.0	0.0	0.0	0.0	0.1	3.5	10.6	31.7
Extreme daily snowfall	18.0	11.4	10.2	0.0	0.0	0.0	0.0	0.0	0.0	2.8	32.5	58.4	
Days with snow	2	1	*	0	0	0	0	0	0	*	*	2	6
Days with precipitation	19	16	16	13	11	8	5	5	9	14	20	19	155

* = Average of less than one but greater than zero

T = Trace

Tahsis 49°55'N 126°39'W
1952 to 1988

Elevation 5 m (16 ft)

	Jan	Feb	Mar	Apr	May	June	July	Aug	Sept	Oct	Nov	Dec	Year
Precipitation													
Rainfall (mm)	483.0	427.0	364.4	260.3	179.3	131.1	90.9	108.4	253.9	521.3	504.5	520.6	3844.7
Extreme daily rainfall	207.5	139.7	138.2	115.0	97.2	106.4	53.8	91.9	139.7	245.2	198.1	199.4	
Days with rain	18	18	18	17	15	12	9	9	12	19	20	18	184
Snowfall (cm)	24.8	10.0	4.6	2.0	0.0	0.0	0.0	0.0	0.0	0.1	4.3	18.4	64.2
Extreme daily snowfall	43.2	19.0	30.5	12.7	0.0	0.0	0.0	0.0	0.0	3.1	17.8	30.5	
Days with snow	3	2	1	*	0	0	0	0	0	*	*	3	10
Days with precipitation	19	18	18	17	15	12	9	9	12	19	20	19	188

* = Average of less than one but greater than zero

Texada Island 49°42'N 124°31'W
1960 to 1990

Elevation 97 m (318 ft)

	Jan	Feb	Mar	Apr	May	June	July	Aug	Sept	Oct	Nov	Dec	Year
Precipitation													
Rainfall (mm)	116	74.7	78.2	52.6	48.0	47.6	33.6	38.8	46.6	108.7	143.2	121.4	909.4
Extreme daily rainfall	60.2	32.5	51.1	28.2	27.0	29.5	34.5	41.7	33.0	41.7	39.9	54.1	
Days with rain	17	13	15	12	10	10	7	7	8	15	18	18	149
Snowfall (cm)	11.1	8.7	1.5	T	0.0	0.0	0.0	0.0	0.0	0.2	4.3	13.6	39.3
Extreme daily snowfall	17.8	25.4	9.1	0.0	0.0	0.0	0.0	0.0	0.0	5.0	17.0	29.2	
Days with snow	2	1	*	0	0	0	0	0	0	*	*	3	7
Days with precipitation	18	N	15	12	10	10	7	7	8	15	19	19	N

* = Average of less than one but greater than zero
N = Some data exists but not enough to derive a value
T = Trace

Tofino 49°05'N 125°46'W
1942 to 1990

Elevation 24 m (79 ft)

	Jan	Feb	Mar	Apr	May	June	July	Aug	Sept	Oct	Nov	Dec	Year
Temperature (°C)													
Daily average	4.2	5.3	5.8	7.3	10.0	12.4	14.2	14.6	13.2	9.8	6.5	4.6	9.0
Daily maximum	7.2	8.5	9.5	11.2	13.9	16.3	18.3	18.6	17.4	13.5	9.7	7.6	12.7
Daily minimum	1.2	1.9	2.1	3.5	6.0	8.5	10.1	10.6	8.9	6.0	3.2	1.6	5.3
Extreme maximum	20.1	18.9	18.3	22.8	27.6	32.2	32.8	32.8	29.4	23.9	21.1	15.6	
Extreme minimum	-15.0	-9.2	-5.5	-1.7	-0.2	2.2	3.9	4.4	-0.6	-3.5	-12.7	-12.2	
Precipitation													
Rainfall (mm)	405.6	363.3	353.7	240.9	154.5	121.7	82.6	92.7	149.5	387.9	455.1	428.3	3235.8
Extreme daily rainfall	174.2	169.2	169.7	126.2	95.5	83.2	98.3	131.3	105.9	154.2	155.4	166.4	
Days with rain	20	19	19	18	14	12	10	11	13	19	22	21	198
Snowfall (cm)	18.8	8.8	6.9	1.8	T	0.0	0.0	0.0	0.0	T	2.9	13.3	52.6
Extreme daily snowfall	31.2	16.6	20.3	14.2	0.0	0.0	0.0	0.0	0.0	1.2	22.6	22.4	
Days with snow	3	2	2	*	0	0	0	0	0	*	*	3	12
Days with precipitation	22	19	20	18	14	12	10	11	13	19	23	23	202

* = Average of less than one but greater than zero
T = Trace

Vancouver International Airport 49°11'N 123°10'W
1937 to 1990

Elevation 3 m (10 ft)

	Jan	Feb	Mar	Apr	May	June	July	Aug	Sept	Oct	Nov	Dec	Year
Temperature (°C)													
Daily average	3.0	4.7	6.3	8.8	12.1	15.2	17.2	17.4	14.3	10.0	6.0	3.5	9.9
Daily maximum	5.7	8.0	9.9	12.7	16.3	19.3	21.7	21.7	18.4	13.5	9.0	6.1	13.5
Daily minimum	0.1	1.4	2.6	4.9	7.9	11.0	12.7	12.9	10.1	6.4	3.0	0.8	6.1
Extreme maximum	15.3	18.4	19.4	25.0	30.4	30.6	31.7	33.3	29.3	23.5	18.4	14.9	
Extreme minimum	-17.8	-16.1	-9.4	-3.3	0.6	3.9	6.7	6.1	0.0	-5.9	-14.3	-17.8	
Precipitation													
Rainfall (mm)	131.6	115.6	105.4	74.9	61.7	45.7	36.1	38.1	64.4	115.3	167.2	161.2	1117.2
Extreme daily rainfall	68.3	64.2	49.3	44.5	29.0	40.4	45.2	31.8	49.5	60.7	65.0	89.4	
Days with rain	17	15	16	13	12	10	7	7	9	15	19	19	159
Snowfall (cm)	20.6	8.6	4.1	0.5	T	0.0	0.0	0.0	0.0	T	2.6	18.6	54.9
Extreme daily snowfall	29.7	28.6	25.9	3.8	0.0	0.0	0.0	0.0	0.0	0.3	22.1	31.2	
Days with snow	5	2	1	*	0	0	0	0	0	*	*	4	13
Days with precipitation	19	16	16	13	12	10	7	7	9	15	19	21	164
Sunshine (hours)	54.9	86.9	131.6	171.9	237.3	242.2	295.9	264.9	188.9	124.4	66.7	53.6	1919.3
Wind (knots)													
Speed	6	6	7	7	6	6	6	6	5	6	6	6	6
Most frequent direction	E	E	E	E	E	E	E	E	E	E	E	E	E
Maximum hourly speed	37	48	42	39	33	28	26	25	35	41	48	38	
Direction	W	W	W	W	W	W	W	W	W	SE	W	W	
Maximum gust speed	52	64	58	54	49	37	38	46	47	68	70	54	
Direction	SW	W	W	W	W	NW	W	NW	W	SE	W	SE	

* = Average of less than one but greater than zero
T = Trace

Victoria International Airport 48°39'N 123°26'W
1940 to 1990

Elevation 20 m (66 ft)

	Jan	Feb	Mar	Apr	May	June	July	Aug	Sept	Oct	Nov	Dec	Year
Temperature (°C)													
Daily average	3.4	4.8	6.1	8.4	11.4	14.3	16.2	16.2	13.8	9.7	6.0	3.8	9.5
Daily maximum	6.5	8.4	10.2	12.9	16.3	19.3	21.8	21.8	19.1	14.1	9.4	6.8	13.9
Daily minimum	0.3	1.2	1.9	3.8	6.5	9.3	10.7	10.6	8.4	5.3	2.5	0.8	5.1
Extreme maximum	15.4	18.3	20.0	24.4	31.5	33.3	36.1	34.4	31.1	27.6	18.3	16.1	
Extreme minimum	-15.6	-15.0	-10.0	-3.9	-1.1	2.2	4.1	4.4	-1.1	-4.4	-13.3	-14.4	
Precipitation													
Rainfall (mm)	124.1	91.2	68.2	41.8	33.4	27.3	17.6	23.7	36.6	74.4	136.4	138.0	812.8
Extreme daily rainfall	92.8	55.9	53.6	31.2	38.1	40.9	20.3	32.5	45.2	57.4	68.3	72.9	
Days with rain	16	15	16	13	11	9	5	6	8	14	18	18	148
Snowfall (cm)	17.2	8.1	3.7	T	T	0.0	0.0	0.0	T	T	3.4	14.5	46.9
Extreme daily snowfall	29.2	26.0	21.3	5.1	0.0	0.0	0.0	0.0	0.0	0.0	16.4	34.8	
Days with snow	4	2	*	*	0	0	0	0	0	0	*	3	11
Days with precipitation	18	16	16	13	11	9	5	6	8	14	18	19	153
Sunshine (hours)	63.7	89.4	142.6	186.8	250.3	257.4	324.4	289.3	207.2	138.7	75.5	56.7	2081.9

* = Average of less than one but greater than zero
T = Trace

Victoria, Gonzales Heights 48°25'N 123°19'W
1898 to 1988

Elevation 69 m (226 ft)

	Jan	Feb	Mar	Apr	May	June	July	Aug	Sept	Oct	Nov	Dec	Year
Temperature (°C)													
Daily average	4.6	6.2	7.3	9.1	11.8	13.8	15.3	15.6	14.2	10.8	7.1	5.0	10.1
Daily maximum	6.6	8.6	10.3	12.5	15.6	17.7	19.5	19.6	17.9	13.6	9.3	6.9	13.2
Daily minimum	2.5	3.8	4.3	5.7	8.0	9.9	11.2	11.5	10.4	7.8	5.0	3.0	6.9
Extreme maximum	14.4	17.4	20.6	23.9	29.5	35.0	35.0	32.8	31.7	25.0	18.9	15.0	
Extreme minimum	-14.4	-12.8	-7.2	-2.2	1.1	3.9	6.1	4.4	1.7	-2.8	-11.1	-15.6	
Precipitation													
Rainfall (mm)	92.6	66.8	42.2	32.1	24.0	18.7	14.0	20.0	32.4	58.8	91.9	99.4	592.9
Extreme daily rainfall	77.5	80.8	67.8	36.8	37.6	33.5	21.8	27.9	43.2	50.8	68.8	83.3	
Days with rain	15	14	13	11	8	7	5	5	8	13	16	17	131
Snowfall (cm)	10.5	2.8	2.4	T	0.0	0.0	0.0	0.0	0.0	T	2.9	9.4	28.1
Extreme daily snowfall	27.9	53.3	17.8	7.4	0.0	0.0	0.0	0.0	0.0	1.2	21.6	26.4	
Days with snow	3	1	1	*	0	0	0	0	0	*	*	3	9
Days with precipitation	17	14	13	11	8	7	5	5	8	13	16	18	135
Sunshine (hours)	71.5	98.9	151.8	193.8	272.4	278.9	328.0	292.3	205.9	147.4	81.2	62.8	2185.1

* = Average of less than one but greater than zero
T = Trace

White Rock 49°01'N 122°46'W
1964 to 1990

Elevation 15 m (49 ft)

	Jan	Feb	Mar	Apr	May	June	July	Aug	Sept	Oct	Nov	Dec	Year
Precipitation													
Rainfall (mm)	129.5	104.1	94.6	71.8	60.4	50.1	36.7	43.8	61.1	107.6	154.1	138.5	1052.4
Extreme daily rainfall	60.2	54.6	40.0	46.0	37.0	44.2	37.3	57.7	34.0	57.4	59.2	56.6	
Days with rain	17	15	16	14	12	10	7	7	10	15	18	17	158
Snowfall (cm)	16.8	7.4	1.5	T	0.0	0.0	0.0	0.0	0.0	T	3.6	16.5	45.8
Extreme daily snowfall	21.6	11.7	10.2	0.6	0.0	0.0	0.0	0.0	0.0	2.4	13.7	19.3	
Days with snow	4	2	*	*	0	0	0	0	0	*	1	4	12
Days with precipitation	19	16	16	14	12	10	7	7	10	15	19	19	164

* = Average of less than one but greater than zero
T = Trace

Woodfibre 49°40'N 123°15'W
1960 to 1990

Elevation 3 m (10 ft)

	Jan	Feb	Mar	Apr	May	June	July	Aug	Sept	Oct	Nov	Dec	Year
Precipitation													
Rainfall (mm)	309.2	299.8	273.4	195.1	140.5	102.4	77.8	74.4	N	326.5	441.2	N	N
Extreme daily rainfall	197.1	115.0	99.0	72.4	60.2	77.0	86.4	111.5	112.8	114.3	144.0	132.8	
Days with rain	13	13	15	14	12	10	7	8	9	14	17	14	145
Snowfall (cm)	50.9	16.8	5.5	0.4	0.0	0.0	0.0	0.0	0.0	0.5	10.4	43.8	128.2
Extreme daily snowfall	53.3	56.0	34.3	5.1	0.0	0.0	0.0	0.0	0.0	11.0	30.0	61.0	
Days with snow	5	2	*	*	0	0	0	0	0	*	1	5	14
Days with precipitation	16	14	15	14	12	10	7	8	9	14	17	17	153

* = Average of less than one but greater than zero
N = Some data exists but not enough to derive a value

FREQUENCY OF FOG

Station	Observations		Percentage of observations when fog was present											
	Years	No.Per Day	Jan	Feb	Mar	Apr	May	June	July	Aug	Sept	Oct	Nov	Dec
Alert Bay 50°35'N 126°57'W	1954-81	6	3.2	2.6	2.3	2.2	2.7	5.0	7.7	14.1	13.4	8.0	3.9	3.9
Bull Harbour 50°55'N 127°56'W	1953-81	6	6.3	5.6	4.7	5.0	6.1	9.4	13.9	18.5	16.8	10.2	7.0	7.6
Campbell River 49°57'N 125°16'W	1979-81	16	20.1	35.7	6.6	7.4	6.6	3.2	3.2	4.4	14.6	24.8	29.4	35.5
Cape St. James 51°56'N 131°01'W	1953-80	24	22.3	24.1	16.8	16.1	14.9	18.6	21.5	20.5	23.3	26.3	19.5	24.3
Cape Scott 50°47'N 128°26'W	1966-81	8	12.3	11.1	11.8	10.6	12.3	14.7	19.3	24.7	20.0	17.7	13.4	14.4
Estevan Point 49°23'N 126°33'W	1953-79	14	22.5	21.5	16.2	11.1	10.3	12.8	14.8	21.4	18.4	23.6	18.9	22.4
Ethelda Bay 53°03'N 129°41'W	1957-80	4	12.3	13.8	11.4	9.2	9.8	10.8	12.3	14.7	16.6	20.0	14.0	14.3
Langara 54°15'N 133°03'W	1954-80	4	4.9	4.3	4.4	4.3	4.2	8.5	14.6	13.8	9.9	6.1	5.1	5.3
McInnes Island 52°16'N 128°43'W	1955-80	6	6.9	5.2	4.7	5.0	5.6	7.1	9.4	13.9	13.7	10.5	7.6	6.6
Merry Island 49°28'N 123°54'W	1954-79	11	4.7	3.8	1.0	0.3	0.1	0.2	0.4	0.4	3.1	6.5	5.0	2.7
Port Hardy 50°41'N 127°22'W	1953-81	24	6.5	4.8	3.8	3.0	2.8	5.0	7.1	13.3	17.2	12.1	7.8	6.8
Prince Rupert 54°17'N 130°23'W	1961-80	24	11.5	11.4	10.6	10.8	7.8	12.8	16.8	20.6	17.9	13.5	10.3	12.4
Sandspit 53°15'N 131°49'W	1953-80	24	9.4	10.8	7.4	6.2	5.4	6.2	5.4	5.4	8.2	12.7	12.2	11.2
Spring Island 50°00'N 127°25'W	1953-79	24	20.2	19.2	13.8	12.2	10.6	11.5	11.6	16.5	15.2	20.3	16.5	20.0
Tofino 49°05'N 125°46'W	1960-81	24	25.7	23.4	20.5	16.4	14.1	18.1	21.8	29.8	26.8	29.0	23.4	27.6
Triple Islands 54°18'N 130°53'W	1953-67	4	1.2	1.8	0.9	1.2	2.6	5.2	7.1	8.5	6.9	1.3	0.9	1.6
Vancouver Airport 49°11'N 123°10'W	1953-81	24	25.3	21.0	9.1	4.4	3.5	3.7	3.0	7.4	16.7	25.7	24.3	25.5
Vancouver Harbour 49°18'N 123°07'W	1976-81	14	37.1	24.1	13.0	7.8	7.5	7.6	3.8	7.6	13.0	20.9	18.8	20.8
Victoria 48°25'N 123°19'W	1953-81	24	11.0	9.2	3.4	2.8	1.9	2.6	2.6	5.4	12.7	17.4	13.4	10.8

Frequency of Fog by Month and Time of Day

Alert Bay

50°35'N 126°56'W   Years of Observations 1954-1981

Month	Total Hours of Observations	Percentage of observations when fog (visibility 0.5 mile or less) was present								
		0400	0700	1000	1300	1600	2200			Average
January	4990	2.0	2.5	4.9	4.1	3.9	1.7			3.2
February	4547	2.4	2.8	2.9	2.5	3.3	1.4			2.6
March	4991	2.4	3.0	2.4	2.5	1.4	2.0			2.3
April	4829	2.7	2.6	2.7	1.7	1.6	2.0			2.2
May	5019	4.1	6.1	2.3	0.9	0.8	2.1			2.7
June	4860	9.1	10.0	4.2	1.1	1.6	4.2			5.0
July	5022	14.2	18.1	5.7	1.5	1.2	5.1			7.7
August	5020	23.4	31.6	14.6	4.0	2.3	8.6			14.1
September	4860	19.6	24.5	15.7	6.4	4.0	9.7			13.4
October	4801	10.6	10.0	9.2	6.8	5.9	5.6			8.0
November	4833	2.9	3.5	4.6	4.4	5.5	2.8			3.9
December	5021	3.8	2.9	4.8	4.6	4.5	2.7			3.9

Frequency of Fog by Month and Time of Day

Bull Harbour

50°55'N 127°57'W   Years of Observations 1953-1981

Month	Total Hours of Observations	Percentage of observations when fog (visibility 0.5 mile or less) was present								
		0400	0700	1000	1300	1600	2200			Average
January	5392	4.4	6.1	6.9	6.8	7.4	5.9			6.3
February	4900	5.0	5.0	5.8	6.4	6.4	4.8			5.6
March	5390	5.1	6.1	4.8	4.1	4.7	3.7			4.7
April	5219	3.6	7.0	5.5	4.6	5.1	4.0			5.0
May	5392	5.6	8.8	6.3	6.2	4.3	5.5			6.1
June	5215	10.0	14.4	11.5	7.8	6.1	6.7			9.4
July	5393	13.1	19.1	17.2	12.4	11.0	10.3			13.9
August	5377	16.8	24.5	21.9	18.0	16.0	13.6			18.5
September	5217	16.6	23.9	19.9	14.4	12.5	13.8			16.8
October	5340	9.7	12.0	10.8	11.2	9.4	8.2			10.2
November	5188	4.4	6.0	7.7	7.5	9.5	6.7			7.0
December	5392	5.5	6.3	8.7	8.7	9.7	6.6			7.6

APPENDICES

Frequency of Fog by Month and Time of Day

Campbell River

49°57'N 125°16'W

Years of Observations 1979-1981

Month	Total Hours of Observations	Percentage of observations when fog (visibility 0.5 mile or less) was present								
		0600	0900	1200	1500	1800				Average
January	992	21.0	19.4	17.7	11.3	21.0				20.1
February	911	42.1	38.6	31.6	29.8	31.6				35.7
March	1489	6.4	7.5	6.5	3.2	6.4				6.6
April	1441	10.0	10.0	3.3	5.6	7.8				7.4
May	1488	12.9	8.6	2.1	4.3	5.4				6.6
June	1446	3.3	5.6	2.2	3.3	1.1				3.2
July	1478	8.6	5.5	1.1	0.0	2.2				3.2
August	1481	5.4	5.4	5.5	2.1	2.2				4.4
September	1438	18.9	23.3	10.0	11.1	12.2				14.6
October	1284	28.4	28.0	23.2	17.5	25.6				24.8
November	1369	25.9	28.2	32.9	27.9	33.7				29.4
December	1489	29.0	33.3	39.8	37.6	35.5				35.5

Frequency of Fog by Month and Time of Day

Cape Scott

50°57'N 128°26'W

Years of Observations 1966-1981

Month	Total Hours of Observations	Percentage of observations when fog (visibility 0.5 mile or less) was present								
		0100	0400	0700	1000	1300	1600	1900	2200	Average
January	3380	11.7	11.5	11.6	11.6	13.3	13.1	14.8	11.6	12.3
February	3101	14.2	11.1	10.6	9.9	10.1	11.3	12.0	10.8	11.1
March	3400	12.5	13.6	11.8	11.4	10.5	11.0	13.5	10.5	11.8
April	3277	11.5	10.9	9.8	10.4	9.1	10.0	14.1	10.7	10.6
May	3155	17.2	13.2	12.7	10.8	12.7	9.9	13.6	10.8	12.3
June	3472	20.1	16.5	17.9	17.9	11.9	10.2	12.0	12.5	14.7
July	3581	21.9	23.9	21.5	21.1	16.6	14.6	16.5	18.6	19.3
August	3580	32.5	26.6	26.0	24.8	22.2	21.0	25.5	22.6	24.7
September	3465	23.1	20.3	19.6	20.6	19.4	15.7	21.7	21.5	20.0
October	3609	20.7	20.4	17.4	17.8	16.2	15.2	19.5	16.3	17.7
November	3494	13.9	12.2	12.1	12.7	11.9	14.4	18.2	13.3	13.4
December	3622	15.5	13.4	15.5	14.3	14.5	14.3	16.7	11.9	14.4

Frequency of Fog by Month and Time of Day

Estevan Point

49°23'N 126°33'W   Years of Observations 1953-1979

Month	Total Hours Of Observations	Percentage of observations when fog (visibility 0.5 mile or less) was present								
		0100	0400	0700	1000	1300	1600	1900	2200	Average
January	10196	24.1	23.1	24.1	19.4	22.5	17.1	22.9	20.4	22.5
February	9235	25.8	24.4	25.6	19.1	17.6	16.3	22.0	20.3	21.5
March	10032	18.9	18.4	17.7	15.5	16.1	11.7	13.5	13.8	16.2
April	9479	16.1	12.8	11.4	9.3	8.6	9.1	9.9	12.3	11.1
May	9795	14.4	11.3	12.5	9.3	8.8	7.8	9.5	10.5	10.3
June	9479	18.0	15.5	14.9	12.7	11.3	7.9	9.9	10.8	12.8
July	9795	19.7	18.4	20.3	16.0	11.2	9.1	11.5	12.0	14.8
August	9876	25.8	26.5	29.6	22.0	15.9	14.2	16.9	21.4	21.4
September	9600	20.7	22.1	20.1	16.5	15.3	14.7	15.6	18.3	18.4
October	9916	26.5	24.1	23.1	21.5	21.6	20.4	22.8	21.6	23.6
November	9600	20.8	18.3	17.4	16.2	17.6	17.8	20.7	18.6	18.9
December	10031	22.1	22.6	23.4	19.6	20.3	17.3	20.9	18.7	22.4

Frequency of Fog by Month and Time of Day

Merry Island

49°28'N 123°54'W   Years of Observations 1954-1979

Month	Total Hours of Observations	Percentage of observations when fog (visibility 0.5 mile or less) was present								
		0400	0700	0900	1100	1300	1600	2000	2200	Average
January	2924	16.1	1.8	11.8	2.6	6.9	3.8	8.1	2.8	4.7
February	2663	8.3	4.6	3.6	4.9	3.5	3.1	3.6	3.5	3.8
March	2821	1.7	1.7	1.7	0.7	1.2	0.8	0.8	0.5	1.0
April	2852	0.0	1.3	0.0	0.7	0.0	0.2	0.0	0.0	0.3
May	2964	0.0	0.0	0.8	0.0	0.4	0.2	0.0	0.0	0.1
June	2872	1.7	0.3	0.0	1.1	0.0	0.0	0.0	0.0	0.2
July	2968	0.0	1.2	0.0	1.0	0.4	0.2	0.0	0.2	0.4
August	2968	0.0	0.5	2.4	0.6	0.0	0.0	0.0	0.2	0.4
September	2786	1.7	6.0	6.7	5.7	0.8	1.9	1.7	1.7	3.1
October	2964	8.1	8.5	12.9	10.3	5.2	4.3	6.5	3.7	6.5
November	2857	5.8	8.1	9.2	5.3	0.8	2.8	5.8	3.3	5.0
December	2956	4.0	1.9	5.6	1.3	2.8	2.4	2.4	2.1	2.7

Frequency of Fog by Month and Time of Day

Port Hardy

50°41'N 127°22'W

Years of Observations 1953-1981

Month	Total Hours of Observations	Percentage of observations when fog (visibility 0.5 mile or less) was present								
		0100	0400	0700	1000	1300	1600	1900	2200	Average
January	21576	6.1	6.6	6.4	7.2	7.3	6.6	6.8	5.2	6.5
February	19656	4.6	4.8	5.7	4.8	4.5	4.4	4.8	4.5	4.8
March	21576	3.4	5.0	4.9	3.8	3.3	3.8	3.0	3.3	3.8
April	20880	2.4	2.2	3.8	3.3	3.0	3.2	2.9	2.3	3.0
May	21576	2.6	3.2	6.8	4.0	1.6	1.4	0.9	1.1	2.8
June	20880	5.4	6.7	10.2	6.9	2.3	2.5	2.3	3.6	5.0
July	21575	6.4	11.1	18.0	10.0	2.7	2.4	2.2	3.9	7.1
August	21575	14.3	20.6	28.0	19.4	6.2	4.9	5.1	9.7	13.3
September	20880	19.0	26.1	27.7	23.4	11.3	6.6	9.5	14.4	17.2
October	21576	12.9	16.1	15.9	12.7	10.3	9.8	9.9	11.0	12.1
November	20880	6.8	8.6	8.3	8.9	8.2	7.5	7.2	7.1	7.8
December	21576	5.0	6.7	6.6	8.1	7.6	7.1	7.0	6.6	6.8

Frequency of Fog by Month and Time of Day

Spring Island

50°00'N 127°25'W

Years of Observations 1953-1979

Month	Total Hours of Observations	Percentage of observations when fog (visibility 0.5 mile or less) was present								
		0100	0400	0700	1000	1300	1600	1900	2200	Average
January	20085	19.7	19.8	18.6	21.5	22.3	22.1	20.9	19.0	20.2
February	18287	18.8	20.9	19.7	19.4	19.4	19.4	19.0	17.6	19.2
March	20085	12.2	13.3	16.5	14.9	15.3	15.9	12.8	12.4	13.8
April	19435	13.0	12.6	12.2	12.7	11.7	10.4	12.1	12.6	12.2
May	20085	10.4	11.6	13.3	10.4	8.6	9.8	9.5	9.6	10.6
June	19438	8.9	14.9	16.2	13.2	10.0	10.5	10.0	10.6	11.5
July	20079	10.3	13.4	14.8	14.1	10.6	10.4	8.4	9.6	11.6
August	20087	15.1	17.4	20.2	17.7	15.2	13.5	15.7	15.5	16.5
September	19431	13.5	13.0	17.2	16.5	15.1	14.8	16.0	14.3	15.2
October	20080	19.9	19.7	21.4	21.5	18.9	20.8	21.7	21.3	20.3
November	19383	15.5	14.1	15.8	17.0	17.6	18.3	17.2	16.0	16.5
December	20084	17.8	18.6	17.0	22.1	20.8	23.3	20.2	18.5	20.0

Frequency of Fog by Month and Time of Day

Tofino

49°05'N 125°46'W   Years of Observations 1960-1981

Month	Total Hours of Observations	Percentage of observations when fog (visibility 0.5 mile or less) was present								
		0100	0400	0700	1000	1300	1600	1900	2200	Average
January	15853	25.5	25.5	22.1	27.4	27.9	27.3	23.9	23.8	25.7
February	14454	26.1	25.6	26.0	31.0	27.0	25.4	24.0	22.7	23.4
March	15848	19.7	21.2	23.0	22.6	20.2	19.8	18.3	16.3	20.5
April	14758	15.8	19.3	22.2	16.2	13.5	15.7	14.0	15.0	16.4
May	15720	13.4	17.4	21.3	14.8	9.5	11.1	11.7	11.8	14.1
June	15064	18.2	22.3	28.6	18.8	13.6	12.4	14.4	16.2	18.1
July	15560	22.6	31.1	41.0	26.8	13.3	10.7	12.2	15.8	21.8
August	15559	32.1	41.1	50.7	34.6	19.5	15.4	20.4	26.3	29.8
September	15056	28.5	34.8	39.8	29.1	21.2	18.2	20.6	22.2	26.8
October	15471	31.5	32.4	34.1	26.6	25.8	26.1	27.6	29.4	29.0
November	15077	21.4	23.6	21.6	21.1	24.8	26.7	23.2	21.9	23.4
December	15621	26.5	25.4	26.2	30.5	29.9	31.0	25.5	24.4	27.6

Frequency of Fog by Month and Time of Day

Vancouver Airport

49°11'N 123°10'W   Years of Observations 1953-1981

Month	Total Hours of Observations	Percentage of observations when fog (visibility 0.5 mile or less) was present								
		0100	0400	0700	1000	1300	1600	1900	2200	Average
January	21576	26.1	26.2	25.8	31.2	21.2	19.8	21.0	26.8	25.3
February	19656	26.1	27.8	32.0	27.8	14.5	12.3	12.8	15.9	21.0
March	21576	8.7	11.7	22.0	11.1	5.6	5.0	6.0	4.7	9.1
April	20880	3.3	6.1	11.3	4.3	2.5	2.1	2.4	2.3	4.4
May	21576	2.9	6.8	7.8	3.3	2.1	1.2	1.9	1.8	3.5
June	20880	2.3	9.3	7.8	4.1	1.8	1.0	1.6	2.2	3.7
July	21576	1.0	7.7	6.8	3.0	1.8	1.2	1.4	0.9	3.0
August	21576	5.0	12.9	20.5	5.7	3.4	3.1	3.0	2.4	7.4
September	20880	18.8	26.8	45.1	16.4	6.7	5.3	6.1	10.1	16.7
October	21576	29.5	35.6	47.2	30.1	15.2	13.6	15.4	22.7	25.7
November	20880	27.0	26.7	31.4	31.0	18.8	17.9	17.5	23.6	24.3
December	21576	27.0	25.8	24.6	32.6	22.1	23.0	20.6	25.7	25.5

Frequency of Fog by Month and Time of Day

Vancouver Harbour

49°18'N 123°07'W

Years of Observations 1976-1981

Month	Total Hours of Observations	Percentage of observations when fog (visibility 0.5 mile or less) was present								Average
		0600	0900	1200	1500	1800				
January	2209	41.5	45.2	38.9	31.1	33.5				37.1
February	2265	17.8	30.6	24.1	21.8	21.2				24.1
March	2478	17.7	16.1	10.2	11.8	12.9				13.0
April	2205	13.1	13.9	8.3	3.3	3.3				7.8
May	2353	12.4	10.3	7.7	3.9	4.5				7.5
June	2760	14.4	13.3	6.1	4.4	1.7				7.6
July	2852	7.5	6.4	2.7	2.2	0.5				3.8
August	2851	12.4	13.4	5.9	5.4	2.7				7.6
September	2729	26.2	21.1	12.2	5.0	6.1				13.0
October	2766	25.3	34.4	16.7	13.4	12.9				20.9
November	2399	30.0	23.3	17.2	20.0	16.7				18.8
December	2475	20.0	22.6	26.3	23.1	15.1				20.8

FREQUENCY OF FOG BY MONTH AND TIME OF DAY

Victoria

48°25'N 123°19'W

Years of Observations 1953-1981

Month	Total Hours of Observations	Percentage of observations when fog (visibility 0.5 mile or less) was present								Average
		0100	0400	0700	1000	1300	1600	1900	2200	
January	16383	11.1	8.9	10.7	12.4	11.2	11.0	10.3	10.9	11.0
February	14982	9.5	9.3	10.8	12.0	7.5	6.4	8.4	8.4	9.2
March	16464	3.6	3.6	5.8	5.2	2.0	1.9	2.8	1.8	3.4
April	15895	2.7	3.5	5.3	3.6	1.6	1.4	2.1	1.7	2.8
May	16056	1.3	3.0	3.9	2.7	1.2	1.2	0.6	1.3	1.9
June	15502	1.8	3.3	4.2	3.9	2.2	0.8	1.3	1.1	2.6
July	16020	2.2	4.1	4.6	3.2	1.6	1.7	0.9	2.1	2.6
August	15984	3.7	7.1	11.0	7.9	3.4	2.5	1.9	1.5	5.4
September	15491	10.9	16.2	23.8	17.3	9.3	5.5	4.7	7.1	12.7
October	15916	18.7	19.6	27.4	22.6	12.2	11.5	13.3	13.8	17.4
November	15294	11.3	11.8	14.9	15.1	12.3	12.4	12.9	11.8	13.4
December	15927	10.8	10.8	9.8	12.5	9.8	10.1	9.5	10.1	10.8

D

G

I

J

U

Y

Z